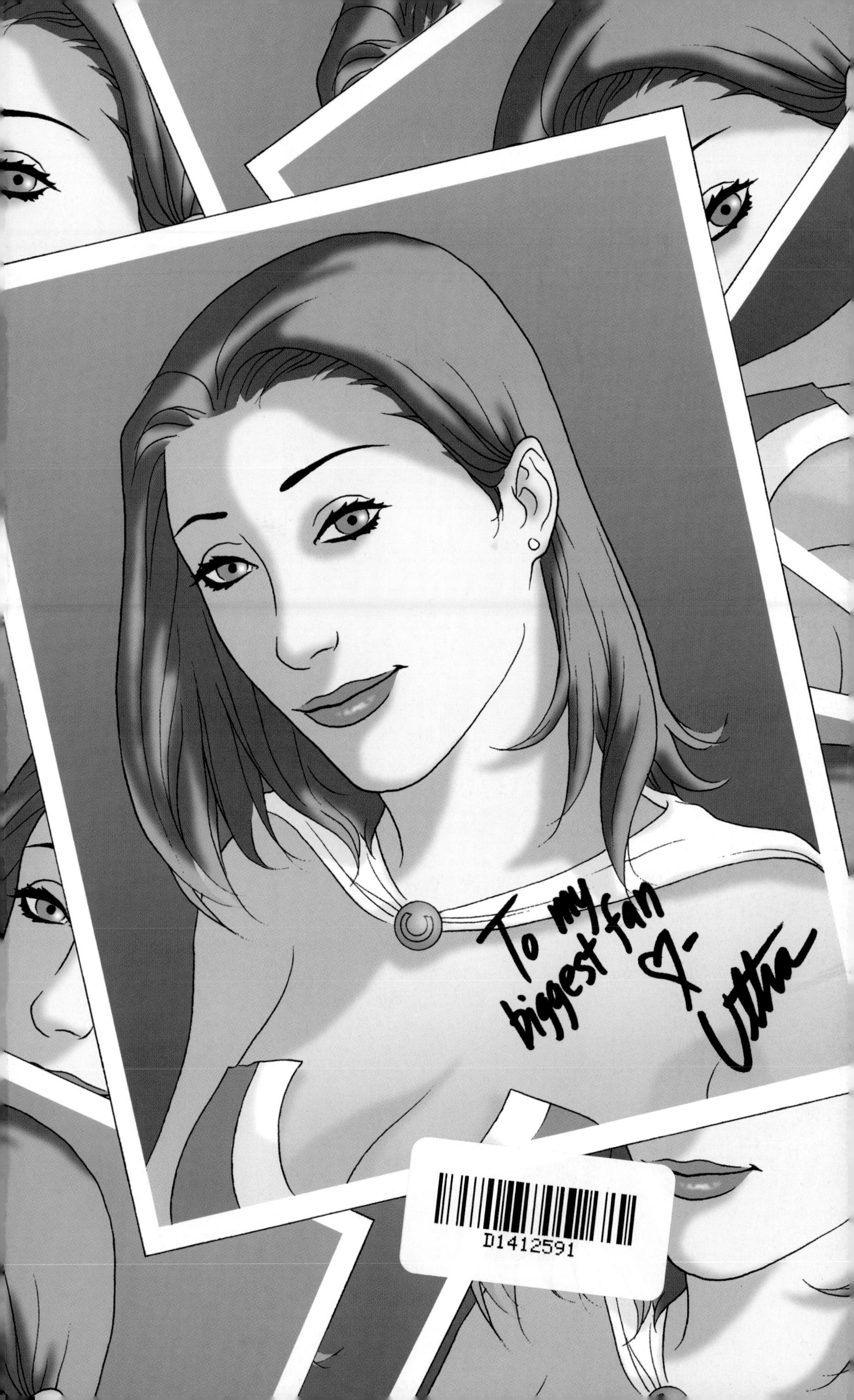
To my biggest fan

ULTRA™

SEVEN DAYS

Image Comics, Inc.

Erik Larsen
Publisher

Todd McFarlane
President

Marc Silvestri
CEO

Jim Valentino
Vice-President

Eric Stephenson
Executive Director

Missie Miranda
Controller

Brett Evans
Production Manager

Jim Demonakos
PR & Marketing Coordinator

Allen Hui
Production Artist

Joe Keatinge
Traffic Manager

Mia MacHatton
Administrative Assistant

Jonathan Chan
Production Assistant

Joshua Luna
Plot, Script, Layouts

Jonathan Luna
Plot, Art, Colors, Letters

AUGUST, 2004, ISSUE #1
ULTRA™
CREATED BY
THE LUNA BROTHERS
THE PRIVATE LIFE OF A SUPER HEROINE
#BXBJLEX *************5-DIGIT 10019
#1920 3881 111#TD 9879CA05 B APR05
Pearl Penalosa 0007
#02734
22194 Crescent Ave #P2 P00267
Spring City 10019 USA

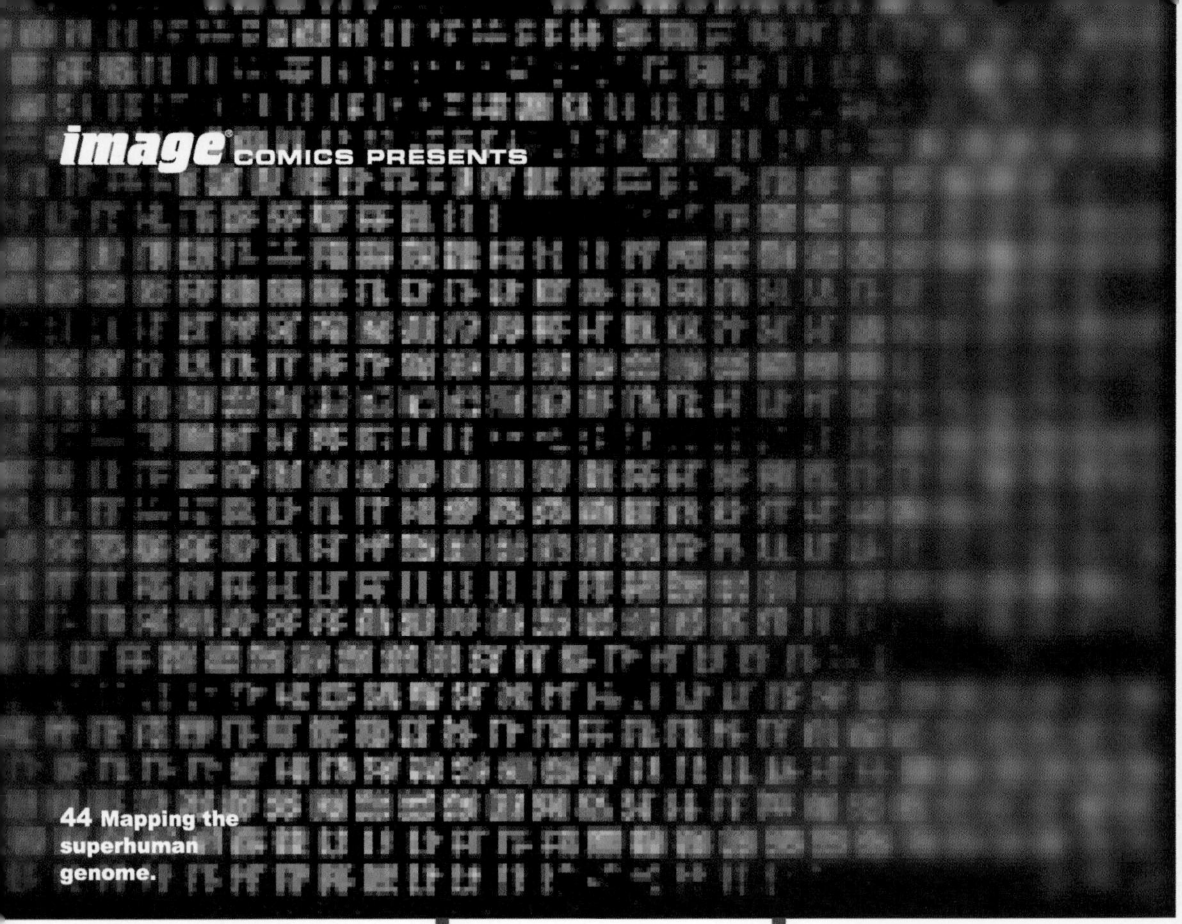

image COMICS PRESENTS

44 Mapping the superhuman genome.

ULTRA

SEVEN DAYS part one
August 2004
Vol. 1, No. 1

CREATED BY
The Luna Brothers

Jonathan Luna:
co-writer, artist, colorist, letterer

Joshua Luna:
co-writer

COVER STORY
The Private Life of a Super Heroine 3

54 ▲ Mayor Jameson Janus prosposes tougher laws against anti-superhuman hate crimes.

62 ▲ Nominations for this year's Superhero Awards.

the official website is **www.LunaBrothers.com**

For Image Comics

Erik Larsen - Publisher
Todd McFarlane - President
Marc Silvestri - CEO
Jim Valentino - Vice-President

Eric Stephenson - Executive Director
Missie Miranda - Controller
Brett Evans - Production Manager
B. Clay Moore - PR & Marketing Coordinator

Allen Hui - Production Artist
Joe Keatinge - Inventory Controller
Mia Machatton - Administrative Assistant

www.imagecomics.com

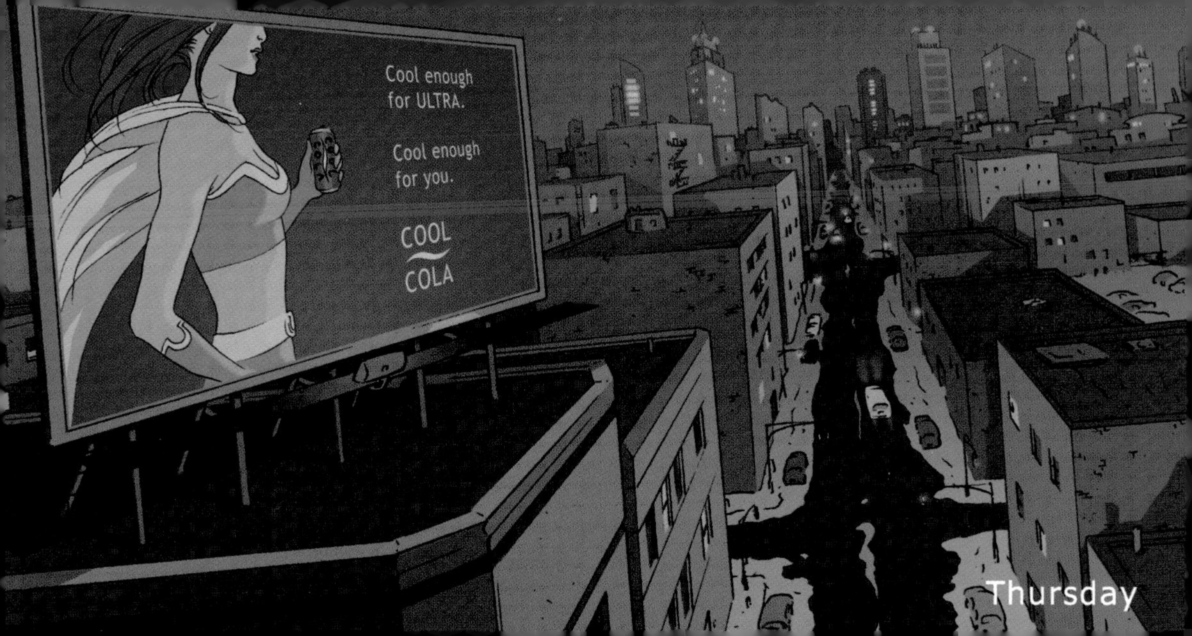
Cool enough
for ULTRA.
Cool enough
for you.
COOL
COLA
Thursday

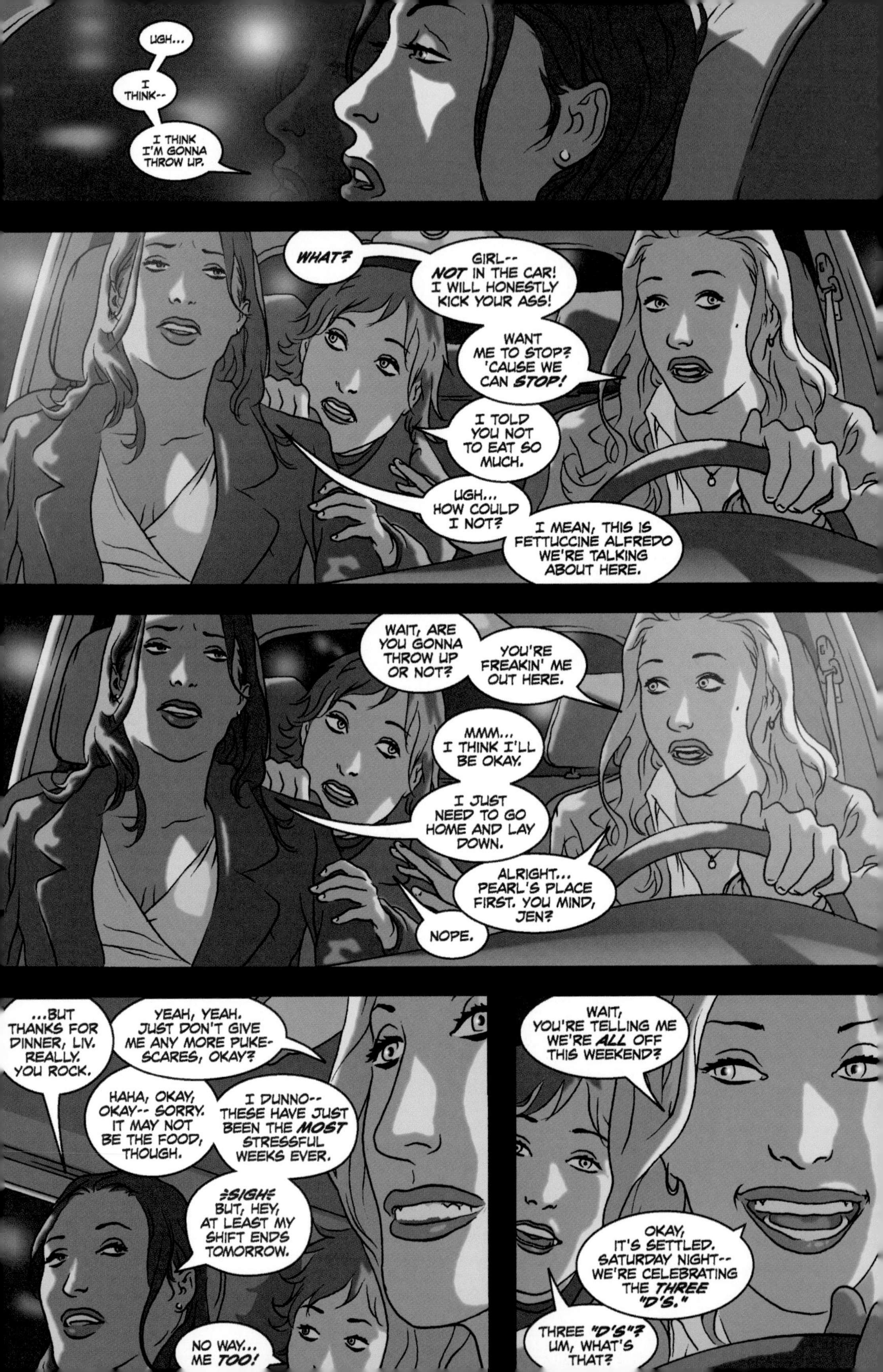
UGH...
I THINK--
I THINK I'M GONNA THROW UP.
WHAT?
GIRL-- NOT IN THE CAR! I WILL HONESTLY KICK YOUR ASS!
WANT ME TO STOP? 'CAUSE WE CAN STOP!
I TOLD YOU NOT TO EAT SO MUCH.
UGH... HOW COULD I NOT?
I MEAN, THIS IS FETTUCCINE ALFREDO WE'RE TALKING ABOUT HERE.
WAIT, ARE YOU GONNA THROW UP OR NOT?
YOU'RE FREAKIN' ME OUT HERE.
MMM... I THINK I'LL BE OKAY.
I JUST NEED TO GO HOME AND LAY DOWN.
ALRIGHT... PEARL'S PLACE FIRST. YOU MIND, JEN?
NOPE.
...BUT THANKS FOR DINNER, LIV. REALLY. YOU ROCK.
YEAH, YEAH. JUST DON'T GIVE ME ANY MORE PUKE-SCARES, OKAY?
HAHA, OKAY, OKAY-- SORRY. IT MAY NOT BE THE FOOD, THOUGH.
I DUNNO-- THESE HAVE JUST BEEN THE MOST STRESSFUL WEEKS EVER.
SIGH BUT, HEY, AT LEAST MY SHIFT ENDS TOMORROW.
NO WAY... ME TOO!
WAIT, YOU'RE TELLING ME WE'RE ALL OFF THIS WEEKEND?
OKAY, IT'S SETTLED. SATURDAY NIGHT-- WE'RE CELEBRATING THE THREE "D'S."
THREE "D'S"? UM, WHAT'S THAT?

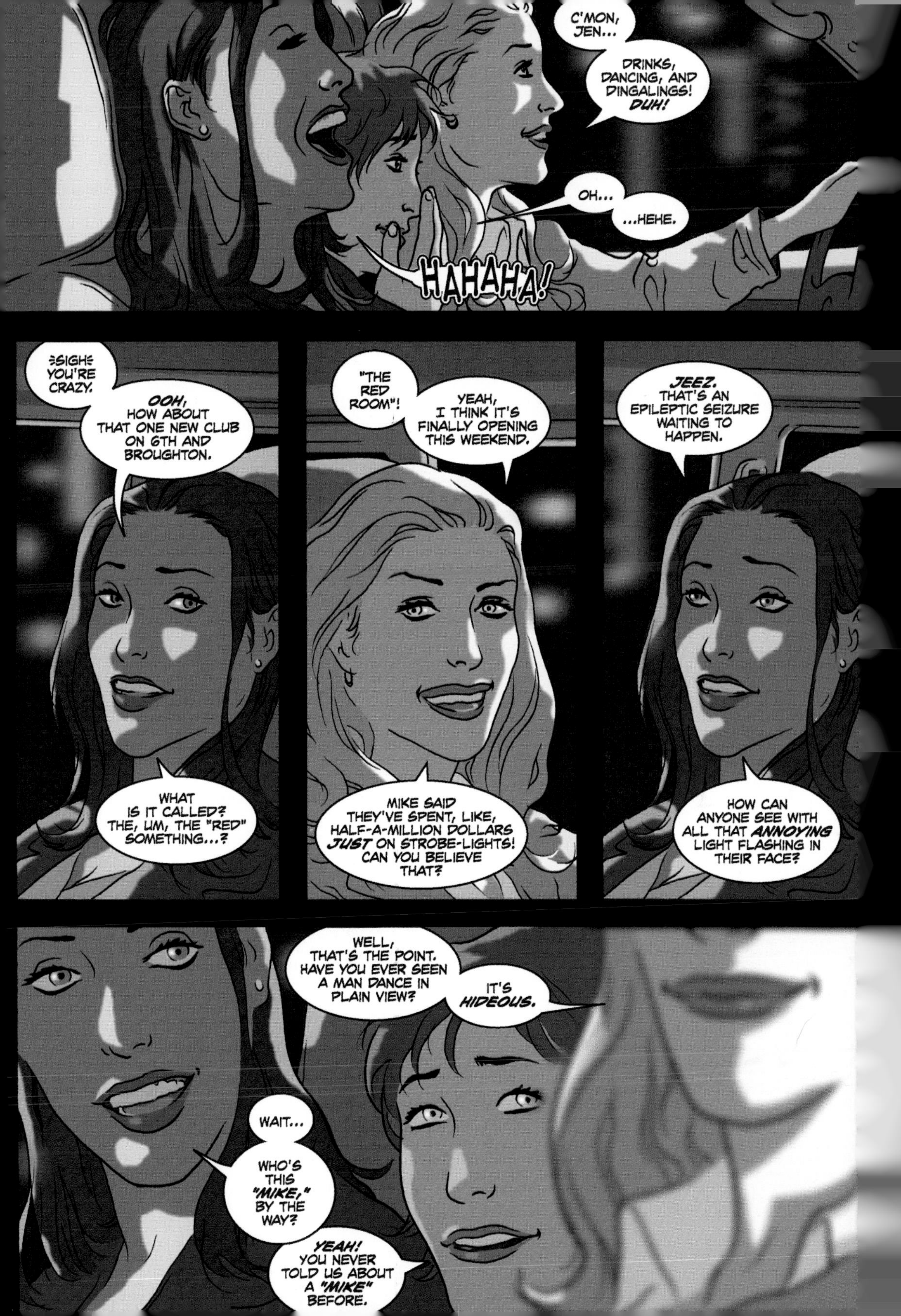
C'MON, JEN...
DRINKS, DANCING, AND DINGALINGS! DUH!
OH...
...HEHE.
HAHAHA!
≡SIGH≡ YOU'RE CRAZY.
OOH, HOW ABOUT THAT ONE NEW CLUB ON 6TH AND BROUGHTON.
WHAT IS IT CALLED? THE, UM, THE "RED" SOMETHING...?
"THE RED ROOM"!
YEAH, I THINK IT'S FINALLY OPENING THIS WEEKEND.
MIKE SAID THEY'VE SPENT, LIKE, HALF-A-MILLION DOLLARS JUST ON STROBE-LIGHTS! CAN YOU BELIEVE THAT?
JEEZ. THAT'S AN EPILEPTIC SEIZURE WAITING TO HAPPEN.
HOW CAN ANYONE SEE WITH ALL THAT ANNOYING LIGHT FLASHING IN THEIR FACE?
WELL, THAT'S THE POINT. HAVE YOU EVER SEEN A MAN DANCE IN PLAIN VIEW?
IT'S HIDEOUS.
WAIT...
WHO'S THIS "MIKE," BY THE WAY?
YEAH! YOU NEVER TOLD US ABOUT A "MIKE" BEFORE.

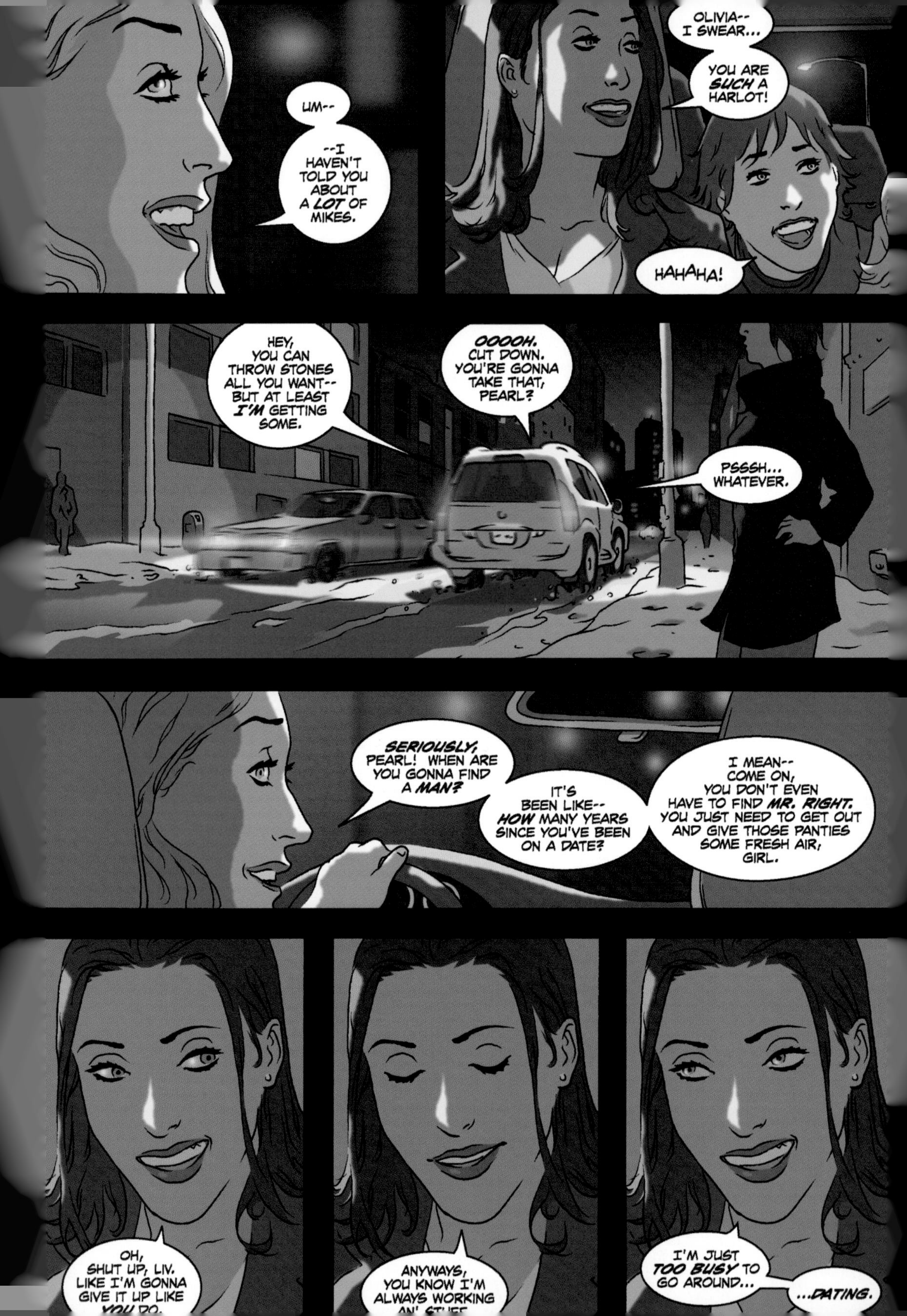
UM--
--I HAVEN'T TOLD YOU ABOUT A LOT OF MIKES.
OLIVIA-- I SWEAR...
YOU ARE SUCH A HARLOT!
HAHAHA!
HEY, YOU CAN THROW STONES ALL YOU WANT-- BUT AT LEAST I'M GETTING SOME.
OOOOH. CUT DOWN. YOU'RE GONNA TAKE THAT, PEARL?
PSSSH... WHATEVER.
SERIOUSLY, PEARL! WHEN ARE YOU GONNA FIND A MAN?
IT'S BEEN LIKE-- HOW MANY YEARS SINCE YOU'VE BEEN ON A DATE?
I MEAN-- COME ON, YOU DON'T EVEN HAVE TO FIND MR. RIGHT. YOU JUST NEED TO GET OUT AND GIVE THOSE PANTIES SOME FRESH AIR, GIRL.
OH, SHUT UP, LIV. LIKE I'M GONNA GIVE IT UP LIKE
ANYWAYS, YOU KNOW I'M ALWAYS WORKING
I'M JUST TOO BUSY TO GO AROUND...
...DATING.

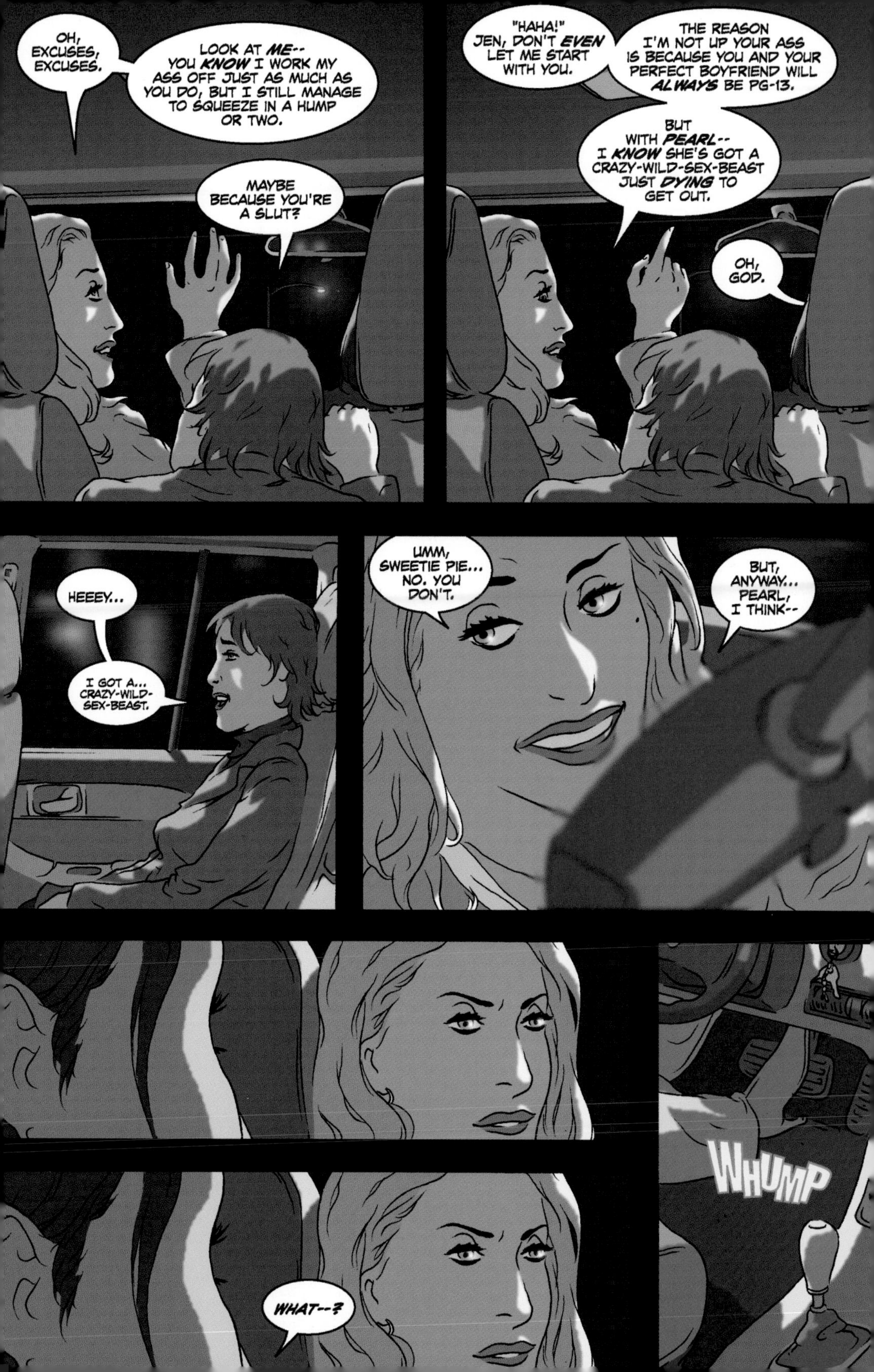

OH, EXCUSES, EXCUSES.
LOOK AT ME-- YOU KNOW I WORK MY ASS OFF JUST AS MUCH AS YOU DO, BUT I STILL MANAGE TO SQUEEZE IN A HUMP OR TWO.
MAYBE BECAUSE YOU'RE A SLUT?
"HAHA!" JEN, DON'T EVEN LET ME START WITH YOU.
THE REASON I'M NOT UP YOUR ASS IS BECAUSE YOU AND YOUR PERFECT BOYFRIEND WILL ALWAYS BE PG-13.
BUT WITH PEARL-- I KNOW SHE'S GOT A CRAZY-WILD-SEX-BEAST JUST DYING TO GET OUT.
OH, GOD.
HEEEY...
I GOT A... CRAZY-WILD-SEX-BEAST.
UMM, SWEETIE PIE... NO. YOU DON'T.
BUT, ANYWAY... PEARL, I THINK--
WHUMP
WHAT--?

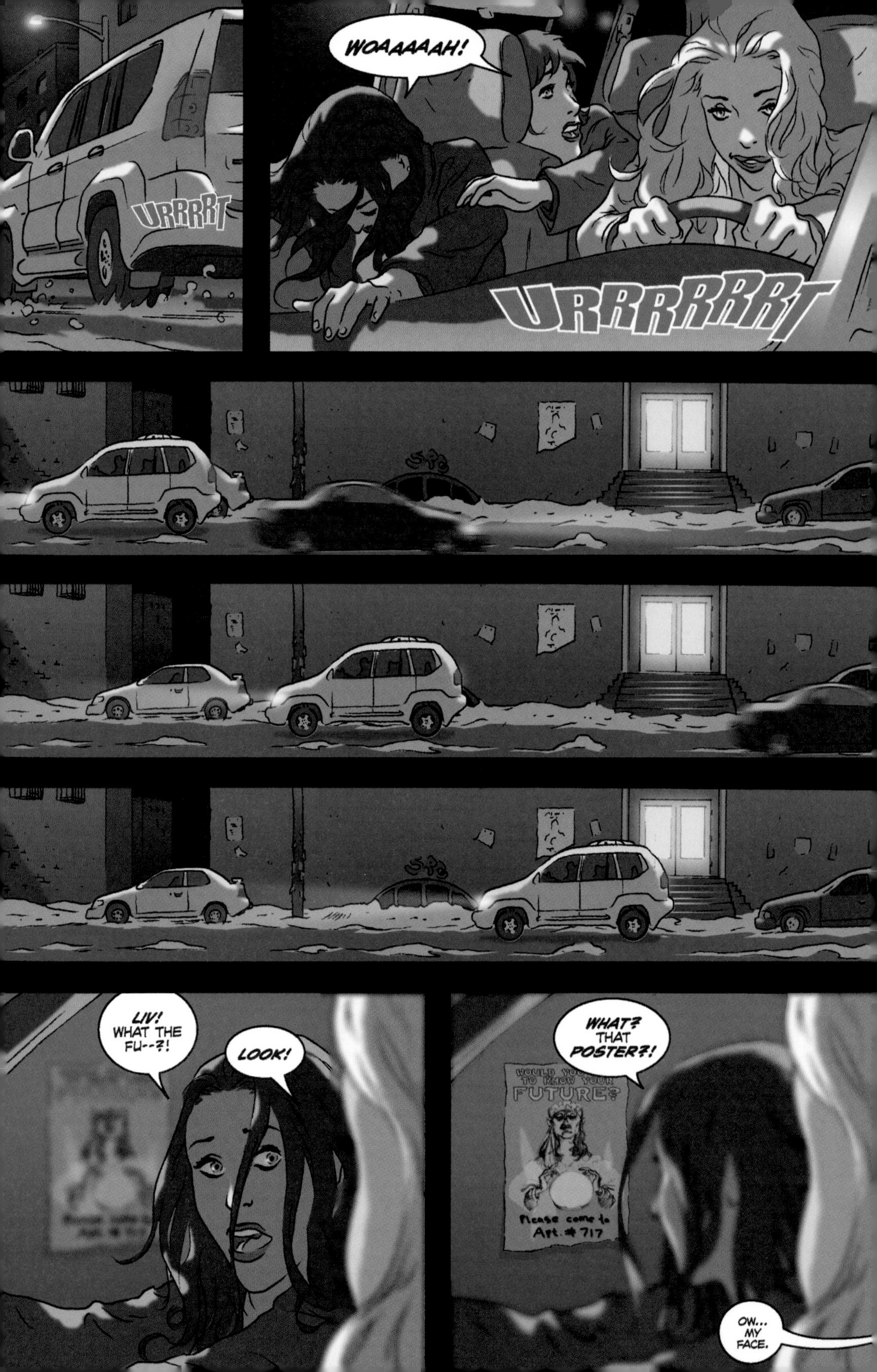
URRRRT
WOAAAAAH!
URRRRRRRT
LIV! WHAT THE FU--?!
LOOK!
WHAT? THAT POSTER?!
WOULD YOU LIKE TO KNOW YOUR FUTURE?
Please come to Apt. # 717
OW... MY FACE.

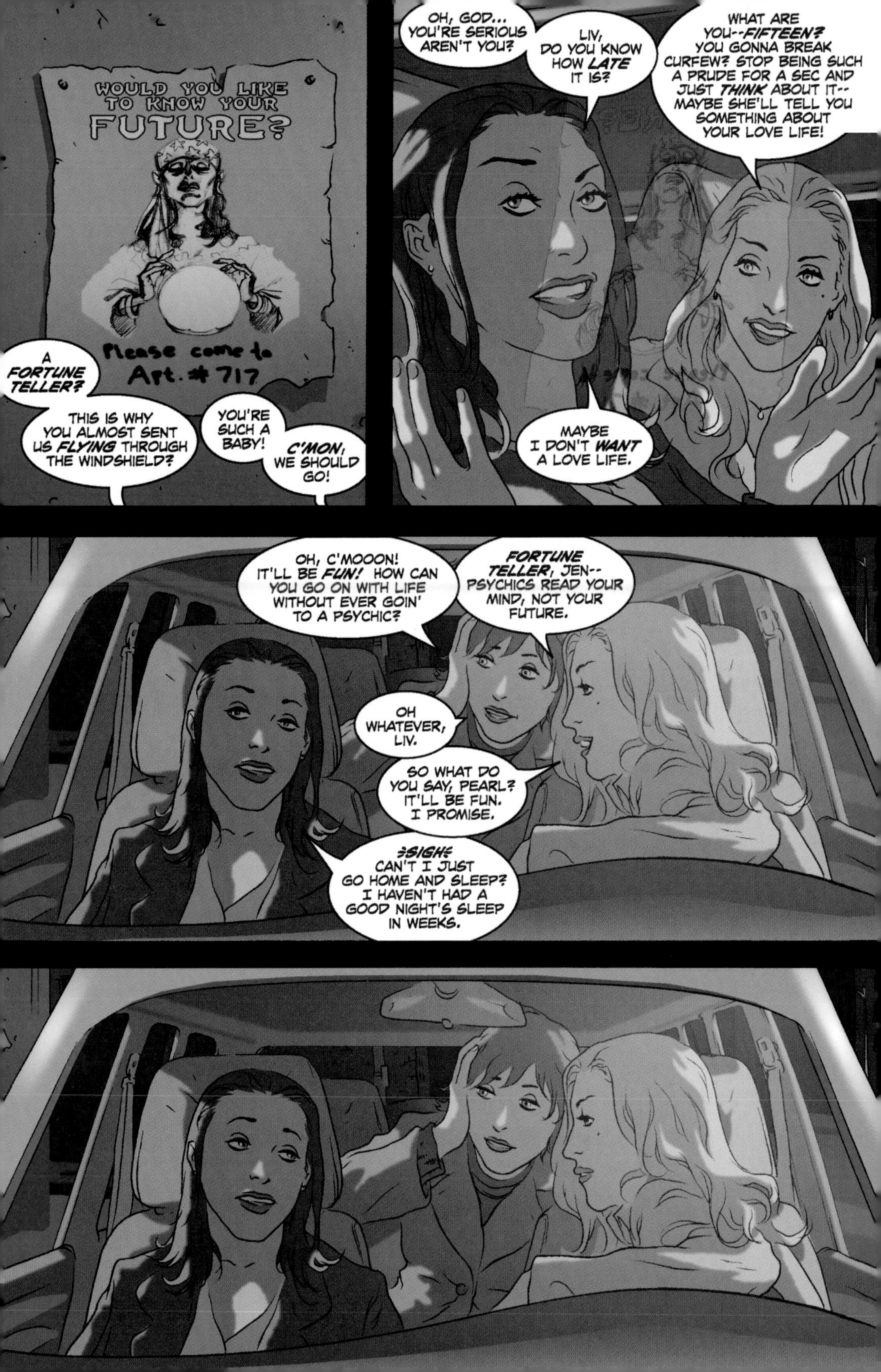

WOULD YOU LIKE TO KNOW YOUR FUTURE?
Please come to Apt. #717
A FORTUNE TELLER?
THIS IS WHY YOU ALMOST SENT US FLYING THROUGH THE WINDSHIELD?
YOU'RE SUCH A BABY!
C'MON, WE SHOULD GO!
OH, GOD... YOU'RE SERIOUS AREN'T YOU?
LIV, DO YOU KNOW HOW LATE IT IS?
WHAT ARE YOU--FIFTEEN? YOU GONNA BREAK CURFEW? STOP BEING SUCH A PRUDE FOR A SEC AND JUST THINK ABOUT IT-- MAYBE SHE'LL TELL YOU SOMETHING ABOUT YOUR LOVE LIFE!
MAYBE I DON'T WANT A LOVE LIFE.
OH, C'MOOON! IT'LL BE FUN! HOW CAN YOU GO ON WITH LIFE WITHOUT EVER GOIN' TO A PSYCHIC?
FORTUNE TELLER, JEN-- PSYCHICS READ YOUR MIND, NOT YOUR FUTURE.
OH WHATEVER, LIV.
SO WHAT DO YOU SAY, PEARL? IT'LL BE FUN. I PROMISE.
SIGH CAN'T I JUST GO HOME AND SLEEP? I HAVEN'T HAD A GOOD NIGHT'S SLEEP IN WEEKS.

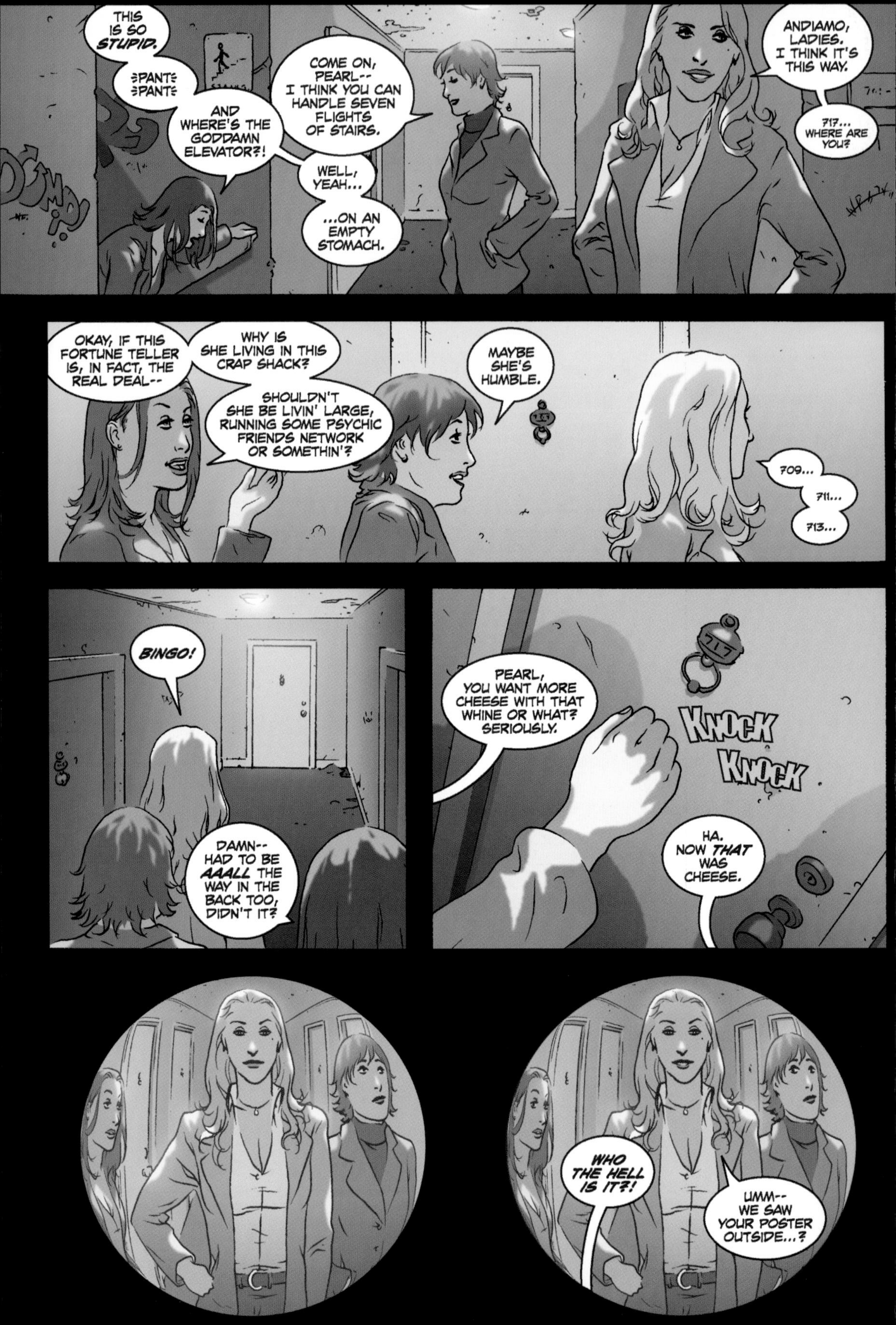
THIS IS SO *STUPID.*
PANT PANT
AND WHERE'S THE GODDAMN ELEVATOR?!
COME ON, PEARL-- I THINK YOU CAN HANDLE SEVEN FLIGHTS OF STAIRS.
WELL, YEAH...
...ON AN EMPTY STOMACH.
ANDIAMO, LADIES. I THINK IT'S THIS WAY.
717... WHERE ARE YOU?
OKAY, IF THIS FORTUNE TELLER IS, IN FACT, THE REAL DEAL--
WHY IS SHE LIVING IN THIS CRAP SHACK?
SHOULDN'T SHE BE LIVIN' LARGE, RUNNING SOME PSYCHIC FRIENDS NETWORK OR SOMETHIN'?
MAYBE SHE'S HUMBLE.
709...
711...
713...
BINGO!
DAMN-- HAD TO BE *AAALL* THE WAY IN THE BACK TOO, DIDN'T IT?
717
PEARL, YOU WANT MORE CHEESE WITH THAT WHINE OR WHAT? SERIOUSLY.
KNOCK KNOCK
HA. NOW *THAT* WAS CHEESE.
WHO THE HELL IS IT?!
UMM-- WE SAW YOUR POSTER OUTSIDE...?

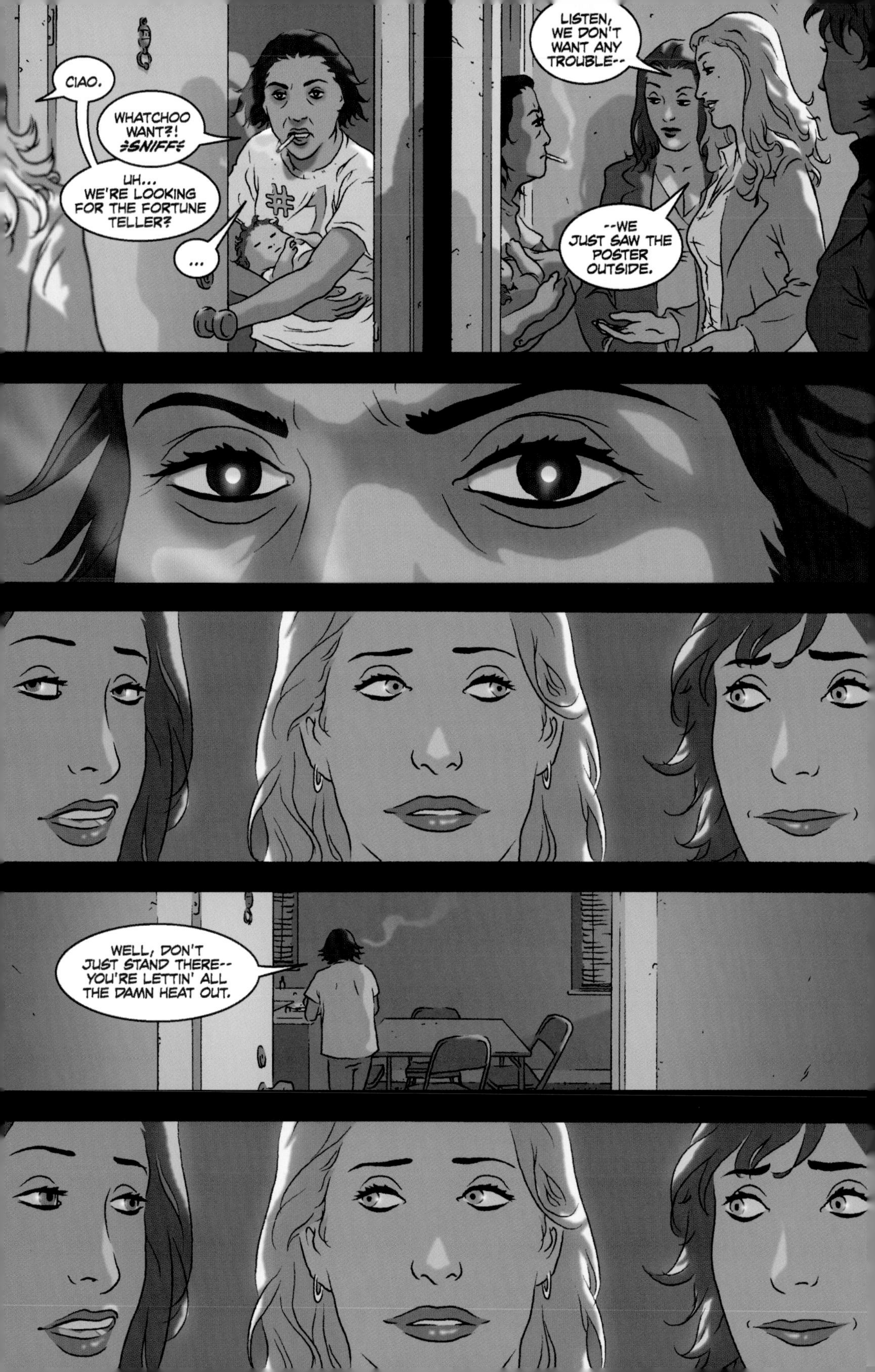
CIAO.
WHATCHOO WANT?! *SNIFF*
UH... WE'RE LOOKING FOR THE FORTUNE TELLER?
...
LISTEN, WE DON'T WANT ANY TROUBLE--
--WE JUST SAW THE POSTER OUTSIDE.
WELL, DON'T JUST STAND THERE-- YOU'RE LETTIN' ALL THE DAMN HEAT OUT.

LLAMA
MOROCCAN BLENDS
Fine Moroccan Tobaccos. Distinctively...
...Moroccan.
MOROCCAN SILVER: 10 mg. "tar", 0.8 mg. nicotine, MOROCCAN KING: 13 mg. "tar", 1.1mg. nicotine, MOROCCAN MINT: 17 mg. "tar", 1.1 mg. nicotine, av. per cigarette by FTC method. Parody.
SURGEON GENERAL'S WARNING: Prolonged Smoking May Cause Death.
SINCE 1910

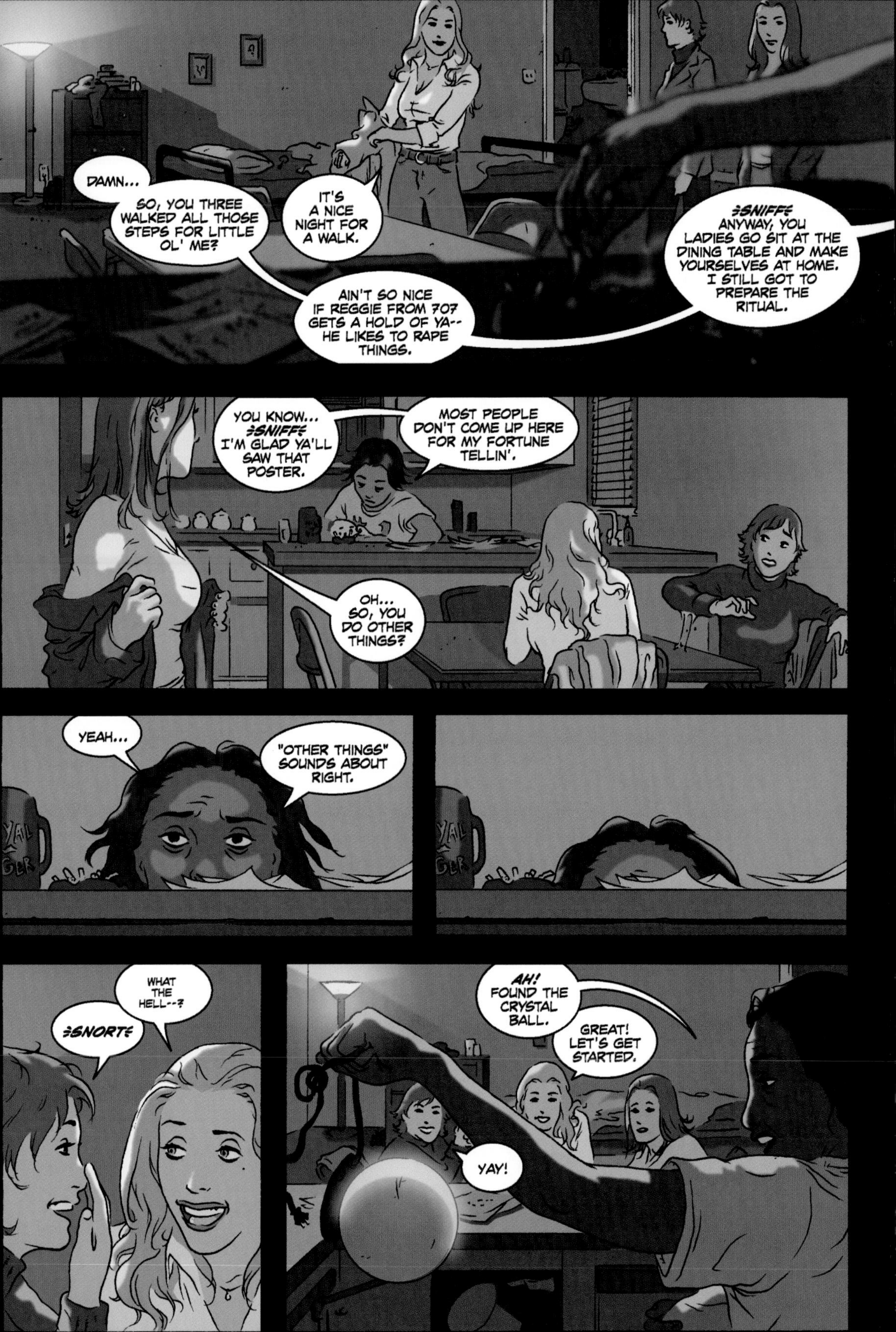
DAMN...
SO, YOU THREE WALKED ALL THOSE STEPS FOR LITTLE OL' ME?
IT'S A NICE NIGHT FOR A WALK.
AIN'T SO NICE IF REGGIE FROM 707 GETS A HOLD OF YA-- HE LIKES TO RAPE THINGS.
SNIFF ANYWAY, YOU LADIES GO SIT AT THE DINING TABLE AND MAKE YOURSELVES AT HOME. I STILL GOT TO PREPARE THE RITUAL.
YOU KNOW... *SNIFF* I'M GLAD YA'LL SAW THAT POSTER.
MOST PEOPLE DON'T COME UP HERE FOR MY FORTUNE TELLIN'.
OH... SO, YOU DO OTHER THINGS?
YEAH...
"OTHER THINGS" SOUNDS ABOUT RIGHT.
SNORT
WHAT THE HELL--?
AH! FOUND THE CRYSTAL BALL.
GREAT! LET'S GET STARTED.
YAY!

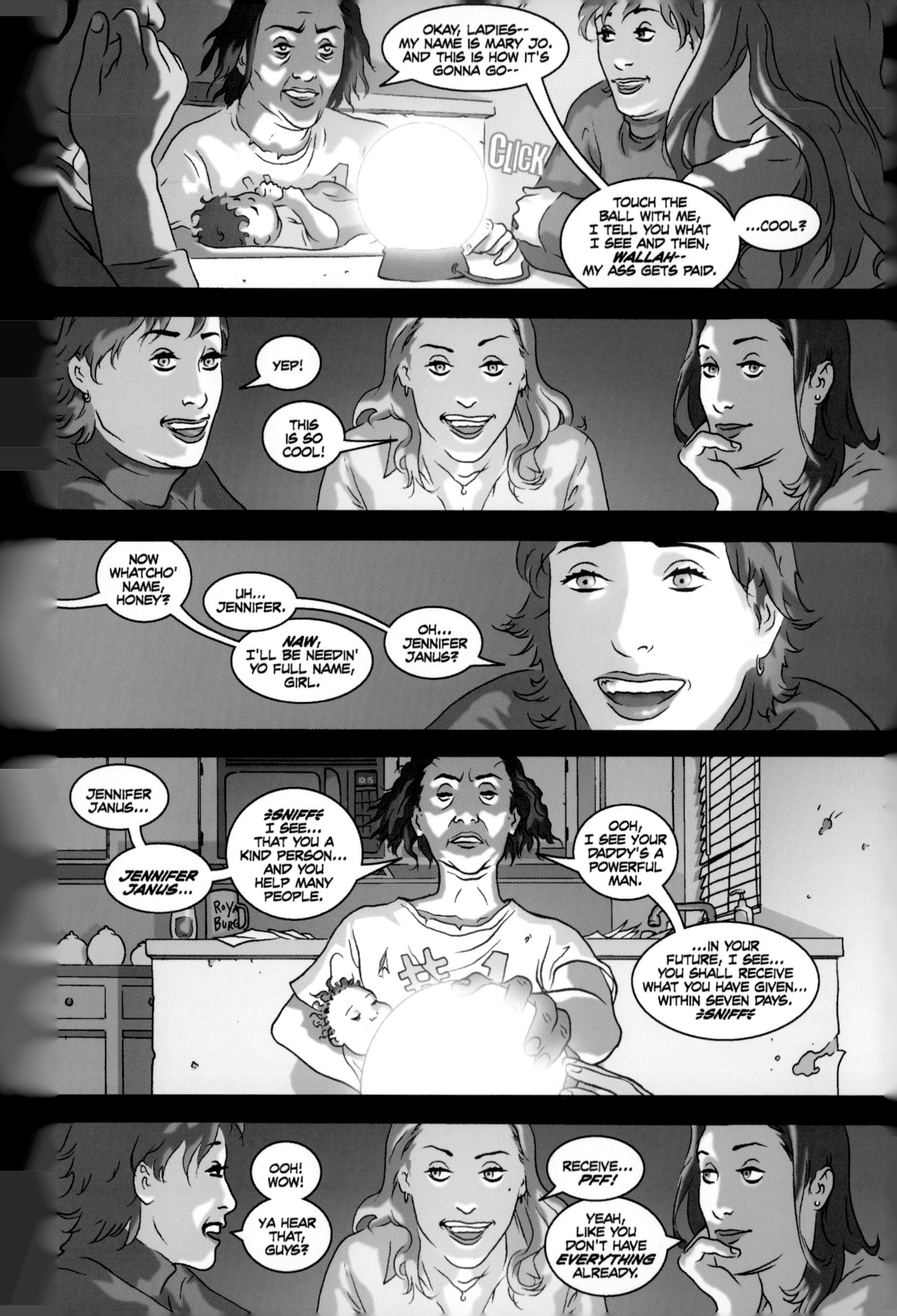
OKAY, LADIES-- MY NAME IS MARY JO. AND THIS IS HOW IT'S GONNA GO--
CLICK
TOUCH THE BALL WITH ME, I TELL YOU WHAT I SEE AND THEN, WALLAH-- MY ASS GETS PAID.
...COOL?
YEP!
THIS IS SO COOL!
NOW WHATCHO' NAME, HONEY?
UH... JENNIFER.
NAW, I'LL BE NEEDIN' YO FULL NAME, GIRL.
OH... JENNIFER JANUS?
JENNIFER JANUS...
JENNIFER JANUS...
SNIFF I SEE... THAT YOU A KIND PERSON... AND YOU HELP MANY PEOPLE.
OOH, I SEE YOUR DADDY'S A POWERFUL MAN.
...IN YOUR FUTURE, I SEE... YOU SHALL RECEIVE WHAT YOU HAVE GIVEN... WITHIN SEVEN DAYS. SNIFF
OOH! WOW!
YA HEAR THAT, GUYS?
RECEIVE... PFF!
YEAH, LIKE YOU DON'T HAVE EVERYTHING ALREADY.

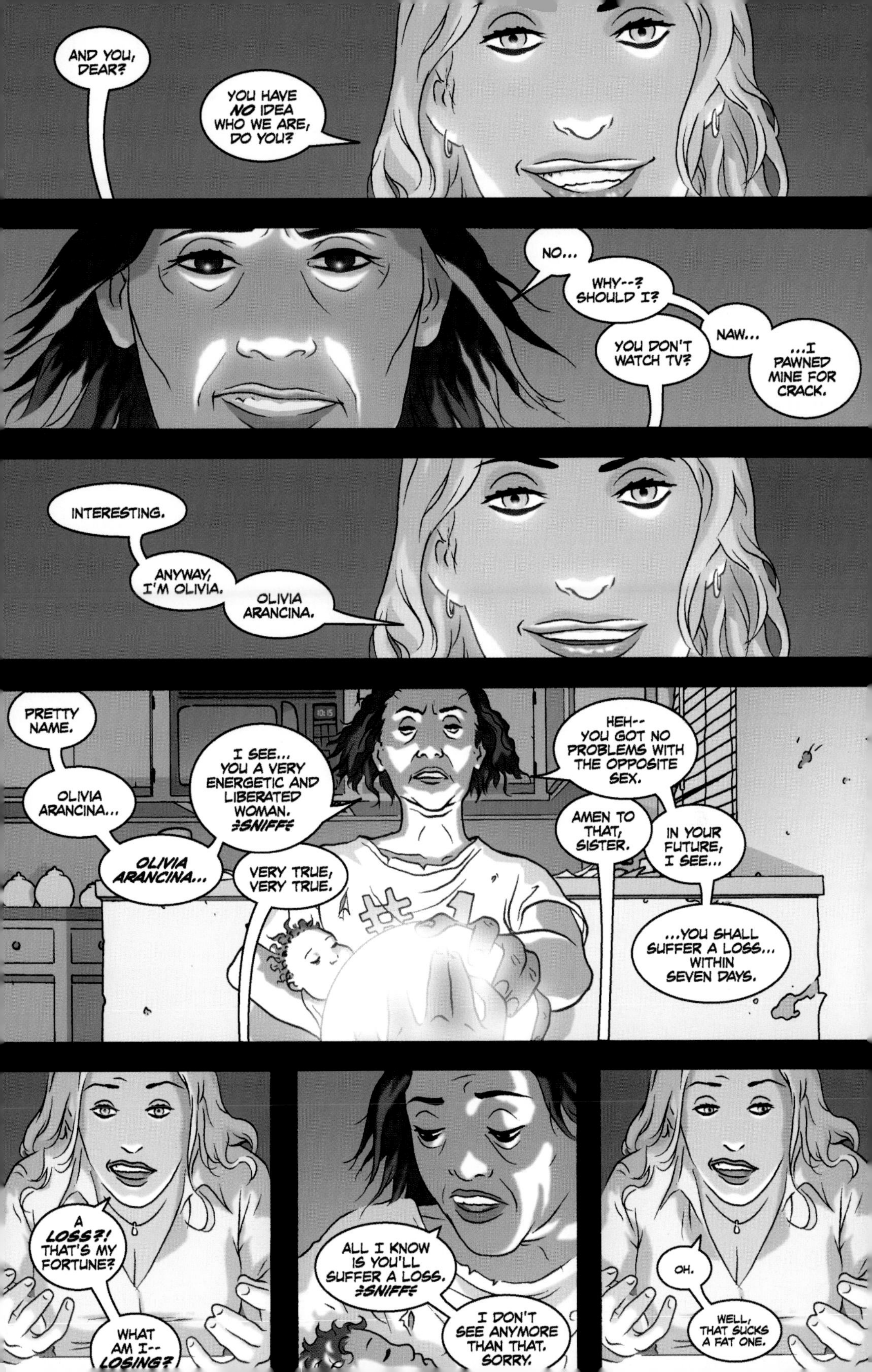

AND YOU, DEAR?
YOU HAVE NO IDEA WHO WE ARE, DO YOU?
NO...
WHY--? SHOULD I?
YOU DON'T WATCH TV?
NAW...
...I PAWNED MINE FOR CRACK.
INTERESTING.
ANYWAY, I'M OLIVIA.
OLIVIA ARANCINA.
PRETTY NAME.
OLIVIA ARANCINA...
OLIVIA ARANCINA...
I SEE... YOU A VERY ENERGETIC AND LIBERATED WOMAN. SNIFF
VERY TRUE, VERY TRUE.
HEH-- YOU GOT NO PROBLEMS WITH THE OPPOSITE SEX.
AMEN TO THAT, SISTER.
IN YOUR FUTURE, I SEE...
...YOU SHALL SUFFER A LOSS... WITHIN SEVEN DAYS.
A LOSS?! THAT'S MY FORTUNE?
WHAT AM I-- LOSING?
ALL I KNOW IS YOU'LL SUFFER A LOSS. SNIFF
I DON'T SEE ANYMORE THAN THAT. SORRY.
OH.
WELL, THAT SUCKS A FAT ONE.

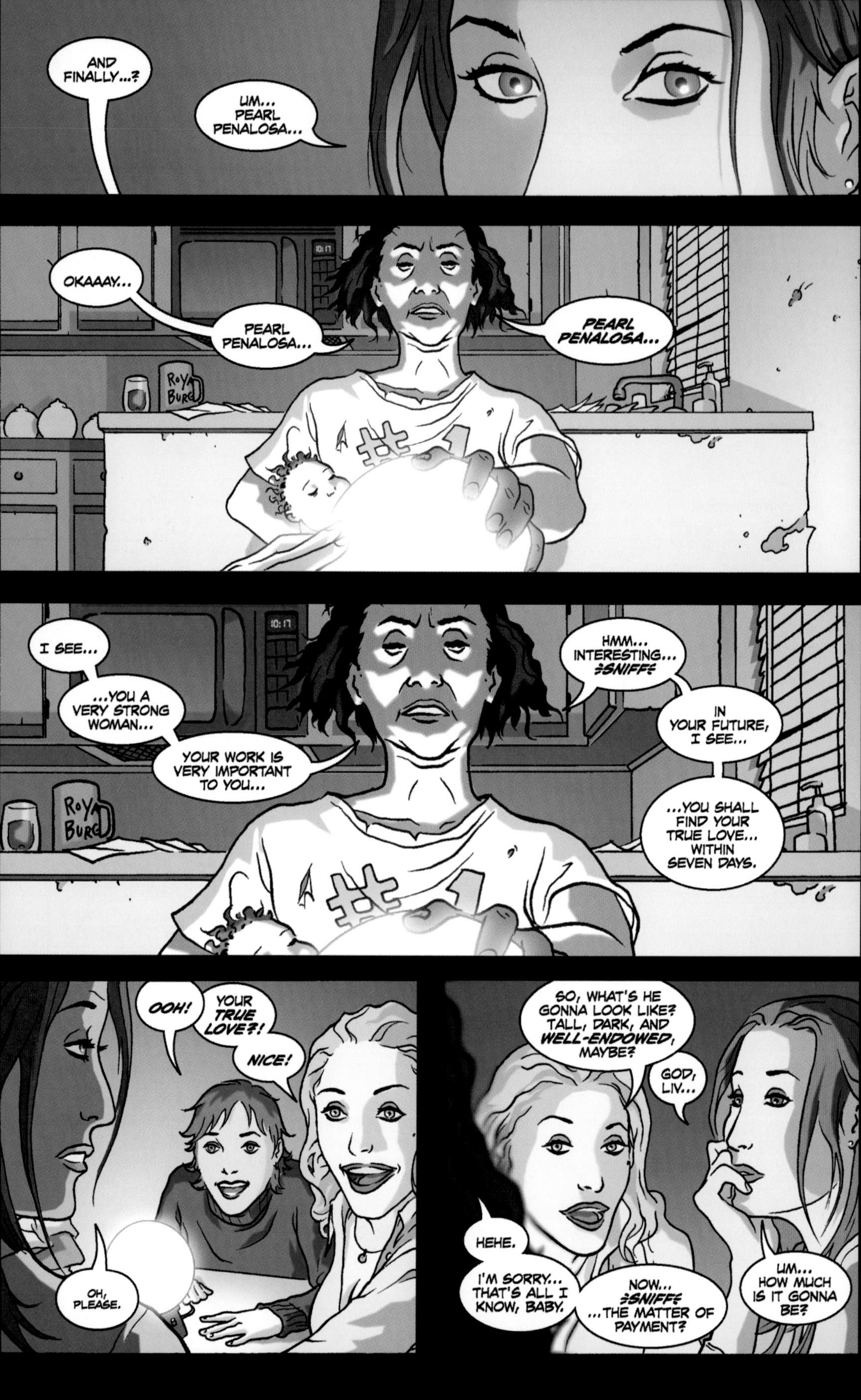
AND FINALLY...?
UM... PEARL PENALOSA...
OKAAAY...
PEARL PENALOSA...
PEARL PENALOSA...
I SEE...
...YOU A VERY STRONG WOMAN...
YOUR WORK IS VERY IMPORTANT TO YOU...
HMM... INTERESTING... SNIFF
IN YOUR FUTURE, I SEE...
...YOU SHALL FIND YOUR TRUE LOVE... WITHIN SEVEN DAYS.
OOH!
YOUR TRUE LOVE?!
NICE!
OH, PLEASE.
SO, WHAT'S HE GONNA LOOK LIKE? TALL, DARK, AND WELL-ENDOWED, MAYBE?
GOD, LIV...
HEHE.
I'M SORRY... THAT'S ALL I KNOW, BABY.
NOW... SNIFF ...THE MATTER OF PAYMENT?
UM... HOW MUCH IS IT GONNA BE?

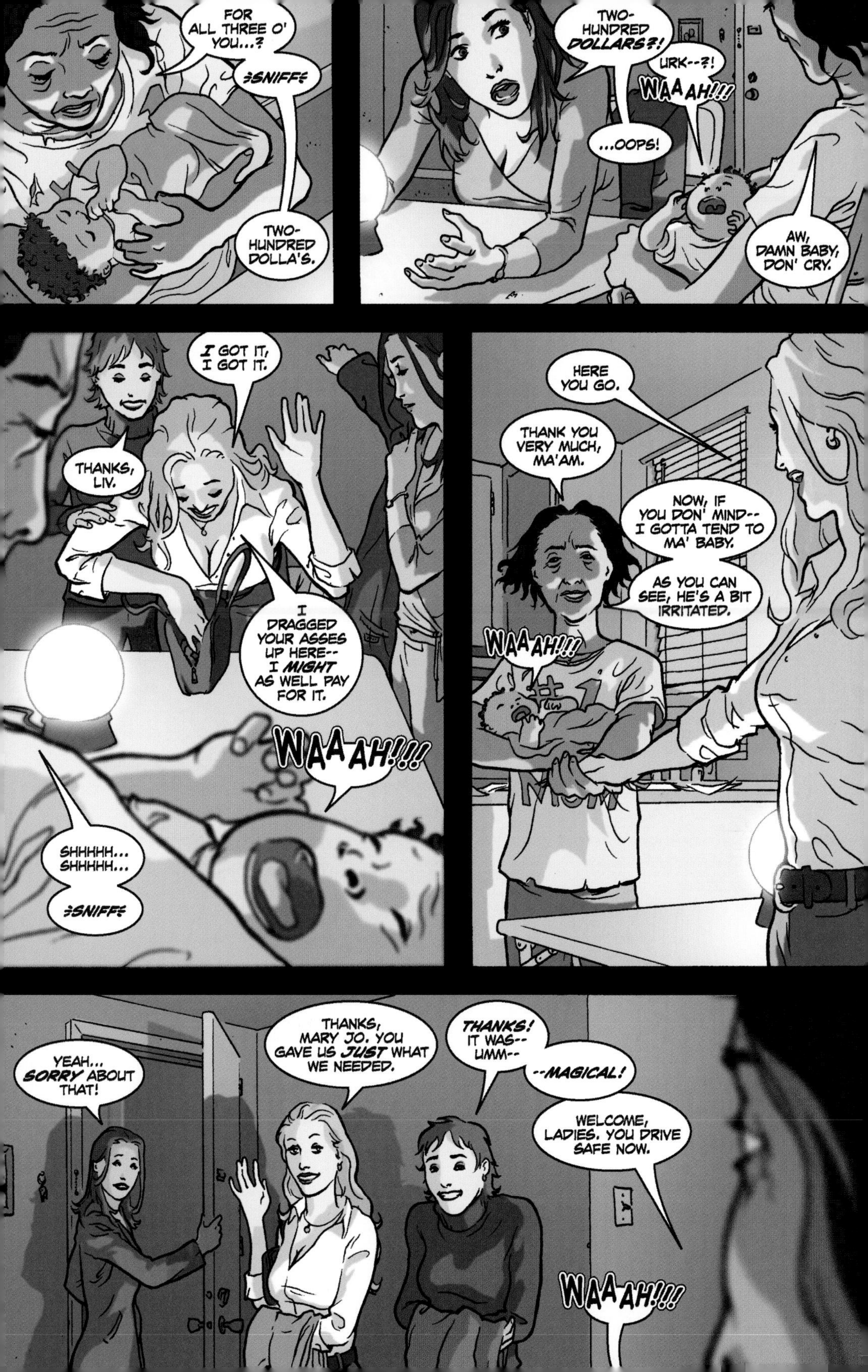
FOR ALL THREE O' YOU...?
SNIFF
TWO-HUNDRED DOLLA'S.
TWO-HUNDRED DOLLARS?!
...OOPS!
URK--?!
WAAAH!!!
AW, DAMN BABY, DON' CRY.
I GOT IT, I GOT IT.
THANKS, LIV.
I DRAGGED YOUR ASSES UP HERE-- I MIGHT AS WELL PAY FOR IT.
WAAAH!!!
SHHHHH... SHHHHH...
SNIFF
HERE YOU GO.
THANK YOU VERY MUCH, MA'AM.
NOW, IF YOU DON' MIND-- I GOTTA TEND TO MA' BABY.
AS YOU CAN SEE, HE'S A BIT IRRITATED.
WAAAH!!!
YEAH... SORRY ABOUT THAT!
THANKS, MARY JO. YOU GAVE US JUST WHAT WE NEEDED.
THANKS! IT WAS-- UMM--
--MAGICAL!
WELCOME, LADIES. YOU DRIVE SAFE NOW.
WAAAH!!!

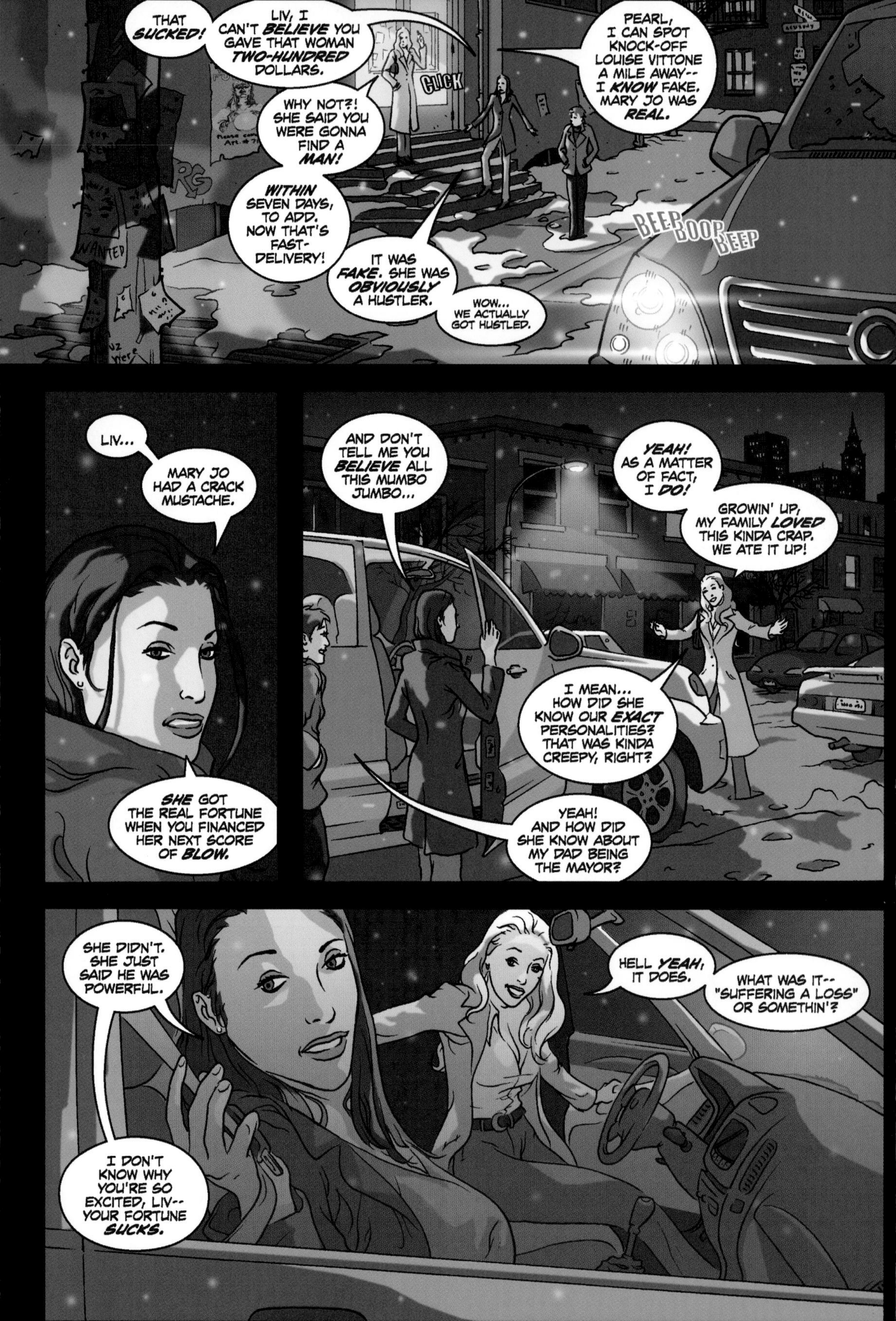

THAT SUCKED!
LIV, I CAN'T BELIEVE YOU GAVE THAT WOMAN TWO-HUNDRED DOLLARS.
CLICK
WHY NOT?! SHE SAID YOU WERE GONNA FIND A MAN!
WITHIN SEVEN DAYS, TO ADD. NOW THAT'S FAST-DELIVERY!
IT WAS FAKE. SHE WAS OBVIOUSLY A HUSTLER.
WOW... WE ACTUALLY GOT HUSTLED.
PEARL, I CAN SPOT KNOCK-OFF LOUISE VITTONE A MILE AWAY-- I KNOW FAKE. MARY JO WAS REAL.
BEEP BOOP BEEP
WANTED
LIV...
MARY JO HAD A CRACK MUSTACHE.
SHE GOT THE REAL FORTUNE WHEN YOU FINANCED HER NEXT SCORE OF BLOW.
AND DON'T TELL ME YOU BELIEVE ALL THIS MUMBO JUMBO...
YEAH! AS A MATTER OF FACT, I DO!
GROWIN' UP, MY FAMILY LOVED THIS KINDA CRAP. WE ATE IT UP!
I MEAN... HOW DID SHE KNOW OUR EXACT PERSONALITIES? THAT WAS KINDA CREEPY, RIGHT?
YEAH! AND HOW DID SHE KNOW ABOUT MY DAD BEING THE MAYOR?
SHE DIDN'T. SHE JUST SAID HE WAS POWERFUL.
HELL YEAH, IT DOES.
WHAT WAS IT-- "SUFFERING A LOSS" OR SOMETHIN'?
I DON'T KNOW WHY YOU'RE SO EXCITED, LIV-- YOUR FORTUNE SUCKS.

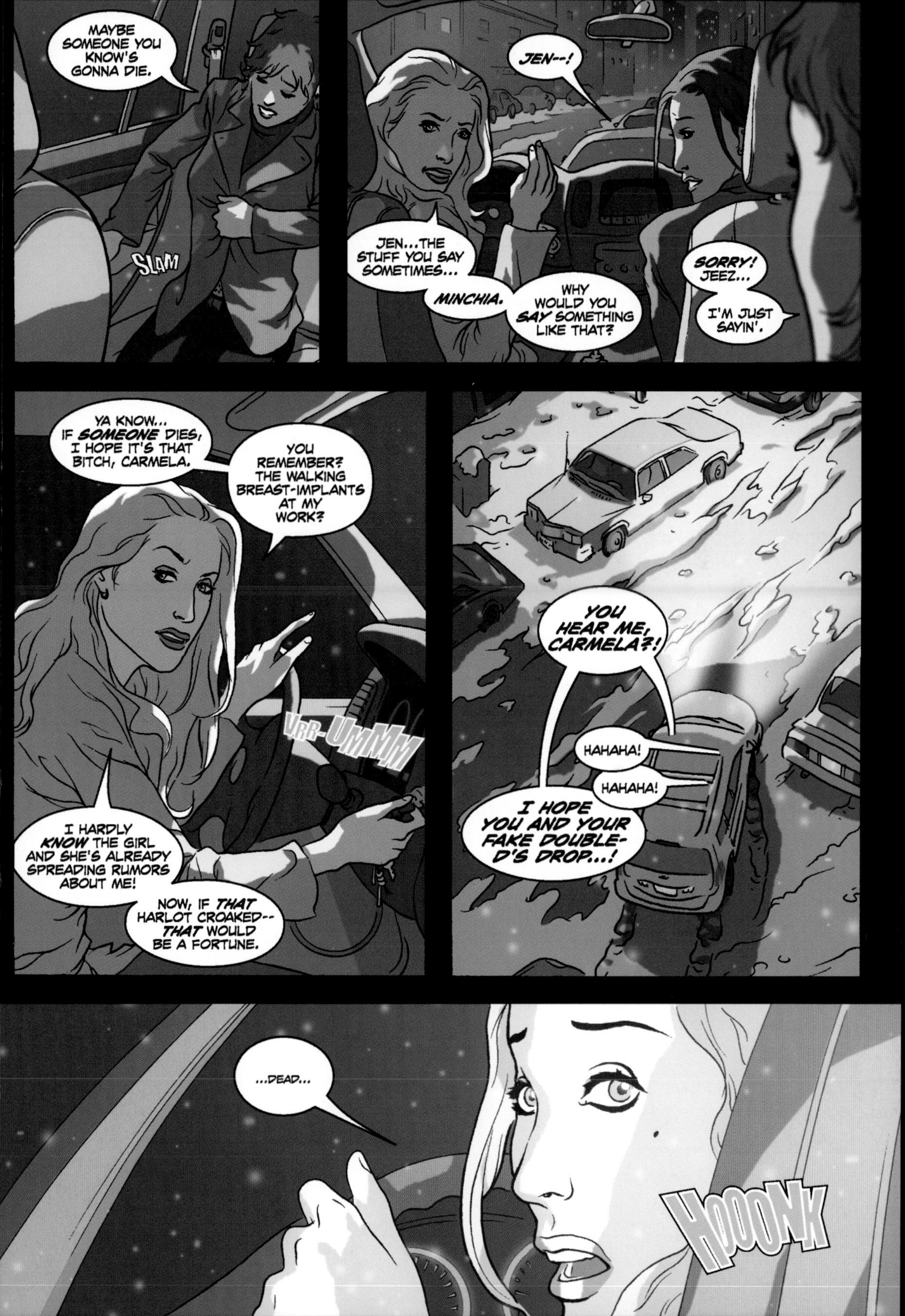
MAYBE SOMEONE YOU KNOW'S GONNA DIE.
SLAM
JEN--!
JEN...THE STUFF YOU SAY SOMETIMES...
MINCHIA.
WHY WOULD YOU SAY SOMETHING LIKE THAT?
SORRY! JEEZ...
I'M JUST SAYIN'.
YA KNOW... IF SOMEONE DIES, I HOPE IT'S THAT BITCH, CARMELA.
YOU REMEMBER? THE WALKING BREAST-IMPLANTS AT MY WORK?
VRR-UMMM
I HARDLY KNOW THE GIRL AND SHE'S ALREADY SPREADING RUMORS ABOUT ME!
NOW, IF THAT HARLOT CROAKED--THAT WOULD BE A FORTUNE.
YOU HEAR ME, CARMELA?!
HAHAHA!
HAHAHA!
I HOPE YOU AND YOUR FAKE DOUBLE-D'S DROP...!
...DEAD...
HOOONK

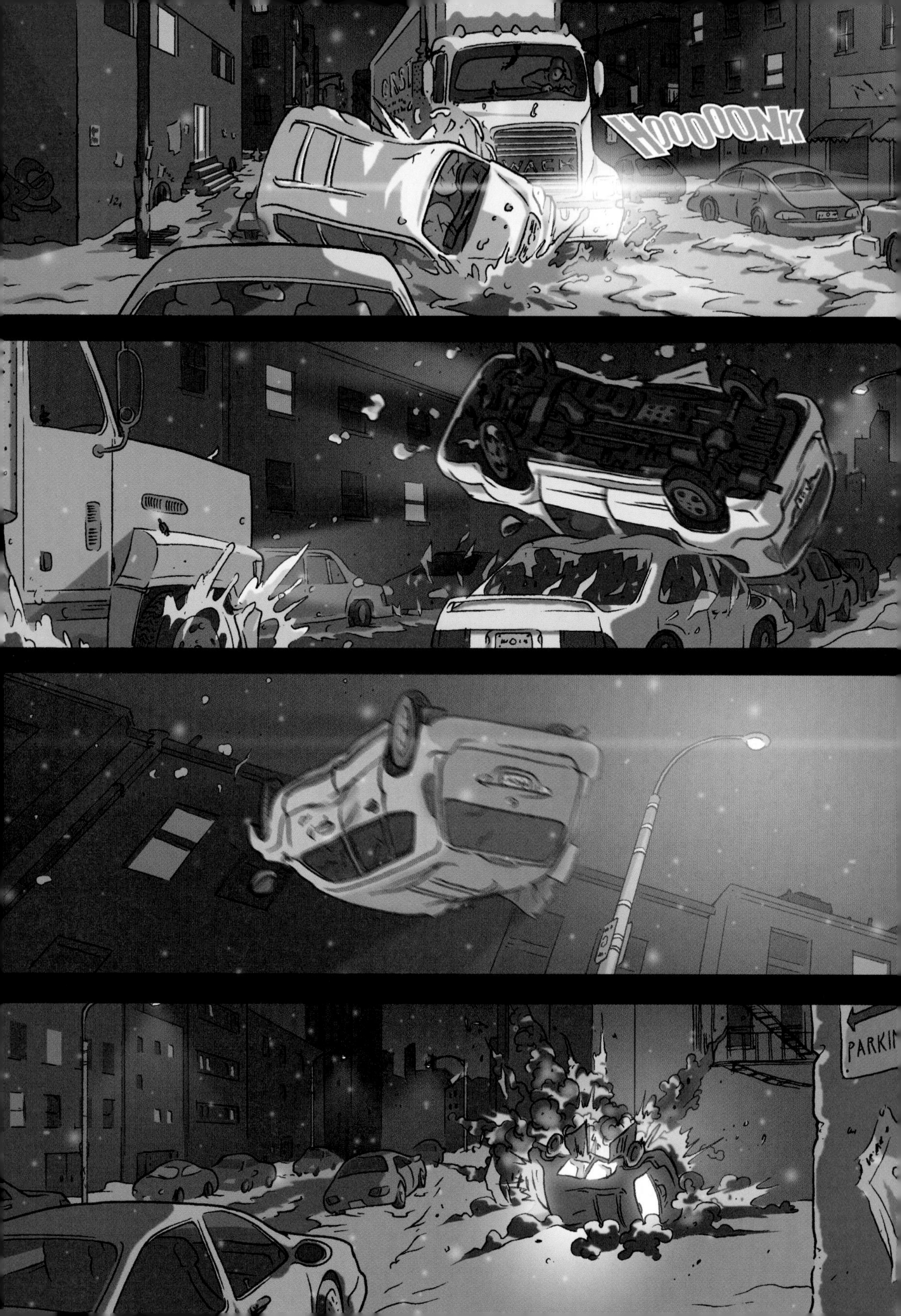
HOOOOONK
PARKIN

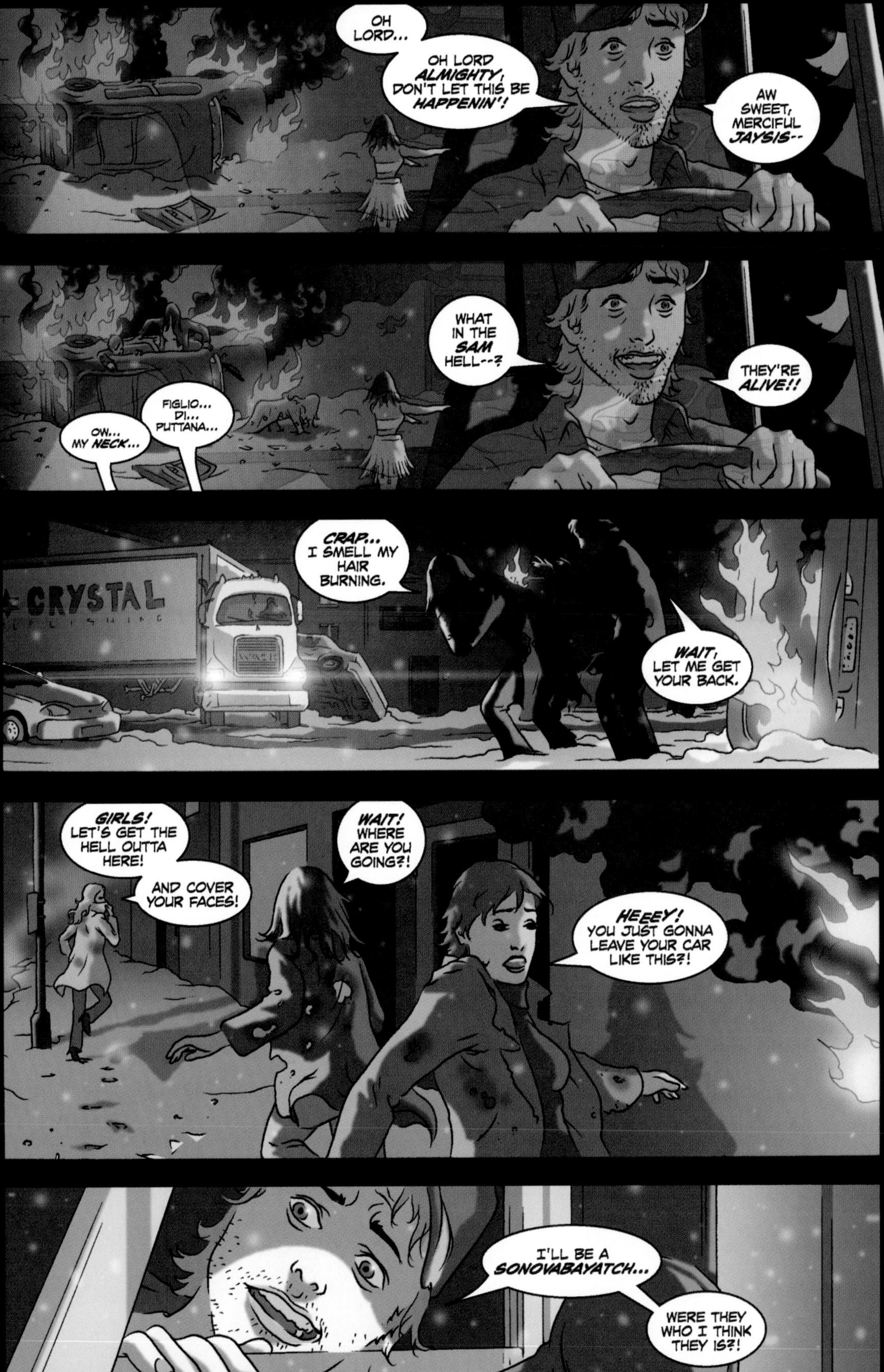
OH LORD...
OH LORD ALMIGHTY, DON'T LET THIS BE HAPPENIN'!
AW SWEET, MERCIFUL JAYSIS--
WHAT IN THE SAM HELL--?
THEY'RE ALIVE!!
FIGLIO... DI... PUTTANA...
OW... MY NECK...
CRYSTAL
CRAP... I SMELL MY HAIR BURNING.
WAIT, LET ME GET YOUR BACK.
GIRLS! LET'S GET THE HELL OUTTA HERE!
AND COVER YOUR FACES!
WAIT! WHERE ARE YOU GOING?!
HEEEY! YOU JUST GONNA LEAVE YOUR CAR LIKE THIS?!
I'LL BE A SONOVABAYATCH...
WERE THEY WHO I THINK THEY IS?!

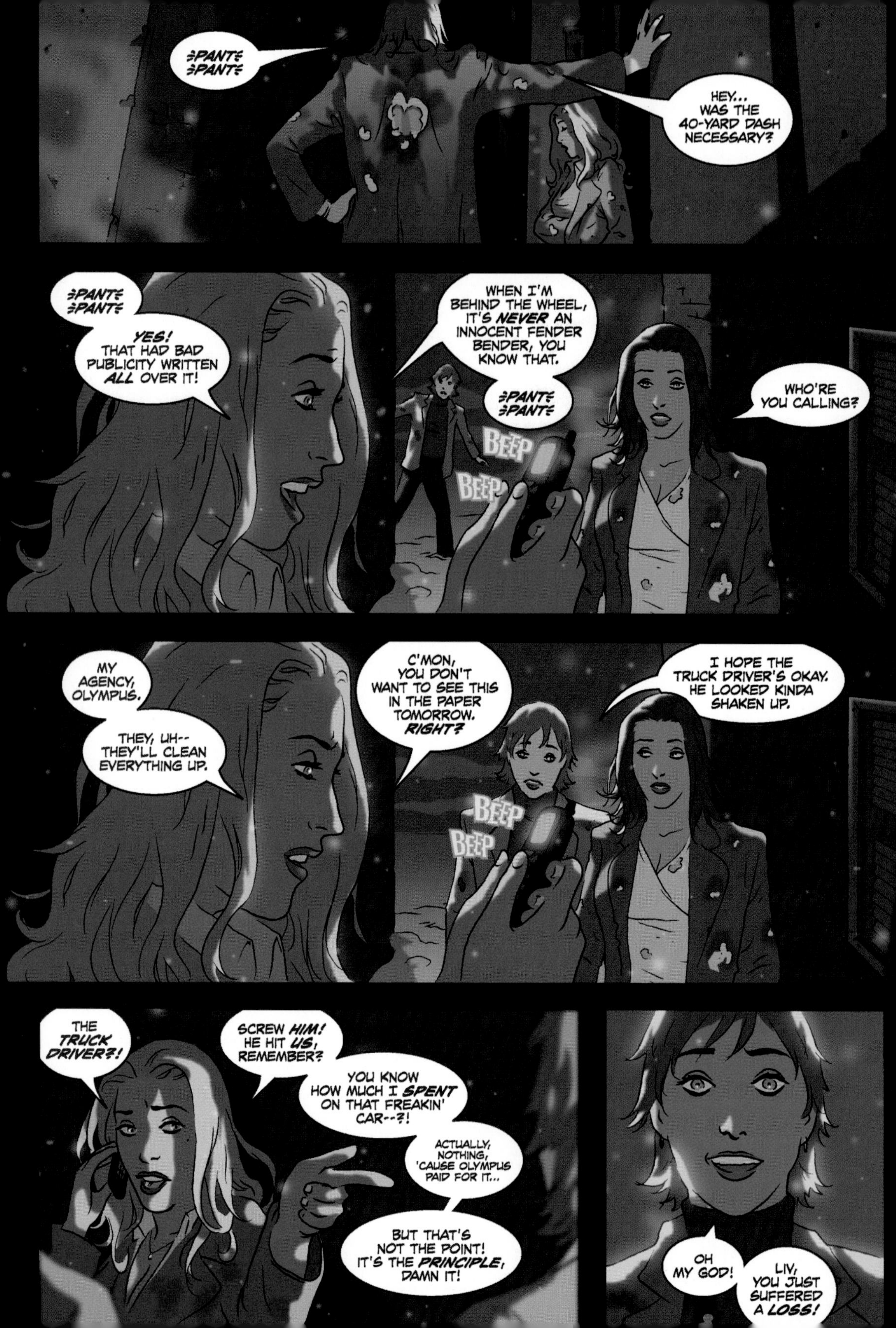

≥PANT≤ ≥PANT≤
HEY... WAS THE 40-YARD DASH NECESSARY?
≥PANT≤ ≥PANT≤
YES! THAT HAD BAD PUBLICITY WRITTEN ALL OVER IT!
WHEN I'M BEHIND THE WHEEL, IT'S NEVER AN INNOCENT FENDER BENDER, YOU KNOW THAT.
≥PANT≤ ≥PANT≤
BEEP
BEEP
WHO'RE YOU CALLING?
MY AGENCY, OLYMPUS.
THEY, UH-- THEY'LL CLEAN EVERYTHING UP.
C'MON, YOU DON'T WANT TO SEE THIS IN THE PAPER TOMORROW. RIGHT?
BEEP
BEEP
I HOPE THE TRUCK DRIVER'S OKAY. HE LOOKED KINDA SHAKEN UP.
THE TRUCK DRIVER?!
SCREW HIM! HE HIT US, REMEMBER?
YOU KNOW HOW MUCH I SPENT ON THAT FREAKIN' CAR--?!
ACTUALLY, NOTHING, 'CAUSE OLYMPUS PAID FOR IT...
BUT THAT'S NOT THE POINT! IT'S THE PRINCIPLE, DAMN IT!
OH MY GOD!
LIV, YOU JUST SUFFERED A LOSS!

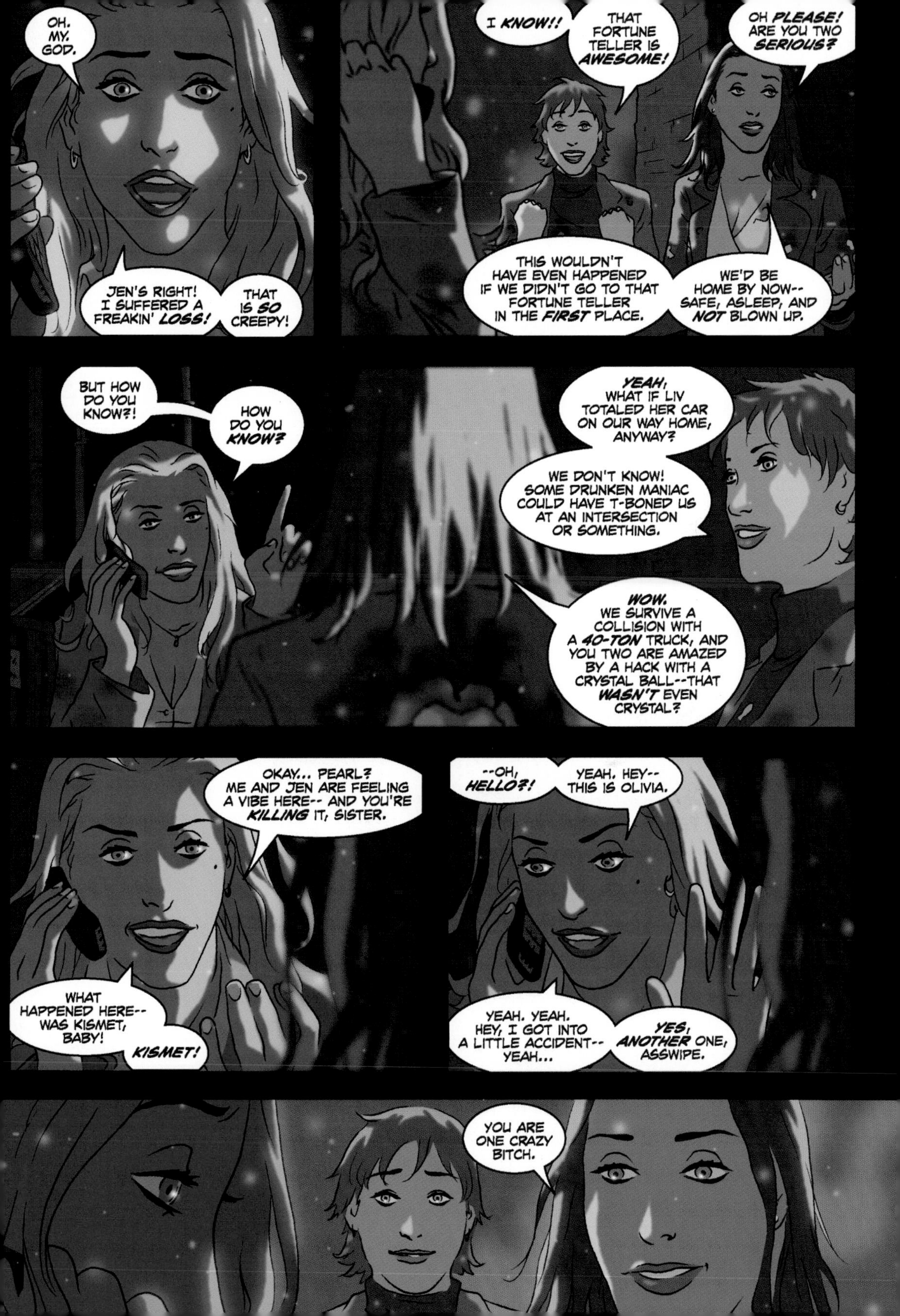
OH. MY. GOD.
JEN'S RIGHT! I SUFFERED A FREAKIN' LOSS!
THAT IS SO CREEPY!
I KNOW!!
THAT FORTUNE TELLER IS AWESOME!
OH PLEASE! ARE YOU TWO SERIOUS?
THIS WOULDN'T HAVE EVEN HAPPENED IF WE DIDN'T GO TO THAT FORTUNE TELLER IN THE FIRST PLACE.
WE'D BE HOME BY NOW-- SAFE, ASLEEP, AND NOT BLOWN UP.
BUT HOW DO YOU KNOW?!
HOW DO YOU KNOW?
YEAH, WHAT IF LIV TOTALED HER CAR ON OUR WAY HOME, ANYWAY?
WE DON'T KNOW! SOME DRUNKEN MANIAC COULD HAVE T-BONED US AT AN INTERSECTION OR SOMETHING.
WOW. WE SURVIVE A COLLISION WITH A 40-TON TRUCK, AND YOU TWO ARE AMAZED BY A HACK WITH A CRYSTAL BALL--THAT WASN'T EVEN CRYSTAL?
OKAY... PEARL? ME AND JEN ARE FEELING A VIBE HERE-- AND YOU'RE KILLING IT, SISTER.
WHAT HAPPENED HERE-- WAS KISMET, BABY!
KISMET!
--OH, HELLO?!
YEAH. HEY-- THIS IS OLIVIA.
YEAH. YEAH. HEY, I GOT INTO A LITTLE ACCIDENT-- YEAH...
YES, ANOTHER ONE, ASSWIPE.
YOU ARE ONE CRAZY BITCH.

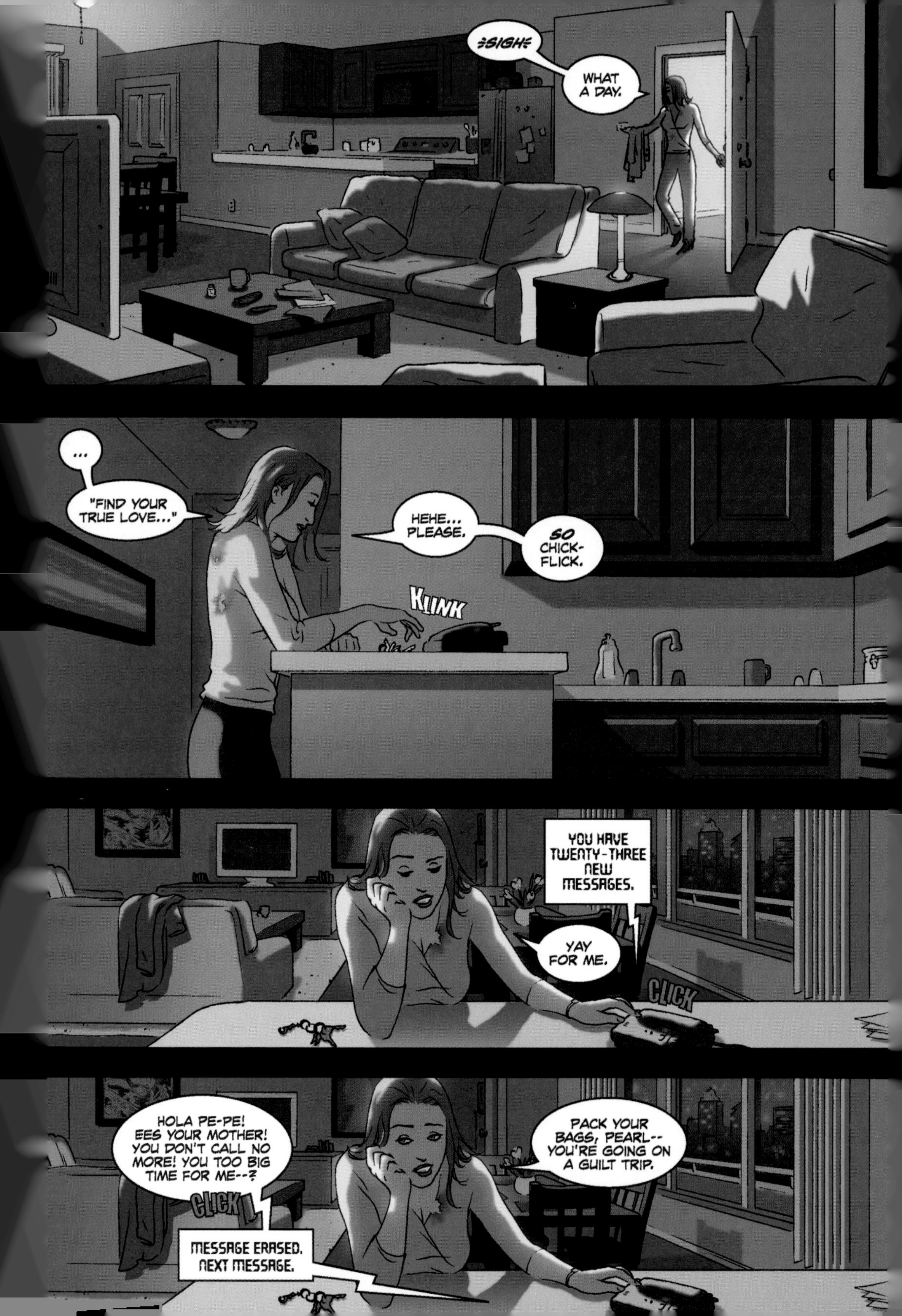

SIGH
WHAT A DAY.
...
"FIND YOUR TRUE LOVE..."
HEHE... PLEASE.
SO CHICK-FLICK.
KLINK
YOU HAVE TWENTY-THREE NEW MESSAGES.
YAY FOR ME.
CLICK
HOLA PE-PE! EES YOUR MOTHER! YOU DON'T CALL NO MORE! YOU TOO BIG TIME FOR ME--?
CLICK
MESSAGE ERASED. NEXT MESSAGE.
PACK YOUR BAGS, PEARL-- YOU'RE GOING ON A GUILT TRIP.

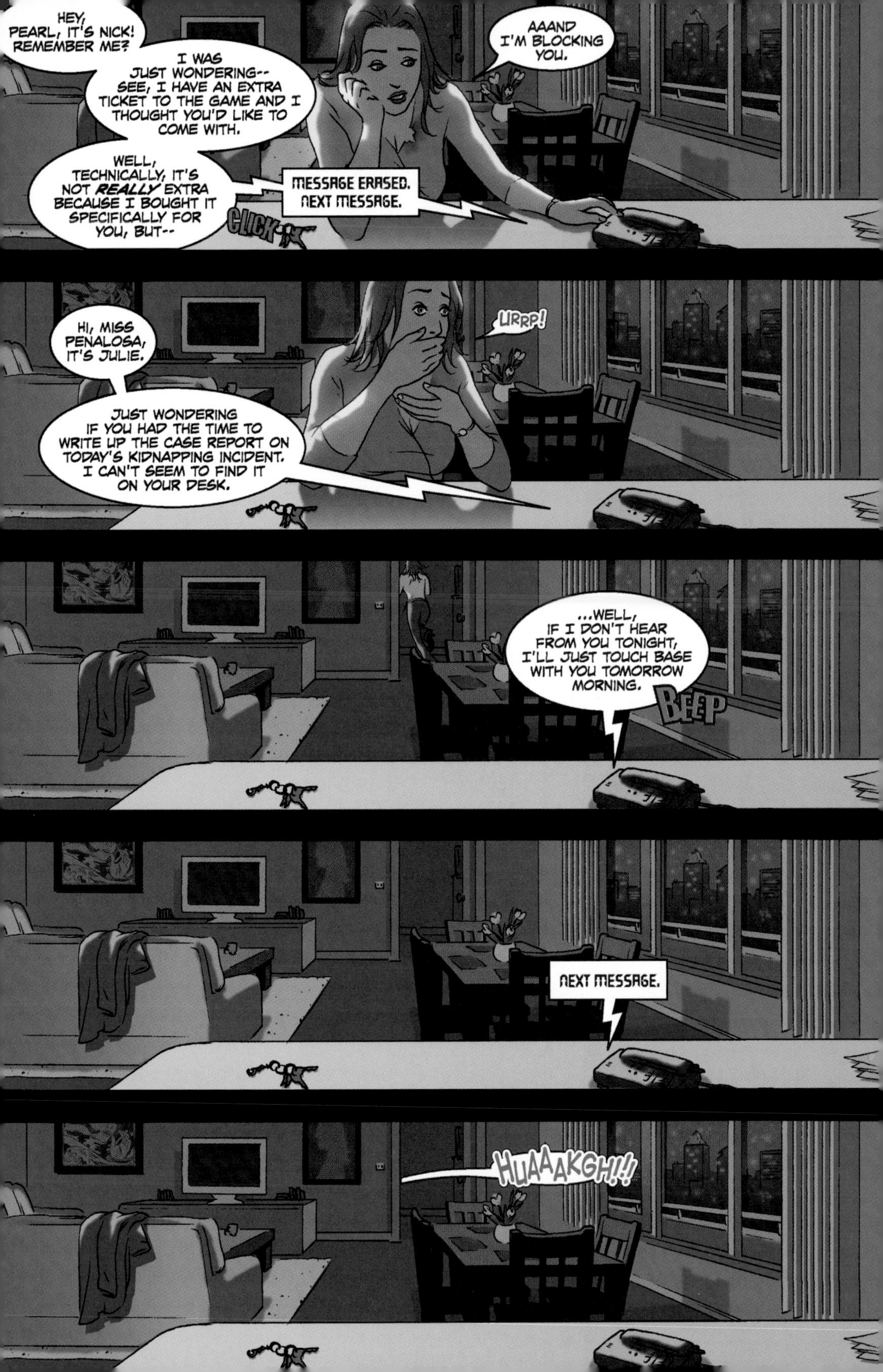
HEY, PEARL, IT'S NICK! REMEMBER ME?
I WAS JUST WONDERING-- SEE, I HAVE AN EXTRA TICKET TO THE GAME AND I THOUGHT YOU'D LIKE TO COME WITH.
WELL, TECHNICALLY, IT'S NOT REALLY EXTRA BECAUSE I BOUGHT IT SPECIFICALLY FOR YOU, BUT--
CLICK
MESSAGE ERASED. NEXT MESSAGE.
AAAND I'M BLOCKING YOU.
HI, MISS PENALOSA, IT'S JULIE.
JUST WONDERING IF YOU HAD THE TIME TO WRITE UP THE CASE REPORT ON TODAY'S KIDNAPPING INCIDENT. I CAN'T SEEM TO FIND IT ON YOUR DESK.
URRP!
...WELL, IF I DON'T HEAR FROM YOU TONIGHT, I'LL JUST TOUCH BASE WITH YOU TOMORROW MORNING.
BEEP
NEXT MESSAGE.
HUAAAKGH!!!

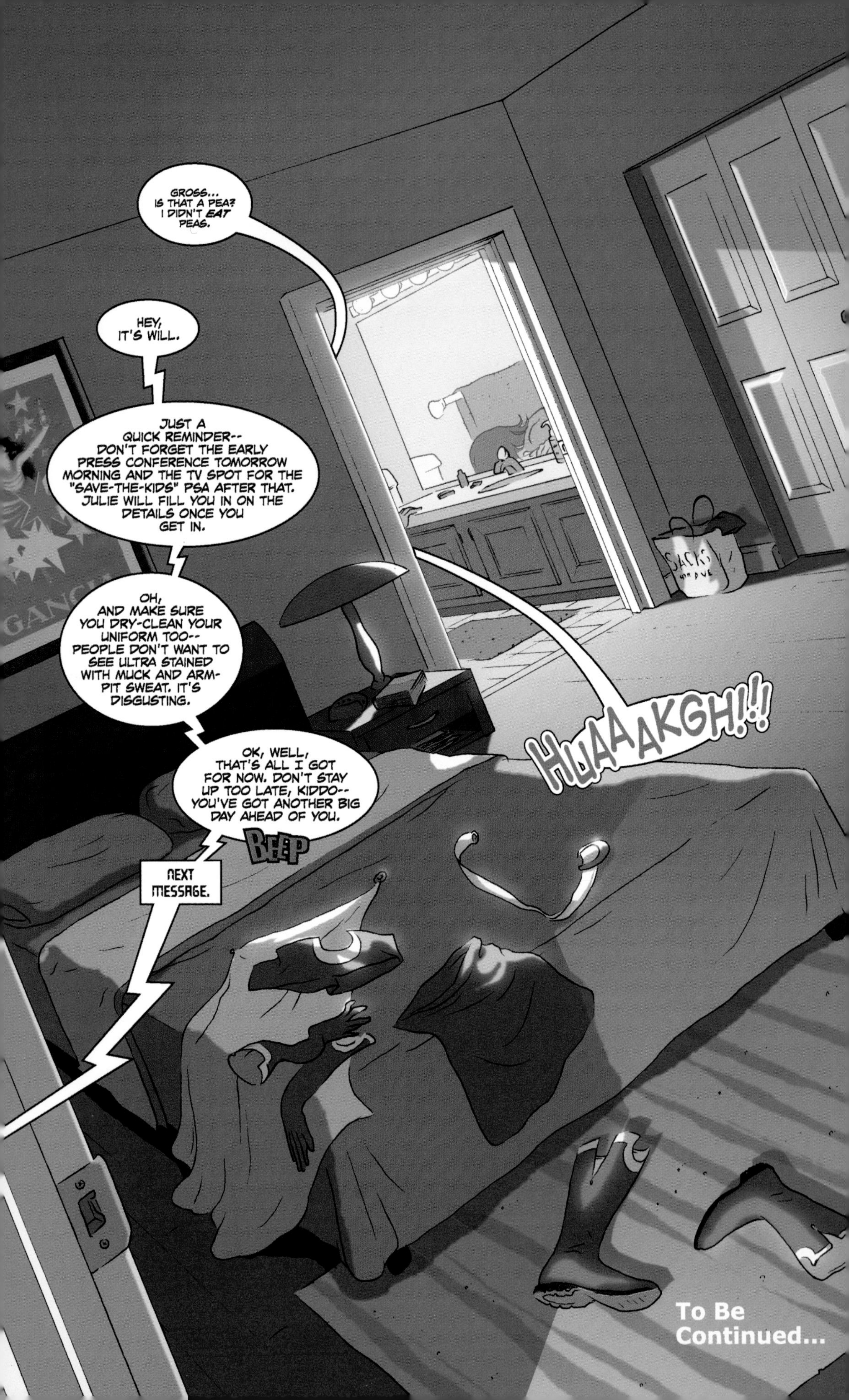
HEY, IT'S WILL.
JUST A QUICK REMINDER-- DON'T FORGET THE EARLY PRESS CONFERENCE TOMORROW MORNING AND THE TV SPOT FOR THE "SAVE-THE-KIDS" PSA AFTER THAT. JULIE WILL FILL YOU IN ON THE DETAILS ONCE YOU GET IN.
OH, AND MAKE SURE YOU DRY-CLEAN YOUR UNIFORM TOO-- PEOPLE DON'T WANT TO SEE ULTRA STAINED WITH MUCK AND ARM-PIT SWEAT. IT'S DISGUSTING.
OK, WELL, THAT'S ALL I GOT FOR NOW. DON'T STAY UP TOO LATE, KIDDO-- YOU'VE GOT ANOTHER BIG DAY AHEAD OF YOU.
BEEEP
NEXT MESSAGE.
GROSS... IS THAT A PEA? I DIDN'T EAT PEAS.
HUAAAKGH!!!
To Be Continued...

10 ANSWERS FROM
ULTRA

DAY IN AND DAY OUT, OUR SENSORY FORTITUDES ARE assaulted, challenged and trial-tested by the superhero media epidemic that perpetually satiates our nation's star-struck appetites. So why do we insist on second servings? Whether it be the perilous exploits, water-cooler rumors of scandalous romps, tantalizing billboard-spreads on 66th and Lexington, or the impossibly, congenial caped-crusader silk-screened onto your child's jammies, their presence is ubiquitous and, dare I say, contagious. Pearl Penalosa, AKA Ultra, the superhero world's latest "It Girl," reminds us why the masses just can't get enough of those titans-in-tights. Rebecca Hurt sits down with Ultra.

PHOTO BY JONATHAN LUNA

The Editor in Chief of Mutant Magazine recently praised your tireless campaign against the escalating gang activity in Spring City saying, "For those unfortunate enough to face Ultra in mortal combat, I pity you. This chick is one tough bitch." How do you respond to this rather, aggressive portrayal?
Well, I'm flattered by the vote of confidence there, but my intent was never to invoke that type of fear into people. It's a big cliché, but I really believe that with more power, comes more responsibility; so when my abilities come into play, they're reserved for extreme, emergency situations only. Our agency works very closely with local and federal law enforcement to ensure proper procedure and safety on all fronts. So yeah, I'd prefer the title "Safe Bitch" instead.

———

Do you feel the media's portrayal of superheroes teeters on the two-dimensional?
It's understandable. See, we're naturally misunderstood so the general consensus of superheroes will always be wrapped in a proverbial question mark. We're different and people don't really know us yet. The underwear-over-the-pants doesn't help matters either. But it's really refreshing to see more and more open-minded film makers or television execs take a stab at more intimate portraits of real, superhero life. Take that indy film "Supermoron" for example. That was moving stuff.

———

You, like many other superheroes, are open with your true identity and reject the conventional methods of anonymous crime-fighting such as dual identities, split personalities, masks, etc. This act of unveiling ultimately broke a cultural wall between our worlds and advanced the superhero movement. Was this a conscious effort on your part?
Not exactly. Being a female, Hispanic Superhero--a triple minority--I can sympathize with superhumans who continue to deconstruct stereotypes, but my reasons for going public were more about personal preference.

See, I don't do masks because: A, they mess up my hair and B, they kinda creep me out--too "serial-killer." Secret identities are out of the question as well. I mean, what am I gonna do--put on a pair of coke-bottle glasses and expect to fool people?

———

And do you ever resent the ones who choose not to follow suit?
Oh no. Anonymity isn't frowned upon in my book. As long as the individual is registered and abides lawfully by the superhero code, identity should remain a personal issue. People wear masks for all kinds of different reasons.

———

Let's face it. People love you. Although your scope of appeal reaches all demographics, you seem to cater largely to the younger, 16-30 female audiences. In fact, two teenagers in Columbus, Ohio, were so obsessed with you, they attempted to "fly" by leaping off an eight story building.
Yeah, I heard about that. My prayers and condolences go out to the victims and their families. But seriously, kids, if you can't fly-- don't.

———

I was preparing my next question when Ultra abruptly excused herself to save a small boy, trapped inside a mining well in rural Spring City.
Yeah. Seriously. ∎

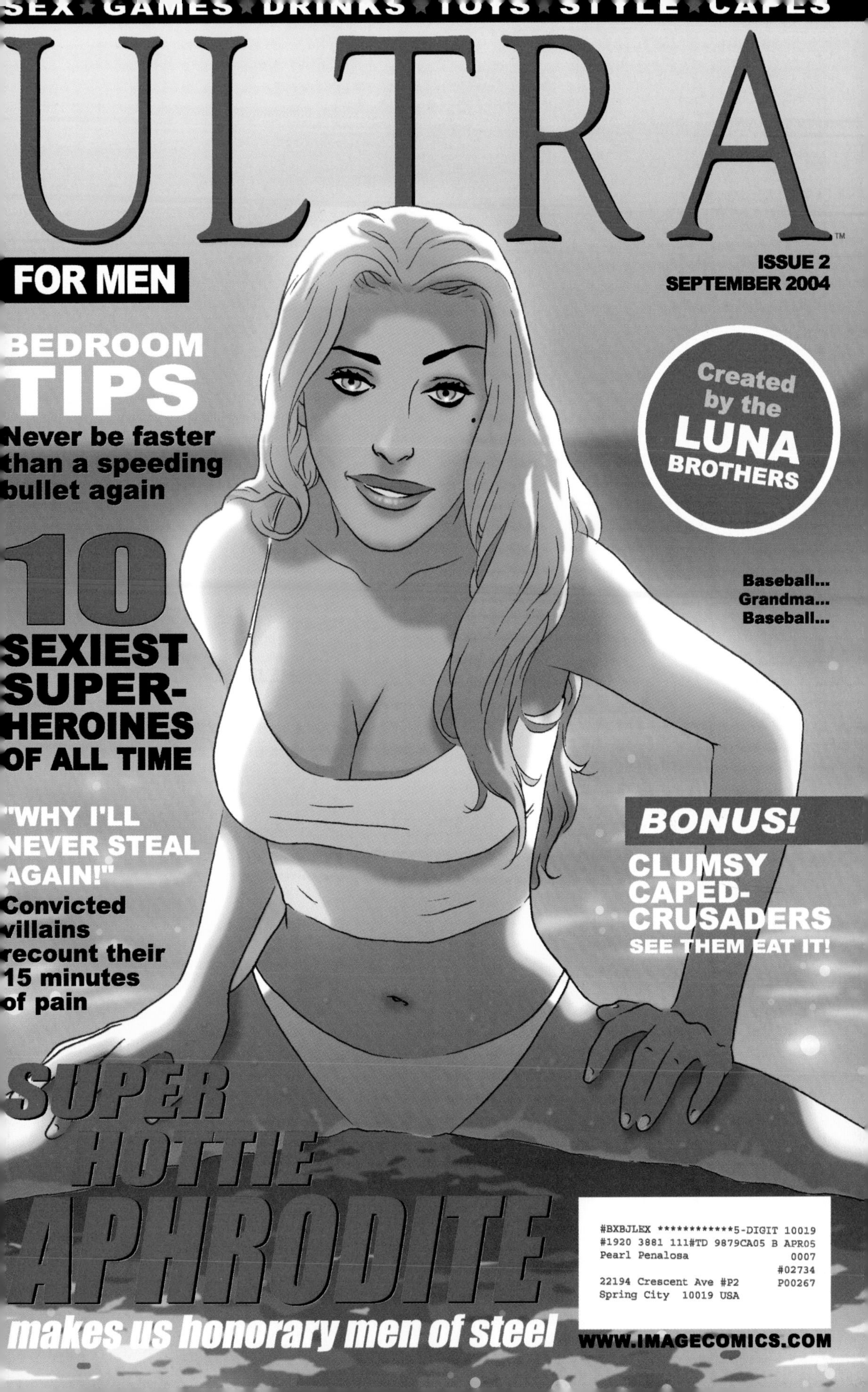
SEX ★ GAMES ★ DRINKS ★ TOYS ★ STYLE ★ CAPES
ULTRA™
FOR MEN
ISSUE 2
SEPTEMBER 2004
BEDROOM TIPS
Never be faster than a speeding bullet again
Created by the LUNA BROTHERS
10 SEXIEST SUPER-HEROINES OF ALL TIME
Baseball...
Grandma...
Baseball...
"WHY I'LL NEVER STEAL AGAIN!"
Convicted villains recount their 15 minutes of pain
BONUS!
CLUMSY CAPED-CRUSADERS
SEE THEM EAT IT!
SUPER HOTTIE APHRODITE
makes us honorary men of steel
#BXBJLEX ************5-DIGIT 10019
#1920 3881 111#TD 9879CA05 B APR05
Pearl Penalosa 0007
#02734
22194 Crescent Ave #P2 P00267
Spring City 10019 USA
WWW.IMAGECOMICS.COM

image® COMICS PRESENTS

119

FEMME FATALES

Meet the
10 sexiest
superheroines
of all time.

"Up, up, and--
aw crap!"
p.150

Superheroes-
turned-80's
revival
rock
stars.
p.160

"I think they
plugged my
guitar into the
wrong hole!"

Green, with
superhero
envy.
p.158

THIS ISSUE
3 SEVEN DAYS, PART TWO

CREATED BY
112 THE LUNA BROTHERS

CREDITS
114 JONATHAN LUNA
Plot, Artist, Colorist, Letterer
114 JOSHUA LUNA
Writer, Layout Assists

OFFICIAL WEBSITE
120 www.LunaBrothers.com

For Image Comics

Erik Larsen - Publisher
Todd McFarlane - President
Marc Silvestri - CEO
Jim Valentino - Vice-President

Eric Stephenson - Executive Director
Missie Miranda - Controller
Brett Evans - Production Manager
B. Clay Moore - PR & Marketing
　Coordinator
Allen Hui - Production Artist
Joe Keatinge - Inventory
　Controller
Mia Machatton - Administrative
　Assistant

www.imagecomics.com

Caption Contest Winner - Brian Hogg

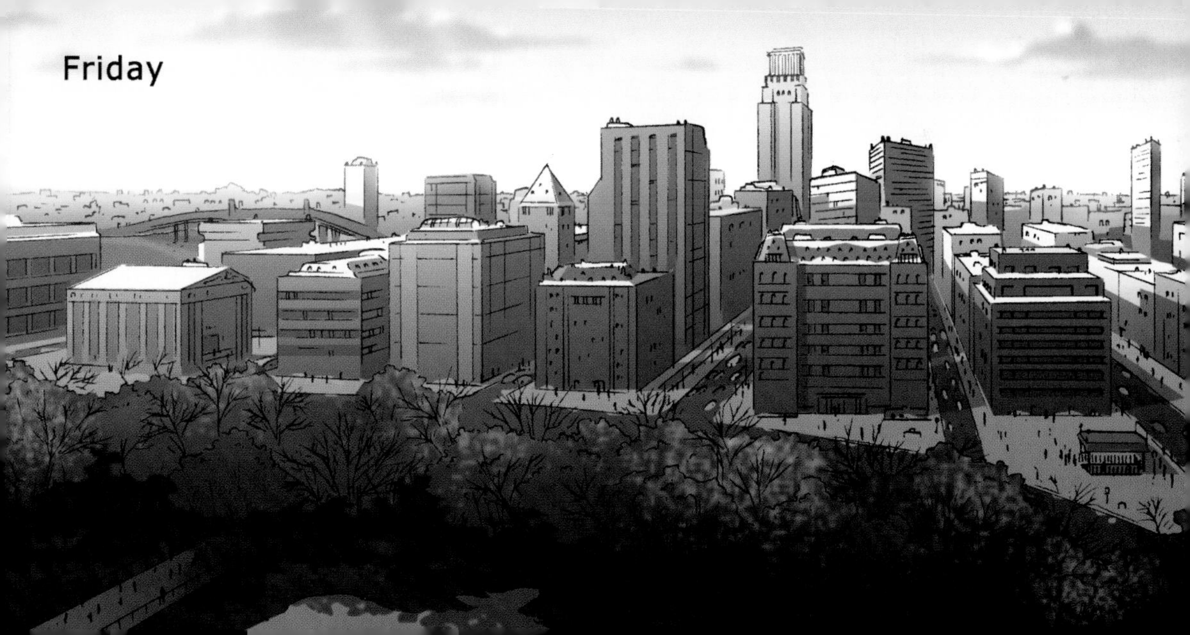
Friday

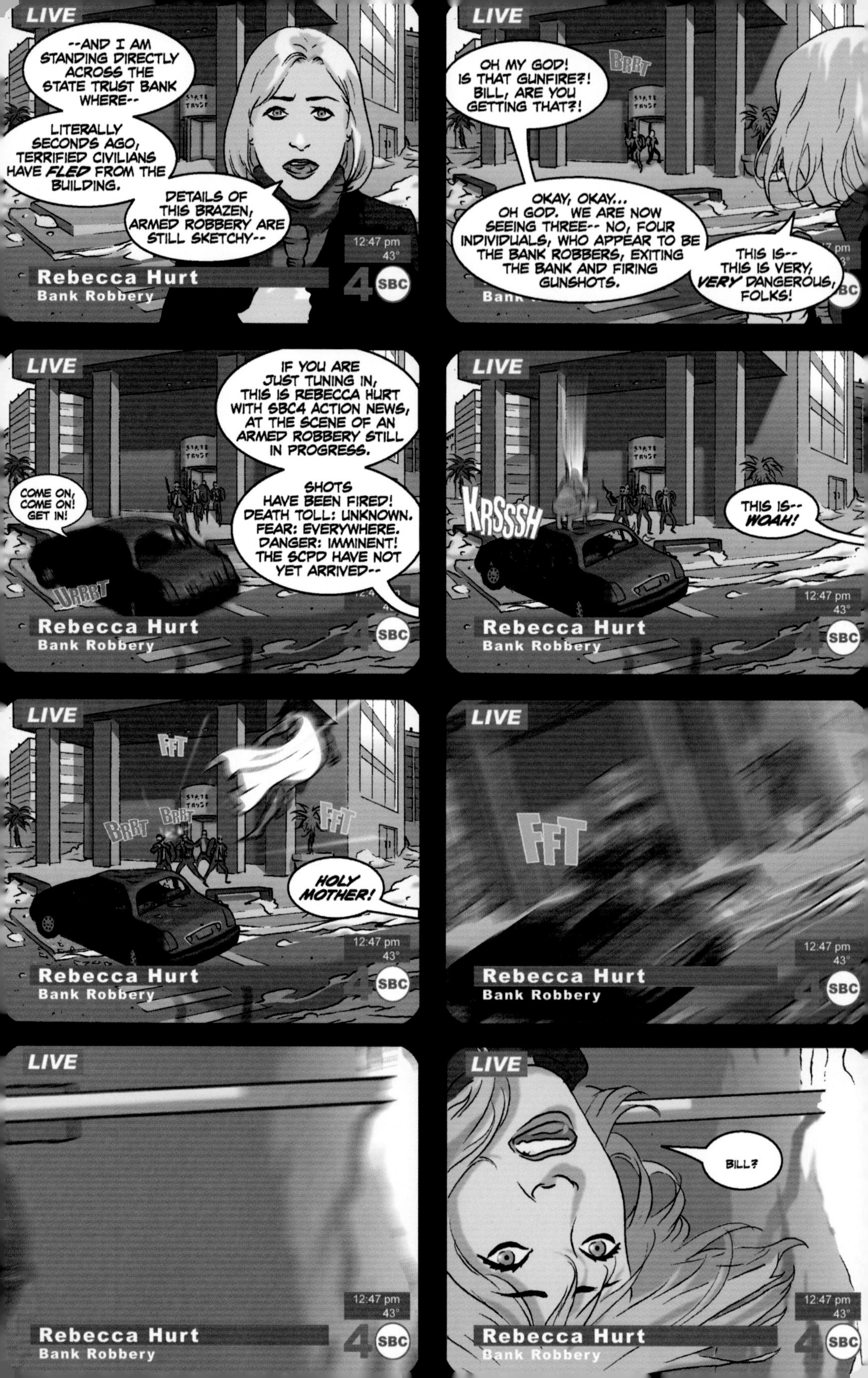
LIVE
--AND I AM STANDING DIRECTLY ACROSS THE STATE TRUST BANK WHERE--
LITERALLY SECONDS AGO, TERRIFIED CIVILIANS HAVE FLED FROM THE BUILDING.
DETAILS OF THIS BRAZEN, ARMED ROBBERY ARE STILL SKETCHY--
12:47 pm
43°
Rebecca Hurt
Bank Robbery
4 SBC
LIVE
OH MY GOD! IS THAT GUNFIRE?! BILL, ARE YOU GETTING THAT?!
BRRT
OKAY, OKAY... OH GOD. WE ARE NOW SEEING THREE-- NO, FOUR INDIVIDUALS, WHO APPEAR TO BE THE BANK ROBBERS, EXITING THE BANK AND FIRING GUNSHOTS.
THIS IS-- THIS IS VERY, VERY DANGEROUS, FOLKS!
LIVE
IF YOU ARE JUST TUNING IN, THIS IS REBECCA HURT WITH SBC4 ACTION NEWS, AT THE SCENE OF AN ARMED ROBBERY STILL IN PROGRESS.
COME ON, COME ON! GET IN!
SHOTS HAVE BEEN FIRED! DEATH TOLL: UNKNOWN. FEAR: EVERYWHERE. DANGER: IMMINENT! THE SCPD HAVE NOT YET ARRIVED--
URRRT
Rebecca Hurt
Bank Robbery
SBC
LIVE
KRSSSH
THIS IS-- WOAH!
12:47 pm
43°
Rebecca Hurt
Bank Robbery
SBC
LIVE
FFT
BRRT
BRRT
FFT
HOLY MOTHER!
12:47 pm
43°
Rebecca Hurt
Bank Robbery
SBC
LIVE
FFT
12:47 pm
43°
Rebecca Hurt
Bank Robbery
SBC
LIVE
12:47 pm
43°
Rebecca Hurt
Bank Robbery
4 SBC
LIVE
BILL?
12:47 pm
43°
Rebecca Hurt
Bank Robbery
4 SBC

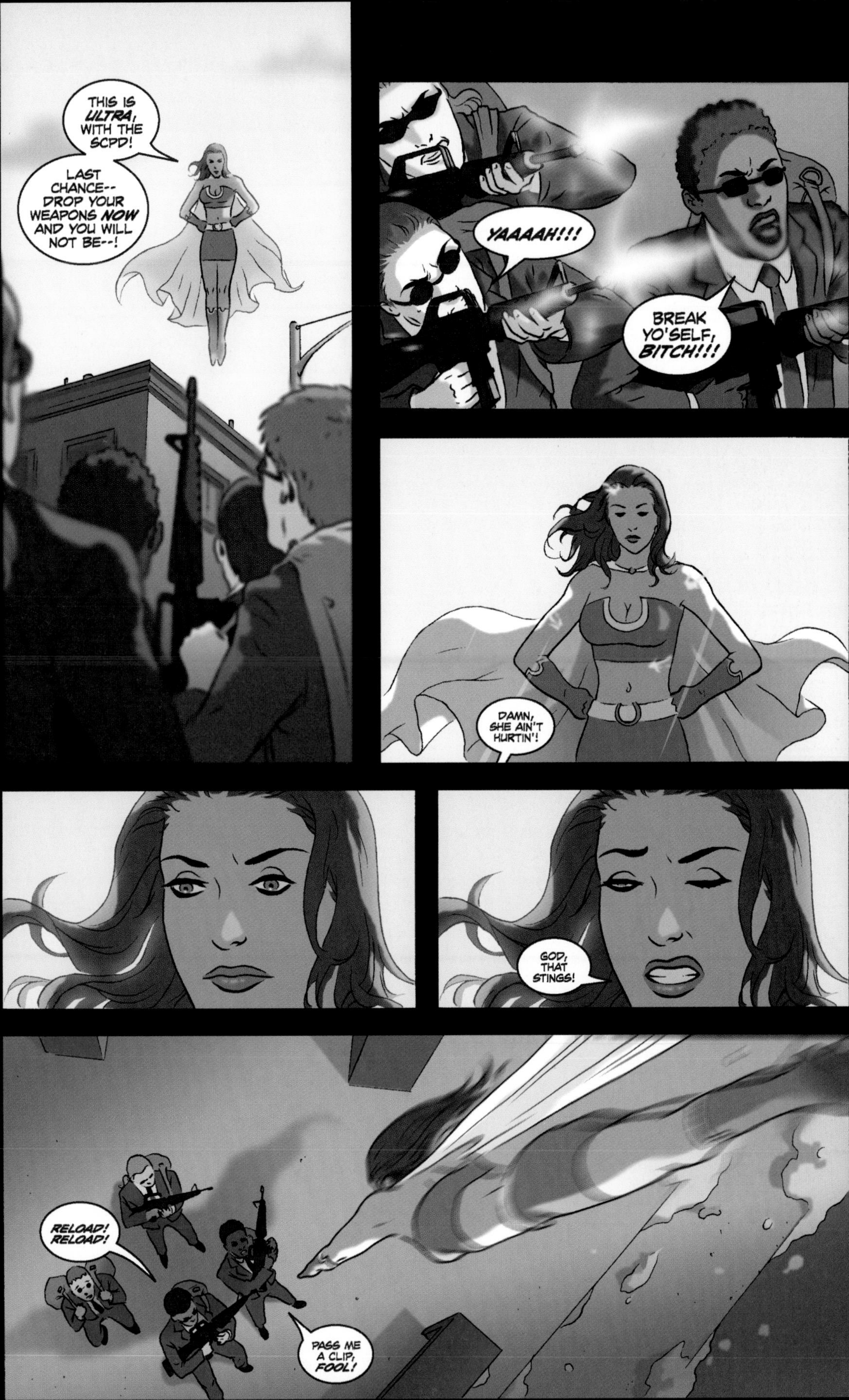
THIS IS *ULTRA*, WITH THE SCPD!
LAST CHANCE-- DROP YOUR WEAPONS *NOW* AND YOU WILL NOT BE--!
YAAAAH!!!
BREAK YO'SELF, *BITCH!!!*
DAMN, SHE AIN'T HURTIN'!
GOD, THAT STINGS!
RELOAD! RELOAD!
PASS ME A CLIP, *FOOL!*

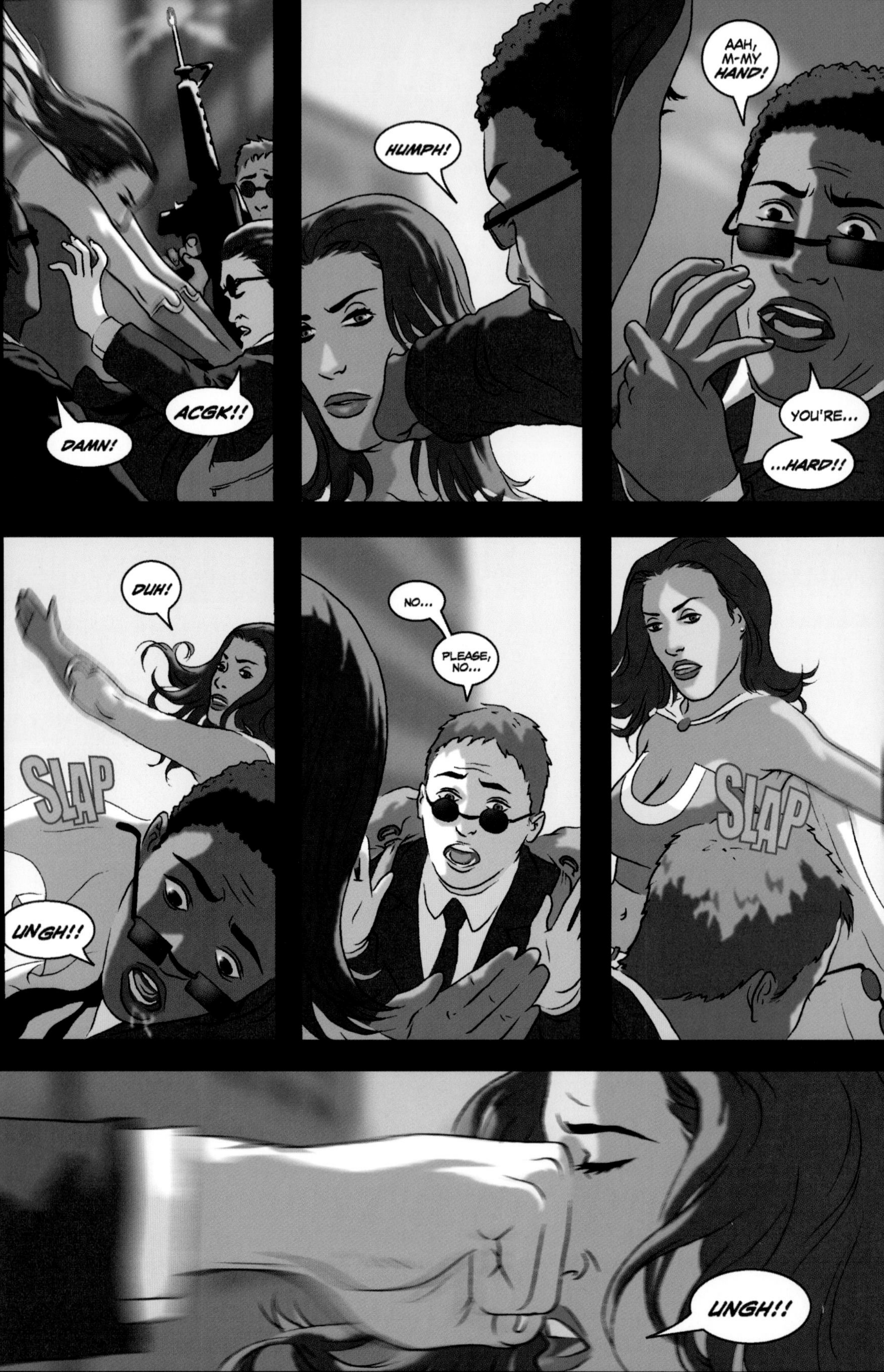
ACGK!!
DAMN!
HUMPH!
AAH, M-MY HAND!
YOU'RE...
...HARD!!
DUH!
SLAP
UNGH!!
NO...
PLEASE, NO...
SLAP
UNGH!!

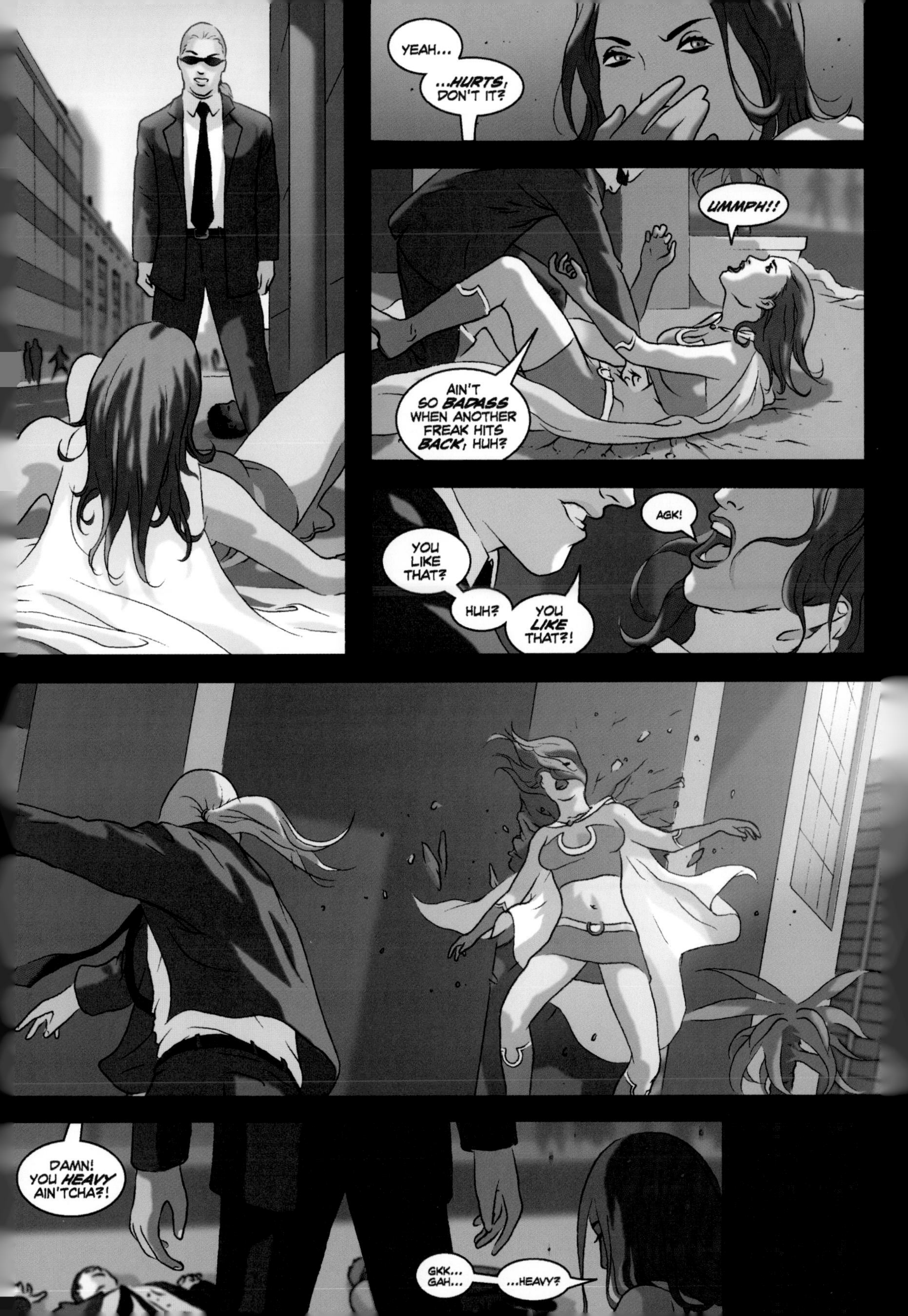
YEAH...
...HURTS, DON'T IT?
UMMPH!!
AIN'T SO BADASS WHEN ANOTHER FREAK HITS BACK, HUH?
AGK!
YOU LIKE THAT?
HUH?
YOU LIKE THAT?!
DAMN! YOU HEAVY AIN'TCHA?!
GKK... GAH...
...HEAVY?

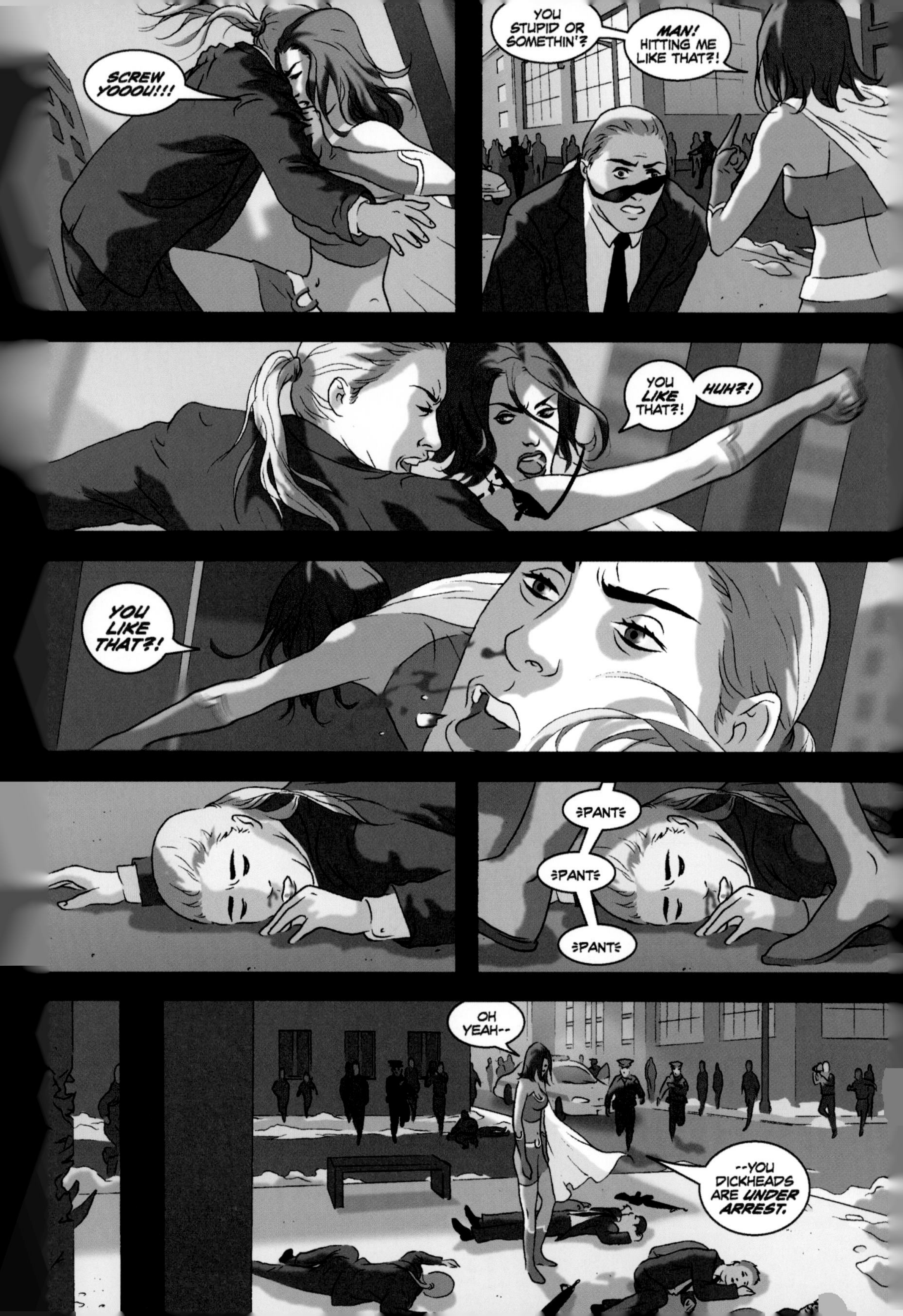
SCREW YOOOU!!!
YOU STUPID OR SOMETHIN'?
MAN! HITTING ME LIKE THAT?!
YOU LIKE THAT?!
HUH?!
YOU LIKE THAT?!
PANT
PANT
PANT
OH YEAH--
--YOU DICKHEADS ARE UNDER ARREST.

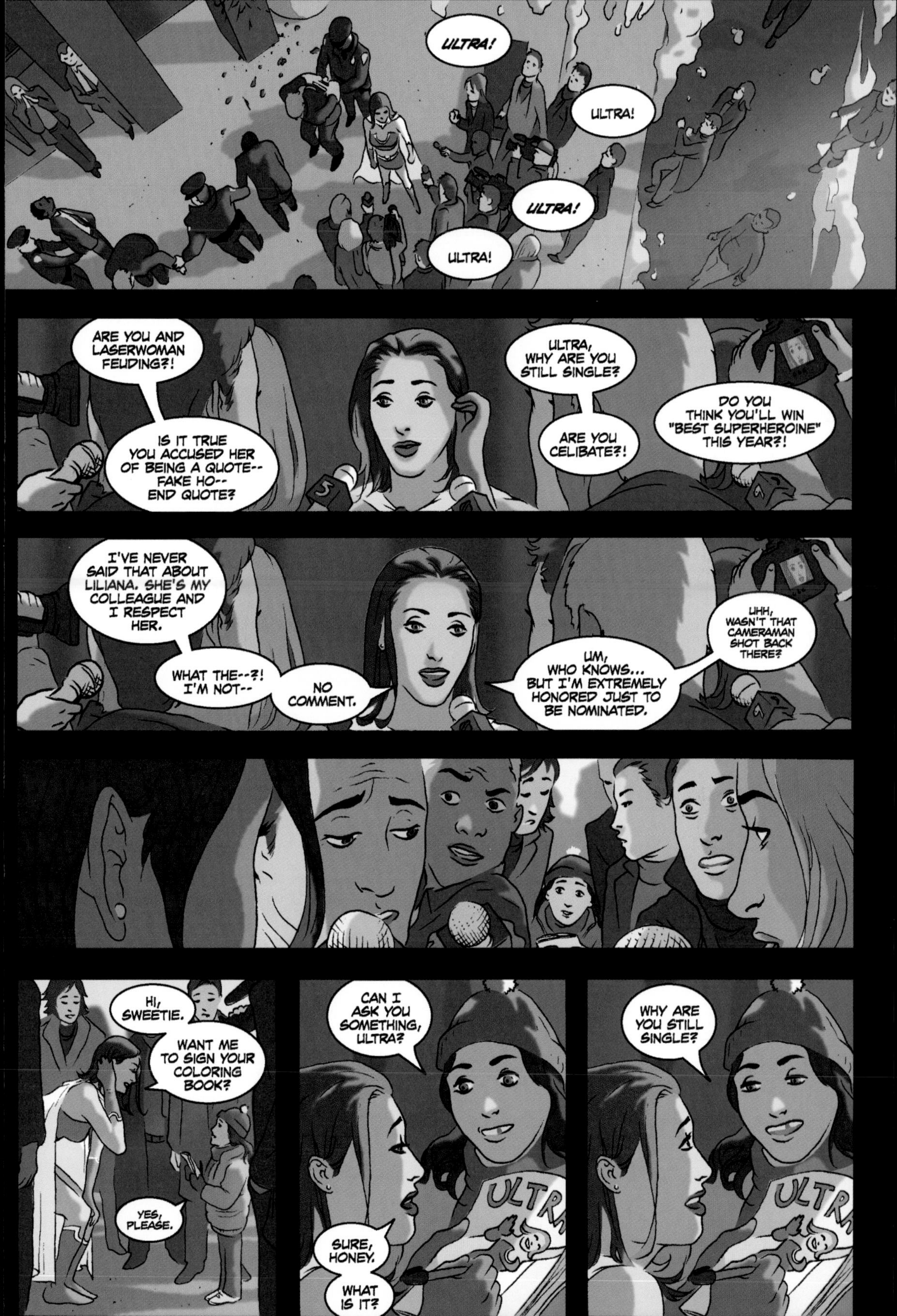
ULTRA!
ULTRA!
ULTRA!
ULTRA!
ARE YOU AND LASERWOMAN FEUDING?!
IS IT TRUE YOU ACCUSED HER OF BEING A QUOTE-- FAKE HO-- END QUOTE?
ULTRA, WHY ARE YOU STILL SINGLE?
ARE YOU CELIBATE?!
DO YOU THINK YOU'LL WIN "BEST SUPERHEROINE" THIS YEAR?!
I'VE NEVER SAID THAT ABOUT LILIANA. SHE'S MY COLLEAGUE AND I RESPECT HER.
WHAT THE--?! I'M NOT--
NO COMMENT.
UM, WHO KNOWS... BUT I'M EXTREMELY HONORED JUST TO BE NOMINATED.
UHH, WASN'T THAT CAMERAMAN SHOT BACK THERE?
HI, SWEETIE.
WANT ME TO SIGN YOUR COLORING BOOK?
YES, PLEASE.
CAN I ASK YOU SOMETHING, ULTRA?
SURE, HONEY.
WHAT IS IT?
ULTRA
WHY ARE YOU STILL SINGLE?
ULTRA

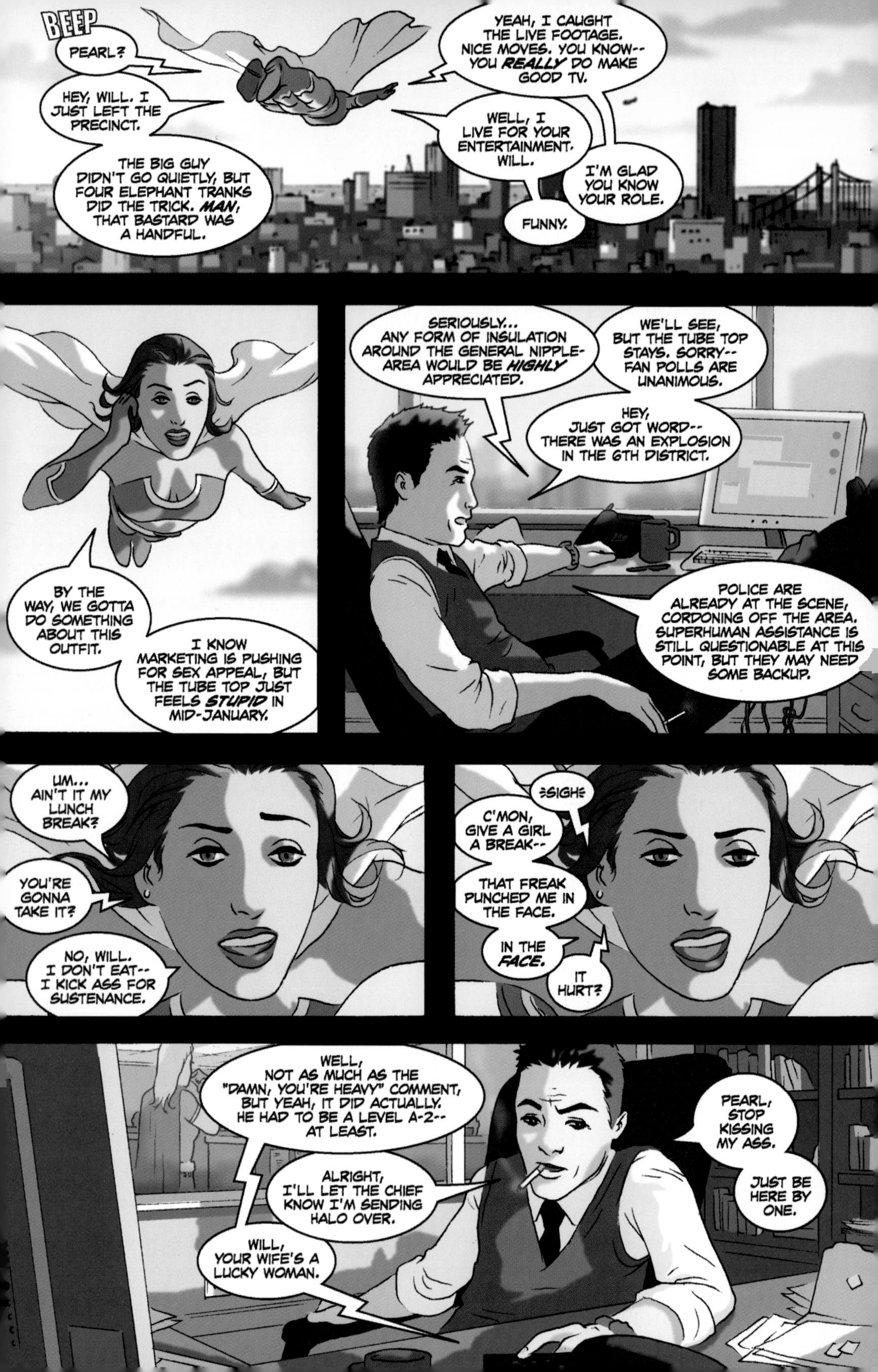
BEEP
PEARL?
HEY, WILL. I JUST LEFT THE PRECINCT.
THE BIG GUY DIDN'T GO QUIETLY, BUT FOUR ELEPHANT TRANKS DID THE TRICK. MAN, THAT BASTARD WAS A HANDFUL.
YEAH, I CAUGHT THE LIVE FOOTAGE. NICE MOVES. YOU KNOW-- YOU REALLY DO MAKE GOOD TV.
WELL, I LIVE FOR YOUR ENTERTAINMENT, WILL.
I'M GLAD YOU KNOW YOUR ROLE.
FUNNY.
BY THE WAY, WE GOTTA DO SOMETHING ABOUT THIS OUTFIT.
I KNOW MARKETING IS PUSHING FOR SEX APPEAL, BUT THE TUBE TOP JUST FEELS STUPID IN MID-JANUARY.
SERIOUSLY... ANY FORM OF INSULATION AROUND THE GENERAL NIPPLE-AREA WOULD BE HIGHLY APPRECIATED.
WE'LL SEE, BUT THE TUBE TOP STAYS. SORRY-- FAN POLLS ARE UNANIMOUS.
HEY, JUST GOT WORD-- THERE WAS AN EXPLOSION IN THE 6TH DISTRICT.
POLICE ARE ALREADY AT THE SCENE, CORDONING OFF THE AREA. SUPERHUMAN ASSISTANCE IS STILL QUESTIONABLE AT THIS POINT, BUT THEY MAY NEED SOME BACKUP.
UM... AIN'T IT MY LUNCH BREAK?
YOU'RE GONNA TAKE IT?
NO, WILL. I DON'T EAT-- I KICK ASS FOR SUSTENANCE.
SIGH
C'MON, GIVE A GIRL A BREAK--
THAT FREAK PUNCHED ME IN THE FACE.
IN THE FACE.
IT HURT?
WELL, NOT AS MUCH AS THE "DAMN, YOU'RE HEAVY" COMMENT, BUT YEAH, IT DID ACTUALLY. HE HAD TO BE A LEVEL A-2-- AT LEAST.
ALRIGHT, I'LL LET THE CHIEF KNOW I'M SENDING HALO OVER.
WILL, YOUR WIFE'S A LUCKY WOMAN.
PEARL, STOP KISSING MY ASS.
JUST BE HERE BY ONE.

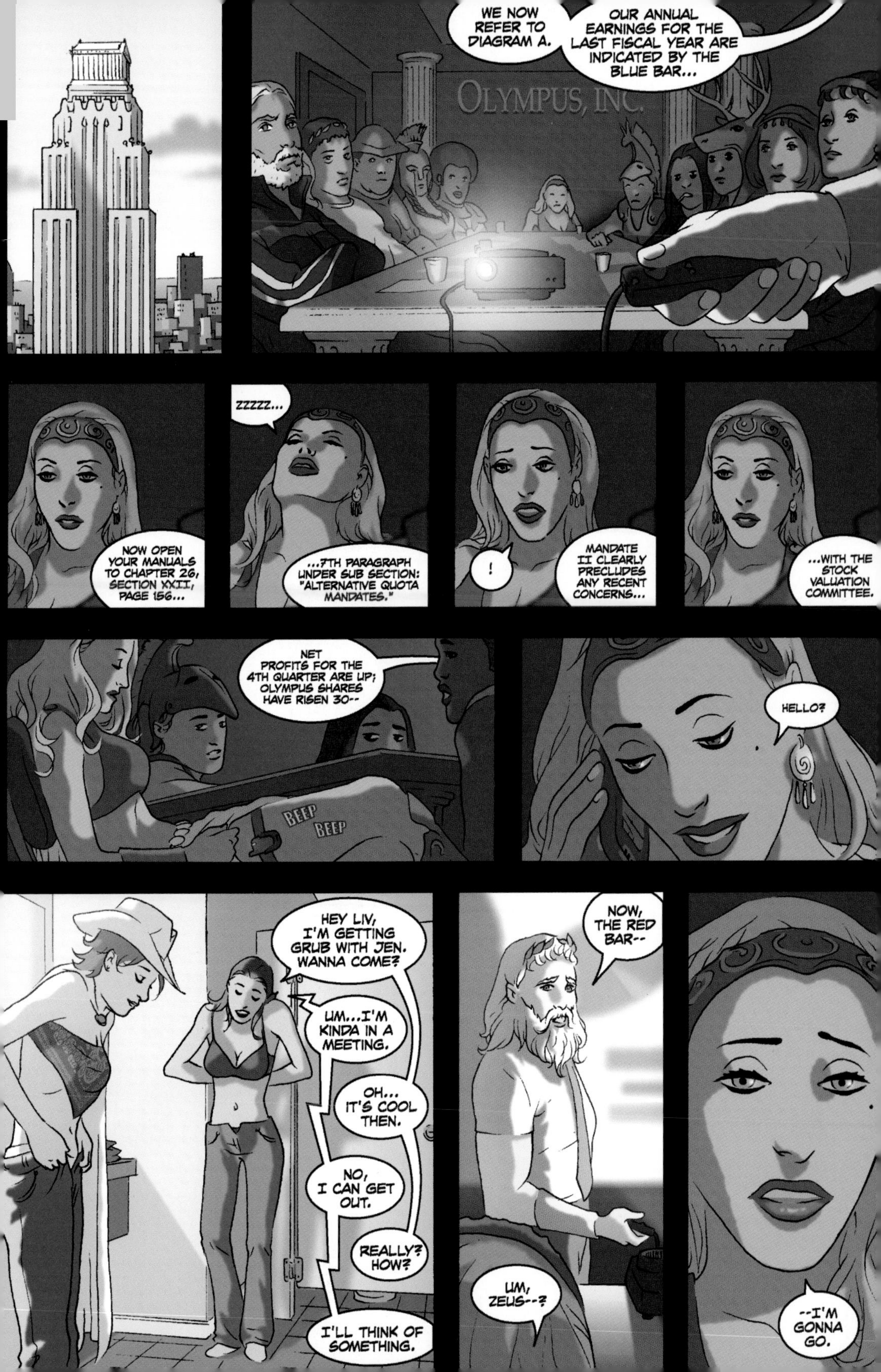
WE NOW REFER TO DIAGRAM A.
OUR ANNUAL EARNINGS FOR THE LAST FISCAL YEAR ARE INDICATED BY THE BLUE BAR...
OLYMPUS, INC.
NOW OPEN YOUR MANUALS TO CHAPTER 26, SECTION XXII, PAGE 156...
ZZZZZ...
...7TH PARAGRAPH UNDER SUB SECTION: "ALTERNATIVE QUOTA MANDATES."
!
MANDATE II CLEARLY PRECLUDES ANY RECENT CONCERNS...
...WITH THE STOCK VALUATION COMMITTEE.
NET PROFITS FOR THE 4TH QUARTER ARE UP; OLYMPUS SHARES HAVE RISEN 30--
BEEP
BEEP
HELLO?
HEY LIV, I'M GETTING GRUB WITH JEN. WANNA COME?
UM...I'M KINDA IN A MEETING.
OH... IT'S COOL THEN.
NO, I CAN GET OUT.
REALLY? HOW?
I'LL THINK OF SOMETHING.
NOW, THE RED BAR--
UM, ZEUS--?
--I'M GONNA GO.

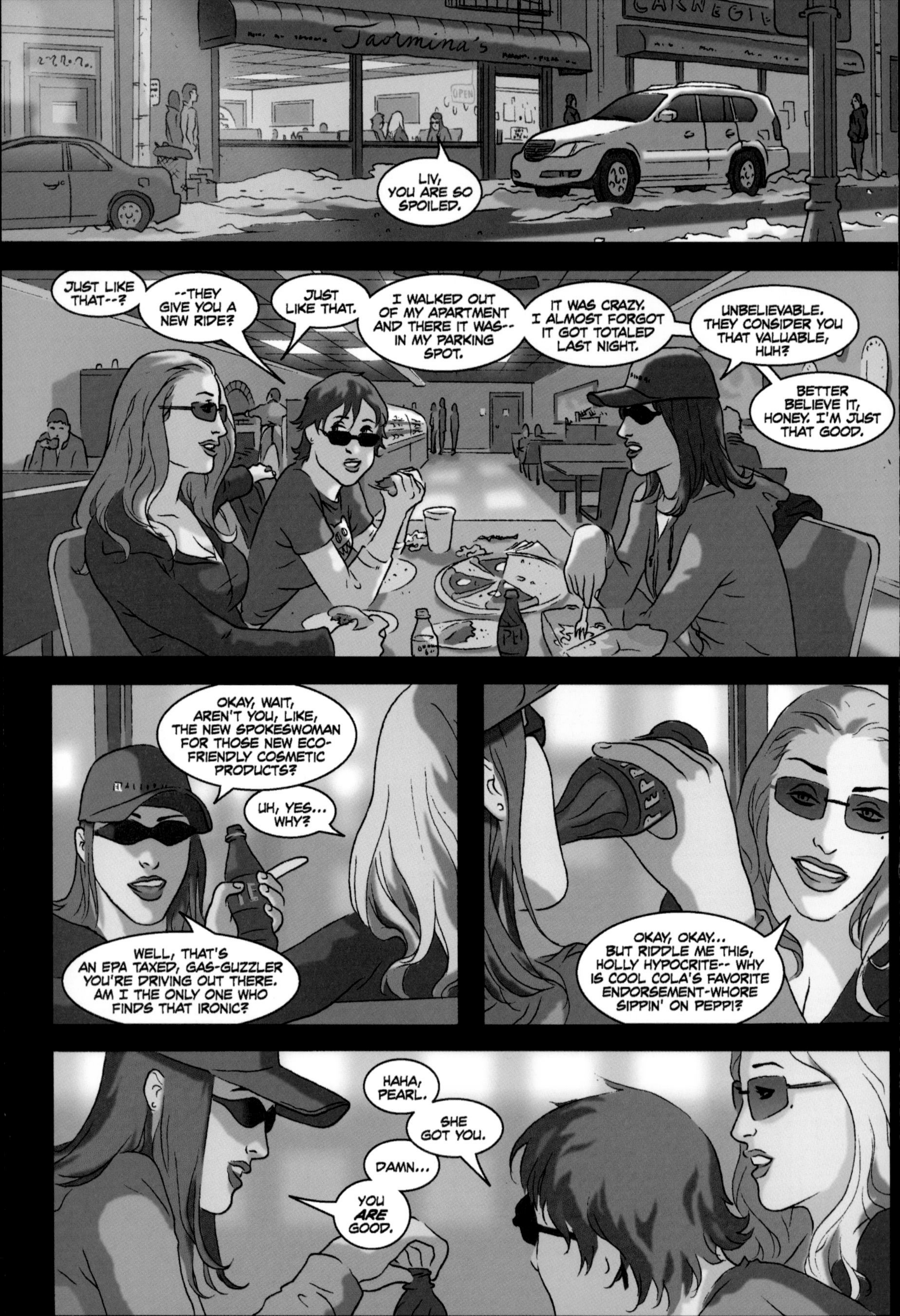

LIV, YOU ARE SO SPOILED.
JUST LIKE THAT--?
--THEY GIVE YOU A NEW RIDE?
JUST LIKE THAT.
I WALKED OUT OF MY APARTMENT AND THERE IT WAS-- IN MY PARKING SPOT.
IT WAS CRAZY. I ALMOST FORGOT IT GOT TOTALED LAST NIGHT.
UNBELIEVABLE. THEY CONSIDER YOU THAT VALUABLE, HUH?
BETTER BELIEVE IT, HONEY. I'M JUST THAT GOOD.
OKAY, WAIT, AREN'T YOU, LIKE, THE NEW SPOKESWOMAN FOR THOSE NEW ECO-FRIENDLY COSMETIC PRODUCTS?
UH, YES... WHY?
WELL, THAT'S AN EPA TAXED, GAS-GUZZLER YOU'RE DRIVING OUT THERE. AM I THE ONLY ONE WHO FINDS THAT IRONIC?
OKAY, OKAY... BUT RIDDLE ME THIS, HOLLY HYPOCRITE-- WHY IS COOL COLA'S FAVORITE ENDORSEMENT-WHORE SIPPIN' ON PEPPI?
HAHA, PEARL.
SHE GOT YOU.
DAMN...
YOU *ARE* GOOD.

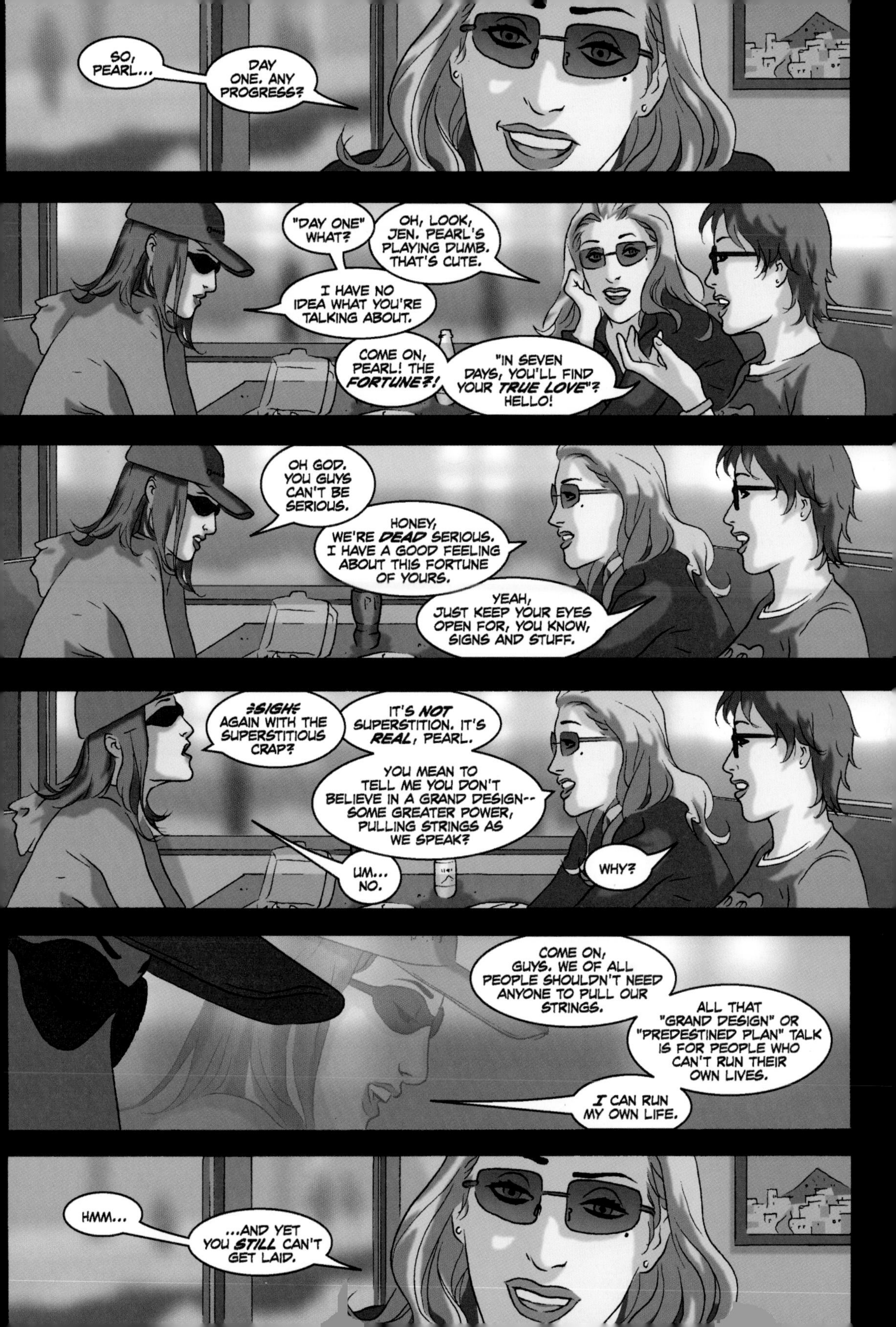
SO, PEARL...
DAY ONE. ANY PROGRESS?
"DAY ONE" WHAT?
OH, LOOK, JEN. PEARL'S PLAYING DUMB. THAT'S CUTE.
I HAVE NO IDEA WHAT YOU'RE TALKING ABOUT.
COME ON, PEARL! THE *FORTUNE?!*
"IN SEVEN DAYS, YOU'LL FIND YOUR *TRUE LOVE*"? HELLO!
OH GOD. YOU GUYS CAN'T BE SERIOUS.
HONEY, WE'RE *DEAD* SERIOUS. I HAVE A GOOD FEELING ABOUT THIS FORTUNE OF YOURS.
YEAH, JUST KEEP YOUR EYES OPEN FOR, YOU KNOW, SIGNS AND STUFF.
SIGH AGAIN WITH THE SUPERSTITIOUS CRAP?
IT'S *NOT* SUPERSTITION. IT'S *REAL*, PEARL.
YOU MEAN TO TELL ME YOU DON'T BELIEVE IN A GRAND DESIGN-- SOME GREATER POWER, PULLING STRINGS AS WE SPEAK?
UM... NO.
WHY?
COME ON, GUYS. WE OF ALL PEOPLE SHOULDN'T NEED ANYONE TO PULL OUR STRINGS.
ALL THAT "GRAND DESIGN" OR "PREDESTINED PLAN" TALK IS FOR PEOPLE WHO CAN'T RUN THEIR OWN LIVES.
I CAN RUN MY OWN LIFE.
HMM...
...AND YET YOU *STILL* CAN'T GET LAID.

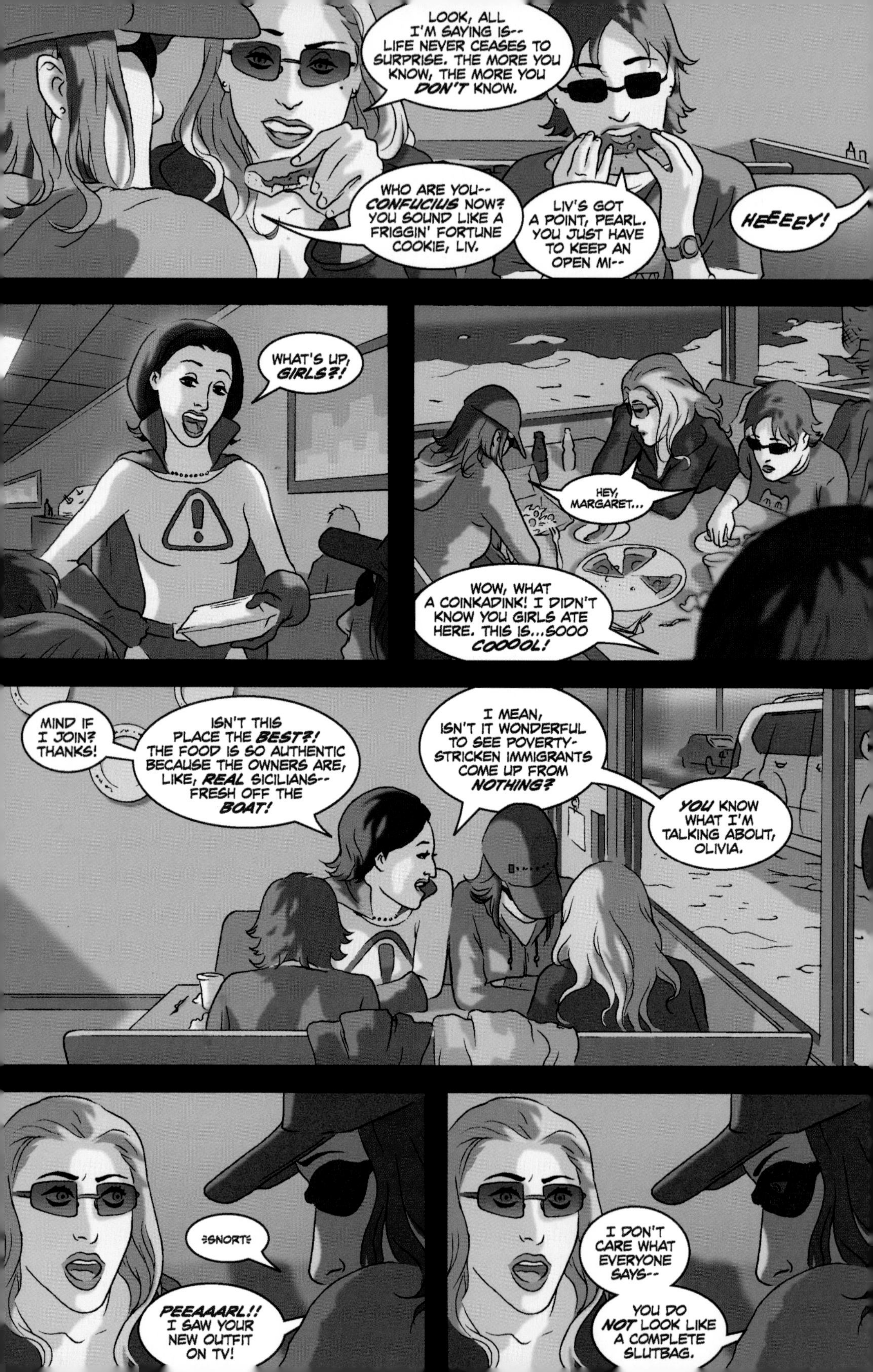

LOOK, ALL I'M SAYING IS-- LIFE NEVER CEASES TO SURPRISE. THE MORE YOU KNOW, THE MORE YOU DON'T KNOW.
WHO ARE YOU-- CONFUCIUS NOW? YOU SOUND LIKE A FRIGGIN' FORTUNE COOKIE, LIV.
LIV'S GOT A POINT, PEARL. YOU JUST HAVE TO KEEP AN OPEN MI--
HEEEEY!
WHAT'S UP, GIRLS?!
HEY, MARGARET...
WOW, WHAT A COINKADINK! I DIDN'T KNOW YOU GIRLS ATE HERE. THIS IS...SOOO COOOOL!
MIND IF I JOIN? THANKS!
ISN'T THIS PLACE THE BEST?! THE FOOD IS SO AUTHENTIC BECAUSE THE OWNERS ARE, LIKE, REAL SICILIANS-- FRESH OFF THE BOAT!
I MEAN, ISN'T IT WONDERFUL TO SEE POVERTY-STRICKEN IMMIGRANTS COME UP FROM NOTHING?
YOU KNOW WHAT I'M TALKING ABOUT, OLIVIA.
SNORT
PEEAAARL!! I SAW YOUR NEW OUTFIT ON TV!
I DON'T CARE WHAT EVERYONE SAYS--
YOU DO NOT LOOK LIKE A COMPLETE SLUTBAG.

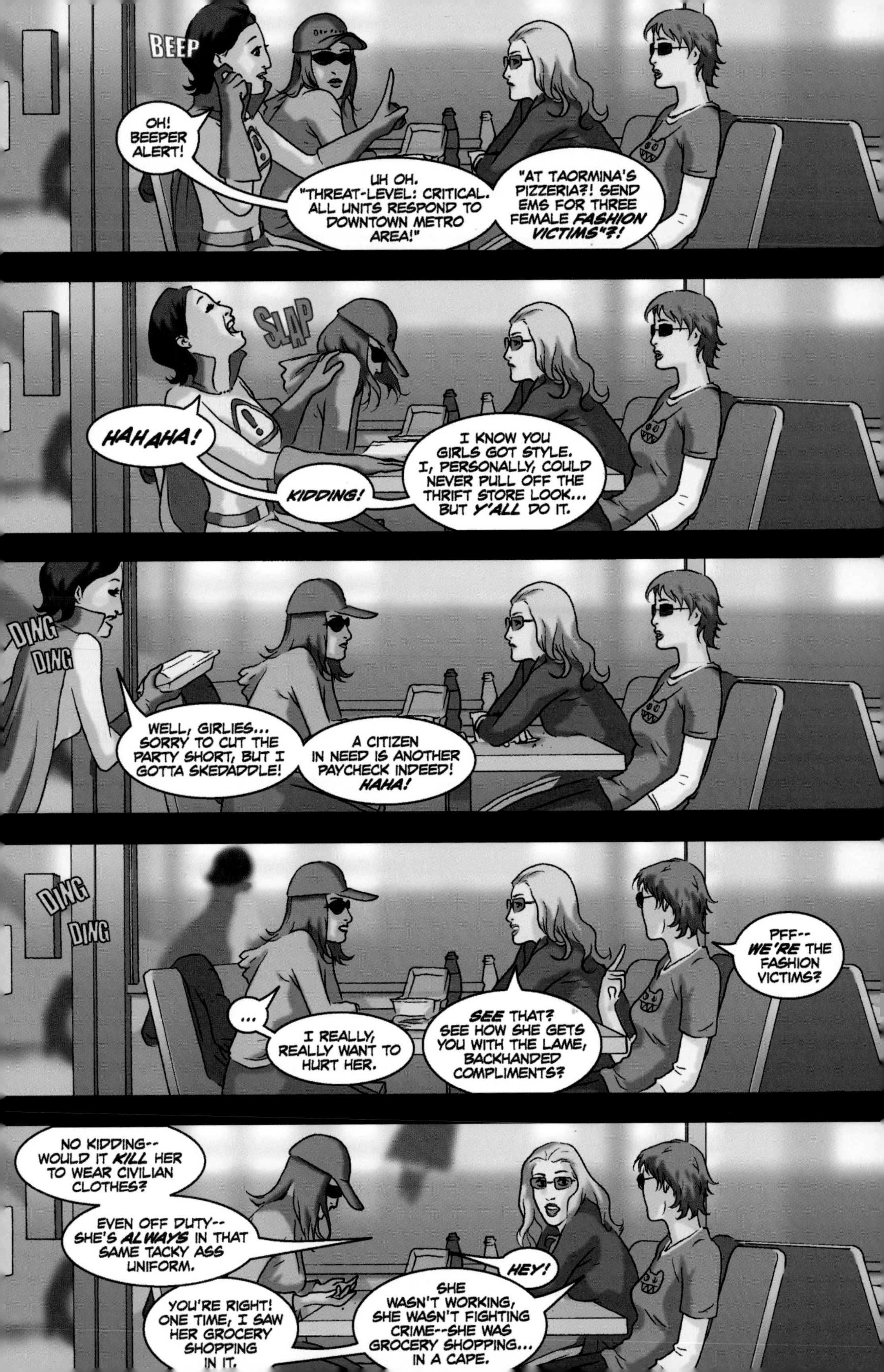
BEEP
OH! BEEPER ALERT!
UH OH. "THREAT-LEVEL: CRITICAL. ALL UNITS RESPOND TO DOWNTOWN METRO AREA!"
"AT TAORMINA'S PIZZERIA?! SEND EMS FOR THREE FEMALE *FASHION VICTIMS*"?!
SLAP
HAHAHA!
KIDDING!
I KNOW YOU GIRLS GOT STYLE. I, PERSONALLY, COULD NEVER PULL OFF THE THRIFT STORE LOOK... BUT *Y'ALL* DO IT.
DING
DING
WELL, GIRLIES... SORRY TO CUT THE PARTY SHORT, BUT I GOTTA SKEDADDLE!
A CITIZEN IN NEED IS ANOTHER PAYCHECK INDEED! *HAHA!*
DING
DING
...
I REALLY, REALLY WANT TO HURT HER.
SEE THAT? SEE HOW SHE GETS YOU WITH THE LAME, BACKHANDED COMPLIMENTS?
PFF-- *WE'RE* THE FASHION VICTIMS?
NO KIDDING-- WOULD IT *KILL* HER TO WEAR CIVILIAN CLOTHES?
EVEN OFF DUTY-- SHE'S *ALWAYS* IN THAT SAME TACKY ASS UNIFORM.
HEY!
YOU'RE RIGHT! ONE TIME, I SAW HER GROCERY SHOPPING IN IT.
SHE WASN'T WORKING, SHE WASN'T FIGHTING CRIME--SHE WAS GROCERY SHOPPING... IN A CAPE.

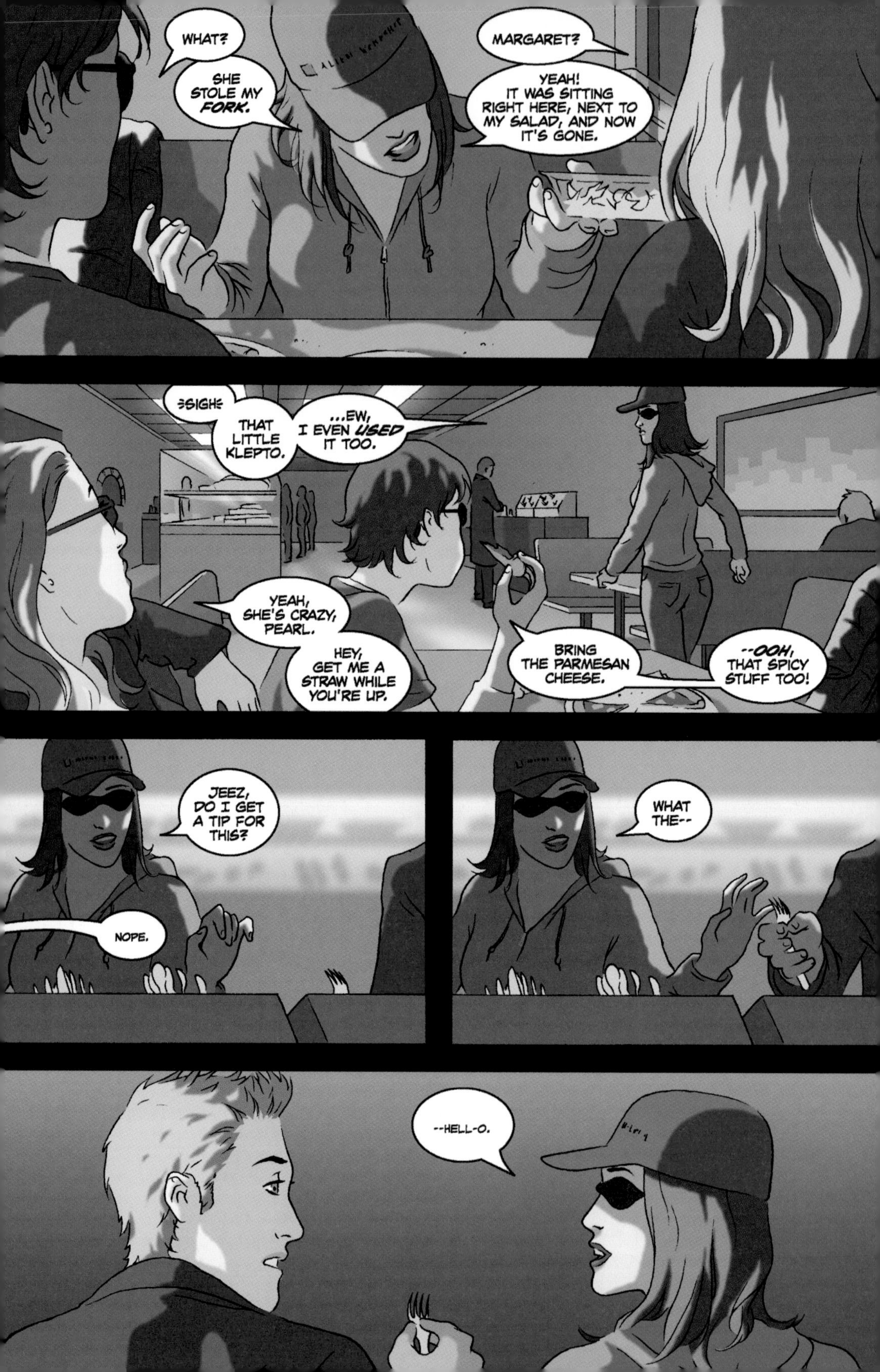
WHAT?
SHE STOLE MY FORK.
MARGARET?
YEAH! IT WAS SITTING RIGHT HERE, NEXT TO MY SALAD, AND NOW IT'S GONE.
SIGH
THAT LITTLE KLEPTO.
...EW, I EVEN USED IT TOO.
YEAH, SHE'S CRAZY, PEARL.
HEY, GET ME A STRAW WHILE YOU'RE UP.
BRING THE PARMESAN CHEESE.
--OOH, THAT SPICY STUFF TOO!
JEEZ, DO I GET A TIP FOR THIS?
NOPE.
WHAT THE--
--HELL-O.

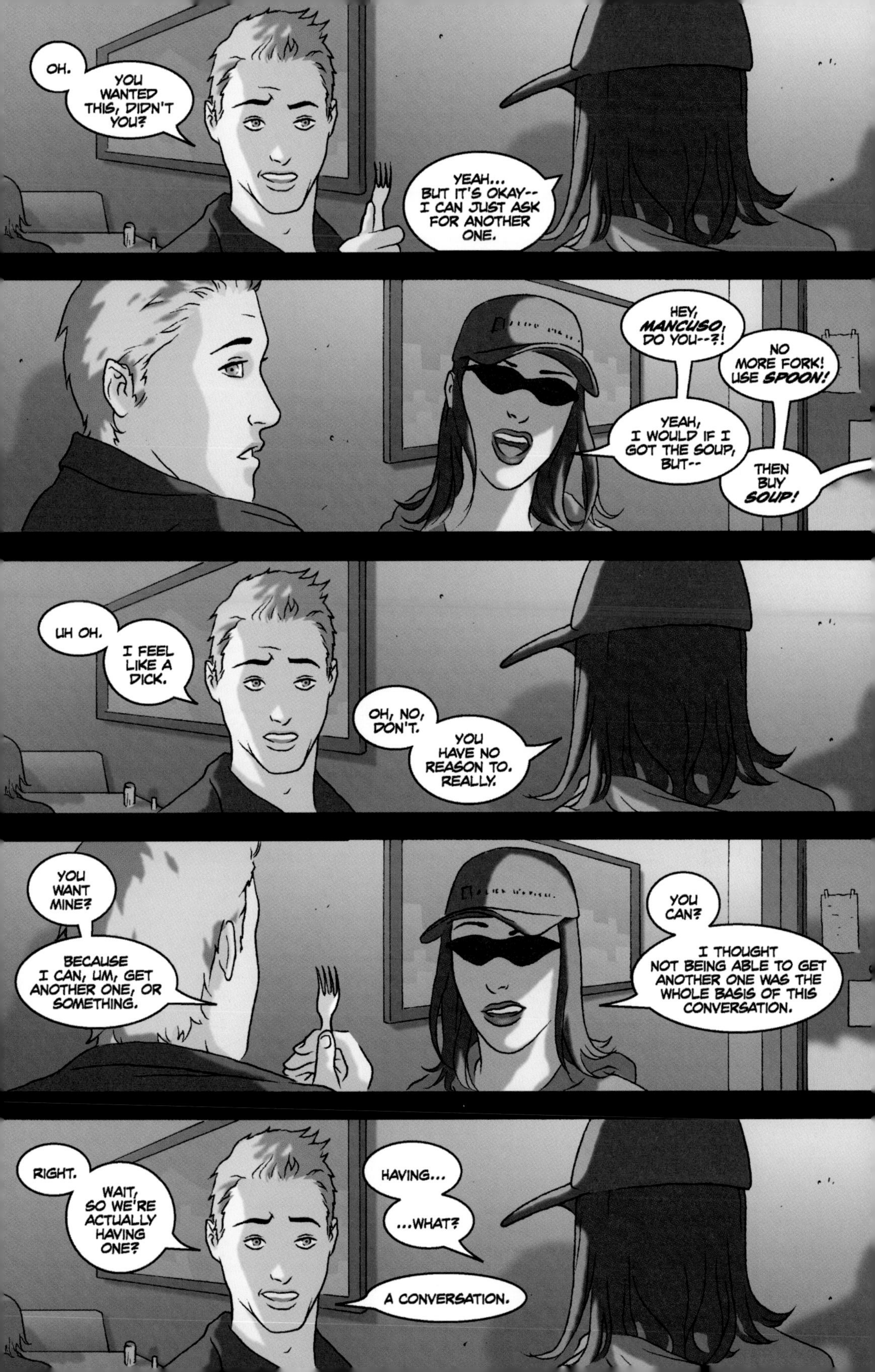
OH.
YOU WANTED THIS, DIDN'T YOU?
YEAH... BUT IT'S OKAY-- I CAN JUST ASK FOR ANOTHER ONE.
HEY, MANCUSO! DO YOU--?!
NO MORE FORK! USE SPOON!
YEAH, I WOULD IF I GOT THE SOUP, BUT--
THEN BUY SOUP!
UH OH.
I FEEL LIKE A DICK.
OH, NO, DON'T.
YOU HAVE NO REASON TO. REALLY.
YOU WANT MINE?
BECAUSE I CAN, UM, GET ANOTHER ONE, OR SOMETHING.
YOU CAN?
I THOUGHT NOT BEING ABLE TO GET ANOTHER ONE WAS THE WHOLE BASIS OF THIS CONVERSATION.
RIGHT.
WAIT, SO WE'RE ACTUALLY HAVING ONE?
HAVING...
...WHAT?
A CONVERSATION.

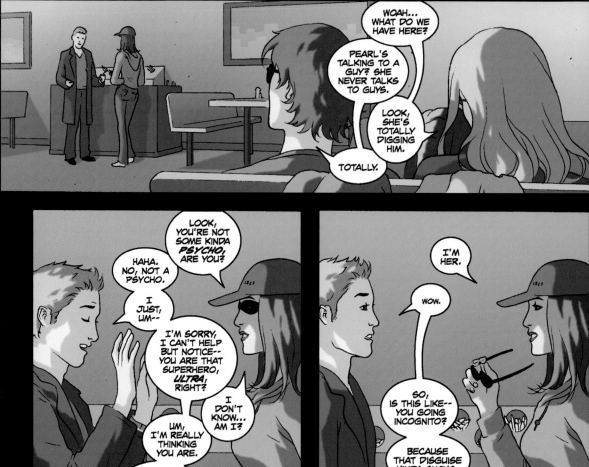

WOAH... WHAT DO WE HAVE HERE?

PEARL'S TALKING TO A GUY? SHE NEVER TALKS TO GUYS.

LOOK, SHE'S TOTALLY DIGGING HIM.

TOTALLY.

LOOK, YOU'RE NOT SOME KINDA *PSYCHO*, ARE YOU?

HAHA. NO, NOT A PSYCHO.

I JUST, UM--

I'M SORRY, I CAN'T HELP BUT NOTICE-- YOU ARE THAT SUPERHERO, *ULTRA*, RIGHT?

I DON'T KNOW... AM I?

UM, I'M REALLY THINKING YOU ARE.

I'M KIND OF A FAN, SO IF YOU *ARE* HER, I'D KINDA LIKE TO COMPLIMENT YOU.

YOU KNOW...AS A FAN.

I'M HER.

WOW.

SO, IS THIS LIKE-- YOU GOING INCOGNITO?

BECAUSE THAT DISGUISE KINDA SUCKS.

SO, WHEN SHOULD I EXPECT THE COMPLIMENTS, BUDDY.

OH, *HA!* ...I'M SORRY. THAT DIDN'T COME OUT RIGHT--

SEE, I HAVE A TENDENCY TO SAY STUPID THINGS WHEN I'M NERVOUS.

OH, DON'T BE NERVOUS.

I'M JUST A REGULAR GAL.

YEAH...

...BUT YOU CAN KICK MY *ASS.*

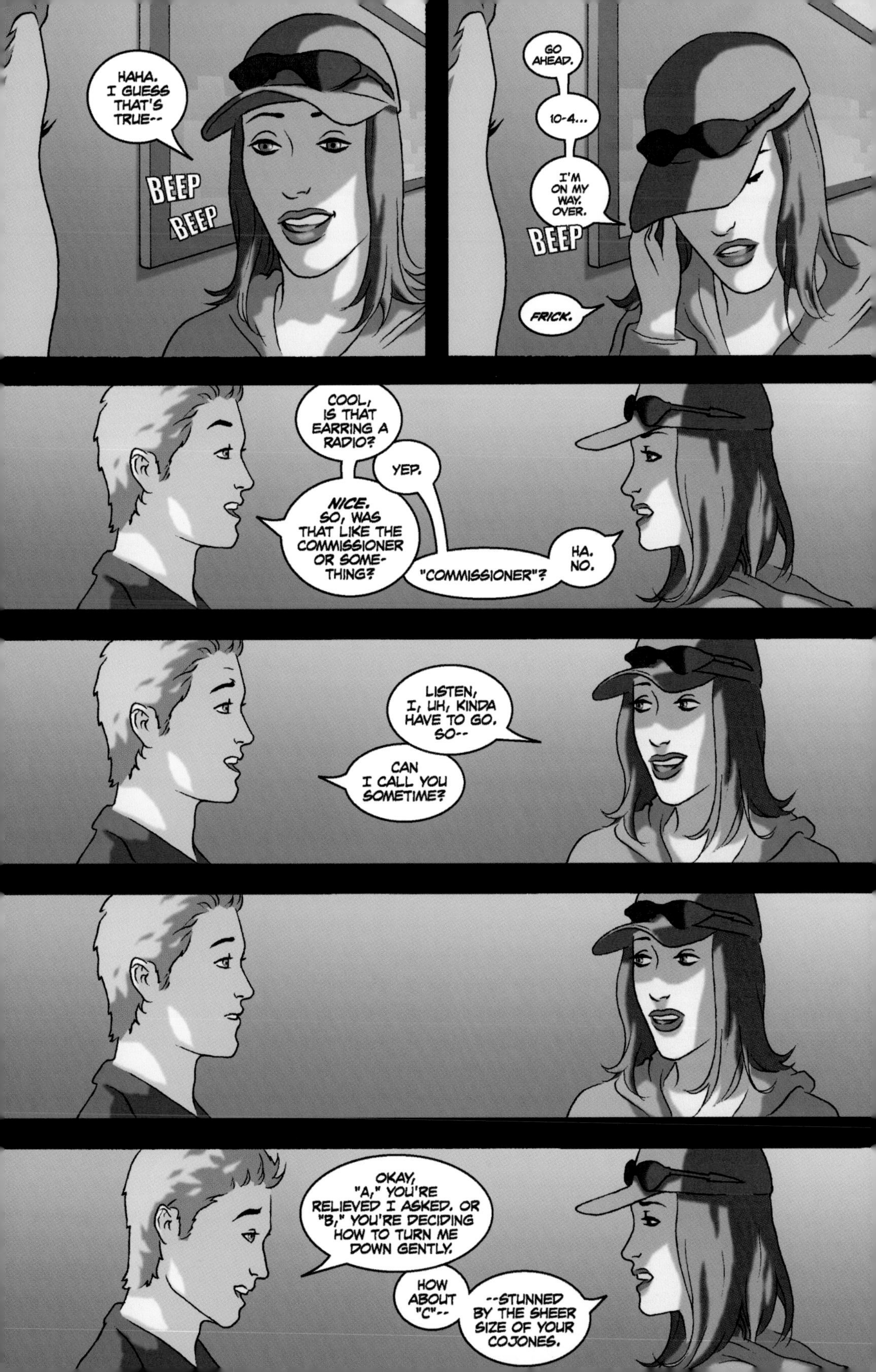
HAHA. I GUESS THAT'S TRUE--
BEEP
BEEP
GO AHEAD.
10-4...
I'M ON MY WAY. OVER.
BEEP
FRICK.
COOL, IS THAT EARRING A RADIO?
YEP.
NICE. SO, WAS THAT LIKE THE COMMISSIONER OR SOME-THING?
"COMMISSIONER"?
HA. NO.
LISTEN, I, UH, KINDA HAVE TO GO. SO--
CAN I CALL YOU SOMETIME?
OKAY, "A," YOU'RE RELIEVED I ASKED. OR "B," YOU'RE DECIDING HOW TO TURN ME DOWN GENTLY.
HOW ABOUT "C"--
--STUNNED BY THE SHEER SIZE OF YOUR COJONES.

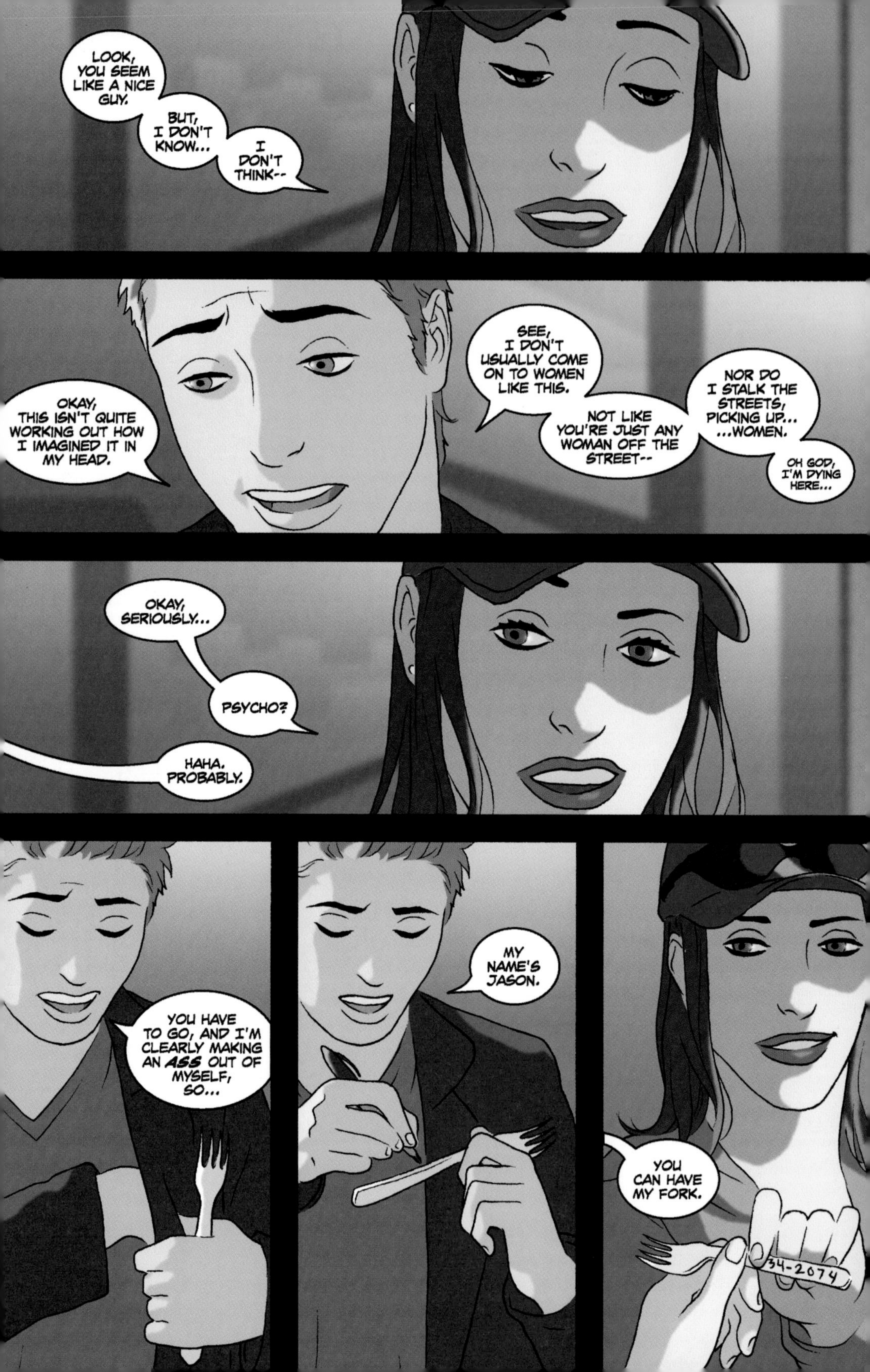
LOOK, YOU SEEM LIKE A NICE GUY.
BUT, I DON'T KNOW...
I DON'T THINK--
OKAY, THIS ISN'T QUITE WORKING OUT HOW I IMAGINED IT IN MY HEAD.
SEE, I DON'T USUALLY COME ON TO WOMEN LIKE THIS.
NOT LIKE YOU'RE JUST ANY WOMAN OFF THE STREET--
NOR DO I STALK THE STREETS, PICKING UP... ...WOMEN.
OH GOD, I'M DYING HERE...
OKAY, SERIOUSLY...
PSYCHO?
HAHA. PROBABLY.
YOU HAVE TO GO, AND I'M CLEARLY MAKING AN ***ASS*** OUT OF MYSELF, SO...
MY NAME'S JASON.
YOU CAN HAVE MY FORK.
34-2074

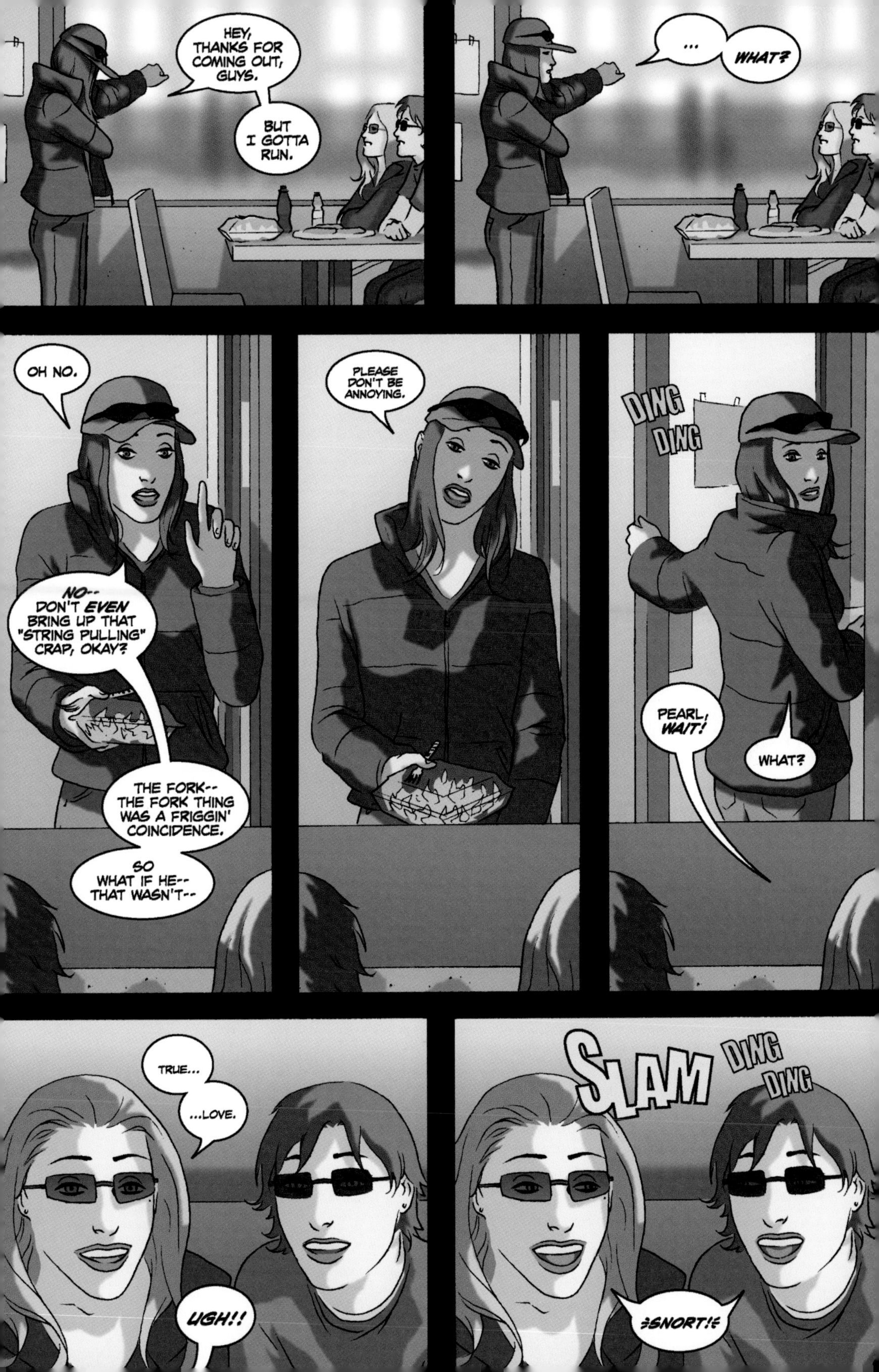

HEY, THANKS FOR COMING OUT, GUYS.
BUT I GOTTA RUN.
...
WHAT?
OH NO.
NO-- DON'T EVEN BRING UP THAT "STRING PULLING" CRAP, OKAY?
THE FORK-- THE FORK THING WAS A FRIGGIN' COINCIDENCE.
SO WHAT IF HE-- THAT WASN'T--
PLEASE DON'T BE ANNOYING.
DING DING
PEARL, WAIT!
WHAT?
TRUE...
...LOVE.
UGH!!
SLAM
DING DING
SNORT!

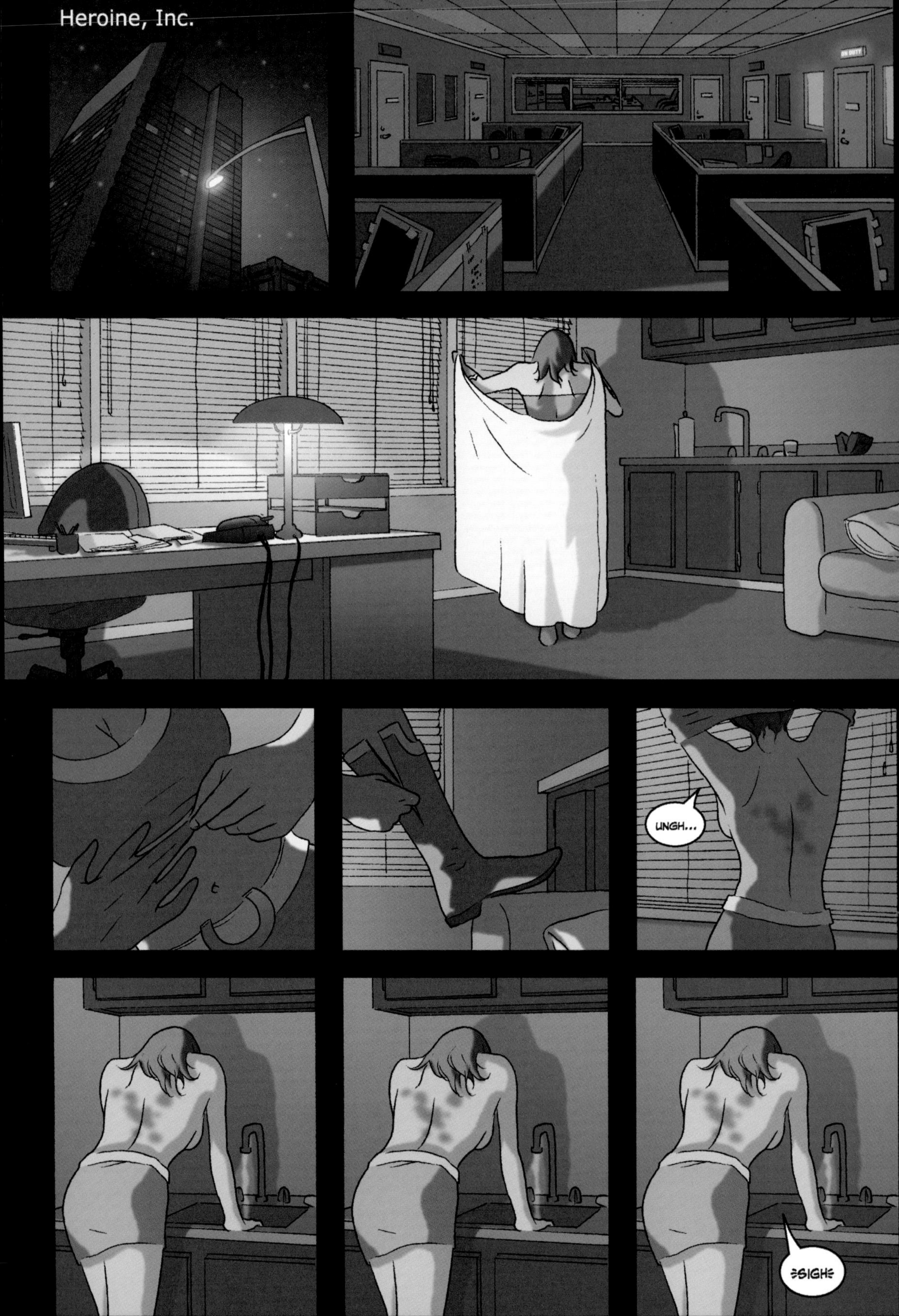
ON DUTY
UNGH...
SIGH

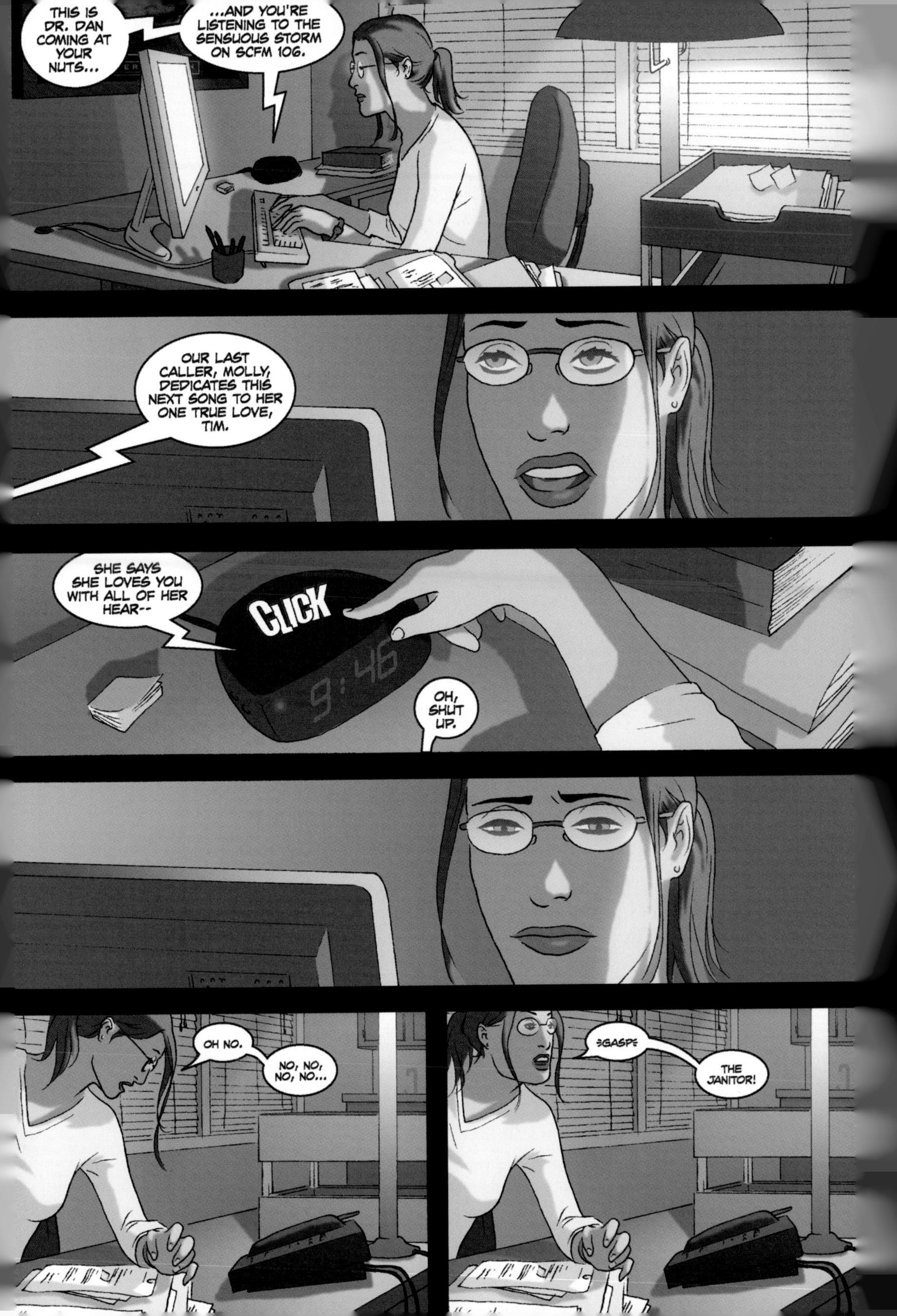
THIS IS DR. DAN COMING AT YOUR NUTS...
...AND YOU'RE LISTENING TO THE SENSUOUS STORM ON SCFM 106.
OUR LAST CALLER, MOLLY, DEDICATES THIS NEXT SONG TO HER ONE TRUE LOVE, TIM.
SHE SAYS SHE LOVES YOU WITH ALL OF HER HEAR--
CLICK
9:46
OH, SHUT UP.
OH NO.
NO, NO, NO, NO...
=GASP=
THE JANITOR!

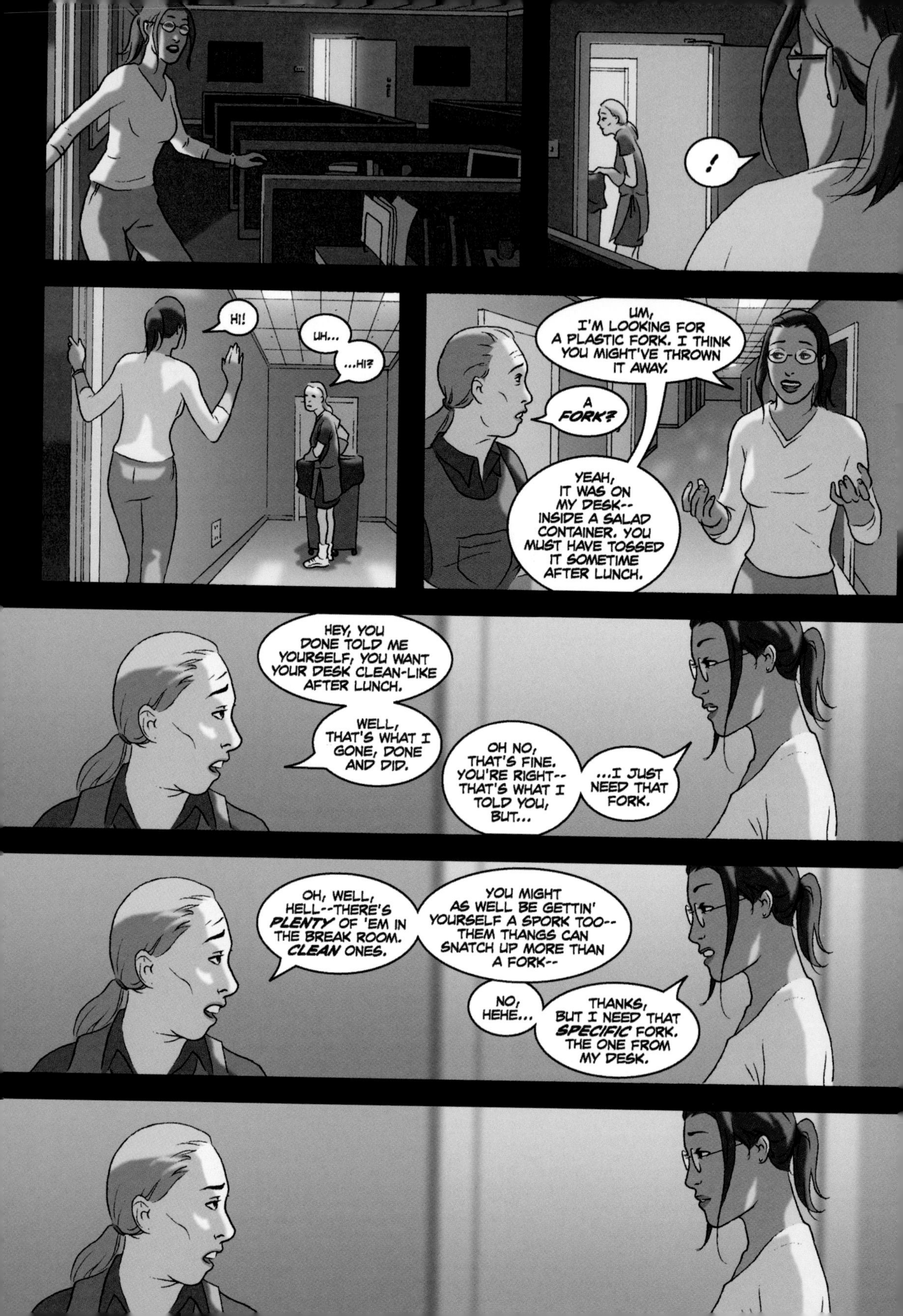
!
HI!
UH...
...HI?
UM, I'M LOOKING FOR A PLASTIC FORK. I THINK YOU MIGHT'VE THROWN IT AWAY.
A FORK?
YEAH, IT WAS ON MY DESK-- INSIDE A SALAD CONTAINER. YOU MUST HAVE TOSSED IT SOMETIME AFTER LUNCH.
HEY, YOU DONE TOLD ME YOURSELF, YOU WANT YOUR DESK CLEAN-LIKE AFTER LUNCH.
WELL, THAT'S WHAT I GONE, DONE AND DID.
OH NO, THAT'S FINE. YOU'RE RIGHT-- THAT'S WHAT I TOLD YOU, BUT...
...I JUST NEED THAT FORK.
OH, WELL, HELL--THERE'S PLENTY OF 'EM IN THE BREAK ROOM. CLEAN ONES.
YOU MIGHT AS WELL BE GETTIN' YOURSELF A SPORK TOO-- THEM THANGS CAN SNATCH UP MORE THAN A FORK--
NO, HEHE...
THANKS, BUT I NEED THAT SPECIFIC FORK. THE ONE FROM MY DESK.

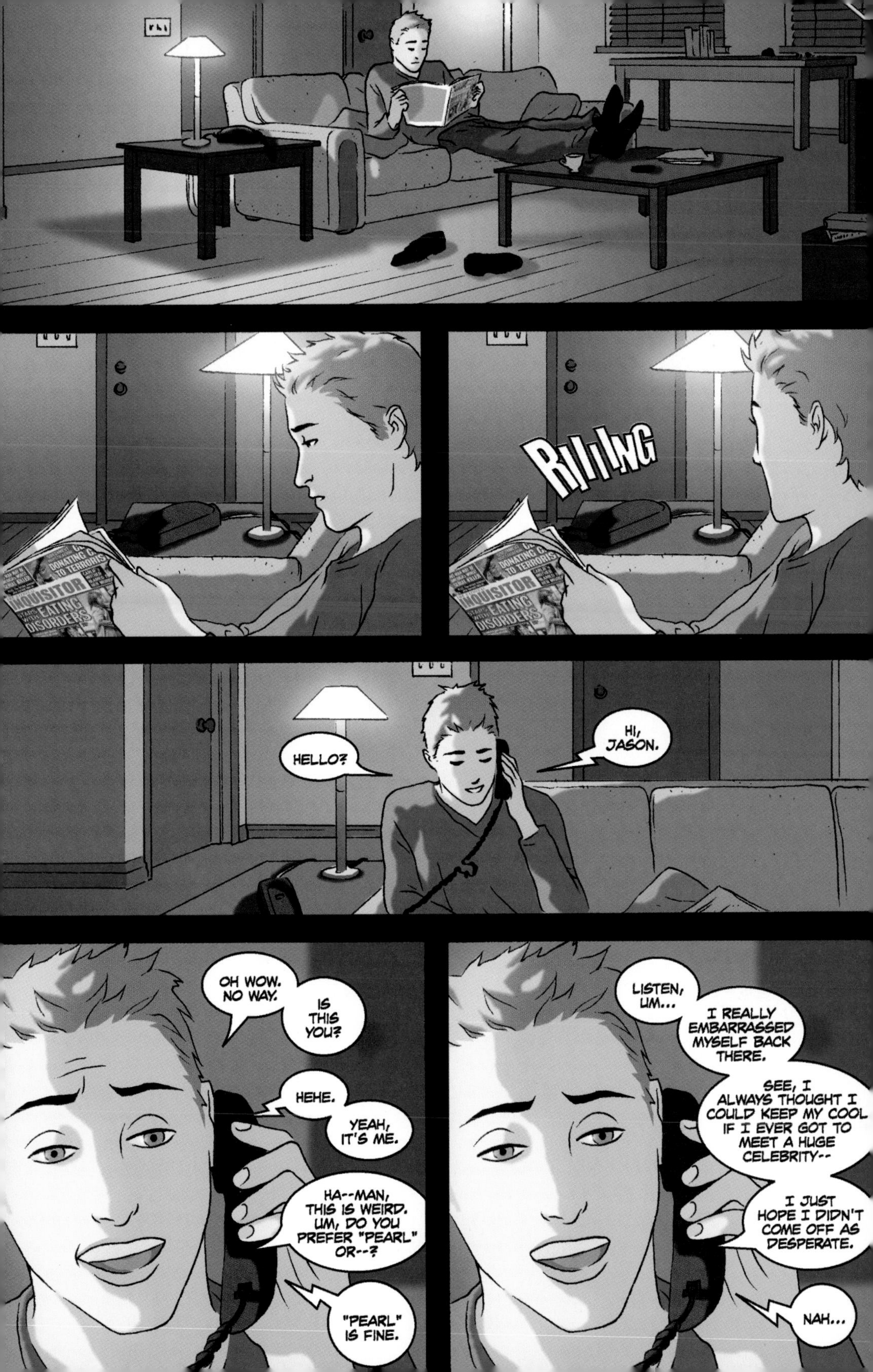
RIIIING
INQUISITOR
DONATING
TO TERRORIS
EATING DISORDERS
HELLO?
HI, JASON.
OH WOW. NO WAY.
IS THIS YOU?
HEHE.
YEAH, IT'S ME.
HA--MAN, THIS IS WEIRD. UM, DO YOU PREFER "PEARL" OR--?
"PEARL" IS FINE.
LISTEN, UM...
I REALLY EMBARRASSED MYSELF BACK THERE.
SEE, I ALWAYS THOUGHT I COULD KEEP MY COOL IF I EVER GOT TO MEET A HUGE CELEBRITY--
I JUST HOPE I DIDN'T COME OFF AS DESPERATE.
NAH...

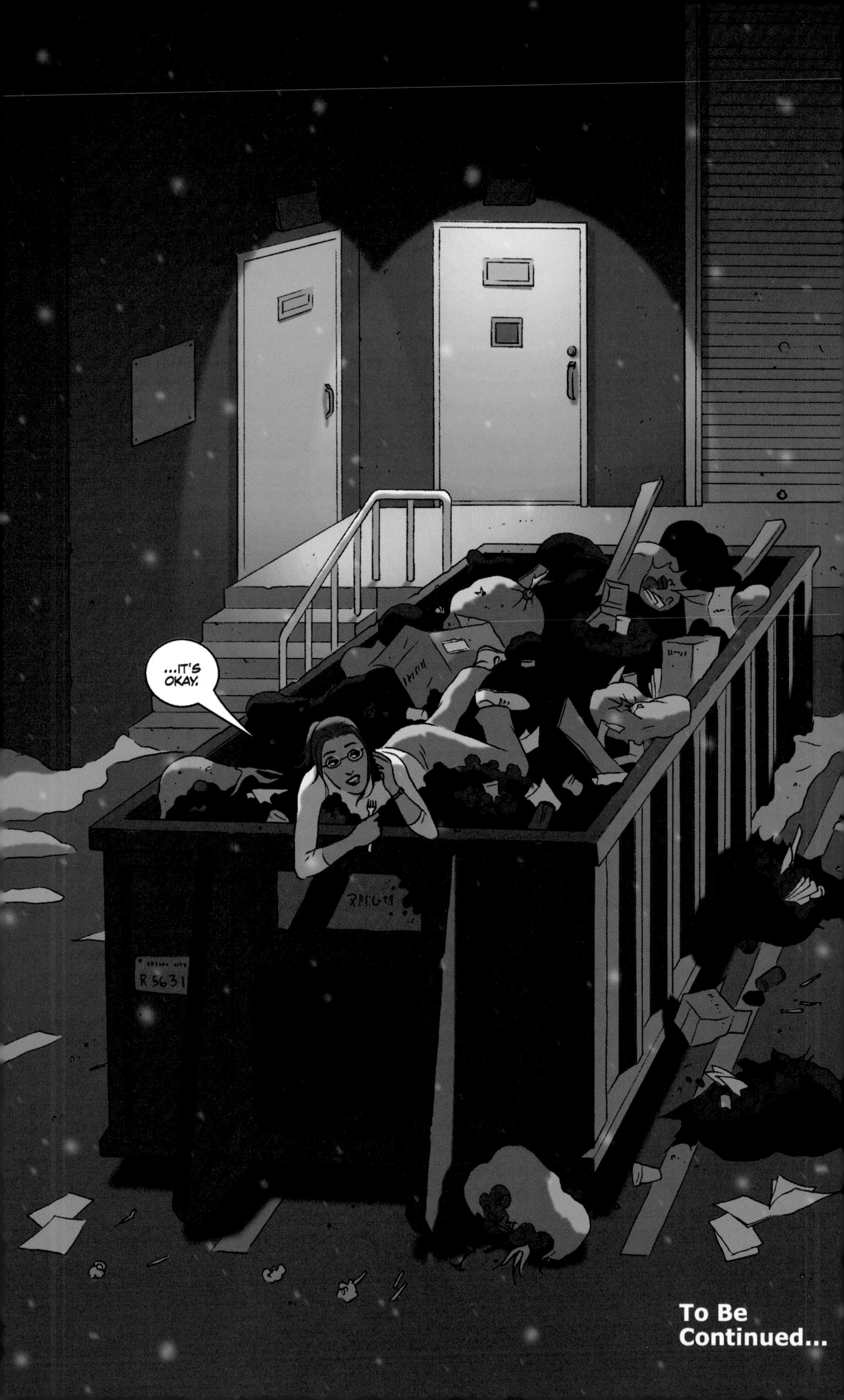
...IT'S OKAY.
R 5631
To Be Continued...

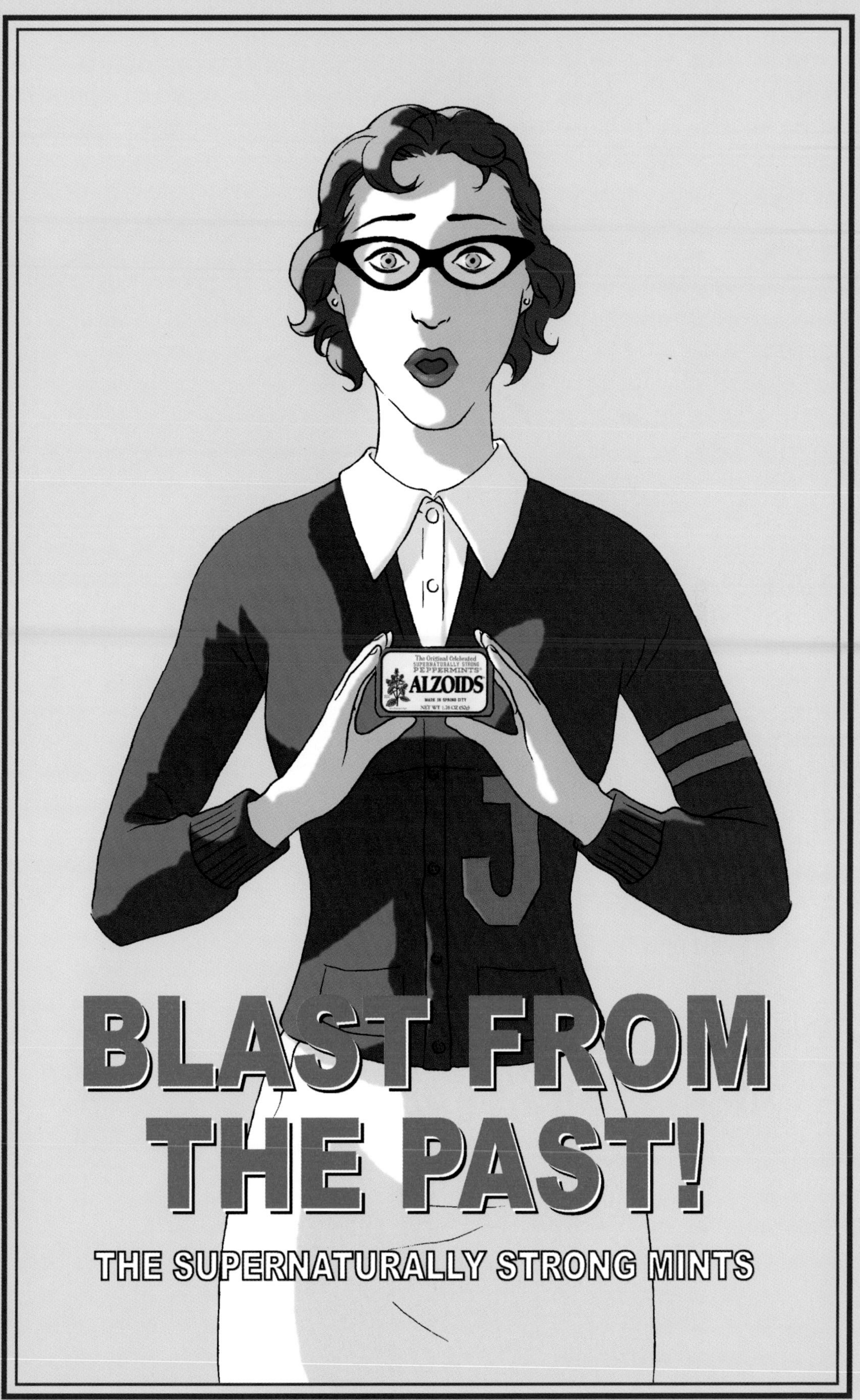
The Original Celebrated
SUPERNATURALLY STRONG
PEPPERMINTS
ALZOIDS
MADE IN SPRING CITY
BLAST FROM THE PAST!
THE SUPERNATURALLY STRONG MINTS

Jennifer Janus, Heroine Inc.'s "Cowgirl"

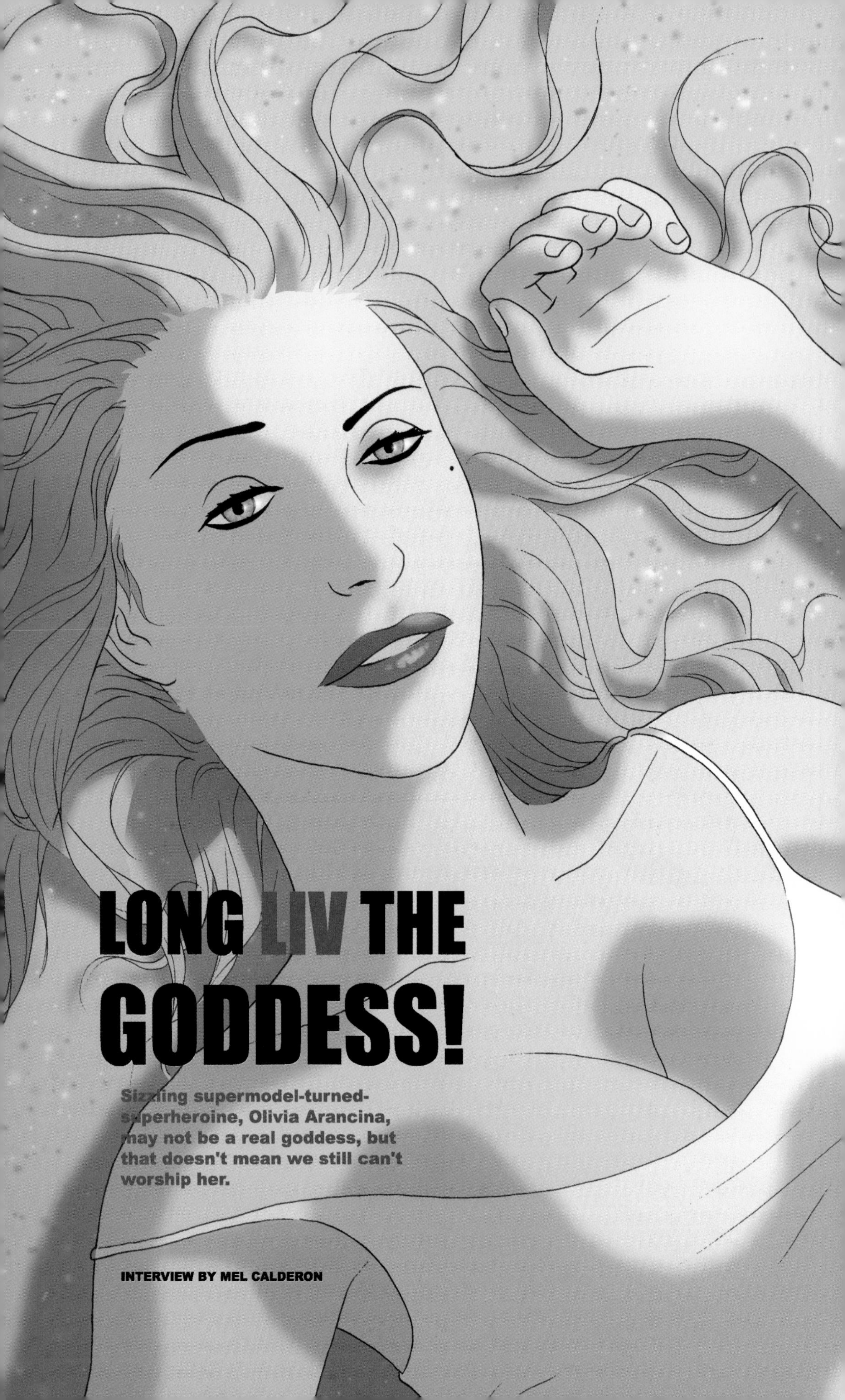

LONG LIV THE GODDESS!

Sizzling supermodel-turned-superheroine, Olivia Arancina, may not be a real goddess, but that doesn't mean we still can't worship her.

INTERVIEW BY MEL CALDERON

Normally, we laugh at celebrity crossovers because, let's face it-- they're destined to suck. But when supermodel, Olivia Arancina, made the leap from international catwalker to caped crusader as *Olympus Inc.'s* new Aphrodite, we reconsidered once she tickled our other "funny bone." With a body built for Greek mythology, and a spellbinding sensuality to match, the Italian bombshell is quickly making superhero spandex oh-so-hot again. We caught up with Liv at *Platinum's Superhuman Training Facility* in downtown Spring City, where the 5'11" hard-body effortlessly firmed her glutes, and we effortlessly enjoyed the view.

First off, let's get the formalities out of the way-- SWEET JESUS, YOU'RE HOT!
[laughs] Grazie.

So were you always this smoking or were you one of those ugly-duckling-turned-swan stories us guys don't really believe anyway?
Yeah, no one likes a beautiful girl with a sob story but, hey, when it's true, it's true. In my case, it was the insane growth spurt scenario-- by age 12, I was already 5'-friggin-8". So there was definitely that awkward phase of growing into my own body. It wasn't until my early twenties that I started to fill out and pack on some substantial meat.

And you certainly wear your meat well-- particularly in the revamped Aphrodite costume. I mean-- BOING! HELLO!
[smiling] Well... gee, I never knew I could stir up such emotion.

Yes, you make men very emotional. We can't stop reaching for the tissue. By the way, belated congratulations on the new gig. How cool is that?
Oh thank you! Yeah, it is very cool to be Aphrodite. I mean, c'mon-- this is *Olympus, Inc.* we're talking about. How many people get to play a goddess in their lifetime?

Hey, that was only one time, and it was Halloween for Christ's sake. So, tell me, since most people know you as Olivia, the supermodel, how do you think they'll react to the big superhero crossover?
People? Or my fans? Because some people will criticize me no matter what I do, and that just sucks. But I believe the fans will appreciate the transition and understand how important this is to me. Because becoming a superheroine wasn't just some marketing ploy, or shameless self-promotion-- not entirely. It was about becoming the real me. I'll never regret the modeling career because it played a huge part in my life. But at the same time, it was holding me back. I'm a superheroine-- this is who I

am now. And for the unfortunate ones who can't accept me, well then... I got two buns. Kiss 'em both.

[raising hand] Um, I totally can't accept you.
Nice try.

> **'I'm not trying to be sexy-- I'm just open-minded.'**

You're quite new to the superhero game. How come it took so long to come out?
Well, it wasn't really a matter of "coming out" because, even throughout my modeling days, I was quite open with my superhuman abilities. I just wasn't sure whether I wanted to pursue the actual superhero business. See, at first, it all seemed so...hmm, how should I say-- stupid? [laughs] I mean, these guys are really out there doing this hero stuff-- they can seriously get hurt. But one night, I met a couple *Heroine* girls at a party, and God-- they were just so cool and down to Earth. They completely won my respect. And at that moment, I just knew that no matter how far I got as a supermodel, I could always go farther as a superheroine.

So, is it weird replacing the last Aphrodite, Dana Samson, only months after her untimely death?
I hate to use the word "replace" when it comes to Dana because... well, you can't replace someone like her. She not only set the bar for Aphrodite, but for superheroes in general. I wasn't in the business yet, so I never knew her personally. But you didn't have to, to see what she's done for the community. And she paid the ultimate sacrifice when she fell to that vicious drive-by shooting last August. It really affected people, because they realized that not all superhumans are impervious. It was a tragedy but, at the same time, we have to go on with our lives and move

forward.

Now that you have *Olympus* status, can you give us the dirt on the other 11 gods?
Damn, you're trying to get me in trouble, huh? [laughs] No, I'm the new girl on the block, so I can't say I know the guys too well. Plus, keep in mind-- our agency is a fortune 500, corporate powerhouse. That means we're dealing with a lot of politics. So basically, I can't blame the gods when they get introverted. But yeah, eventually, I'd like to find some dirt on these guys, but for now, they're virtually perfect. Well, come to think of it... I have bumped into Athena in the bathroom from time to time and the girl definitely doesn't flush.

Youch. I bet that girl can crap a brick. So tell me, what do you look for in a guy?
I like shy guys. I know most girls usually go for the alpha males and the extroverts, but to me, those types can get old-- fast. Shy guys have a certain, subdued charm that's really underrated these days. The challenge of peeling through the layers intrigues me. And, as generic as it sounds, a sense of humor can go a long way. I just love it when a man can make me laugh. Well... as long as I'm not laughing in bed.

You've always been frank about sex. Were you just sexy since utero, or what?
I was born in the states, but my parents were immigrants and brought me up very Italian. I'm not saying Italians are the sexiest people who have ever walked the planet-- we were just a very close-knit unit. I could literally talk to them about anything--including sex--and not once have I ever felt ashamed or uncomfortable about it. I'm not trying to be sexy-- I'm just open-minded. Now as for Americans, I hate to generalize and clump people together, but from my experience, sex seems to be a rather taboo subject for most families.

It's true. My mother still thinks I'm a virgin... because... I am. Anyway, let's get serious here for a minute. Inquiring minds need to know. Can a normal human dude survive a night in the sack with you?
Loving the hard-hitting journalism here, guy. [laughs] Well, I don't know-- depends on the guy.

Oh, mama mia!
Don't get too excited. I'd most likely break you. [U]

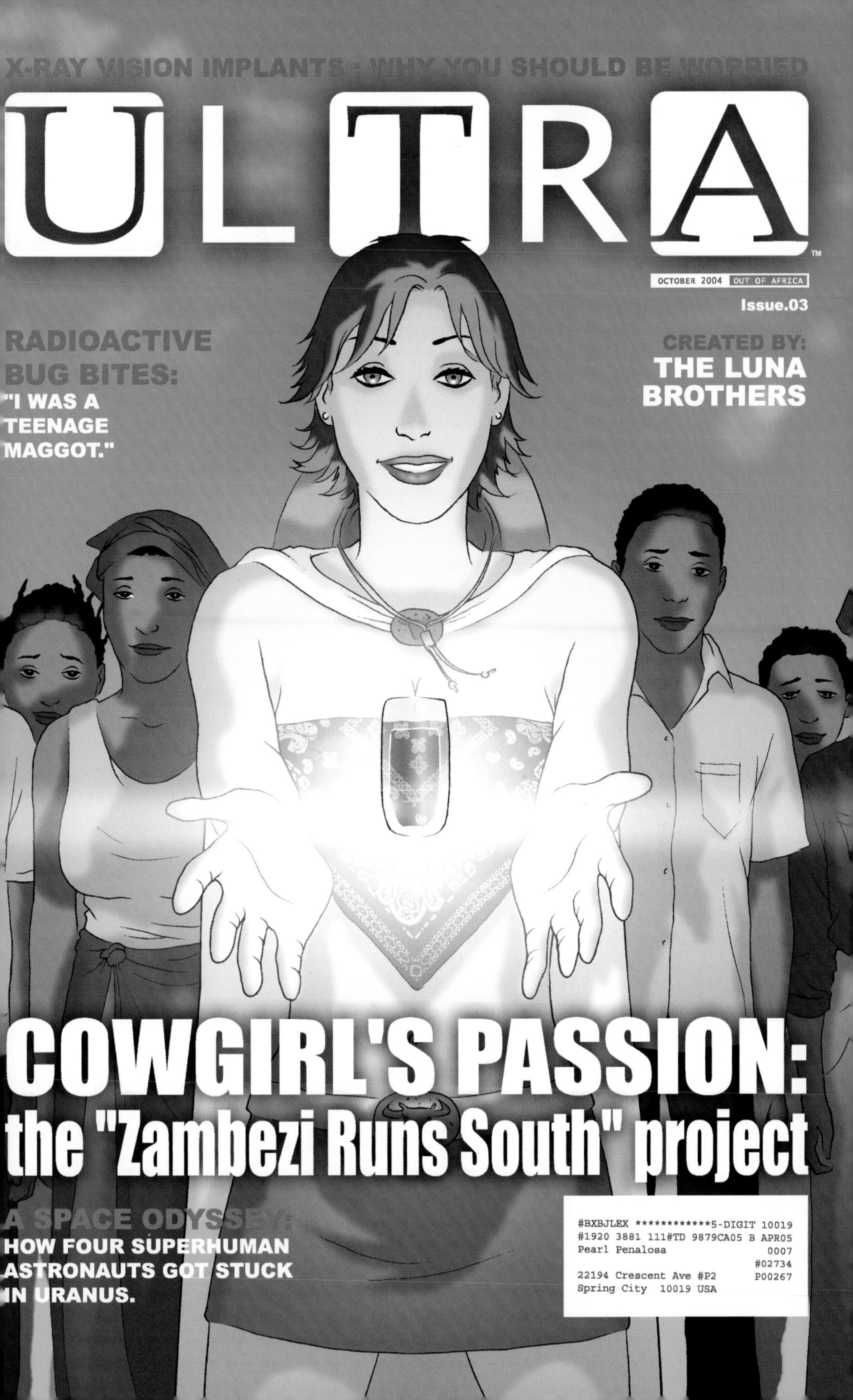
X-RAY VISION IMPLANTS : WHY YOU SHOULD BE WORRIED
ULTRA
TM
OCTOBER 2004 OUT OF AFRICA
Issue.03
RADIOACTIVE BUG BITES:
"I WAS A TEENAGE MAGGOT."
CREATED BY:
THE LUNA BROTHERS
COWGIRL'S PASSION:
the "Zambezi Runs South" project
A SPACE ODYSSEY:
HOW FOUR SUPERHUMAN ASTRONAUTS GOT STUCK IN URANUS.
#BXBJLEX ************5-DIGIT 10019
#1920 3881 111#TD 9879CA05 B APR05
Pearl Penalosa 0007
#02734
22194 Crescent Ave #P2 P00267
Spring City 10019 USA

126

94

134

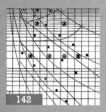

142

136

146

image® COMICS PRESENTS

THIS ISSUE
3   SEVEN DAYS, PART THREE

CREATED BY
112   **THE LUNA BROTHERS**

CREDITS
114   **JONATHAN LUNA**
     Plot, Art, Colors, Letters

114   **JOSHUA LUNA**
     Plot, Script, Layout Assists

OFFICIAL WEBSITE
120   **www.LunaBrothers.com**

For Image Comics

Erik Larsen - Publisher
Todd McFarlane - President
Marc Silvestri - CEO
Jim Valentino - Vice-President

Eric Stephenson - Executive Director
Missie Miranda - Controller
Brett Evans - Production Manager
B. Clay Moore - PR & Marketing
   Coordinator
Allen Hui - Production Artist
Joe Keatinge - Inventory
   Controller
Mia Machatton - Administrative
   Assistant

www.imagecomics.com

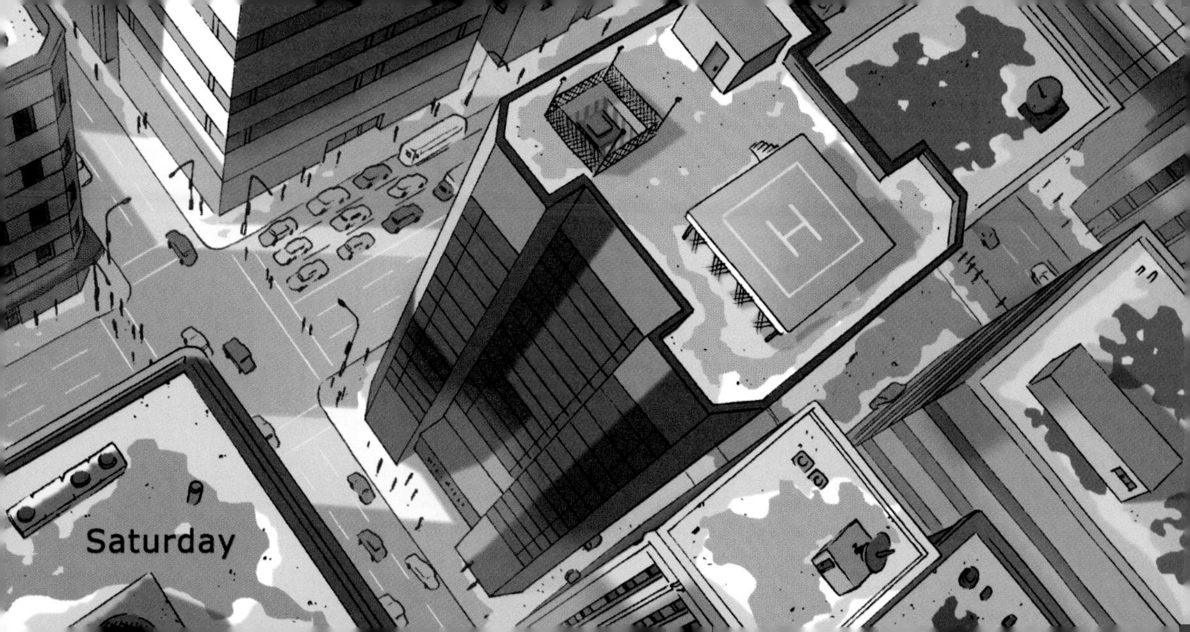
Saturday

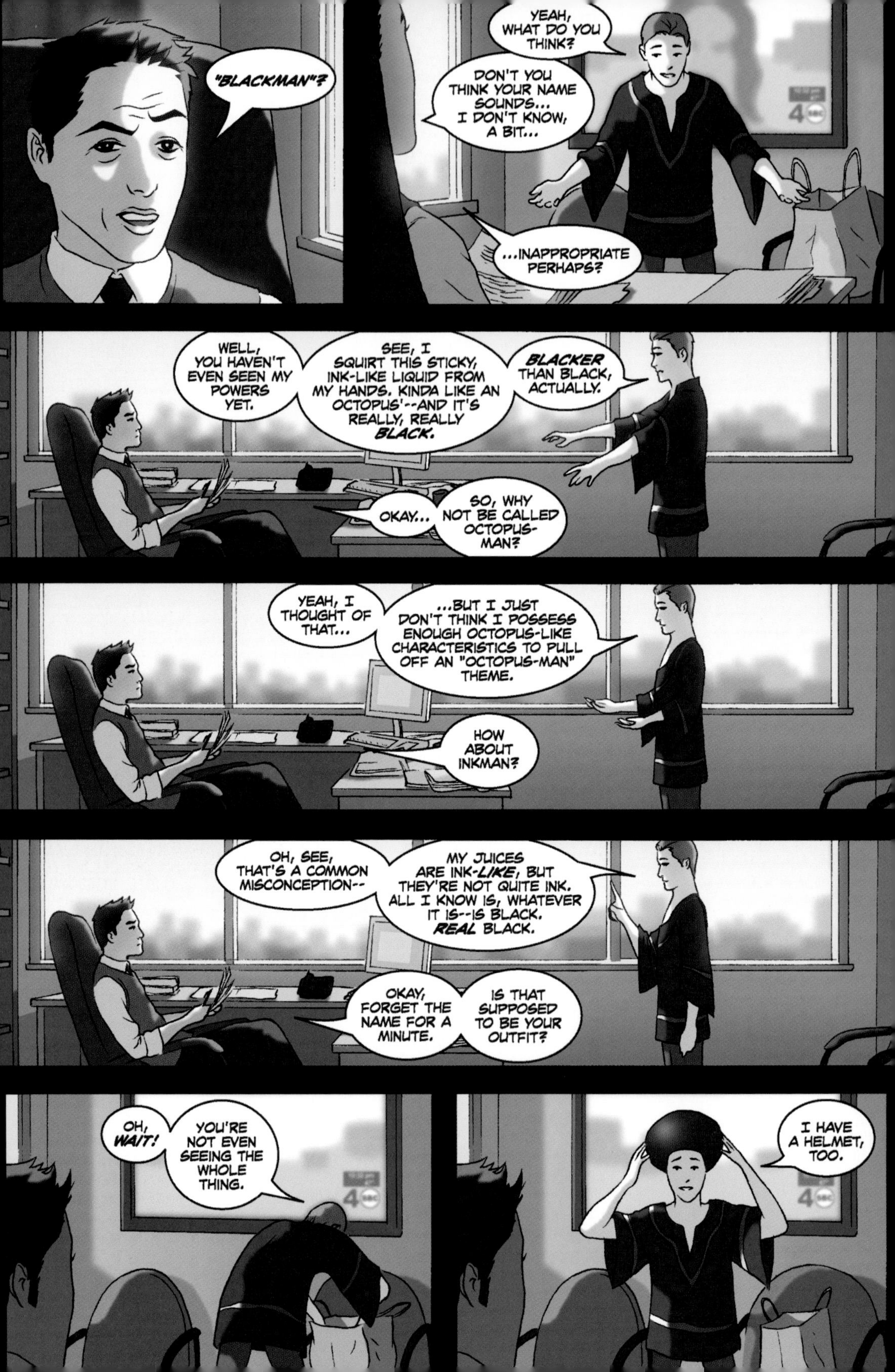
"BLACKMAN"?
YEAH, WHAT DO YOU THINK?
DON'T YOU THINK YOUR NAME SOUNDS... I DON'T KNOW, A BIT...
...INAPPROPRIATE PERHAPS?
WELL, YOU HAVEN'T EVEN SEEN MY POWERS YET.
SEE, I SQUIRT THIS STICKY, INK-LIKE LIQUID FROM MY HANDS. KINDA LIKE AN OCTOPUS'--AND IT'S REALLY, REALLY BLACK.
BLACKER THAN BLACK, ACTUALLY.
OKAY...
SO, WHY NOT BE CALLED OCTOPUS-MAN?
YEAH, I THOUGHT OF THAT...
...BUT I JUST DON'T THINK I POSSESS ENOUGH OCTOPUS-LIKE CHARACTERISTICS TO PULL OFF AN "OCTOPUS-MAN" THEME.
HOW ABOUT INKMAN?
OH, SEE, THAT'S A COMMON MISCONCEPTION--
MY JUICES ARE INK-LIKE, BUT THEY'RE NOT QUITE INK. ALL I KNOW IS, WHATEVER IT IS--IS BLACK. REAL BLACK.
OKAY, FORGET THE NAME FOR A MINUTE.
IS THAT SUPPOSED TO BE YOUR OUTFIT?
OH, WAIT!
YOU'RE NOT EVEN SEEING THE WHOLE THING.
I HAVE A HELMET, TOO.

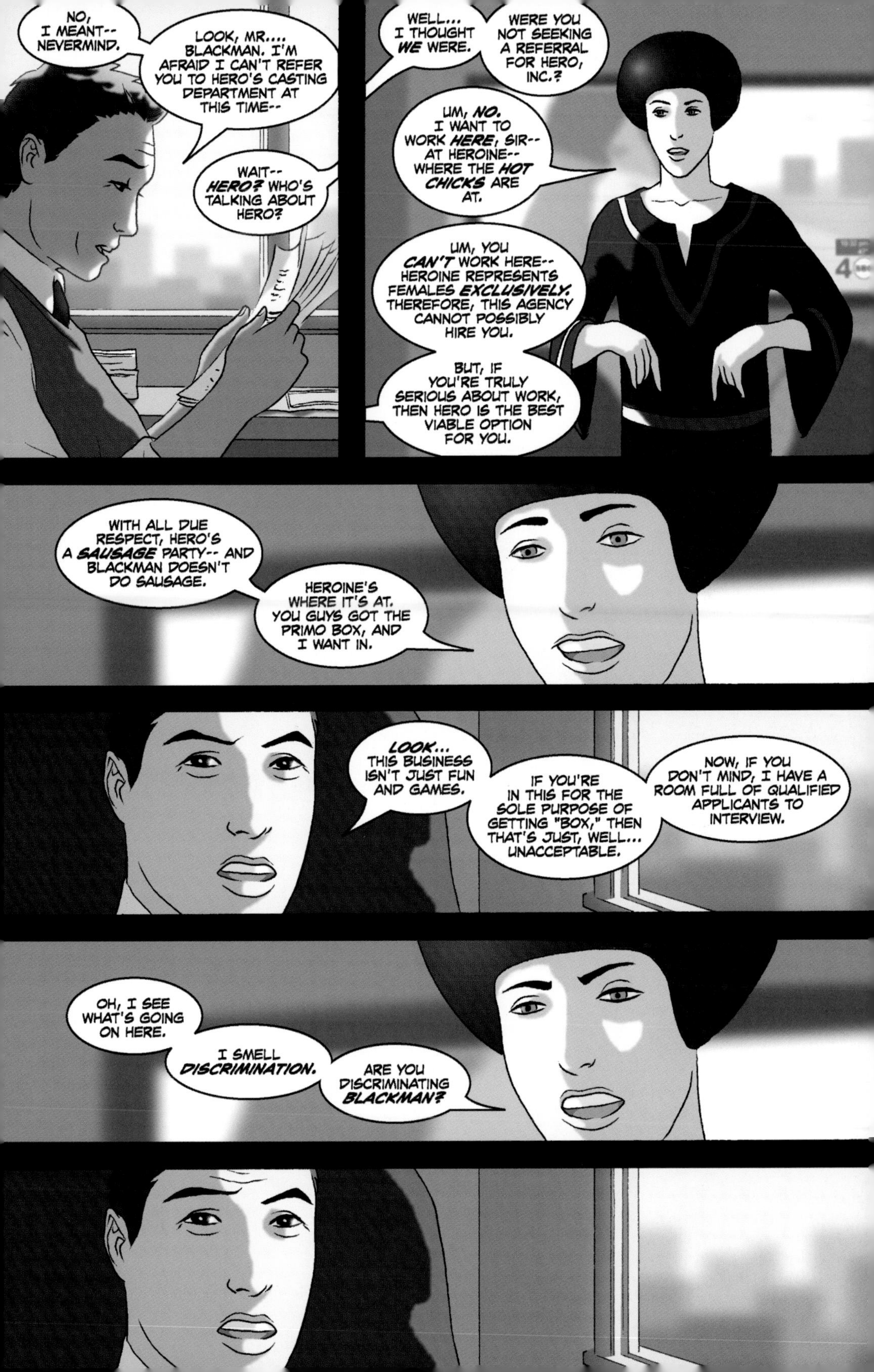
NO, I MEANT-- NEVERMIND.
LOOK, MR.... BLACKMAN. I'M AFRAID I CAN'T REFER YOU TO HERO'S CASTING DEPARTMENT AT THIS TIME--
WAIT-- HERO? WHO'S TALKING ABOUT HERO?
WELL... I THOUGHT WE WERE.
WERE YOU NOT SEEKING A REFERRAL FOR HERO, INC.?
UM, NO. I WANT TO WORK HERE, SIR-- AT HEROINE-- WHERE THE HOT CHICKS ARE AT.
UM, YOU CAN'T WORK HERE-- HEROINE REPRESENTS FEMALES EXCLUSIVELY. THEREFORE, THIS AGENCY CANNOT POSSIBLY HIRE YOU.
BUT, IF YOU'RE TRULY SERIOUS ABOUT WORK, THEN HERO IS THE BEST VIABLE OPTION FOR YOU.
WITH ALL DUE RESPECT, HERO'S A SAUSAGE PARTY-- AND BLACKMAN DOESN'T DO SAUSAGE.
HEROINE'S WHERE IT'S AT. YOU GUYS GOT THE PRIMO BOX, AND I WANT IN.
LOOK... THIS BUSINESS ISN'T JUST FUN AND GAMES.
IF YOU'RE IN THIS FOR THE SOLE PURPOSE OF GETTING "BOX," THEN THAT'S JUST, WELL... UNACCEPTABLE.
NOW, IF YOU DON'T MIND, I HAVE A ROOM FULL OF QUALIFIED APPLICANTS TO INTERVIEW.
OH, I SEE WHAT'S GOING ON HERE.
I SMELL DISCRIMINATION.
ARE YOU DISCRIMINATING BLACKMAN?

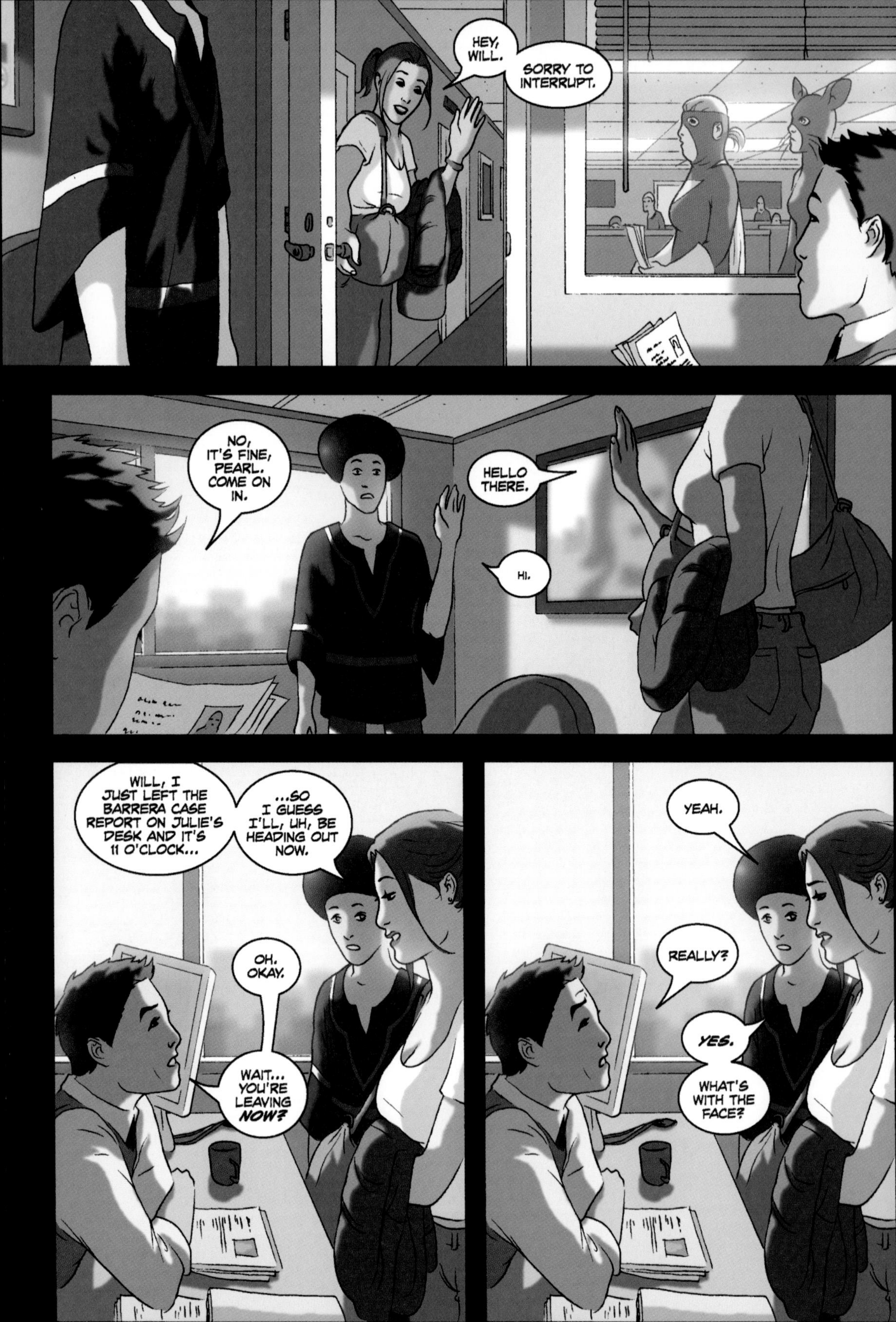
HEY, WILL.
SORRY TO INTERRUPT.
NO, IT'S FINE, PEARL. COME ON IN.
HELLO THERE.
HI.
WILL, I JUST LEFT THE BARRERA CASE REPORT ON JULIE'S DESK AND IT'S 11 O'CLOCK...
...SO I GUESS I'LL, UH, BE HEADING OUT NOW.
OH. OKAY.
WAIT... YOU'RE LEAVING *NOW?*
YEAH.
REALLY?
YES.
WHAT'S WITH THE FACE?

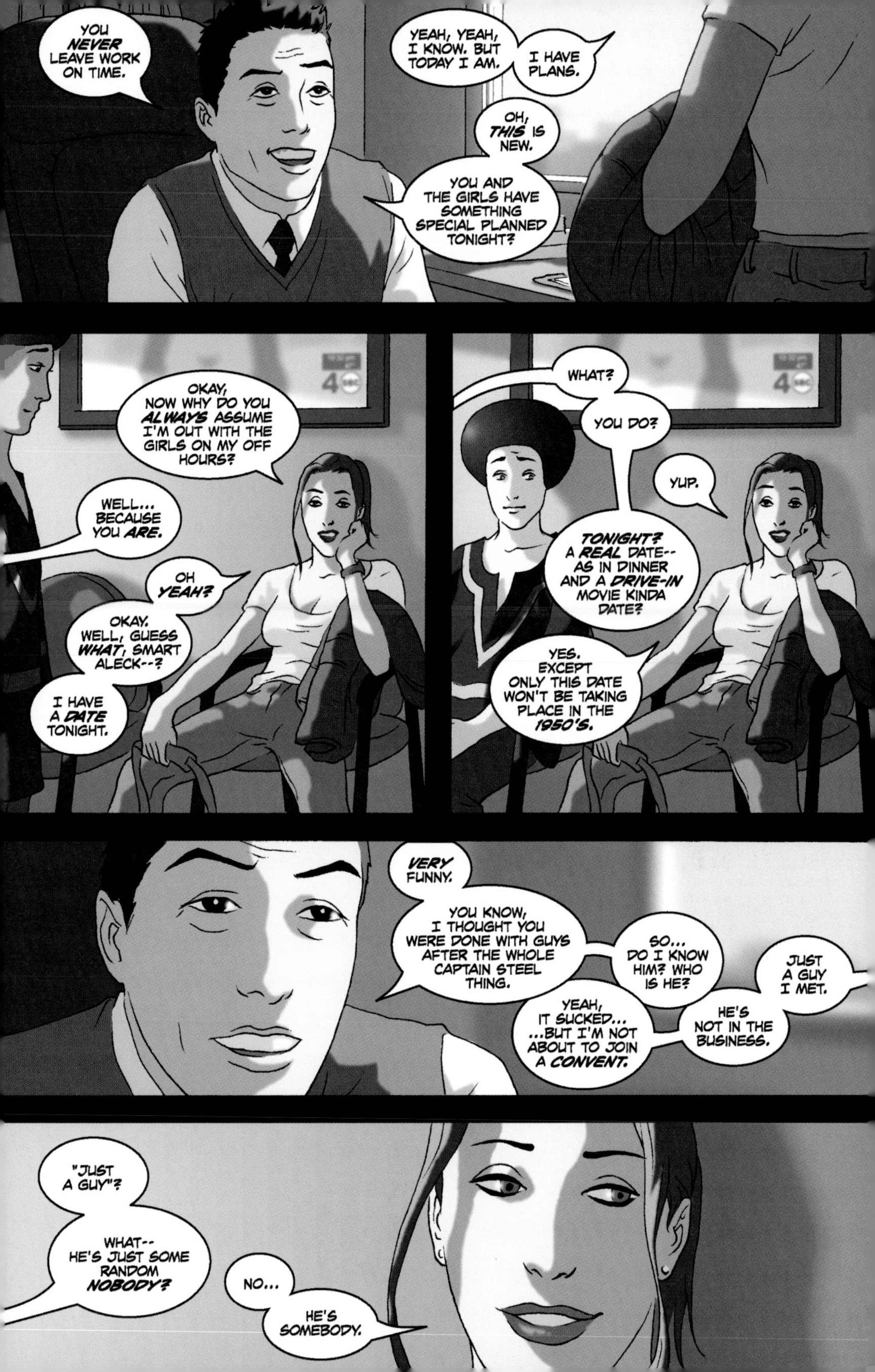

YOU NEVER LEAVE WORK ON TIME.
YEAH, YEAH, I KNOW. BUT TODAY I AM.
I HAVE PLANS.
OH, THIS IS NEW.
YOU AND THE GIRLS HAVE SOMETHING SPECIAL PLANNED TONIGHT?
OKAY, NOW WHY DO YOU ALWAYS ASSUME I'M OUT WITH THE GIRLS ON MY OFF HOURS?
WELL... BECAUSE YOU ARE.
OH YEAH?
OKAY. WELL, GUESS WHAT, SMART ALECK--?
I HAVE A DATE TONIGHT.
WHAT?
YOU DO?
YUP.
TONIGHT? A REAL DATE--AS IN DINNER AND A DRIVE-IN MOVIE KINDA DATE?
YES. EXCEPT ONLY THIS DATE WON'T BE TAKING PLACE IN THE 1950'S.
VERY FUNNY.
YOU KNOW, I THOUGHT YOU WERE DONE WITH GUYS AFTER THE WHOLE CAPTAIN STEEL THING.
YEAH, IT SUCKED... ...BUT I'M NOT ABOUT TO JOIN A CONVENT.
SO... DO I KNOW HIM? WHO IS HE?
HE'S NOT IN THE BUSINESS.
JUST A GUY I MET.
"JUST A GUY"?
WHAT--HE'S JUST SOME RANDOM NOBODY?
NO...
HE'S SOMEBODY.

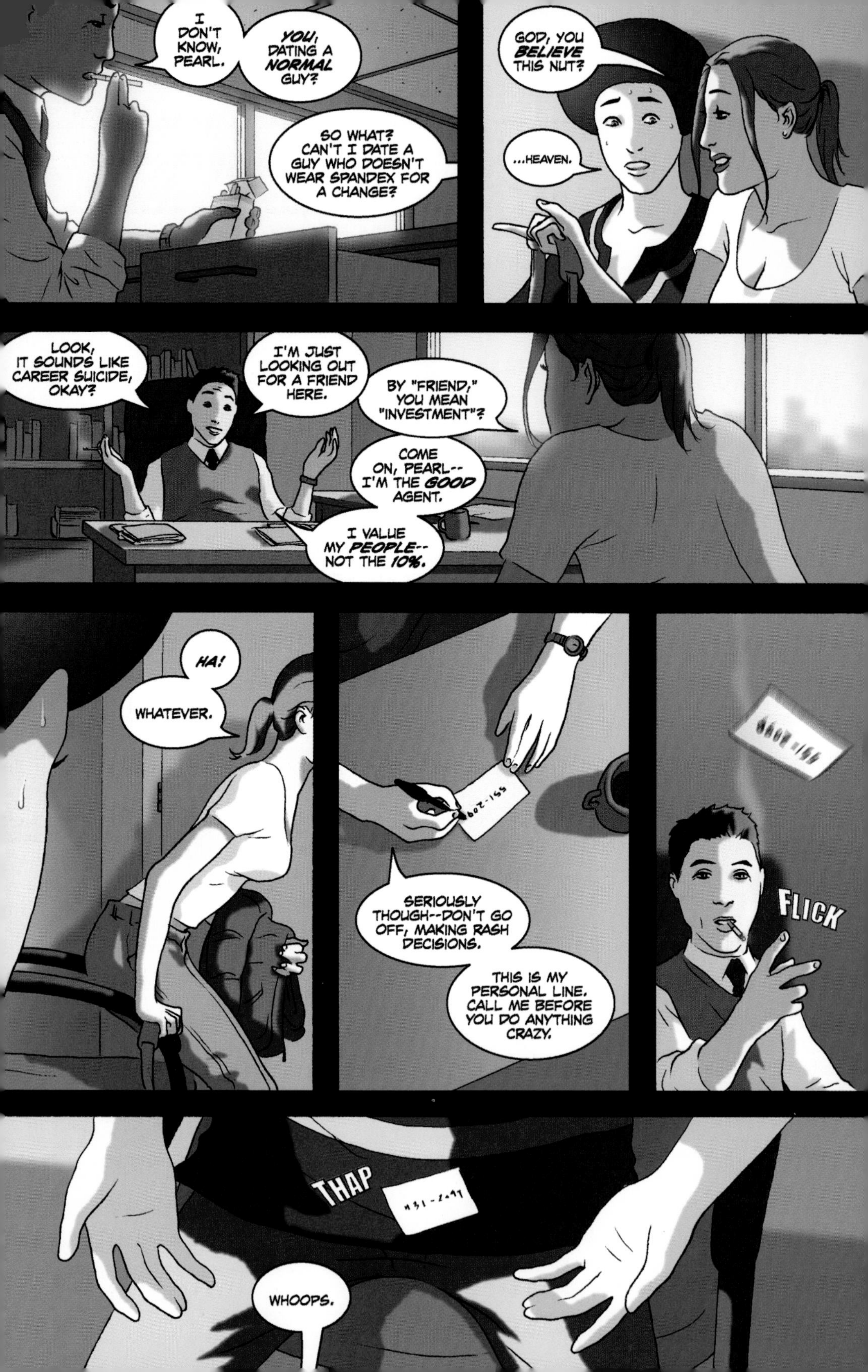

I DON'T KNOW, PEARL.
YOU, DATING A NORMAL GUY?
SO WHAT? CAN'T I DATE A GUY WHO DOESN'T WEAR SPANDEX FOR A CHANGE?
GOD, YOU BELIEVE THIS NUT?
...HEAVEN.
LOOK, IT SOUNDS LIKE CAREER SUICIDE, OKAY?
I'M JUST LOOKING OUT FOR A FRIEND HERE.
BY "FRIEND," YOU MEAN "INVESTMENT"?
COME ON, PEARL-- I'M THE GOOD AGENT.
I VALUE MY PEOPLE-- NOT THE 10%.
HA!
WHATEVER.
SERIOUSLY THOUGH--DON'T GO OFF, MAKING RASH DECISIONS.
THIS IS MY PERSONAL LINE. CALL ME BEFORE YOU DO ANYTHING CRAZY.
FLICK
THAP
431-2097
WHOOPS.

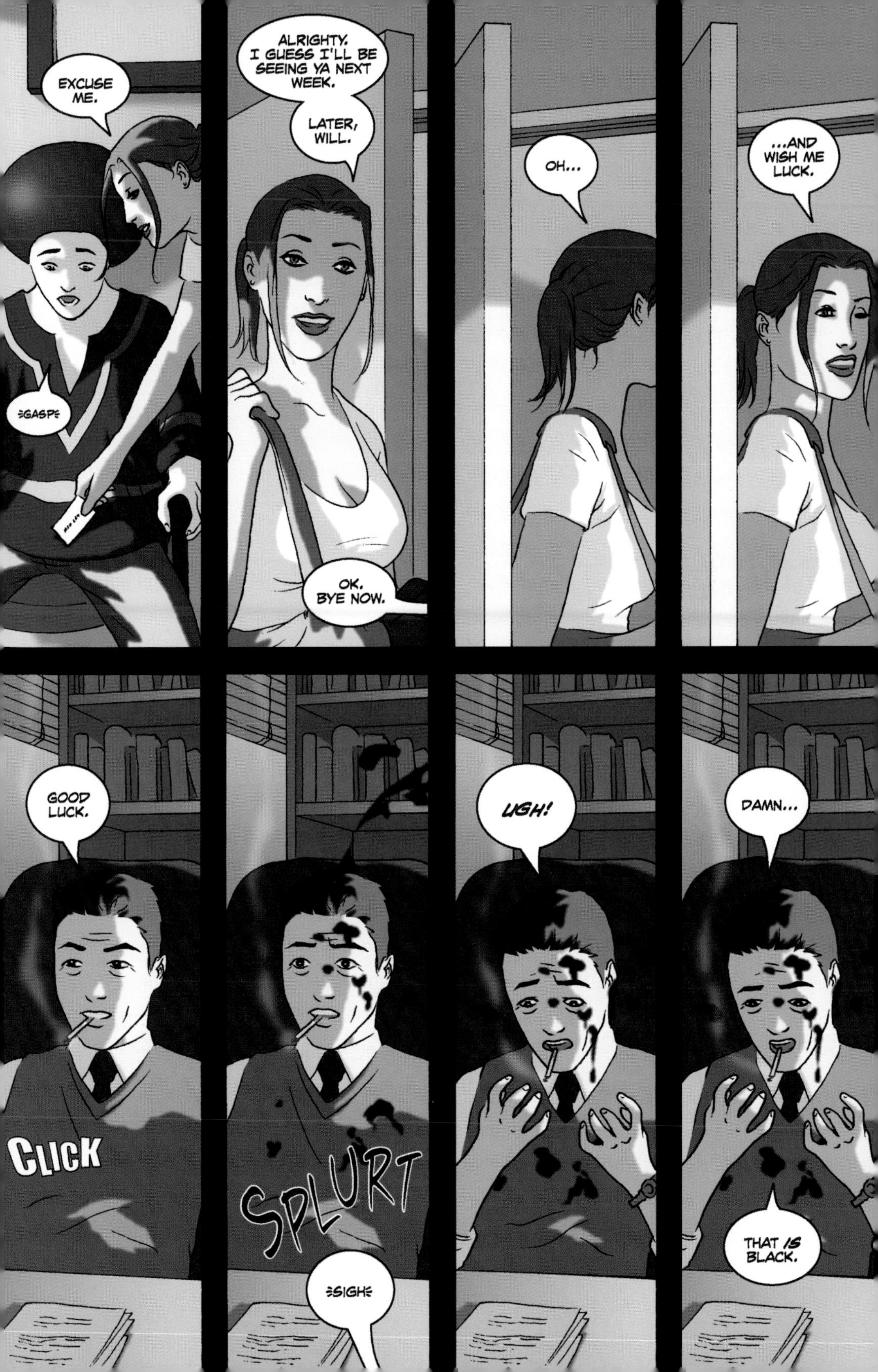
EXCUSE ME.
=GASP=
ALRIGHTY. I GUESS I'LL BE SEEING YA NEXT WEEK.
LATER, WILL.
OK. BYE NOW.
OH...
...AND WISH ME LUCK.
GOOD LUCK.
CLICK
SPLURT
=SIGH=
UGH!
DAMN...
THAT IS BLACK.

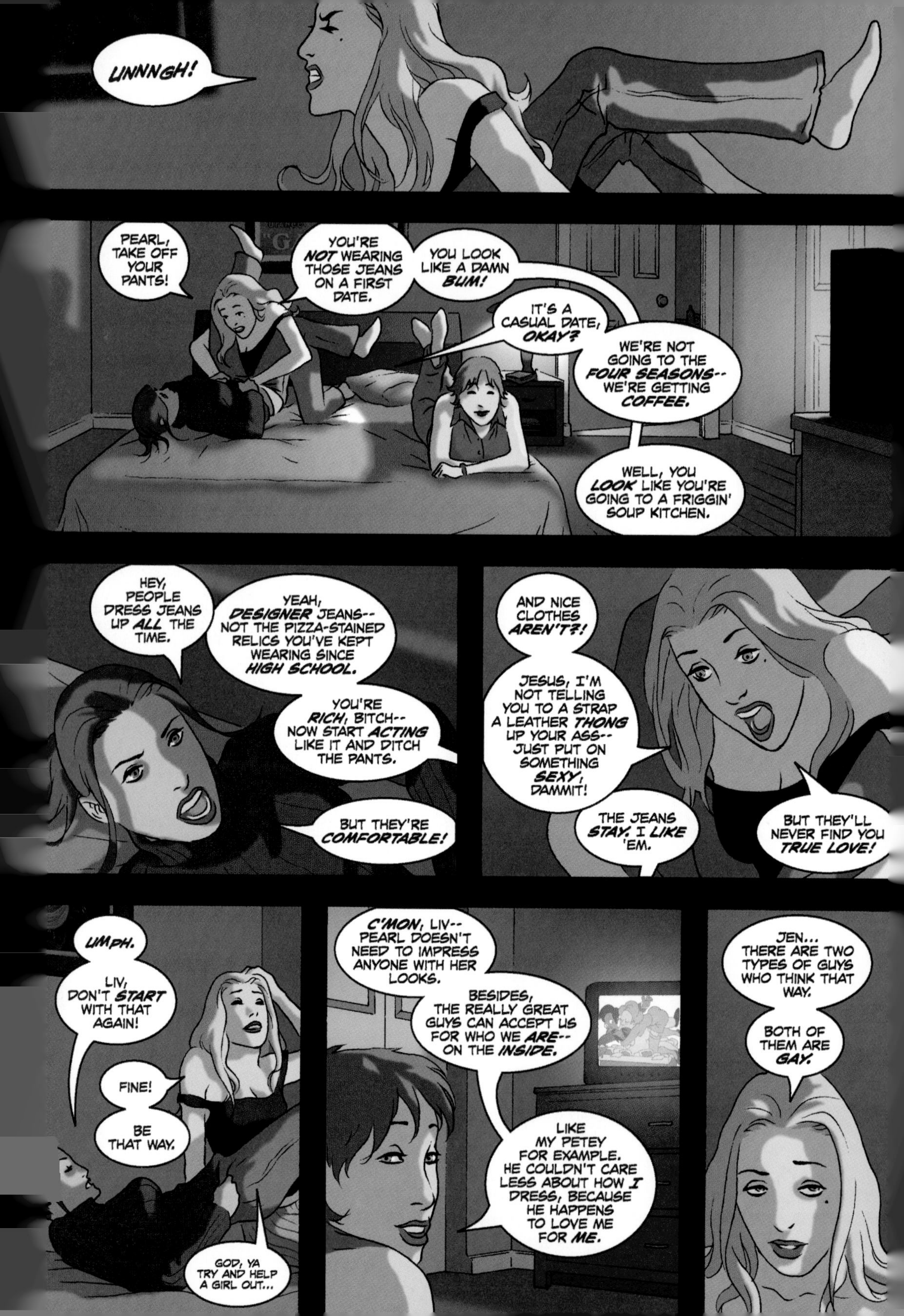
UNNNGH!
PEARL, TAKE OFF YOUR PANTS!
YOU'RE NOT WEARING THOSE JEANS ON A FIRST DATE.
YOU LOOK LIKE A DAMN BUM!
IT'S A CASUAL DATE, OKAY?
WE'RE NOT GOING TO THE FOUR SEASONS-- WE'RE GETTING COFFEE.
WELL, YOU LOOK LIKE YOU'RE GOING TO A FRIGGIN' SOUP KITCHEN.
HEY, PEOPLE DRESS JEANS UP ALL THE TIME.
YEAH, DESIGNER JEANS-- NOT THE PIZZA-STAINED RELICS YOU'VE KEPT WEARING SINCE HIGH SCHOOL.
YOU'RE RICH, BITCH-- NOW START ACTING LIKE IT AND DITCH THE PANTS.
BUT THEY'RE COMFORTABLE!
AND NICE CLOTHES AREN'T?!
JESUS, I'M NOT TELLING YOU TO A STRAP A LEATHER THONG UP YOUR ASS-- JUST PUT ON SOMETHING SEXY, DAMMIT!
THE JEANS STAY. I LIKE 'EM.
BUT THEY'LL NEVER FIND YOU TRUE LOVE!
UMPH.
LIV, DON'T START WITH THAT AGAIN!
FINE!
BE THAT WAY.
GOD, YA TRY AND HELP A GIRL OUT...
C'MON, LIV-- PEARL DOESN'T NEED TO IMPRESS ANYONE WITH HER LOOKS.
BESIDES, THE REALLY GREAT GUYS CAN ACCEPT US FOR WHO WE ARE-- ON THE INSIDE.
LIKE MY PETEY FOR EXAMPLE. HE COULDN'T CARE LESS ABOUT HOW I DRESS, BECAUSE HE HAPPENS TO LOVE ME FOR ME.
JEN... THERE ARE TWO TYPES OF GUYS WHO THINK THAT WAY.
BOTH OF THEM ARE GAY.

BY GAY, I HOPE YOU MEAN *MERRY*.

WELL, YEAH, THAT CAN APPLY TOO.

EXCUSE ME? ARE YOU CALLING PETEY A *HOMOSEXUAL*?

NO, I *NEVER* SAID YOUR BOYFRIEND WAS A HOMOSEXUAL.

I MEAN, HE *IS* ONE... BUT, FOR THE RECORD, I *NEVER* OPENLY STATED THAT.

OKAY, I'M *SERIOUSLY* GONNA SEAL YOUR LIPS SHUT WITH A LASER BEAM RIGHT NOW.

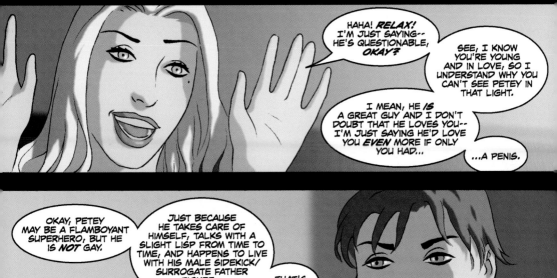

HAHA! *RELAX!* I'M JUST SAYING-- HE'S QUESTIONABLE, *OKAY?*

SEE, I KNOW YOU'RE YOUNG AND IN LOVE, SO I UNDERSTAND WHY YOU CAN'T SEE PETEY IN THAT LIGHT.

I MEAN, HE *IS* A GREAT GUY AND I DON'T DOUBT THAT HE LOVES YOU-- I'M JUST SAYING HE'D LOVE YOU *EVEN* MORE IF ONLY YOU HAD...

...A PENIS.

OKAY, PETEY MAY BE A FLAMBOYANT SUPERHERO, BUT HE IS *NOT* GAY.

JUST BECAUSE HE TAKES CARE OF HIMSELF, TALKS WITH A SLIGHT LISP FROM TIME TO TIME, AND HAPPENS TO LIVE WITH HIS MALE SIDEKICK/ SURROGATE FATHER FIGURE-- HE'S *GAY?!*

THAT'S *ABSURD*.

JEN, THEIR TEAM NAME IS "*SWEET AND SOUR*."

PETER'S "*SWEET*."

IT'S *OBVIOUSLY* A CLASSIC "GOOD COP, BAD COP" GIMMICK, DUH! *JEEZ!*

COME ON, LIV. PETER'S NOT GAY.

SUPERHEROES JUST TEND TO BE A LITTLE... COMPLICATED.

COMPLICATED LIKE YOUR *EX*, YOU MEAN?

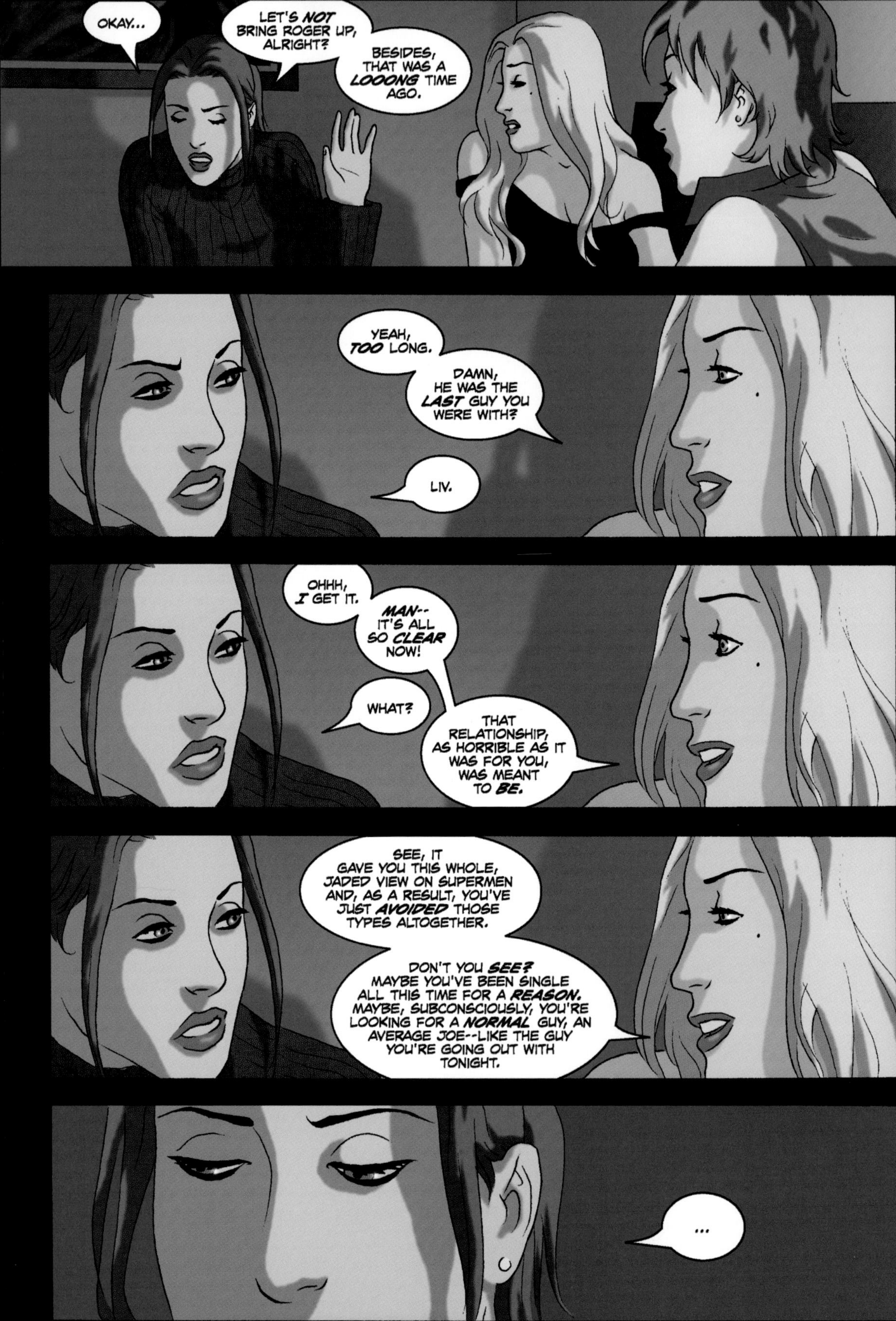

OKAY...
LET'S NOT BRING ROGER UP, ALRIGHT?
BESIDES, THAT WAS A LOOONG TIME AGO.
YEAH, TOO LONG.
DAMN, HE WAS THE LAST GUY YOU WERE WITH?
LIV.
OHHH, I GET IT.
MAN-- IT'S ALL SO CLEAR NOW!
WHAT?
THAT RELATIONSHIP, AS HORRIBLE AS IT WAS FOR YOU, WAS MEANT TO BE.
SEE, IT GAVE YOU THIS WHOLE, JADED VIEW ON SUPERMEN AND, AS A RESULT, YOU'VE JUST AVOIDED THOSE TYPES ALTOGETHER.
DON'T YOU SEE? MAYBE YOU'VE BEEN SINGLE ALL THIS TIME FOR A REASON. MAYBE, SUBCONSCIOUSLY, YOU'RE LOOKING FOR A NORMAL GUY, AN AVERAGE JOE--LIKE THE GUY YOU'RE GOING OUT WITH TONIGHT.
...

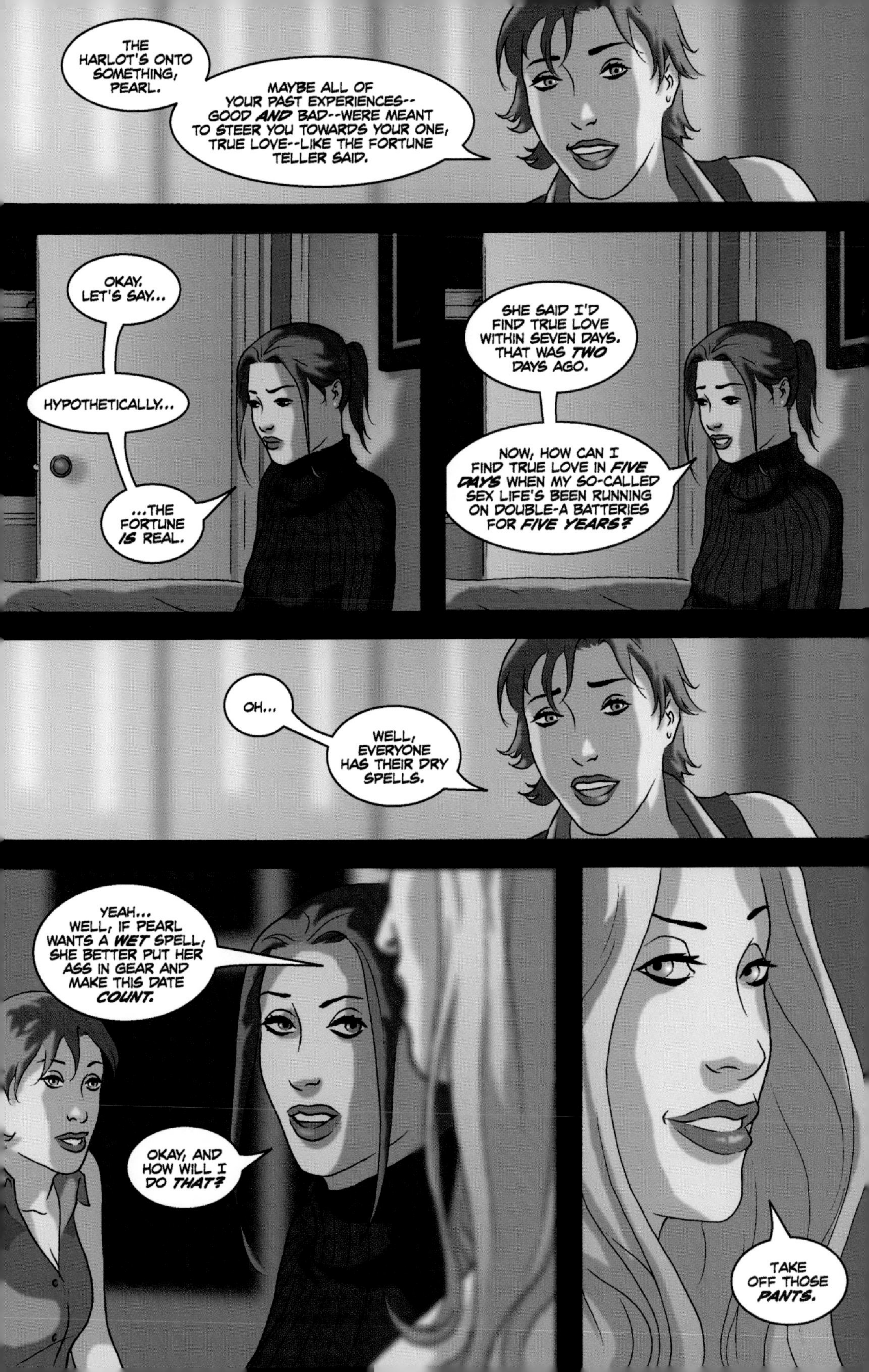
THE HARLOT'S ONTO SOMETHING, PEARL.
MAYBE ALL OF YOUR PAST EXPERIENCES-- GOOD AND BAD--WERE MEANT TO STEER YOU TOWARDS YOUR ONE, TRUE LOVE--LIKE THE FORTUNE TELLER SAID.
OKAY. LET'S SAY...
HYPOTHETICALLY...
...THE FORTUNE IS REAL.
SHE SAID I'D FIND TRUE LOVE WITHIN SEVEN DAYS. THAT WAS TWO DAYS AGO.
NOW, HOW CAN I FIND TRUE LOVE IN FIVE DAYS WHEN MY SO-CALLED SEX LIFE'S BEEN RUNNING ON DOUBLE-A BATTERIES FOR FIVE YEARS?
OH...
WELL, EVERYONE HAS THEIR DRY SPELLS.
YEAH... WELL, IF PEARL WANTS A WET SPELL, SHE BETTER PUT HER ASS IN GEAR AND MAKE THIS DATE COUNT.
OKAY, AND HOW WILL I DO THAT?
TAKE OFF THOSE PANTS.

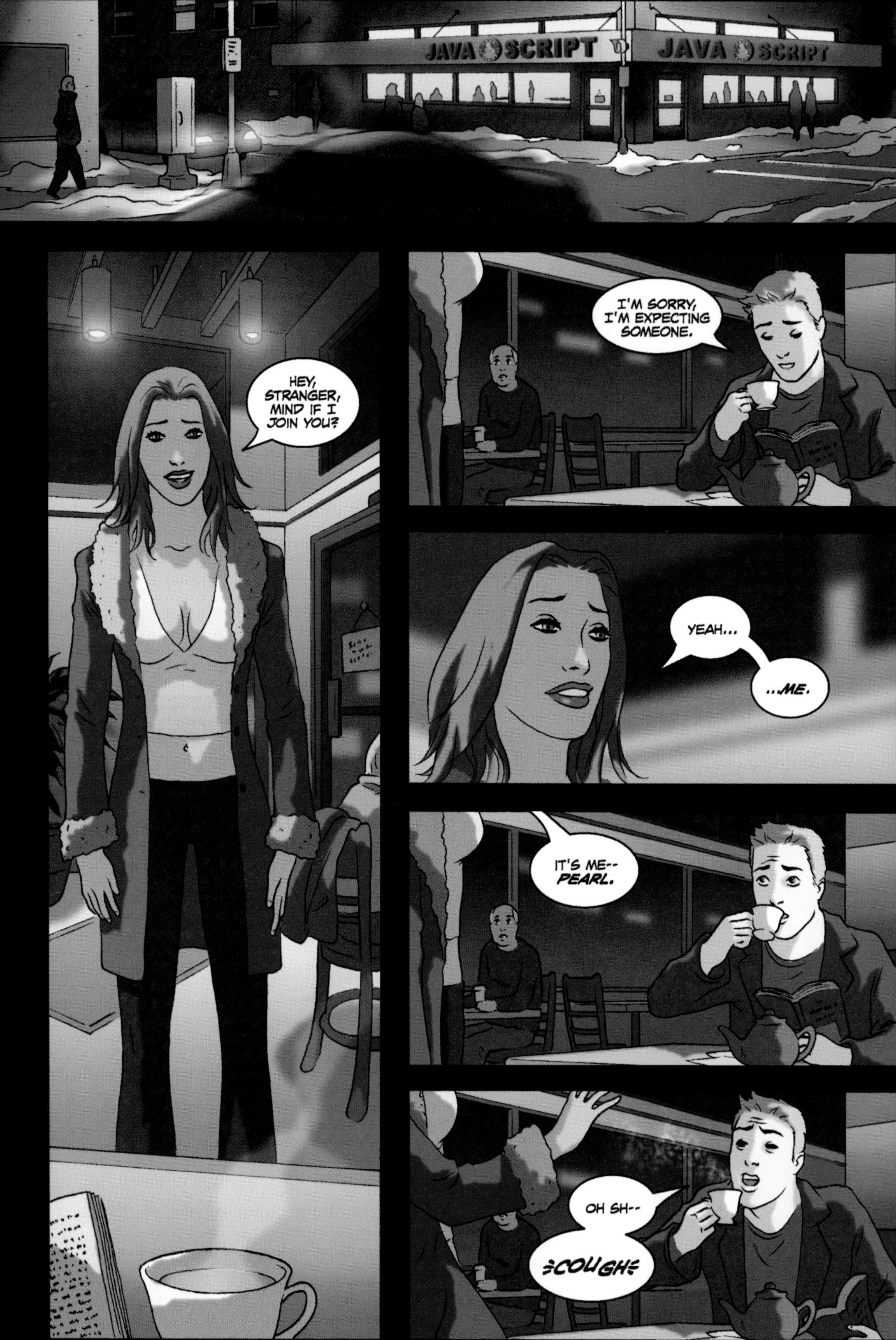
JAVA SCRIPT
JAVA SCRIPT
HEY, STRANGER, MIND IF I JOIN YOU?
I'M SORRY, I'M EXPECTING SOMEONE.
YEAH...
...ME.
IT'S ME-- PEARL.
OH SH--
COUGH

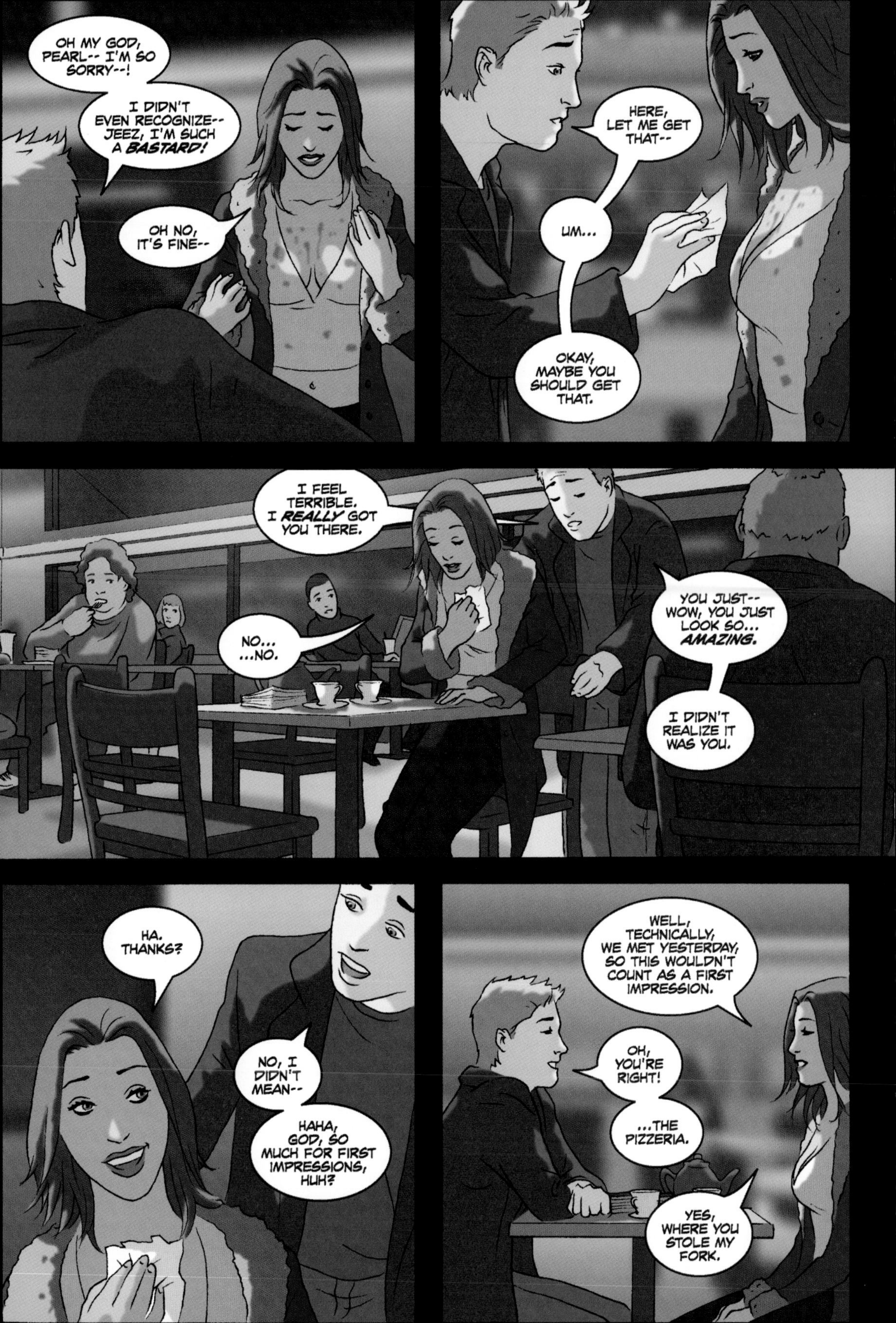
OH MY GOD, PEARL-- I'M SO SORRY--!
I DIDN'T EVEN RECOGNIZE-- JEEZ, I'M SUCH A ***BASTARD!***
OH NO, IT'S FINE--
HERE, LET ME GET THAT--
UM...
OKAY, MAYBE YOU SHOULD GET THAT.
I FEEL TERRIBLE. I ***REALLY*** GOT YOU THERE.
NO... ...NO.
YOU JUST-- WOW, YOU JUST LOOK SO... ***AMAZING.***
I DIDN'T REALIZE IT WAS YOU.
HA. THANKS?
NO, I DIDN'T MEAN--
HAHA, GOD, SO MUCH FOR FIRST IMPRESSIONS, HUH?
WELL, TECHNICALLY, WE MET YESTERDAY, SO THIS WOULDN'T COUNT AS A FIRST IMPRESSION.
OH, YOU'RE RIGHT!
...THE PIZZERIA.
YES, WHERE YOU STOLE MY FORK.

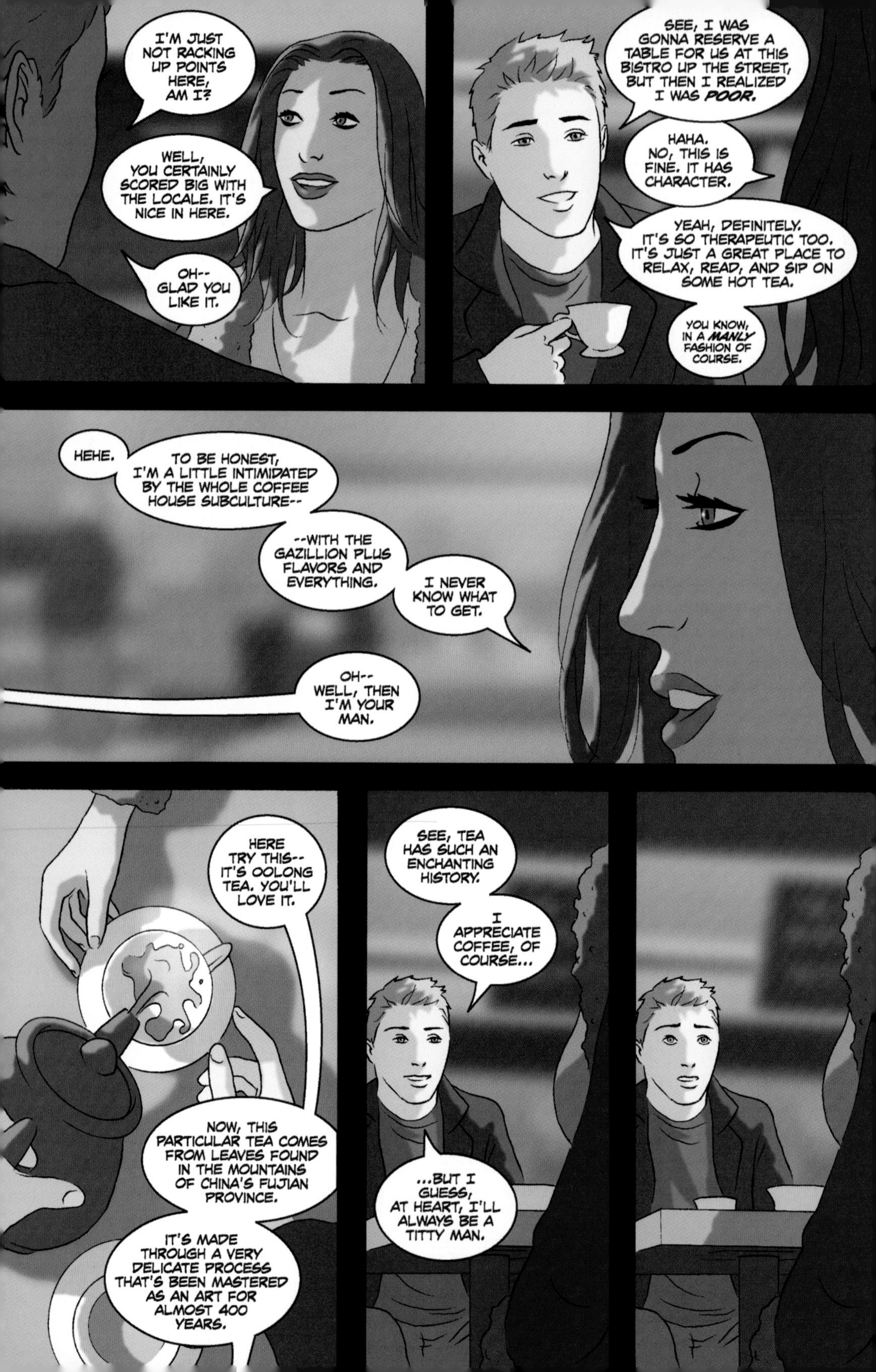
I'M JUST NOT RACKING UP POINTS HERE, AM I?
WELL, YOU CERTAINLY SCORED BIG WITH THE LOCALE. IT'S NICE IN HERE.
OH-- GLAD YOU LIKE IT.
SEE, I WAS GONNA RESERVE A TABLE FOR US AT THIS BISTRO UP THE STREET, BUT THEN I REALIZED I WAS POOR.
HAHA. NO, THIS IS FINE. IT HAS CHARACTER.
YEAH, DEFINITELY. IT'S SO THERAPEUTIC TOO. IT'S JUST A GREAT PLACE TO RELAX, READ, AND SIP ON SOME HOT TEA.
YOU KNOW, IN A MANLY FASHION OF COURSE.
HEHE.
TO BE HONEST, I'M A LITTLE INTIMIDATED BY THE WHOLE COFFEE HOUSE SUBCULTURE--
--WITH THE GAZILLION PLUS FLAVORS AND EVERYTHING.
I NEVER KNOW WHAT TO GET.
OH-- WELL, THEN I'M YOUR MAN.
HERE TRY THIS-- IT'S OOLONG TEA. YOU'LL LOVE IT.
NOW, THIS PARTICULAR TEA COMES FROM LEAVES FOUND IN THE MOUNTAINS OF CHINA'S FUJIAN PROVINCE.
IT'S MADE THROUGH A VERY DELICATE PROCESS THAT'S BEEN MASTERED AS AN ART FOR ALMOST 400 YEARS.
SEE, TEA HAS SUCH AN ENCHANTING HISTORY.
I APPRECIATE COFFEE, OF COURSE...
...BUT I GUESS, AT HEART, I'LL ALWAYS BE A TITTY MAN.

OH!

I MEANT, "TITTY"!

NO—!

HA.

JASON, RELAX.

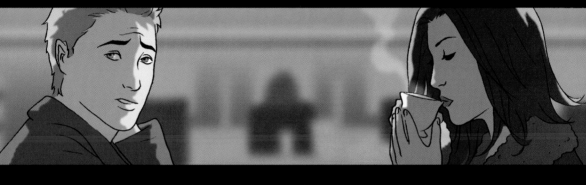

MMM...

OKAY, I'M OFFICIALLY HOOKED. THIS TEA IS DELICIOUS.

OH, COOL!

MAN...

...NO ONE'S EVER GONNA BELIEVE YOU WERE HERE, SLUMMING IT WITH ME.

NO, THIS ISN'T SLUMMING. I LIKE IT LIKE THIS.

SOMETIMES I NEED TO DISAPPEAR—

—MOMMY, LOOK! IT'S ULTRA!!

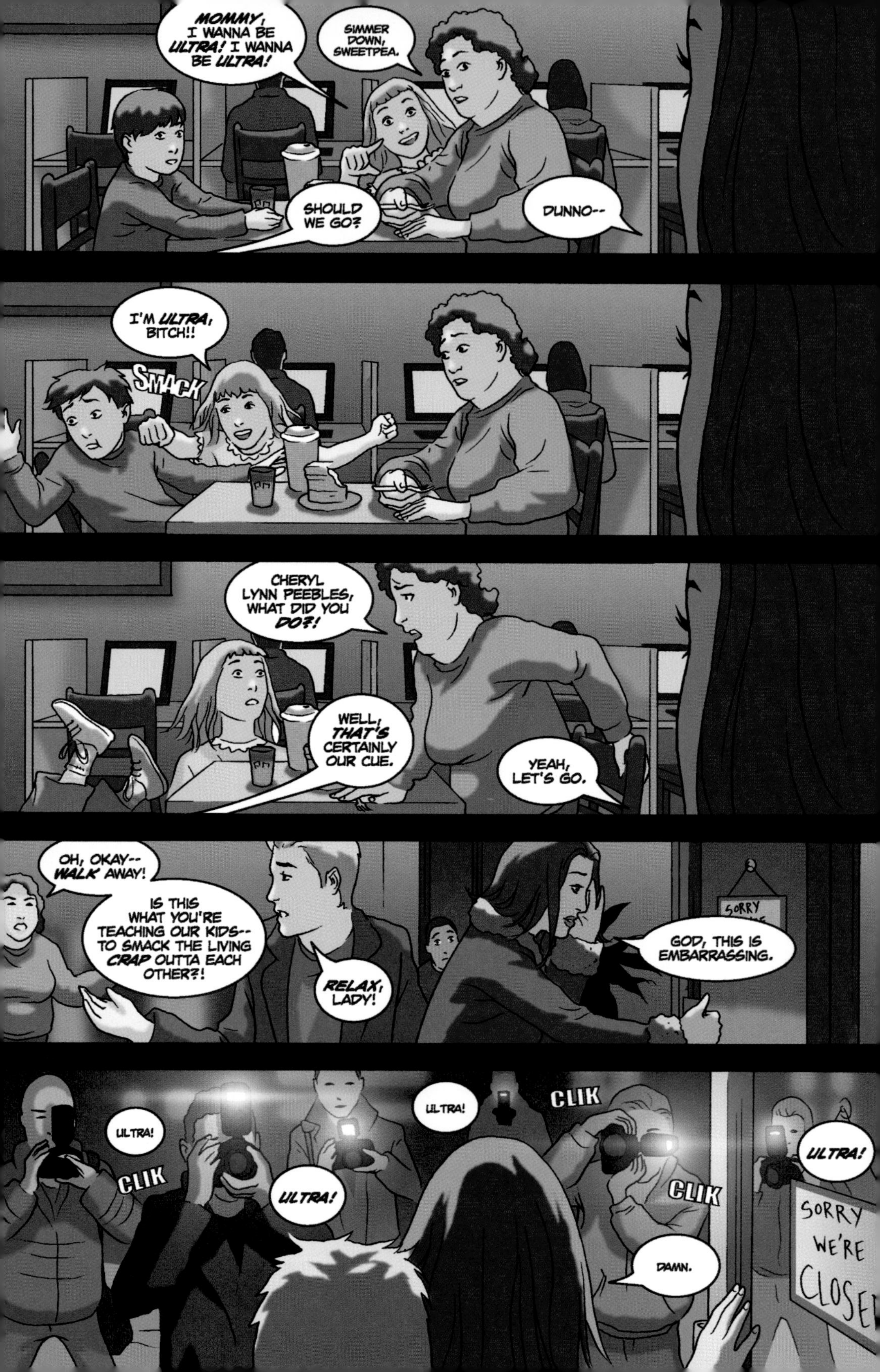
MOMMY, I WANNA BE ULTRA! I WANNA BE ULTRA!
SIMMER DOWN, SWEETPEA.
SHOULD WE GO?
DUNNO--
I'M ULTRA, BITCH!!
SMACK
CHERYL LYNN PEEBLES, WHAT DID YOU DO?!
WELL, THAT'S CERTAINLY OUR CUE.
YEAH, LET'S GO.
OH, OKAY-- WALK AWAY!
IS THIS WHAT YOU'RE TEACHING OUR KIDS-- TO SMACK THE LIVING CRAP OUTTA EACH OTHER?!
RELAX, LADY!
SORRY
GOD, THIS IS EMBARRASSING.
ULTRA!
CLIK
ULTRA!
ULTRA!
CLIK
ULTRA!
CLIK
DAMN.
SORRY WE'RE CLOSE

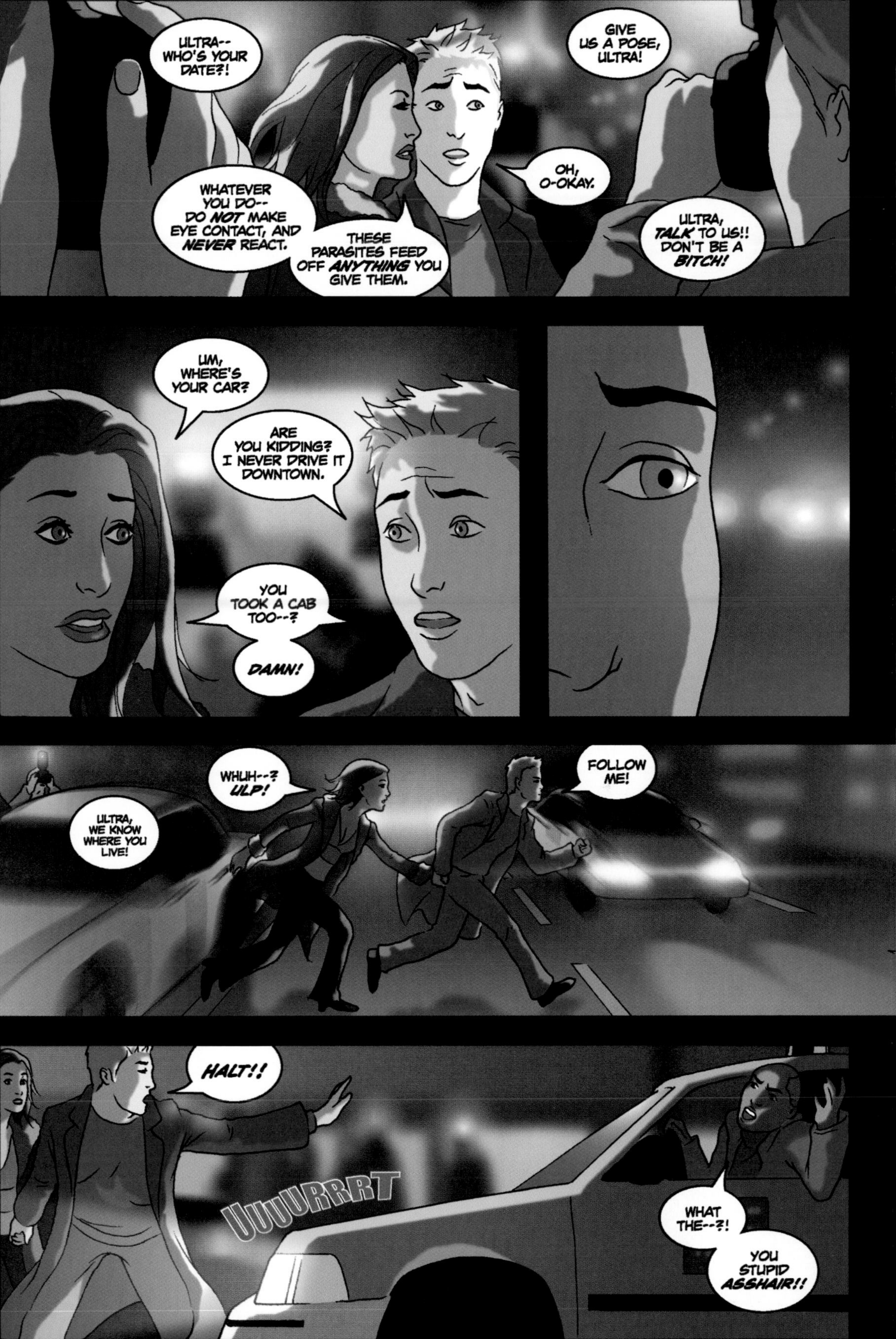
ULTRA-- WHO'S YOUR DATE?!
GIVE US A POSE, ULTRA!
OH, O-OKAY.
WHATEVER YOU DO-- DO NOT MAKE EYE CONTACT, AND NEVER REACT.
THESE PARASITES FEED OFF ANYTHING YOU GIVE THEM.
ULTRA, TALK TO US!! DON'T BE A BITCH!
UM, WHERE'S YOUR CAR?
ARE YOU KIDDING? I NEVER DRIVE IT DOWNTOWN.
YOU TOOK A CAB TOO--?
DAMN!
WHUH--? ULP!
FOLLOW ME!
ULTRA, WE KNOW WHERE YOU LIVE!
HALT!!
UUUURRRT
WHAT THE--?!
YOU STUPID ASSHAIR!!

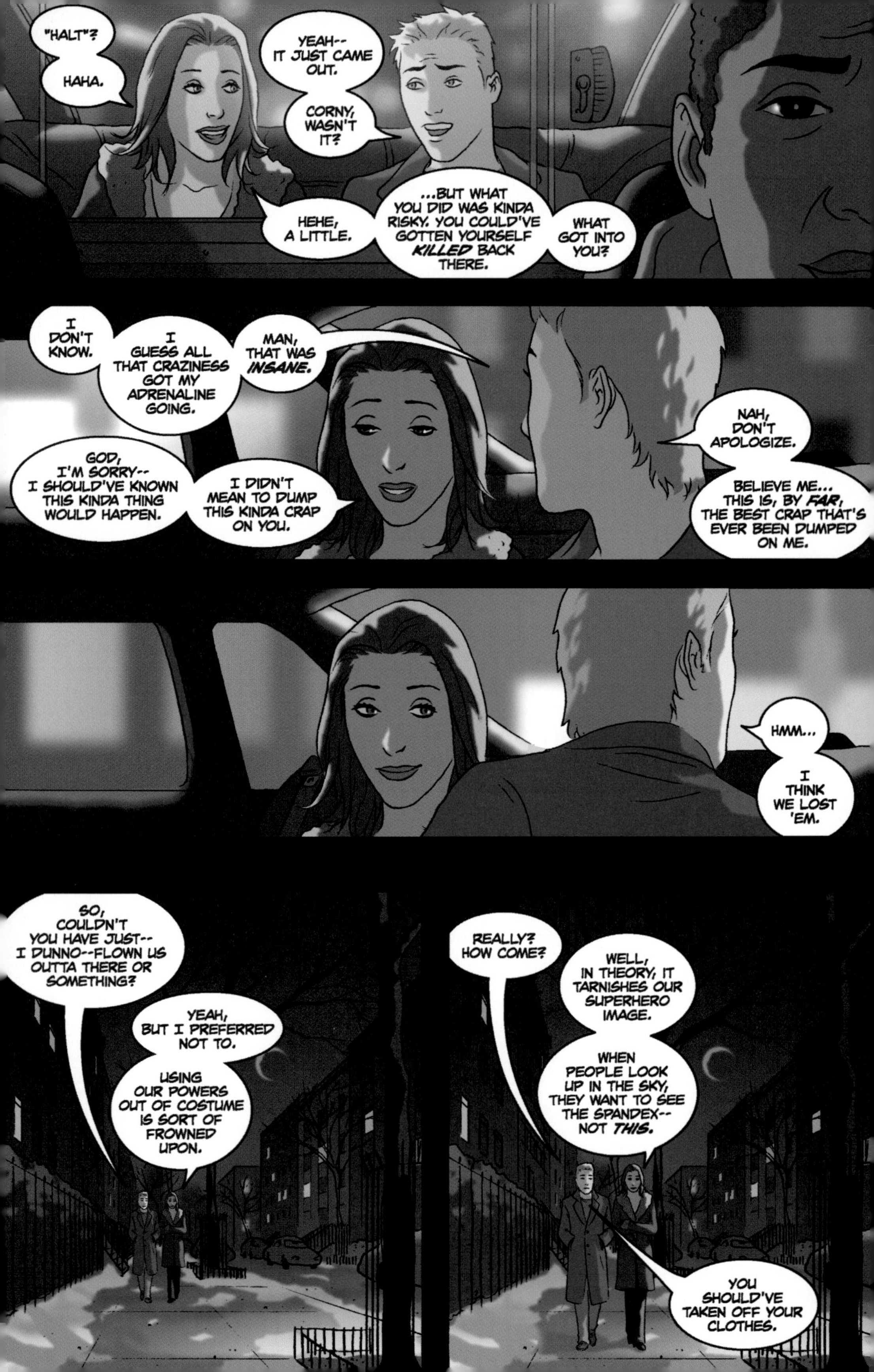
"HALT"?
HAHA.
YEAH-- IT JUST CAME OUT.
CORNY, WASN'T IT?
HEHE, A LITTLE.
...BUT WHAT YOU DID WAS KINDA RISKY. YOU COULD'VE GOTTEN YOURSELF KILLED BACK THERE.
WHAT GOT INTO YOU?
I DON'T KNOW.
I GUESS ALL THAT CRAZINESS GOT MY ADRENALINE GOING.
MAN, THAT WAS INSANE.
GOD, I'M SORRY-- I SHOULD'VE KNOWN THIS KINDA THING WOULD HAPPEN.
I DIDN'T MEAN TO DUMP THIS KINDA CRAP ON YOU.
NAH, DON'T APOLOGIZE.
BELIEVE ME... THIS IS, BY FAR, THE BEST CRAP THAT'S EVER BEEN DUMPED ON ME.
HMM...
I THINK WE LOST 'EM.
SO, COULDN'T YOU HAVE JUST-- I DUNNO--FLOWN US OUTTA THERE OR SOMETHING?
YEAH, BUT I PREFERRED NOT TO.
USING OUR POWERS OUT OF COSTUME IS SORT OF FROWNED UPON.
REALLY? HOW COME?
WELL, IN THEORY, IT TARNISHES OUR SUPERHERO IMAGE.
WHEN PEOPLE LOOK UP IN THE SKY, THEY WANT TO SEE THE SPANDEX-- NOT THIS.
YOU SHOULD'VE TAKEN OFF YOUR CLOTHES.

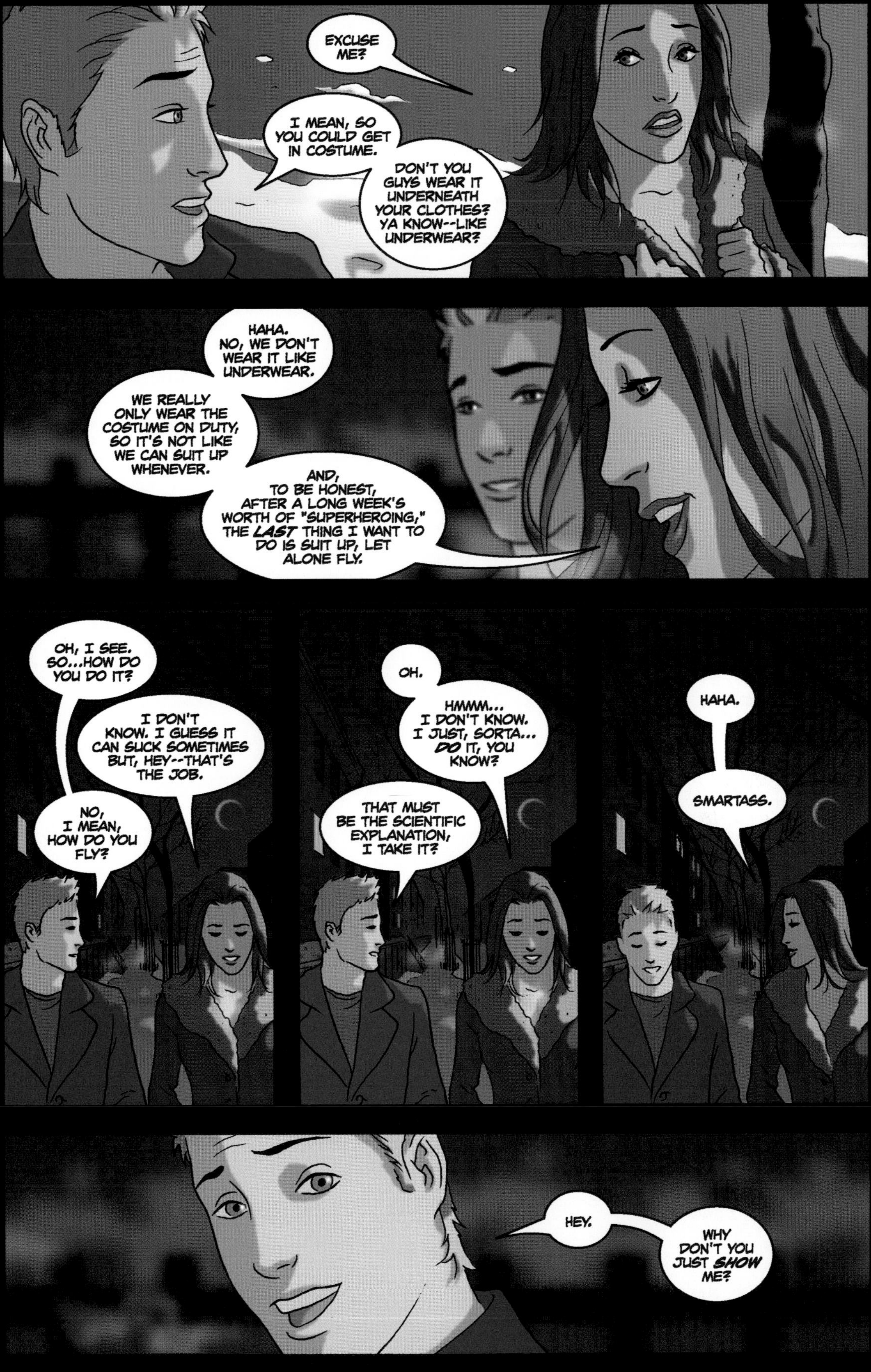
EXCUSE ME?
I MEAN, SO YOU COULD GET IN COSTUME.
DON'T YOU GUYS WEAR IT UNDERNEATH YOUR CLOTHES? YA KNOW--LIKE UNDERWEAR?
HAHA. NO, WE DON'T WEAR IT LIKE UNDERWEAR.
WE REALLY ONLY WEAR THE COSTUME ON DUTY, SO IT'S NOT LIKE WE CAN SUIT UP WHENEVER.
AND, TO BE HONEST, AFTER A LONG WEEK'S WORTH OF "SUPERHEROING," THE *LAST* THING I WANT TO DO IS SUIT UP, LET ALONE FLY.
OH, I SEE. SO...HOW DO YOU DO IT?
I DON'T KNOW. I GUESS IT CAN SUCK SOMETIMES BUT, HEY--THAT'S THE JOB.
NO, I MEAN, HOW DO YOU FLY?
OH.
HMMM... I DON'T KNOW. I JUST, SORTA... *DO* IT, YOU KNOW?
THAT MUST BE THE SCIENTIFIC EXPLANATION, I TAKE IT?
HAHA.
SMARTASS.
HEY.
WHY DON'T YOU JUST *SHOW* ME?

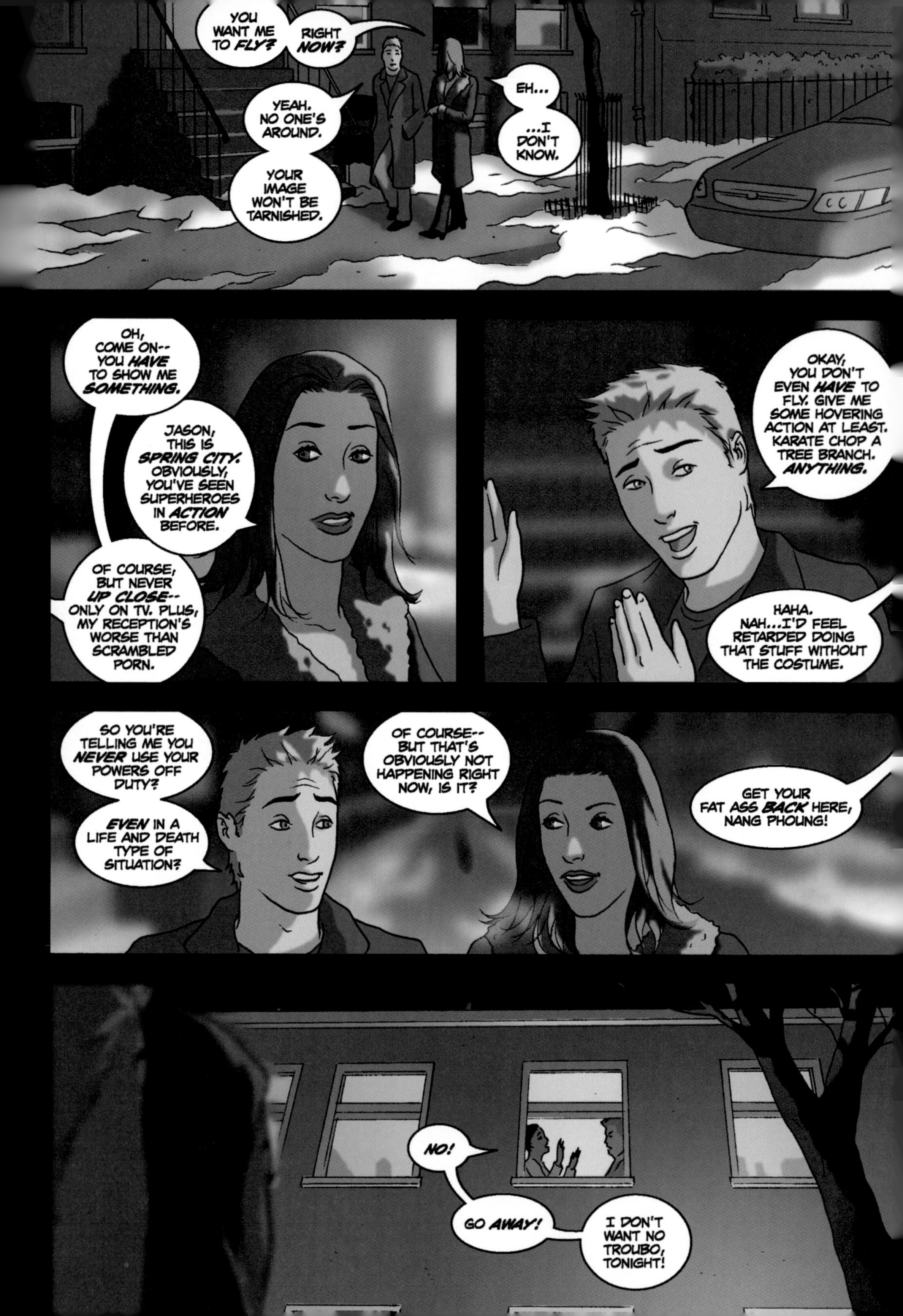
YOU WANT ME TO FLY?
RIGHT NOW?
YEAH. NO ONE'S AROUND.
YOUR IMAGE WON'T BE TARNISHED.
EH...
...I DON'T KNOW.
OH, COME ON-- YOU HAVE TO SHOW ME SOMETHING.
JASON, THIS IS SPRING CITY. OBVIOUSLY, YOU'VE SEEN SUPERHEROES IN ACTION BEFORE.
OF COURSE, BUT NEVER UP CLOSE-- ONLY ON TV. PLUS, MY RECEPTION'S WORSE THAN SCRAMBLED PORN.
OKAY, YOU DON'T EVEN HAVE TO FLY. GIVE ME SOME HOVERING ACTION AT LEAST. KARATE CHOP A TREE BRANCH. ANYTHING.
HAHA. NAH...I'D FEEL RETARDED DOING THAT STUFF WITHOUT THE COSTUME.
SO YOU'RE TELLING ME YOU NEVER USE YOUR POWERS OFF DUTY?
EVEN IN A LIFE AND DEATH TYPE OF SITUATION?
OF COURSE-- BUT THAT'S OBVIOUSLY NOT HAPPENING RIGHT NOW, IS IT?
GET YOUR FAT ASS BACK HERE, NANG PHOUNG!
NO!
GO AWAY!
I DON'T WANT NO TROUBO, TONIGHT!

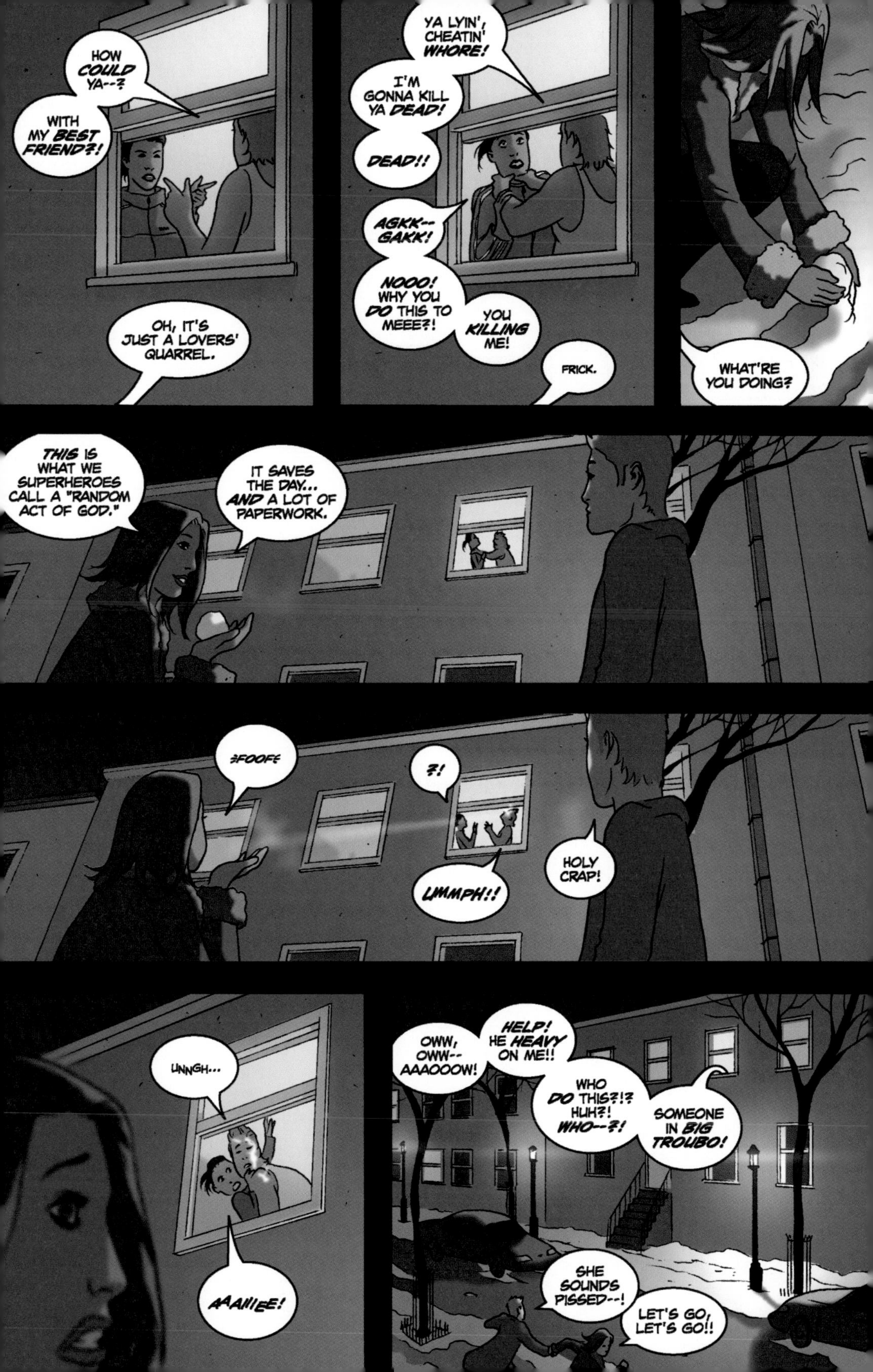
HOW COULD YA--?
WITH MY BEST FRIEND?!
OH, IT'S JUST A LOVERS' QUARREL.
YA LYIN', CHEATIN' WHORE!
I'M GONNA KILL YA DEAD!
DEAD!!
AGKK--GAKK!
NOOO! WHY YOU DO THIS TO MEEE?!
YOU KILLING ME!
FRICK.
WHAT'RE YOU DOING?
THIS IS WHAT WE SUPERHEROES CALL A "RANDOM ACT OF GOD."
IT SAVES THE DAY... AND A LOT OF PAPERWORK.
FOOF
?!
UMMPH!!
HOLY CRAP!
UNNGH...
AAAIIEE!
OWW, OWW--AAAOOOW!
HELP! HE HEAVY ON ME!!
WHO DO THIS?!? HUH?! WHO--?!
SOMEONE IN BIG TROUBO!
SHE SOUNDS PISSED--!
LET'S GO, LET'S GO!!

WELL... THIS IS ME.

YEP.

YOU SURE YOU DON'T WANNA RIDE HOME? IT'S NO PROBLEM, REALLY--

OH NO. IT'S OKAY-- I CAN CATCH A CAB.

...

WHAT?

...THIS IS INSANE.

WHAT IS?

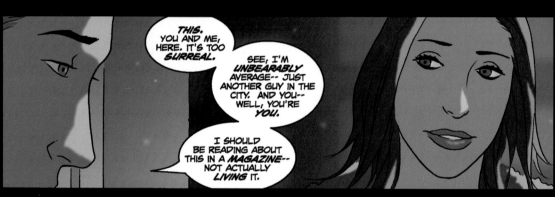

THIS. YOU AND ME, HERE. IT'S TOO SURREAL.

SEE, I'M UNBEARABLY AVERAGE-- JUST ANOTHER GUY IN THE CITY. AND YOU-- WELL, YOU'RE YOU.

I SHOULD BE READING ABOUT THIS IN A MAGAZINE-- NOT ACTUALLY LIVING IT.

DON'T GET ME WRONG-- THIS IS AMAZING. IT'S JUST THAT-- SEE, I HATE DATING.

THERE'S ALL THIS PRESSURE AND EXPECTATION. IT'S JUST SO... COMPLICATED.

AND IF DATING AVERAGE GIRLS IS HARD ENOUGH AS IT IS-- THEN, WELL, DATING YOU IS LIKE WORKING ON A WHOLE NEW LEVEL.

I MEAN, WAY BACK THEN, IT WAS SO SIMPLE-- CAVEMEN GOT TO BONK THE GIRL WITH A CLUB AND THAT WAS IT.

OKAAAY.

SO... LEMME GET THIS STRAIGHT.

YOU WANNA BONK ME?

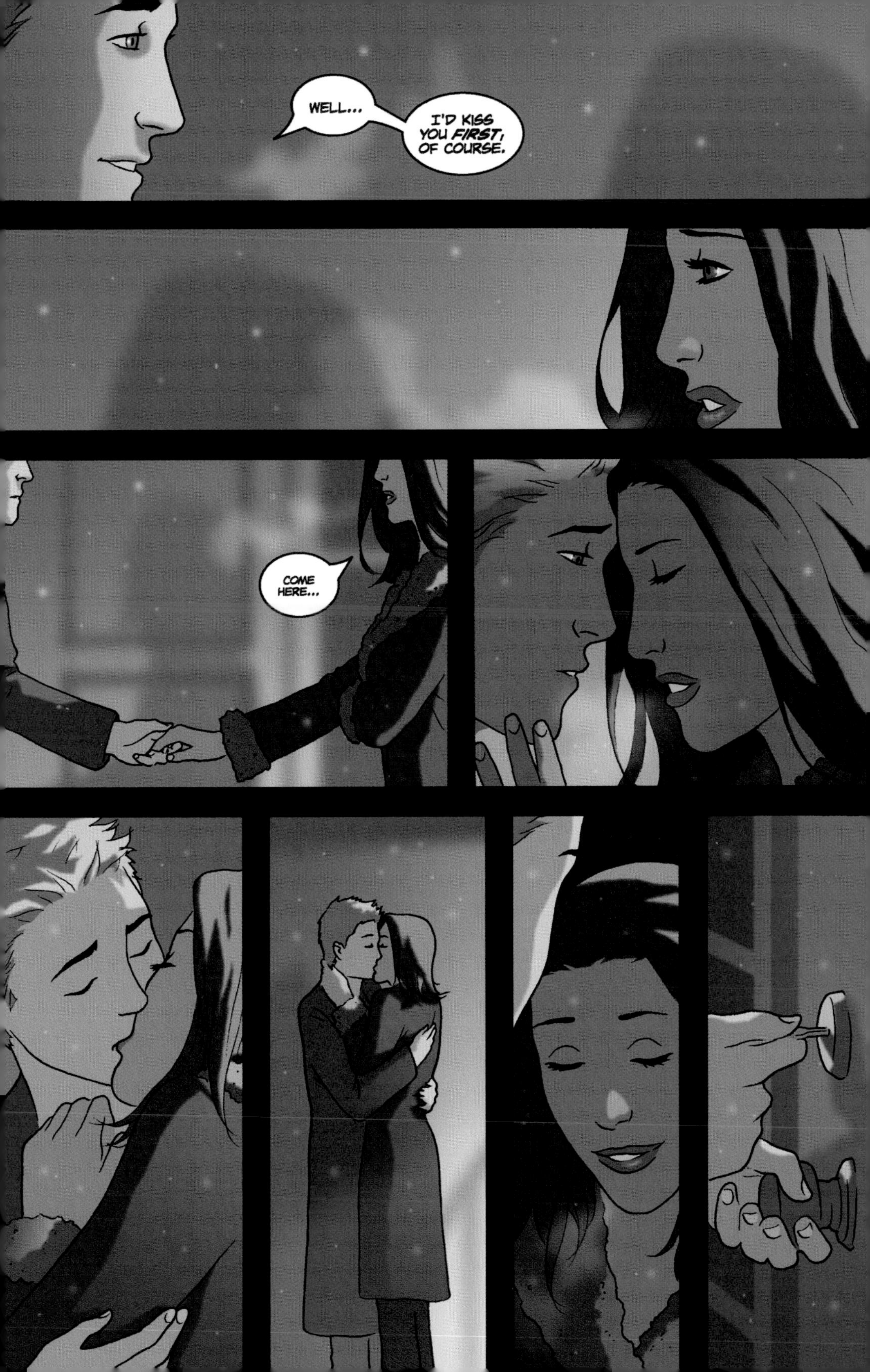
WELL...
I'D KISS YOU FIRST, OF COURSE.
COME HERE...

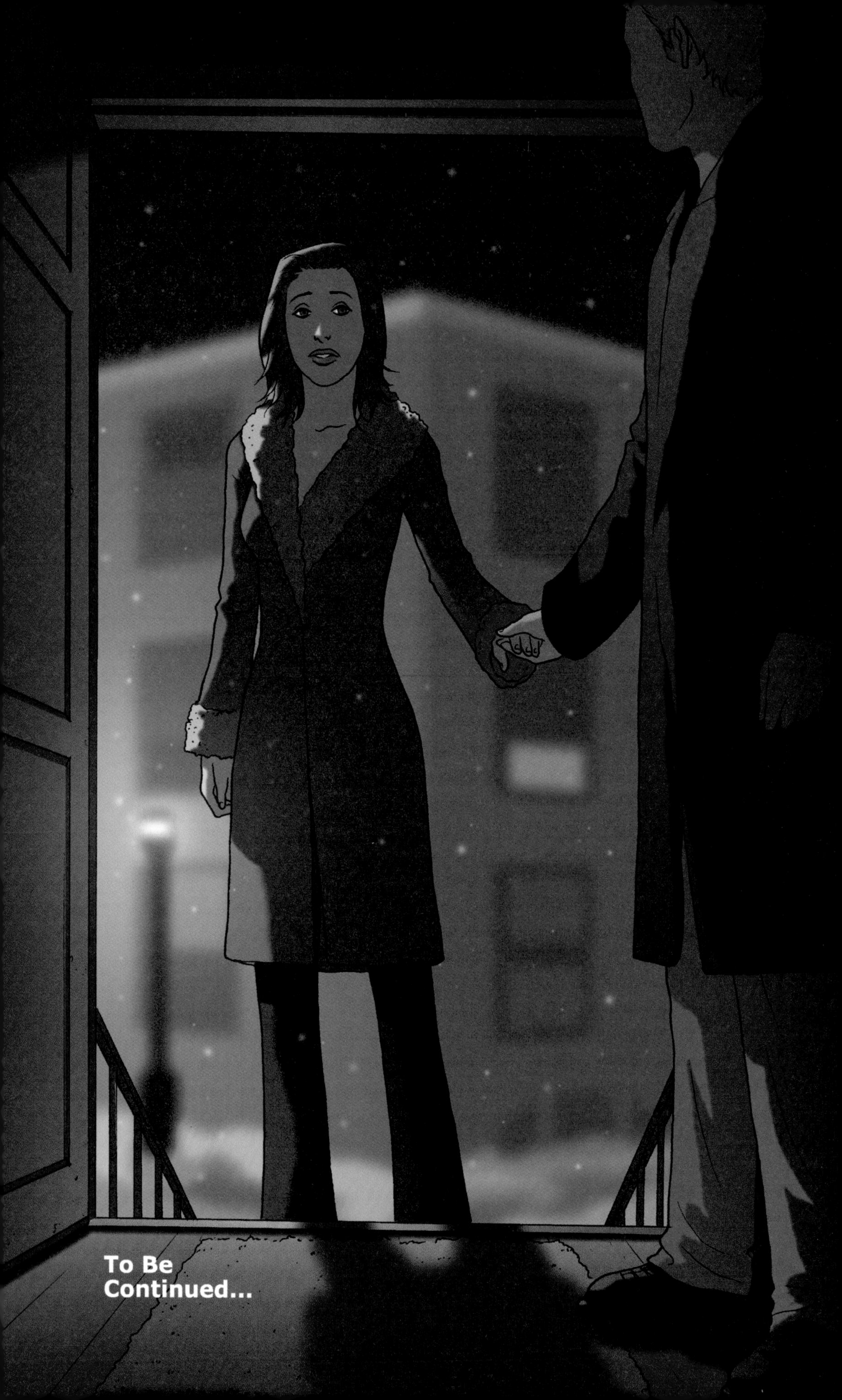
To Be
Continued...

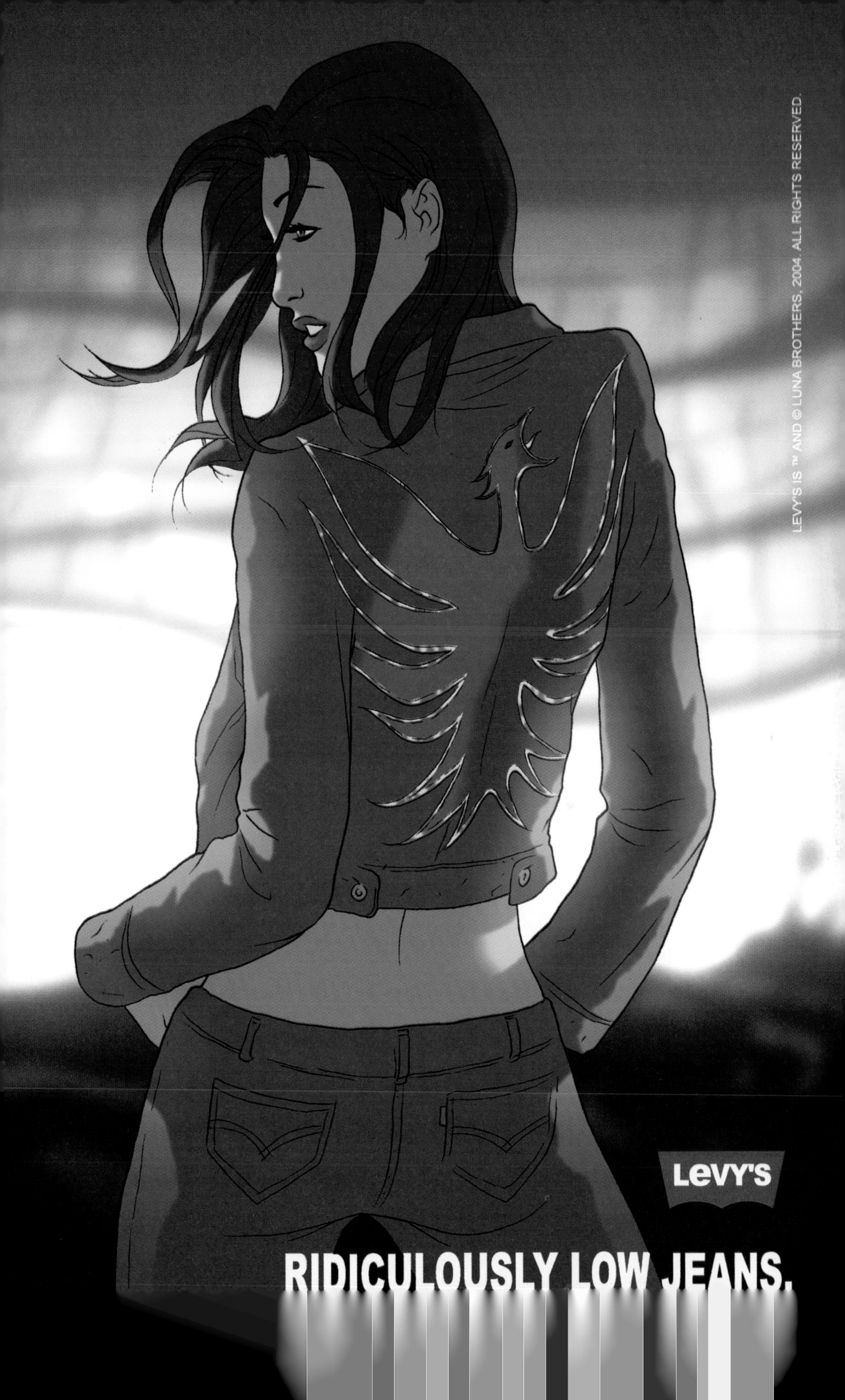

LEVY'S
RIDICULOUSLY LOW JEANS.

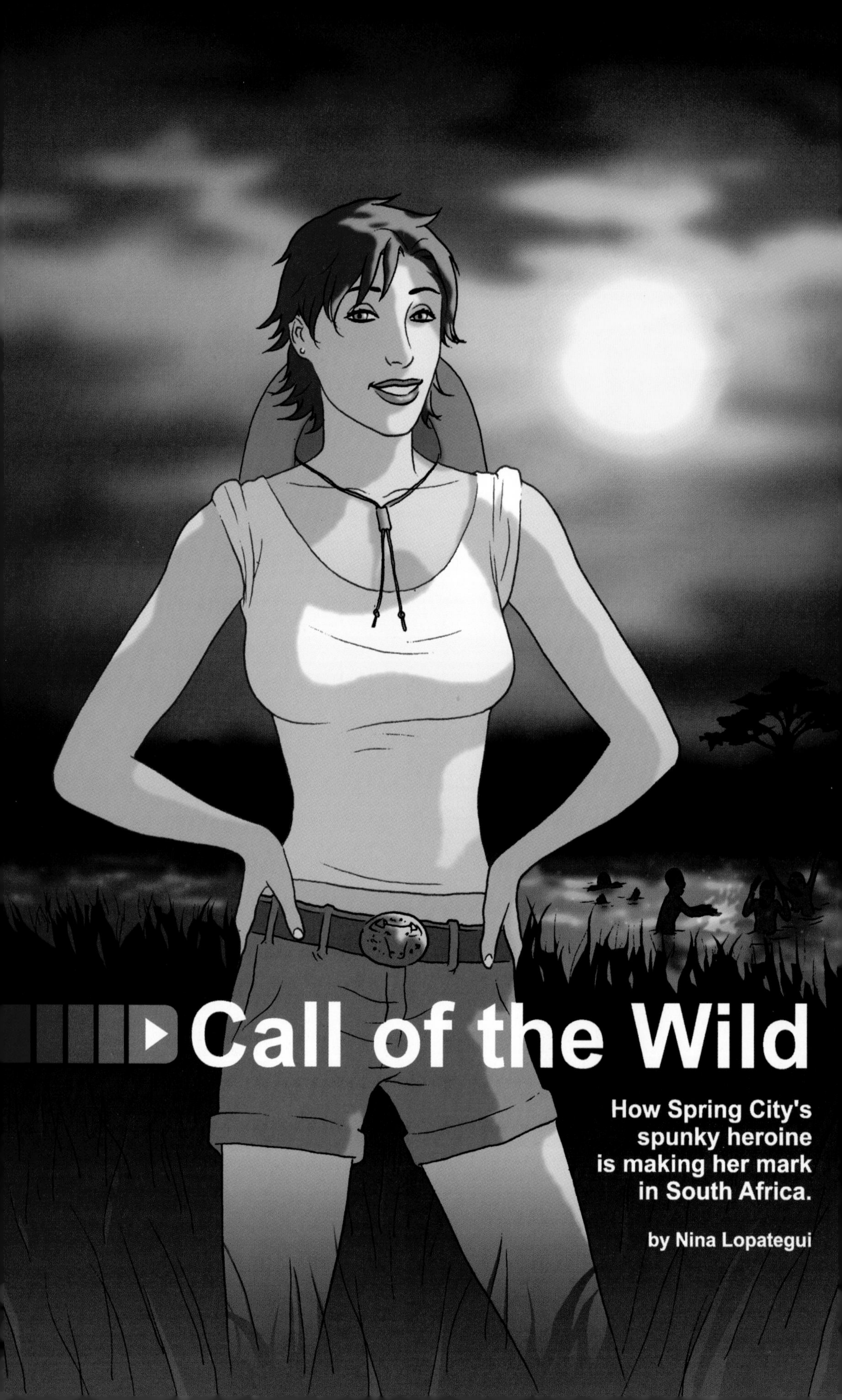

Call of the Wild

How Spring City's spunky heroine is making her mark in South Africa.

by Nina Lopategui

Cowgirl should have been a spoiled brat.

As daughter of Spring City's mayor, Jameson Janus, and legendary sexpot superheroine, Marilyn Mansfield, Jennifer Janus (Cowgirl) was born into wealth, raised as a blue-blooded debutante, but blossomed into everything but. She first silenced critics with her superheroine debut, defiantly deviating from her mother's footsteps by becoming less of a sexploitative pinup girl and more of a full-fledged heroine, utilizing her abilities to emit raw light for the good of mankind. Though as impressive as her elemental levels are, they are only second to the innate diplomatic skills she used to gain highly acclaimed success in a cutthroat superhero industry, mending stronger interagency bonds with federal and local law enforcement, locking up Spring City's worst by the bus loads and advocating limitless opportunities for the underprivileged. When advised to stick to a winning formula, she continuously rejects the easy road and pursues the challenge, proving time after time that her only arch-nemesis is complacency. Now she's taking another dramatic leap, launching the single most ambitious humanitarian effort to date: diverting South Africa's major rivers towards the continent's driest regions. To pull off such a feat, Cowgirl hooked up with a team of cutting-edge experts and scientists led by Nobel Prize winner, Albert Harris, to prove she means business. Now approaching their final week of the project, her spirits remain high as ever. We caught up with the wide-eyed, girl-wonder where she looked more at home, basking under the hot African sun--not the limelight.

Ultra: It's a long way from Spring City. Everybody knows you like to take on the impossible, but why Africa?

Cowgirl: It's funny because, ironically enough, I came here to take time off work. My boyfriend wanted to see a fashion show here in South Africa, and since I've never been, we just decided to make a weekend out of it. I knew Africa had problems and needed help-- I just didn't think I'd be doing anything about it, at first. See, when our lives aren't directly affected by something this overwhelming, it's hard to believe we can make a difference. Besides, I've always assumed Uprah or Bonno had it covered. But when I actually experienced South Africa up close, I finally saw the big picture. Africa is just this tragic paradox of a place--a continent enriched with vast beauty, history and amazing culture, yet underscored by all this needless suffering. But these people are more than just faceless, charity cases--they are tangible, complex human beings like you and I. And the thought of them living in such horrible conditions no longer became acceptable to me. I had to help them because they've helped me reorganize my perspective on the world. Everything happens for a reason and I believe my visit here isn't a coincidence.

We know Africa is a continent riddled with numerous problems so what made the water crisis, in particular, such a priority for you?

Well, water is such a basic necessity yet millions are deprived. It's something a lot of us tend to take for granted. Some women, here in Africa, are walking ten miles a day to fetch water while we have the luxury of filling our glasses on tap. Regions in Southern Africa are so dry, their soil can no longer harvest crops and countless people are starving to death. Neighboring countries are forced to share a single river basin and, unfortunately, this often leads to violence and "water wars." And it's sickening but the water these people fight over is not even sanitary--they're virtually cesspools. Cholera is spreading through people like an epidemic because major sources of drinking water are being used as toilets. So, for me, making the water crisis a priority wasn't a matter of finding Africa's biggest problem because all of their troubles are equally significant. I just thought that any start was a good start when it came to helping these people.

Because of your full-time obligations to Spring City, you obviously couldn't cover the entire African continent. So how did you decide on which countries you were going to divert the rivers to?

Well, the crazy thing about Africa is its erratic weather. There'll be severe droughts from lack of rain in one region and intense

flooding from torrential storms and cyclones in others. And you'd think flooding would answer these people's prayers but millions actually die when inadequate pumping stations are swept away, leaving filthy water to stagnate and breed disease-carrying mosquitoes. So in a basic sense, our goal was to simply balance these specific regions out. Diverting water from areas that had excess amounts to areas that had none would kill two birds with one stone. So once we got the green light from the proper authorities and consulted with the good people of UNEP, Department of Water Affairs, and the local Trans-boundary water officials, our crew first set up shop along the Zambezi River and got to work on that bad boy right away. I began blasting the ground with my lasers, branching off the Zambezi, and leading the river's surplus flow into countries where water was dangerously scarce. Just a few weeks into the project, we've already managed to create the longest, most elaborate network of man-made rivers in recorded history. It's such an awesome sight. Now with rivers branching south from the Zambezi River into the four crucial countries (southern Zimbabwe, southern Mozambique, eastern Botswana and northeastern South Africa) we're wrapping up the final stages of the project.

Within shooting distance: Standing atop a crane for added support and accuracy, Janus uses her laser blasts to create the crevasses the Zambezi will divert to.

I know your team had the latest advances of hydrological technology at their disposal. How did you get a handle on all the high-tech gadgetry?

Oh, believe me, I didn't! I'm such a ditz when it comes to that stuff. The technicians, the engineers and the thinkers are the real superheroes here. Without them, this project wouldn't have even been a possibility. The technology these fellas developed is insane-- It will actually revolutionize the way we irrigate soil and treat polluted water. So the South Africans are in good hands with this crew. See, I had the easy job. They just told me where to shoot, and I zapped away at it.

With the Superhero awards around the corner, critics have been questioning your motives in Africa. How do you respond to the trash-talkers who call your efforts a publicity stunt?

Well, in a sense, they're right because I do want publicity--not for me, but for these people. Everyone should be informed on what's going on down here and if my celebrity can lead fans to a good cause then, hey, I'm all for it. See, superheroes have a tremendous opportunity to change lives for the better and as long as we're helping those who can't help themselves, I don't see any reason why we shouldn't do everything in our power to do so. The problems out there, and not just in Africa, aren't about me, or superheroes, or award shows--they're bigger than us. Because they're our problems too.

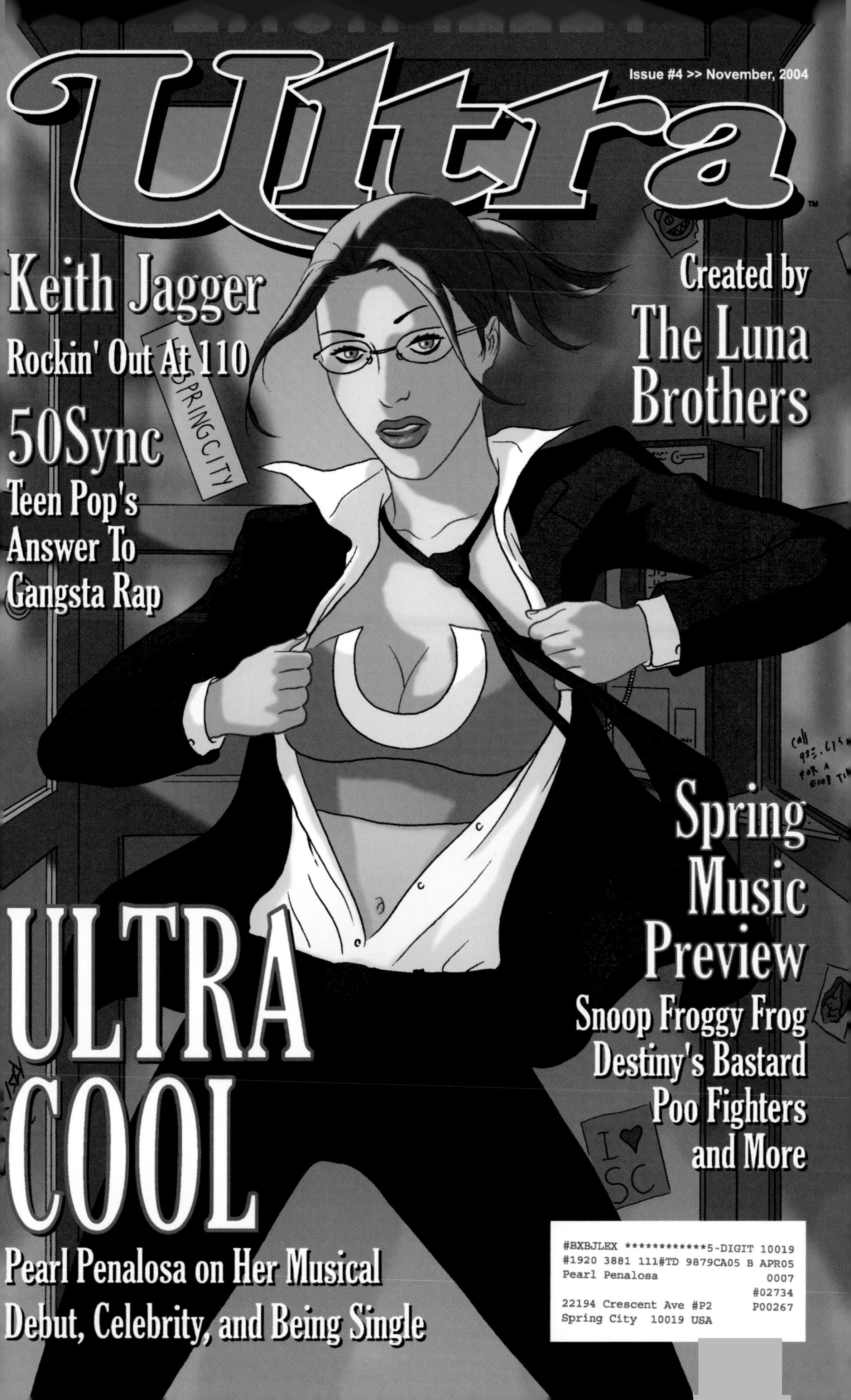

Ultra
Issue #4 >> November, 2004
Keith Jagger
Rockin' Out At 110
50Sync
Teen Pop's
Answer To
Gangsta Rap
Created by
The Luna
Brothers
SPRINGCITY
Spring
Music
Preview
Snoop Froggy Frog
Destiny's Bastard
Poo Fighters
and More
I ♥ SC
ULTRA
COOL
Pearl Penalosa on Her Musical
Debut, Celebrity, and Being Single
#BXBJLEX ************5-DIGIT 10019
#1920 3881 111#TD 9879CA05 B APR05
Pearl Penalosa 0007
#02734
22194 Crescent Ave #P2 P00267
Spring City 10019 USA

>>IN HERE

THIS ISSUE
3 SEVEN DAYS, PART FOUR

CREATED BY
112 THE LUNA BROTHERS

CREDITS
114 JONATHAN LUNA
Plot, Art, Colors, Letters

114 JOSHUA LUNA
Plot, Script, Layout Assists

OFFICIAL WEBSITE
120 www.LunaBrothers.com

For Image Comics

Erik Larsen - Publisher
Todd McFarlane - President
Marc Silvestri - CEO
Jim Valentino - Vice-President

Eric Stephenson - Executive Director
Missie Miranda - Controller
Brett Evans - Production Manager
B. Clay Moore - PR & Marketing
  Coordinator
Allen Hui - Production Artist
Joe Keatinge - Inventory
  Controller
Mia Machatton - Administrative
  Assistant

www.imagecomics.com

image

> **Reviews**

140 We'll tell you what's cool, and you'll believe us.

50Sync: Bustin' caps and breakin' hearts. p.130

Strawberry Syphilis, 10:30 Club, Spring City. p.138

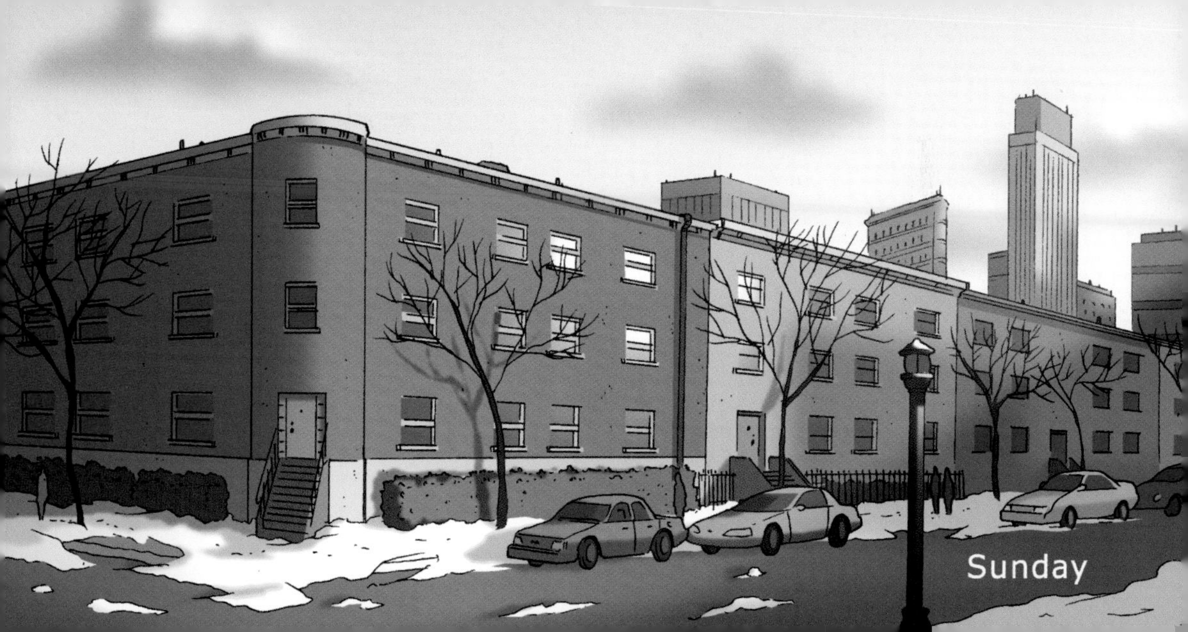
Sunday

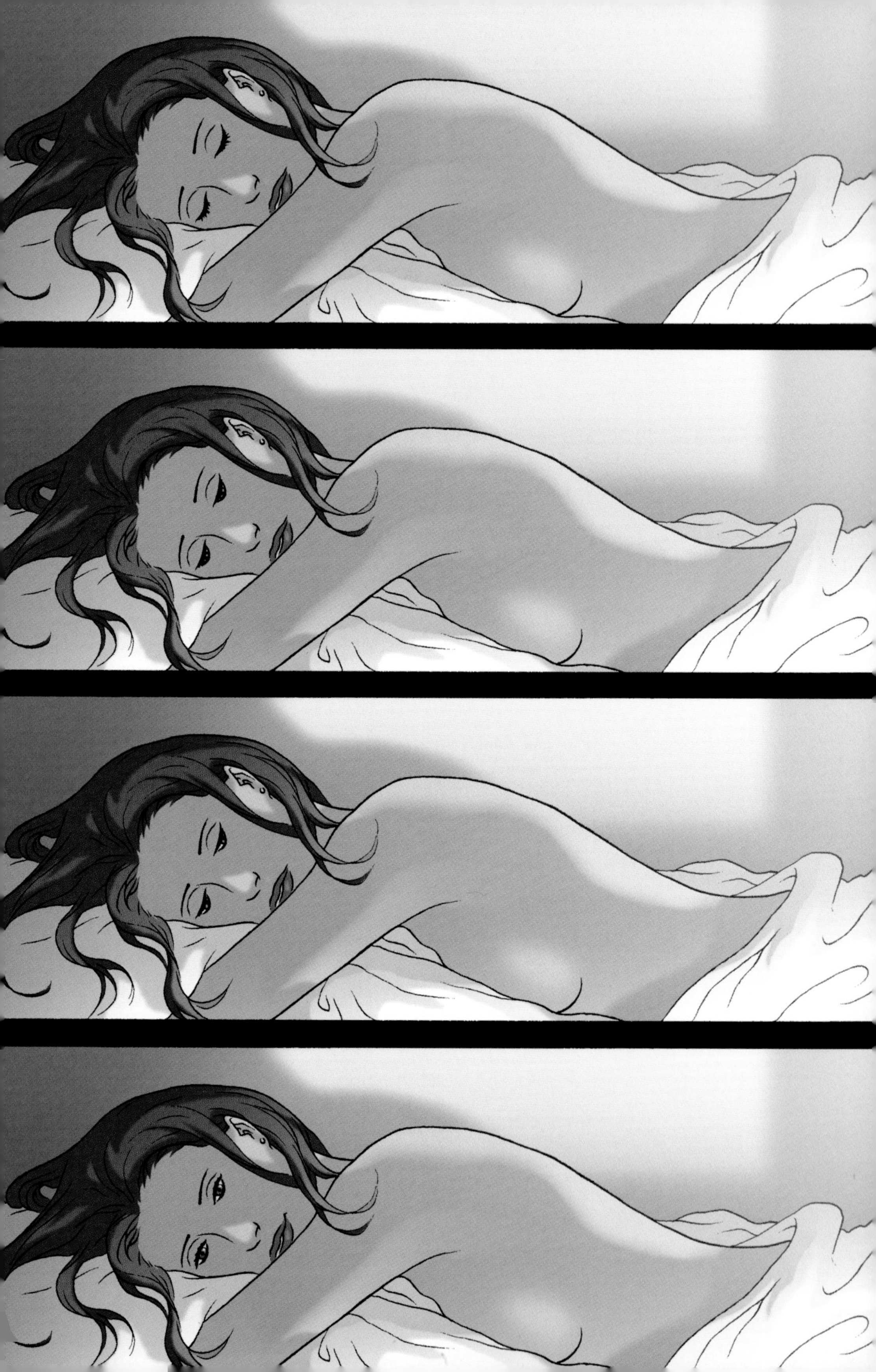

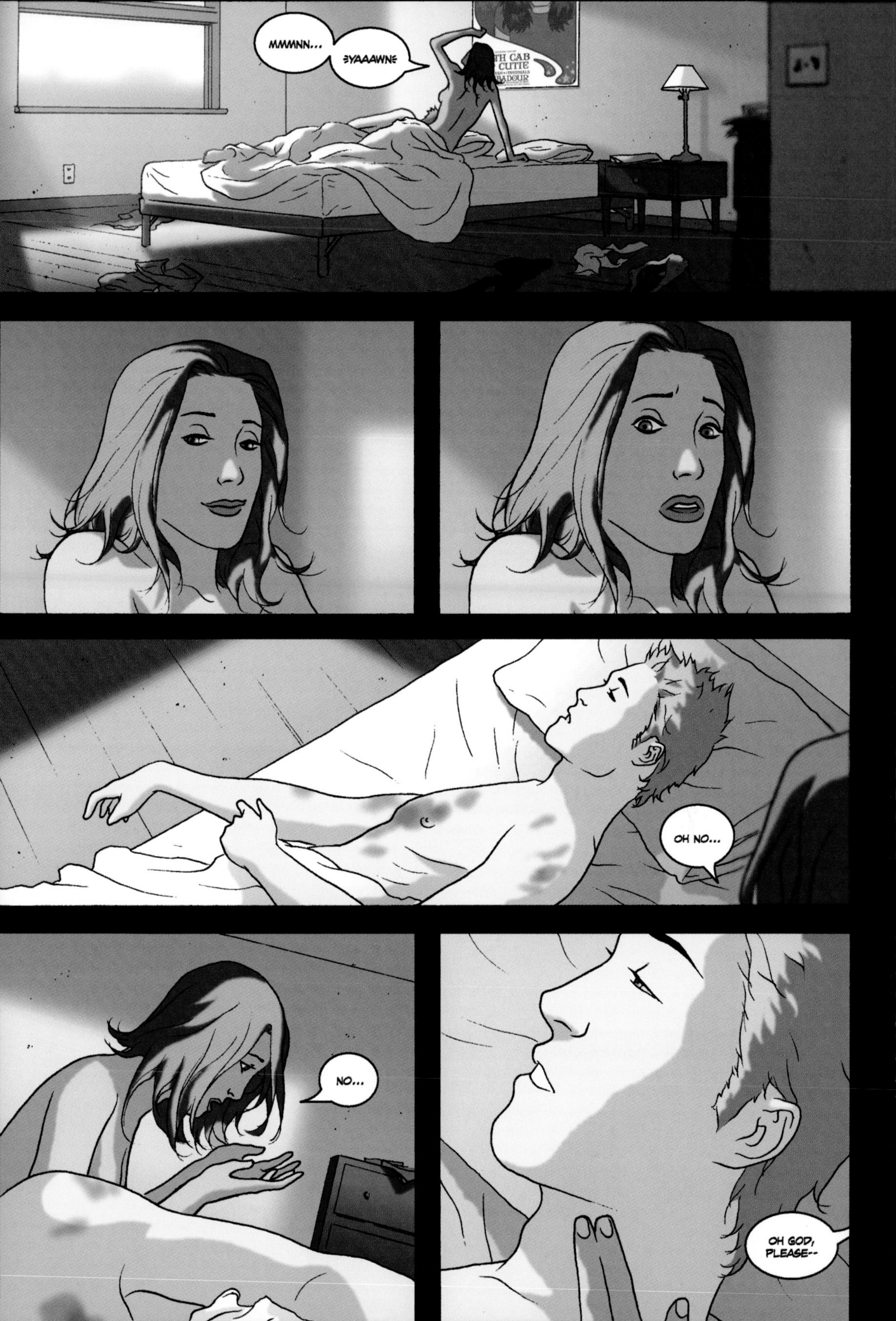
MMMNN...
YAAAWN
OH NO...
NO...
OH GOD, PLEASE--

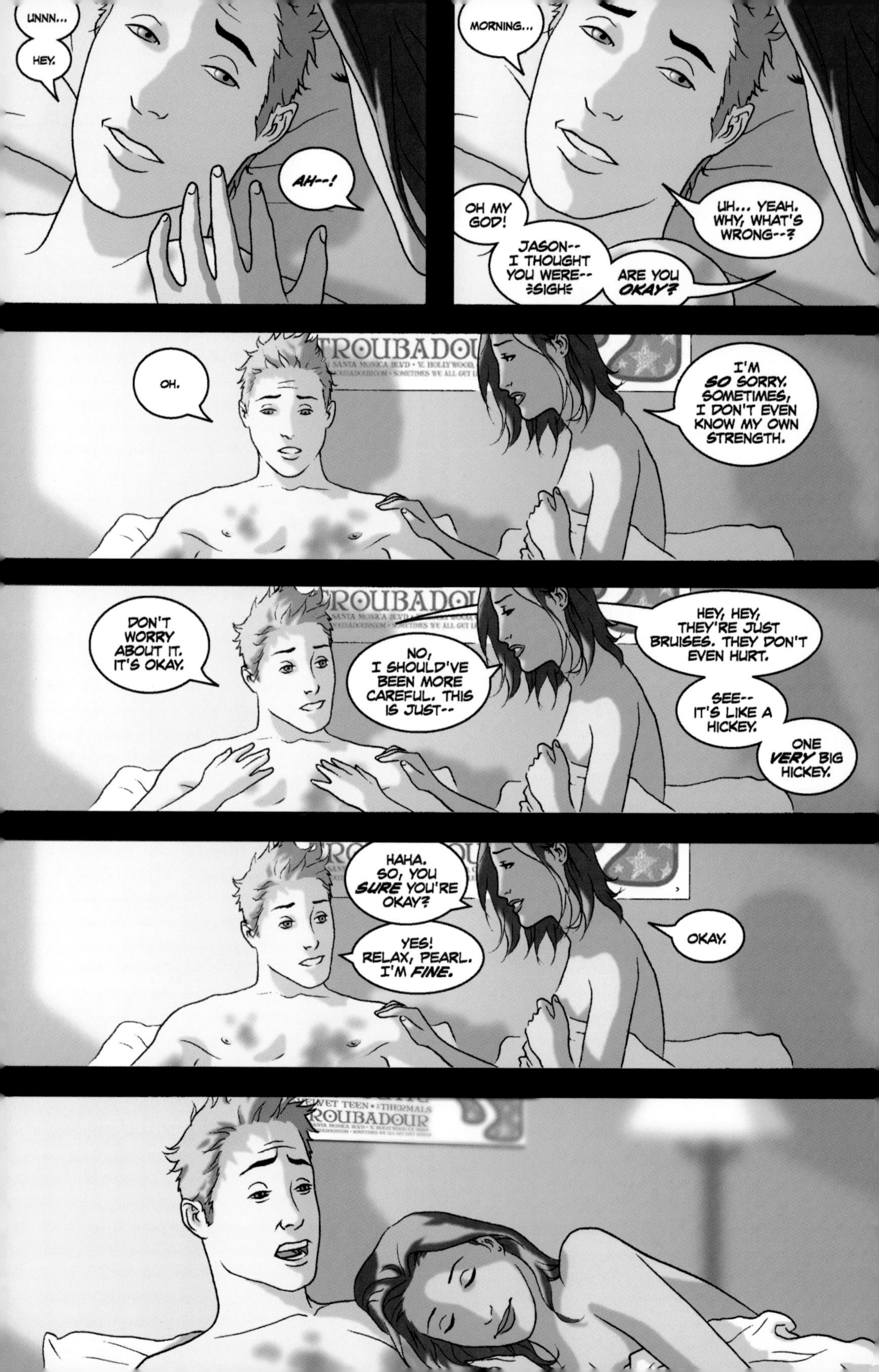
UNNN...
HEY.
AH--!
MORNING...
OH MY GOD!
JASON-- I THOUGHT YOU WERE-- ≶SIGH≶
UH... YEAH. WHY, WHAT'S WRONG--?
ARE YOU OKAY?
TROUBADOUR
OH.
I'M SO SORRY. SOMETIMES, I DON'T EVEN KNOW MY OWN STRENGTH.
DON'T WORRY ABOUT IT. IT'S OKAY.
NO, I SHOULD'VE BEEN MORE CAREFUL. THIS IS JUST--
HEY, HEY, THEY'RE JUST BRUISES. THEY DON'T EVEN HURT.
SEE-- IT'S LIKE A HICKEY.
ONE VERY BIG HICKEY.
HAHA. SO, YOU SURE YOU'RE OKAY?
YES! RELAX, PEARL. I'M FINE.
OKAY.
VELVET TEEN THERMALS
TROUBADOUR

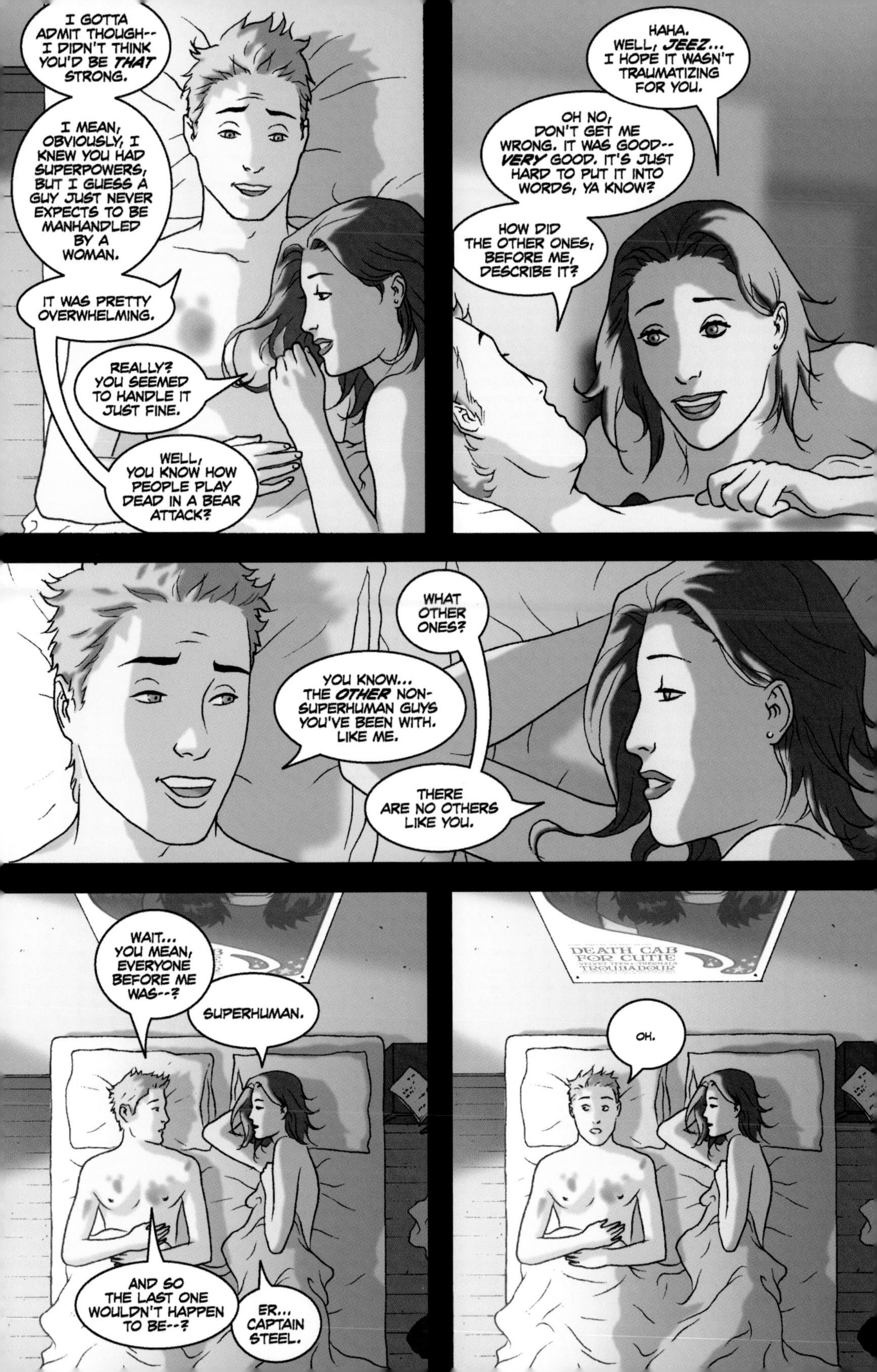
I GOTTA ADMIT THOUGH-- I DIDN'T THINK YOU'D BE *THAT* STRONG.
I MEAN, OBVIOUSLY, I KNEW YOU HAD SUPERPOWERS, BUT I GUESS A GUY JUST NEVER EXPECTS TO BE MANHANDLED BY A WOMAN.
IT WAS PRETTY OVERWHELMING.
REALLY? YOU SEEMED TO HANDLE IT JUST FINE.
WELL, YOU KNOW HOW PEOPLE PLAY DEAD IN A BEAR ATTACK?
HAHA. WELL, *JEEZ*... I HOPE IT WASN'T TRAUMATIZING FOR YOU.
OH NO, DON'T GET ME WRONG. IT WAS GOOD-- *VERY* GOOD. IT'S JUST HARD TO PUT IT INTO WORDS, YA KNOW?
HOW DID THE OTHER ONES, BEFORE ME, DESCRIBE IT?
WHAT OTHER ONES?
YOU KNOW... THE *OTHER* NON-SUPERHUMAN GUYS YOU'VE BEEN WITH. LIKE ME.
THERE ARE NO OTHERS LIKE YOU.
WAIT... YOU MEAN, EVERYONE BEFORE ME WAS--?
SUPERHUMAN.
AND SO THE LAST ONE WOULDN'T HAPPEN TO BE--?
ER... CAPTAIN STEEL.
DEATH CAB FOR CUTIE
TROUBADOUR
OH.

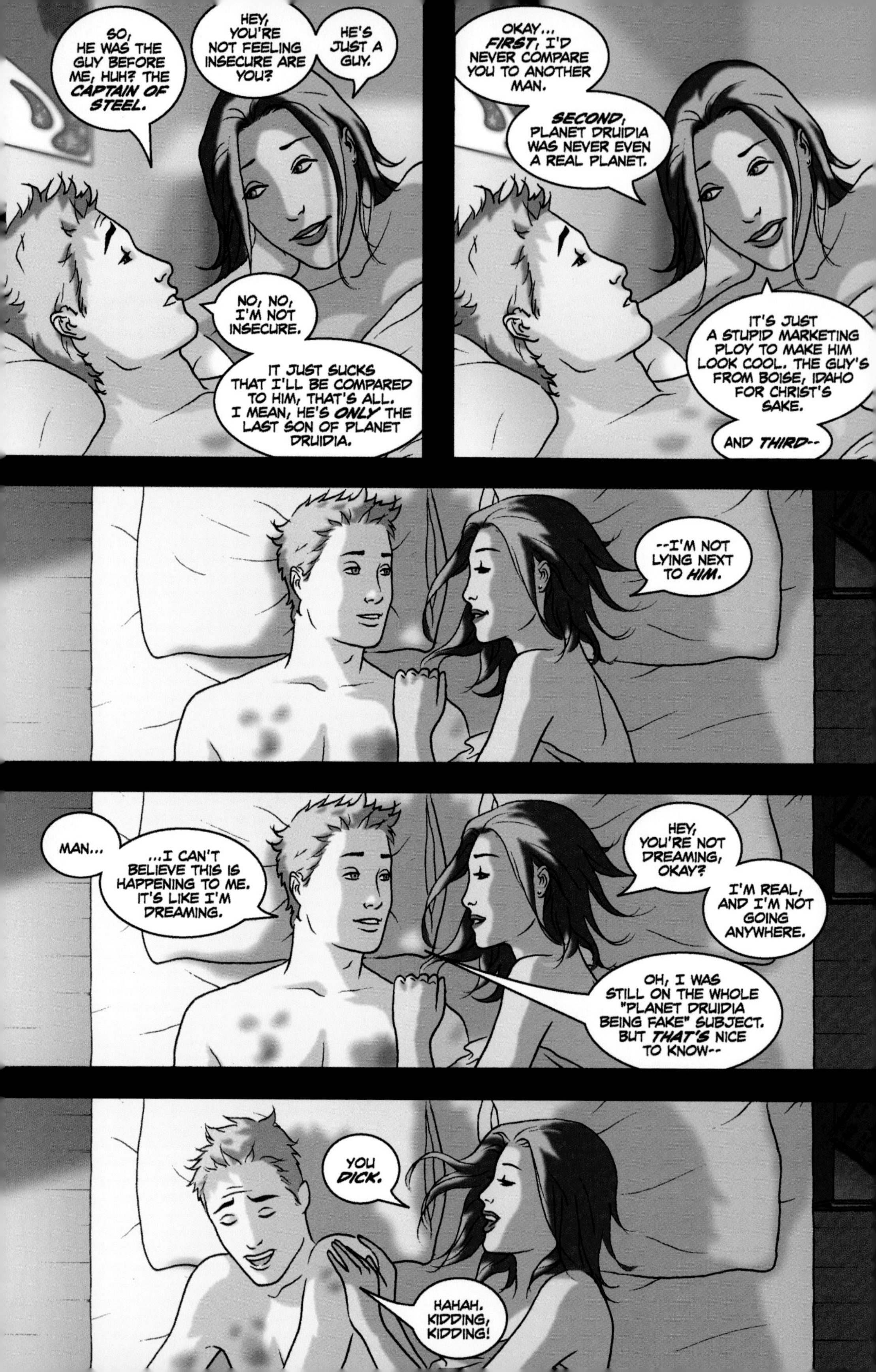
SO, HE WAS THE GUY BEFORE ME, HUH? THE CAPTAIN OF STEEL.
HEY, YOU'RE NOT FEELING INSECURE ARE YOU?
HE'S JUST A GUY.
NO, NO, I'M NOT INSECURE.
IT JUST SUCKS THAT I'LL BE COMPARED TO HIM, THAT'S ALL. I MEAN, HE'S ONLY THE LAST SON OF PLANET DRUIDIA.
OKAY... FIRST, I'D NEVER COMPARE YOU TO ANOTHER MAN.
SECOND, PLANET DRUIDIA WAS NEVER EVEN A REAL PLANET.
IT'S JUST A STUPID MARKETING PLOY TO MAKE HIM LOOK COOL. THE GUY'S FROM BOISE, IDAHO FOR CHRIST'S SAKE.
AND THIRD--
--I'M NOT LYING NEXT TO HIM.
MAN...
...I CAN'T BELIEVE THIS IS HAPPENING TO ME. IT'S LIKE I'M DREAMING.
HEY, YOU'RE NOT DREAMING, OKAY?
I'M REAL, AND I'M NOT GOING ANYWHERE.
OH, I WAS STILL ON THE WHOLE "PLANET DRUIDIA BEING FAKE" SUBJECT. BUT THAT'S NICE TO KNOW--
YOU DICK.
HAHAH. KIDDING, KIDDING!

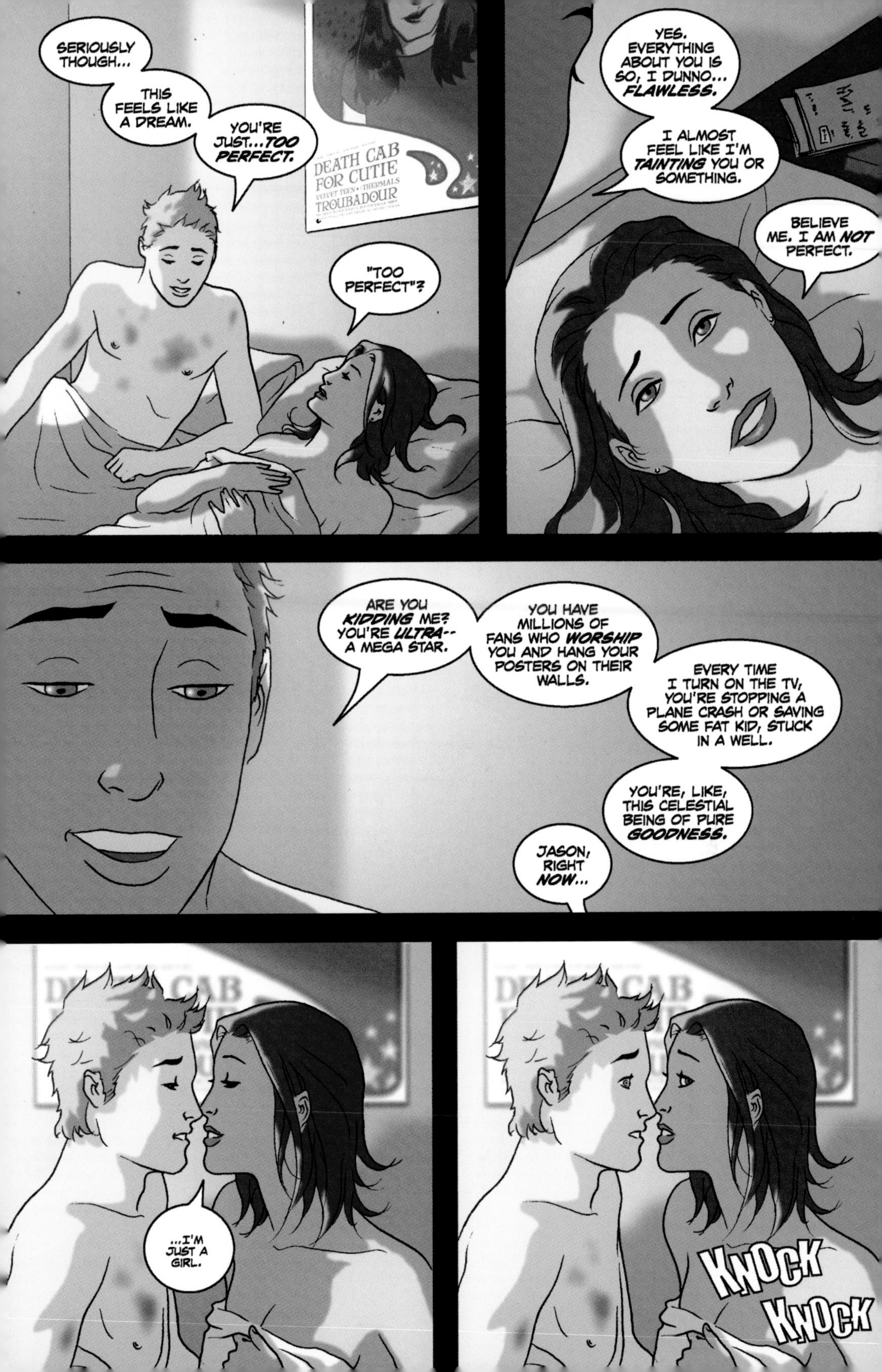
SERIOUSLY THOUGH...
THIS FEELS LIKE A DREAM.
YOU'RE JUST...TOO PERFECT.
DEATH CAB FOR CUTIE
VELVET TEEN • THERMALS
TROUBADOUR
"TOO PERFECT"?
YES. EVERYTHING ABOUT YOU IS SO, I DUNNO... FLAWLESS.
I ALMOST FEEL LIKE I'M TAINTING YOU OR SOMETHING.
BELIEVE ME. I AM NOT PERFECT.
ARE YOU KIDDING ME? YOU'RE ULTRA-- A MEGA STAR.
YOU HAVE MILLIONS OF FANS WHO WORSHIP YOU AND HANG YOUR POSTERS ON THEIR WALLS.
EVERY TIME I TURN ON THE TV, YOU'RE STOPPING A PLANE CRASH OR SAVING SOME FAT KID, STUCK IN A WELL.
YOU'RE, LIKE, THIS CELESTIAL BEING OF PURE GOODNESS.
JASON, RIGHT NOW...
...I'M JUST A GIRL.
KNOCK
KNOCK

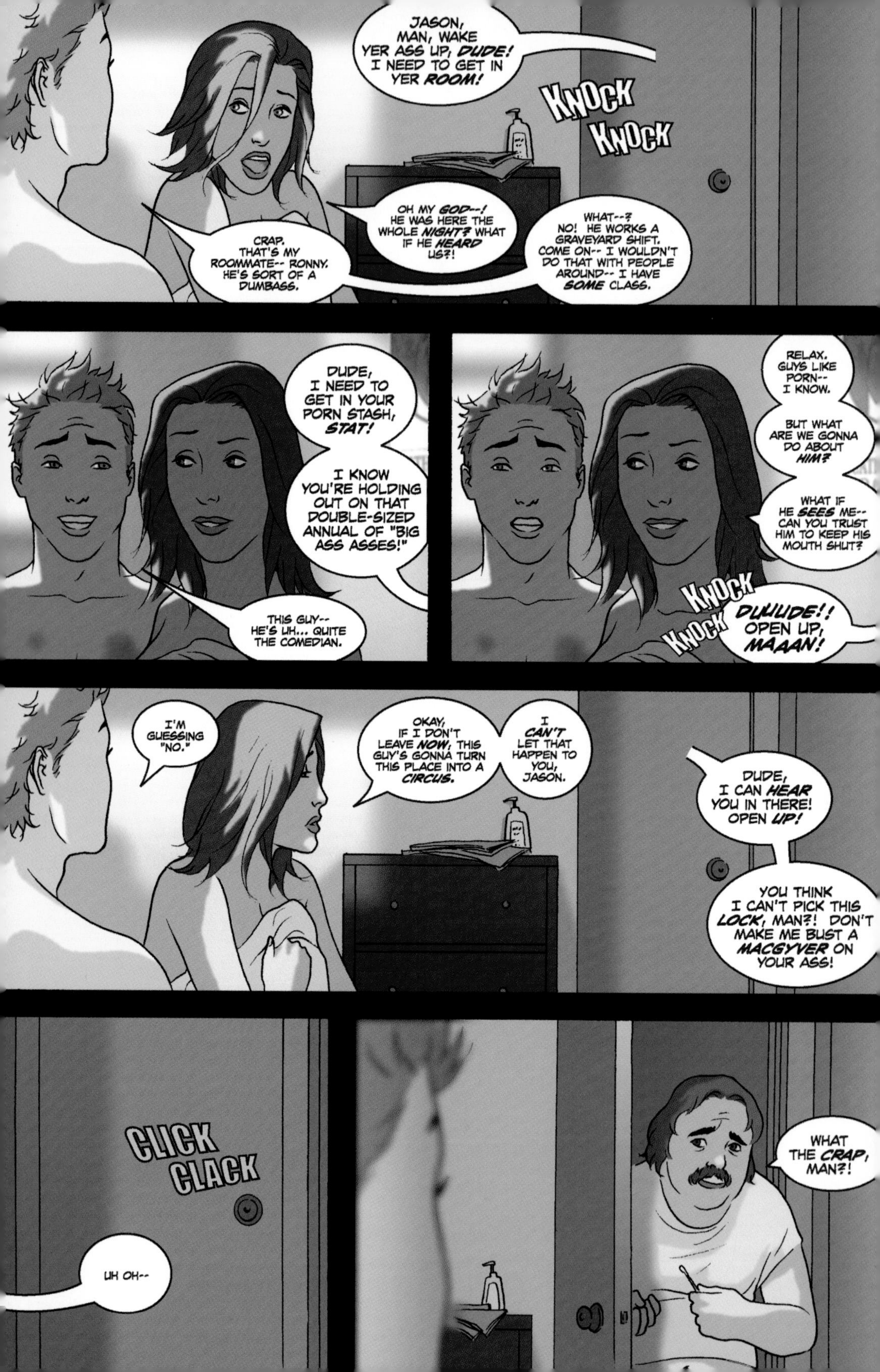
JASON, MAN, WAKE YER ASS UP, DUDE! I NEED TO GET IN YER ROOM!
KNOCK KNOCK
CRAP. THAT'S MY ROOMMATE-- RONNY. HE'S SORT OF A DUMBASS.
OH MY GOD--! HE WAS HERE THE WHOLE NIGHT? WHAT IF HE HEARD US?!
WHAT--? NO! HE WORKS A GRAVEYARD SHIFT. COME ON-- I WOULDN'T DO THAT WITH PEOPLE AROUND-- I HAVE SOME CLASS.
DUDE, I NEED TO GET IN YOUR PORN STASH, STAT!
I KNOW YOU'RE HOLDING OUT ON THAT DOUBLE-SIZED ANNUAL OF "BIG ASS ASSES!"
THIS GUY-- HE'S UH... QUITE THE COMEDIAN.
RELAX. GUYS LIKE PORN-- I KNOW.
BUT WHAT ARE WE GONNA DO ABOUT HIM?
WHAT IF HE SEES ME-- CAN YOU TRUST HIM TO KEEP HIS MOUTH SHUT?
KNOCK KNOCK
DUUUDE!! OPEN UP, MAAAN!
I'M GUESSING "NO."
OKAY, IF I DON'T LEAVE NOW, THIS GUY'S GONNA TURN THIS PLACE INTO A CIRCUS.
I CAN'T LET THAT HAPPEN TO YOU, JASON.
DUDE, I CAN HEAR YOU IN THERE! OPEN UP!
YOU THINK I CAN'T PICK THIS LOCK, MAN?! DON'T MAKE ME BUST A MACGYVER ON YOUR ASS!
CLICK CLACK
UH OH--
WHAT THE CRAP, MAN?!

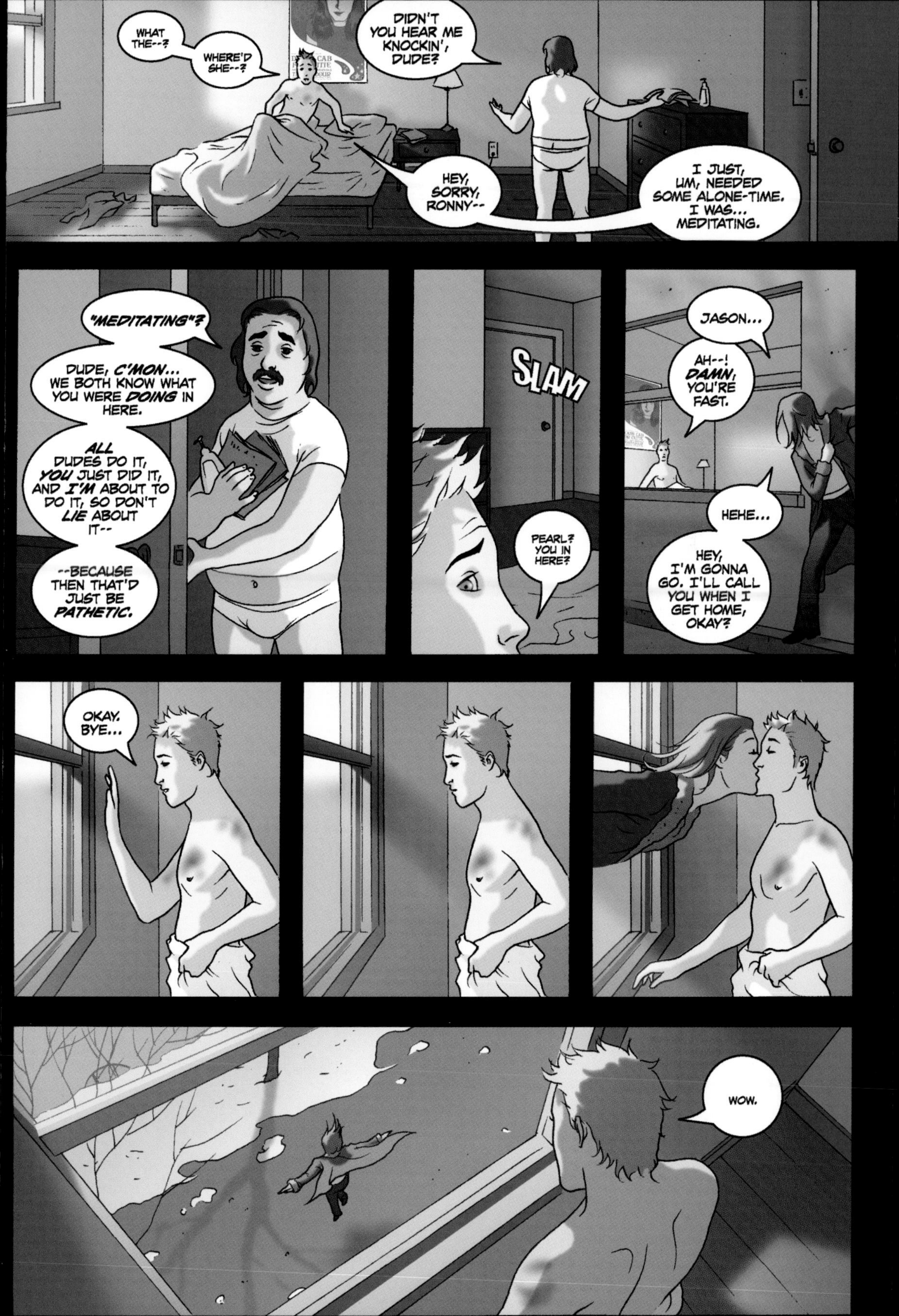
WHAT THE--?
WHERE'D SHE--?
DIDN'T YOU HEAR ME KNOCKIN', DUDE?
HEY, SORRY, RONNY--
I JUST, UM, NEEDED SOME ALONE-TIME. I WAS... MEDITATING.
"MEDITATING"?
DUDE, C'MON... WE BOTH KNOW WHAT YOU WERE DOING IN HERE.
ALL DUDES DO IT, YOU JUST DID IT, AND I'M ABOUT TO DO IT, SO DON'T LIE ABOUT IT--
--BECAUSE THEN THAT'D JUST BE PATHETIC.
SLAM
PEARL? YOU IN HERE?
JASON...
AH--! DAMN, YOU'RE FAST.
HEHE...
HEY, I'M GONNA GO. I'LL CALL YOU WHEN I GET HOME, OKAY?
OKAY. BYE...
WOW.

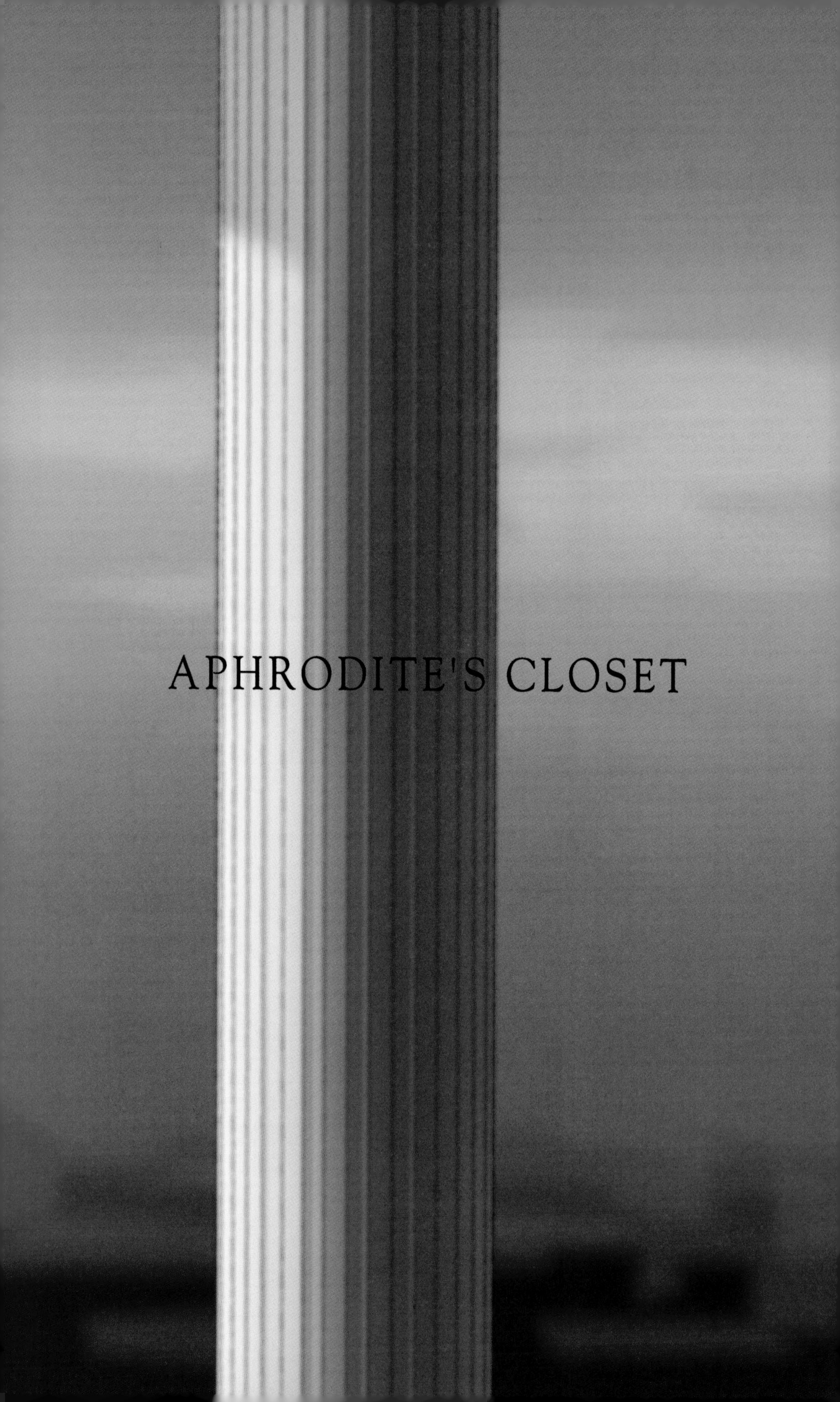

APHRODITE'S CLOSET

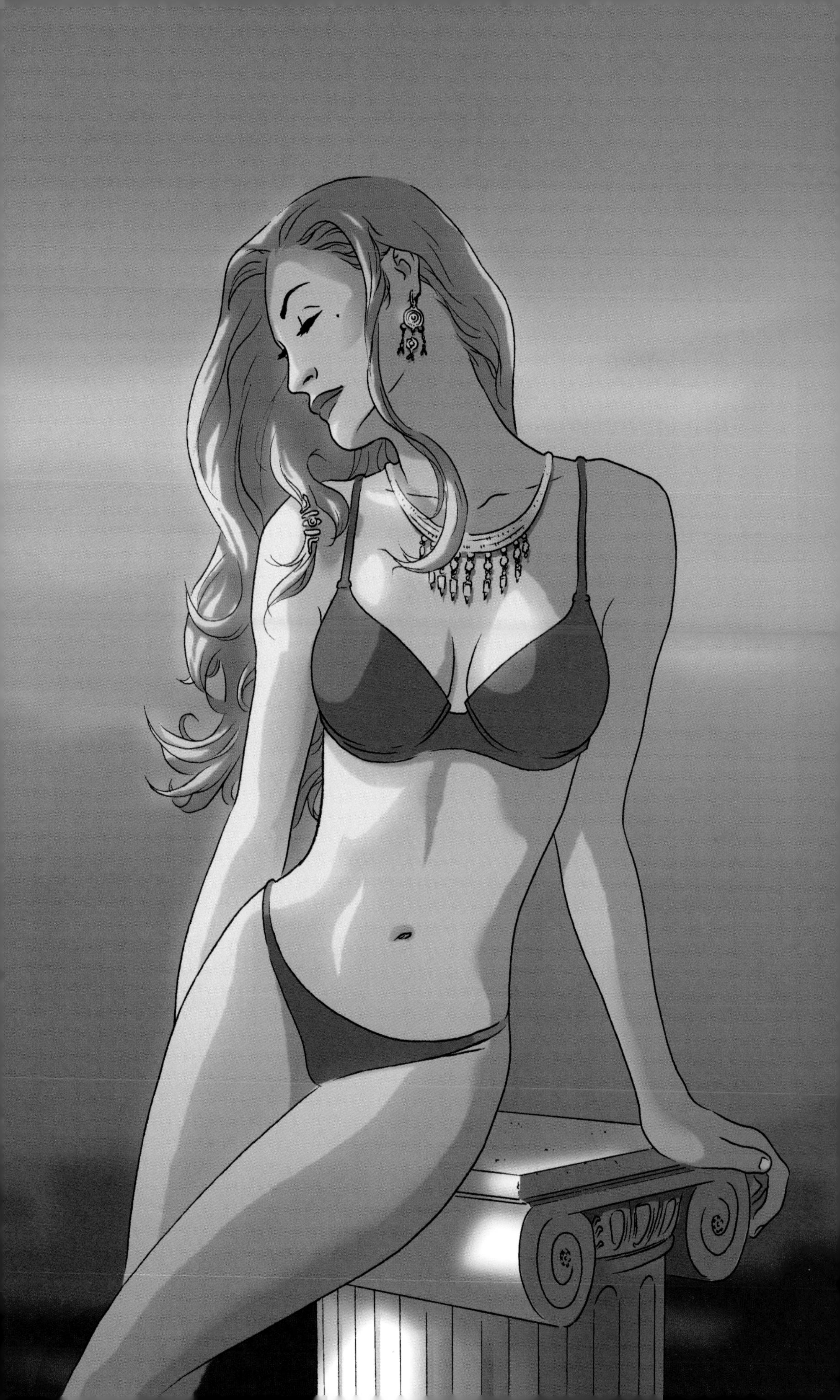

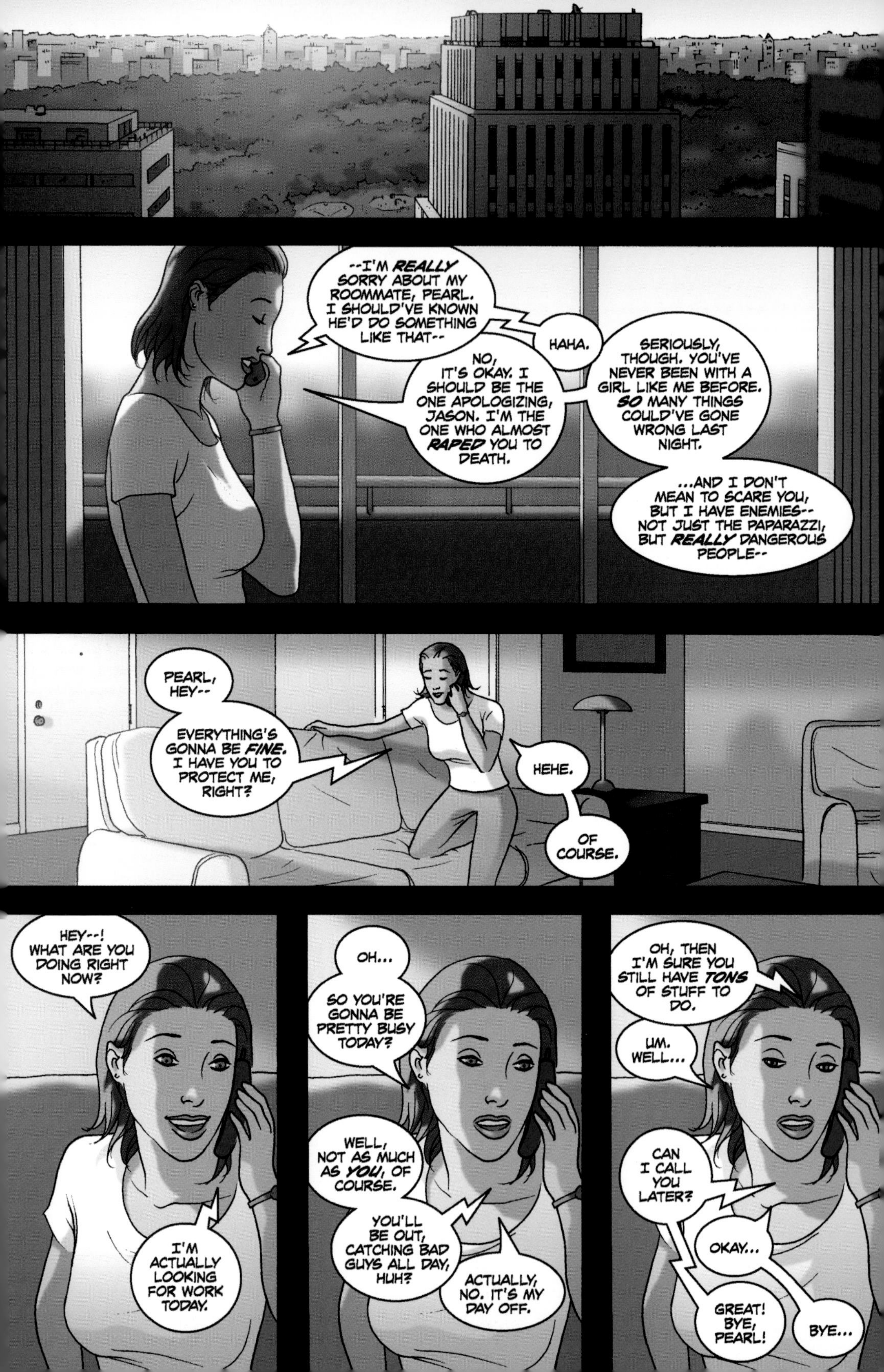
--I'M REALLY SORRY ABOUT MY ROOMMATE, PEARL. I SHOULD'VE KNOWN HE'D DO SOMETHING LIKE THAT--
HAHA.
NO, IT'S OKAY. I SHOULD BE THE ONE APOLOGIZING, JASON. I'M THE ONE WHO ALMOST RAPED YOU TO DEATH.
SERIOUSLY, THOUGH. YOU'VE NEVER BEEN WITH A GIRL LIKE ME BEFORE. SO MANY THINGS COULD'VE GONE WRONG LAST NIGHT.
...AND I DON'T MEAN TO SCARE YOU, BUT I HAVE ENEMIES-- NOT JUST THE PAPARAZZI, BUT REALLY DANGEROUS PEOPLE--
PEARL, HEY--
EVERYTHING'S GONNA BE FINE. I HAVE YOU TO PROTECT ME, RIGHT?
HEHE.
OF COURSE.
HEY--! WHAT ARE YOU DOING RIGHT NOW?
I'M ACTUALLY LOOKING FOR WORK TODAY.
OH...
SO YOU'RE GONNA BE PRETTY BUSY TODAY?
WELL, NOT AS MUCH AS YOU, OF COURSE.
YOU'LL BE OUT, CATCHING BAD GUYS ALL DAY, HUH?
ACTUALLY, NO. IT'S MY DAY OFF.
OH, THEN I'M SURE YOU STILL HAVE TONS OF STUFF TO DO.
UM. WELL...
CAN I CALL YOU LATER?
OKAY...
GREAT! BYE, PEARL!
BYE...

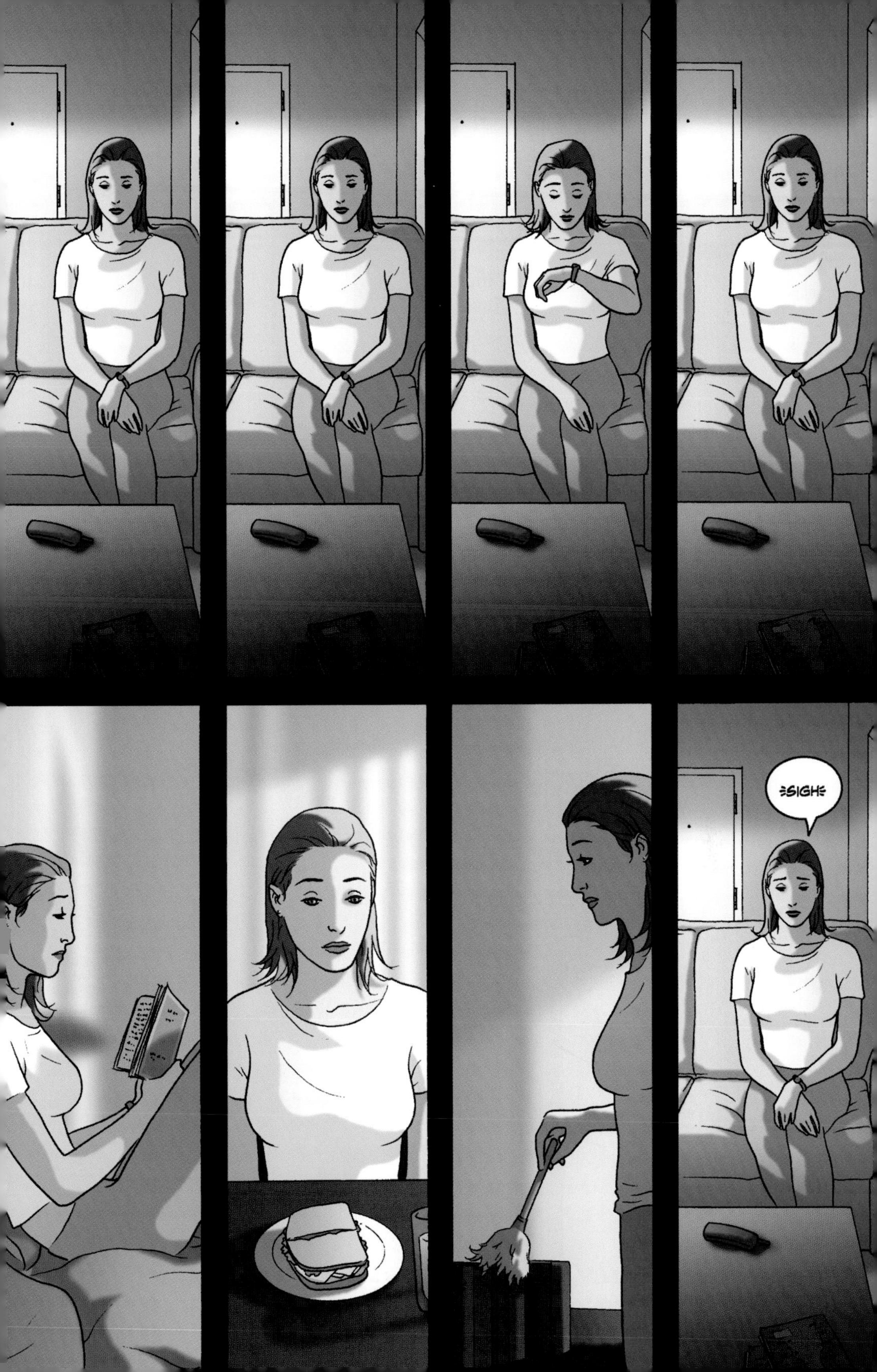
SIGH

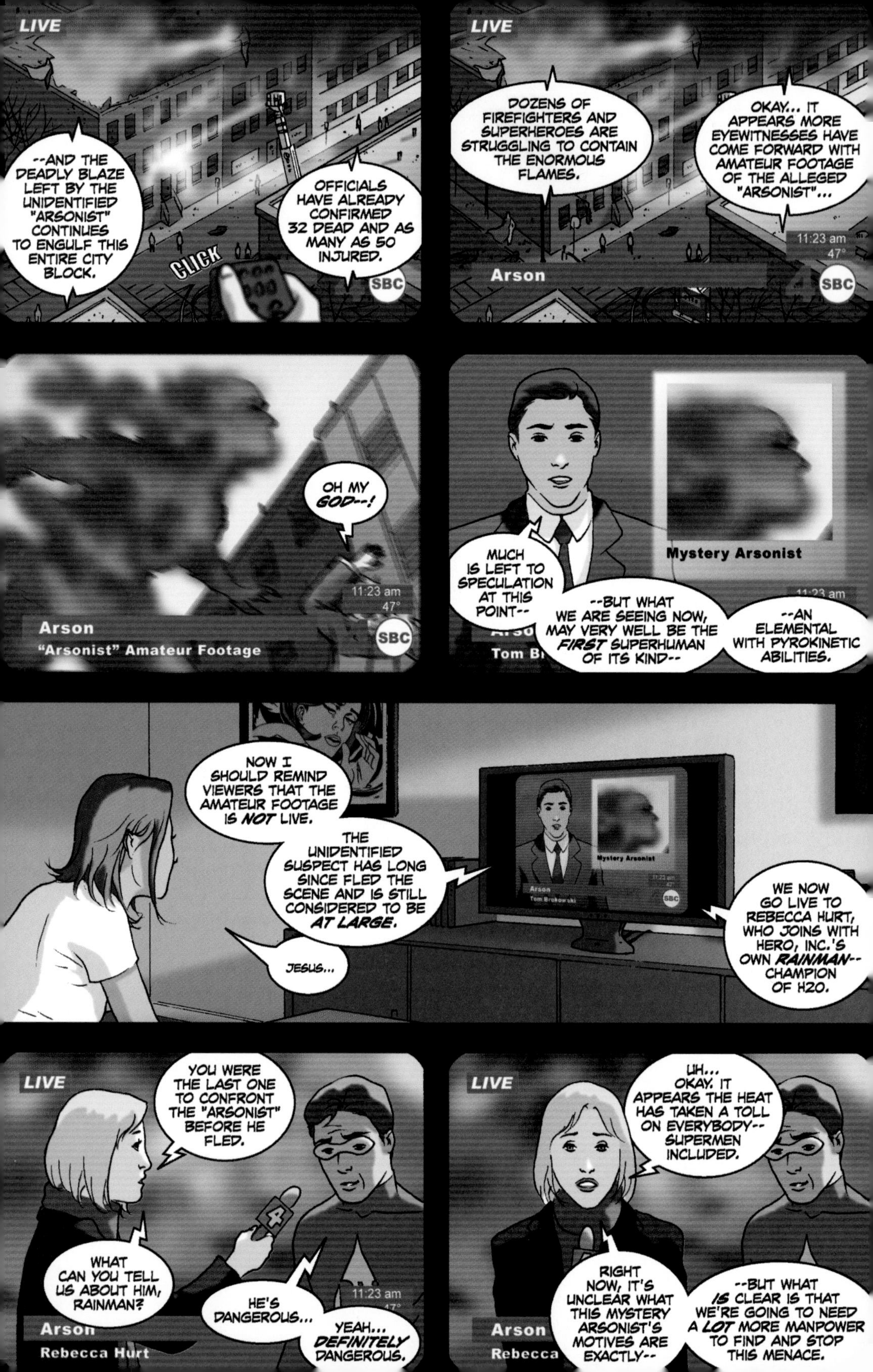

LIVE
--AND THE DEADLY BLAZE LEFT BY THE UNIDENTIFIED "ARSONIST" CONTINUES TO ENGULF THIS ENTIRE CITY BLOCK.
OFFICIALS HAVE ALREADY CONFIRMED 32 DEAD AND AS MANY AS 50 INJURED.
CLICK
SBC
LIVE
DOZENS OF FIREFIGHTERS AND SUPERHEROES ARE STRUGGLING TO CONTAIN THE ENORMOUS FLAMES.
OKAY... IT APPEARS MORE EYEWITNESSES HAVE COME FORWARD WITH AMATEUR FOOTAGE OF THE ALLEGED "ARSONIST"...
11:23 am
47°
Arson
SBC
OH MY GOD--!
11:23 am
47°
Arson
"Arsonist" Amateur Footage
SBC
Mystery Arsonist
MUCH IS LEFT TO SPECULATION AT THIS POINT--
--BUT WHAT WE ARE SEEING NOW, MAY VERY WELL BE THE FIRST SUPERHUMAN OF ITS KIND--
--AN ELEMENTAL WITH PYROKINETIC ABILITIES.
NOW I SHOULD REMIND VIEWERS THAT THE AMATEUR FOOTAGE IS NOT LIVE.
THE UNIDENTIFIED SUSPECT HAS LONG SINCE FLED THE SCENE AND IS STILL CONSIDERED TO BE AT LARGE.
Mystery Arsonist
JESUS...
WE NOW GO LIVE TO REBECCA HURT, WHO JOINS WITH HERO, INC.'S OWN RAINMAN-- CHAMPION OF H2O.
LIVE
YOU WERE THE LAST ONE TO CONFRONT THE "ARSONIST" BEFORE HE FLED.
WHAT CAN YOU TELL US ABOUT HIM, RAINMAN?
HE'S DANGEROUS...
YEAH... DEFINITELY DANGEROUS.
11:23 am
Arson
Rebecca Hurt
LIVE
UH... OKAY. IT APPEARS THE HEAT HAS TAKEN A TOLL ON EVERYBODY-- SUPERMEN INCLUDED.
RIGHT NOW, IT'S UNCLEAR WHAT THIS MYSTERY ARSONIST'S MOTIVES ARE EXACTLY--
--BUT WHAT IS CLEAR IS THAT WE'RE GOING TO NEED A LOT MORE MANPOWER TO FIND AND STOP THIS MENACE.
Arson
Rebecca

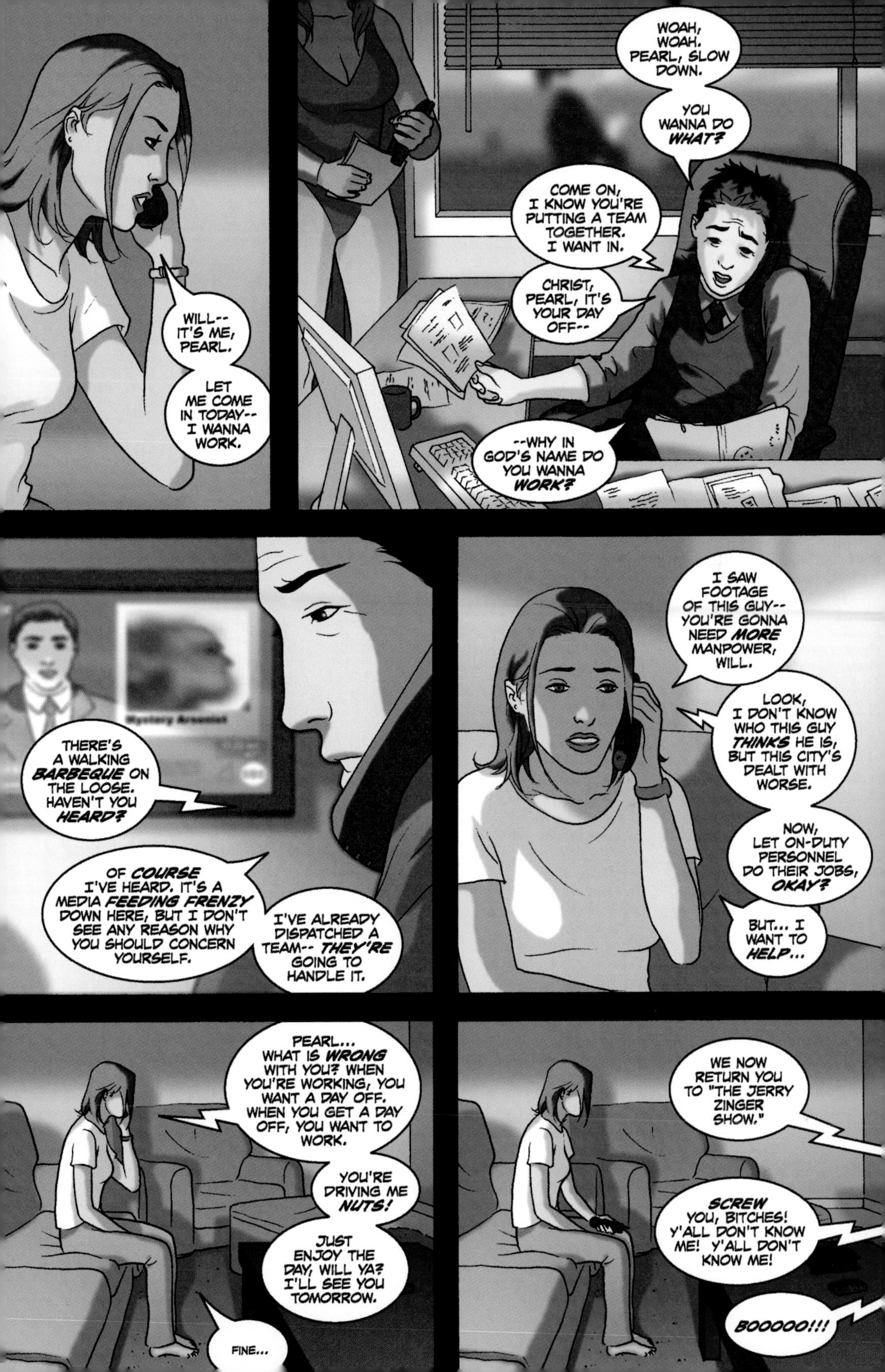
WILL-- IT'S ME, PEARL.
LET ME COME IN TODAY-- I WANNA WORK.
WOAH, WOAH. PEARL, SLOW DOWN.
YOU WANNA DO WHAT?
COME ON, I KNOW YOU'RE PUTTING A TEAM TOGETHER. I WANT IN.
CHRIST, PEARL, IT'S YOUR DAY OFF--
--WHY IN GOD'S NAME DO YOU WANNA WORK?
THERE'S A WALKING BARBEQUE ON THE LOOSE. HAVEN'T YOU HEARD?
OF COURSE I'VE HEARD. IT'S A MEDIA FEEDING FRENZY DOWN HERE, BUT I DON'T SEE ANY REASON WHY YOU SHOULD CONCERN YOURSELF.
I'VE ALREADY DISPATCHED A TEAM-- THEY'RE GOING TO HANDLE IT.
I SAW FOOTAGE OF THIS GUY-- YOU'RE GONNA NEED MORE MANPOWER, WILL.
LOOK, I DON'T KNOW WHO THIS GUY THINKS HE IS, BUT THIS CITY'S DEALT WITH WORSE.
NOW, LET ON-DUTY PERSONNEL DO THEIR JOBS, OKAY?
BUT... I WANT TO HELP...
PEARL... WHAT IS WRONG WITH YOU? WHEN YOU'RE WORKING, YOU WANT A DAY OFF. WHEN YOU GET A DAY OFF, YOU WANT TO WORK.
YOU'RE DRIVING ME NUTS!
JUST ENJOY THE DAY, WILL YA? I'LL SEE YOU TOMORROW.
FINE...
WE NOW RETURN YOU TO "THE JERRY ZINGER SHOW."
SCREW YOU, BITCHES! Y'ALL DON'T KNOW ME! Y'ALL DON'T KNOW ME!
BOOOOO!!!

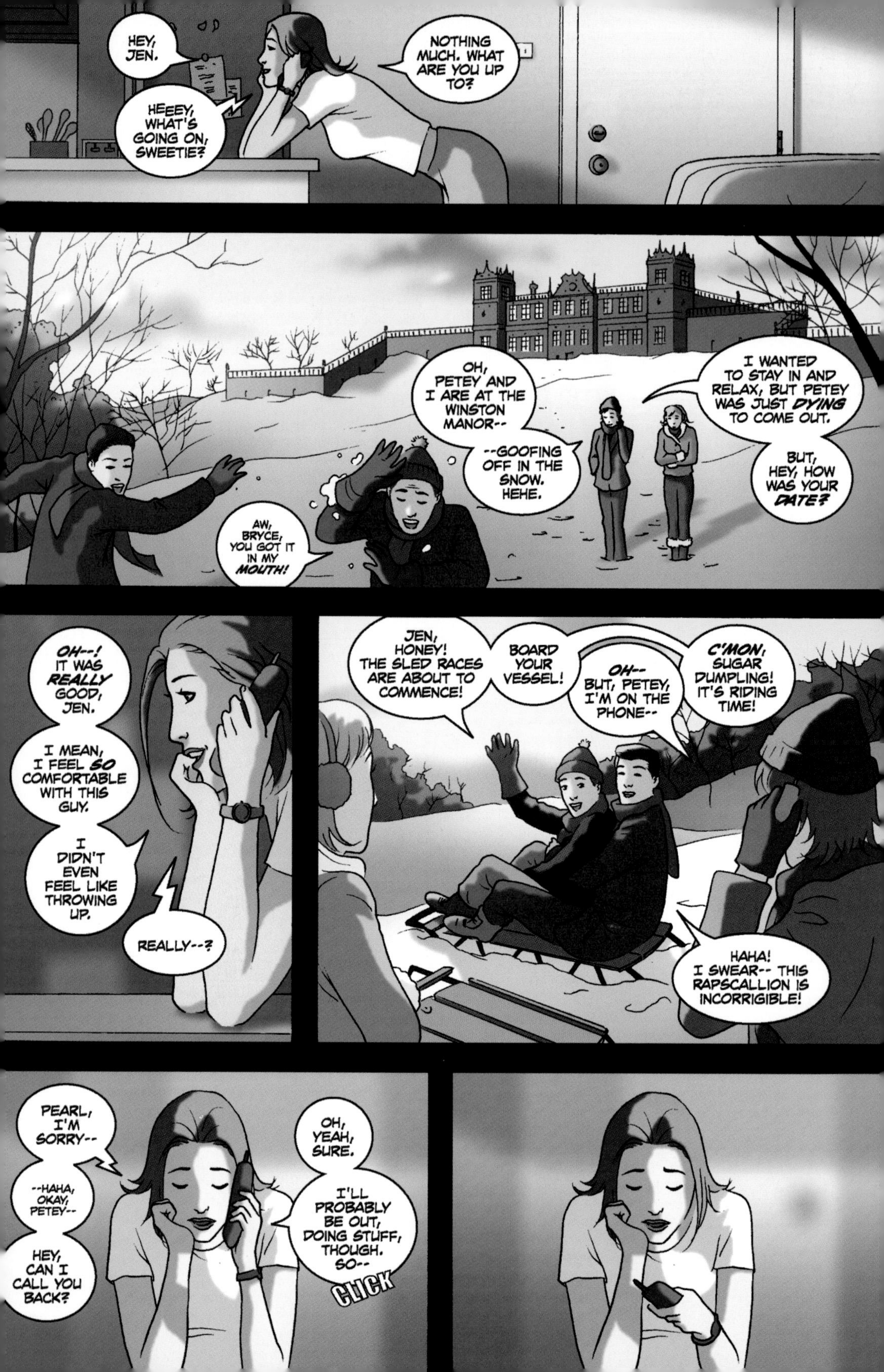
HEY, JEN.
HEEEY, WHAT'S GOING ON, SWEETIE?
NOTHING MUCH. WHAT ARE YOU UP TO?
OH, PETEY AND I ARE AT THE WINSTON MANOR--
--GOOFING OFF IN THE SNOW. HEHE.
I WANTED TO STAY IN AND RELAX, BUT PETEY WAS JUST DYING TO COME OUT.
BUT, HEY, HOW WAS YOUR DATE?
AW, BRYCE, YOU GOT IT IN MY MOUTH!
OH--! IT WAS REALLY GOOD, JEN.
I MEAN, I FEEL SO COMFORTABLE WITH THIS GUY.
I DIDN'T EVEN FEEL LIKE THROWING UP.
REALLY--?
JEN, HONEY! THE SLED RACES ARE ABOUT TO COMMENCE!
BOARD YOUR VESSEL!
OH-- BUT, PETEY, I'M ON THE PHONE--
C'MON, SUGAR DUMPLING! IT'S RIDING TIME!
HAHA! I SWEAR-- THIS RAPSCALLION IS INCORRIGIBLE!
PEARL, I'M SORRY--
--HAHA, OKAY, PETEY--
HEY, CAN I CALL YOU BACK?
OH, YEAH, SURE.
I'LL PROBABLY BE OUT, DOING STUFF, THOUGH. SO--
CLICK

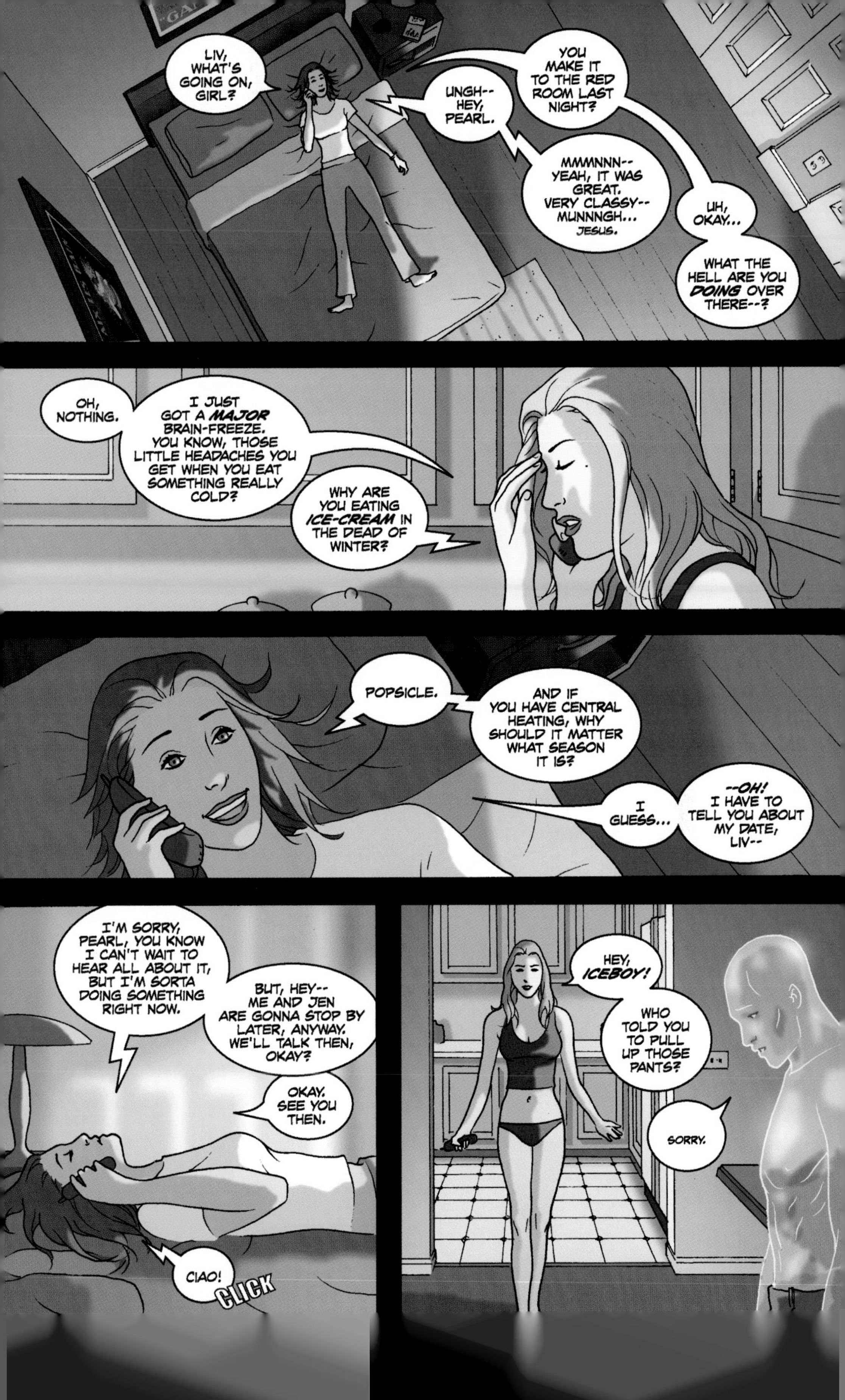
LIV, WHAT'S GOING ON, GIRL?
UNGH-- HEY, PEARL.
YOU MAKE IT TO THE RED ROOM LAST NIGHT?
MMMNNN-- YEAH, IT WAS GREAT. VERY CLASSY-- MUNNNGH... JESUS.
UH, OKAY...
WHAT THE HELL ARE YOU DOING OVER THERE--?
OH, NOTHING.
I JUST GOT A MAJOR BRAIN-FREEZE. YOU KNOW, THOSE LITTLE HEADACHES YOU GET WHEN YOU EAT SOMETHING REALLY COLD?
WHY ARE YOU EATING ICE-CREAM IN THE DEAD OF WINTER?
POPSICLE.
AND IF YOU HAVE CENTRAL HEATING, WHY SHOULD IT MATTER WHAT SEASON IT IS?
I GUESS...
--OH! I HAVE TO TELL YOU ABOUT MY DATE, LIV--
I'M SORRY, PEARL, YOU KNOW I CAN'T WAIT TO HEAR ALL ABOUT IT, BUT I'M SORTA DOING SOMETHING RIGHT NOW.
BUT, HEY-- ME AND JEN ARE GONNA STOP BY LATER, ANYWAY. WE'LL TALK THEN, OKAY?
OKAY. SEE YOU THEN.
CIAO!
CLICK
HEY, ICEBOY!
WHO TOLD YOU TO PULL UP THOSE PANTS?
SORRY.

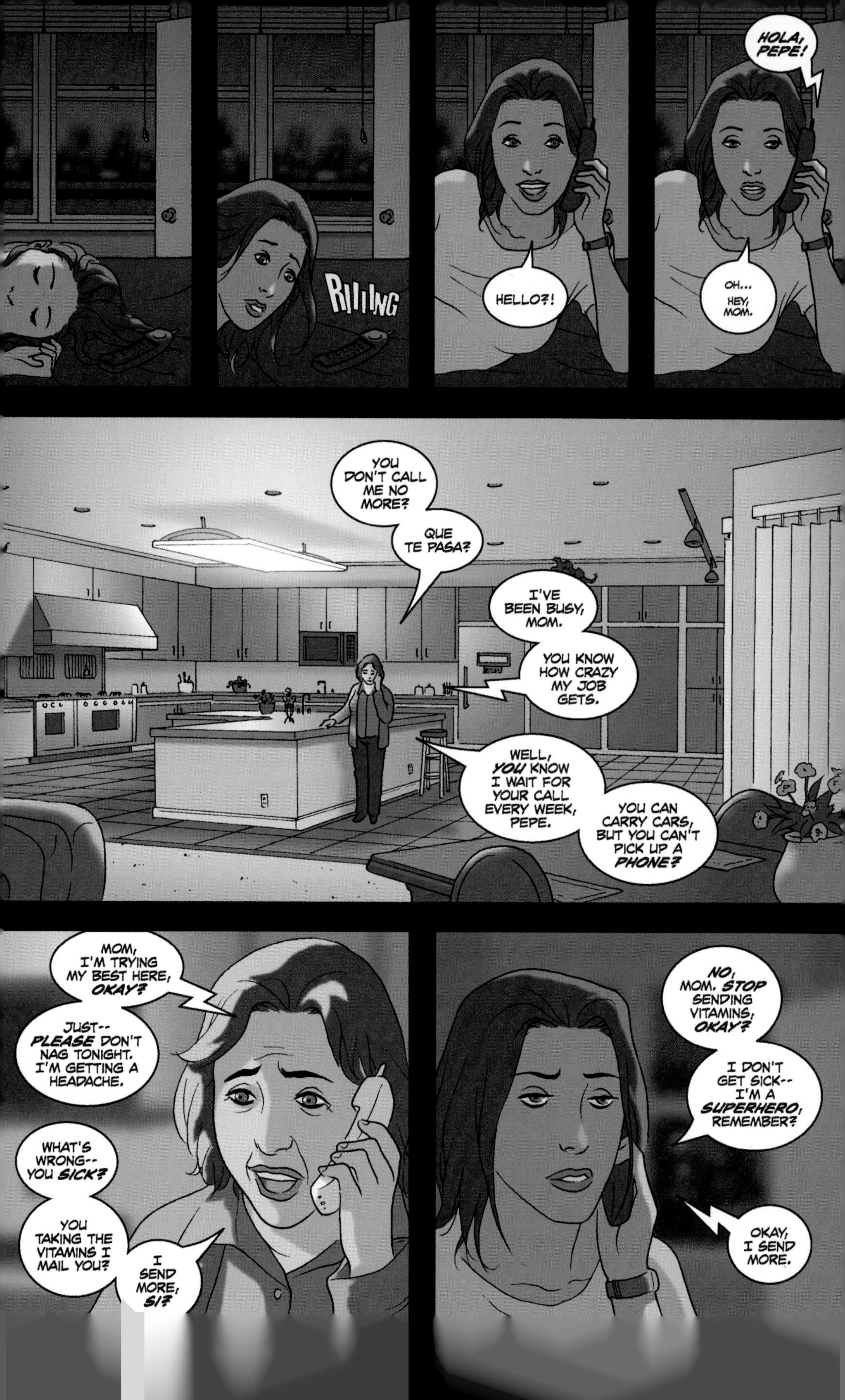
RIIIING
HELLO?!
HOLA, PEPE!
OH... HEY, MOM.
YOU DON'T CALL ME NO MORE?
QUE TE PASA?
I'VE BEEN BUSY, MOM.
YOU KNOW HOW CRAZY MY JOB GETS.
WELL, YOU KNOW I WAIT FOR YOUR CALL EVERY WEEK, PEPE.
YOU CAN CARRY CARS, BUT YOU CAN'T PICK UP A PHONE?
MOM, I'M TRYING MY BEST HERE, OKAY?
JUST-- PLEASE DON'T NAG TONIGHT. I'M GETTING A HEADACHE.
WHAT'S WRONG-- YOU SICK?
YOU TAKING THE VITAMINS I MAIL YOU?
I SEND MORE, SI?
NO, MOM. STOP SENDING VITAMINS, OKAY?
I DON'T GET SICK-- I'M A SUPERHERO, REMEMBER?
OKAY, I SEND MORE.

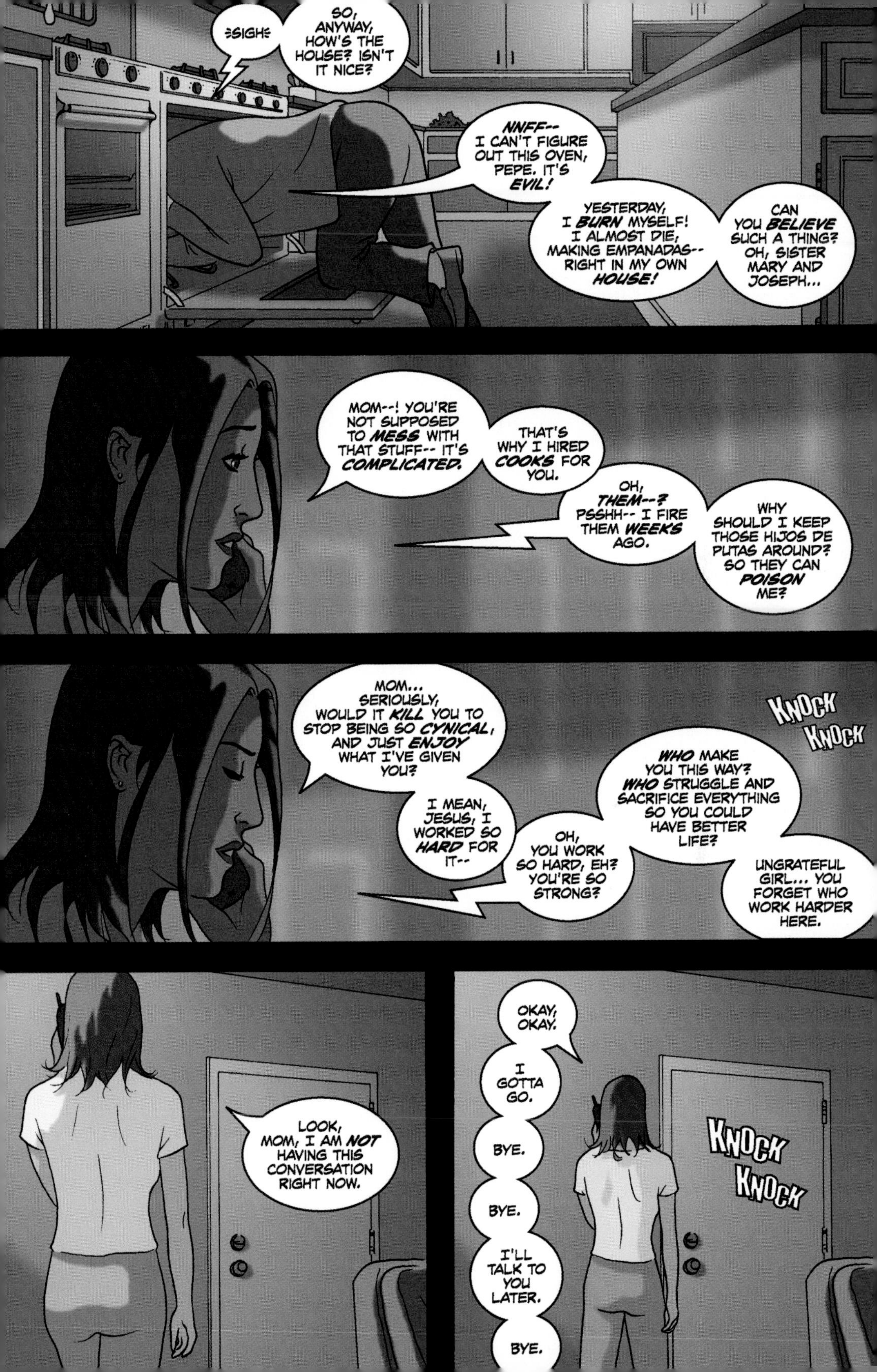

SIGH
SO, ANYWAY, HOW'S THE HOUSE? ISN'T IT NICE?
NNFF-- I CAN'T FIGURE OUT THIS OVEN, PEPE. IT'S EVIL!
YESTERDAY, I BURN MYSELF! I ALMOST DIE, MAKING EMPANADAS-- RIGHT IN MY OWN HOUSE!
CAN YOU BELIEVE SUCH A THING? OH, SISTER MARY AND JOSEPH...
MOM--! YOU'RE NOT SUPPOSED TO MESS WITH THAT STUFF-- IT'S COMPLICATED.
THAT'S WHY I HIRED COOKS FOR YOU.
OH, THEM--? PSSHH-- I FIRE THEM WEEKS AGO.
WHY SHOULD I KEEP THOSE HIJOS DE PUTAS AROUND? SO THEY CAN POISON ME?
MOM... SERIOUSLY, WOULD IT KILL YOU TO STOP BEING SO CYNICAL, AND JUST ENJOY WHAT I'VE GIVEN YOU?
I MEAN, JESUS, I WORKED SO HARD FOR IT--
OH, YOU WORK SO HARD, EH? YOU'RE SO STRONG?
WHO MAKE YOU THIS WAY? WHO STRUGGLE AND SACRIFICE EVERYTHING SO YOU COULD HAVE BETTER LIFE?
UNGRATEFUL GIRL... YOU FORGET WHO WORK HARDER HERE.
KNOCK KNOCK
LOOK, MOM, I AM NOT HAVING THIS CONVERSATION RIGHT NOW.
OKAY, OKAY.
I GOTTA GO.
BYE.
BYE.
I'LL TALK TO YOU LATER.
BYE.
KNOCK KNOCK

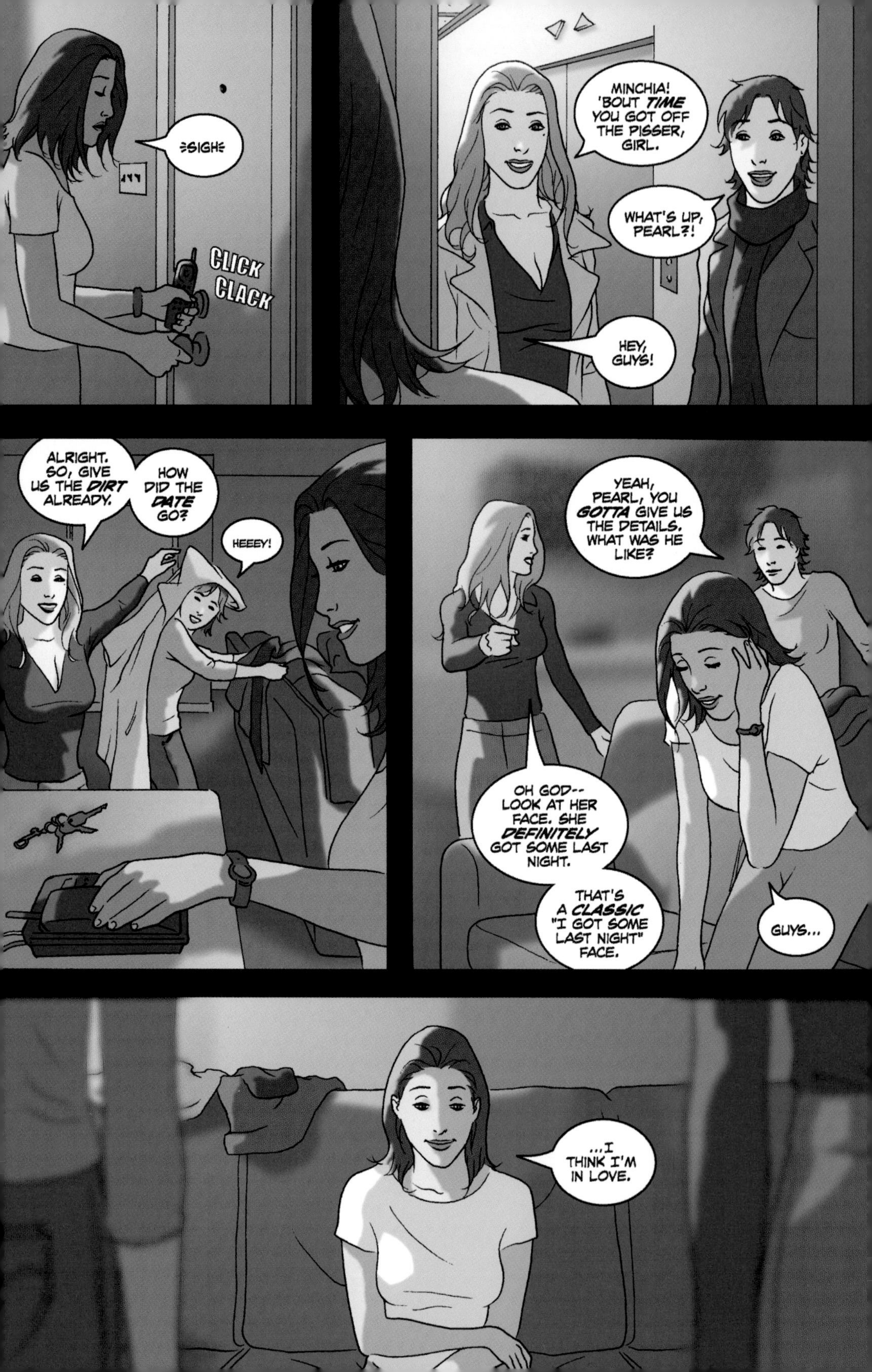

=SIGH=
CLICK
CLACK
MINCHIA! 'BOUT TIME YOU GOT OFF THE PISSER, GIRL.
WHAT'S UP, PEARL?!
HEY, GUYS!
ALRIGHT. SO, GIVE US THE DIRT ALREADY.
HOW DID THE DATE GO?
HEEEY!
YEAH, PEARL, YOU GOTTA GIVE US THE DETAILS. WHAT WAS HE LIKE?
OH GOD-- LOOK AT HER FACE. SHE DEFINITELY GOT SOME LAST NIGHT.
THAT'S A CLASSIC "I GOT SOME LAST NIGHT" FACE.
GUYS...
...I THINK I'M IN LOVE.

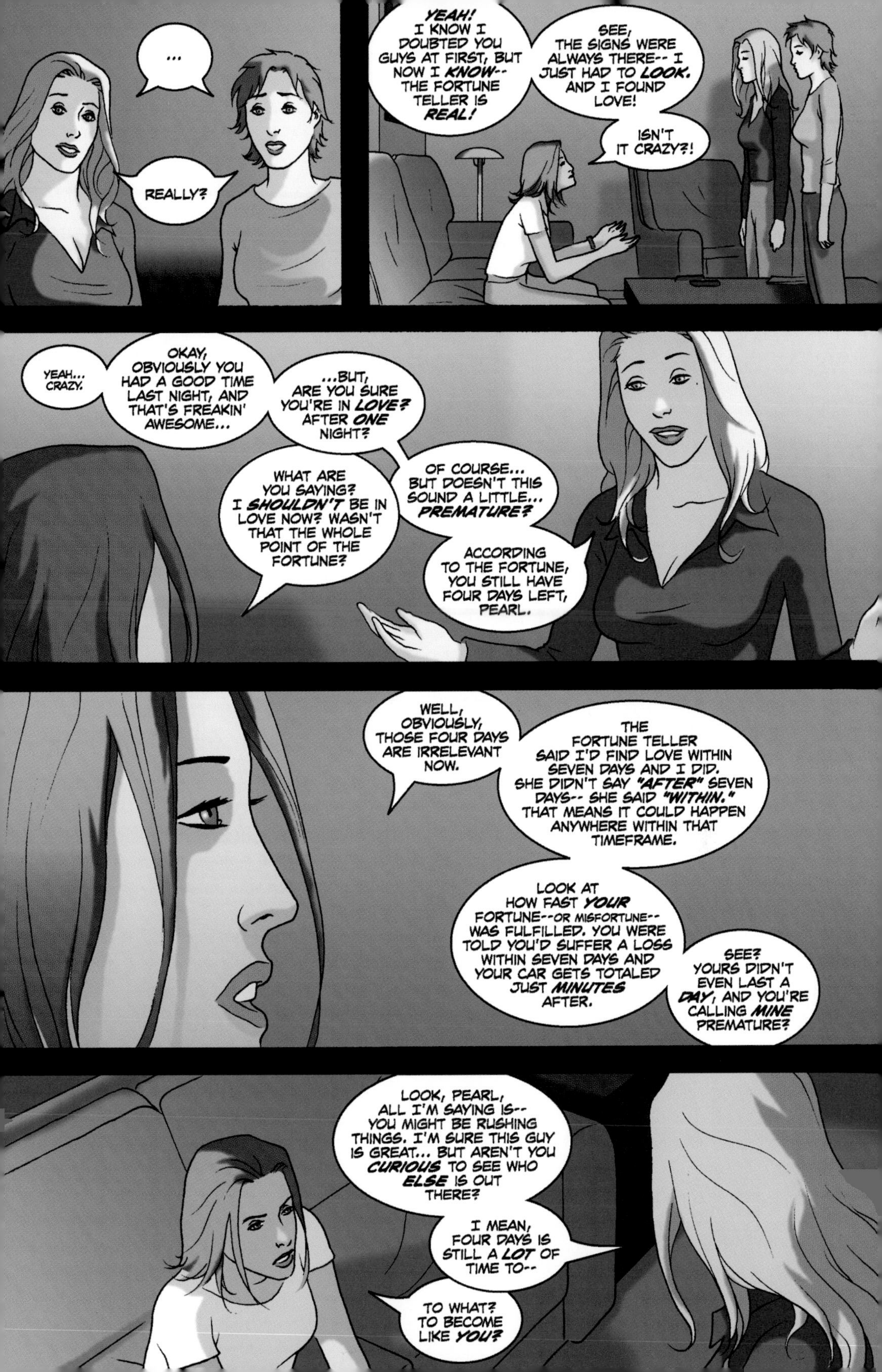
...
REALLY?
YEAH! I KNOW I DOUBTED YOU GUYS AT FIRST, BUT NOW I KNOW-- THE FORTUNE TELLER IS REAL!
SEE, THE SIGNS WERE ALWAYS THERE-- I JUST HAD TO LOOK. AND I FOUND LOVE!
ISN'T IT CRAZY?!
YEAH... CRAZY.
OKAY, OBVIOUSLY YOU HAD A GOOD TIME LAST NIGHT, AND THAT'S FREAKIN' AWESOME...
...BUT, ARE YOU SURE YOU'RE IN LOVE? AFTER ONE NIGHT?
WHAT ARE YOU SAYING? I SHOULDN'T BE IN LOVE NOW? WASN'T THAT THE WHOLE POINT OF THE FORTUNE?
OF COURSE... BUT DOESN'T THIS SOUND A LITTLE... PREMATURE?
ACCORDING TO THE FORTUNE, YOU STILL HAVE FOUR DAYS LEFT, PEARL.
WELL, OBVIOUSLY, THOSE FOUR DAYS ARE IRRELEVANT NOW.
THE FORTUNE TELLER SAID I'D FIND LOVE WITHIN SEVEN DAYS AND I DID. SHE DIDN'T SAY "AFTER" SEVEN DAYS-- SHE SAID "WITHIN." THAT MEANS IT COULD HAPPEN ANYWHERE WITHIN THAT TIMEFRAME.
LOOK AT HOW FAST YOUR FORTUNE--OR MISFORTUNE-- WAS FULFILLED. YOU WERE TOLD YOU'D SUFFER A LOSS WITHIN SEVEN DAYS AND YOUR CAR GETS TOTALED JUST MINUTES AFTER.
SEE? YOURS DIDN'T EVEN LAST A DAY, AND YOU'RE CALLING MINE PREMATURE?
LOOK, PEARL, ALL I'M SAYING IS-- YOU MIGHT BE RUSHING THINGS. I'M SURE THIS GUY IS GREAT... BUT AREN'T YOU CURIOUS TO SEE WHO ELSE IS OUT THERE?
I MEAN, FOUR DAYS IS STILL A LOT OF TIME TO--
TO WHAT? TO BECOME LIKE YOU?

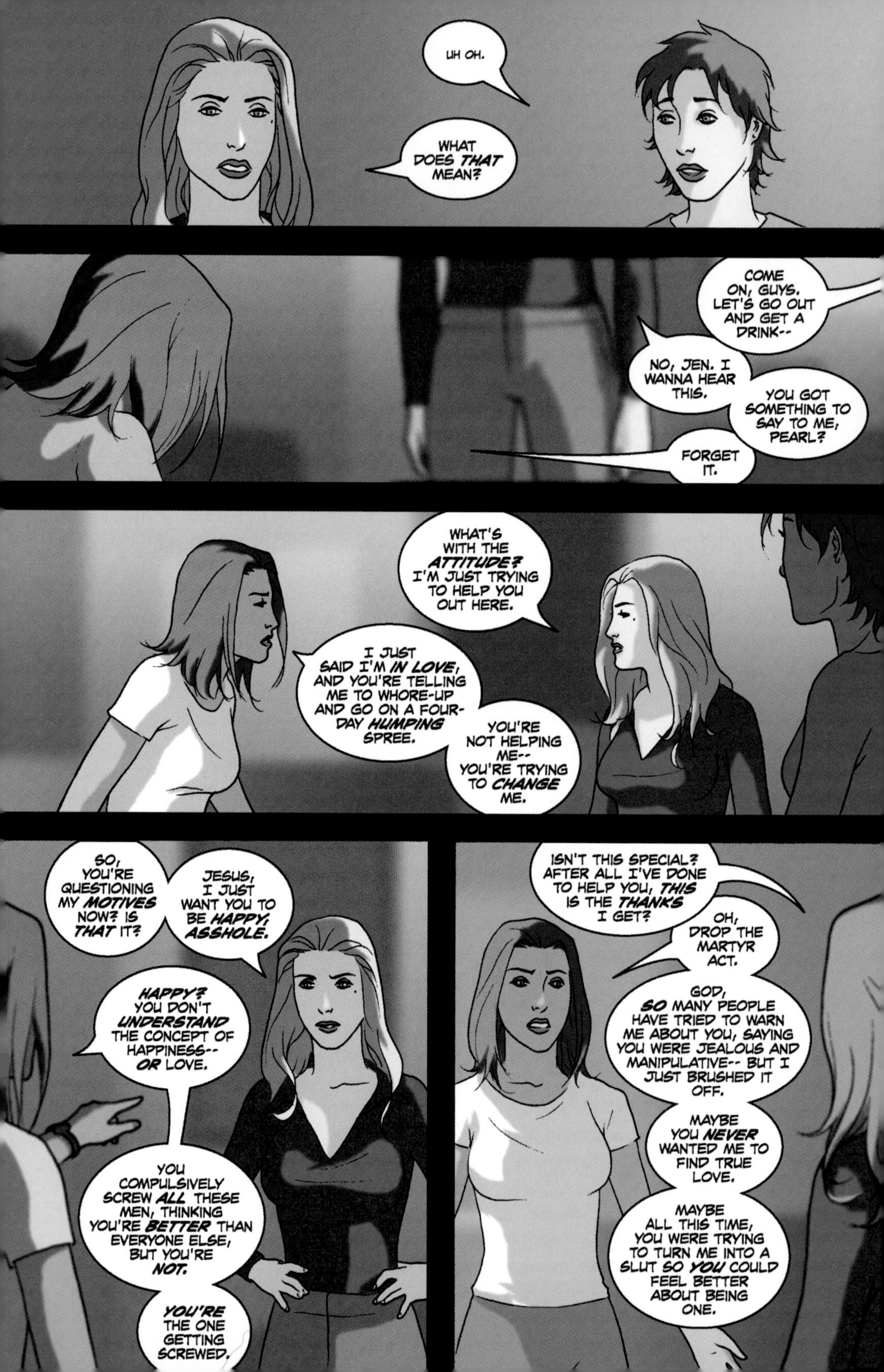
UH OH.
WHAT DOES THAT MEAN?
COME ON, GUYS. LET'S GO OUT AND GET A DRINK--
NO, JEN. I WANNA HEAR THIS.
YOU GOT SOMETHING TO SAY TO ME, PEARL?
FORGET IT.
WHAT'S WITH THE ATTITUDE? I'M JUST TRYING TO HELP YOU OUT HERE.
I JUST SAID I'M IN LOVE, AND YOU'RE TELLING ME TO WHORE-UP AND GO ON A FOUR-DAY HUMPING SPREE.
YOU'RE NOT HELPING ME-- YOU'RE TRYING TO CHANGE ME.
SO, YOU'RE QUESTIONING MY MOTIVES NOW? IS THAT IT?
JESUS, I JUST WANT YOU TO BE HAPPY, ASSHOLE.
HAPPY? YOU DON'T UNDERSTAND THE CONCEPT OF HAPPINESS-- OR LOVE.
YOU COMPULSIVELY SCREW ALL THESE MEN, THINKING YOU'RE BETTER THAN EVERYONE ELSE, BUT YOU'RE NOT.
YOU'RE THE ONE GETTING SCREWED.
ISN'T THIS SPECIAL? AFTER ALL I'VE DONE TO HELP YOU, THIS IS THE THANKS I GET?
OH, DROP THE MARTYR ACT.
GOD, SO MANY PEOPLE HAVE TRIED TO WARN ME ABOUT YOU, SAYING YOU WERE JEALOUS AND MANIPULATIVE-- BUT I JUST BRUSHED IT OFF.
MAYBE YOU NEVER WANTED ME TO FIND TRUE LOVE.
MAYBE ALL THIS TIME, YOU WERE TRYING TO TURN ME INTO A SLUT SO YOU COULD FEEL BETTER ABOUT BEING ONE.

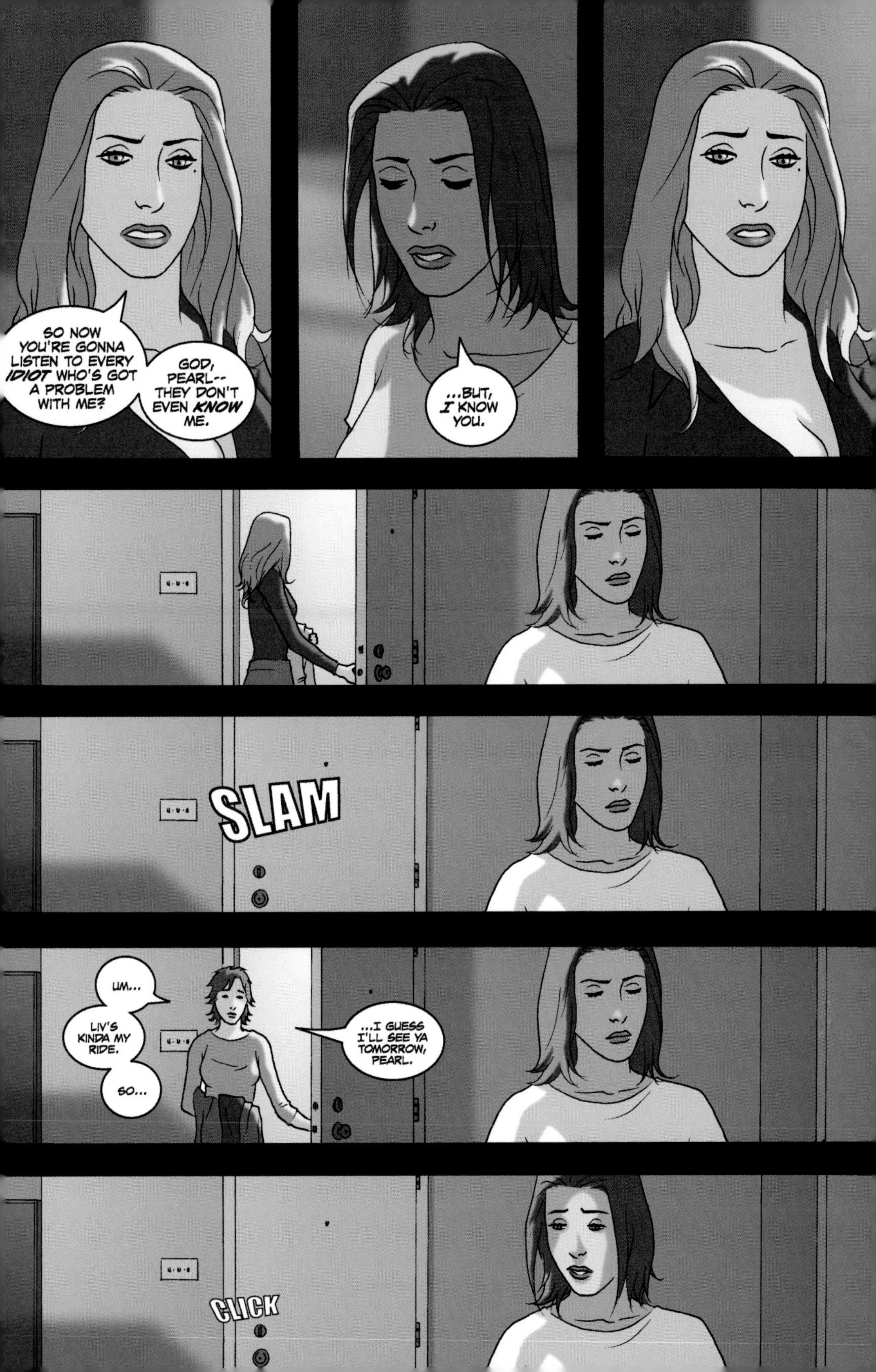
SO NOW YOU'RE GONNA LISTEN TO EVERY IDIOT WHO'S GOT A PROBLEM WITH ME?
GOD, PEARL-- THEY DON'T EVEN KNOW ME.
...BUT, I KNOW YOU.
SLAM
UM...
LIV'S KINDA MY RIDE.
SO...
...I GUESS I'LL SEE YA TOMORROW, PEARL.
CLICK

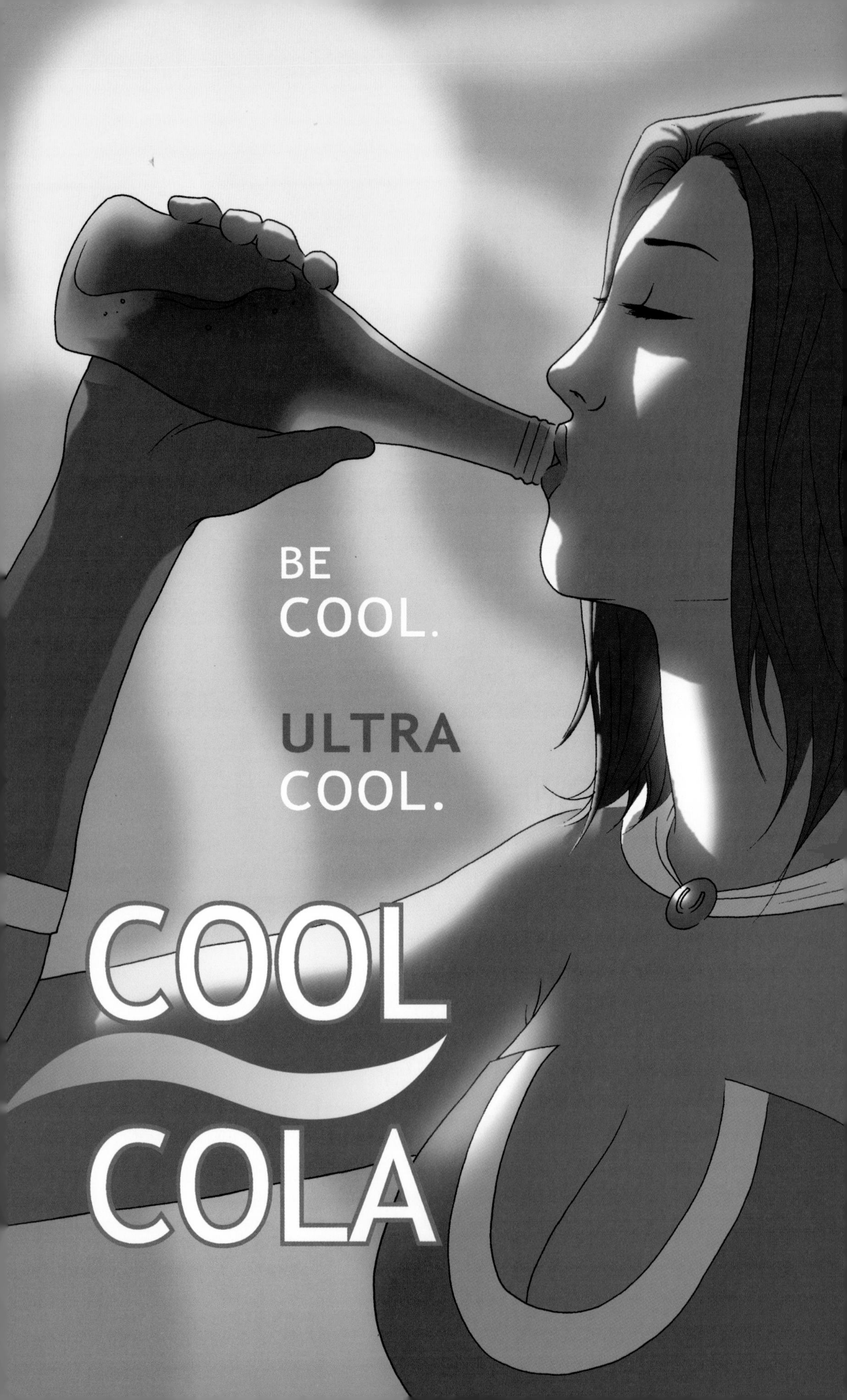
BE
COOL.
ULTRA
COOL.
COOL
COLA

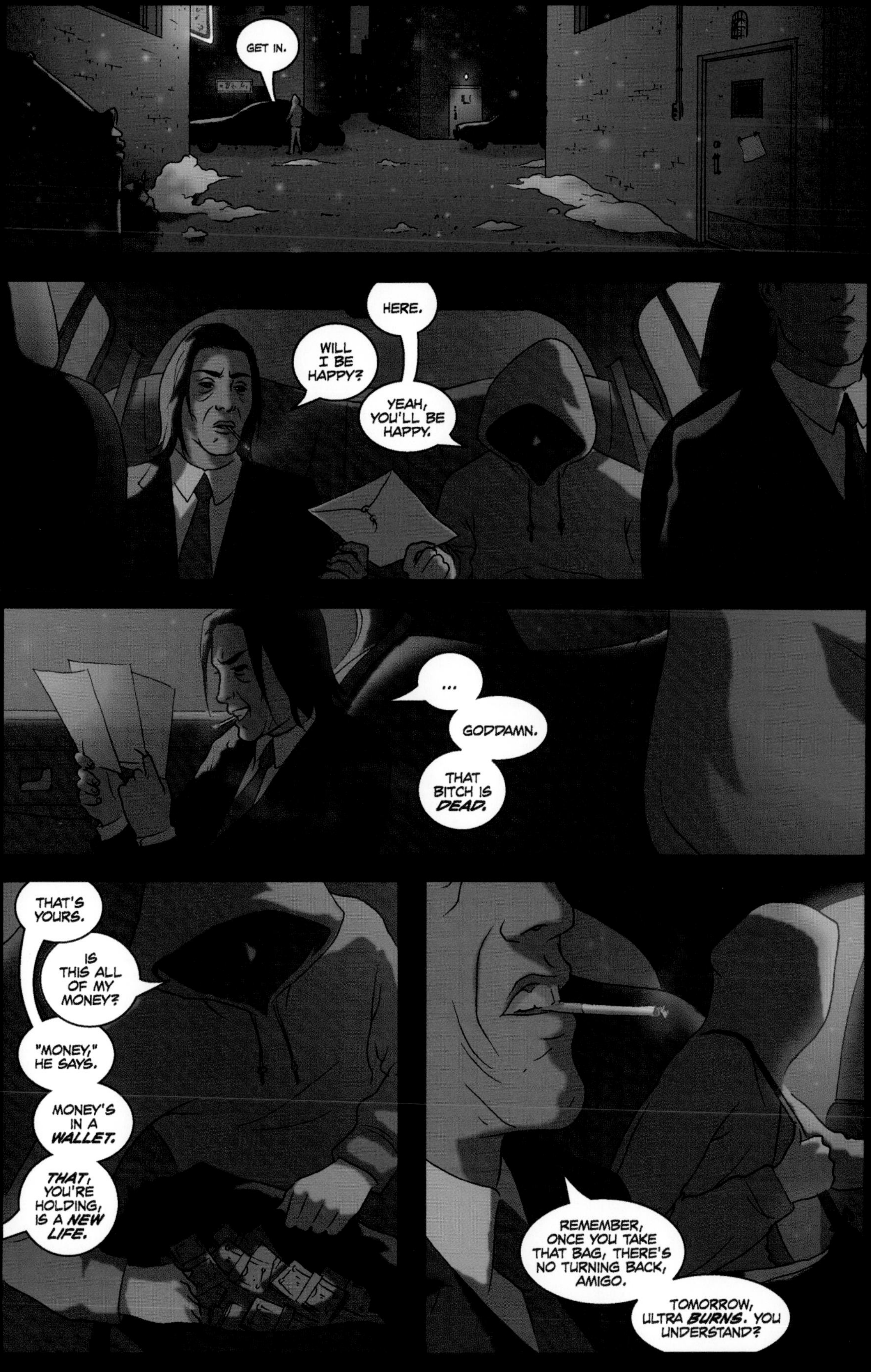
GET IN.
WILL I BE HAPPY?
HERE.
YEAH, YOU'LL BE HAPPY.
...
GODDAMN.
THAT BITCH IS ***DEAD.***
THAT'S YOURS.
IS THIS ALL OF MY MONEY?
"MONEY," HE SAYS.
MONEY'S IN A ***WALLET.***
THAT, YOU'RE HOLDING, IS A ***NEW LIFE.***
REMEMBER, ONCE YOU TAKE THAT BAG, THERE'S NO TURNING BACK, AMIGO.
TOMORROW, ULTRA ***BURNS.*** YOU UNDERSTAND?

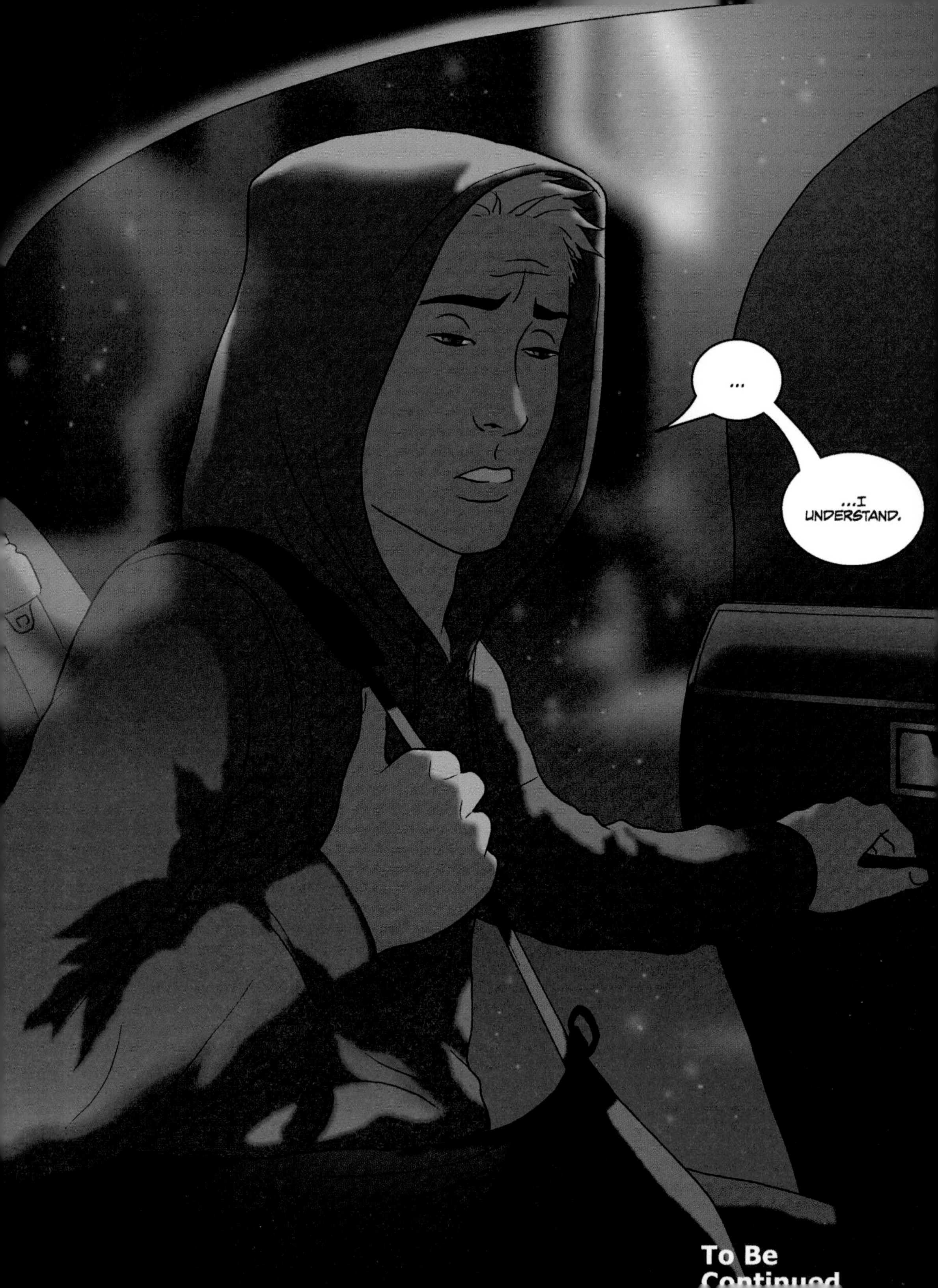
...
...I UNDERSTAND.
To Be Continued

Pearl At Her Peak

Pearl Penalosa's career wasn't always dynamite, but she was certainly destined to blow up.

STORY BY GIANNI CARLO

PEARL PENALOSA, WORLD renowned, superheroine celebrity, defender of Spring City and recent nominee for "Best Superheroine of the Year," wants a burrito. On our way to her ten o'clock photo shoot, she reluctantly decides on taking a detour in her slick yet relatively modest BNW and steers into a Burrito Bell drive-thru, professing how erratic her eating habits can get with a super-busy schedule. Considering the circumstances, I wasn't sure which I found more shocking-- the sight of an uber star, pulling up to a not-so authentic, Mexican fast-food joint, or the fact that a respectable, card-carrying Latina, was actually going to eat this crap. None of this contradictive behavior, however, is to suggest that Penalosa is anything but a classy gal. In fact, it's these particular slips of character-- these random rags-to-riches revelations that endear her, solidifying her much deserved status as Spring City's undisputed It-girl. Basically, as far as first impressions go, I find the only problem with Pearl Penalosa is that she is too cool to be Pearl Penalosa.

Witnessing Penalosa dressed down, minus the Ultra spandex, is an exceptionally, notable event-- a voyeuristic unmasking of sorts. In a surprising discovery, the scantily clad aforementioned costume, provocatively sleek and sexy with aeronautic gloss, pales in comparison to the natural beauty I see before me. The trim, five-foot-nine, no-pretentions superwoman effortlessly conveys a demure--almost utilitarian--sense of femininity, sporting a simple, black cashmere sweater, a beaten pair of rustic jeans and a blue cap-- fit snug over her trademark tangle of chestnut

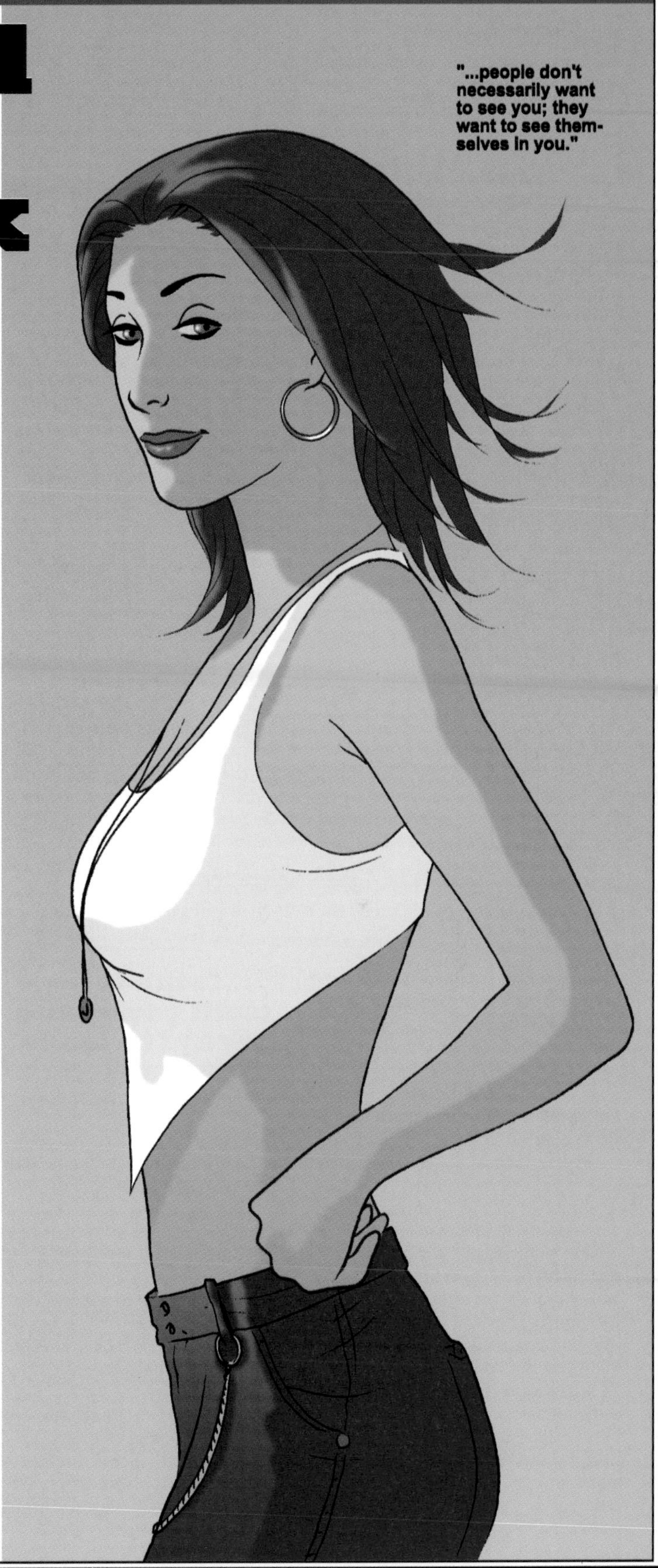
"...people don't necessarily want to see you; they want to see themselves in you."

brown locks. She notices me staring and flashes me a suspicious yet timid, sideways glance which indicates that she doesn't quite get how stunning she actually is. However, the jittery, and slightly greasy, Burrito Bell employee at the drive-thru window obviously does.

The teen flashes a goofy, knowing smile as he leans submissively towards Pearl's side window, proffering a freshly wrapped Beef and Bean Burrito Supreme. He has spotted his celebrity quarry, and in typical awkward, self-effacing fashion, presents Pearl with a spare receipt, asking to have it autographed. It's a critical juncture-- a star trapped in a car, between an adoring fan and the watchful eye of the media, i.e. me. A hit-or-miss situation such as this tests the authenticity of a celebrity's character. With no room for feigning curtsy, every lull or nuance in tone is measured-- every subtle gesture is visually polygraphed and accounted for. But Pearl is savvy enough to know this game because, to her, it isn't a game. The adulation does not compromise or bend her identity-- instead, it reveals it. Without hesitation, she drops her burrito in mid-unwrap, yanks a pen from the glove compartment and dutifully signs away, taking a few more minutes to meet and greet the inevitable, kowtowing mob scene, now accumulating around us by the very second. Like I said: cool.

In between her man-sized bites, the notoriously private superheroine sets the record straight on her red-hot career, her rise to fame, the bumpy road of success, the schadenfreude directed towards her over-publicized breakup with Captain Steel, and the joys of being alone. In an industry that breeds super-sized egos, secret identities, and split personalities, it's refreshing to meet a superheroine who doesn't wear a mask.

After surprising the world with a promising acting debut last year, you shock us yet again, burning up the music charts with the hot, hit single "Supernatural." Is there anything you can't do?

Oh God, yes. I'm not as versatile as people would like to think. I just have a tendency to spread myself thin and dabble in everything. Plus, when you get a one-time chance to collaborate with music legends

such as Prinze and Janet Jacko, you can't let the opportunity slip by. I admit I was a little intimidated at first, singing in a recording studio for the first time, under the watchful eyes of record producers and the industry's heavy-hitters, but working on the single "Supernatural" was a lot of fun. It has a very trance-y kind of vibe-- very beat-heavy and melodic with some reggae and Latin influences. I'd describe the track as strip-club music for the whole family-- an equal opportunity ass-shaker. I'm very pleased with it. And aside from a two-year stint in the church choir when I was twelve, I never had much previous singing experience, but the track came out really, really well. Of course, they tweaked some of my vocals on the computer, but still-- it's damn good. Though, I doubt I'll be switching careers anytime soon. I'll stick to what I do best-- being a superheroine.

So how did you end up in the superhero business anyway?

Well, before I even considered superhero work, I got my start in law enforcement as a police officer with the Spring City PD, working the daily beat in a patrol unit. My father was a cop, and I was always a tomboy so it made sense. I grew up in a strict, working class household where we lived check-to-check, but my dad set such an

> **"...fame is cool until you're too afraid to leave your own house."**

inspiring example for all of us, catching bad guys and still doing his best to put food on the table. He's just a good man who did everything in his power to help others. So for me, leaving the force to pursue superhero work was the next logical step towards helping people in the best way I possibly could. Plus, those police uniforms make your ass look ridiculously huge.

You've come a long way from handing out parking citations.

Just because I chased down some carjackers and knocked out a few crackheads in my day, I thought

this superheroine gig would be a breeze. I was so wrong. It's law enforcement on a whole new level-- the playing field is the same, but the stakes are elevated.

You basically went from zero to overnight multi-million dollar hero. How did you handle the fame?

Not very well. Starting out, I was really naive and had a few misconceptions about fame. I used to think being too famous to walk into a restaurant or a movie theater, for fear of being mobbed, would be so cool. Everyone, at some point, fantasizes about that kind of recognition. But once it happens, you're like, "woah... step back, people." See, fame is cool until you're too afraid to leave your own house. It's insane and inescapable, but it's not like you can take a "time out" and return to normal life again. You're always going to be this persona, and it starts to outgrow you and take a life of its own. It's like everyone suddenly knows you but you don't really know anybody. And unless you're completely full of yourself, I don't think anyone can really be one hundred percent comfortable with that amount of attention. I'm not going to whine about it though, because I chose this, and I'm pretty sure there are much bigger problems in the world today other than being rich and famous.

Speaking of fame-- how uncomfortable were you, dating Captain Steel, the most prominent superhero icon of our time?

As far as the publicity and the constant press coverage went, it sucked. Every day was a media onslaught-- people really wanted to know the minute-by-minute status on us, regardless of how trivial or mundane it was. And believe me, it usually was. I could take a nap in my car or step in a pile of dog crap and that would be breaking news. We literally had more updates on our relationship than a 24-hour weather channel. So that was definitely stressful. Plus, for some reason, the media decided to portray us as this perfect couple-- role models expected to set the bar for this chaste ideal because, to them, we were considered "young, innocent and untouched by the evils of the world." To this day, even after the split, the pressure to live up to these expectations stuck.

Even now, neither one of you have revealed the real reason behind the split.

Okay, I'm aware of the social obligations that come with celebrity, and I know the price of fame means living a life in the spotlight, but somewhere, we have to draw a line. See, what Roger and I had wasn't a gimmick or a publicity stunt-- we were in a real relationship, and there are some things that must remain sacred. And you have to understand that I hardly discussed this relationship even with my closest friends. I'm a

> **"...looking back, maybe I did put dating off too long."**

pretty open girl, but when it comes to matters of the heart, I'm guarded. Relationships aren't easy. They're mysterious and fickle. Sometimes, I don't even know why we didn't work. But when it doesn't work, there's obviously a reason, and you have to accept it gracefully.

Were you surprised by the nationwide backlash caused by your overexposed relationship?

No, I pretty much knew from the get-go that there was going to be a backlash. Our relationship was talked about so much that it just annoyed everyone. I mean, come on, nobody wants to see that much of anybody. But I think the most frustrating part of the backlash was the blatant one-sidedness of it. The people didn't get to see the ones behind the cameras-- the crazed, car-chasing photographers, the paparazzi lurking outside of my window ledge, or the jerks who made nasty comments to provoke me. The only thing people were seeing was me. So, naturally, the general public directed the blame towards what they saw. It's like the old saying goes-- "Familiarity breeds contempt." So, people got sick of me. Hell, even I got sick of me.

Is the paparazzi your archenemy?

I'm just not a big fan of annoying dickheads. I mean, there's valid journalism, and then there's abuse. I know superheroes are public commodities but no one deserves to be harassed. And in all fairness, I'll admit that I'm not completely without blame. I realize, by simply being a celebrity, I'm complicit in my own lack of privacy, but the media just took the spectacle too far. It got to a point where their "scoops" became lower than mere tabloid fodder, let alone journalism. Every tidbit about my personal life overshadowed the professional achievements that mattered, like that little thing I happen to do for a living called-- saving lives. I could rescue orphans from a burning building and all the paparazzi wanted was an ass-shot for the headlining story. That type of behavior eventually led to their loss of credibility, and people slowly, but surely, realized who the real bad guy was. I guess you can say I was vindicated.

So with the brouhaha long since forgiven, how do you feel now, emerging as one of the few celebrities to make a comeback and match, if not surpass, your initial level of fame?

Having the people back on my side is definitely a plus because my career revolves around them. Though looking back, I think the momentary break from that level of celebrity may have been a blessing in disguise because once I stepped out of the spotlight for a while-- and out of Captain Steel's shadow-- I finally had a chance to be my own woman. People started to see me as an individual and not just "The Captain's Chick" anymore. They realized I was just like them, a vulnerable human being, coming out of a bad breakup, and not just some impenetrable caped crusader. You can't have a big ego in the superhero business because the people don't necessarily want to see you; they want to see themselves in you. So, I'm really grateful for all the people who supported me because they played a big part in my comeback. I wouldn't be here without them.

You seriously put off dating after the breakup. Do you just hate men now?

I don't think so. It's funny, because people really start to assume

the worst when you drop out of the dating scene. After the break-up, I was so fed up with the whole ordeal that I decided to put off dating for a while and just concentrate on work. It seemed like a good idea until out of nowhere, I'm unofficially crowned "poster girl" for teenage abstinence. It was sort of humiliating. I suddenly gained this whole new fan following made up of worried mothers who expected me to set the example for their promiscuous teenage daughters. Now when you become internationally known and celebrated for not putting out, it's not the best way to jump start a new love life. So looking back, maybe I did put dating off too long.

Do you like being single?

It has its ups and downs. You no longer have that intimacy you get in a relationship, but on the upside, being alone is the best way to spend quality time with yourself. And no-- not like *that*. **Ⓤ**

Making the Music

Pearl in the recording studio.

In her music video, "Supernatual."

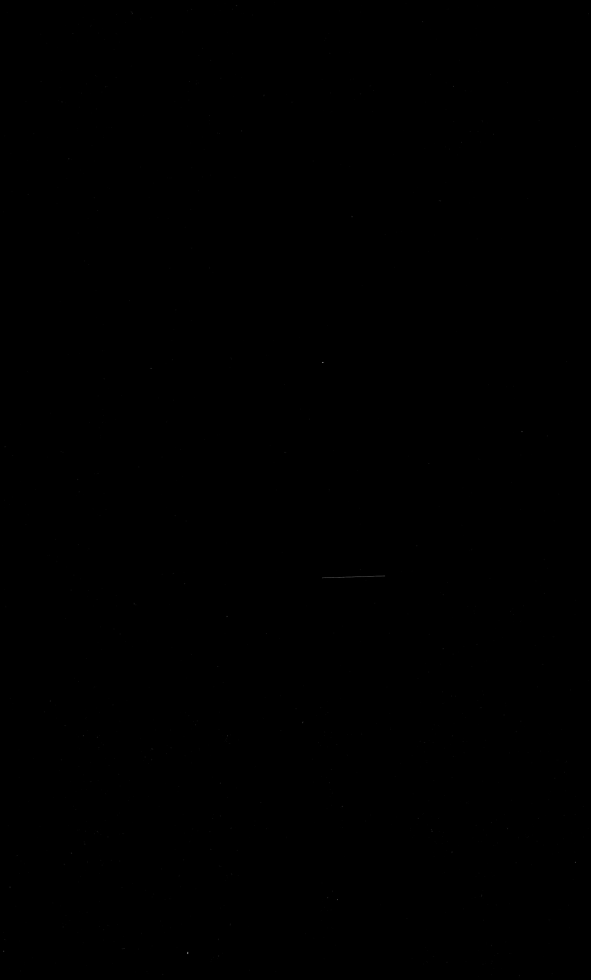

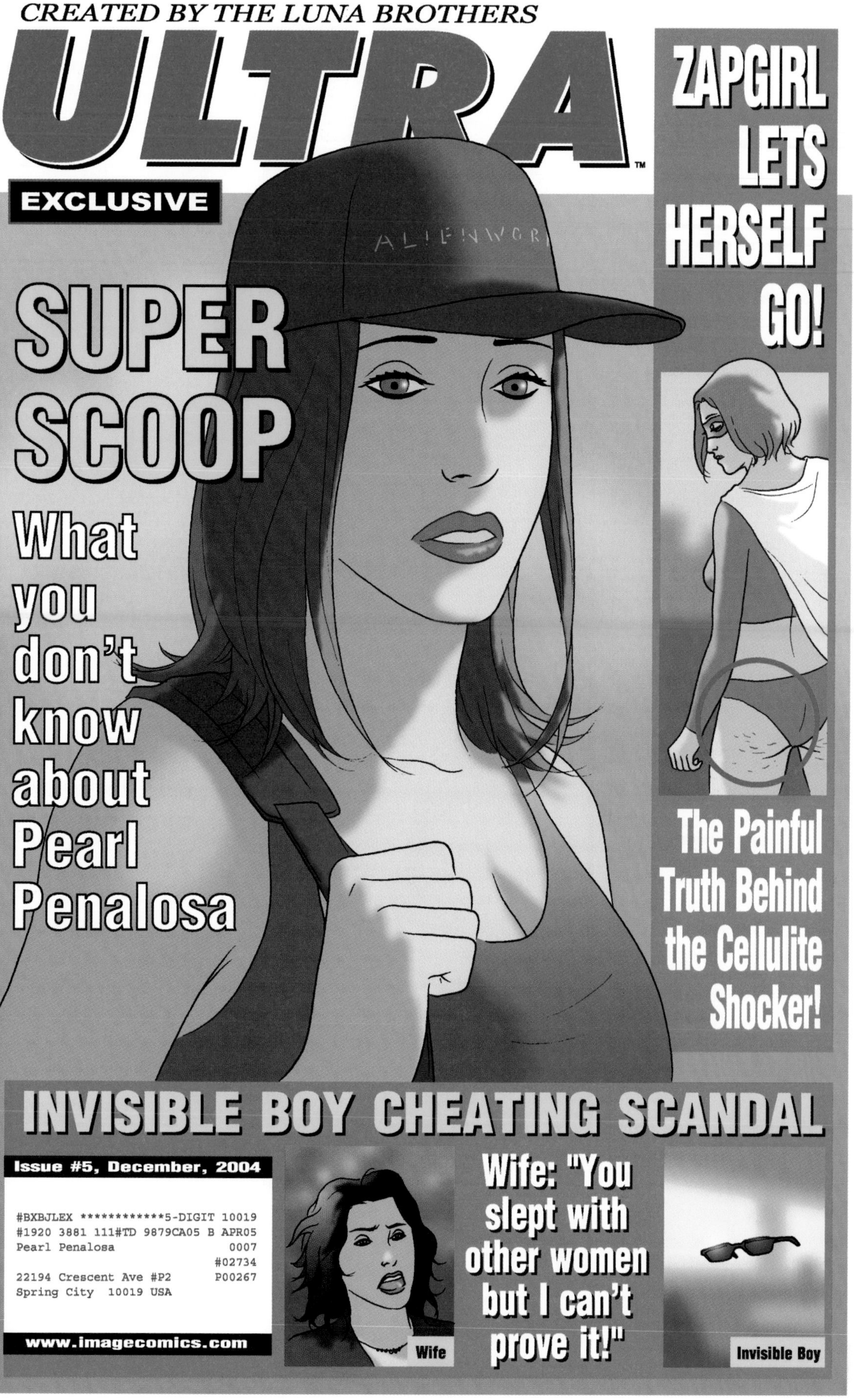
CREATED BY THE LUNA BROTHERS
ULTRA™
EXCLUSIVE
SUPER SCOOP
What you don't know about Pearl Penalosa
ZAPGIRL LETS HERSELF GO!
The Painful Truth Behind the Cellulite Shocker!
INVISIBLE BOY CHEATING SCANDAL
Issue #5, December, 2004
#BXBJLEX ************5-DIGIT 10019
#1920 3881 111#TD 9879CA05 B APR05
Pearl Penalosa 0007
#02734
22194 Crescent Ave #P2 P00267
Spring City 10019 USA
www.imagecomics.com
Wife
Wife: "You slept with other women but I can't prove it!"
Invisible Boy

image COMICS PRESENTS

ULTRA™

THIS ISSUE
SEVEN DAYS, PART FIVE

CREATED BY
THE LUNA BROTHERS

CREDITS
JONATHAN LUNA
Plot, Art, Colors, Letters
JOSHUA LUNA
Plot, Script, Layout Assists

OFFICIAL WEBSITE
www.LunaBrothers.com

For Image Comics

Erik Larsen
Publisher
Todd McFarlane
President
Marc Silvestri
CEO
Jim Valentino
Vice-President

Eric Stephenson
Executive Director
Missie Miranda
Controller
Brett Evans
Production Manager
B. Clay Moore
PR & Marketing Coordinator
Allen Hui
Production Artist
Joe Keatinge
Inventory Controller
Mia Machatton
Administrative Assistant

www.imagecomics.com

GOT A HOT SCOOP?

PHONE OUR NEWS OFFICES
Spring City:
1-555-U-GOSSIP
OR E-MAIL US AT:
letters@fakeemail.com

ULTRA #5, DECEMBER, 2004

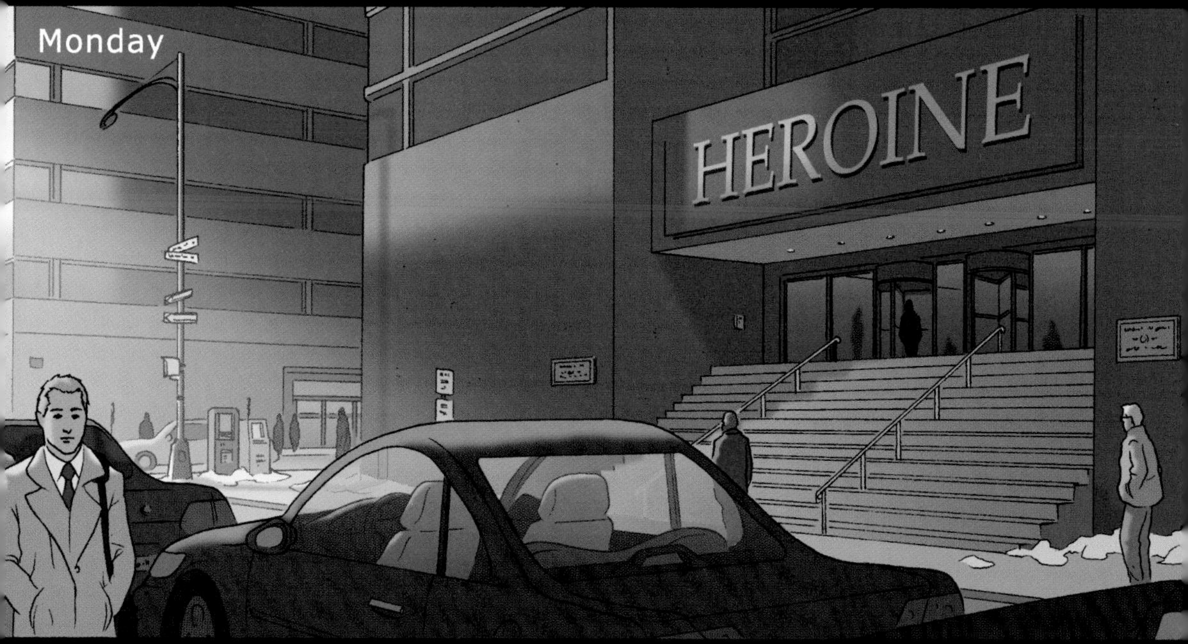
Monday
HEROINE

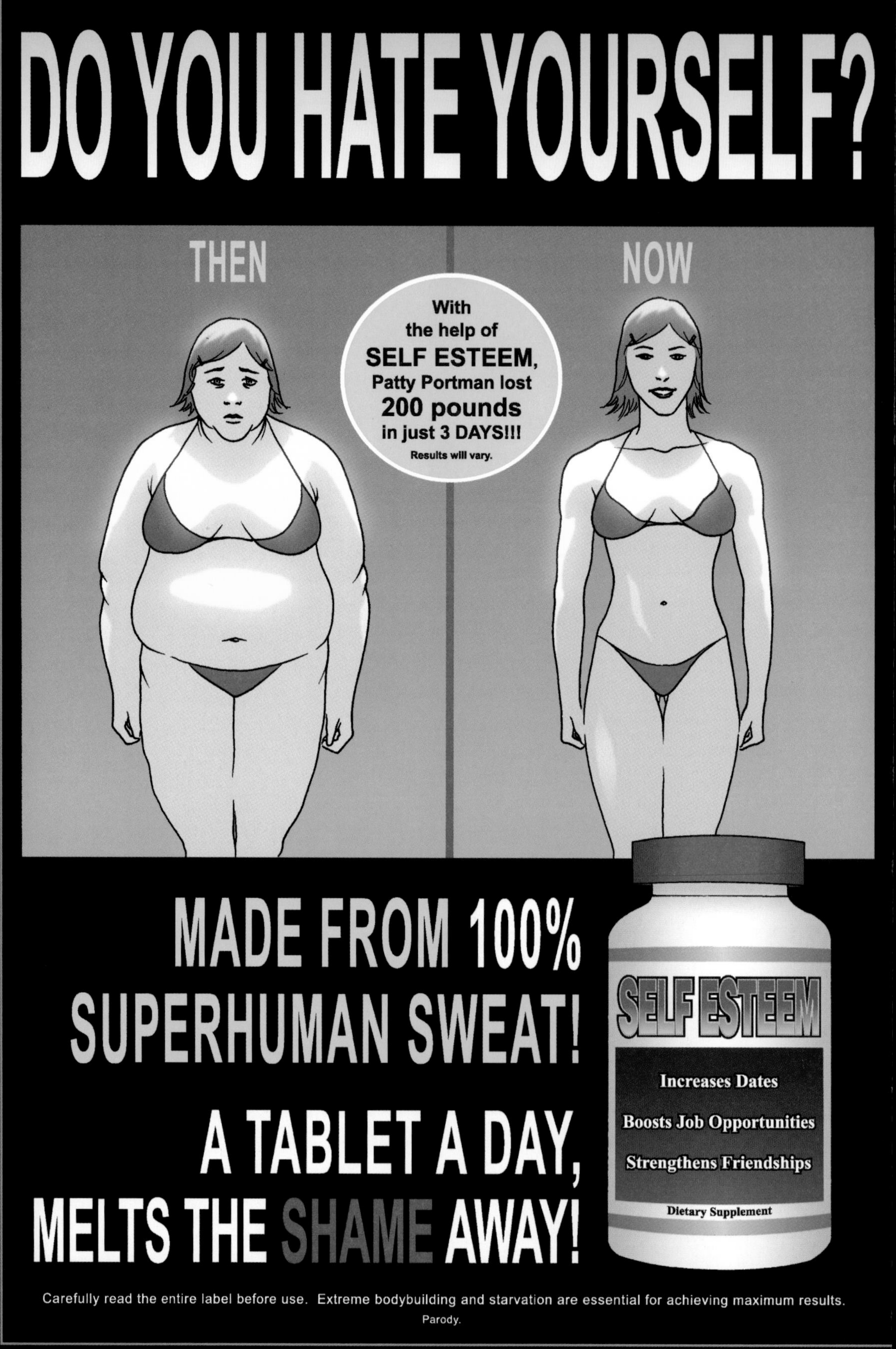
DO YOU HATE YOURSELF?
THEN
NOW
With the help of SELF ESTEEM, Patty Portman lost 200 pounds in just 3 DAYS!!!
Results will vary.
MADE FROM 100% SUPERHUMAN SWEAT!
A TABLET A DAY, MELTS THE SHAME AWAY!
SELF ESTEEM
Increases Dates
Boosts Job Opportunities
Strengthens Friendships
Dietary Supplement
Carefully read the entire label before use. Extreme bodybuilding and starvation are essential for achieving maximum results.
Parody.

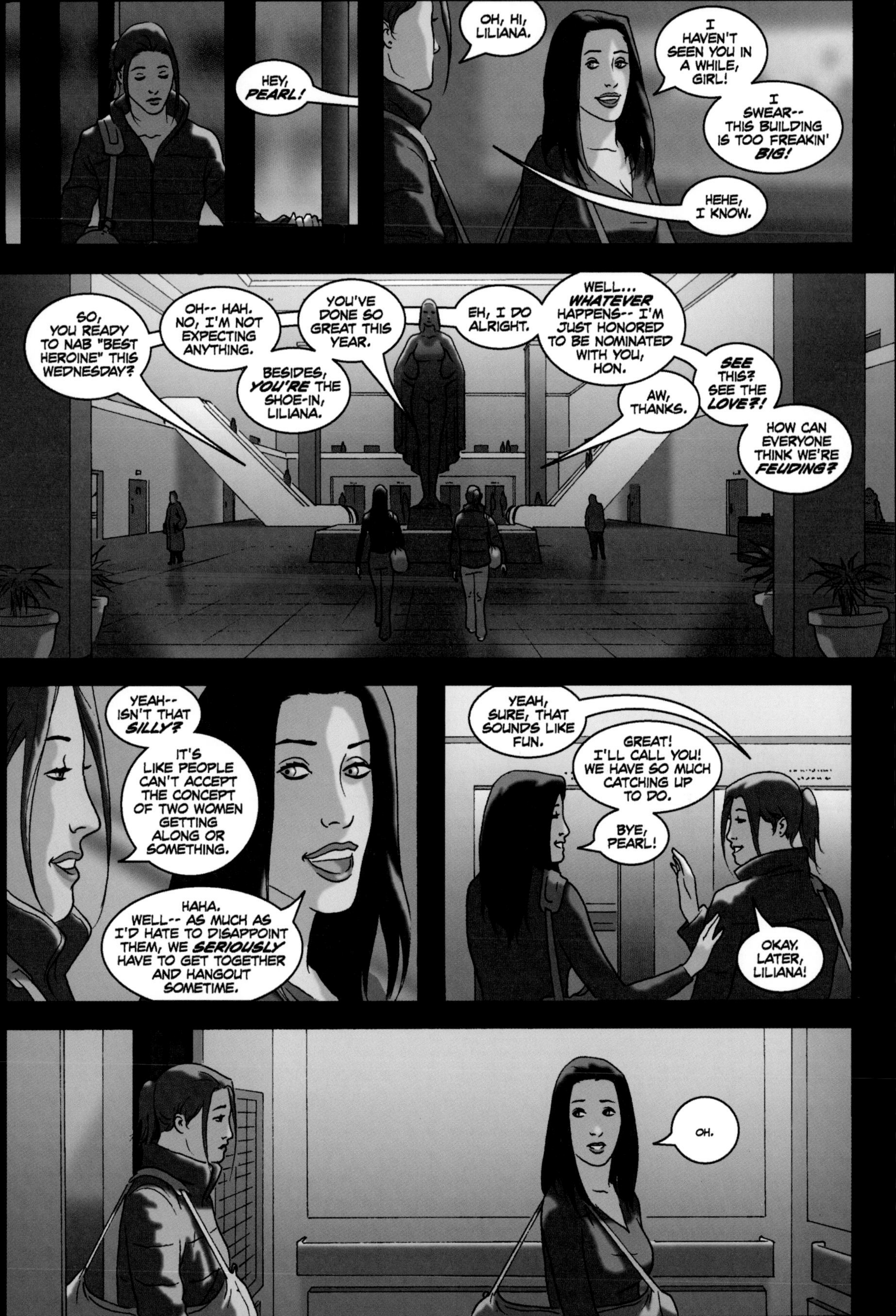
HEY, PEARL!
OH, HI, LILIANA.
I HAVEN'T SEEN YOU IN A WHILE, GIRL!
I SWEAR-- THIS BUILDING IS TOO FREAKIN' BIG!
HEHE, I KNOW.
SO, YOU READY TO NAB "BEST HEROINE" THIS WEDNESDAY?
OH-- HAH. NO, I'M NOT EXPECTING ANYTHING.
BESIDES, YOU'RE THE SHOE-IN, LILIANA.
YOU'VE DONE SO GREAT THIS YEAR.
EH, I DO ALRIGHT.
WELL... WHATEVER HAPPENS-- I'M JUST HONORED TO BE NOMINATED WITH YOU, HON.
AW, THANKS.
SEE THIS? SEE THE LOVE?!
HOW CAN EVERYONE THINK WE'RE FEUDING?
YEAH-- ISN'T THAT SILLY?
IT'S LIKE PEOPLE CAN'T ACCEPT THE CONCEPT OF TWO WOMEN GETTING ALONG OR SOMETHING.
HAHA. WELL-- AS MUCH AS I'D HATE TO DISAPPOINT THEM, WE SERIOUSLY HAVE TO GET TOGETHER AND HANGOUT SOMETIME.
YEAH, SURE, THAT SOUNDS LIKE FUN.
GREAT! I'LL CALL YOU! WE HAVE SO MUCH CATCHING UP TO DO.
BYE, PEARL!
OKAY. LATER, LILIANA!
OH.

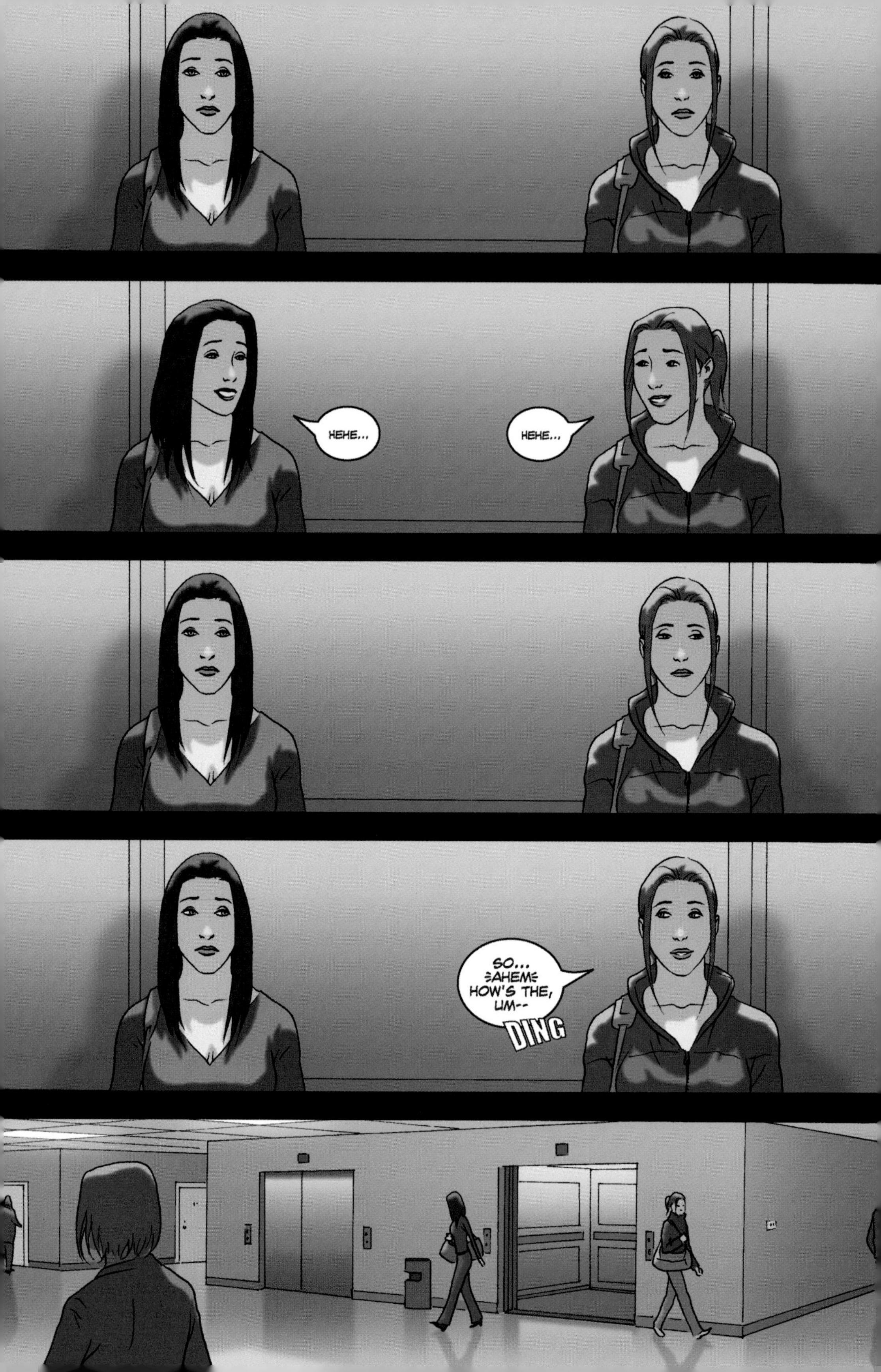
HEHE...
HEHE...
SO... *AHEM* HOW'S THE, UM--
DING

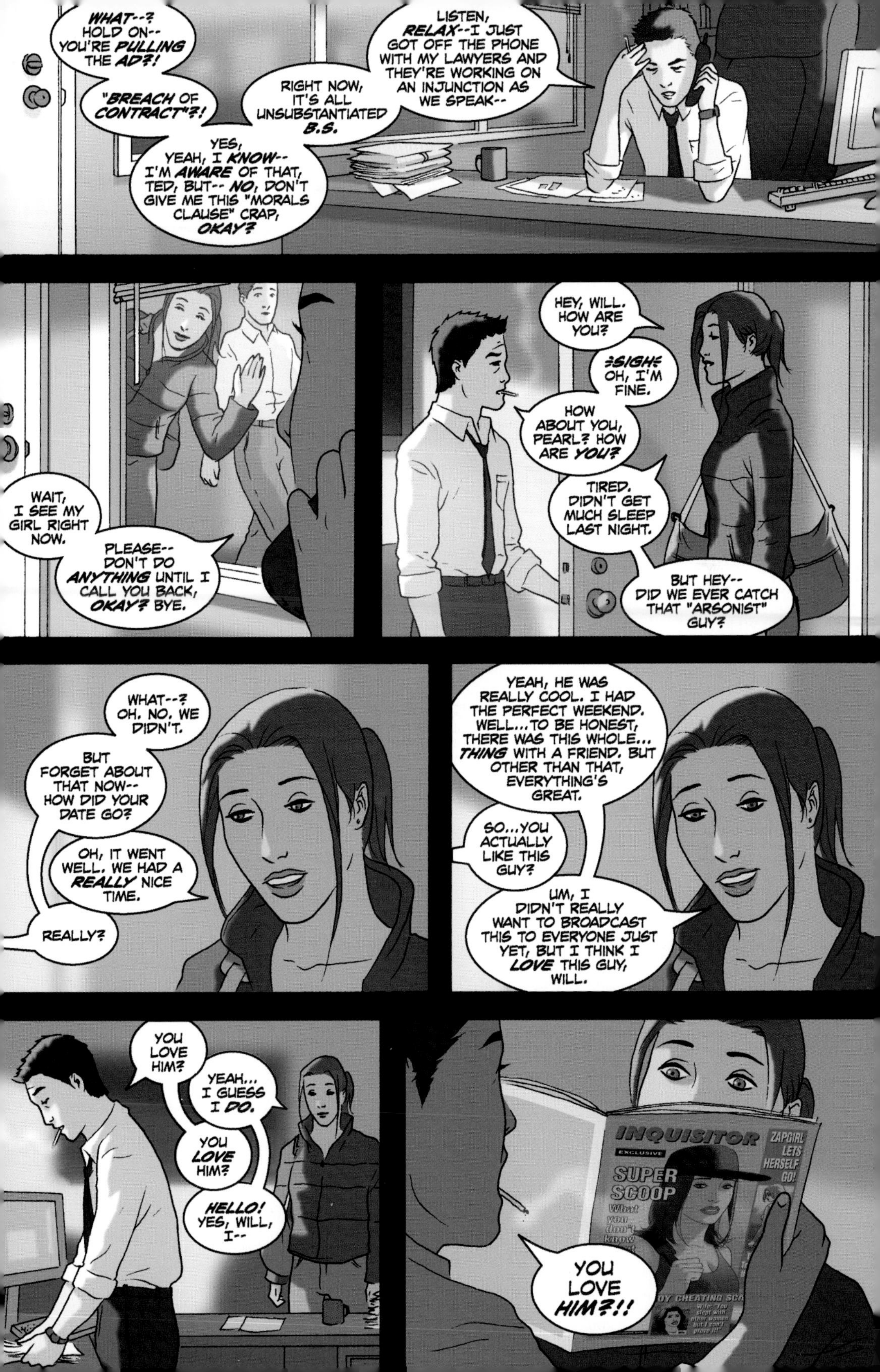

WHAT--? HOLD ON-- YOU'RE PULLING THE AD?!
"BREACH OF CONTRACT"?!
LISTEN, RELAX--I JUST GOT OFF THE PHONE WITH MY LAWYERS AND THEY'RE WORKING ON AN INJUNCTION AS WE SPEAK--
RIGHT NOW, IT'S ALL UNSUBSTANTIATED B.S.
YES, YEAH, I KNOW-- I'M AWARE OF THAT, TED, BUT-- NO, DON'T GIVE ME THIS "MORALS CLAUSE" CRAP, OKAY?
WAIT, I SEE MY GIRL RIGHT NOW.
PLEASE-- DON'T DO ANYTHING UNTIL I CALL YOU BACK, OKAY? BYE.
HEY, WILL. HOW ARE YOU?
:SIGH: OH, I'M FINE.
HOW ABOUT YOU, PEARL? HOW ARE YOU?
TIRED. DIDN'T GET MUCH SLEEP LAST NIGHT.
BUT HEY-- DID WE EVER CATCH THAT "ARSONIST" GUY?
WHAT--? OH. NO. WE DIDN'T.
BUT FORGET ABOUT THAT NOW-- HOW DID YOUR DATE GO?
OH, IT WENT WELL. WE HAD A REALLY NICE TIME.
REALLY?
YEAH, HE WAS REALLY COOL. I HAD THE PERFECT WEEKEND. WELL... TO BE HONEST, THERE WAS THIS WHOLE... THING WITH A FRIEND. BUT OTHER THAN THAT, EVERYTHING'S GREAT.
SO... YOU ACTUALLY LIKE THIS GUY?
UM, I DIDN'T REALLY WANT TO BROADCAST THIS TO EVERYONE JUST YET, BUT I THINK I LOVE THIS GUY, WILL.
YOU LOVE HIM?
YEAH... I GUESS I DO.
YOU LOVE HIM?
HELLO! YES, WILL, I--
INQUISITOR
EXCLUSIVE
SUPER SCOOP
ZAPGIRL LETS HERSELF GO!
YOU LOVE HIM?!!

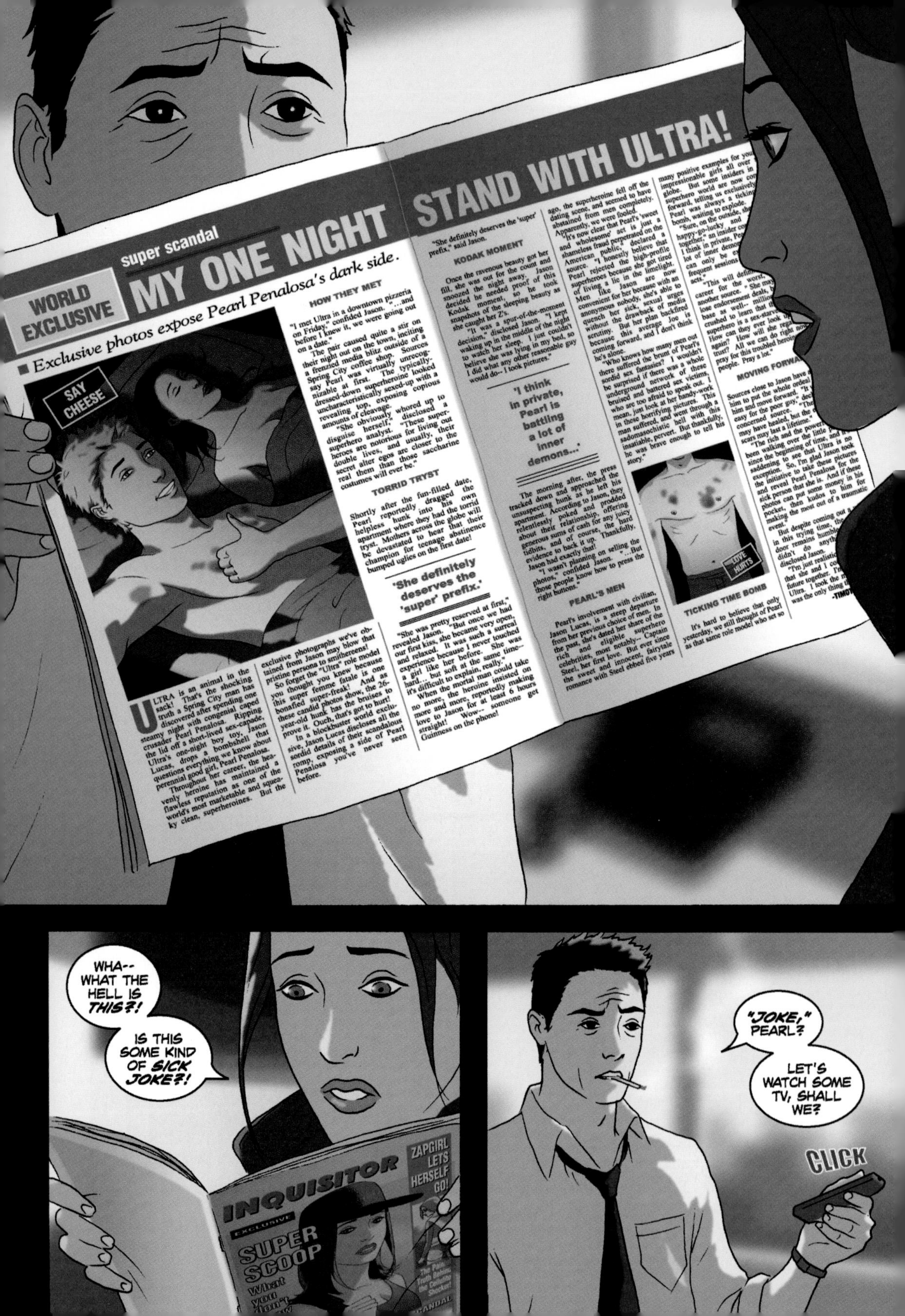

WORLD EXCLUSIVE
super scandal
MY ONE NIGHT STAND WITH ULTRA!
Exclusive photos expose Pearl Penalosa's dark side.
SAY CHEESE
HOW THEY MET
TORRID TRYST
'She definitely deserves the 'super' prefix.'
KODAK MOMENT
'I think in private, Pearl is battling a lot of inner demons...'
PEARL'S MEN
LOVE HURTS
TICKING TIME BOMB
MOVING FORWA
WHA-- WHAT THE HELL IS THIS?!
IS THIS SOME KIND OF SICK JOKE?!
INQUISITOR
EXCLUSIVE
SUPER SCOOP
ZAPGIRL LETS HERSELF GO!
"JOKE," PEARL?
LET'S WATCH SOME TV, SHALL WE?
CLICK

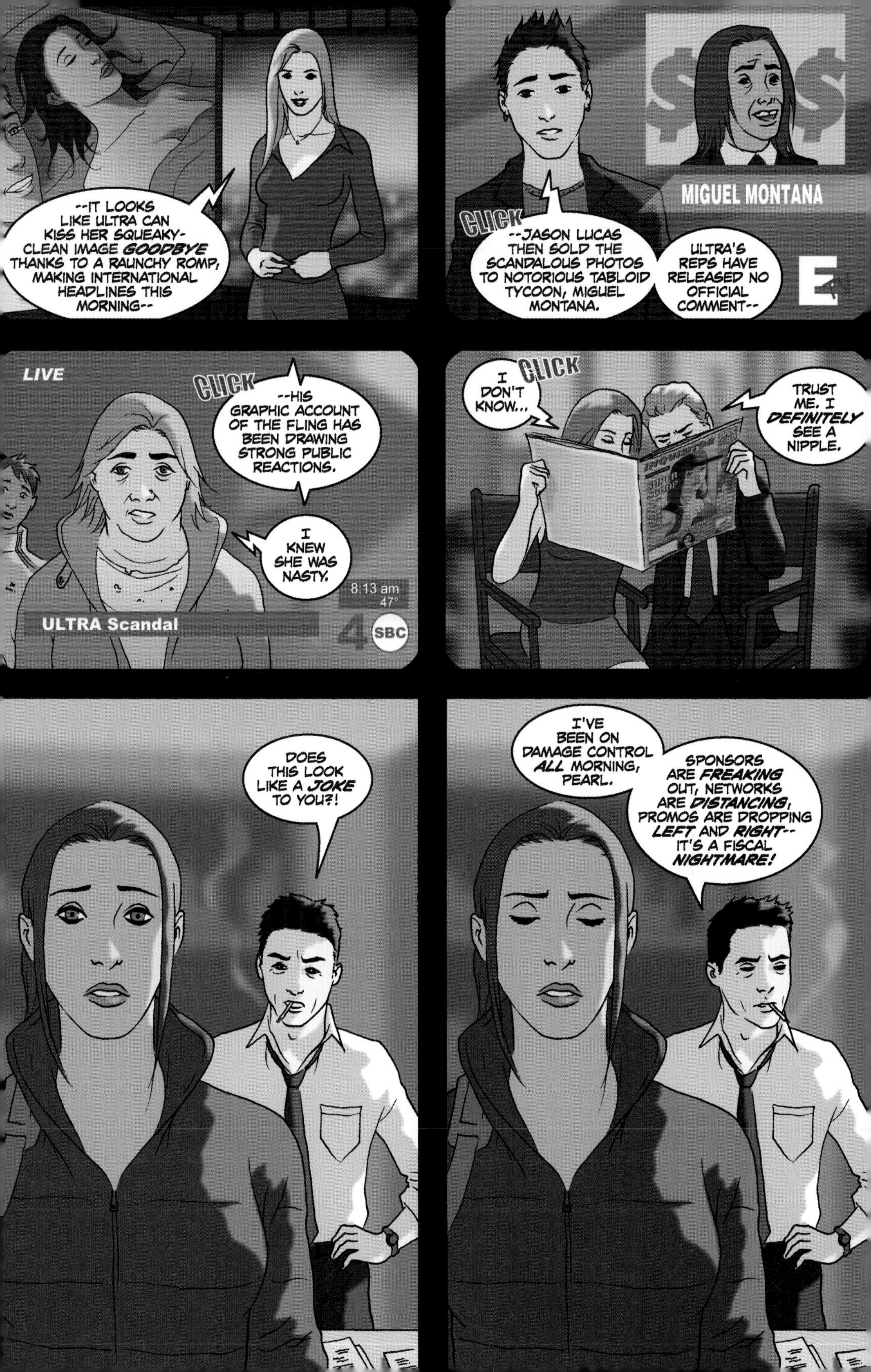
--IT LOOKS LIKE ULTRA CAN KISS HER SQUEAKY-CLEAN IMAGE GOODBYE THANKS TO A RAUNCHY ROMP, MAKING INTERNATIONAL HEADLINES THIS MORNING--
CLICK
MIGUEL MONTANA
--JASON LUCAS THEN SOLD THE SCANDALOUS PHOTOS TO NOTORIOUS TABLOID TYCOON, MIGUEL MONTANA.
ULTRA'S REPS HAVE RELEASED NO OFFICIAL COMMENT--
E
LIVE
CLICK
--HIS GRAPHIC ACCOUNT OF THE FLING HAS BEEN DRAWING STRONG PUBLIC REACTIONS.
I KNEW SHE WAS NASTY.
8:13 am
47°
ULTRA Scandal
4 SBC
CLICK
I DON'T KNOW...
TRUST ME. I DEFINITELY SEE A NIPPLE.
INQUISITOR
SUPER SCOOP
DOES THIS LOOK LIKE A JOKE TO YOU?!
I'VE BEEN ON DAMAGE CONTROL ALL MORNING, PEARL.
SPONSORS ARE FREAKING OUT, NETWORKS ARE DISTANCING, PROMOS ARE DROPPING LEFT AND RIGHT-- IT'S A FISCAL NIGHTMARE!

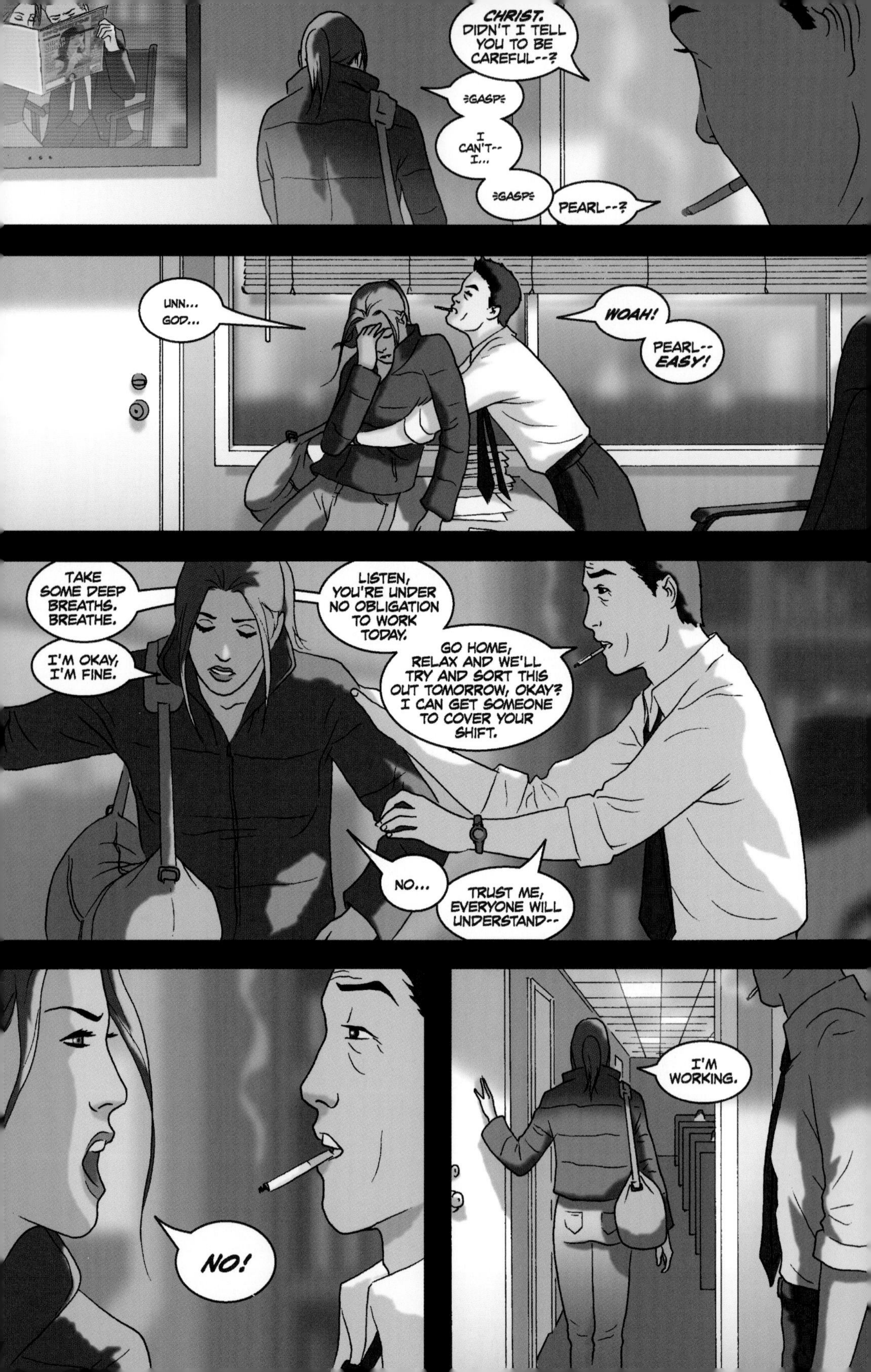
CHRIST. DIDN'T I TELL YOU TO BE CAREFUL--?
≈GASP≈
I CAN'T-- I...
≈GASP≈
PEARL--?
UNN... GOD...
WOAH!
PEARL-- EASY!
TAKE SOME DEEP BREATHS. BREATHE.
I'M OKAY, I'M FINE.
LISTEN, YOU'RE UNDER NO OBLIGATION TO WORK TODAY.
GO HOME, RELAX AND WE'LL TRY AND SORT THIS OUT TOMORROW, OKAY? I CAN GET SOMEONE TO COVER YOUR SHIFT.
NO...
TRUST ME, EVERYONE WILL UNDERSTAND--
NO!
I'M WORKING.

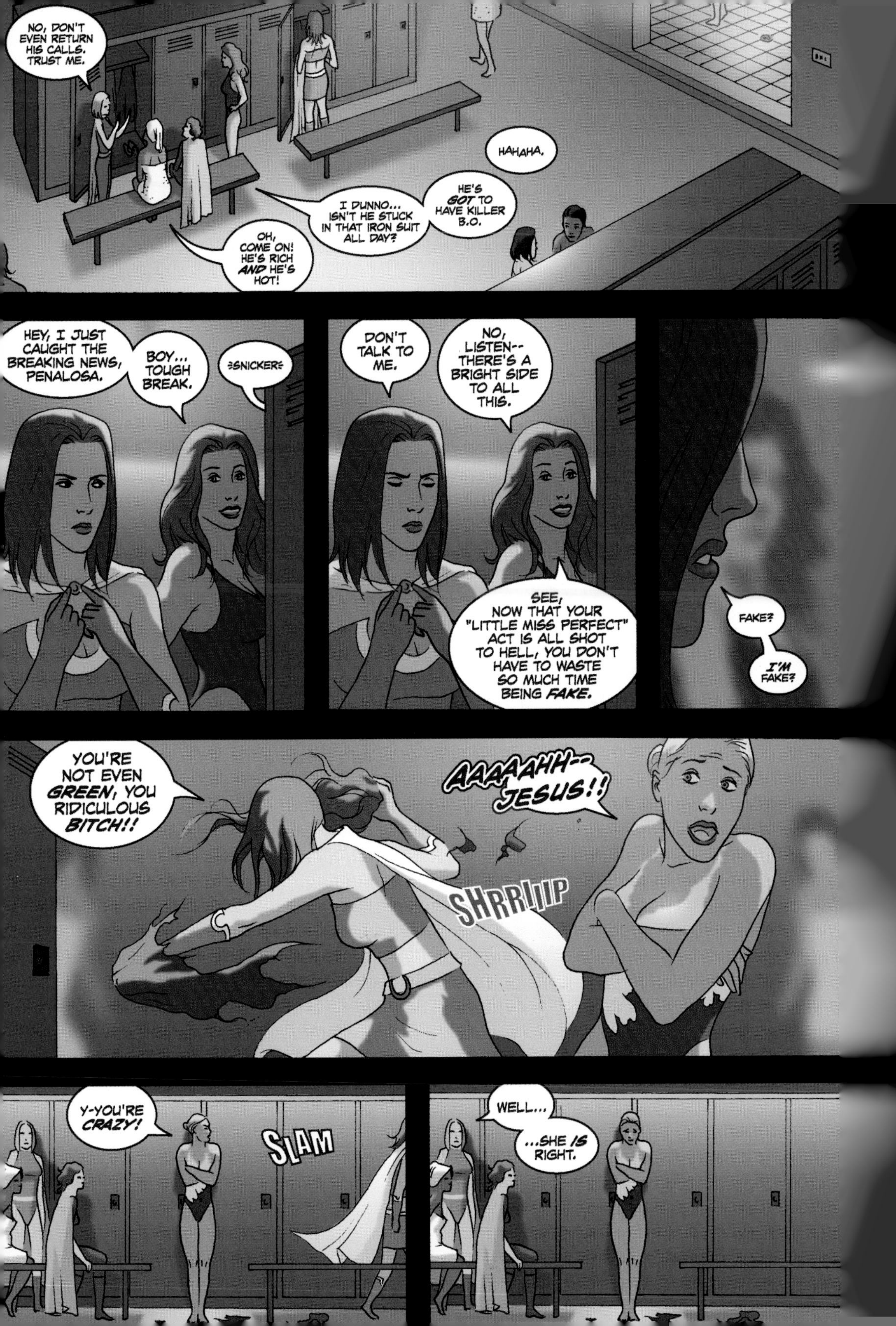
NO, DON'T EVEN RETURN HIS CALLS. TRUST ME.
HAHAHA.
I DUNNO... ISN'T HE STUCK IN THAT IRON SUIT ALL DAY?
HE'S GOT TO HAVE KILLER B.O.
OH, COME ON! HE'S RICH AND HE'S HOT!
HEY, I JUST CAUGHT THE BREAKING NEWS, PENALOSA.
BOY... TOUGH BREAK.
SNICKER
DON'T TALK TO ME.
NO, LISTEN-- THERE'S A BRIGHT SIDE TO ALL THIS.
SEE, NOW THAT YOUR "LITTLE MISS PERFECT" ACT IS ALL SHOT TO HELL, YOU DON'T HAVE TO WASTE SO MUCH TIME BEING FAKE.
FAKE?
I'M FAKE?
YOU'RE NOT EVEN GREEN, YOU RIDICULOUS BITCH!!
AAAAAHH-- JESUS!!
SHRRIIIP
Y-YOU'RE CRAZY!
SLAM
WELL...
...SHE IS RIGHT.

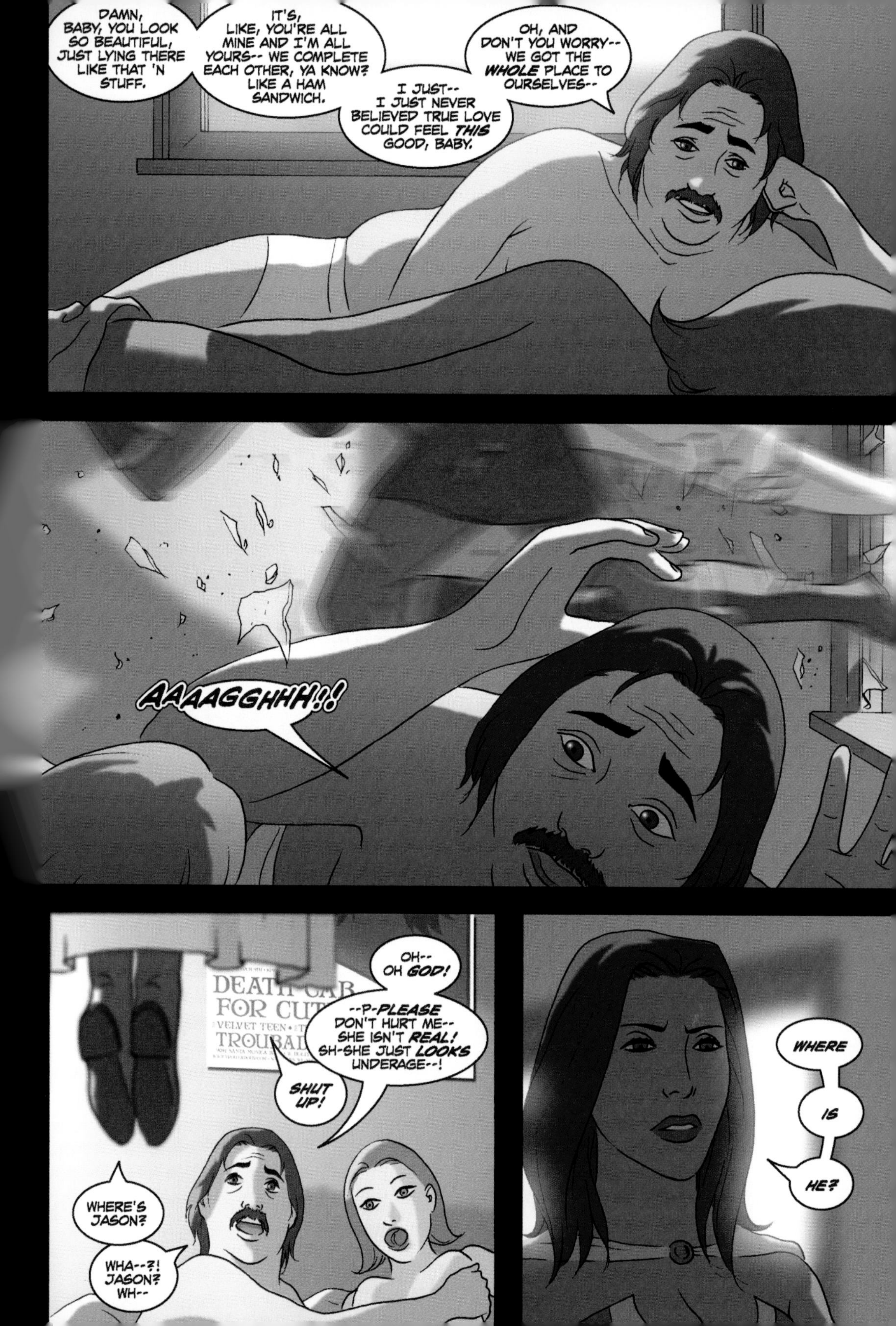
DAMN, BABY, YOU LOOK SO BEAUTIFUL, JUST LYING THERE LIKE THAT 'N STUFF.
IT'S, LIKE, YOU'RE ALL MINE AND I'M ALL YOURS-- WE COMPLETE EACH OTHER, YA KNOW? LIKE A HAM SANDWICH.
I JUST-- I JUST NEVER BELIEVED TRUE LOVE COULD FEEL THIS GOOD, BABY.
OH, AND DON'T YOU WORRY-- WE GOT THE WHOLE PLACE TO OURSELVES--
AAAAGGHHH!!
DEATH CAB FOR CUT
VELVET TEEN
TROUBAD
OH-- OH GOD!
--P-PLEASE DON'T HURT ME-- SHE ISN'T REAL! SH-SHE JUST LOOKS UNDERAGE--!
SHUT UP!
WHERE'S JASON?
WHA--?! JASON? WH--
WHERE IS HE?

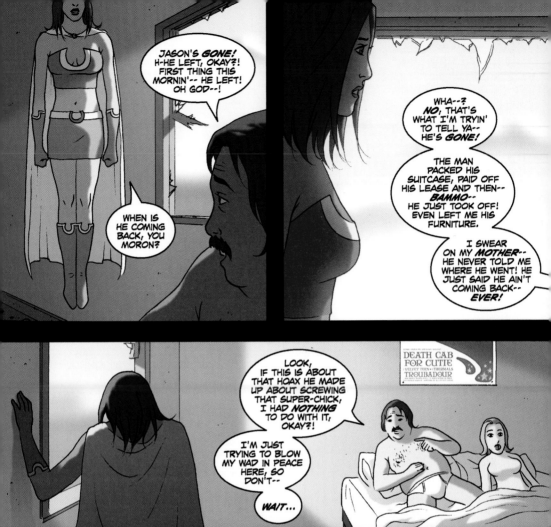

JASON'S *GONE!* H-HE LEFT, OKAY?! FIRST THING THIS MORNIN'-- HE LEFT! OH GOD--!

WHEN IS HE COMING BACK, YOU MORON?

WHA--? *NO,* THAT'S WHAT I'M TRYIN' TO TELL YA-- HE'S *GONE!*

THE MAN PACKED HIS SUITCASE, PAID OFF HIS LEASE AND THEN-- *BAMMO--* HE JUST TOOK OFF! EVEN LEFT ME HIS FURNITURE.

I SWEAR ON MY *MOTHER--* HE NEVER TOLD ME WHERE HE WENT! HE JUST SAID HE AIN'T COMING BACK-- *EVER!*

LOOK, IF THIS IS ABOUT THAT HOAX HE MADE UP ABOUT SCREWING THAT SUPER-CHICK, I HAD *NOTHING* TO DO WITH IT, OKAY?!

I'M JUST TRYING TO BLOW MY WAD IN PEACE HERE, SO DON'T--

WAIT...

DEATH CAB FOR CUTIE · VELVET TEEN · THERMALS
TROUBADOUR

NO WAY.

I-IT'S *YOU!* YOU-YOU'RE *ULTRA!*

SO... IT'S *TRUE?* *YOU* AND JASON REALLY--? WOAH.

WITH *JASON?!*

I MEAN... YOU-- YOU WERE REALLY *HERE?!* ON *THIS* BED?! ON THESE... ≷GULP≷ ...SHEETS?

ULTRA, THIS IS DISPATCH-- DO YOU COPY?

≷SNIIIFF≷

OHHH, BAAABY!

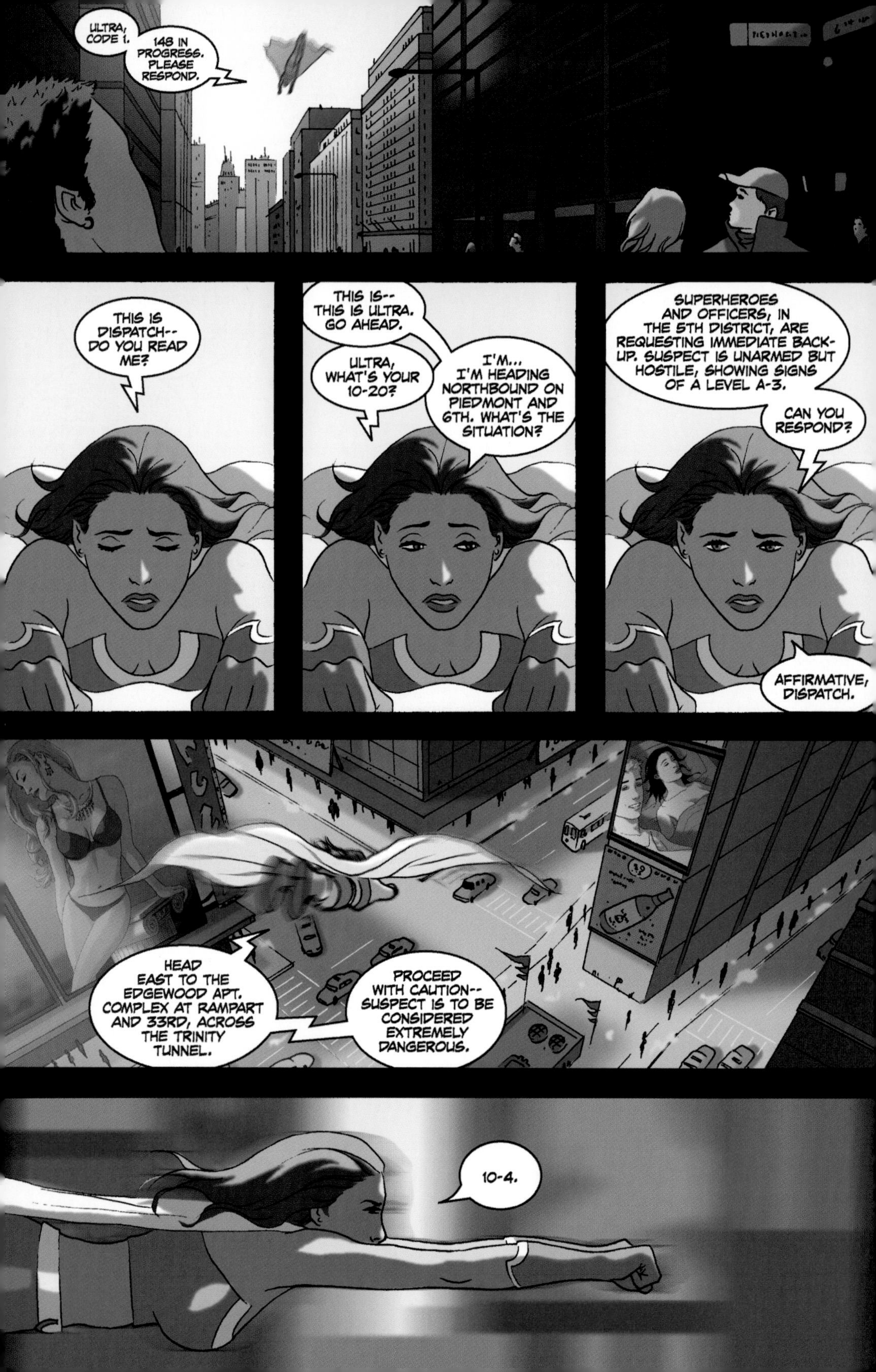
ULTRA, CODE 1.
148 IN PROGRESS. PLEASE RESPOND.
THIS IS DISPATCH-- DO YOU READ ME?
THIS IS-- THIS IS ULTRA. GO AHEAD.
ULTRA, WHAT'S YOUR 10-20?
I'M... I'M HEADING NORTHBOUND ON PIEDMONT AND 6TH. WHAT'S THE SITUATION?
SUPERHEROES AND OFFICERS, IN THE 5TH DISTRICT, ARE REQUESTING IMMEDIATE BACK-UP. SUSPECT IS UNARMED BUT HOSTILE, SHOWING SIGNS OF A LEVEL A-3.
CAN YOU RESPOND?
AFFIRMATIVE, DISPATCH.
HEAD EAST TO THE EDGEWOOD APT. COMPLEX AT RAMPART AND 33RD, ACROSS THE TRINITY TUNNEL.
PROCEED WITH CAUTION-- SUSPECT IS TO BE CONSIDERED EXTREMELY DANGEROUS.
10-4.

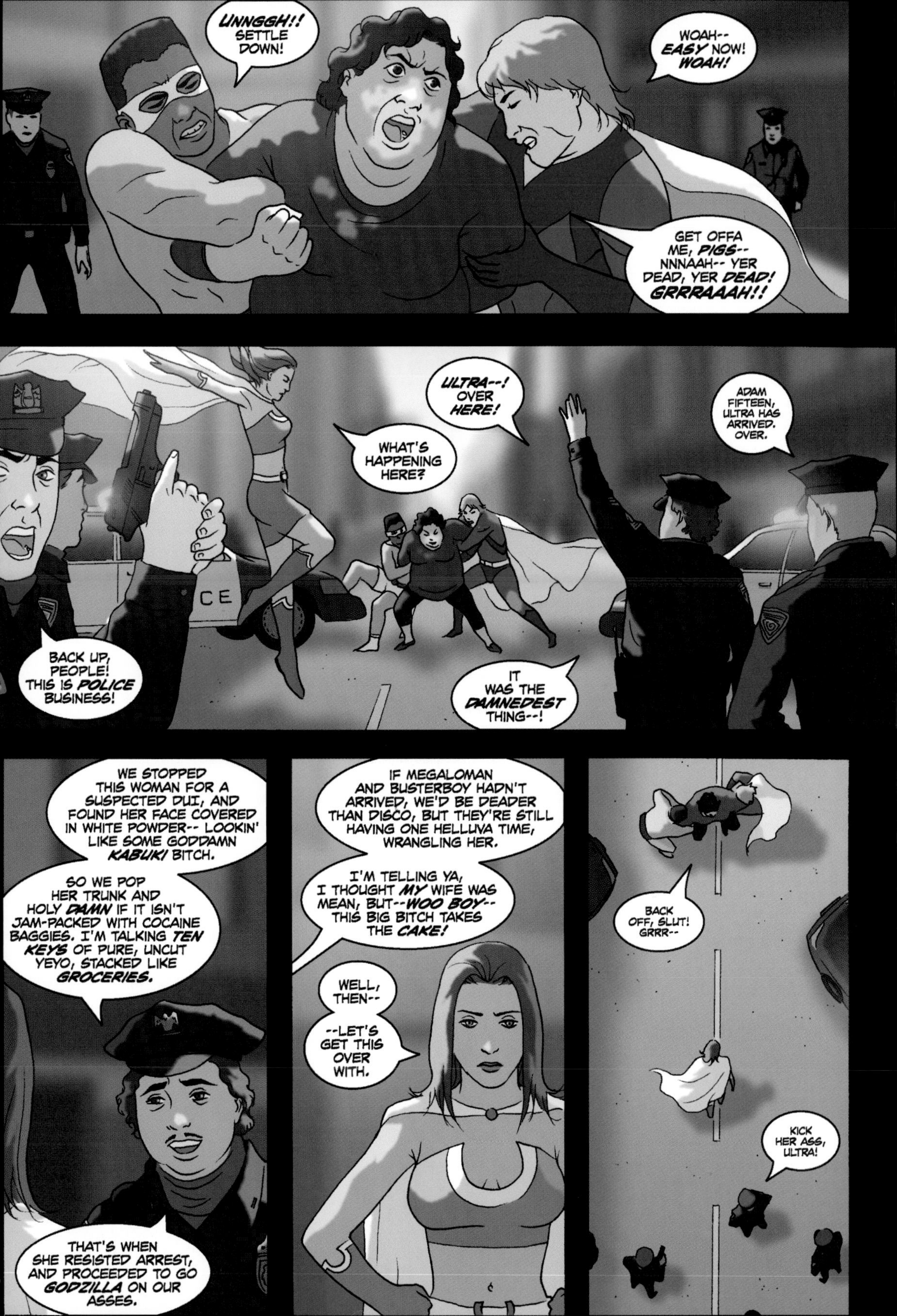
UNNGGH!! SETTLE DOWN!
WOAH-- EASY NOW! WOAH!
GET OFFA ME, PIGS-- NNNAAH-- YER DEAD, YER DEAD! GRRRAAAH!!
WHAT'S HAPPENING HERE?
ULTRA--! OVER HERE!
ADAM FIFTEEN, ULTRA HAS ARRIVED. OVER.
BACK UP, PEOPLE! THIS IS POLICE BUSINESS!
IT WAS THE DAMNEDEST THING--!
WE STOPPED THIS WOMAN FOR A SUSPECTED DUI, AND FOUND HER FACE COVERED IN WHITE POWDER-- LOOKIN' LIKE SOME GODDAMN KABUKI BITCH.
SO WE POP HER TRUNK AND HOLY DAMN IF IT ISN'T JAM-PACKED WITH COCAINE BAGGIES. I'M TALKING TEN KEYS OF PURE, UNCUT YEYO, STACKED LIKE GROCERIES.
THAT'S WHEN SHE RESISTED ARREST, AND PROCEEDED TO GO GODZILLA ON OUR ASSES.
IF MEGALOMAN AND BUSTERBOY HADN'T ARRIVED, WE'D BE DEADER THAN DISCO, BUT THEY'RE STILL HAVING ONE HELLUVA TIME, WRANGLING HER.
I'M TELLING YA, I THOUGHT MY WIFE WAS MEAN, BUT--WOO BOY-- THIS BIG BITCH TAKES THE CAKE!
WELL, THEN--
--LET'S GET THIS OVER WITH.
BACK OFF, SLUT! GRRR--
KICK HER ASS, ULTRA!

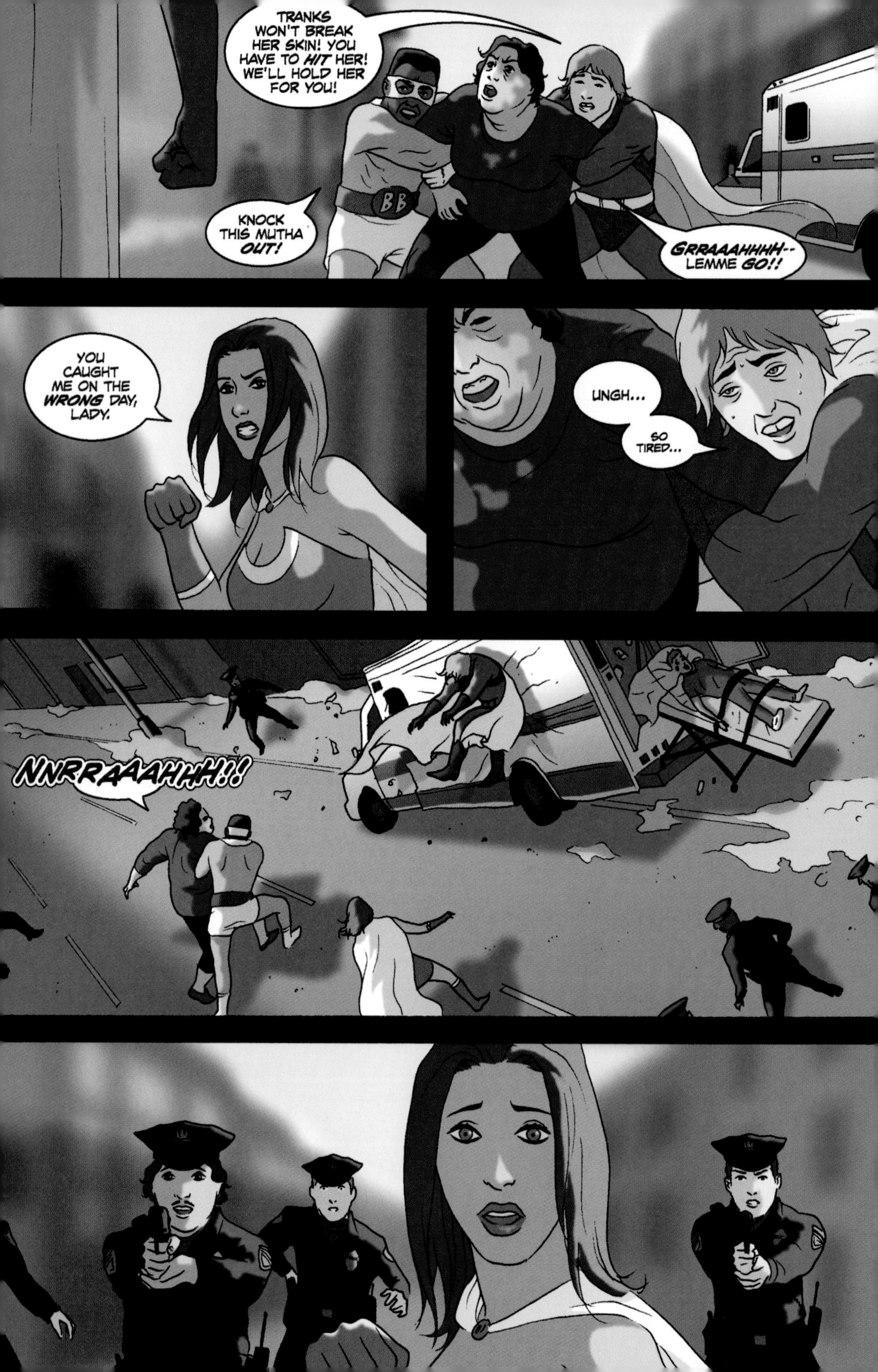
TRANKS WON'T BREAK HER SKIN! YOU HAVE TO HIT HER! WE'LL HOLD HER FOR YOU!
KNOCK THIS MUTHA OUT!
GRRAAAHHHH-- LEMME GO!!
YOU CAUGHT ME ON THE WRONG DAY, LADY.
UNGH...
SO TIRED...
NNRRAAAHHHH!!

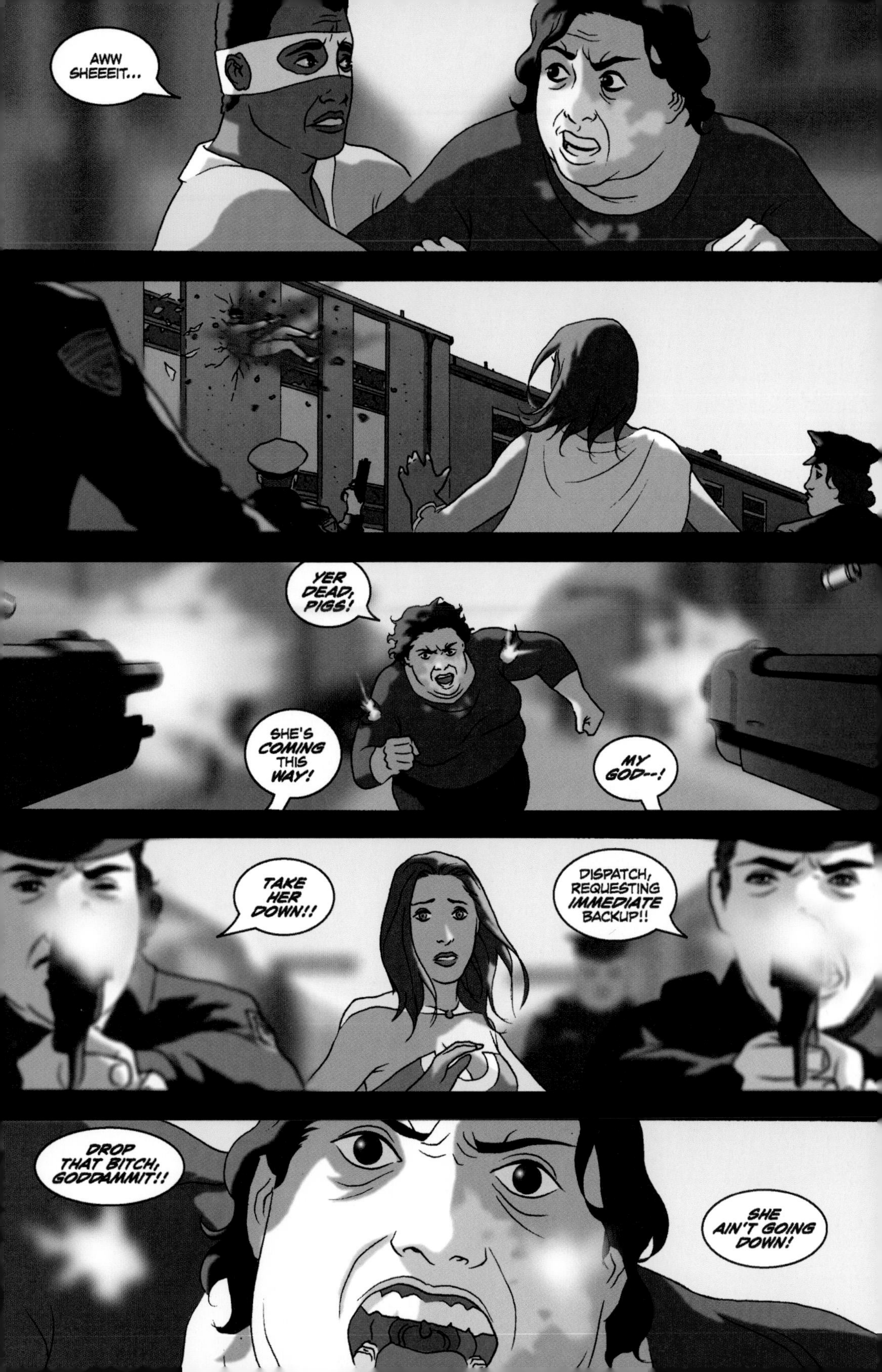
AWW SHEEEIT...
YER DEAD, PIGS!
SHE'S COMING THIS WAY!
MY GOD--!
TAKE HER DOWN!!
DISPATCH, REQUESTING IMMEDIATE BACKUP!!
DROP THAT BITCH, GODDAMMIT!!
SHE AIN'T GOING DOWN!

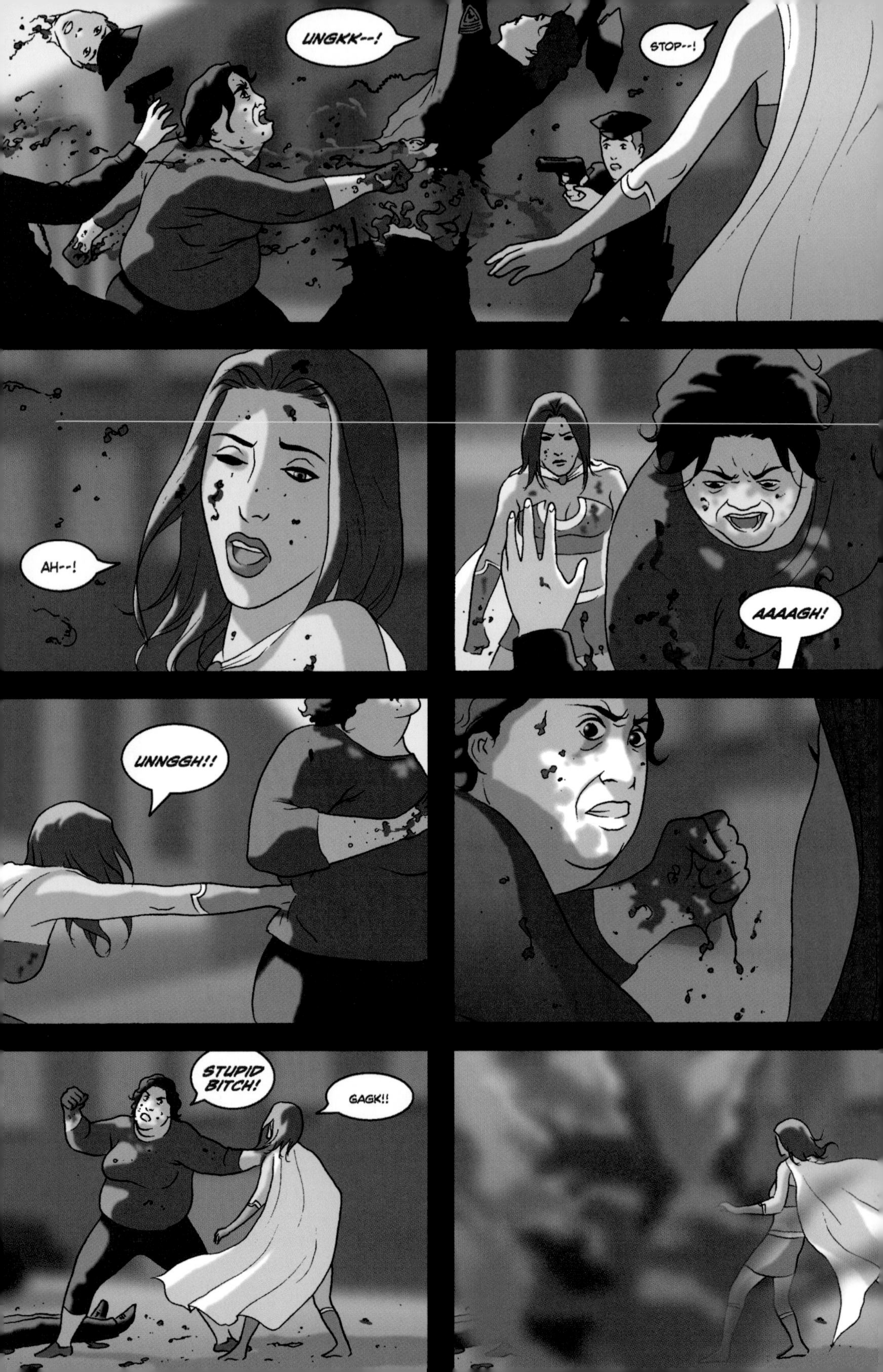
UNGKK--!
STOP--!
AH--!
AAAAGH!
UNNGGH!!
STUPID BITCH!
GAGK!!

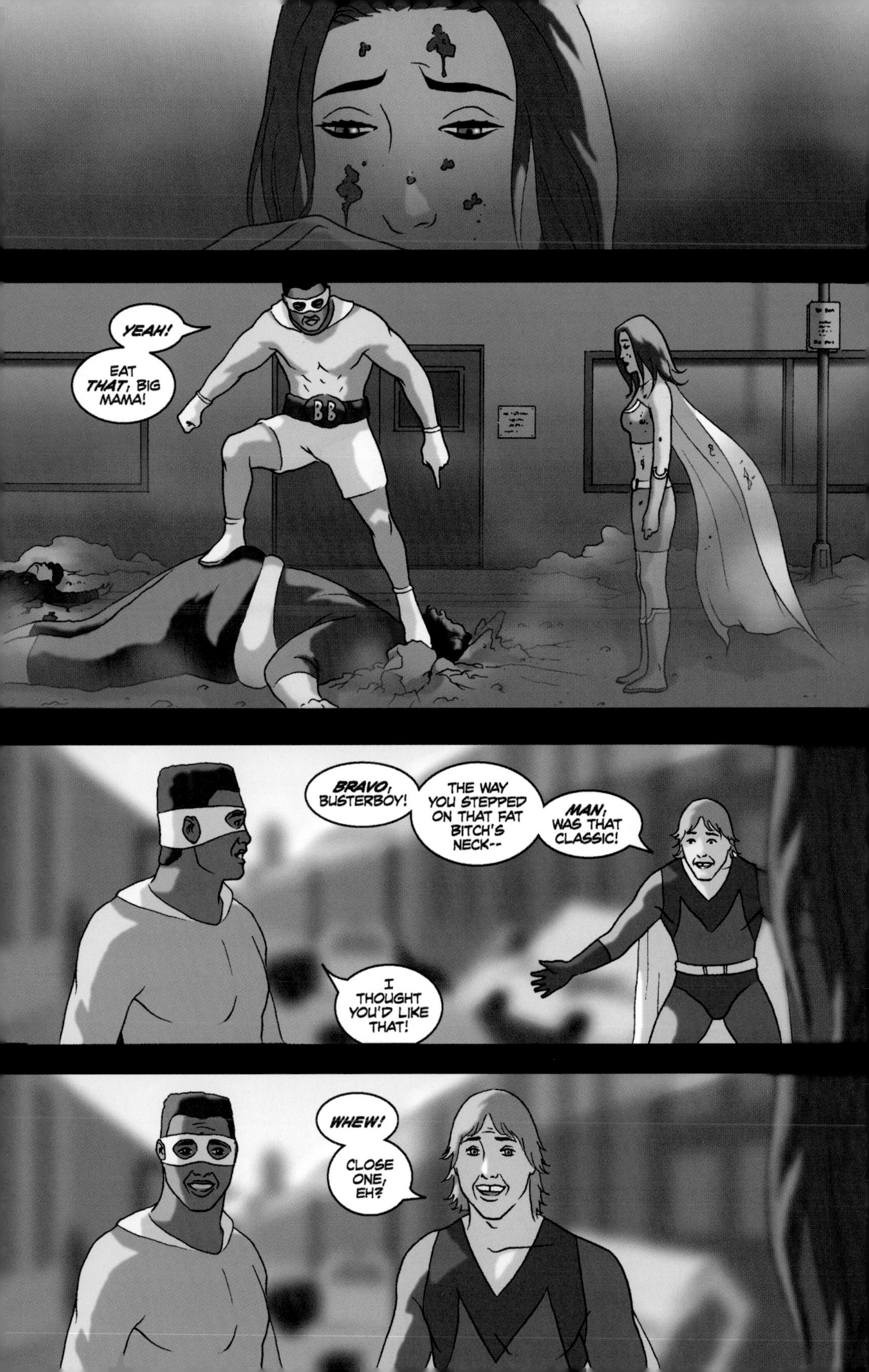
YEAH!
EAT THAT, BIG MAMA!
BB
BRAVO, BUSTERBOY!
THE WAY YOU STEPPED ON THAT FAT BITCH'S NECK--
MAN, WAS THAT CLASSIC!
I THOUGHT YOU'D LIKE THAT!
WHEW!
CLOSE ONE, EH?

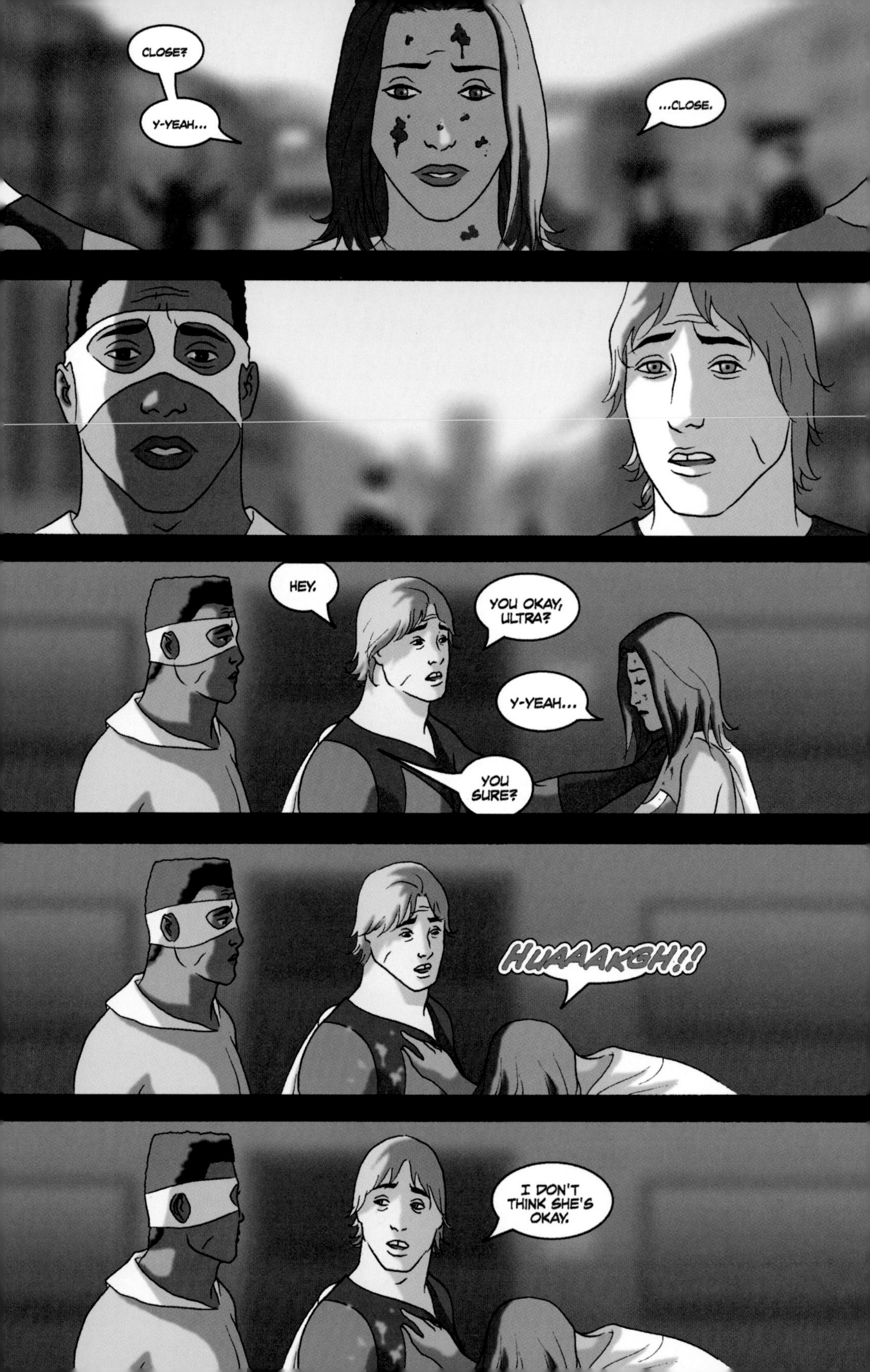
CLOSE?
Y-YEAH...
...CLOSE.
HEY.
YOU OKAY, ULTRA?
Y-YEAH...
YOU SURE?
HUAAAKGH!!
I DON'T THINK SHE'S OKAY.

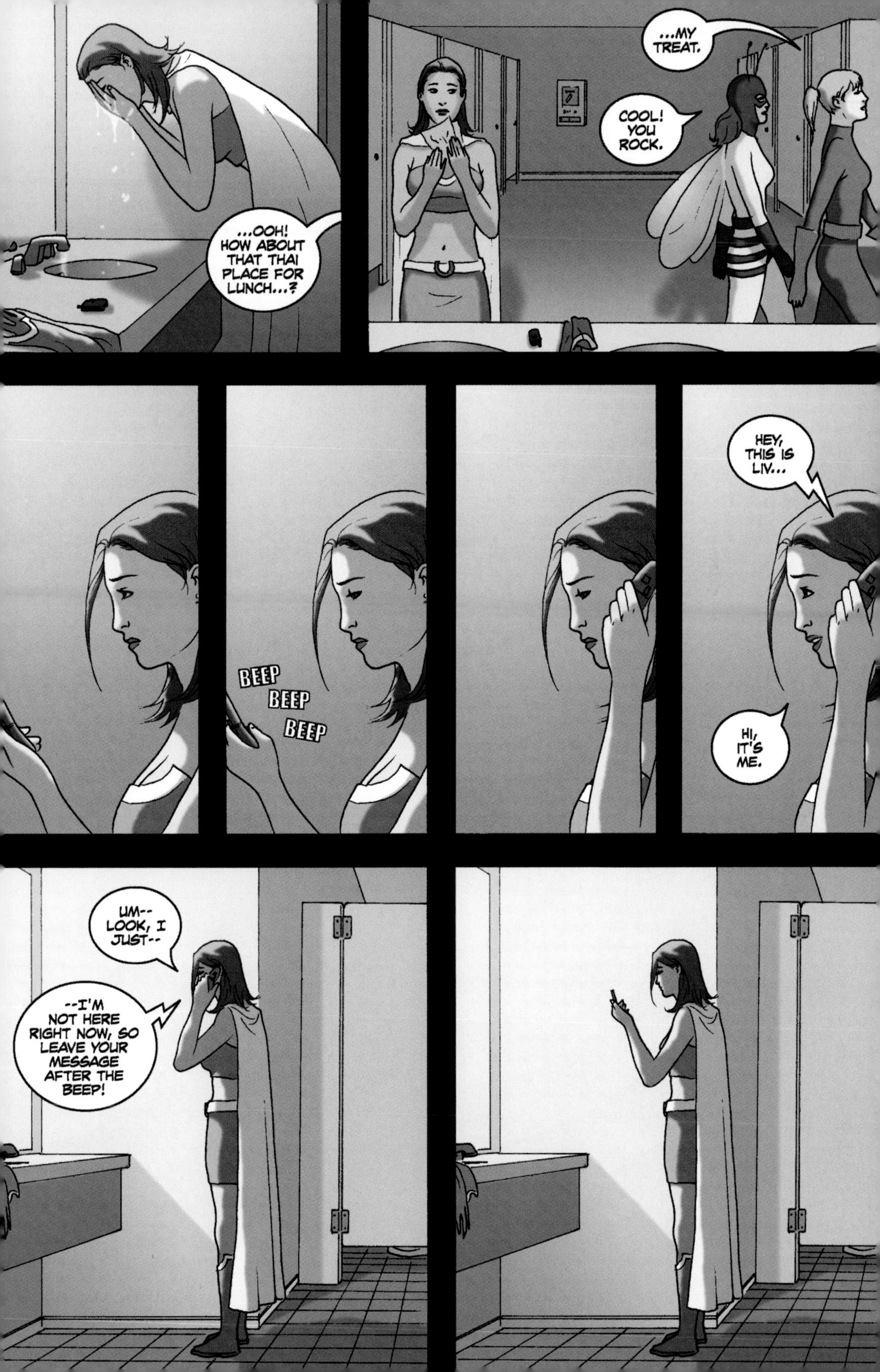
...OOH! HOW ABOUT THAT THAI PLACE FOR LUNCH...?
...MY TREAT.
COOL! YOU ROCK.
BEEP
BEEP
BEEP
HEY, THIS IS LIV...
HI, IT'S ME.
UM-- LOOK, I JUST--
--I'M NOT HERE RIGHT NOW, SO LEAVE YOUR MESSAGE AFTER THE BEEP!

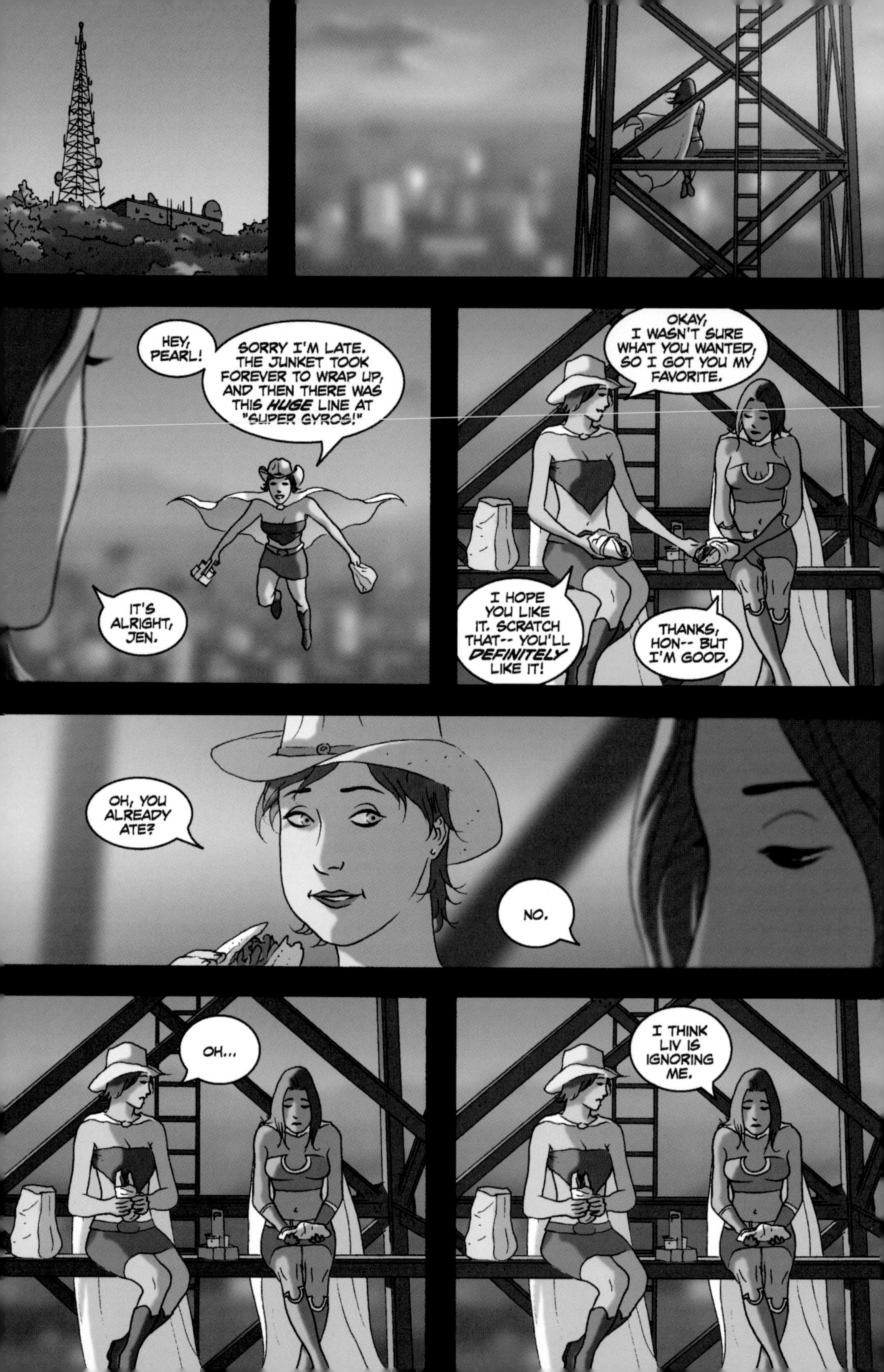
HEY, PEARL!
SORRY I'M LATE. THE JUNKET TOOK FOREVER TO WRAP UP, AND THEN THERE WAS THIS HUGE LINE AT "SUPER GYROS!"
IT'S ALRIGHT, JEN.
OKAY, I WASN'T SURE WHAT YOU WANTED, SO I GOT YOU MY FAVORITE.
I HOPE YOU LIKE IT. SCRATCH THAT-- YOU'LL DEFINITELY LIKE IT!
THANKS, HON-- BUT I'M GOOD.
OH, YOU ALREADY ATE?
NO.
OH...
I THINK LIV IS IGNORING ME.

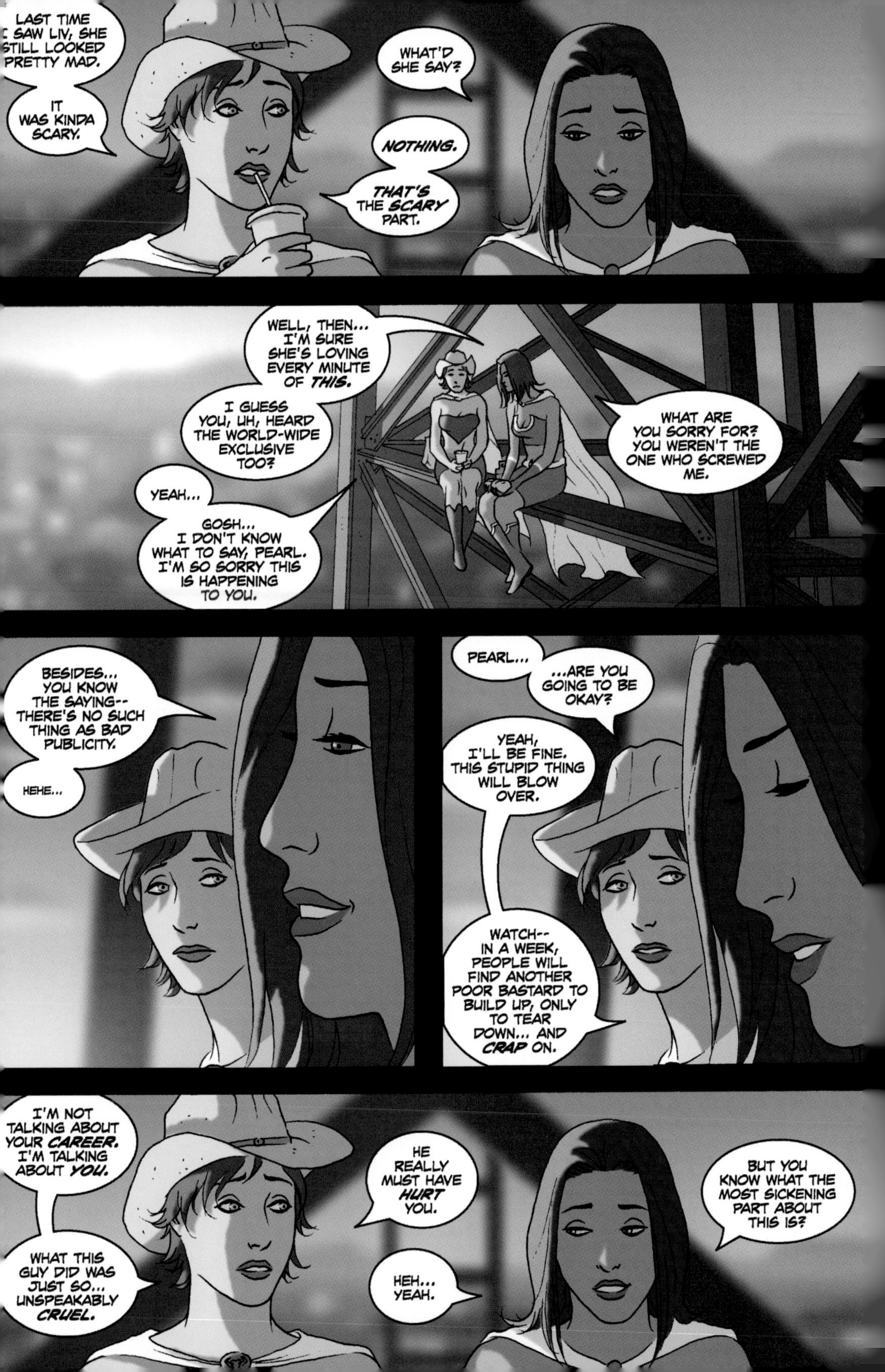
LAST TIME I SAW LIV, SHE STILL LOOKED PRETTY MAD.
IT WAS KINDA SCARY.
WHAT'D SHE SAY?
NOTHING.
THAT'S THE SCARY PART.
WELL, THEN... I'M SURE SHE'S LOVING EVERY MINUTE OF THIS.
I GUESS YOU, UH, HEARD THE WORLD-WIDE EXCLUSIVE TOO?
YEAH...
GOSH... I DON'T KNOW WHAT TO SAY, PEARL. I'M SO SORRY THIS IS HAPPENING TO YOU.
WHAT ARE YOU SORRY FOR? YOU WEREN'T THE ONE WHO SCREWED ME.
BESIDES... YOU KNOW THE SAYING-- THERE'S NO SUCH THING AS BAD PUBLICITY.
HEHE...
PEARL...
...ARE YOU GOING TO BE OKAY?
YEAH, I'LL BE FINE. THIS STUPID THING WILL BLOW OVER.
WATCH-- IN A WEEK, PEOPLE WILL FIND ANOTHER POOR BASTARD TO BUILD UP, ONLY TO TEAR DOWN... AND CRAP ON.
I'M NOT TALKING ABOUT YOUR CAREER. I'M TALKING ABOUT YOU.
WHAT THIS GUY DID WAS JUST SO... UNSPEAKABLY CRUEL.
HE REALLY MUST HAVE HURT YOU.
HEH... YEAH.
BUT YOU KNOW WHAT THE MOST SICKENING PART ABOUT THIS IS?

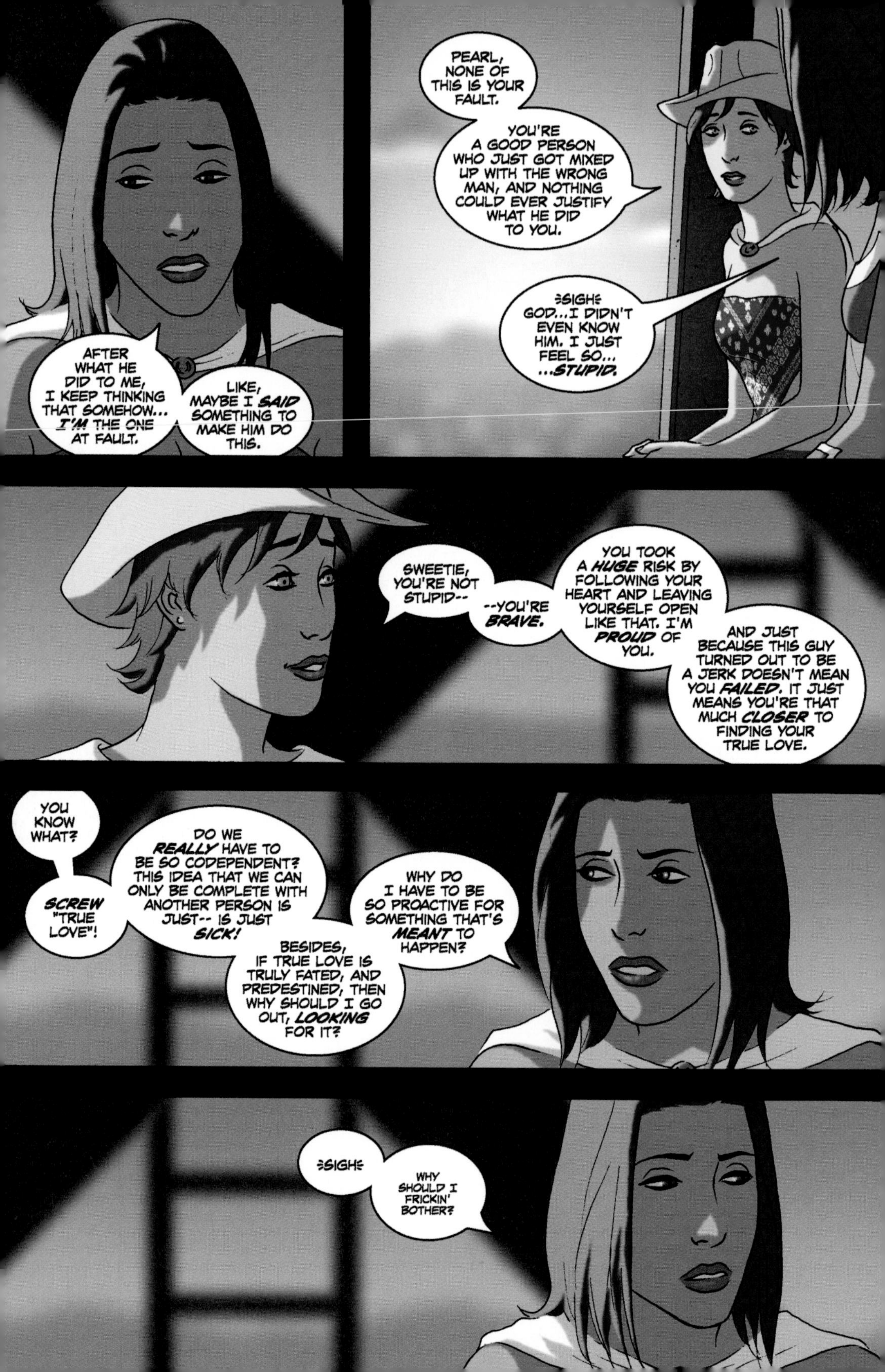
AFTER WHAT HE DID TO ME, I KEEP THINKING THAT SOMEHOW... I'M THE ONE AT FAULT.
LIKE, MAYBE I SAID SOMETHING TO MAKE HIM DO THIS.
PEARL, NONE OF THIS IS YOUR FAULT.
YOU'RE A GOOD PERSON WHO JUST GOT MIXED UP WITH THE WRONG MAN, AND NOTHING COULD EVER JUSTIFY WHAT HE DID TO YOU.
SIGH
GOD...I DIDN'T EVEN KNOW HIM. I JUST FEEL SO... ...STUPID.
SWEETIE, YOU'RE NOT STUPID--
--YOU'RE BRAVE.
YOU TOOK A HUGE RISK BY FOLLOWING YOUR HEART AND LEAVING YOURSELF OPEN LIKE THAT. I'M PROUD OF YOU.
AND JUST BECAUSE THIS GUY TURNED OUT TO BE A JERK DOESN'T MEAN YOU FAILED. IT JUST MEANS YOU'RE THAT MUCH CLOSER TO FINDING YOUR TRUE LOVE.
YOU KNOW WHAT?
SCREW "TRUE LOVE"!
DO WE REALLY HAVE TO BE SO CODEPENDENT? THIS IDEA THAT WE CAN ONLY BE COMPLETE WITH ANOTHER PERSON IS JUST-- IS JUST SICK!
WHY DO I HAVE TO BE SO PROACTIVE FOR SOMETHING THAT'S MEANT TO HAPPEN?
BESIDES, IF TRUE LOVE IS TRULY FATED, AND PREDESTINED, THEN WHY SHOULD I GO OUT, LOOKING FOR IT?
SIGH
WHY SHOULD I FRICKIN' BOTHER?

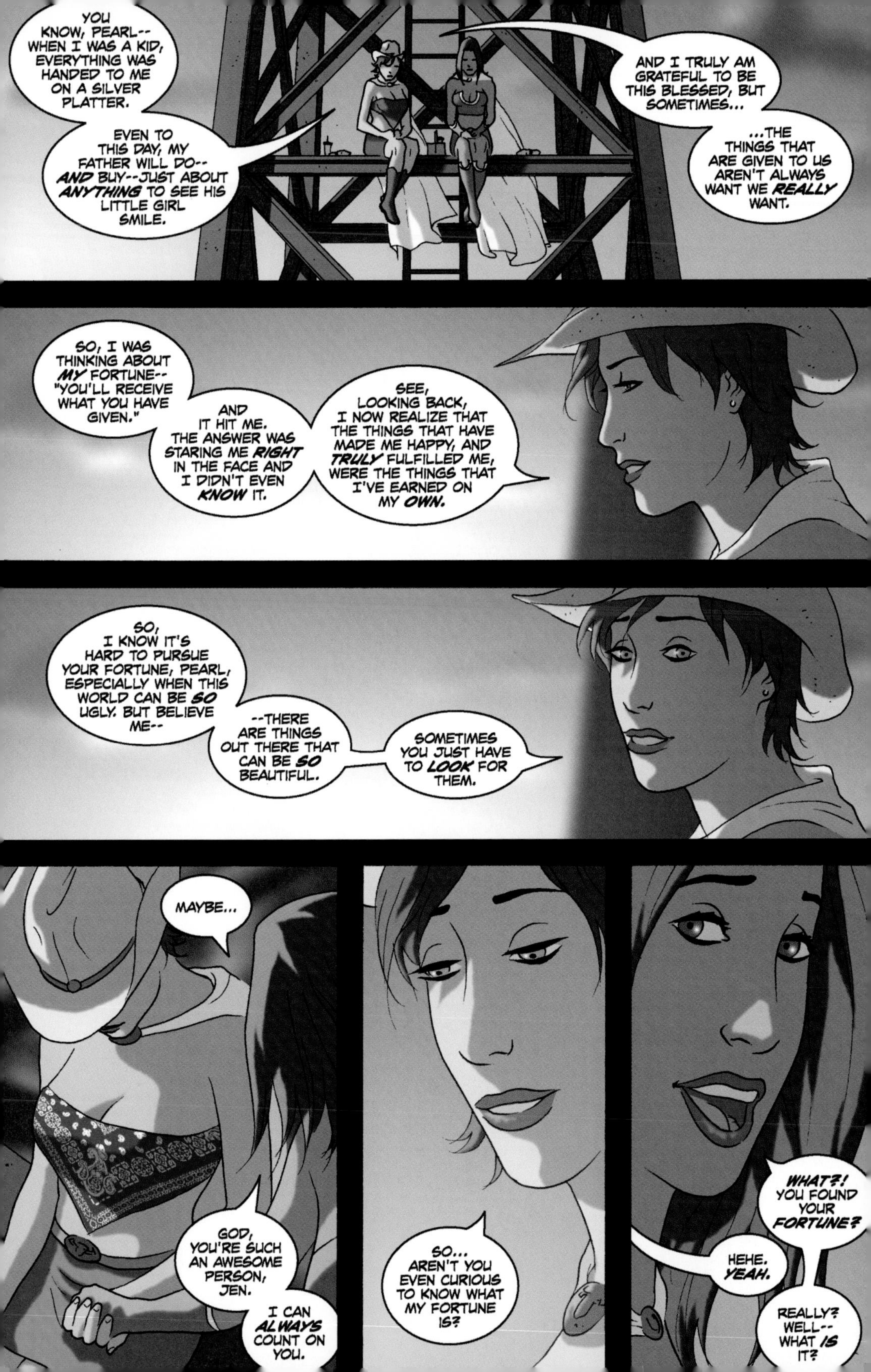
YOU KNOW, PEARL-- WHEN I WAS A KID, EVERYTHING WAS HANDED TO ME ON A SILVER PLATTER.
EVEN TO THIS DAY, MY FATHER WILL DO-- AND BUY--JUST ABOUT ANYTHING TO SEE HIS LITTLE GIRL SMILE.
AND I TRULY AM GRATEFUL TO BE THIS BLESSED, BUT SOMETIMES...
...THE THINGS THAT ARE GIVEN TO US AREN'T ALWAYS WANT WE REALLY WANT.
SO, I WAS THINKING ABOUT MY FORTUNE-- "YOU'LL RECEIVE WHAT YOU HAVE GIVEN."
AND IT HIT ME. THE ANSWER WAS STARING ME RIGHT IN THE FACE AND I DIDN'T EVEN KNOW IT.
SEE, LOOKING BACK, I NOW REALIZE THAT THE THINGS THAT HAVE MADE ME HAPPY, AND TRULY FULFILLED ME, WERE THE THINGS THAT I'VE EARNED ON MY OWN.
SO, I KNOW IT'S HARD TO PURSUE YOUR FORTUNE, PEARL, ESPECIALLY WHEN THIS WORLD CAN BE SO UGLY. BUT BELIEVE ME--
--THERE ARE THINGS OUT THERE THAT CAN BE SO BEAUTIFUL.
SOMETIMES YOU JUST HAVE TO LOOK FOR THEM.
MAYBE...
GOD, YOU'RE SUCH AN AWESOME PERSON, JEN.
I CAN ALWAYS COUNT ON YOU.
SO... AREN'T YOU EVEN CURIOUS TO KNOW WHAT MY FORTUNE IS?
WHAT?! YOU FOUND YOUR FORTUNE?
HEHE. YEAH.
REALLY? WELL-- WHAT IS IT?

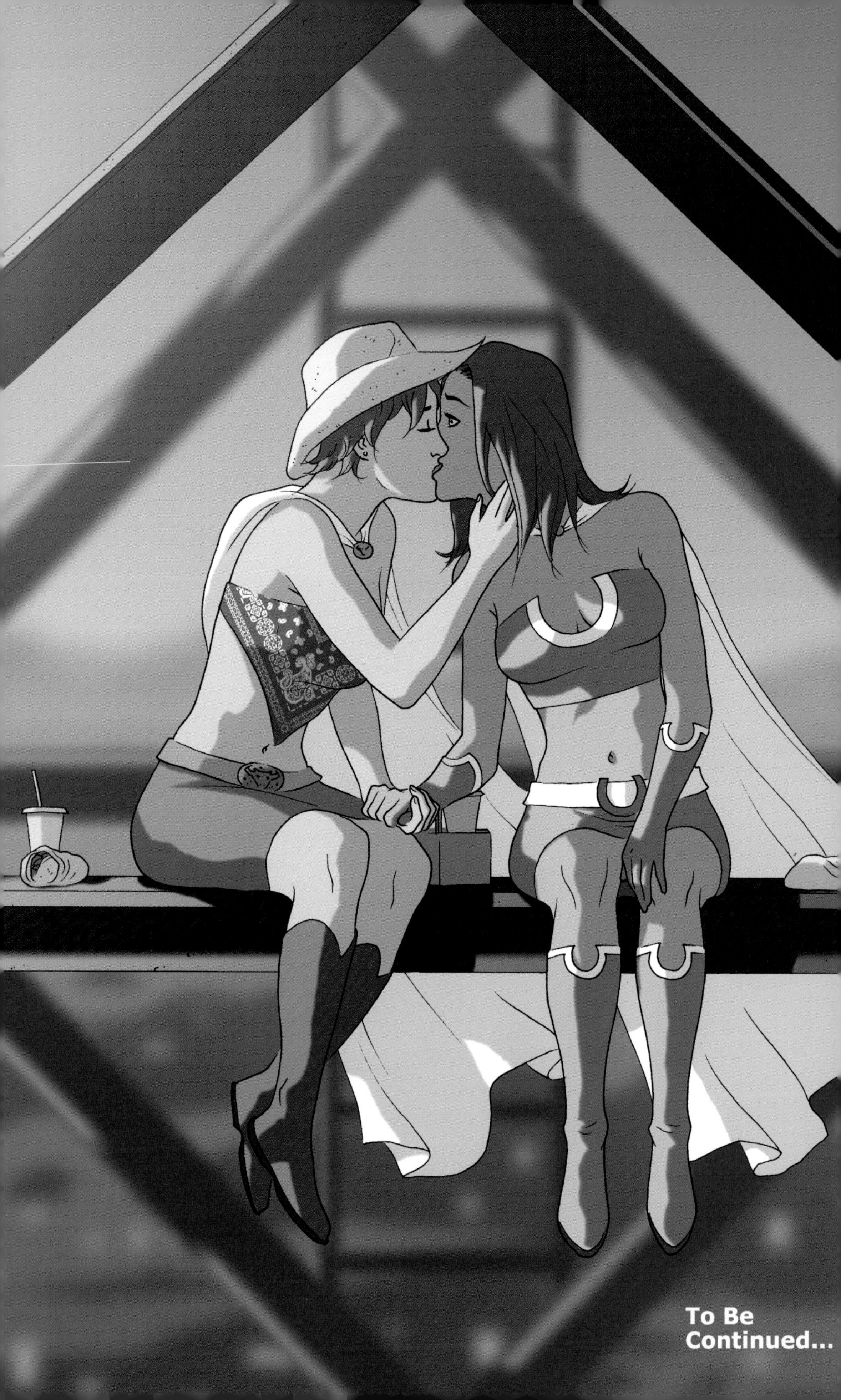

To Be
Continued...

fashion police

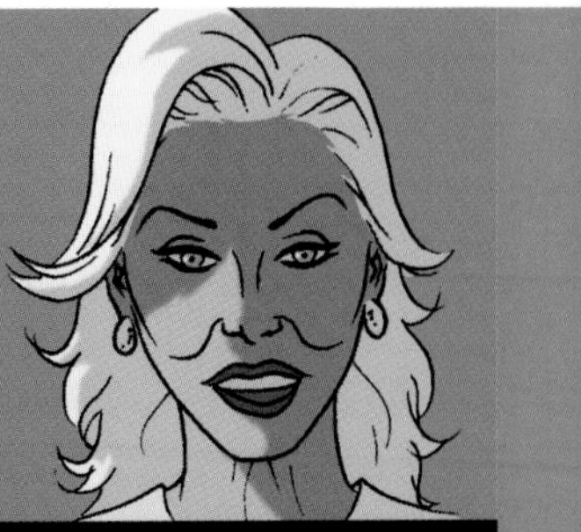

Joanne Shivers
Inquisitor Fashion Editor

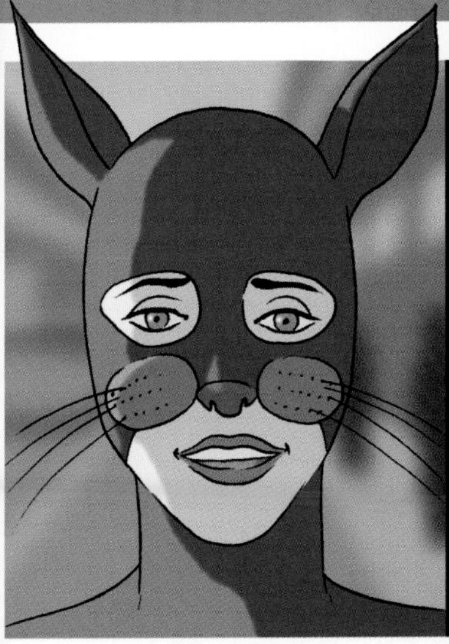

ME-YUCK!

Heroine Inc.'s casting dept. must have been smoking crack when they signed on this ugly feline. Sweet Saint Maria, that's a God-awful outfit. This kitty needs to be put down stat!

This Outfit Rain-BLOWS!

Someone call a medic. It looks like Rainbow Girl has overdosed on fashion acid. With her technicolor tutu and prepubescent pigtails, this super-zero just looks plain creepy, not cute. Gag! No pot of gold at the end of this rainbow!

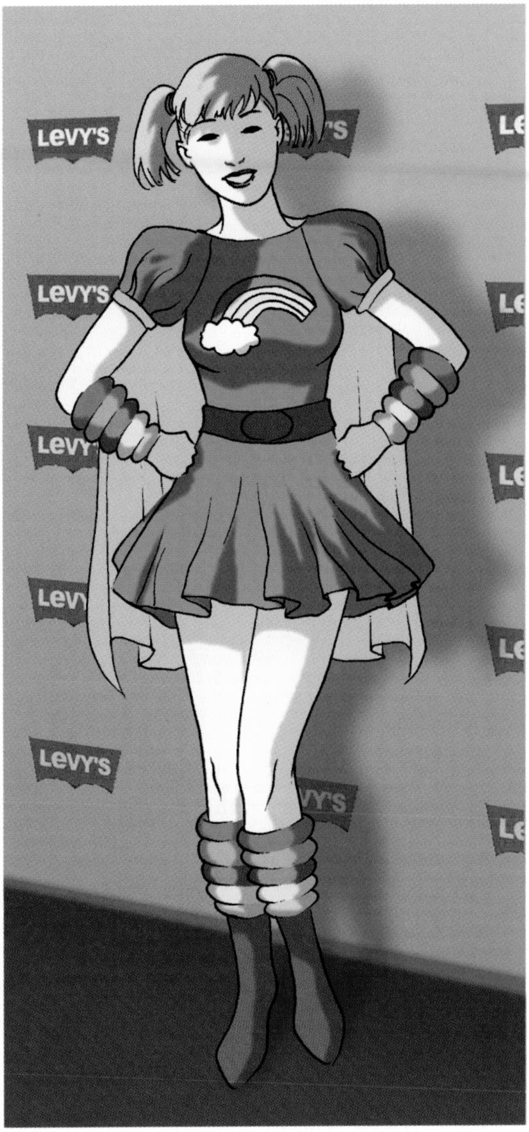
LEVY'S
LEVY'S
LEVY'S

Wonder Wedgie

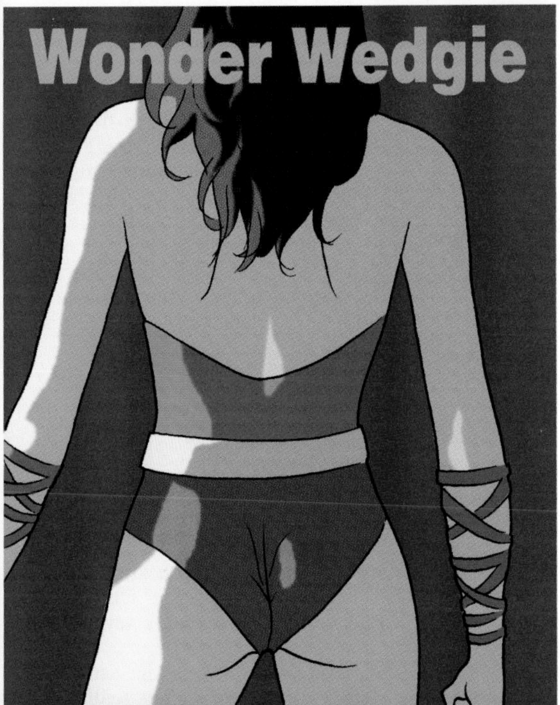

We're going to need the jaws of life because Amazon Woman has her panties in a death grip. Either lose the wedgie-prone getup, or relax the ass cheeks, sister!

WORLD EXCLUSIVE

super scandal

MY ONE NIGHT

■ *Exclusive photos expose Pearl Penalosa's dark side.*

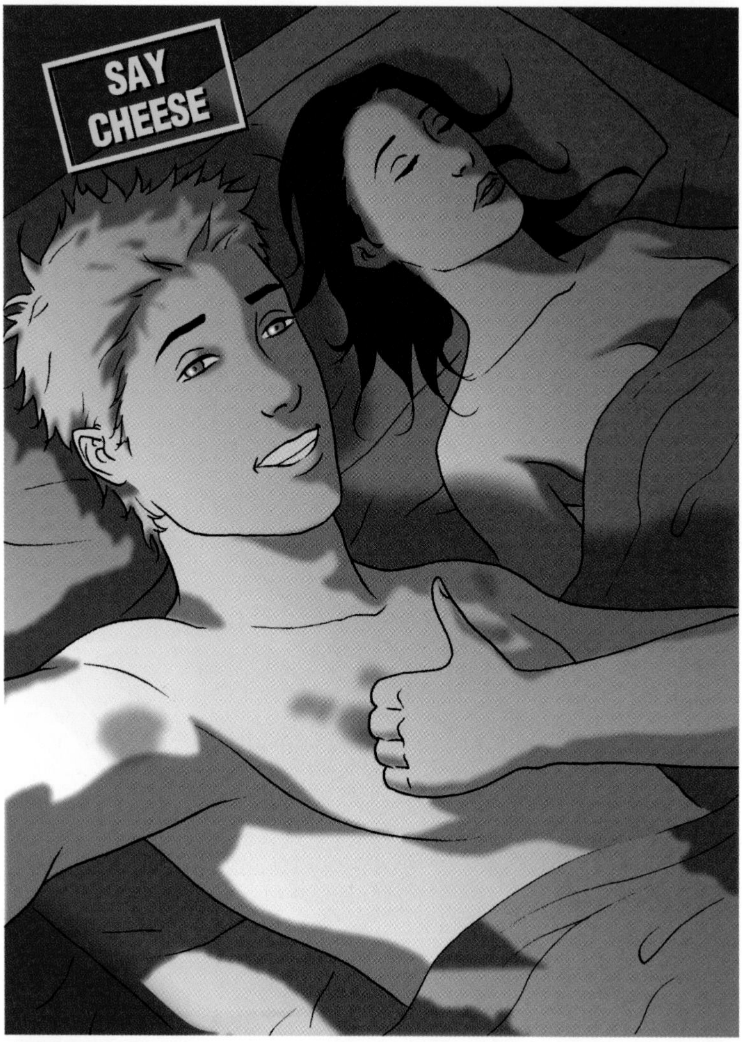
SAY CHEESE

ULTRA is an animal in the sack! That's the shocking truth a Spring City man has discovered after spending one steamy night with congenial caped crusader Pearl Penalosa. Ripping the lid off a short-lived sex-capade, Ultra's one-night boy toy, Jason Lucas, drops a bombshell that questions everything we know about perennial good girl, Pearl Penalosa.

Throughout her career, the heavenly heroine has maintained a flawless reputation as one of the world's most marketable and squeaky clean, superheroines. But the exclusive photographs we've obtained from Jason may blow that pristine persona to smithereens!

So forget the "Ultra" role model you thought you knew because this super femme fatale is one bonafied super-freak! And as these candid photos show, the 26-year-old hunk has the bruises to prove it. Ouch, that's got to hurt!

In a blockbuster world exclusive, Jason Lucas discloses all the sordid details of their scandalous romp, exposing a side of Pearl Penalosa you've never seen before.

HOW THEY MET

"I met Ultra in a downtown pizzeria on Friday," confided Jason. "...and before I knew it, we were going out on a date."

The pair caused quite a stir on their night out on the town, inciting a frenzied media blitz outside of a Spring City coffee shop. Sources say Pearl was virtually unrecognizable at first. The typically-dressed-down superheroine looked uncharacteristically sexed-up with a revealing top, exposing copious amounts of cleavage.

"She obviously whored up to disguise herself," disclosed a superhero analyst. "These superheroes are notorious for living out double lives, and usually, their secret alter egos are closer to the real them than those saccharine costumes will ever be."

TORRID TRYST

Shortly after the fun-filled date, Pearl reportedly dragged the helpless hunk into his own apartment where they had the torrid tryst. Mothers across the globe will be devastated to hear that their champion for teenage abstinence bumped uglies on the first date!

'She definitely deserves the 'super' prefix.'

"She was pretty reserved at first," revealed Jason. "But once we had our first kiss, she became very open, and relaxed. It was such a surreal experience because I never touched a girl like her before. She was hard... but soft at the same time--it's difficult to explain, really."

When the mortal man could take no more, the heroine insisted on more and more, reportedly making love to Jason for at least 6 hours straight! Wow-- someone get Guinness on the phone!

STAND WITH ULTRA!

"She definitely deserves the 'super' prefix," said Jason.

KODAK MOMENT

Once the ravenous beauty got her fill, she was out for the count and snoozed the night away. Jason decided he needed proof of this Kodak moment, so he took snapshots of the sleeping beauty as she caught her Z's.

"It was a spur-of-the-moment decision," disclosed Jason. "I kept waking up in the middle of the night to watch her sleep. I just couldn't believe she was lying in my bed, so I did what any other reasonable guy would do-- I took pictures."

'I think in private, Pearl is battling a lot of inner demons...'

The morning after, the press tracked down and approached the unsuspecting hunk as he left his apartment. According to Jason, they relentlessly poked and prodded about their relationship, offering generous sums of cash for any juicy tidbits, and of course, the hard evidence to back it up. Thankfully, Jason had exactly that!

"I wasn't planning on selling the photos," confided Jason. "...But those people know how to press the right buttons."

PEARL'S MEN

Pearl's involvement with civilian, Jason Lucas, is a steep departure from her previous choice of men. In the past, she's dated her share of the rich and eligible superhero celebrities, most notably-- Captain Steel, her first love. But ever since the sweet and innocent, fairytale romance with Steel ebbed five years ago, the superheroine fell off the dating scene, and seemed to have abstained from men completely. Apparently, we were fooled.

"It's now clear that Pearl's 'sweet and wholesome' act is just a shameless fraud perpetrated on the American public," declared a source. "I honestly believe that Pearl rejected the high-profile superheroes because she got tired of living a lie in the limelight. Men like Jason are now convenient for her because with an anonymous nobody, she's able to quench her sick, sexual urges without the drawback of media scrutiny. But her plan backfired because this average Joe is coming forward, and I don't think he's alone.

"Who knows how many men out there suffered the brunt of Pearl's sordid sex fantasies? I wouldn't be surprised if there was a whole underground network of these bruised and battered sex victims, who are too afraid to speak out. I mean, just look at her handy-work in these horrifying pictures. This man suffered, and went through a sadomasochistic hell with this insatiable, pervert. But thankfully, he was brave enough to tell his story."

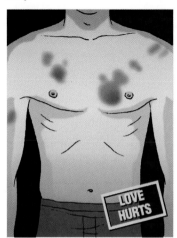

TICKING TIME BOMB

It's hard to believe that only yesterday, we still thought of Pearl as that same role model who set so many positive examples for young, impressionable girls all over the globe. But some insiders in the superhero world are now coming forward, telling us exclusively, that Pearl was always a ticking time bomb, waiting to explode.

"Sure, on the outside, she seems happy-go-lucky and very put-together," an insider confided. "-but I think in private, Pearl is battling a lot of inner demons that she feels can only be exorcised through frequent sessions of dirty, dirty sex acts."

"This will definitely affect her career for the worst," revealed another source. " She may not only lose endorsement deals, but her fan base as well-- millions will be crushed to learn that their favorite superhero is a sex-starved nympho. How can they ever look up to her again? How will she regain their trust? All we can do right now is pray for this troubled heroine. Pray, people. Pray a lot."

MOVING FORWARD

Sources close to Jason have advised him to put the whole ordeal behind him and move forward. "It won't be easy for the poor guy," declared the concerned source. "The bruises may have healed, but the emotional scars may last a lifetime."

"The rich and the powerful have been walking all over the little people since the beginning of time, and it's saddening to see that Ultra is no exception. So, I'm glad Jason took the initiative to take these pictures and reveal Pearl Penalosa for the sick person that she is. And if these photos can put some money in his pocket, then kudos to him for making the most out of a traumatic event."

But despite coming out a winner in this trying time, the guy-next-door remains humble as ever. "I didn't do anything special," disclosed Jason.

"I'm just realistic enough to know that she and I could never have a future together. I'm a nobody. She's Ultra. I took the money because it was the only thing that made sense."

-TIMOTHY INGLEWOOD

ULTRA™
JAN 2005
Issue 6
WHAT TO WEAR WHEN YOU'RE TRAGICALLY UNATTRACTIVE
Created by THE LUNA BROTHERS
BEAUTY CONTEST
Supermodels vs. Superheroines
BEAR IS THE NEW MINK
Top Designers Gear Up for the Hunting Season
MAJOR MAKEOVERS
What is the Price of Perfection?
THE POWER DIET
What Goes Down Must Come Up
OLIVIA ARANCINA
Super Chic
900 Page FASHION SPECTACULAR
#BXBJLEX ***********5-DIGIT 10019
#1920 3881 111#TD 9879CA05 B APR05
Pearl Penalosa 0007
22194 Crescent Ave #P2 #02734
Spring City 10019 USA P00267

ULTRA *january*

SEXIER THAN THE AVERAGE BEAR

p.696

COVER LOOK: *super chic*

Olivia Arancina wears a Salvatore LeTigra smoke-black chiffon dress. Hair, Franco Belaggio of Belaggio Salon. Makeup, Mandrake for Sebastian Vagaras Cosmetics. Details, stores, see In This Issue. Fashion Editor: Ange "Wicky Wicky" Bonet. Photography: Vicky Stein.

image COMICS PRESENTS

THIS ISSUE

3 **SEVEN DAYS, Part Six**

CREATED BY

112 **THE LUNA BROTHERS**

CREDITS

114 **JOSHUA LUNA**
   Plot, Script, Layouts
114 **JONATHAN LUNA**
   Plot, Art, Colors, Letters

OFFICIAL WEBSITE

120 www.LunaBrothers.com

FOR
IMAGE COMICS

Erik Larsen
Publisher

Todd McFarlane
President

Marc Silvestri
CEO

Jim Valentino
Vice-President

Eric Stephenson
Executive Director

Missie Miranda
Controller

Brett Evans
Production Manager

B. Clay Moore
Public Relations &
Marketing Coordinator

Allen Hui
Production Artist

Joe Keatinge
Inventory Controller

Mia Machatton
Administrative Assistant

www.imagecomics.com

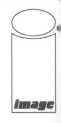

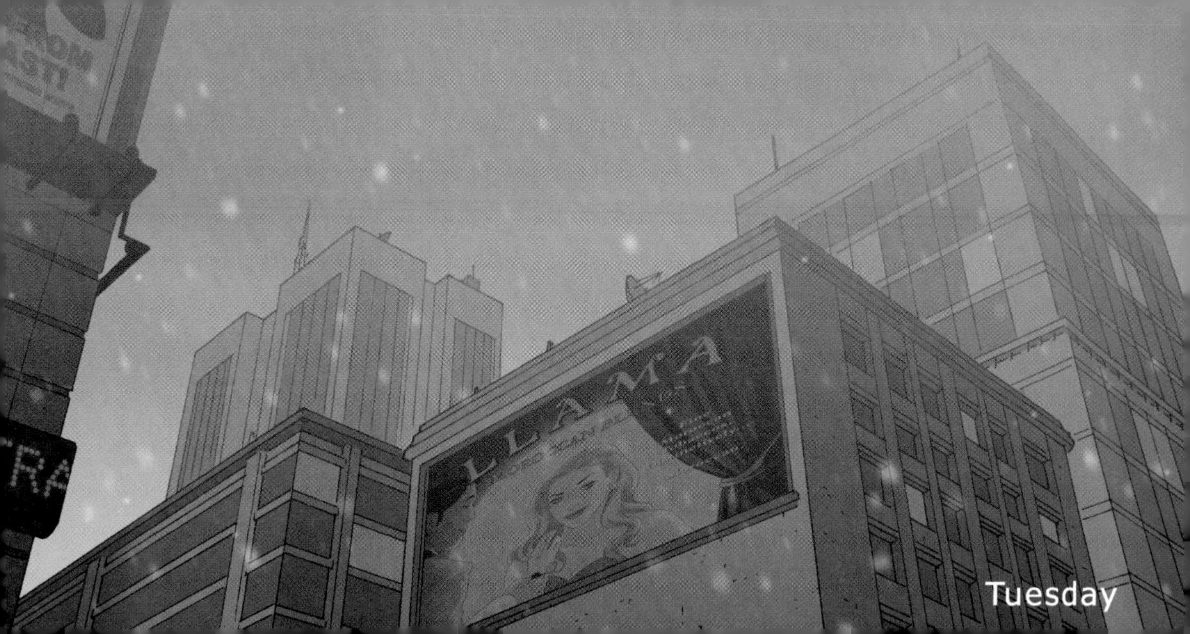
LLAMA
Tuesday

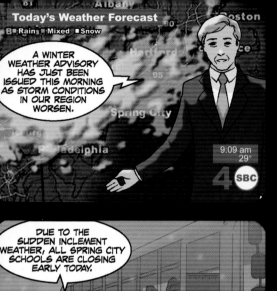
Today's Weather Forecast

Rain ■ Mixed ■ Snow

A WINTER WEATHER ADVISORY HAS JUST BEEN ISSUED THIS MORNING AS STORM CONDITIONS IN OUR REGION WORSEN.

9:09 am
29°

4 SBC

Today's Weather Forecast

Rain ■ Mixed ■ Snow

MODERATE TO HEAVY SNOW IS EXPECTED TO CONTINUE THROUGHOUT THE DAY AND POSSIBLY INTO TOMORROW.

DUE TO THE SUDDEN INCLEMENT WEATHER, ALL SPRING CITY SCHOOLS ARE CLOSING EARLY TODAY.

JOHN HENRY ELEMENTARY

9:09 am
29°

SBC

Today's Weather Forecast

Rain ■ Mixed ■ Snow

SO MAKE NO MISTAKE ABOUT IT-- IT'S GOING TO BE A NASTY DAY, FOLKS. STAY SAFE OUT THERE.

9:09 am
29°

4 SBC

HERE WITH US IS DR. TWOMBLY, OFFERING SOME INSIGHT ON THE CITY'S MOST WANTED FUGITIVE-- THE SERIAL ARSONIST.

DOCTOR, WE KNOW NOTHING OF THIS MENACE. HOW DO YOU THINK THIS MONSTER'S PYROKINETIC ABILITIES EVEN WORK?

GAS, TOM. LOTS AND LOTS OF GAS.

SBC

THAT WOULD EXPLAIN HOW THIS C-LEVEL SUPER-HUMAN--

--COULD FUEL AND SUSTAIN SUCH LONG PERIODS OF INTENSE EXOTHERMIC ACTIVITY.

ALLOW ME TO DEMONSTRATE WITH THIS MODEL, CONTAINING FLAMMABLE GAS.

9:10 am
29°

SBC

IN THEORY, WITH A CONSTANT FLOW OF GASEOUS SECRETIONS, A SINGLE SPARK--

WHOOSH

--IS ALL THIS PYRO REALLY NEEDS TO FULLY IGNITE.

HOLY GOD!!

YES, FASCINATING, ISN'T IT?

9:10 am
29°

SBC

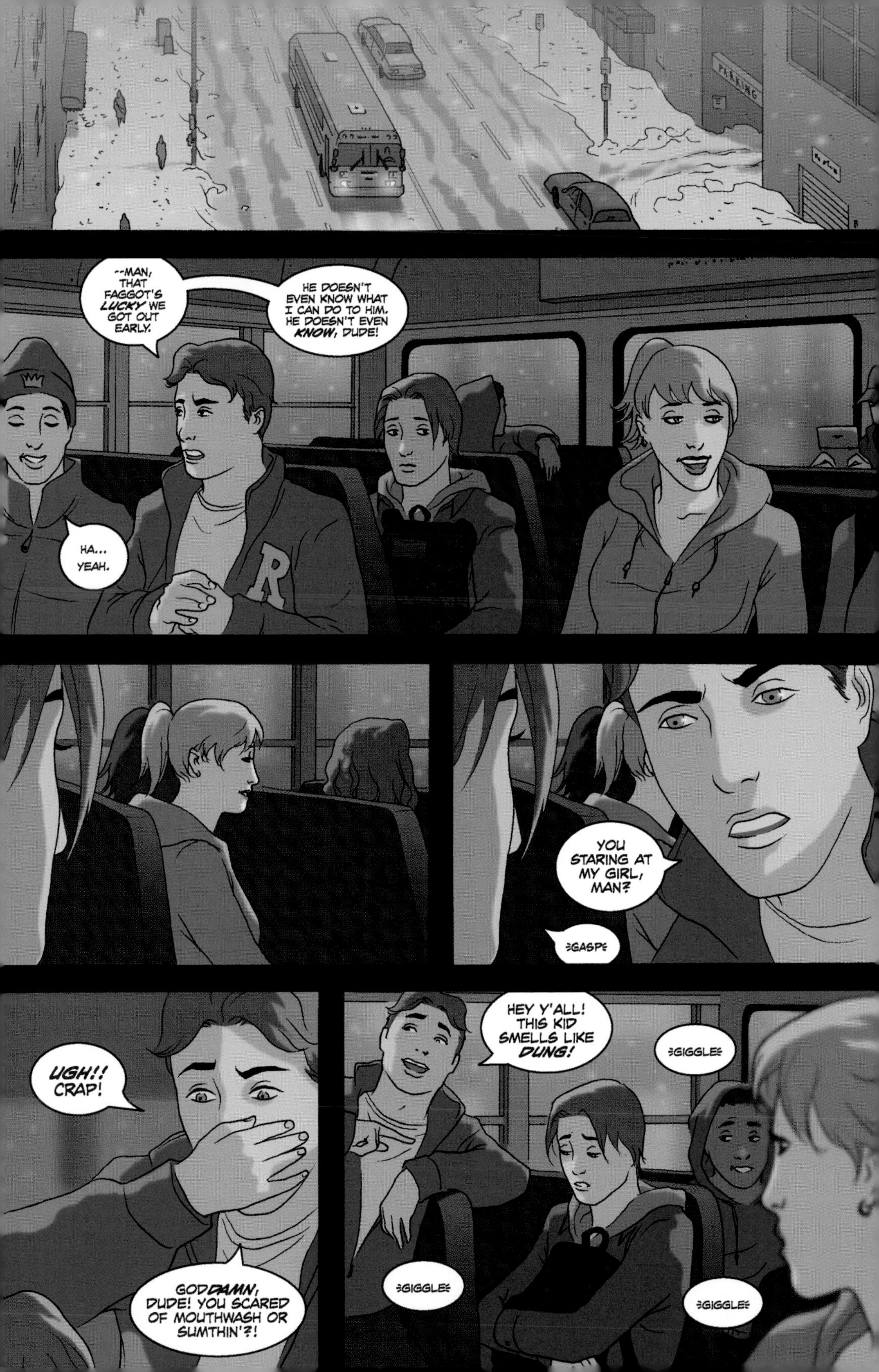
--MAN, THAT FAGGOT'S *LUCKY* WE GOT OUT EARLY.
HE DOESN'T EVEN KNOW WHAT I CAN DO TO HIM. HE DOESN'T EVEN *KNOW*, DUDE!
HA... YEAH.
YOU STARING AT MY GIRL, MAN?
GASP
UGH!! CRAP!
GOD*DAMN*, DUDE! YOU SCARED OF MOUTHWASH OR SUMTHIN'?!
HEY Y'ALL! THIS KID SMELLS LIKE *DUNG!*
GIGGLE
GIGGLE
GIGGLE

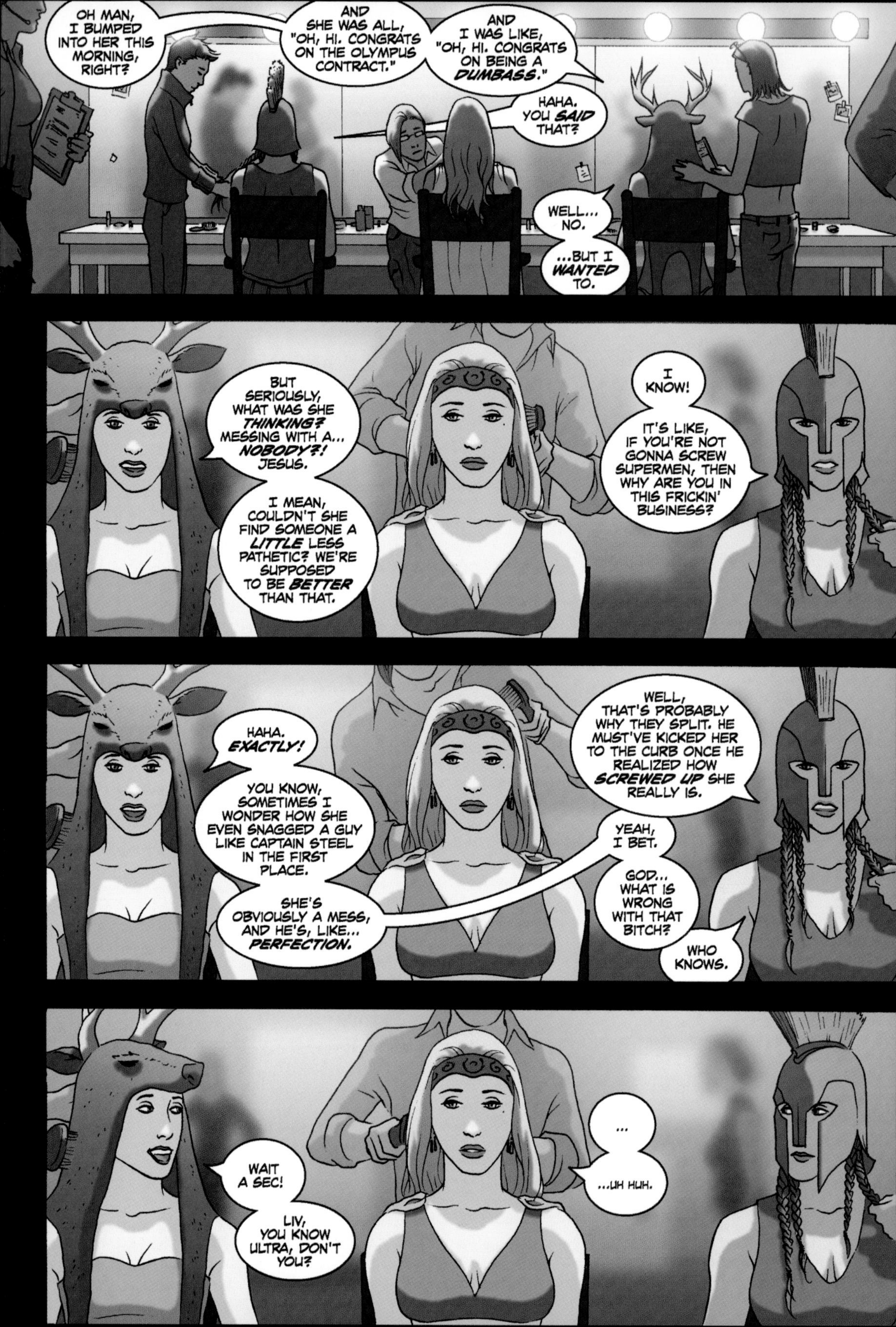
OH MAN, I BUMPED INTO HER THIS MORNING, RIGHT?
AND SHE WAS ALL, "OH, HI. CONGRATS ON THE OLYMPUS CONTRACT."
AND I WAS LIKE, "OH, HI. CONGRATS ON BEING A DUMBASS."
HAHA. YOU SAID THAT?
WELL... NO.
...BUT I WANTED TO.
BUT SERIOUSLY, WHAT WAS SHE THINKING? MESSING WITH A... NOBODY?! JESUS.
I MEAN, COULDN'T SHE FIND SOMEONE A LITTLE LESS PATHETIC? WE'RE SUPPOSED TO BE BETTER THAN THAT.
I KNOW!
IT'S LIKE, IF YOU'RE NOT GONNA SCREW SUPERMEN, THEN WHY ARE YOU IN THIS FRICKIN' BUSINESS?
HAHA. EXACTLY!
YOU KNOW, SOMETIMES I WONDER HOW SHE EVEN SNAGGED A GUY LIKE CAPTAIN STEEL IN THE FIRST PLACE.
SHE'S OBVIOUSLY A MESS, AND HE'S, LIKE... PERFECTION.
WELL, THAT'S PROBABLY WHY THEY SPLIT. HE MUST'VE KICKED HER TO THE CURB ONCE HE REALIZED HOW SCREWED UP SHE REALLY IS.
YEAH, I BET.
GOD... WHAT IS WRONG WITH THAT BITCH?
WHO KNOWS.
WAIT A SEC!
LIV, YOU KNOW ULTRA, DON'T YOU?
...
...UH HUH.

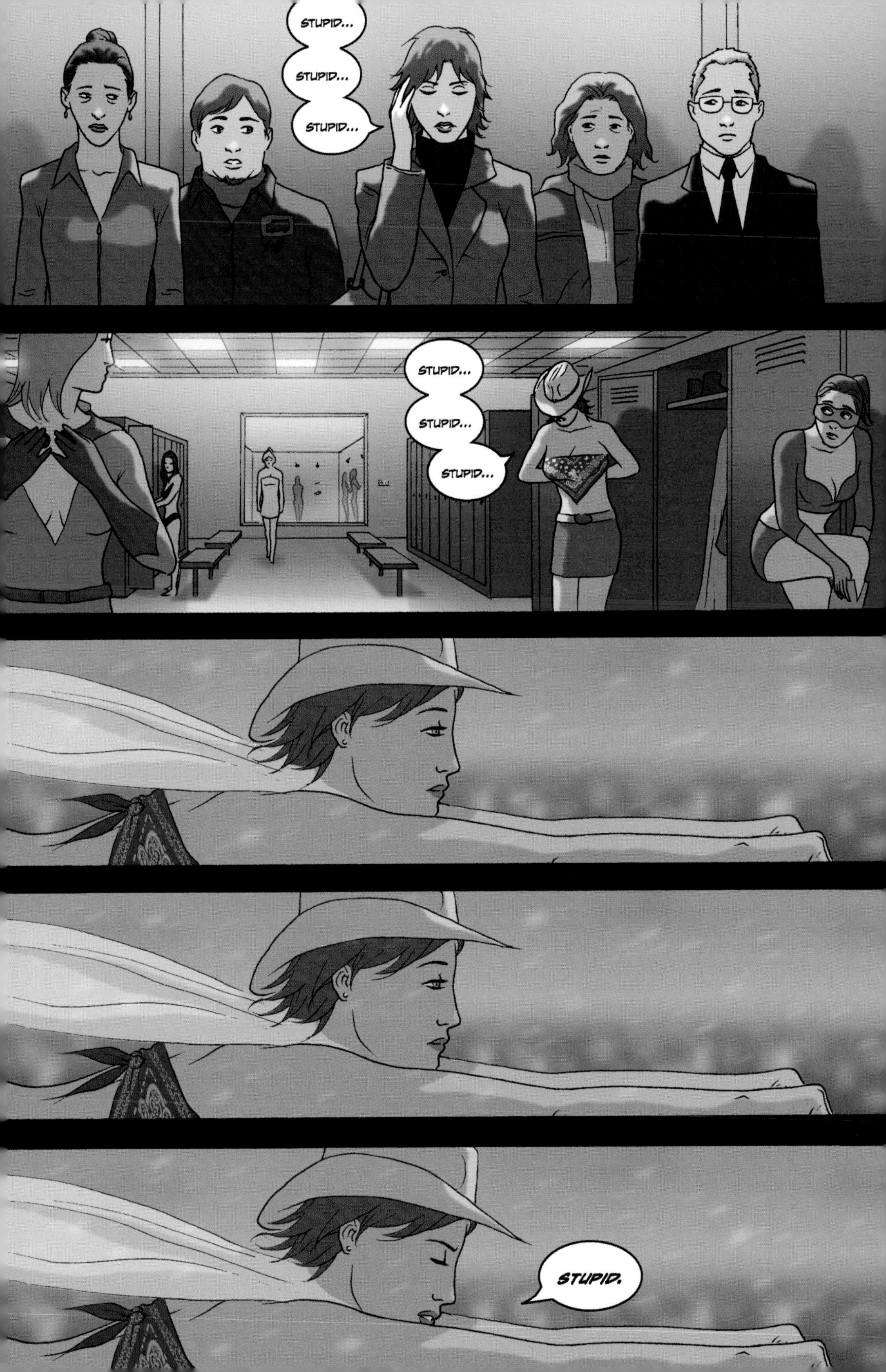
STUPID...
STUPID...
STUPID...
STUPID...
STUPID...
STUPID...
STUPID.

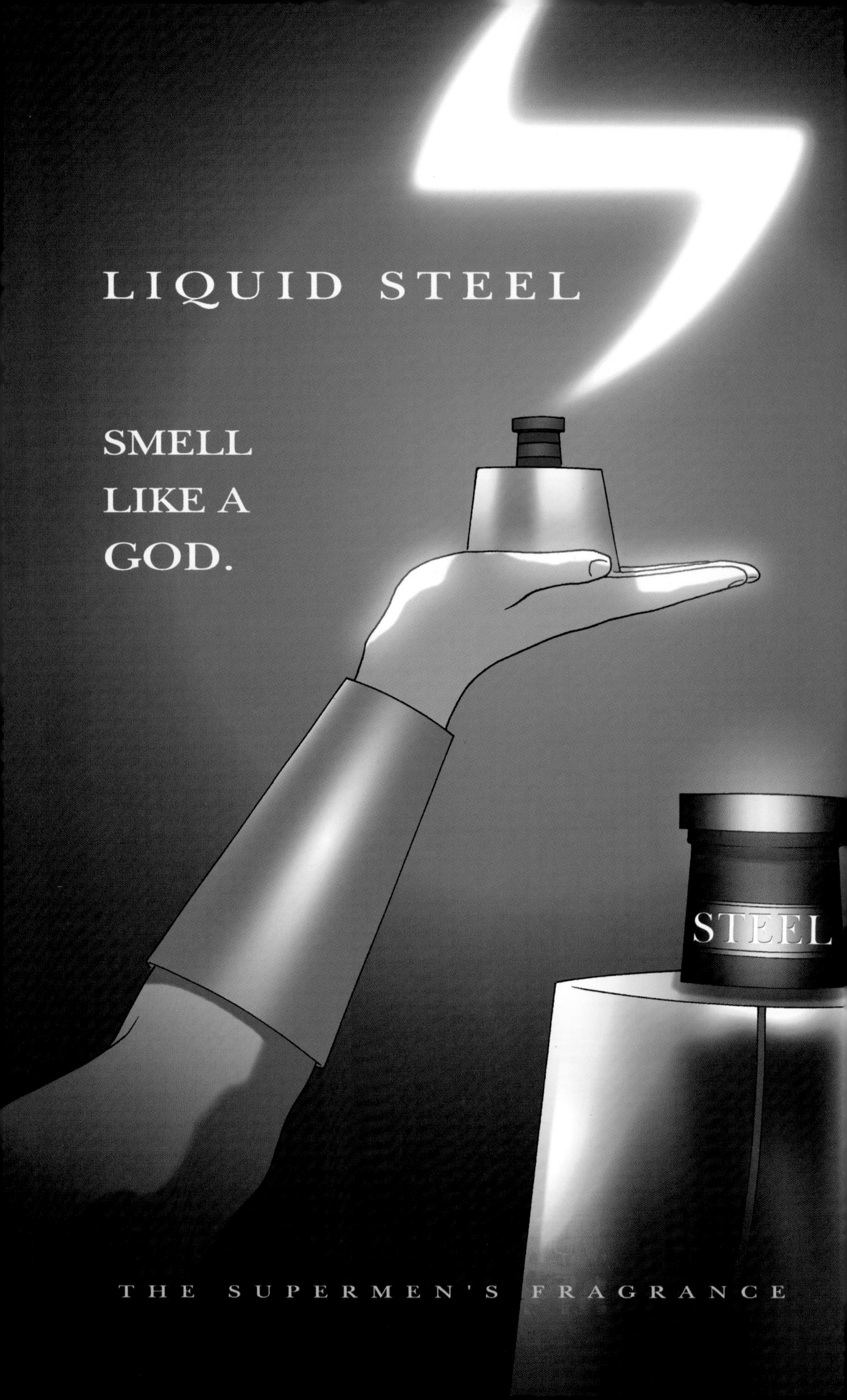
LIQUID STEEL
SMELL
LIKE A
GOD.
STEEL
THE SUPERMEN'S FRAGRANCE

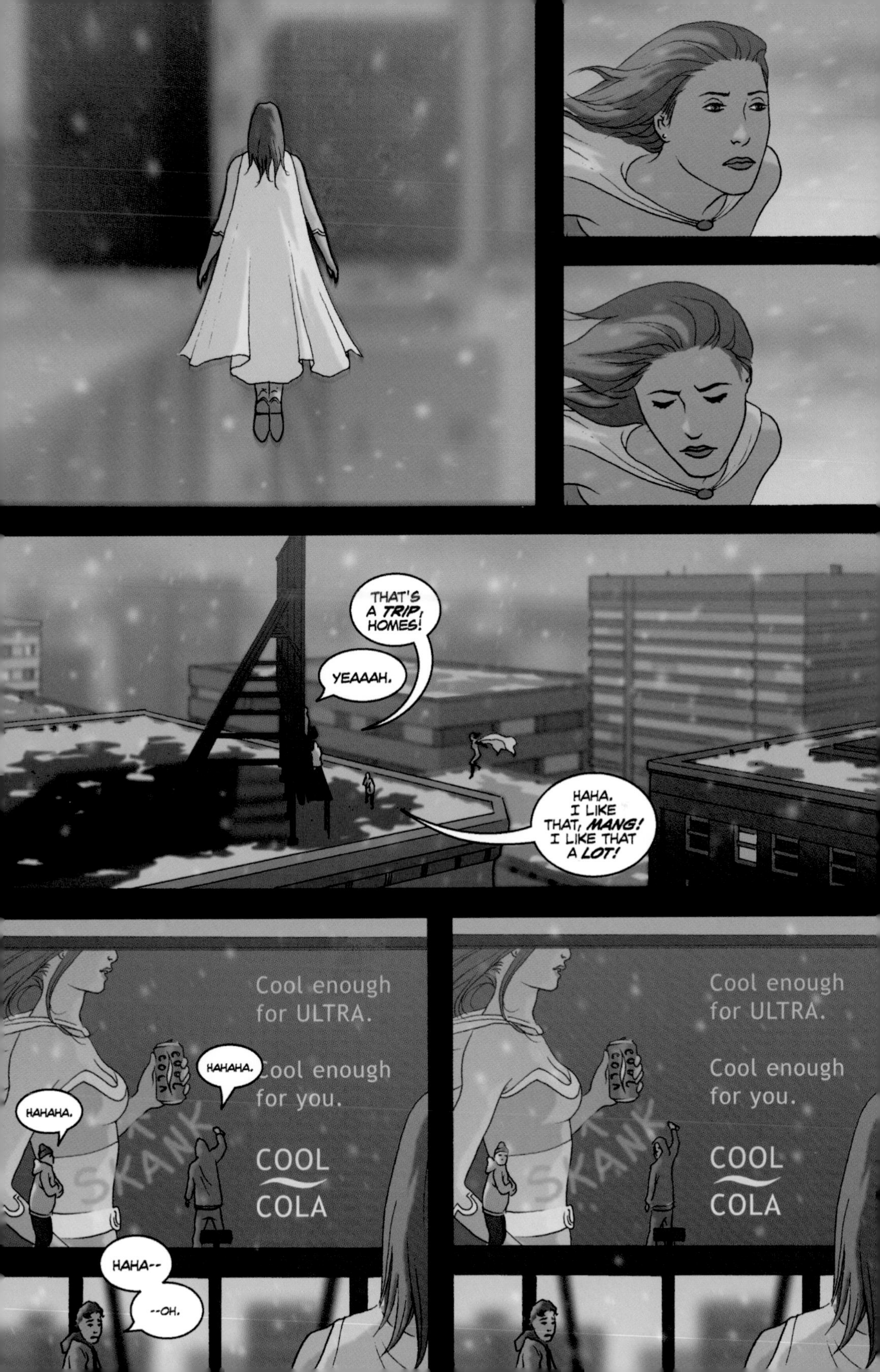
THAT'S A *TRIP*, HOMES!
YEAAAH.
HAHA. I LIKE THAT, *MANG!* I LIKE THAT A *LOT!*
Cool enough for ULTRA.
Cool enough for you.
COOL COLA
SKANK
HAHAHA.
HAHAHA.
HAHA--
--OH.
Cool enough for ULTRA.
Cool enough for you.
COOL COLA

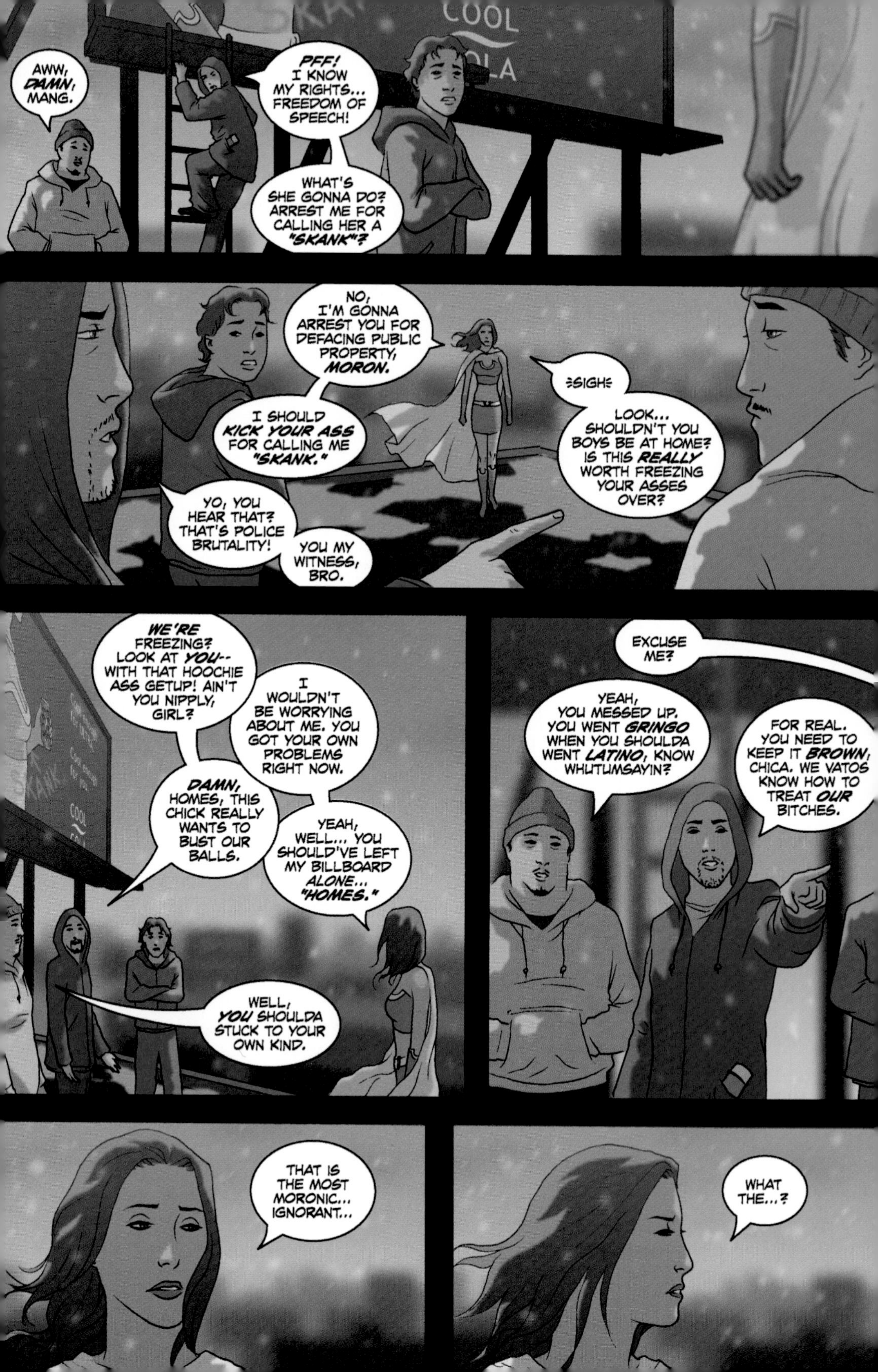
COOL
OLA
AWW, DAMN, MANG.
PFF! I KNOW MY RIGHTS... FREEDOM OF SPEECH!
WHAT'S SHE GONNA DO? ARREST ME FOR CALLING HER A "SKANK"?
NO, I'M GONNA ARREST YOU FOR DEFACING PUBLIC PROPERTY, MORON.
I SHOULD KICK YOUR ASS FOR CALLING ME "SKANK."
YO, YOU HEAR THAT? THAT'S POLICE BRUTALITY!
YOU MY WITNESS, BRO.
SIGH
LOOK... SHOULDN'T YOU BOYS BE AT HOME? IS THIS REALLY WORTH FREEZING YOUR ASSES OVER?
WE'RE FREEZING? LOOK AT YOU-- WITH THAT HOOCHIE ASS GETUP! AIN'T YOU NIPPLY, GIRL?
I WOULDN'T BE WORRYING ABOUT ME. YOU GOT YOUR OWN PROBLEMS RIGHT NOW.
DAMN, HOMES, THIS CHICK REALLY WANTS TO BUST OUR BALLS.
YEAH, WELL... YOU SHOULD'VE LEFT MY BILLBOARD ALONE... "HOMES."
WELL, YOU SHOULDA STUCK TO YOUR OWN KIND.
EXCUSE ME?
YEAH, YOU MESSED UP. YOU WENT GRINGO WHEN YOU SHOULDA WENT LATINO, KNOW WHUTUMSAYIN?
FOR REAL. YOU NEED TO KEEP IT BROWN, CHICA. WE VATOS KNOW HOW TO TREAT OUR BITCHES.
THAT IS THE MOST MORONIC... IGNORANT...
WHAT THE...?

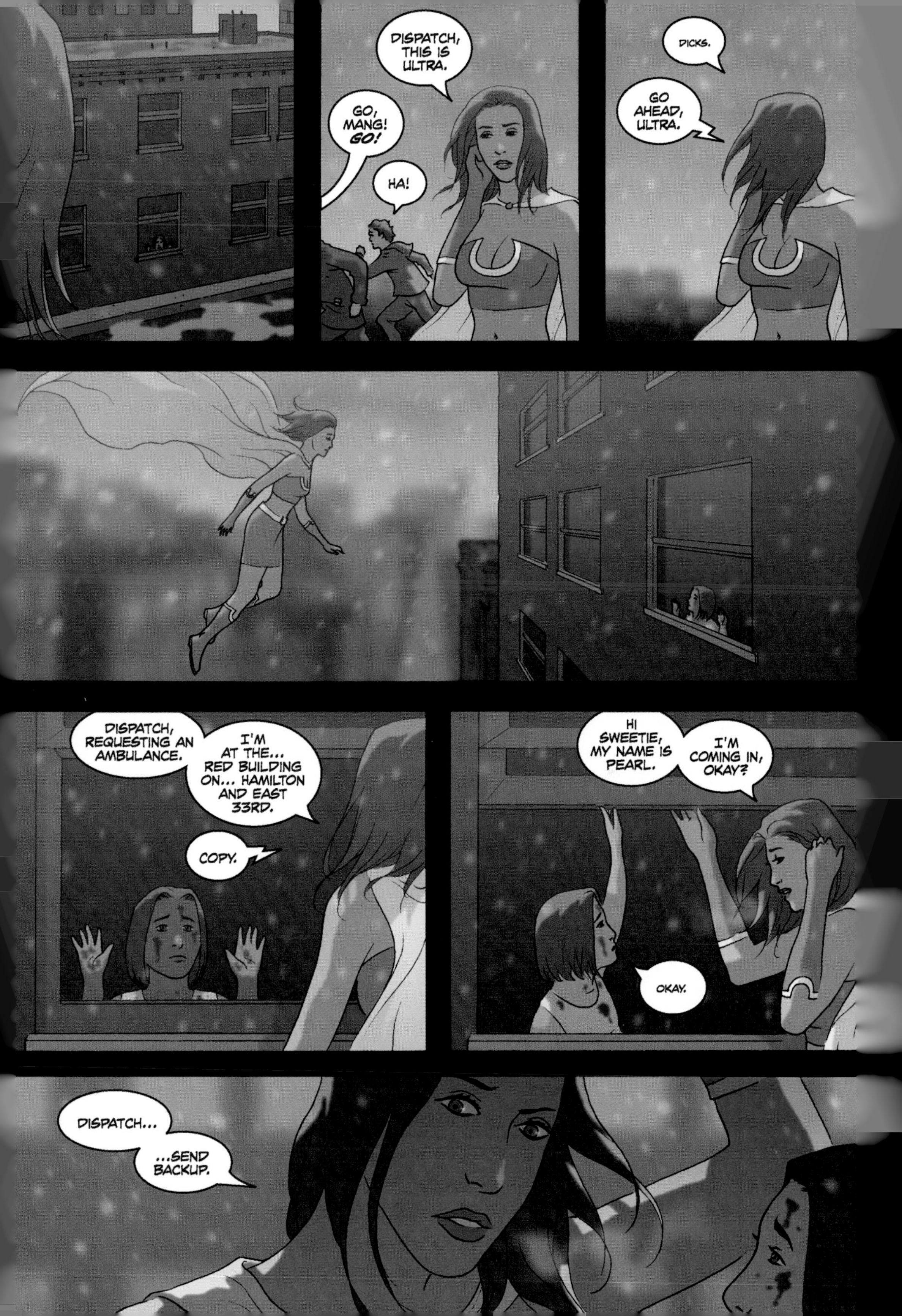
DISPATCH, THIS IS ULTRA.
GO, MANG! GO!
HA!
DICKS.
GO AHEAD, ULTRA.
DISPATCH, REQUESTING AN AMBULANCE.
I'M AT THE... RED BUILDING ON... HAMILTON AND EAST 33RD.
COPY.
HI SWEETIE, MY NAME IS PEARL.
I'M COMING IN, OKAY?
OKAY.
DISPATCH...
...SEND BACKUP.

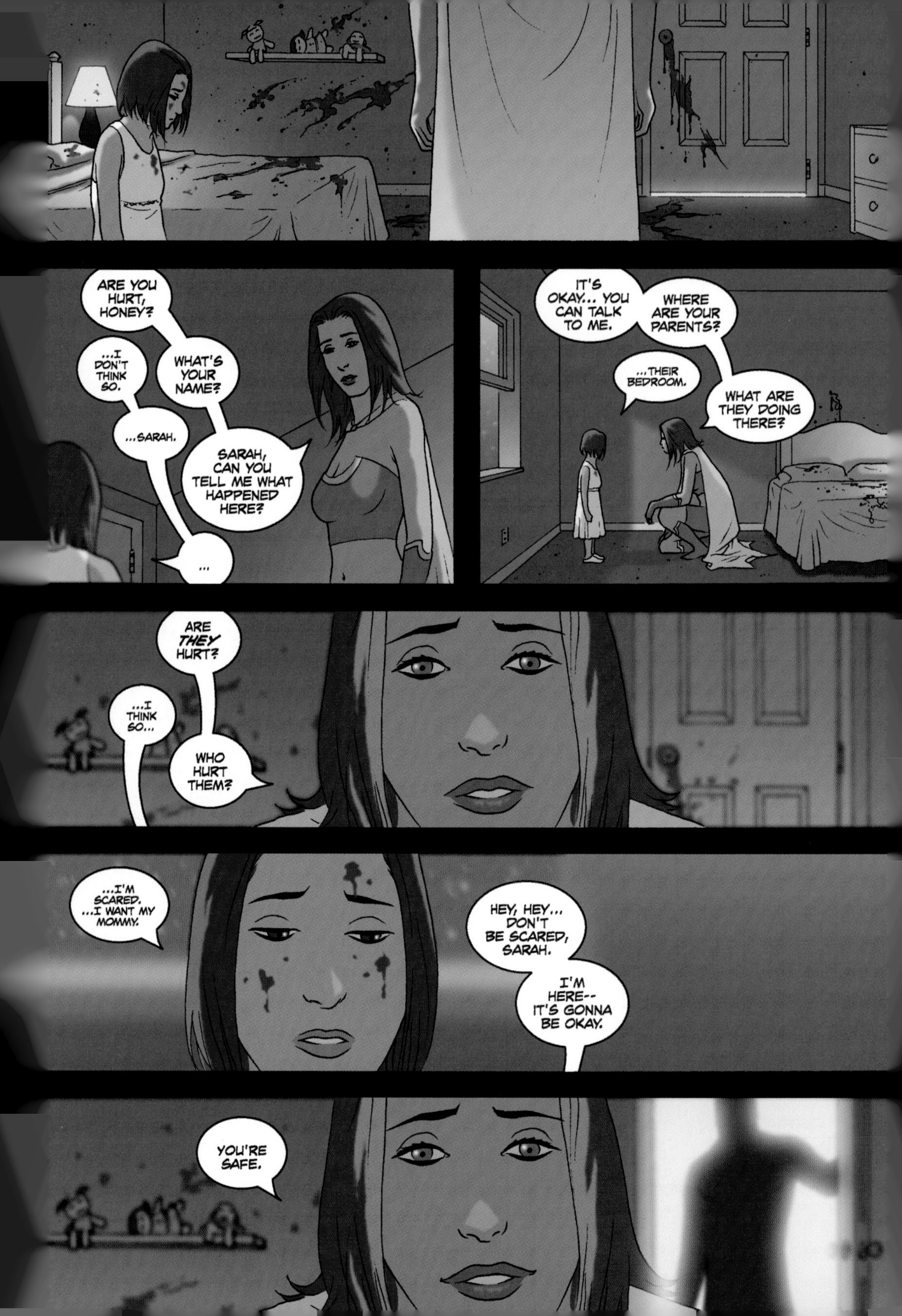
ARE YOU HURT, HONEY?
...I DON'T THINK SO.
WHAT'S YOUR NAME?
...SARAH.
SARAH, CAN YOU TELL ME WHAT HAPPENED HERE?
...
IT'S OKAY... YOU CAN TALK TO ME.
WHERE ARE YOUR PARENTS?
...THEIR BEDROOM.
WHAT ARE THEY DOING THERE?
ARE *THEY* HURT?
...I THINK SO...
WHO HURT THEM?
...I'M SCARED. ...I WANT MY MOMMY.
HEY, HEY... DON'T BE SCARED, SARAH.
I'M HERE-- IT'S GONNA BE OKAY.
YOU'RE SAFE.

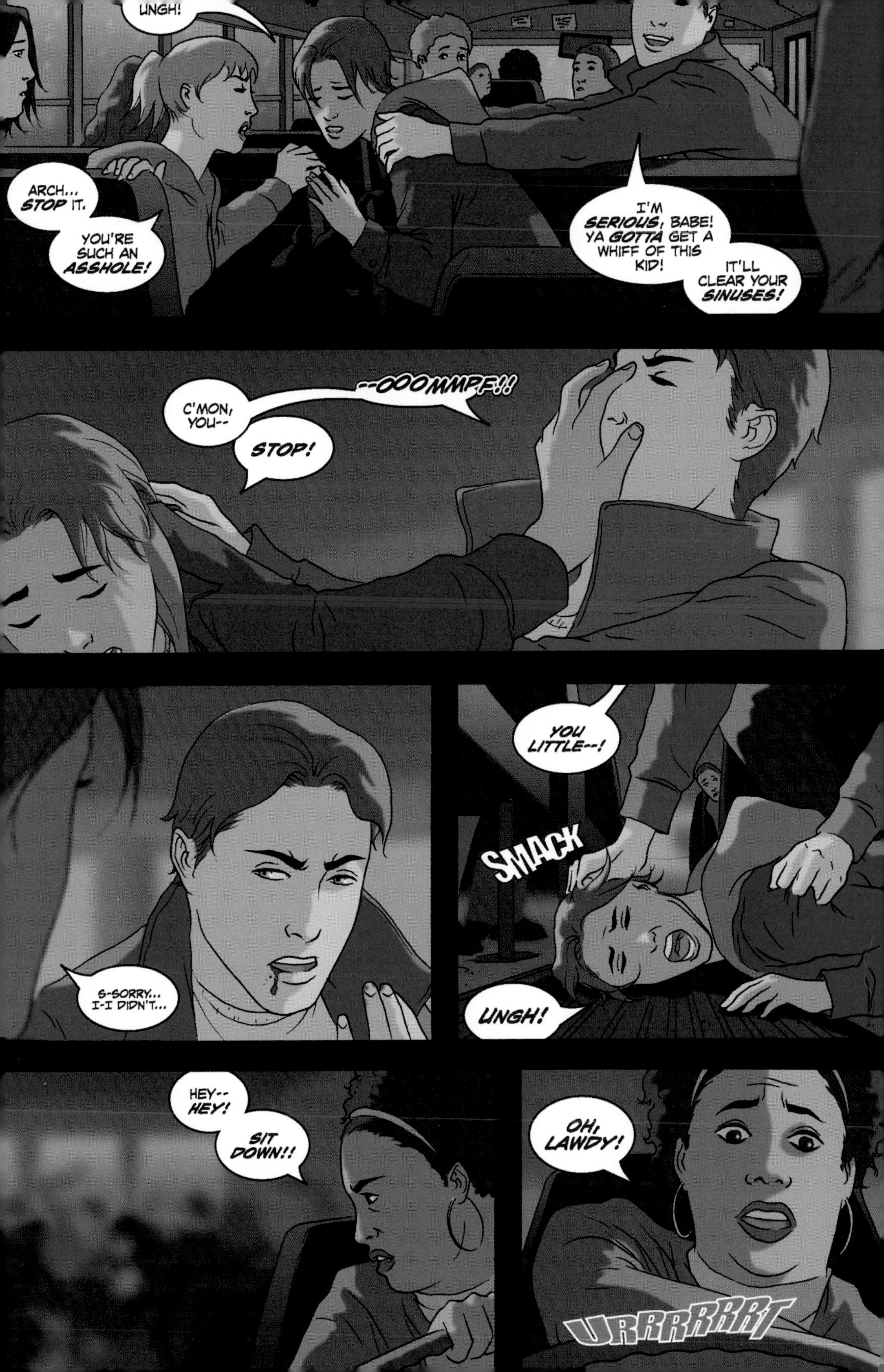
UNGH!
ARCH... STOP IT.
YOU'RE SUCH AN ASSHOLE!
I'M SERIOUS, BABE! YA GOTTA GET A WHIFF OF THIS KID!
IT'LL CLEAR YOUR SINUSES!
C'MON, YOU--
--OOOMMPF!!
STOP!
S-SORRY... I-I DIDN'T...
YOU LITTLE--!
SMACK
UNGH!
HEY-- HEY!
SIT DOWN!!
OH, LAWDY!
URRRRRRT

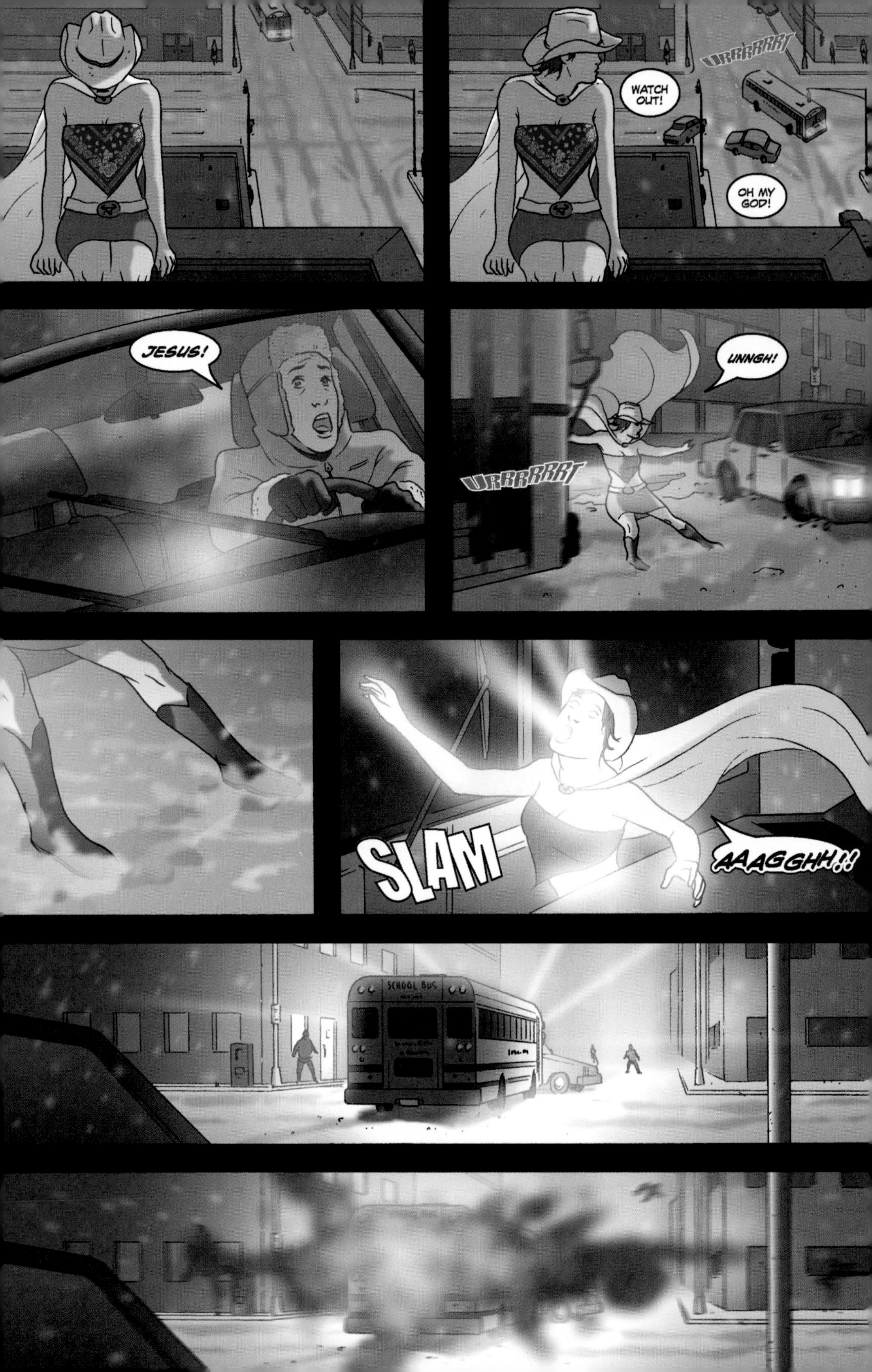
URRRRRRT
WATCH OUT!
OH MY GOD!
JESUS!
UNNGH!
URRRRRRT
SLAM
AAAGGHH!!
SCHOOL BUS

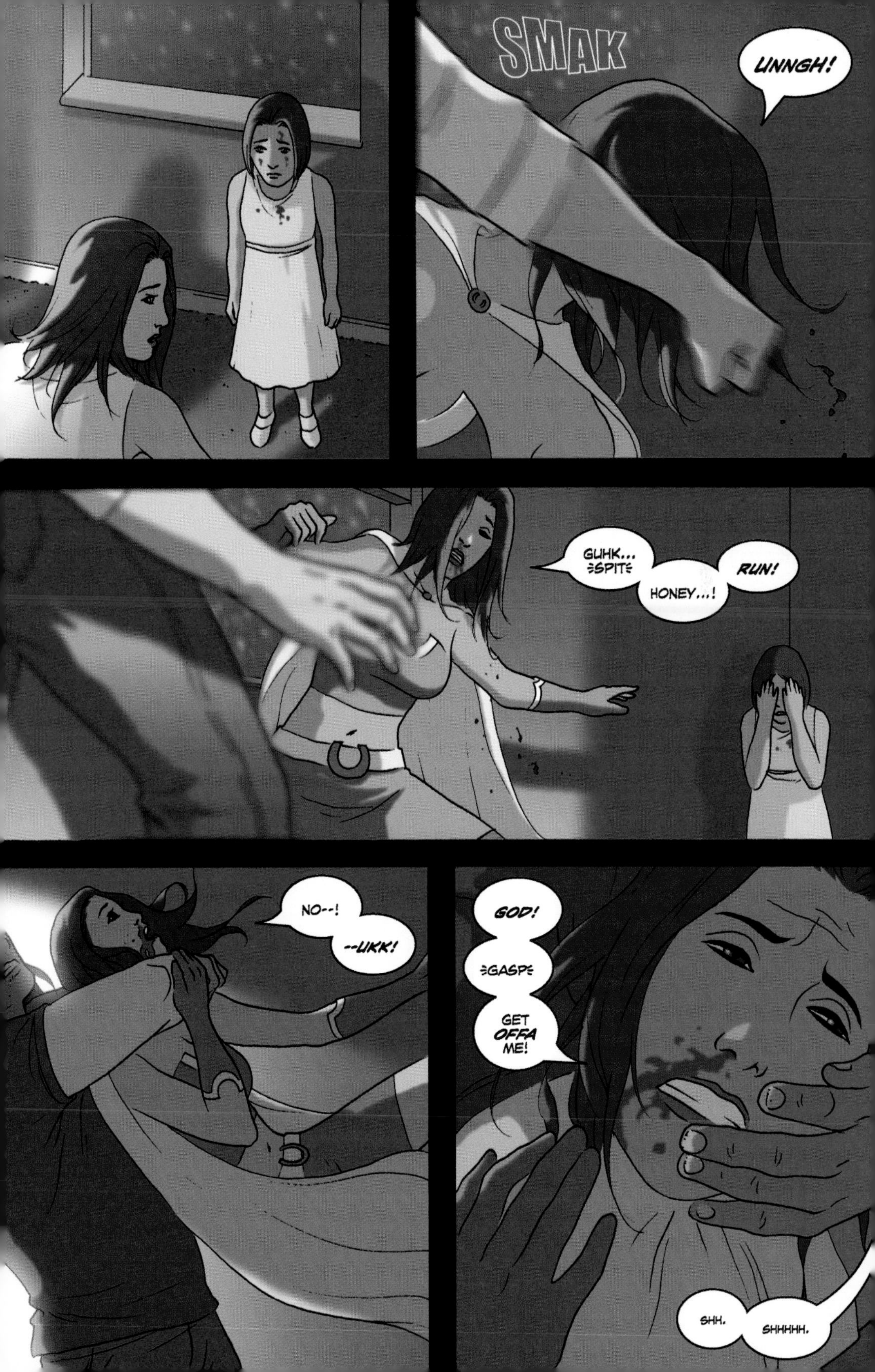
SMAK
UNNGH!
GUHK... SPIT
HONEY...!
RUN!
NO--!
--UKK!
GOD!
GASP
GET OFFA ME!
SHH.
SHHHHH.

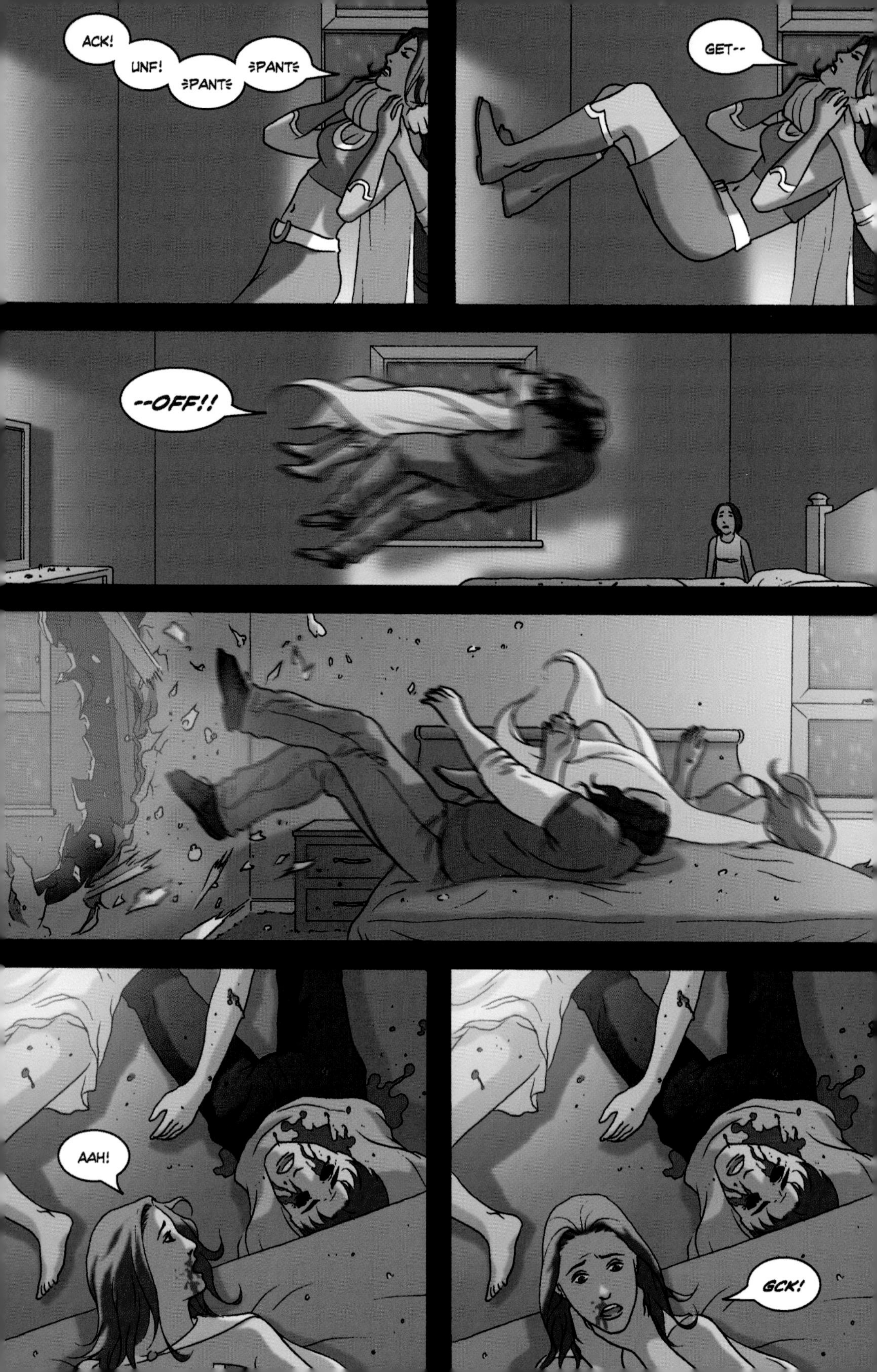
ACK!
UNF!
PANT
PANT
GET--
--OFF!!
AAH!
GCK!

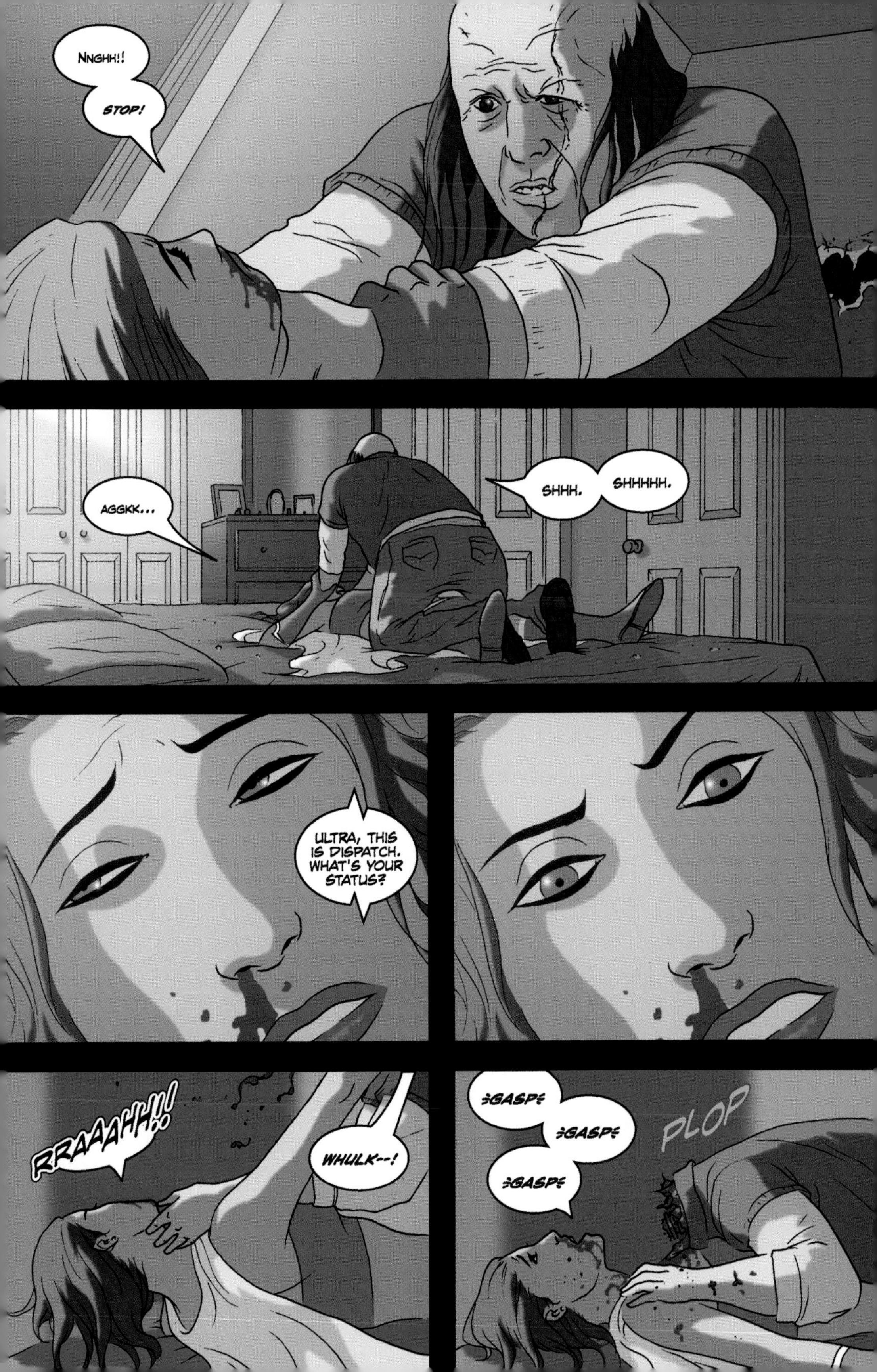
NNGHH!!
STOP!
AGGKK...
SHHH.
SHHHHH.
ULTRA, THIS IS DISPATCH. WHAT'S YOUR STATUS?
RRAAAHH!!
WHULK--!
PLOP
GASP
GASP
GASP

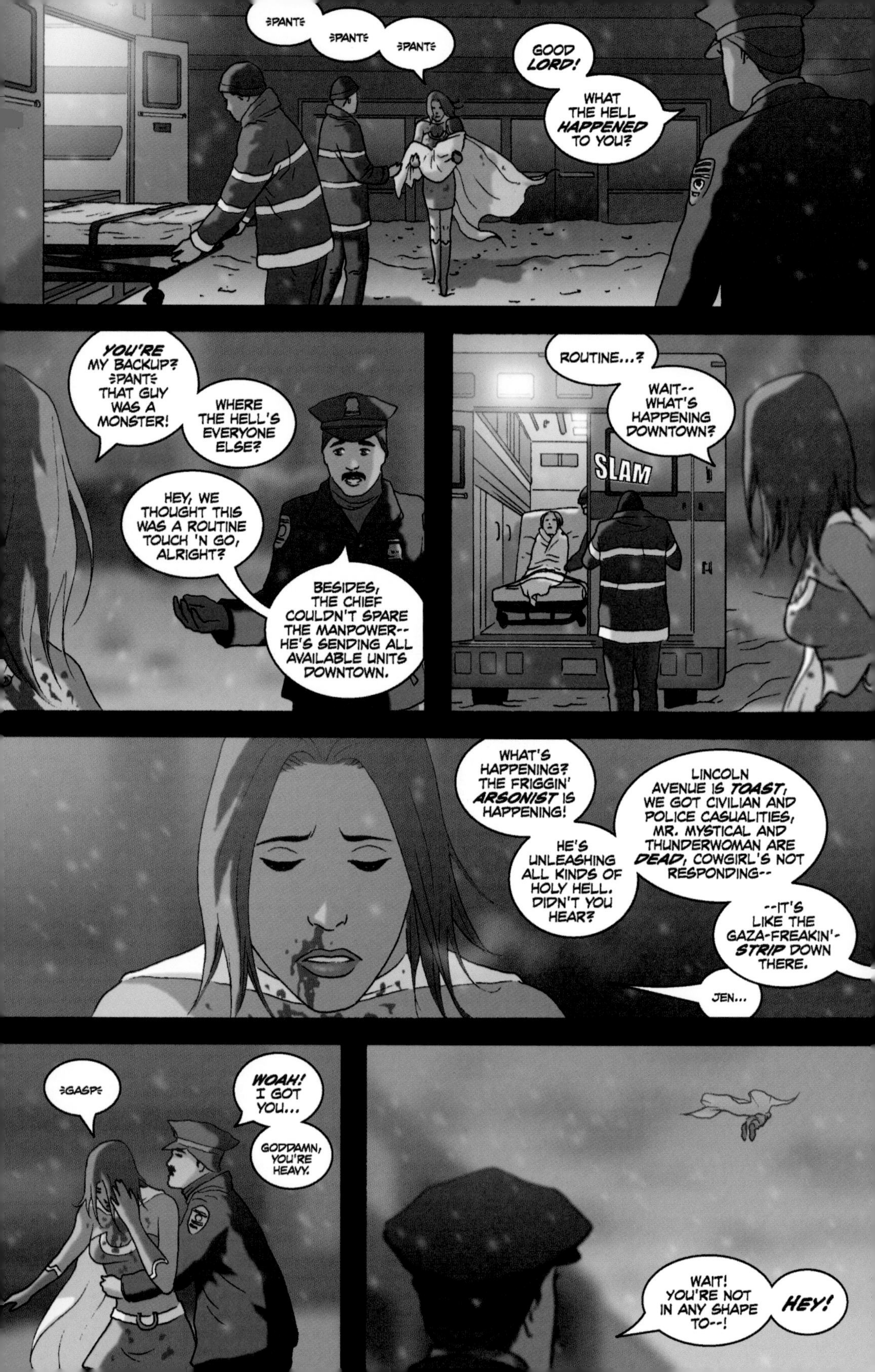

≥PANT≤
≥PANT≤
≥PANT≤
GOOD LORD!
WHAT THE HELL HAPPENED TO YOU?
YOU'RE MY BACKUP? ≥PANT≤ THAT GUY WAS A MONSTER!
WHERE THE HELL'S EVERYONE ELSE?
HEY, WE THOUGHT THIS WAS A ROUTINE TOUCH 'N GO, ALRIGHT?
BESIDES, THE CHIEF COULDN'T SPARE THE MANPOWER-- HE'S SENDING ALL AVAILABLE UNITS DOWNTOWN.
ROUTINE...?
WAIT-- WHAT'S HAPPENING DOWNTOWN?
SLAM
WHAT'S HAPPENING? THE FRIGGIN' ARSONIST IS HAPPENING!
HE'S UNLEASHING ALL KINDS OF HOLY HELL. DIDN'T YOU HEAR?
LINCOLN AVENUE IS TOAST, WE GOT CIVILIAN AND POLICE CASUALITIES, MR. MYSTICAL AND THUNDERWOMAN ARE DEAD, COWGIRL'S NOT RESPONDING--
--IT'S LIKE THE GAZA-FREAKIN'-STRIP DOWN THERE.
JEN...
≥GASP≤
WOAH! I GOT YOU...
GODDAMN, YOU'RE HEAVY.
WAIT! YOU'RE NOT IN ANY SHAPE TO--!
HEY!

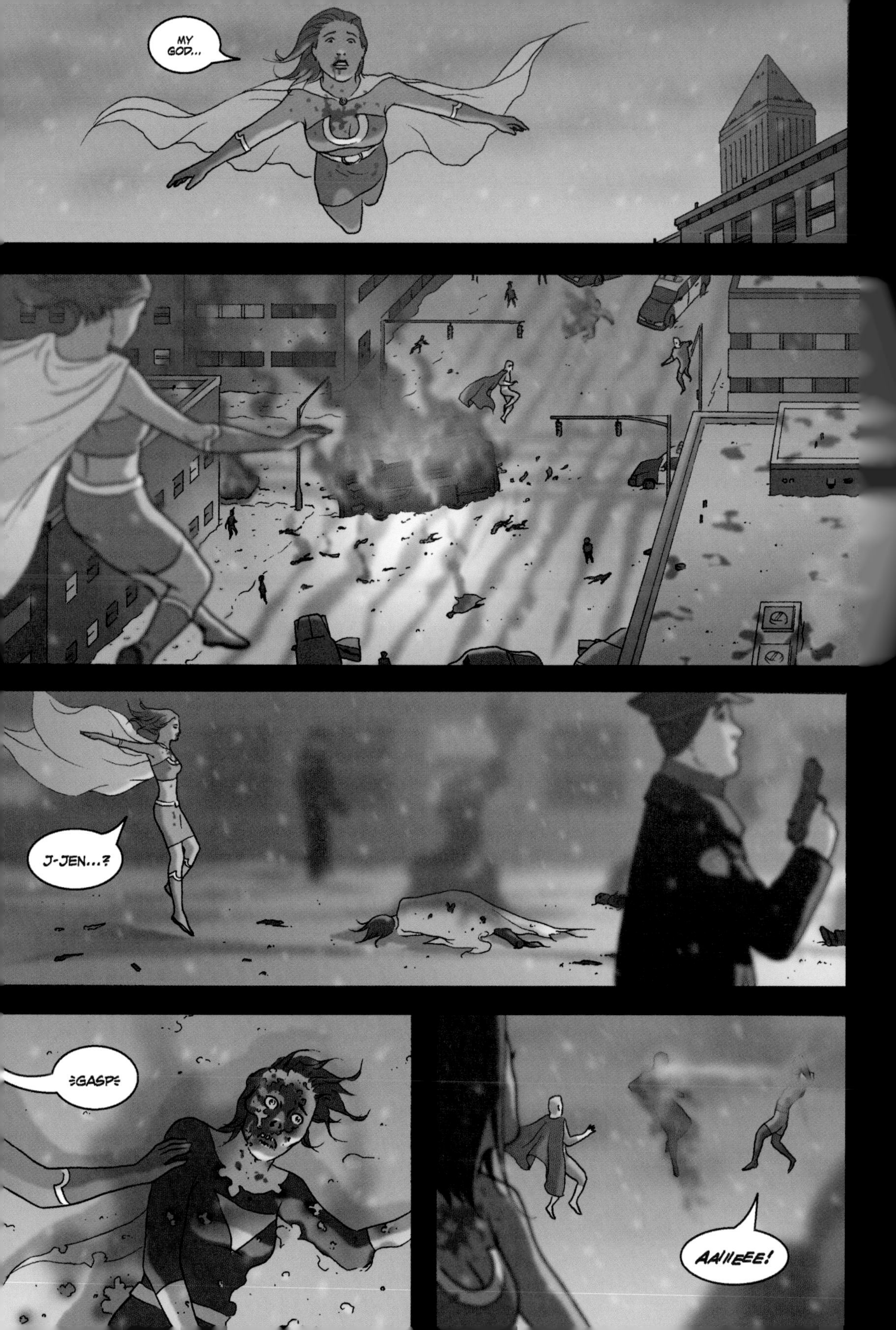
MY GOD...
J-JEN...?
≠GASP≠
AAIIEEE!

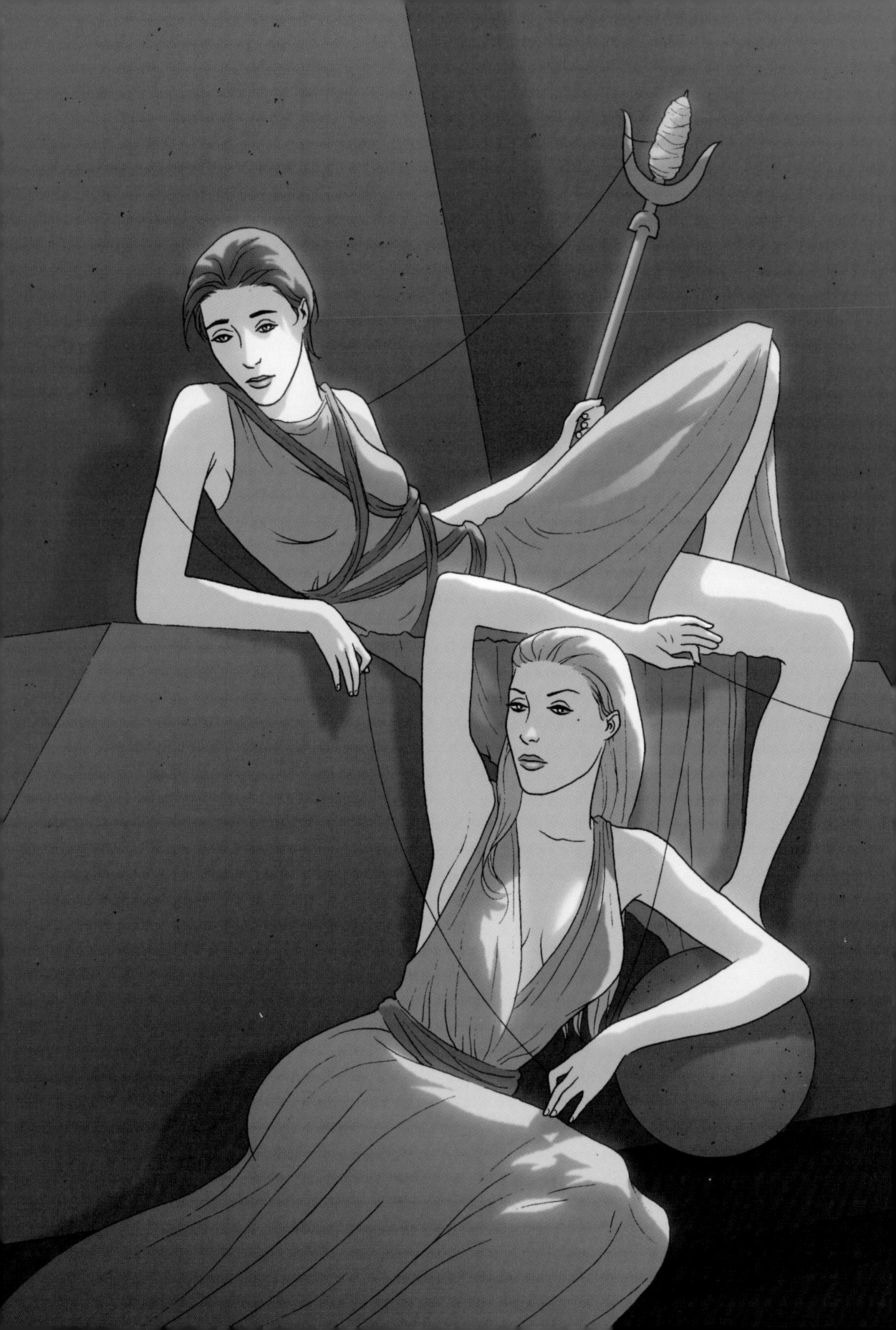

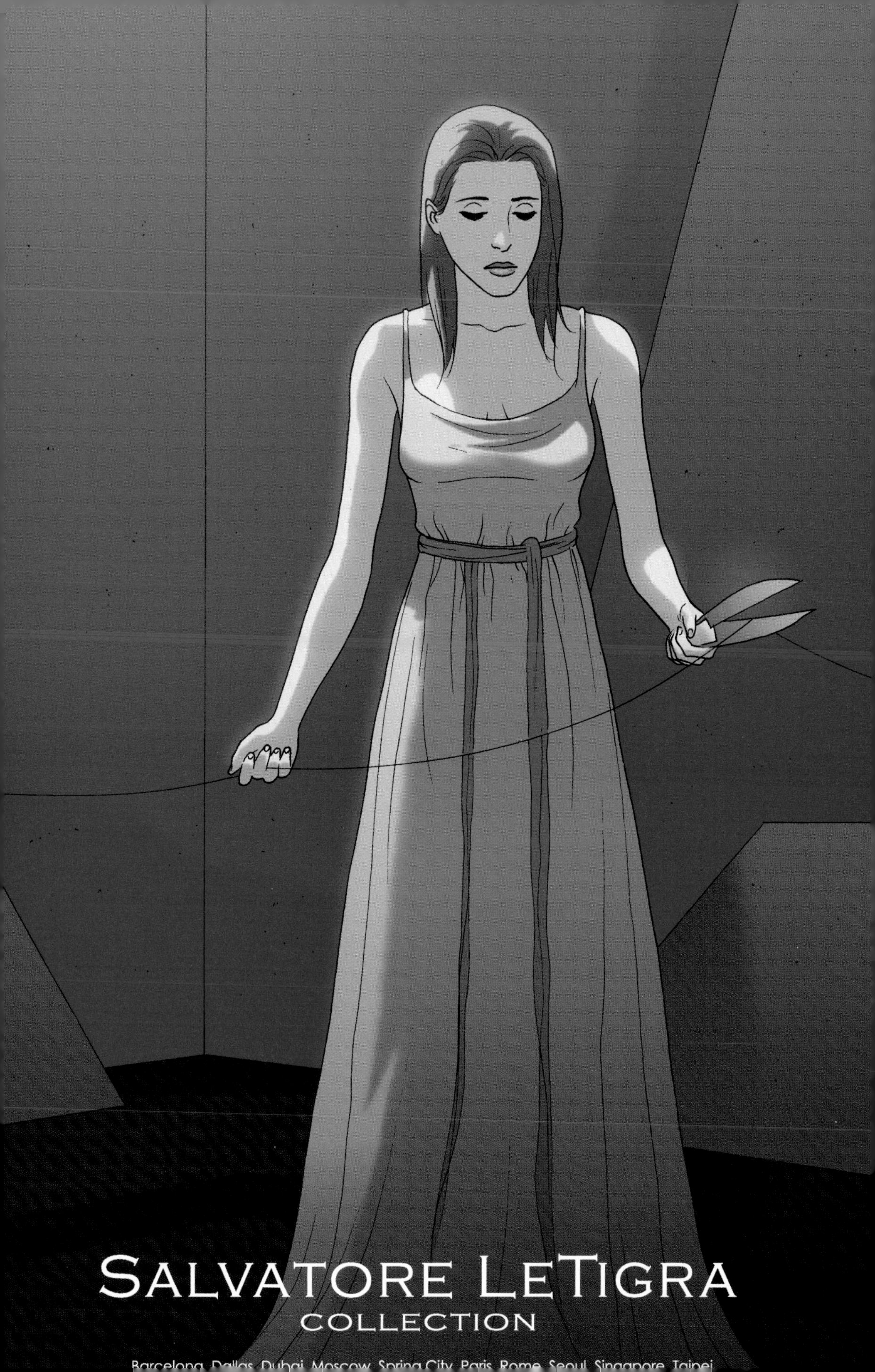
SALVATORE LETIGRA
COLLECTION
Barcelona Dallas Dubai Moscow Spring City Paris Rome Seoul Singapore Taipei

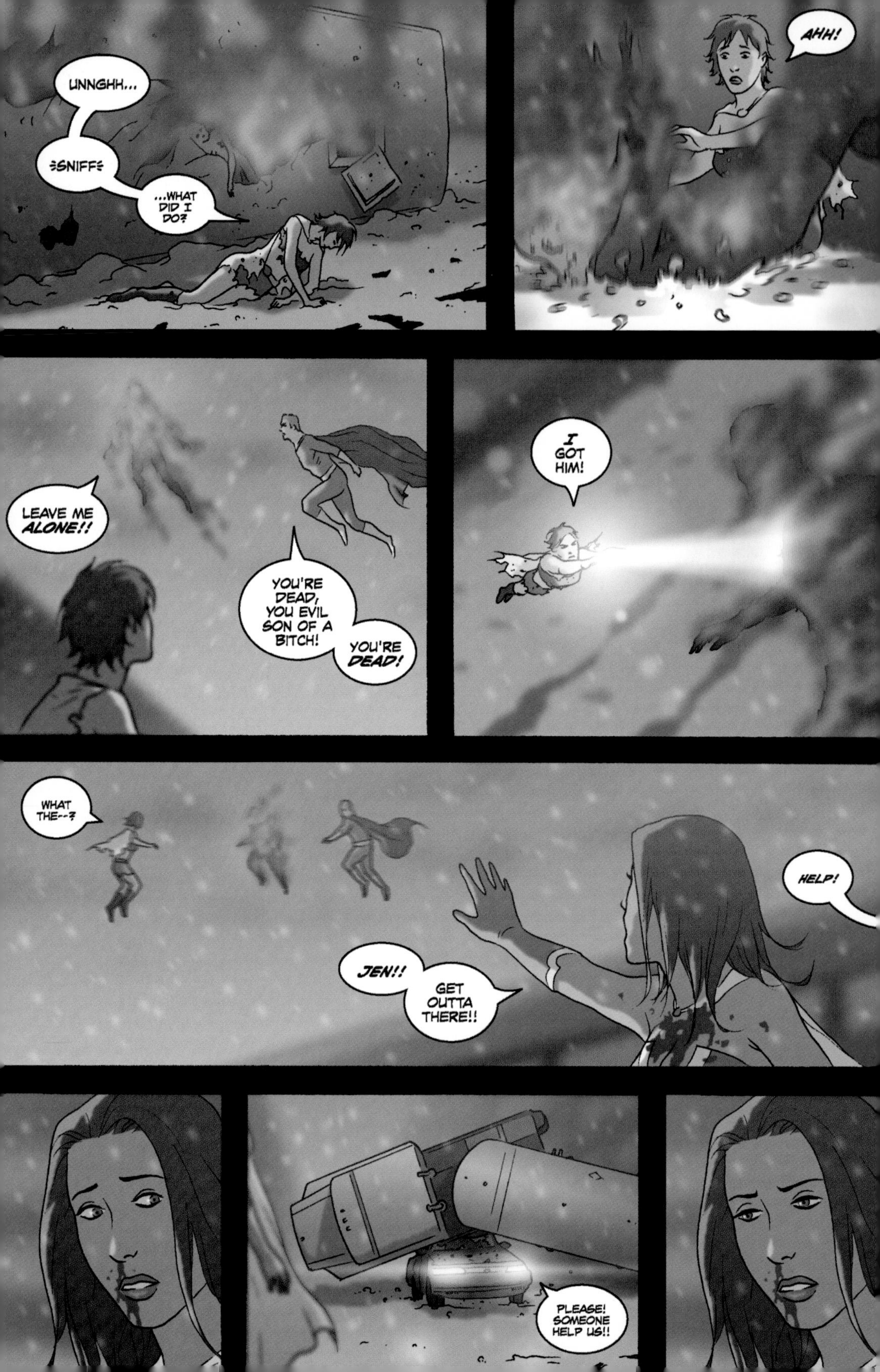
UNNGHH...
SNIFF
...WHAT DID I DO?
AHH!
LEAVE ME ALONE!!
YOU'RE DEAD, YOU EVIL SON OF A BITCH!
YOU'RE DEAD!
I GOT HIM!
WHAT THE--?
HELP!
JEN!!
GET OUTTA THERE!!
PLEASE! SOMEONE HELP US!!

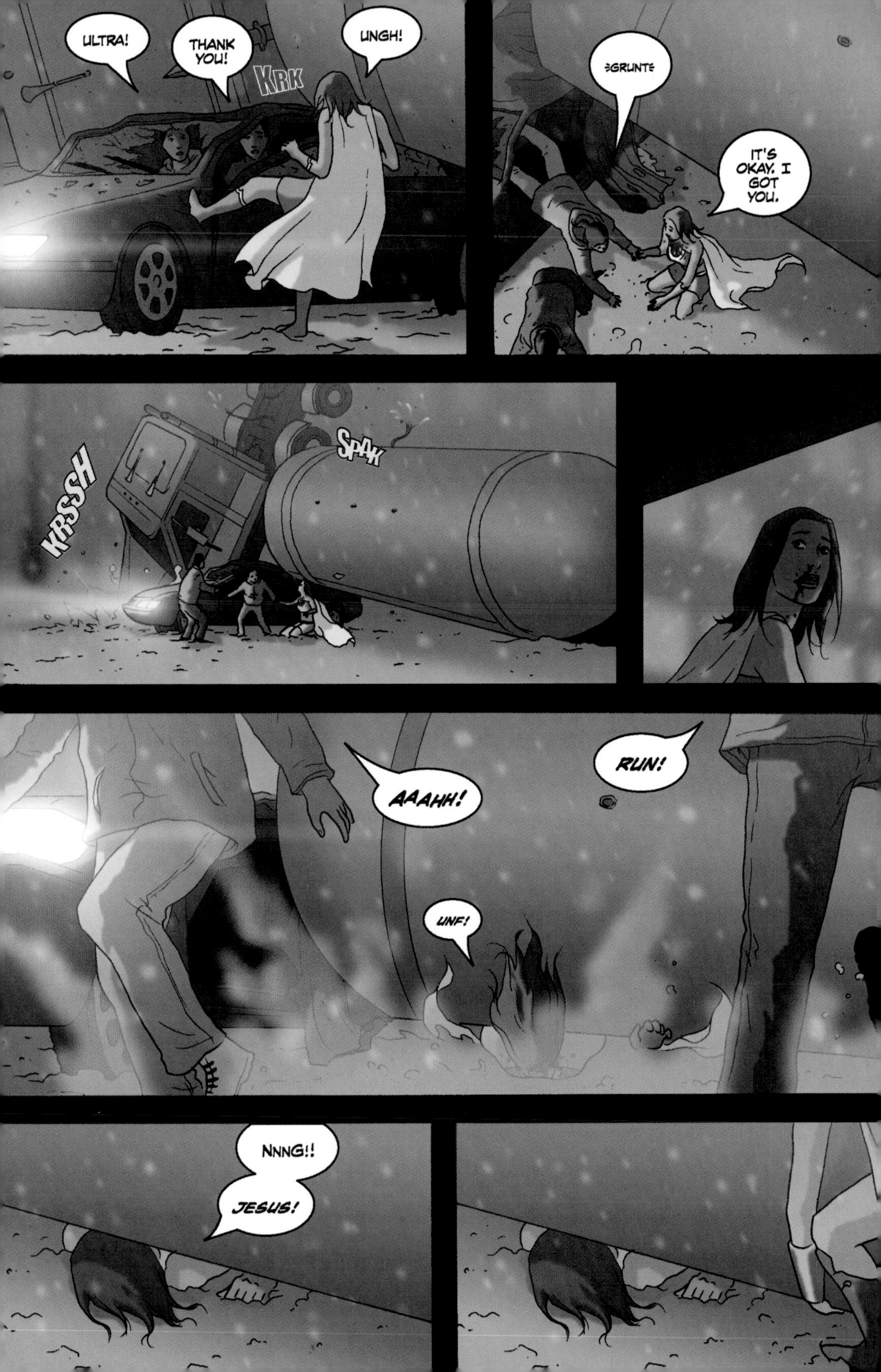
ULTRA!
THANK YOU!
UNGH!
KRK
≡GRUNT≡
IT'S OKAY. I GOT YOU.
KRSSH
SPAK
AAAHH!
RUN!
UNF!
NNNG!!
JESUS!

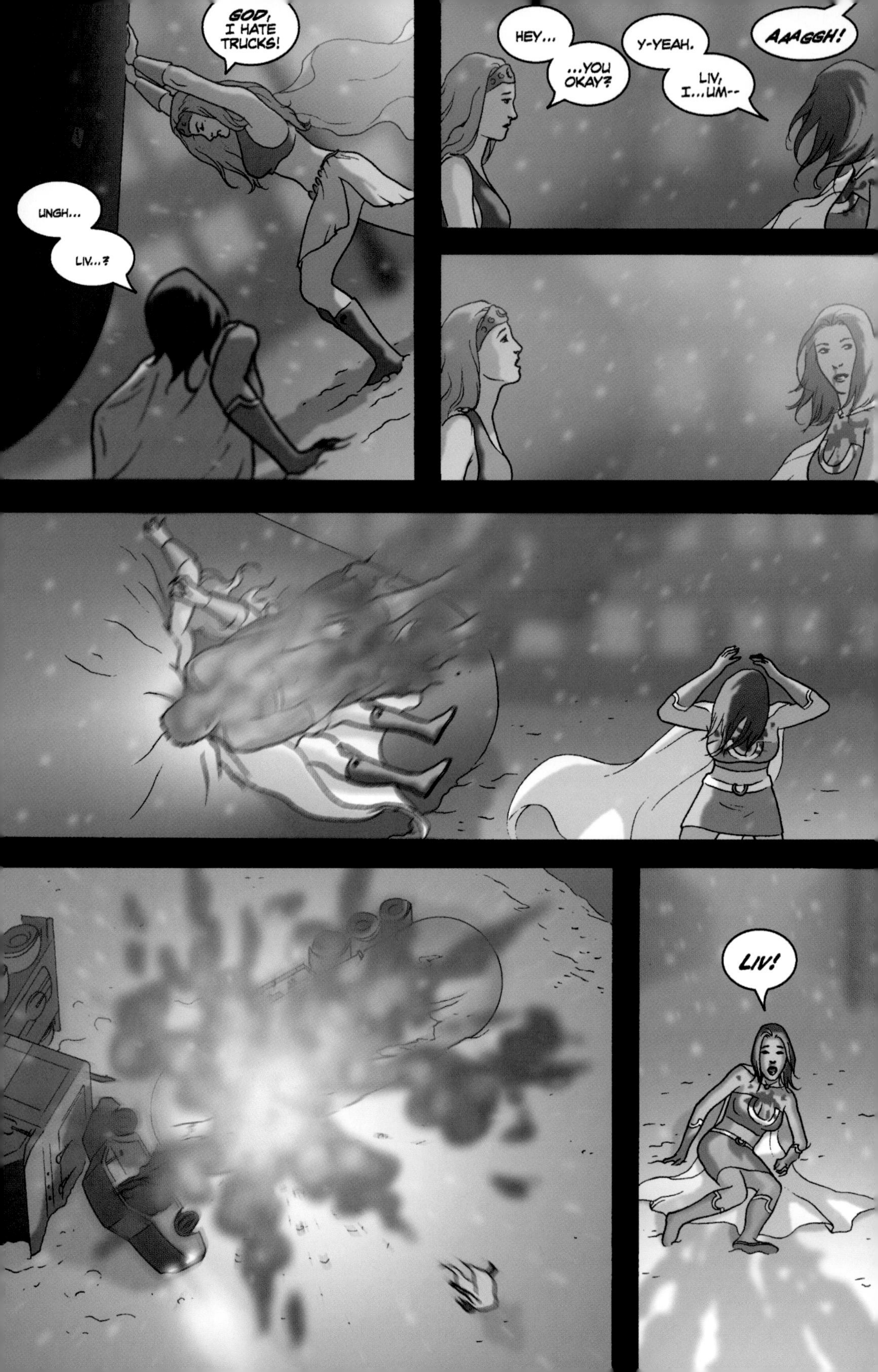
GOD, I HATE TRUCKS!
UNGH...
LIV...?
HEY...
...YOU OKAY?
Y-YEAH.
LIV, I...UM--
AAAGGH!
LIV!

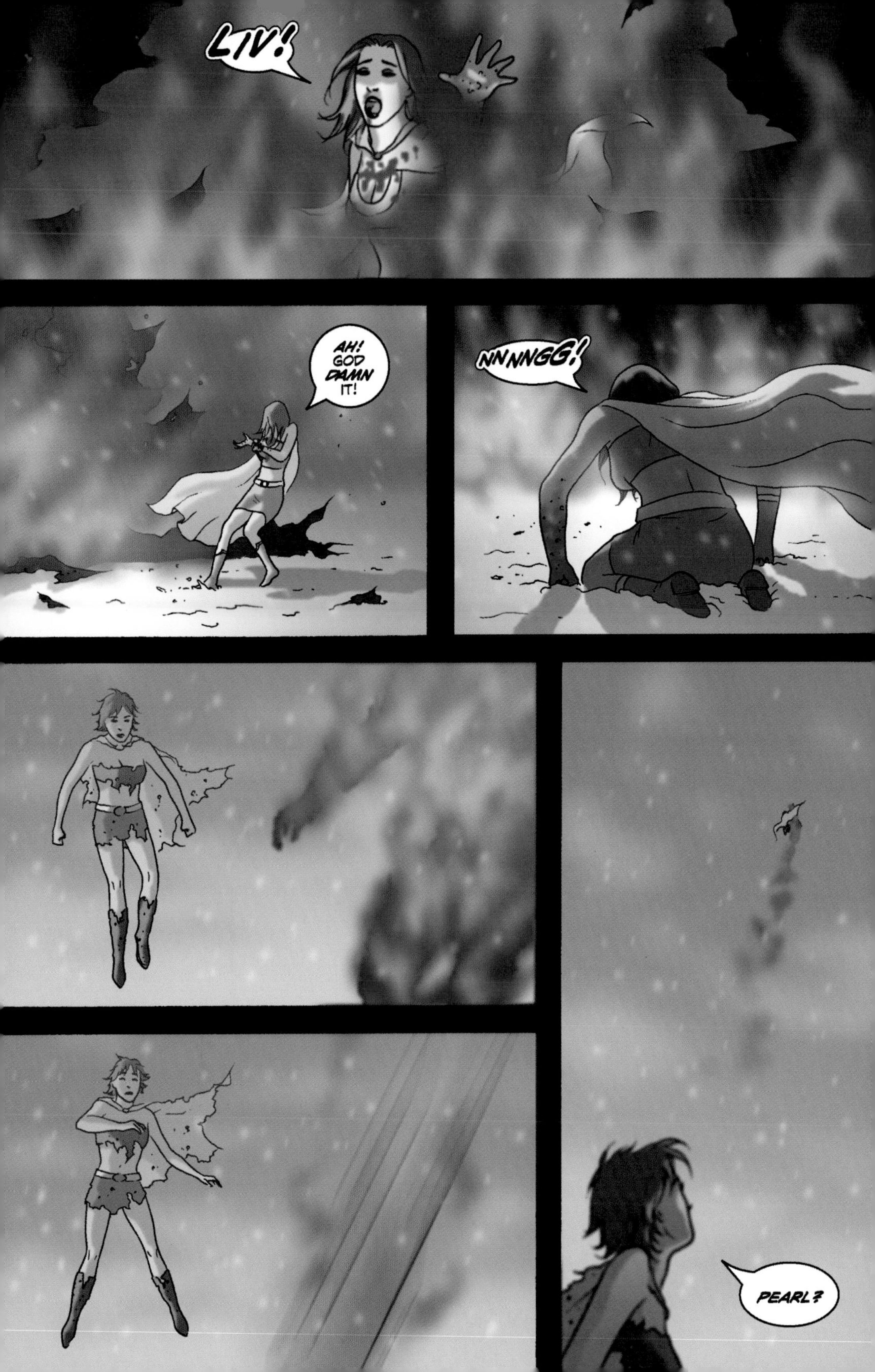
LIV!
AH! GOD DAMN IT!
NNNNGG!
PEARL?

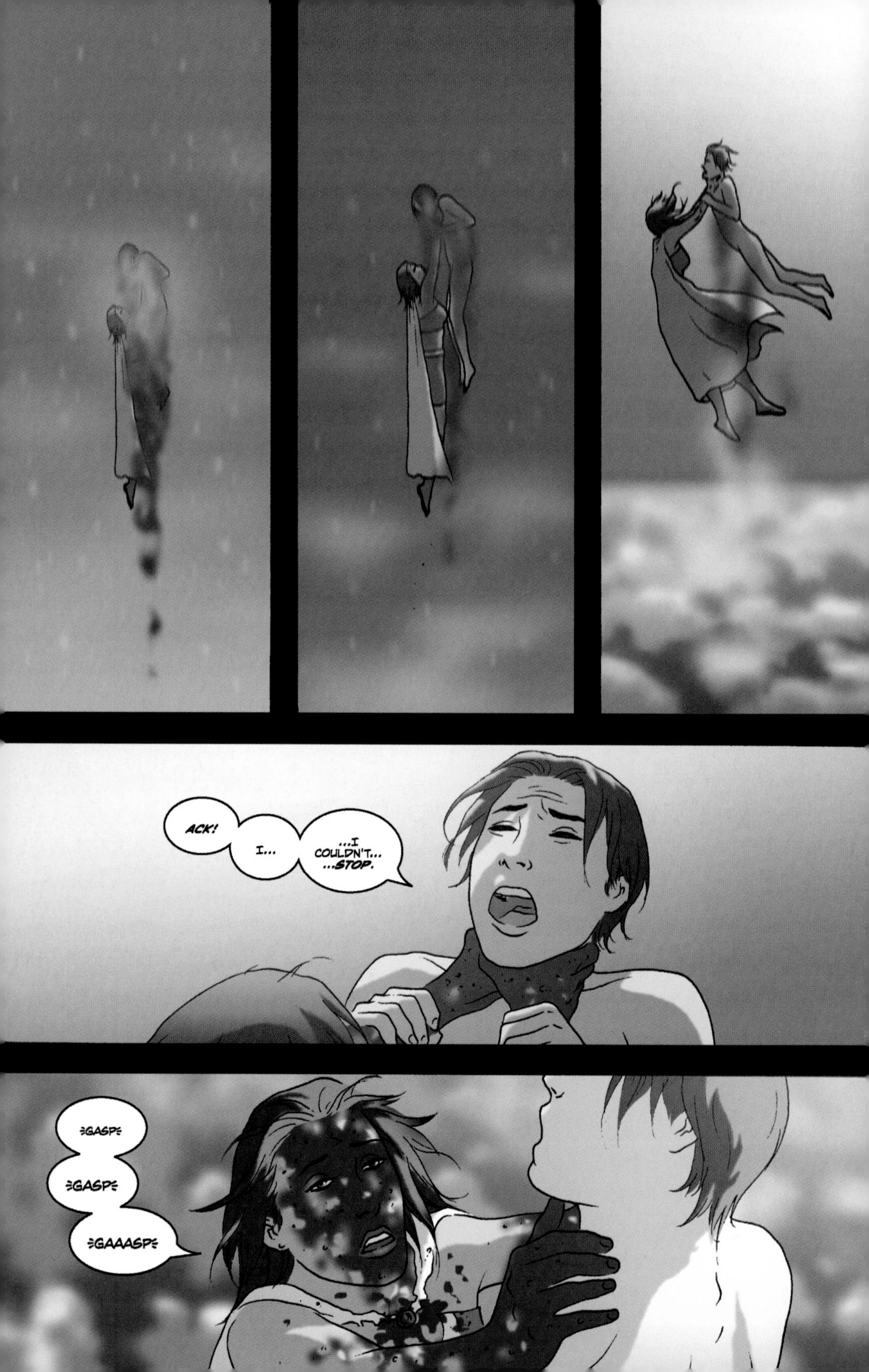
ACK!
I...
...I COULDN'T... ...STOP.
GASP
GASP
GAAASP

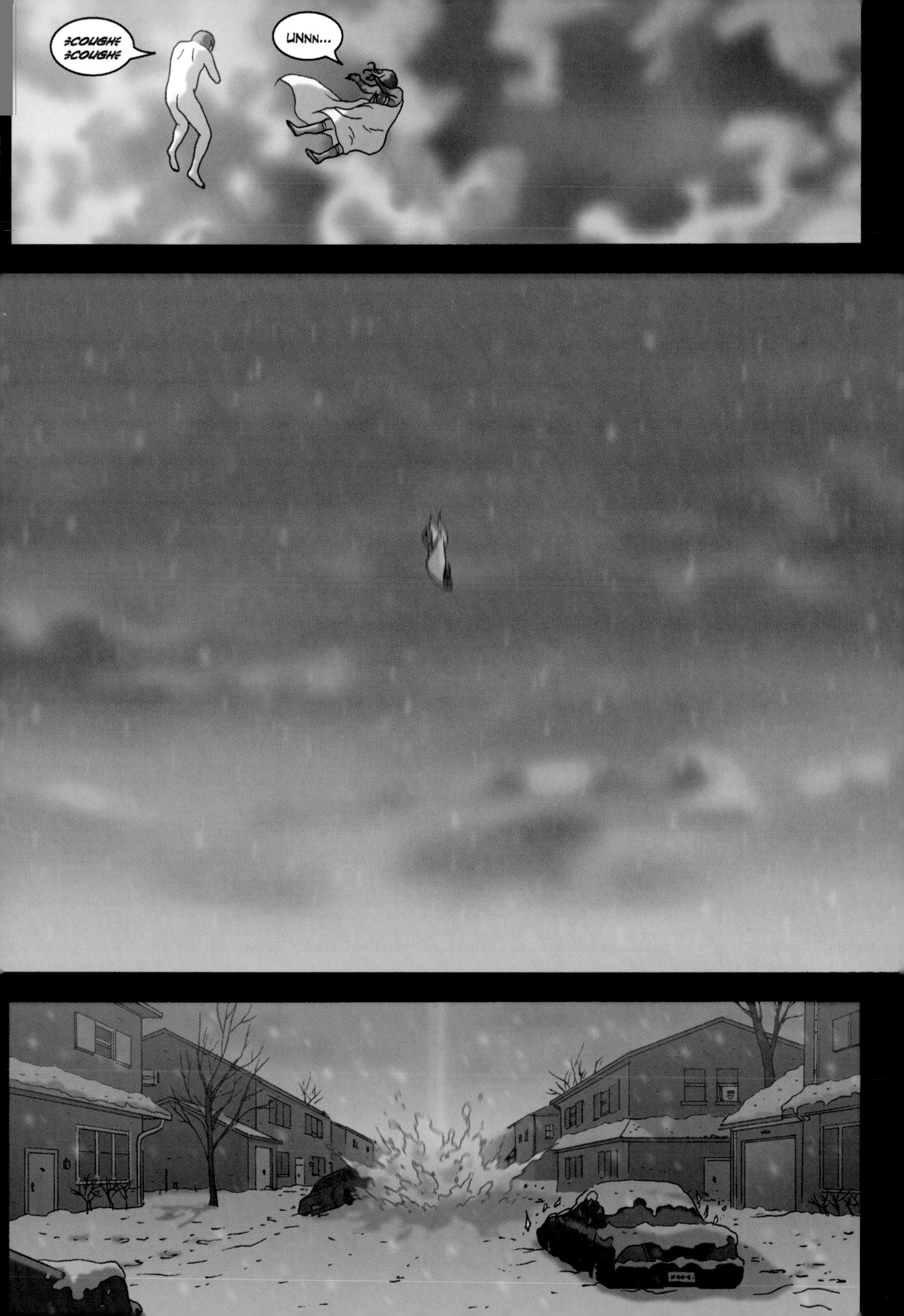

COUGH
COUGH
UNNN...

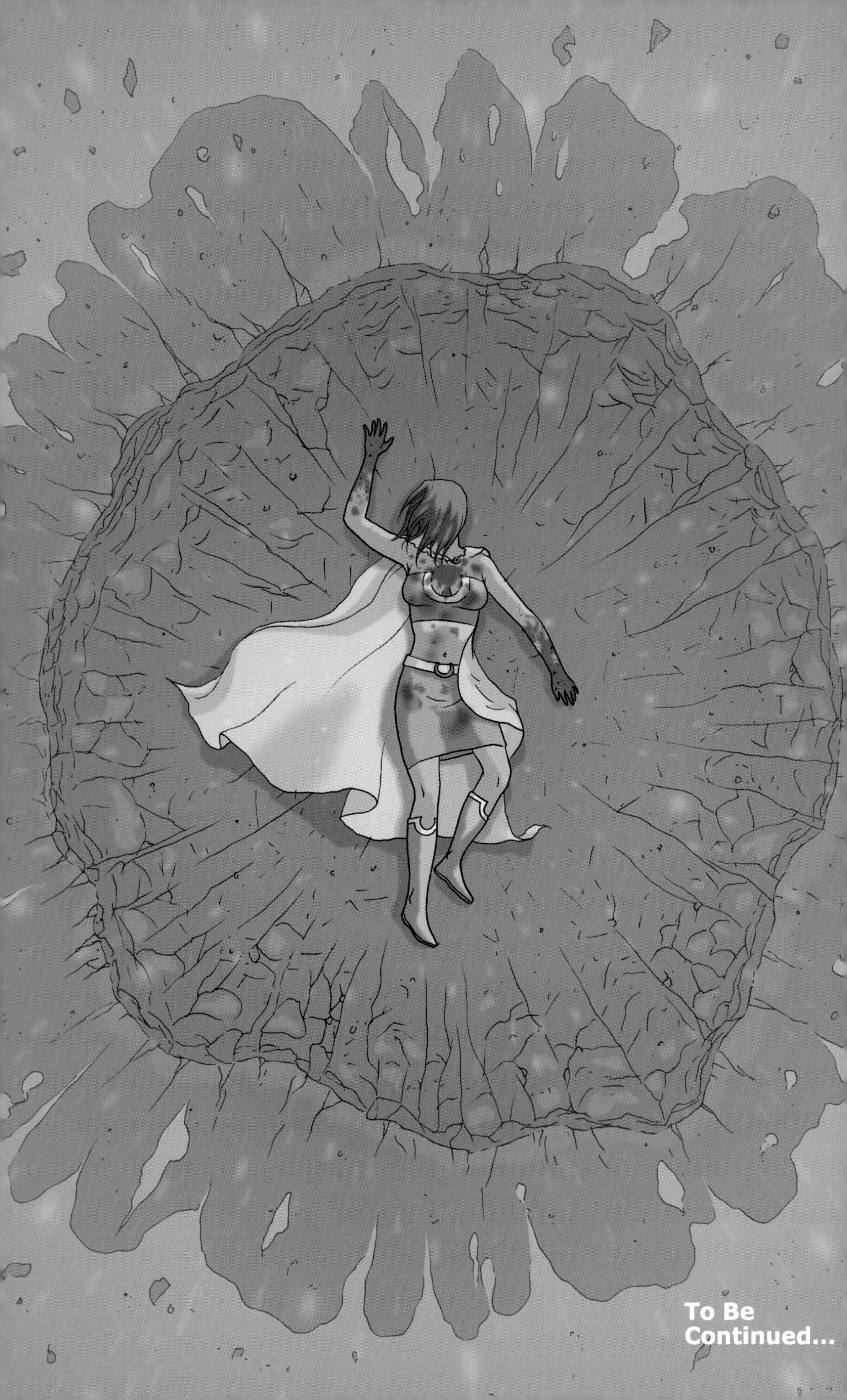
To Be
Continued...

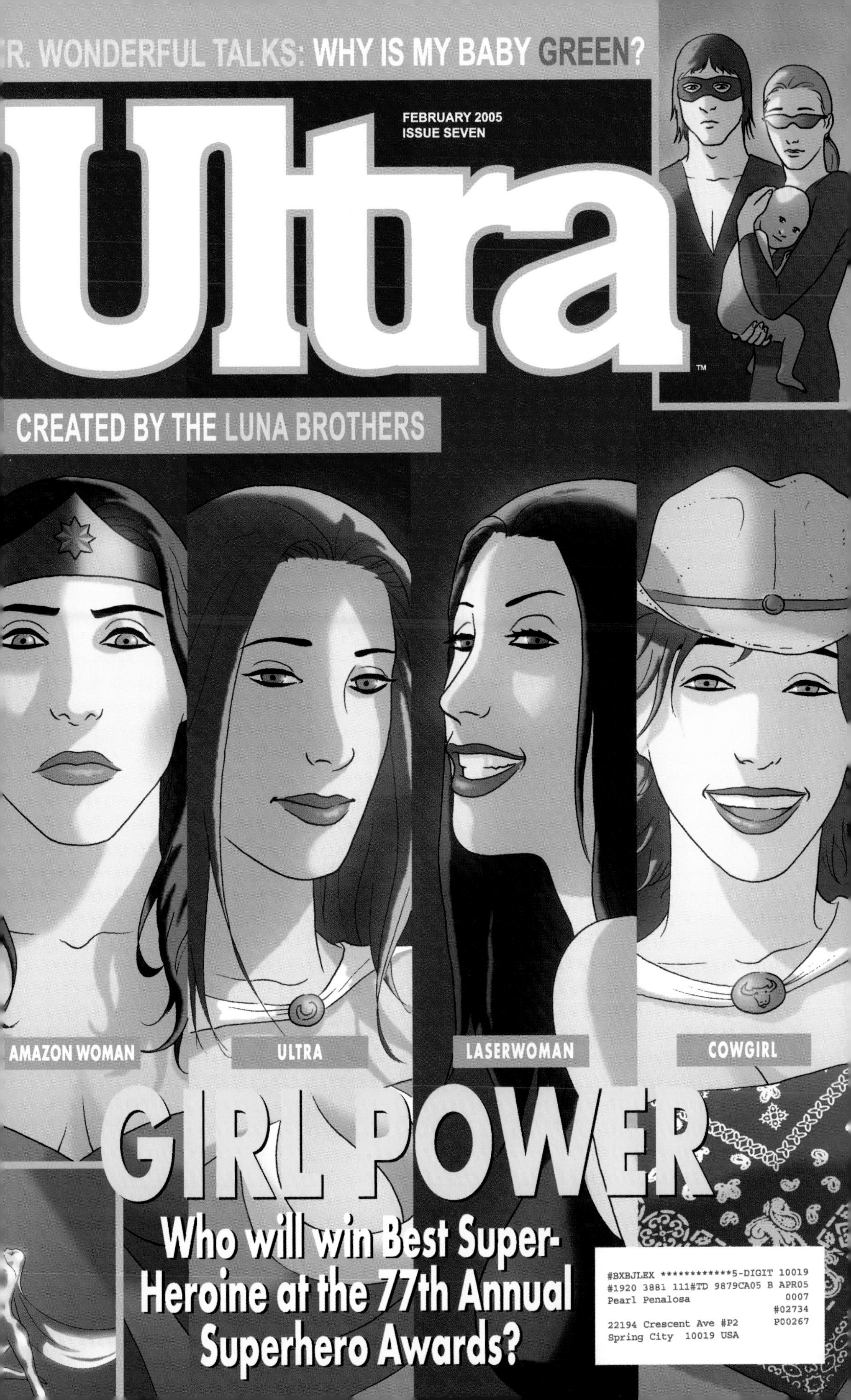
R. WONDERFUL TALKS: WHY IS MY BABY GREEN?
Ultra™
FEBRUARY 2005
ISSUE SEVEN
CREATED BY THE LUNA BROTHERS
AMAZON WOMAN
ULTRA
LASERWOMAN
COWGIRL
GIRL POWER
Who will win Best Super-Heroine at the 77th Annual Superhero Awards?
#BXBJLEX ************5-DIGIT 10019
#1920 3881 111#TD 9879CA05 B APR05
Pearl Penalosa 0007
#02734
22194 Crescent Ave #P2 P00267
Spring City 10019 USA

FEBRUARY 2005 • VOL. 1 • ISSUE 7

Ultra™

image® COMICS PRESENTS

3 THIS ISSUE
SEVEN DAYS, Part Seven

112 CREATED BY
THE LUNA BROTHERS

114 CREDITS
JOSHUA LUNA
    Plot, Script, Layouts
JONATHAN LUNA
    Plot, Art, Colors, Letters

120 OFFICIAL WEBSITE
www.LunaBrothers.com

148 **SWEET AND SOUR** still scaling walls despite having elevators at their disposal.

60 **CAPED CASTAWAYS,** the hit reality show featuring stranded superheroes who can leave the island whenever they want.

FOR IMAGE COMICS

Erik Larsen
Publisher

Todd McFarlane
President

Marc Silvestri
CEO

Jim Valentino
Vice-President

Eric Stephenson
Executive Director

Missie Miranda
Controller

Brett Evans
Production Manager

B. Clay Moore
Public Relations &
Marketing Coordinator

Allen Hui
Production Artist

Joe Keatinge
Inventory Controller

Mia Machatton
Administrative Assistant

image

www.ImageComics.com

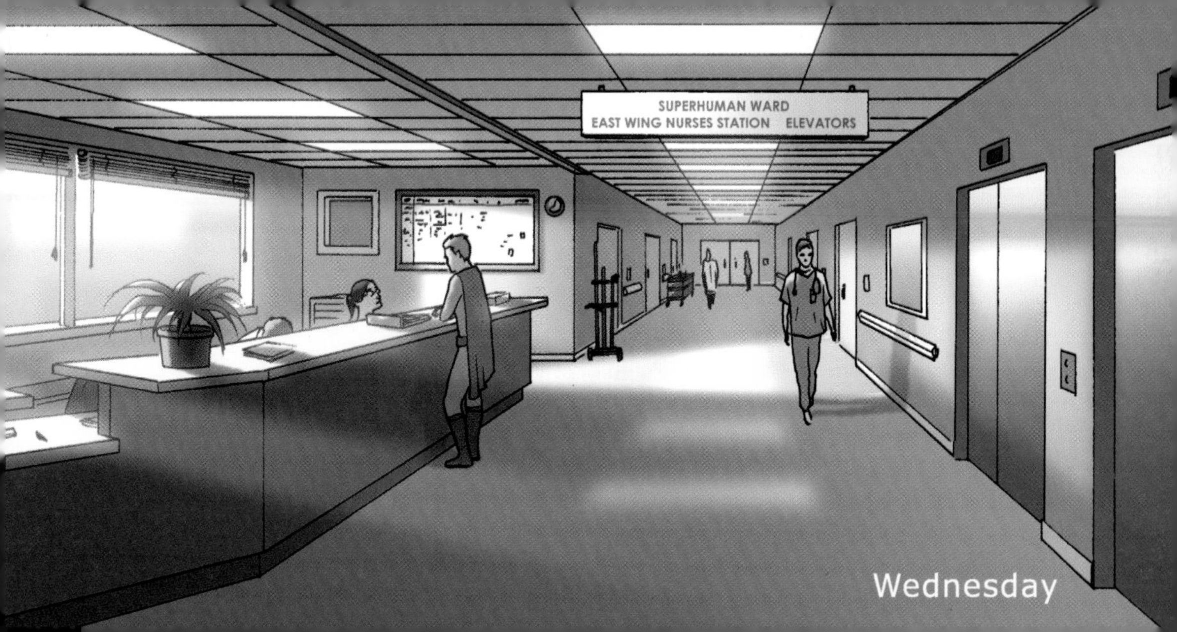
SUPERHUMAN WARD
EAST WING NURSES STATION ELEVATORS
Wednesday

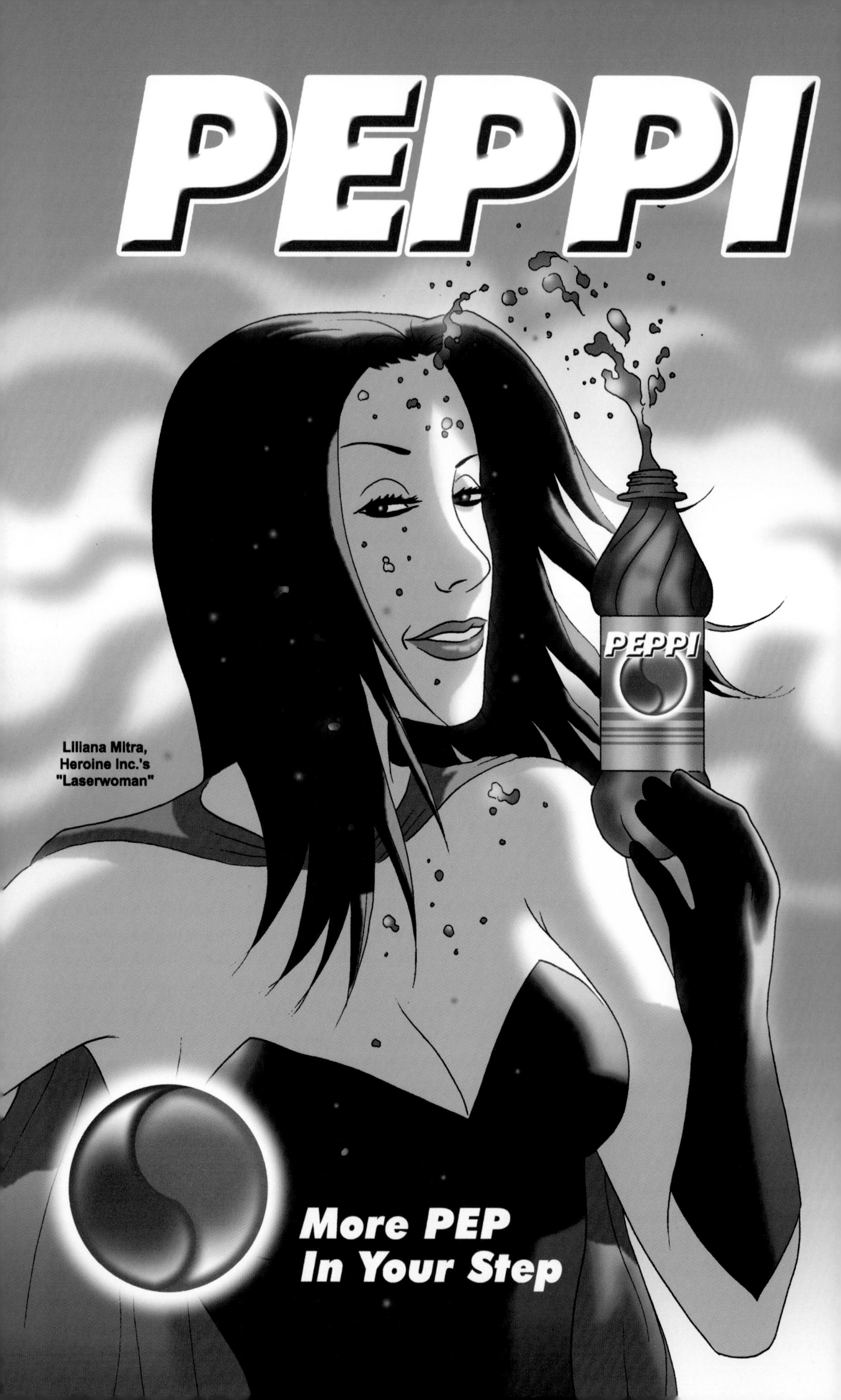

PEPPI
PEPPI
Liliana Mitra,
Heroine Inc.'s
"Laserwoman"
More PEP
In Your Step

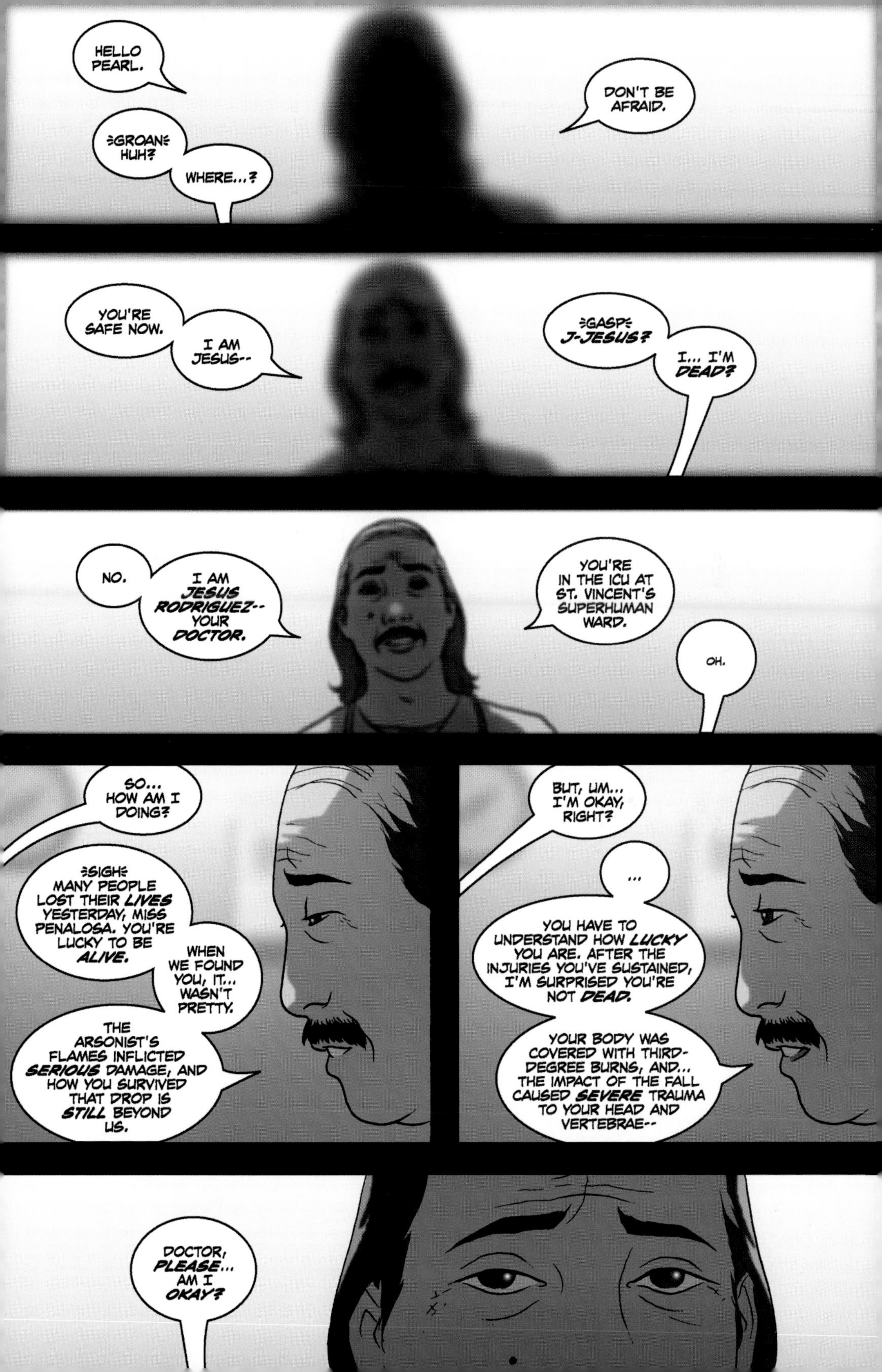
HELLO PEARL.
=GROAN= HUH?
WHERE...?
DON'T BE AFRAID.
YOU'RE SAFE NOW.
I AM JESUS--
=GASP= J-JESUS?
I... I'M DEAD?
NO.
I AM JESUS RODRIGUEZ-- YOUR DOCTOR.
YOU'RE IN THE ICU AT ST. VINCENT'S SUPERHUMAN WARD.
OH.
SO... HOW AM I DOING?
=SIGH= MANY PEOPLE LOST THEIR LIVES YESTERDAY, MISS PENALOSA. YOU'RE LUCKY TO BE ALIVE.
WHEN WE FOUND YOU, IT... WASN'T PRETTY.
THE ARSONIST'S FLAMES INFLICTED SERIOUS DAMAGE, AND HOW YOU SURVIVED THAT DROP IS STILL BEYOND US.
BUT, UM... I'M OKAY, RIGHT?
...
YOU HAVE TO UNDERSTAND HOW LUCKY YOU ARE. AFTER THE INJURIES YOU'VE SUSTAINED, I'M SURPRISED YOU'RE NOT DEAD.
YOUR BODY WAS COVERED WITH THIRD-DEGREE BURNS, AND... THE IMPACT OF THE FALL CAUSED SEVERE TRAUMA TO YOUR HEAD AND VERTEBRAE--
DOCTOR, PLEASE... AM I OKAY?

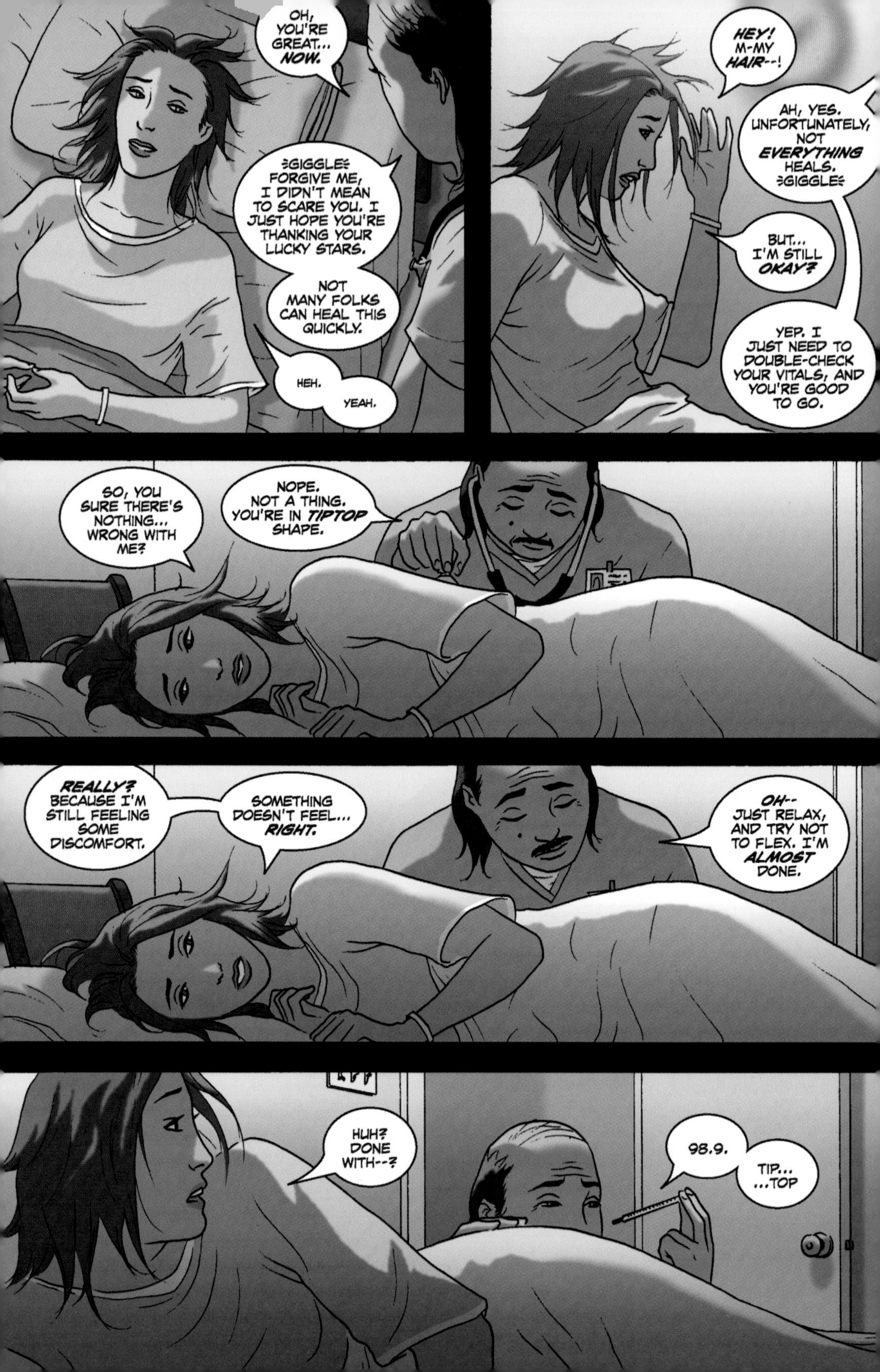
OH, YOU'RE GREAT... NOW.
≡GIGGLE≡ FORGIVE ME, I DIDN'T MEAN TO SCARE YOU. I JUST HOPE YOU'RE THANKING YOUR LUCKY STARS.
NOT MANY FOLKS CAN HEAL THIS QUICKLY.
HEH.
YEAH.
HEY! M-MY HAIR--!
AH, YES. UNFORTUNATELY, NOT EVERYTHING HEALS. ≡GIGGLE≡
BUT... I'M STILL OKAY?
YEP. I JUST NEED TO DOUBLE-CHECK YOUR VITALS, AND YOU'RE GOOD TO GO.
SO, YOU SURE THERE'S NOTHING... WRONG WITH ME?
NOPE. NOT A THING. YOU'RE IN TIPTOP SHAPE.
REALLY? BECAUSE I'M STILL FEELING SOME DISCOMFORT.
SOMETHING DOESN'T FEEL... RIGHT.
OH-- JUST RELAX, AND TRY NOT TO FLEX. I'M ALMOST DONE.
HUH? DONE WITH--?
98.9.
TIP... ...TOP

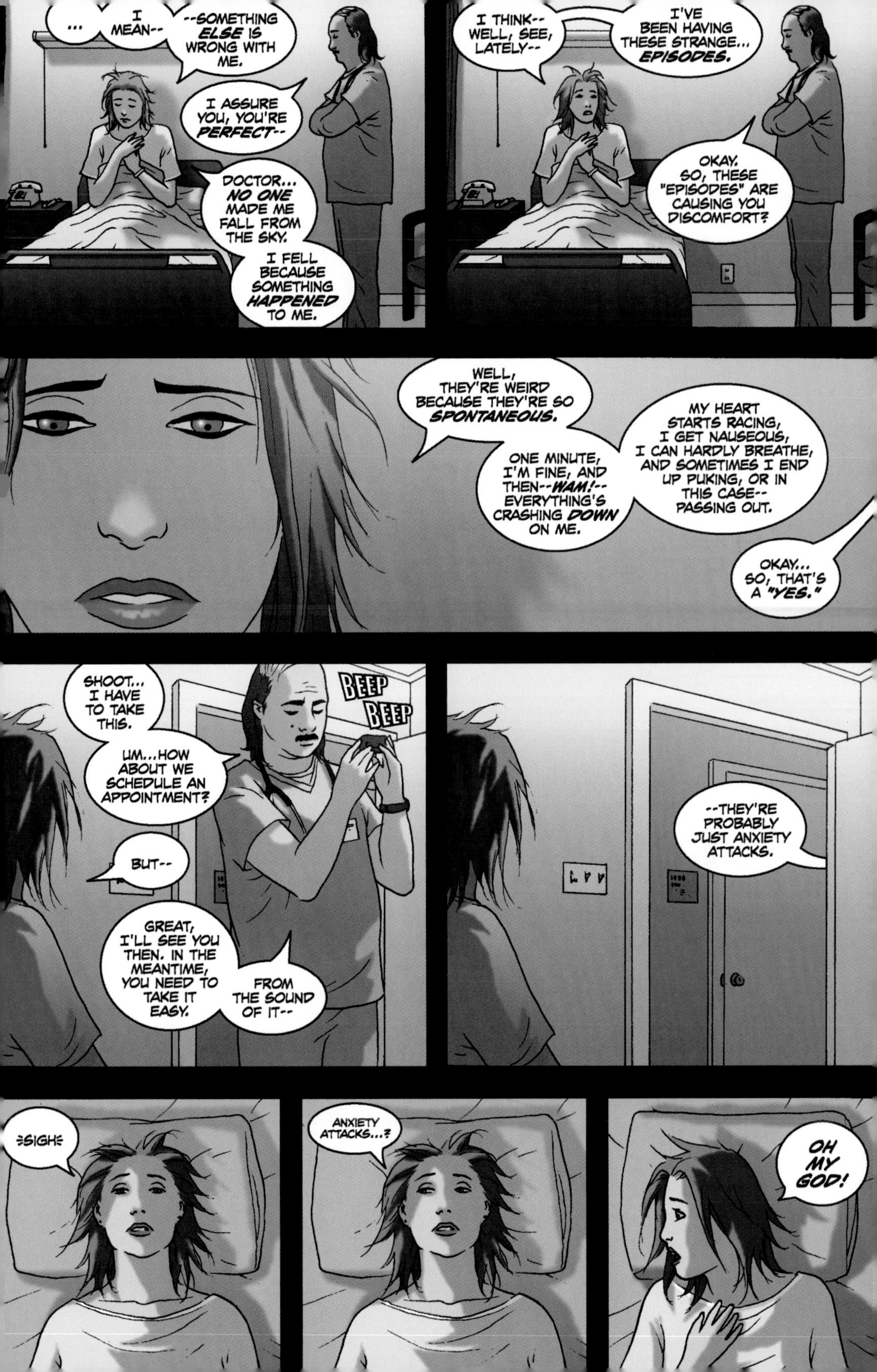
...
I MEAN--
--SOMETHING ELSE IS WRONG WITH ME.
I ASSURE YOU, YOU'RE PERFECT--
DOCTOR... NO ONE MADE ME FALL FROM THE SKY.
I FELL BECAUSE SOMETHING HAPPENED TO ME.
I THINK--WELL, SEE, LATELY--
I'VE BEEN HAVING THESE STRANGE... EPISODES.
OKAY. SO, THESE "EPISODES" ARE CAUSING YOU DISCOMFORT?
WELL, THEY'RE WEIRD BECAUSE THEY'RE SO SPONTANEOUS.
ONE MINUTE, I'M FINE, AND THEN--WAM!--EVERYTHING'S CRASHING DOWN ON ME.
MY HEART STARTS RACING, I GET NAUSEOUS, I CAN HARDLY BREATHE, AND SOMETIMES I END UP PUKING, OR IN THIS CASE--PASSING OUT.
OKAY... SO, THAT'S A "YES."
SHOOT... I HAVE TO TAKE THIS.
BEEP
BEEP
UM...HOW ABOUT WE SCHEDULE AN APPOINTMENT?
BUT--
GREAT, I'LL SEE YOU THEN. IN THE MEANTIME, YOU NEED TO TAKE IT EASY.
FROM THE SOUND OF IT--
--THEY'RE PROBABLY JUST ANXIETY ATTACKS.
SIGH
ANXIETY ATTACKS...?
OH MY GOD!

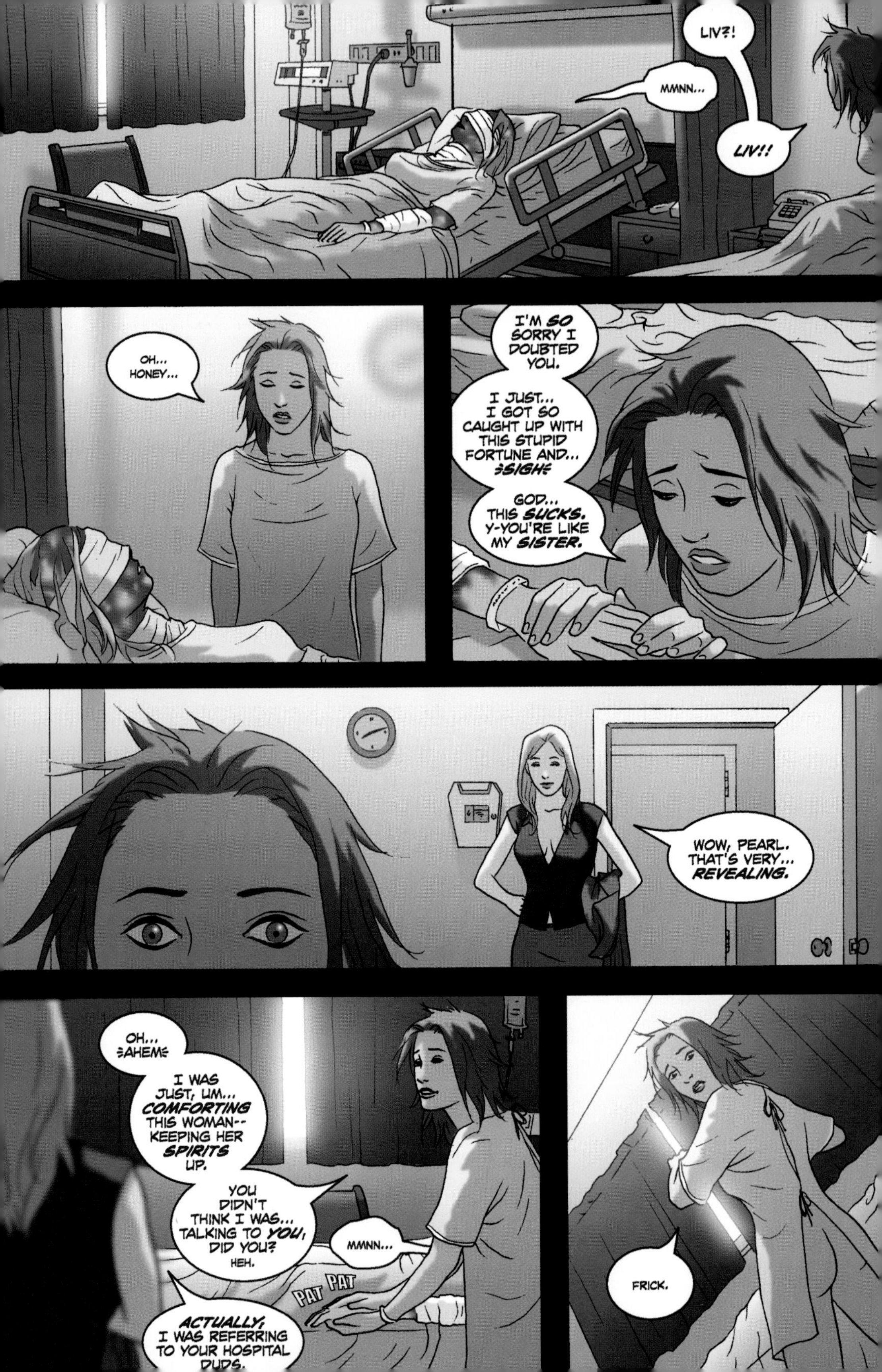
LIV?!
MMNN...
LIV!!
OH... HONEY...
I'M SO SORRY I DOUBTED YOU.
I JUST... I GOT SO CAUGHT UP WITH THIS STUPID FORTUNE AND... SIGH
GOD... THIS SUCKS. Y-YOU'RE LIKE MY SISTER.
WOW, PEARL. THAT'S VERY... REVEALING.
OH... AHEM
I WAS JUST, UM... COMFORTING THIS WOMAN-- KEEPING HER SPIRITS UP.
YOU DIDN'T THINK I WAS... TALKING TO YOU, DID YOU? HEH.
MMNN...
PAT PAT
ACTUALLY, I WAS REFERRING TO YOUR HOSPITAL DUDS.
FRICK.

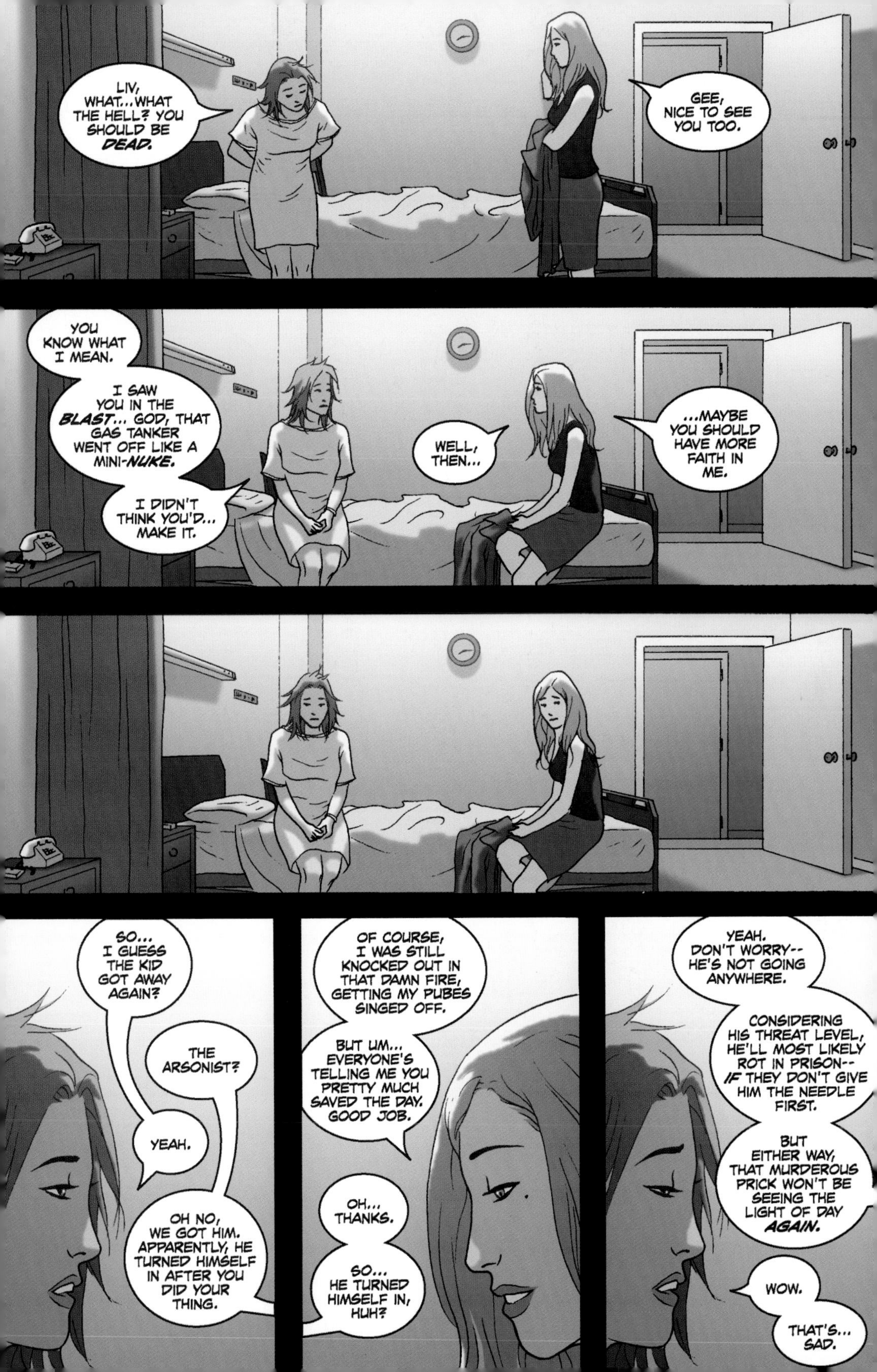
LIV, WHAT...WHAT THE HELL? YOU SHOULD BE DEAD.
GEE, NICE TO SEE YOU TOO.
YOU KNOW WHAT I MEAN.
I SAW YOU IN THE BLAST... GOD, THAT GAS TANKER WENT OFF LIKE A MINI-NUKE.
I DIDN'T THINK YOU'D... MAKE IT.
WELL, THEN...
...MAYBE YOU SHOULD HAVE MORE FAITH IN ME.
SO... I GUESS THE KID GOT AWAY AGAIN?
THE ARSONIST?
YEAH.
OH NO, WE GOT HIM. APPARENTLY, HE TURNED HIMSELF IN AFTER YOU DID YOUR THING.
OF COURSE, I WAS STILL KNOCKED OUT IN THAT DAMN FIRE, GETTING MY PUBES SINGED OFF.
BUT UM... EVERYONE'S TELLING ME YOU PRETTY MUCH SAVED THE DAY. GOOD JOB.
OH... THANKS.
SO... HE TURNED HIMSELF IN, HUH?
YEAH. DON'T WORRY-- HE'S NOT GOING ANYWHERE.
CONSIDERING HIS THREAT LEVEL, HE'LL MOST LIKELY ROT IN PRISON-- IF THEY DON'T GIVE HIM THE NEEDLE FIRST.
BUT EITHER WAY, THAT MURDEROUS PRICK WON'T BE SEEING THE LIGHT OF DAY AGAIN.
WOW.
THAT'S... SAD.

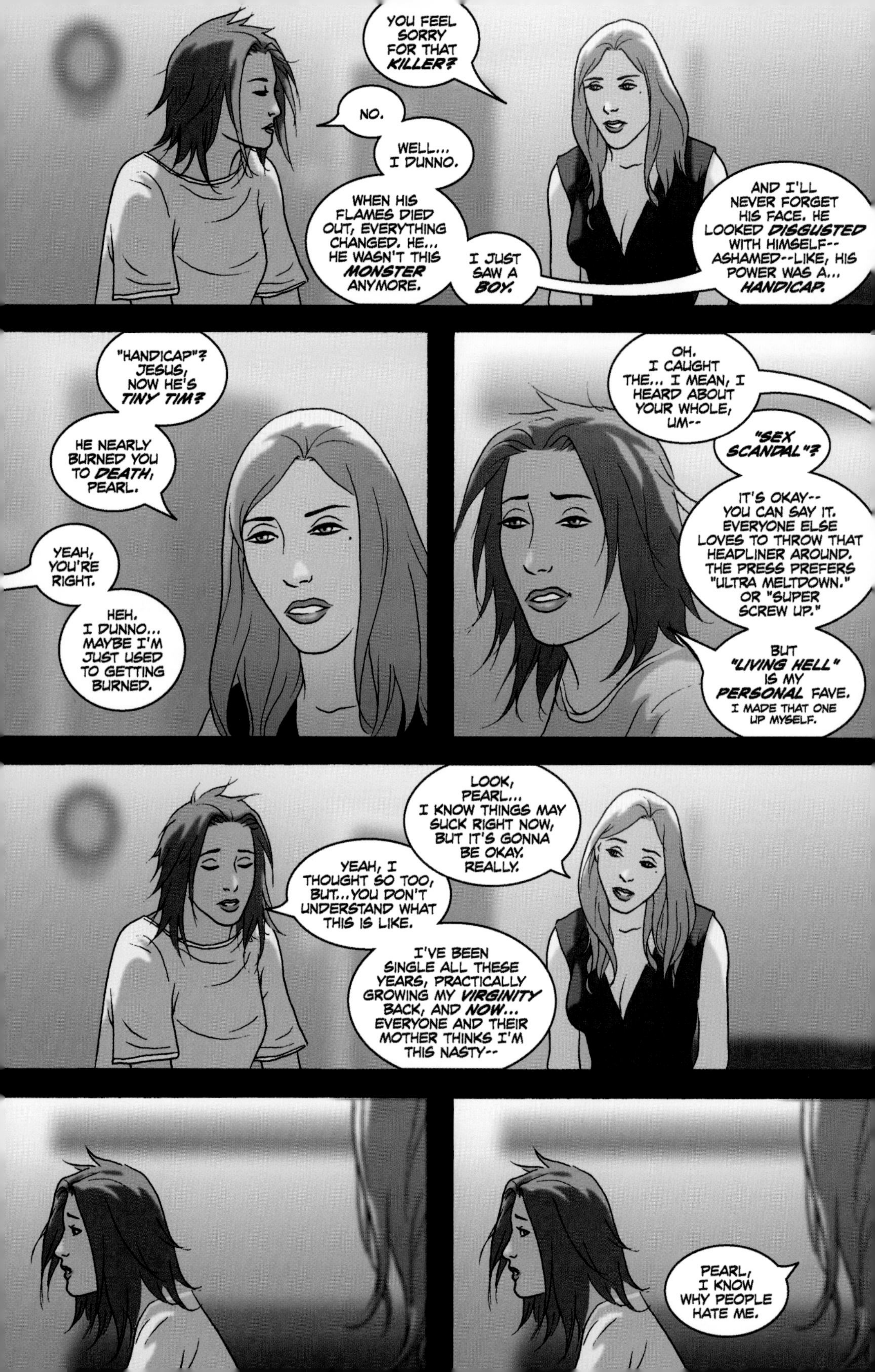
YOU FEEL SORRY FOR THAT KILLER?
NO.
WELL... I DUNNO.
WHEN HIS FLAMES DIED OUT, EVERYTHING CHANGED. HE... HE WASN'T THIS MONSTER ANYMORE.
I JUST SAW A BOY.
AND I'LL NEVER FORGET HIS FACE. HE LOOKED DISGUSTED WITH HIMSELF--ASHAMED--LIKE, HIS POWER WAS A... HANDICAP.
"HANDICAP"? JESUS, NOW HE'S TINY TIM?
HE NEARLY BURNED YOU TO DEATH, PEARL.
YEAH, YOU'RE RIGHT.
HEH. I DUNNO... MAYBE I'M JUST USED TO GETTING BURNED.
OH. I CAUGHT THE... I MEAN, I HEARD ABOUT YOUR WHOLE, UM--
"SEX SCANDAL"?
IT'S OKAY-- YOU CAN SAY IT. EVERYONE ELSE LOVES TO THROW THAT HEADLINER AROUND. THE PRESS PREFERS "ULTRA MELTDOWN." OR "SUPER SCREW UP."
BUT "LIVING HELL" IS MY PERSONAL FAVE. I MADE THAT ONE UP MYSELF.
LOOK, PEARL... I KNOW THINGS MAY SUCK RIGHT NOW, BUT IT'S GONNA BE OKAY. REALLY.
YEAH, I THOUGHT SO TOO, BUT...YOU DON'T UNDERSTAND WHAT THIS IS LIKE.
I'VE BEEN SINGLE ALL THESE YEARS, PRACTICALLY GROWING MY VIRGINITY BACK, AND NOW... EVERYONE AND THEIR MOTHER THINKS I'M THIS NASTY--
PEARL, I KNOW WHY PEOPLE HATE ME.

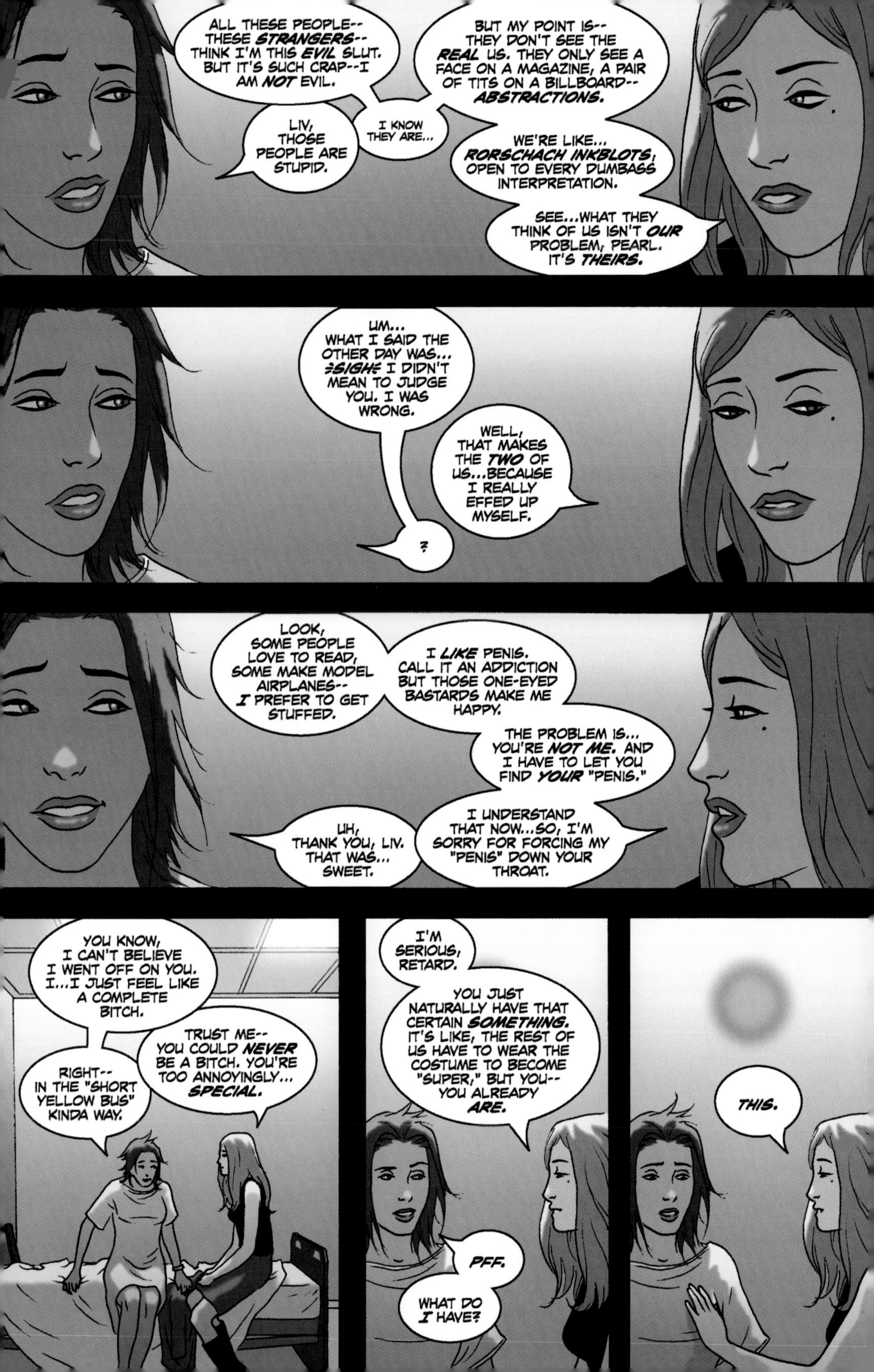
ALL THESE PEOPLE-- THESE STRANGERS-- THINK I'M THIS EVIL SLUT. BUT IT'S SUCH CRAP--I AM NOT EVIL.
LIV, THOSE PEOPLE ARE STUPID.
I KNOW THEY ARE...
BUT MY POINT IS-- THEY DON'T SEE THE REAL US. THEY ONLY SEE A FACE ON A MAGAZINE, A PAIR OF TITS ON A BILLBOARD-- ABSTRACTIONS.
WE'RE LIKE... RORSCHACH INKBLOTS, OPEN TO EVERY DUMBASS INTERPRETATION.
SEE...WHAT THEY THINK OF US ISN'T OUR PROBLEM, PEARL. IT'S THEIRS.
UM... WHAT I SAID THE OTHER DAY WAS... SIGH I DIDN'T MEAN TO JUDGE YOU. I WAS WRONG.
WELL, THAT MAKES THE TWO OF US...BECAUSE I REALLY EFFED UP MYSELF.
?
LOOK, SOME PEOPLE LOVE TO READ, SOME MAKE MODEL AIRPLANES-- I PREFER TO GET STUFFED.
I LIKE PENIS. CALL IT AN ADDICTION BUT THOSE ONE-EYED BASTARDS MAKE ME HAPPY.
THE PROBLEM IS... YOU'RE NOT ME. AND I HAVE TO LET YOU FIND YOUR "PENIS."
I UNDERSTAND THAT NOW...SO, I'M SORRY FOR FORCING MY "PENIS" DOWN YOUR THROAT.
UH, THANK YOU, LIV. THAT WAS... SWEET.
YOU KNOW, I CAN'T BELIEVE I WENT OFF ON YOU. I...I JUST FEEL LIKE A COMPLETE BITCH.
TRUST ME-- YOU COULD NEVER BE A BITCH. YOU'RE TOO ANNOYINGLY... SPECIAL.
RIGHT-- IN THE "SHORT YELLOW BUS" KINDA WAY.
I'M SERIOUS, RETARD.
YOU JUST NATURALLY HAVE THAT CERTAIN SOMETHING. IT'S LIKE, THE REST OF US HAVE TO WEAR THE COSTUME TO BECOME "SUPER," BUT YOU-- YOU ALREADY ARE.
PFF.
WHAT DO I HAVE?
THIS.

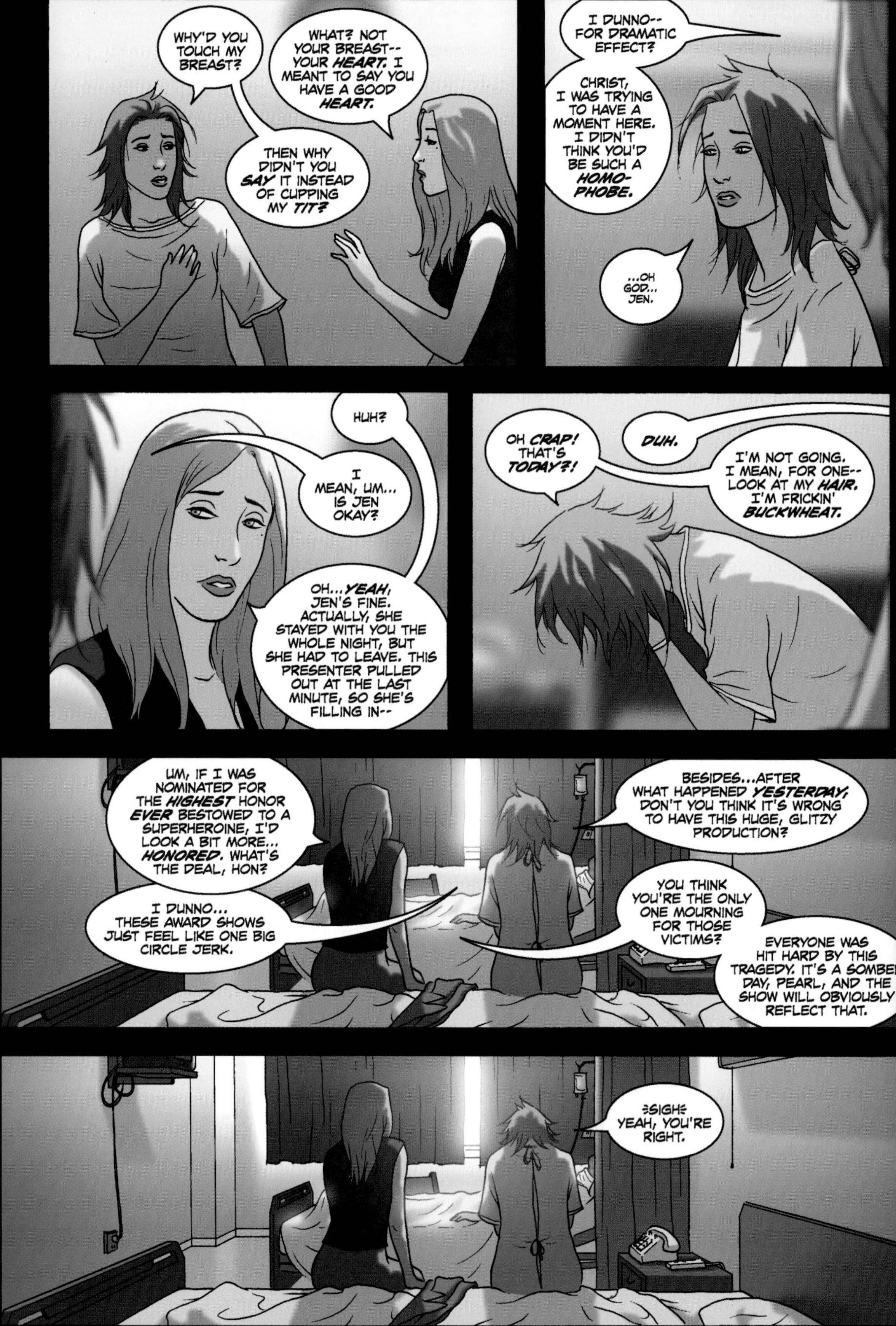
WHY'D YOU TOUCH MY BREAST?
WHAT? NOT YOUR BREAST-- YOUR *HEART.* I MEANT TO SAY YOU HAVE A GOOD *HEART.*
THEN WHY DIDN'T YOU *SAY* IT INSTEAD OF CUPPING MY *TIT?*
I DUNNO-- FOR DRAMATIC EFFECT?
CHRIST, I WAS TRYING TO HAVE A MOMENT HERE. I DIDN'T THINK YOU'D BE SUCH A *HOMO-PHOBE.*
...OH GOD... JEN.
HUH?
I MEAN, UM... IS JEN OKAY?
OH...*YEAH,* JEN'S FINE. ACTUALLY, SHE STAYED WITH YOU THE WHOLE NIGHT, BUT SHE HAD TO LEAVE. THIS PRESENTER PULLED OUT AT THE LAST MINUTE, SO SHE'S FILLING IN--
OH *CRAP!* THAT'S *TODAY?!*
DUH.
I'M NOT GOING. I MEAN, FOR ONE-- LOOK AT MY *HAIR.* I'M FRICKIN' *BUCKWHEAT.*
UM, IF I WAS NOMINATED FOR THE *HIGHEST* HONOR *EVER* BESTOWED TO A SUPERHEROINE, I'D LOOK A BIT MORE... *HONORED.* WHAT'S THE DEAL, HON?
I DUNNO... THESE AWARD SHOWS JUST FEEL LIKE ONE BIG CIRCLE JERK.
BESIDES...AFTER WHAT HAPPENED *YESTERDAY,* DON'T YOU THINK IT'S WRONG TO HAVE THIS HUGE, GLITZY PRODUCTION?
YOU THINK YOU'RE THE ONLY ONE MOURNING FOR THOSE VICTIMS?
EVERYONE WAS HIT HARD BY THIS TRAGEDY. IT'S A SOMBER DAY, PEARL, AND THE SHOW WILL OBVIOUSLY REFLECT THAT.
SIGH YEAH, YOU'RE RIGHT.

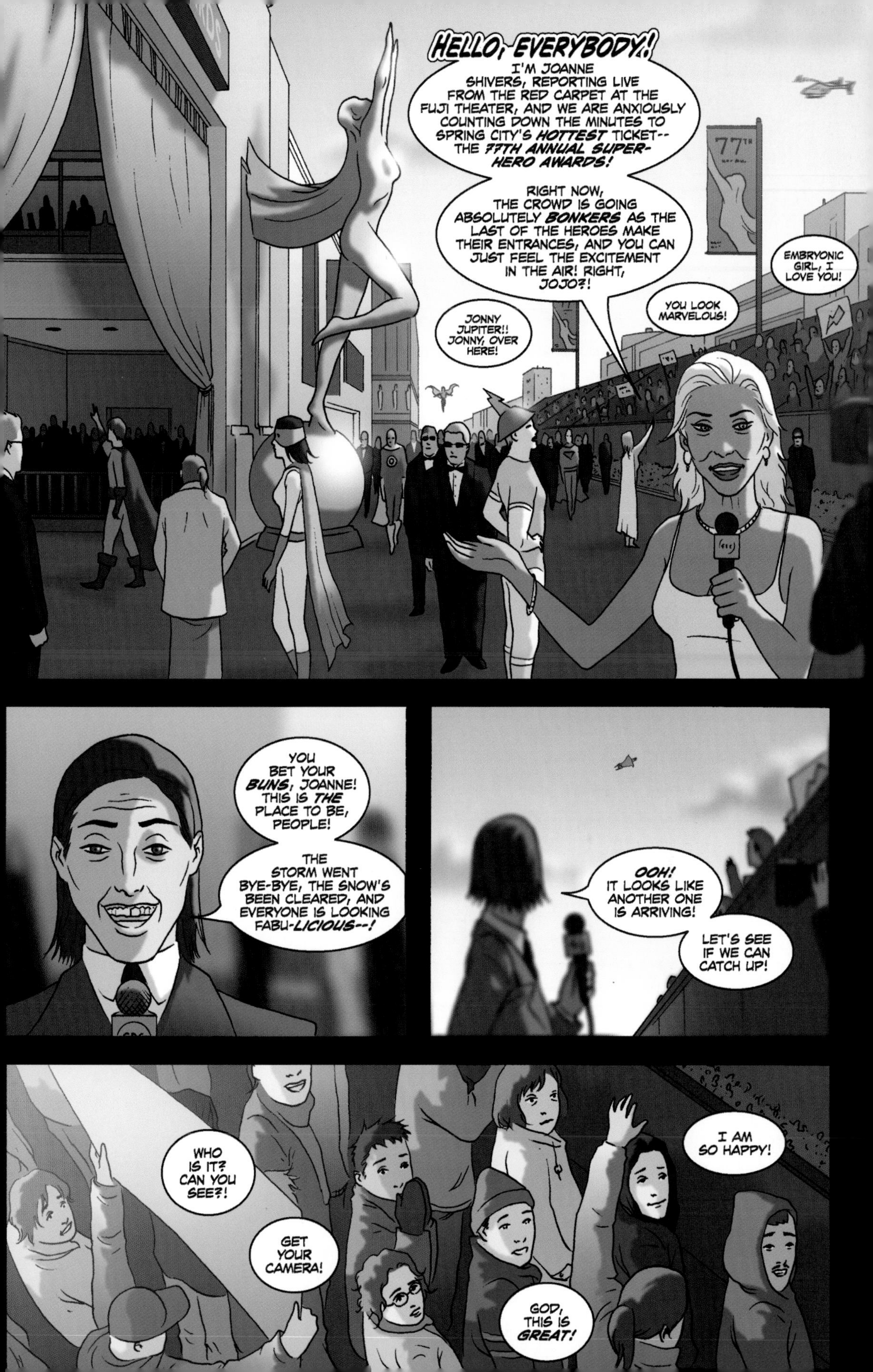
HELLO, EVERYBODY!
I'M JOANNE SHIVERS, REPORTING LIVE FROM THE RED CARPET AT THE FUJI THEATER, AND WE ARE ANXIOUSLY COUNTING DOWN THE MINUTES TO SPRING CITY'S HOTTEST TICKET-- THE 77TH ANNUAL SUPER-HERO AWARDS!
RIGHT NOW, THE CROWD IS GOING ABSOLUTELY BONKERS AS THE LAST OF THE HEROES MAKE THEIR ENTRANCES, AND YOU CAN JUST FEEL THE EXCITEMENT IN THE AIR! RIGHT, JOJO?!
EMBRYONIC GIRL, I LOVE YOU!
YOU LOOK MARVELOUS!
JONNY JUPITER!! JONNY, OVER HERE!
77TH
YOU BET YOUR BUNS, JOANNE! THIS IS THE PLACE TO BE, PEOPLE!
THE STORM WENT BYE-BYE, THE SNOW'S BEEN CLEARED, AND EVERYONE IS LOOKING FABU-LICIOUS--!
OOH! IT LOOKS LIKE ANOTHER ONE IS ARRIVING!
LET'S SEE IF WE CAN CATCH UP!
WHO IS IT? CAN YOU SEE?!
I AM SO HAPPY!
GET YOUR CAMERA!
GOD, THIS IS GREAT!

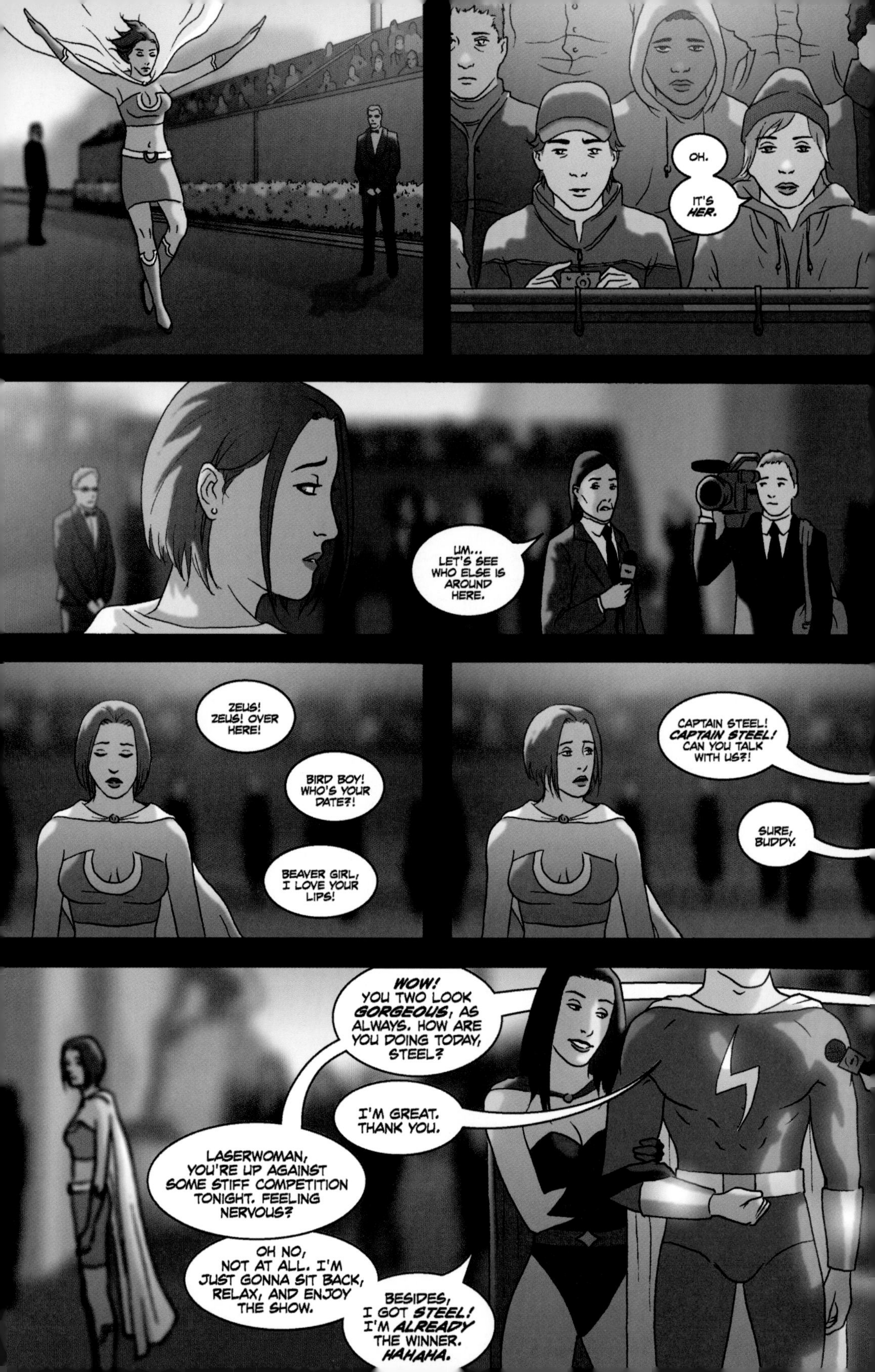
OH.
IT'S HER.
UM... LET'S SEE WHO ELSE IS AROUND HERE.
ZEUS! ZEUS! OVER HERE!
BIRD BOY! WHO'S YOUR DATE?!
BEAVER GIRL, I LOVE YOUR LIPS!
CAPTAIN STEEL! CAPTAIN STEEL! CAN YOU TALK WITH US?!
SURE, BUDDY.
WOW! YOU TWO LOOK GORGEOUS, AS ALWAYS. HOW ARE YOU DOING TODAY, STEEL?
I'M GREAT. THANK YOU.
LASERWOMAN, YOU'RE UP AGAINST SOME STIFF COMPETITION TONIGHT. FEELING NERVOUS?
OH NO, NOT AT ALL. I'M JUST GONNA SIT BACK, RELAX, AND ENJOY THE SHOW.
BESIDES, I GOT STEEL! I'M ALREADY THE WINNER. HAHAHA.

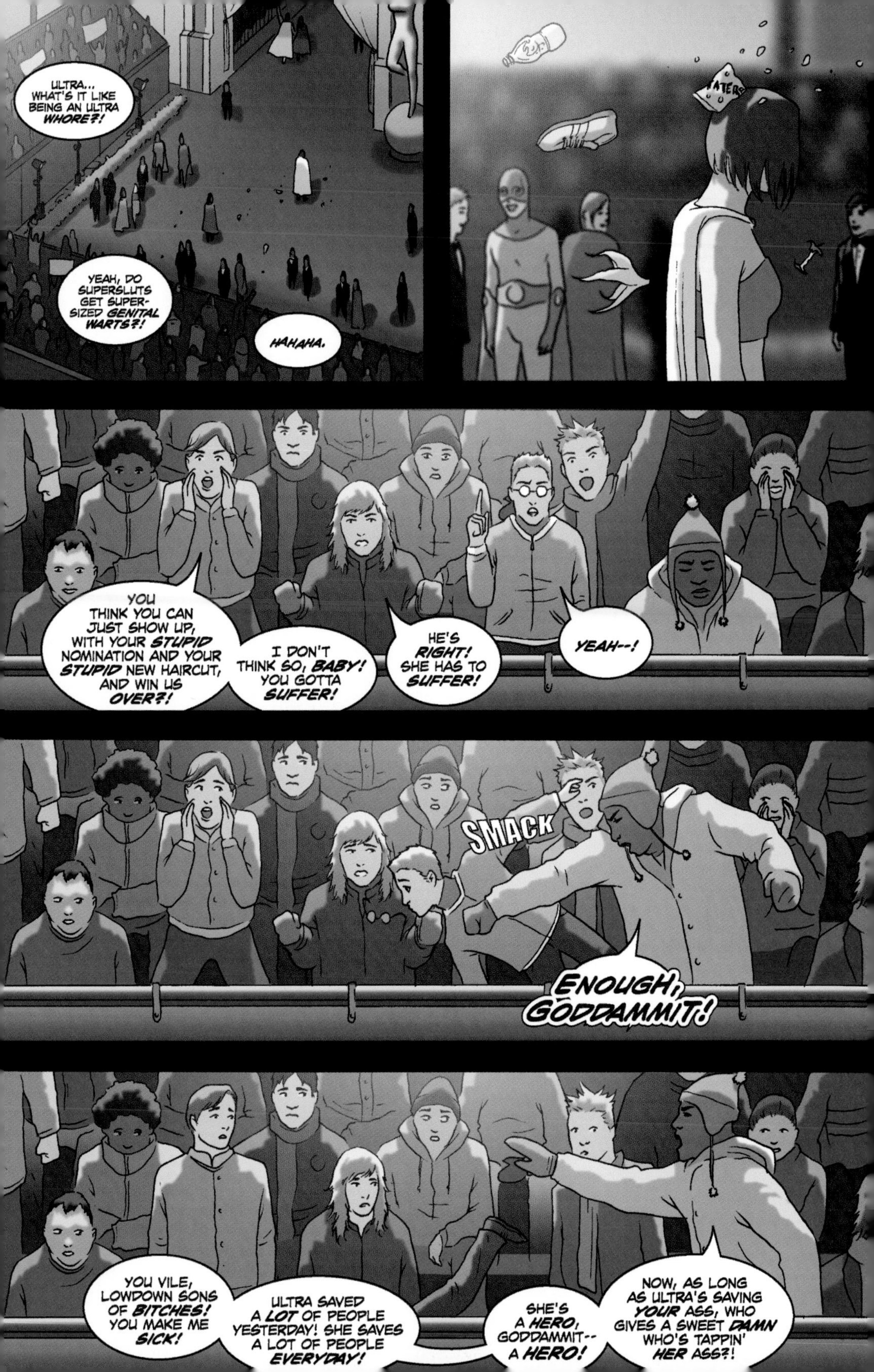
ULTRA... WHAT'S IT LIKE BEING AN ULTRA WHORE?!
YEAH, DO SUPERSLUTS GET SUPER-SIZED GENITAL WARTS?!
HAHAHA.
WATERS
YOU THINK YOU CAN JUST SHOW UP, WITH YOUR STUPID NOMINATION AND YOUR STUPID NEW HAIRCUT, AND WIN US OVER?!
I DON'T THINK SO, BABY! YOU GOTTA SUFFER!
HE'S RIGHT! SHE HAS TO SUFFER!
YEAH--!
SMACK
ENOUGH, GODDAMMIT!
YOU VILE, LOWDOWN SONS OF BITCHES! YOU MAKE ME SICK!
ULTRA SAVED A LOT OF PEOPLE YESTERDAY! SHE SAVES A LOT OF PEOPLE EVERYDAY!
SHE'S A HERO, GODDAMMIT-- A HERO!
NOW, AS LONG AS ULTRA'S SAVING YOUR ASS, WHO GIVES A SWEET DAMN WHO'S TAPPIN' HER ASS?!

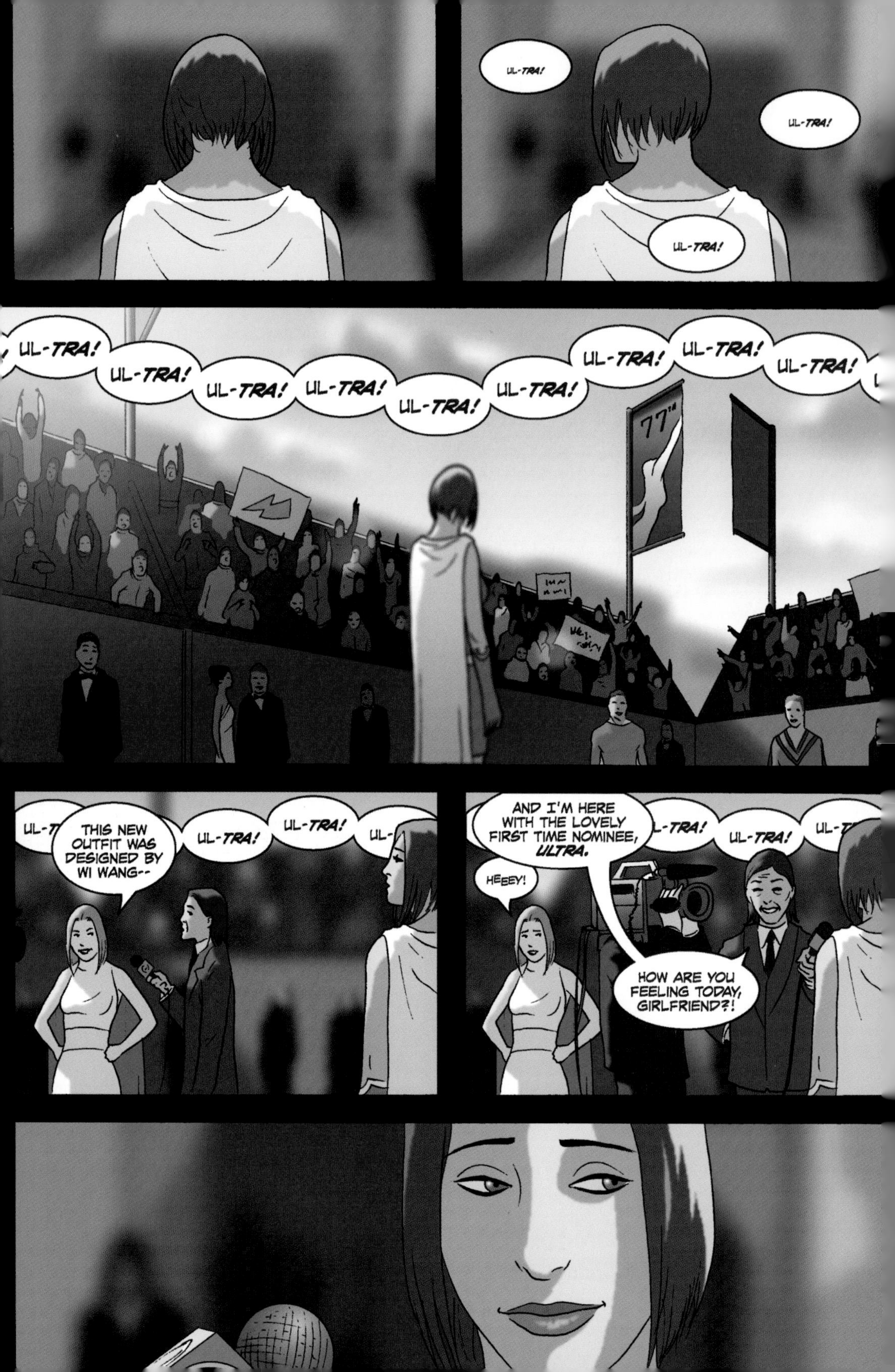
UL-TRA!
UL-TRA!
UL-TRA!
UL-TRA!
UL-TRA!
UL-TRA!
UL-TRA!
UL-TRA!
UL-TRA!
UL-TRA!
UL-TRA!
UL-TRA!
UL-TRA!
THIS NEW OUTFIT WAS DESIGNED BY WI WANG--
UL-TRA!
UL-TRA!
AND I'M HERE WITH THE LOVELY FIRST TIME NOMINEE, ULTRA.
-TRA!
UL-TRA!
HEEEY!
HOW ARE YOU FEELING TODAY, GIRLFRIEND?!

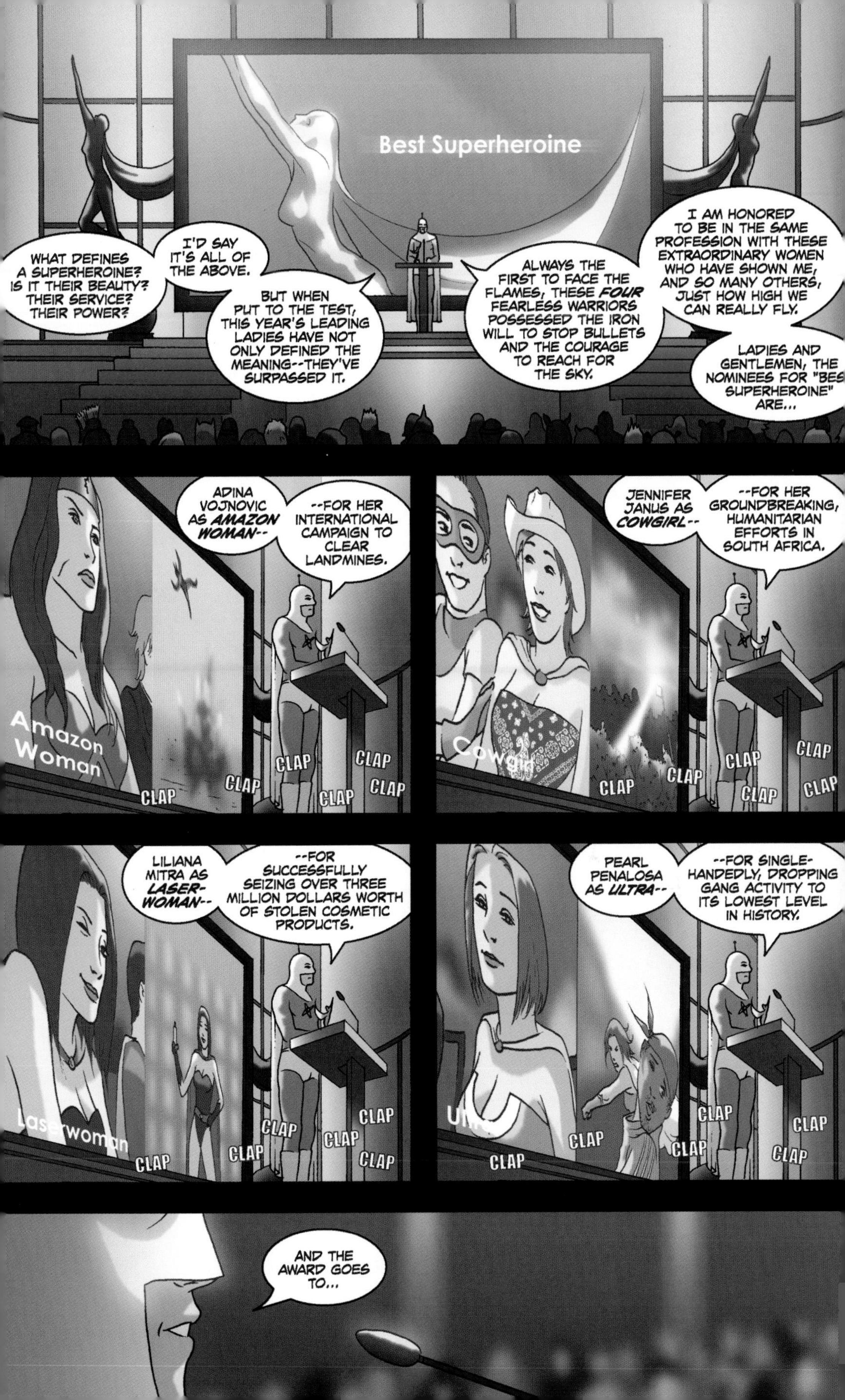

Best Superheroine
WHAT DEFINES A SUPERHEROINE? IS IT THEIR BEAUTY? THEIR SERVICE? THEIR POWER?
I'D SAY IT'S ALL OF THE ABOVE.
BUT WHEN PUT TO THE TEST, THIS YEAR'S LEADING LADIES HAVE NOT ONLY DEFINED THE MEANING--THEY'VE SURPASSED IT.
ALWAYS THE FIRST TO FACE THE FLAMES, THESE FOUR FEARLESS WARRIORS POSSESSED THE IRON WILL TO STOP BULLETS AND THE COURAGE TO REACH FOR THE SKY.
I AM HONORED TO BE IN THE SAME PROFESSION WITH THESE EXTRAORDINARY WOMEN WHO HAVE SHOWN ME, AND SO MANY OTHERS, JUST HOW HIGH WE CAN REALLY FLY.
LADIES AND GENTLEMEN, THE NOMINEES FOR "BES SUPERHEROINE" ARE...
ADINA VOJNOVIC AS AMAZON WOMAN--
--FOR HER INTERNATIONAL CAMPAIGN TO CLEAR LANDMINES.
Amazon Woman
CLAP CLAP CLAP CLAP CLAP CLAP
JENNIFER JANUS AS COWGIRL--
--FOR HER GROUNDBREAKING, HUMANITARIAN EFFORTS IN SOUTH AFRICA.
Cowgirl
CLAP CLAP CLAP CLAP CLAP CLAP
LILIANA MITRA AS LASER-WOMAN--
--FOR SUCCESSFULLY SEIZING OVER THREE MILLION DOLLARS WORTH OF STOLEN COSMETIC PRODUCTS.
Laserwoman
CLAP CLAP CLAP CLAP CLAP CLAP
PEARL PENALOSA AS ULTRA--
--FOR SINGLE-HANDEDLY, DROPPING GANG ACTIVITY TO ITS LOWEST LEVEL IN HISTORY.
Ultra
CLAP CLAP CLAP CLAP CLAP CLAP
AND THE AWARD GOES TO...

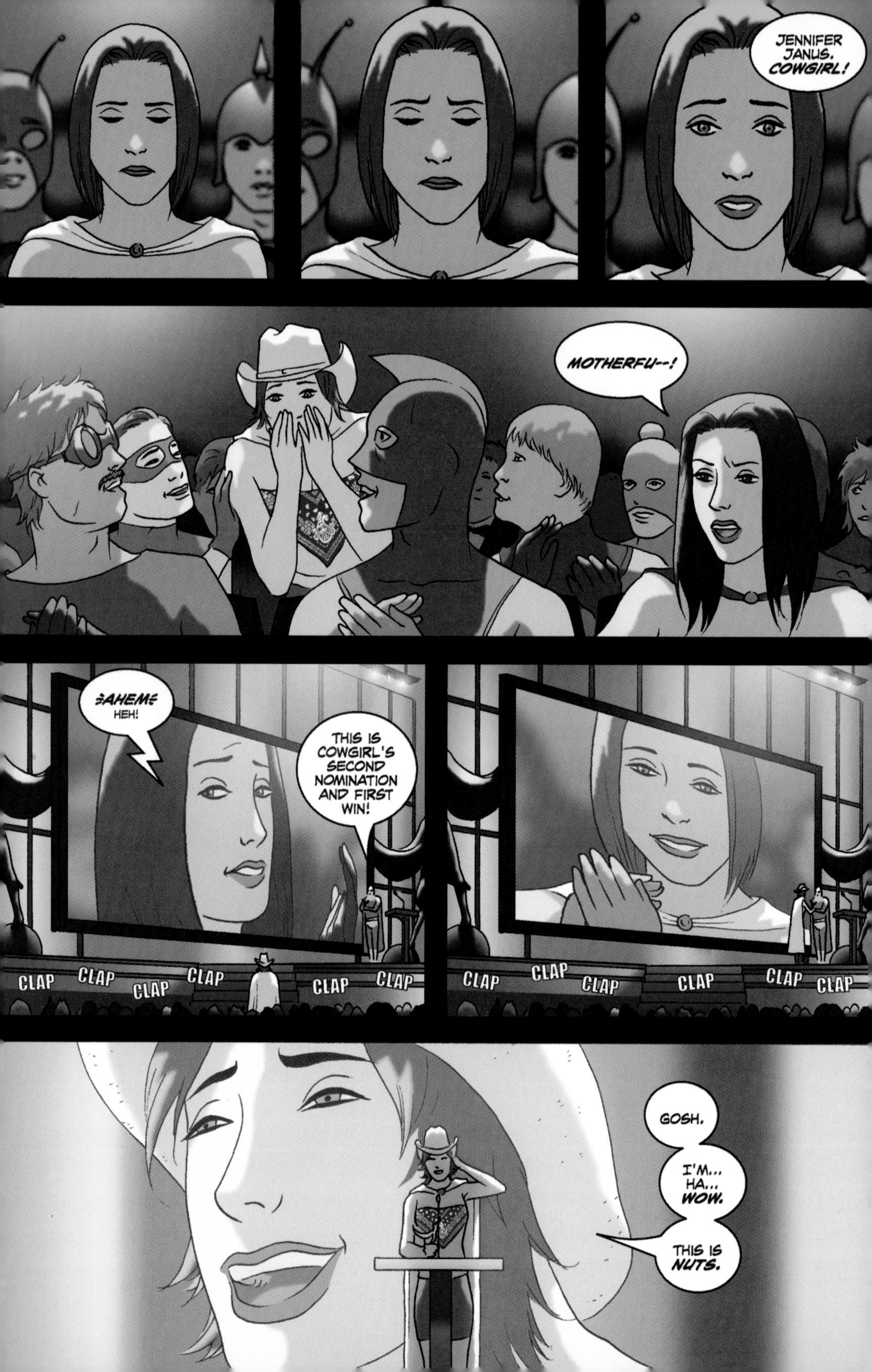
JENNIFER JANUS. COWGIRL!
MOTHERFU--!
≠AHEM≠ HEH!
THIS IS COWGIRL'S SECOND NOMINATION AND FIRST WIN!
CLAP CLAP CLAP CLAP CLAP CLAP
CLAP CLAP CLAP CLAP CLAP CLAP
GOSH.
I'M... HA... WOW.
THIS IS NUTS.

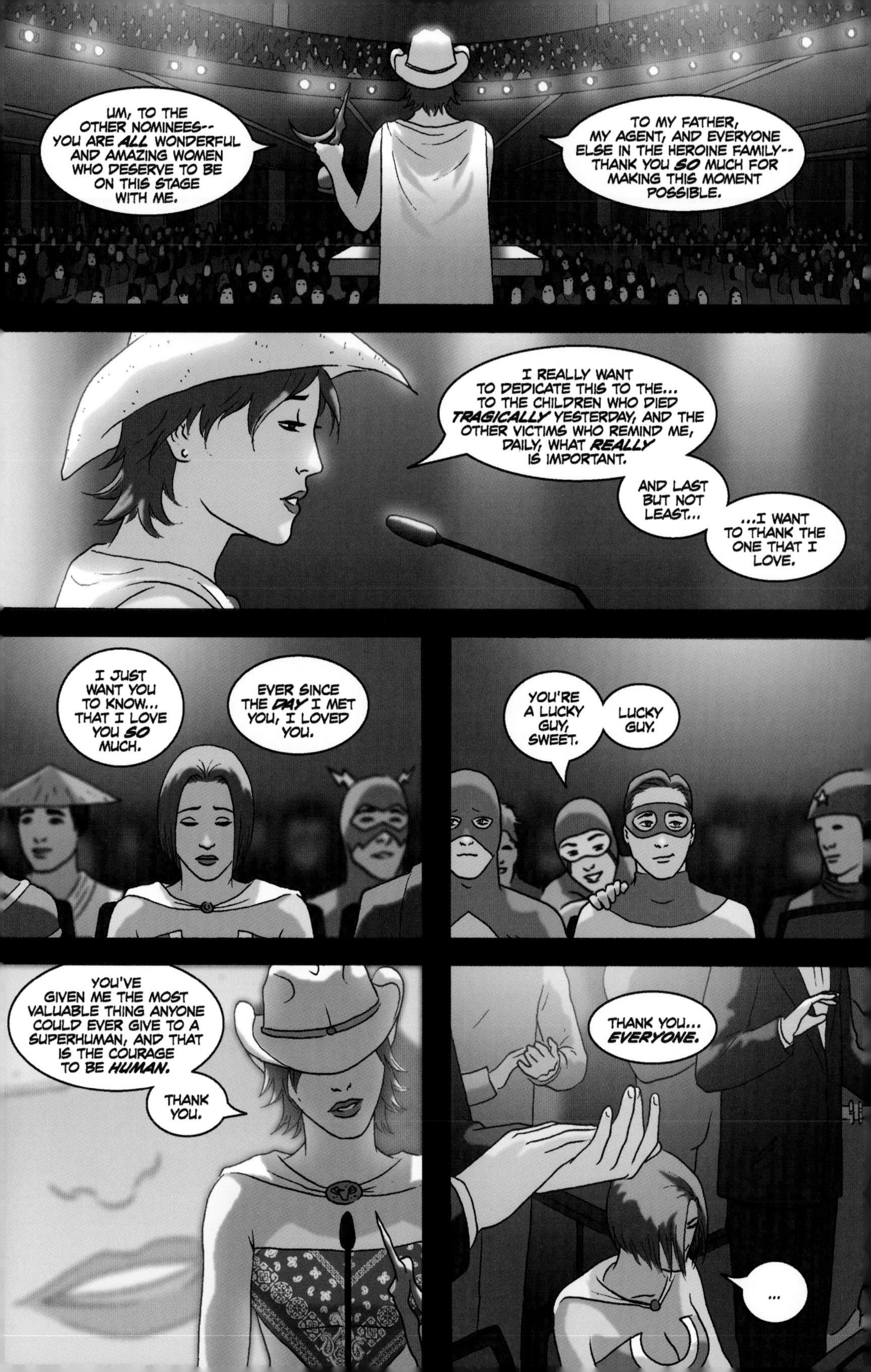
UM, TO THE OTHER NOMINEES-- YOU ARE ALL WONDERFUL AND AMAZING WOMEN WHO DESERVE TO BE ON THIS STAGE WITH ME.
TO MY FATHER, MY AGENT, AND EVERYONE ELSE IN THE HEROINE FAMILY-- THANK YOU SO MUCH FOR MAKING THIS MOMENT POSSIBLE.
I REALLY WANT TO DEDICATE THIS TO THE... TO THE CHILDREN WHO DIED TRAGICALLY YESTERDAY, AND THE OTHER VICTIMS WHO REMIND ME, DAILY, WHAT REALLY IS IMPORTANT.
AND LAST BUT NOT LEAST...
...I WANT TO THANK THE ONE THAT I LOVE.
I JUST WANT YOU TO KNOW... THAT I LOVE YOU SO MUCH.
EVER SINCE THE DAY I MET YOU, I LOVED YOU.
YOU'RE A LUCKY GUY, SWEET.
LUCKY GUY.
YOU'VE GIVEN ME THE MOST VALUABLE THING ANYONE COULD EVER GIVE TO A SUPERHUMAN, AND THAT IS THE COURAGE TO BE HUMAN.
THANK YOU.
THANK YOU... EVERYONE.
...

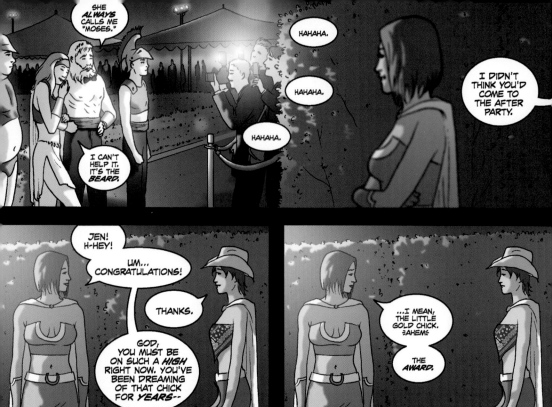

SHE *ALWAYS* CALLS ME "MOSES."

HAHAHA.

HAHAHA.

HAHAHA.

I CAN'T HELP IT. IT'S THE *BEARD.*

I DIDN'T THINK YOU'D COME TO THE AFTER PARTY.

JEN! H-HEY!

UM... CONGRATULATIONS!

THANKS.

GOD, YOU MUST BE ON SUCH A *HIGH* RIGHT NOW. YOU'VE BEEN DREAMING OF THAT CHICK FOR *YEARS*--

...I MEAN, THE LITTLE GOLD CHICK. ≋AHEM≋

THE *AWARD.*

IT'S FUNNY. I FINALLY SEE THIS THING UP CLOSE, AND... IT'S A LOT SMALLER THAN I THOUGHT.

WELL, I'M REALLY HAPPY FOR YOU, JEN. YOU DESERVE THAT AWARD.

SO...I GUESS THIS IS IT--THIS IS MY *FORTUNE.* SHE SAID I'D RECEIVE WHAT I HAVE GIVEN, AND LO AND BEHOLD...I HAVE MOST DEFINITELY *RECEIVED.*

YEAH... DEFINITELY.

PEARL...

...I THINK I KILLED THOSE KIDS.

WHAT?

I MESSED UP. I TRIED TO SAVE THEM, BUT...I *COULDN'T.* I JUST MADE THINGS WORSE, AND THEY...THEY ALL *BURNED.*

JEN, YOU DIDN'T KILL ANYONE. WE JUST...WE CAN'T *ALWAYS* SAVE EVERYONE.

BUT YOU TRIED, RIGHT?

WHAT IF TRYING ISN'T GOOD ENOUGH?

OF *COURSE* IT IS.

I TRIED WITH *YOU,* PEARL.

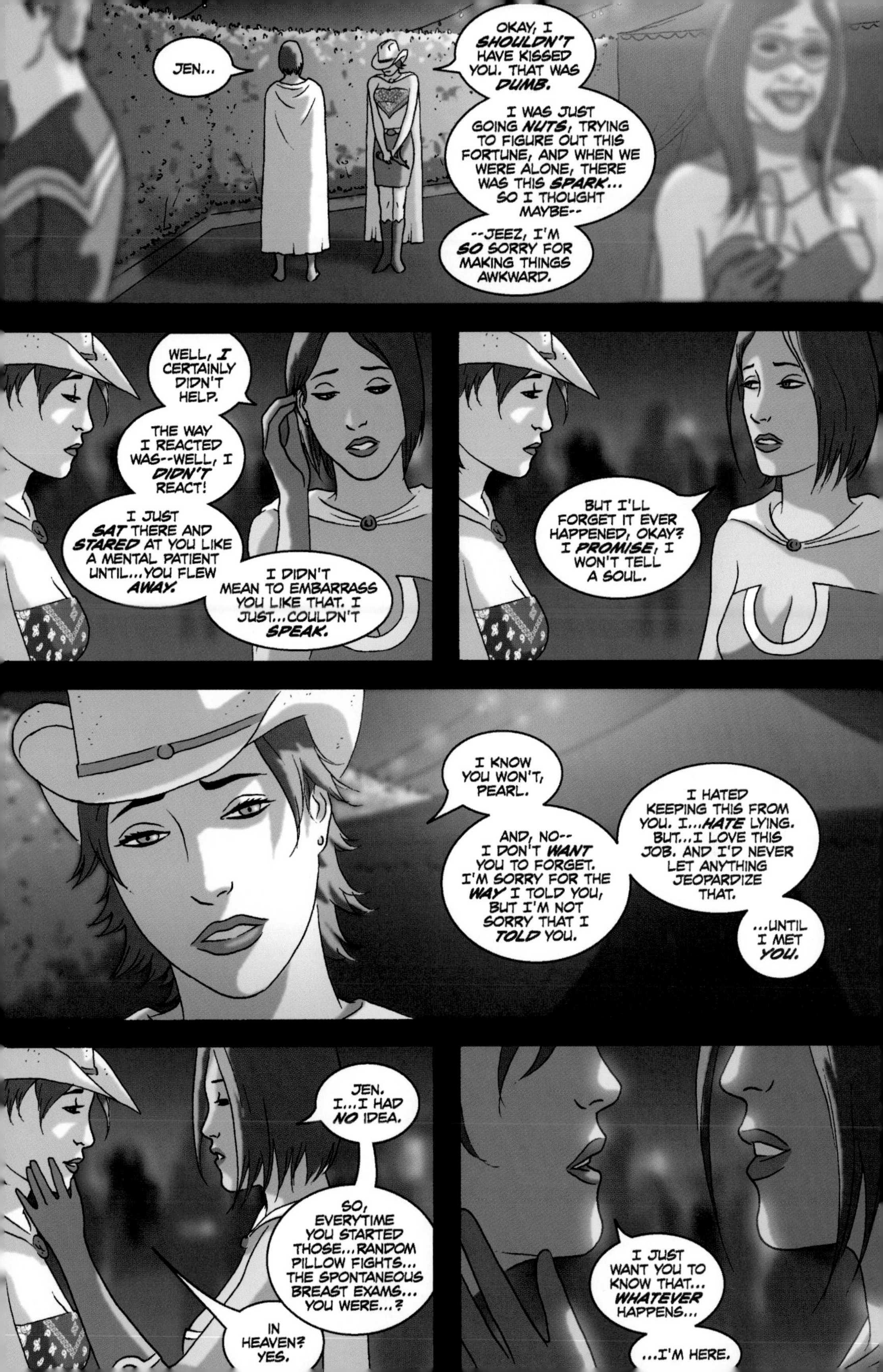
JEN...
OKAY, I SHOULDN'T HAVE KISSED YOU. THAT WAS DUMB.
I WAS JUST GOING NUTS, TRYING TO FIGURE OUT THIS FORTUNE, AND WHEN WE WERE ALONE, THERE WAS THIS SPARK... SO I THOUGHT MAYBE--
--JEEZ, I'M SO SORRY FOR MAKING THINGS AWKWARD.
WELL, I CERTAINLY DIDN'T HELP.
THE WAY I REACTED WAS--WELL, I DIDN'T REACT!
I JUST SAT THERE AND STARED AT YOU LIKE A MENTAL PATIENT UNTIL...YOU FLEW AWAY.
I DIDN'T MEAN TO EMBARRASS YOU LIKE THAT. I JUST...COULDN'T SPEAK.
BUT I'LL FORGET IT EVER HAPPENED, OKAY? I PROMISE, I WON'T TELL A SOUL.
I KNOW YOU WON'T, PEARL.
AND, NO-- I DON'T WANT YOU TO FORGET. I'M SORRY FOR THE WAY I TOLD YOU, BUT I'M NOT SORRY THAT I TOLD YOU.
I HATED KEEPING THIS FROM YOU. I...HATE LYING. BUT...I LOVE THIS JOB. AND I'D NEVER LET ANYTHING JEOPARDIZE THAT.
...UNTIL I MET YOU.
JEN. I...I HAD NO IDEA.
SO, EVERYTIME YOU STARTED THOSE...RANDOM PILLOW FIGHTS... THE SPONTANEOUS BREAST EXAMS... YOU WERE...?
IN HEAVEN? YES.
I JUST WANT YOU TO KNOW THAT... WHATEVER HAPPENS...
...I'M HERE.

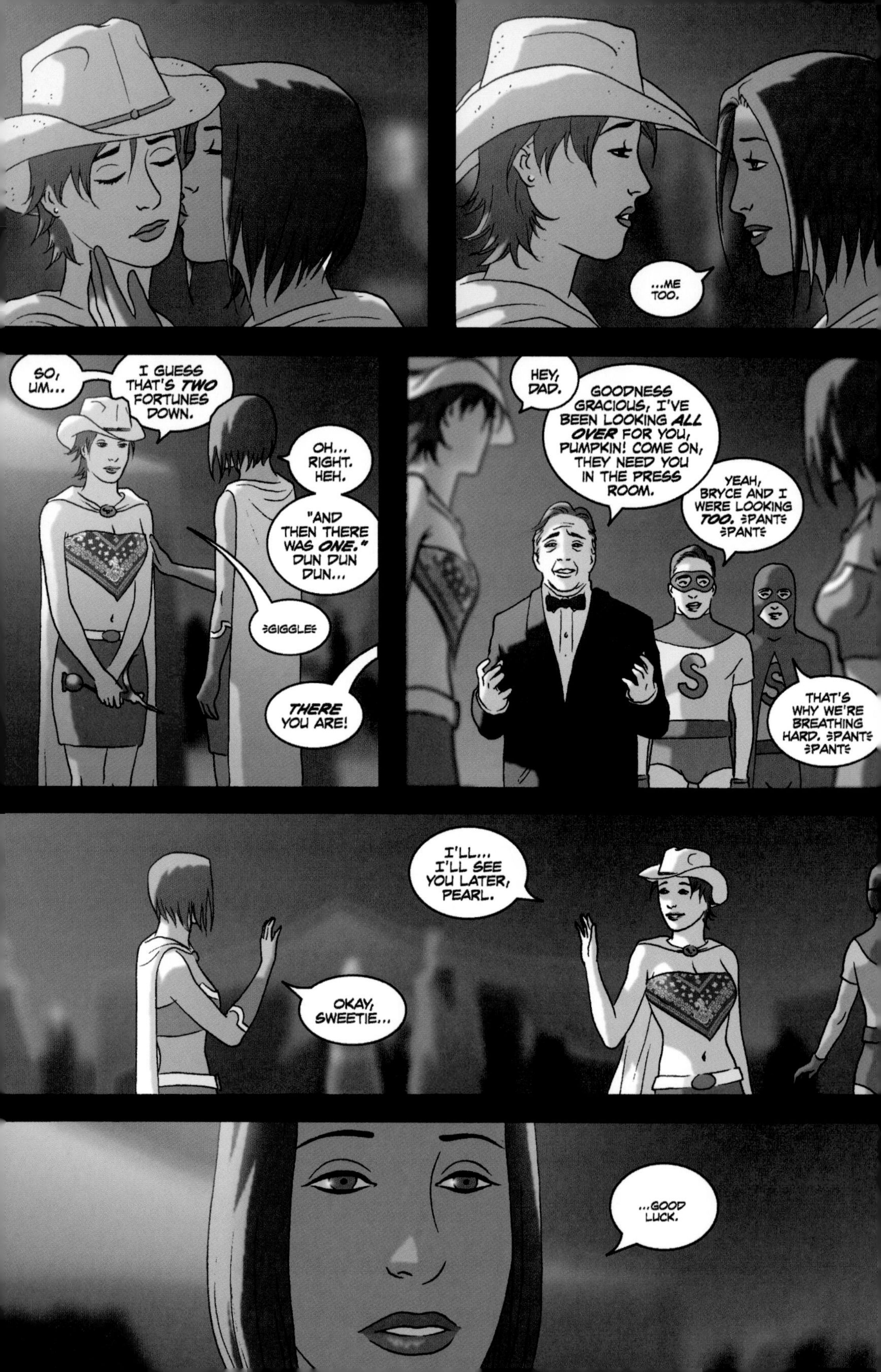
...ME TOO.
SO, UM...
I GUESS THAT'S TWO FORTUNES DOWN.
OH... RIGHT. HEH.
"AND THEN THERE WAS ONE." DUN DUN DUN...
GIGGLE
THERE YOU ARE!
HEY, DAD.
GOODNESS GRACIOUS, I'VE BEEN LOOKING ALL OVER FOR YOU, PUMPKIN! COME ON, THEY NEED YOU IN THE PRESS ROOM.
YEAH, BRYCE AND I WERE LOOKING TOO. PANT PANT
THAT'S WHY WE'RE BREATHING HARD. PANT PANT
I'LL... I'LL SEE YOU LATER, PEARL.
OKAY, SWEETIE...
...GOOD LUCK.

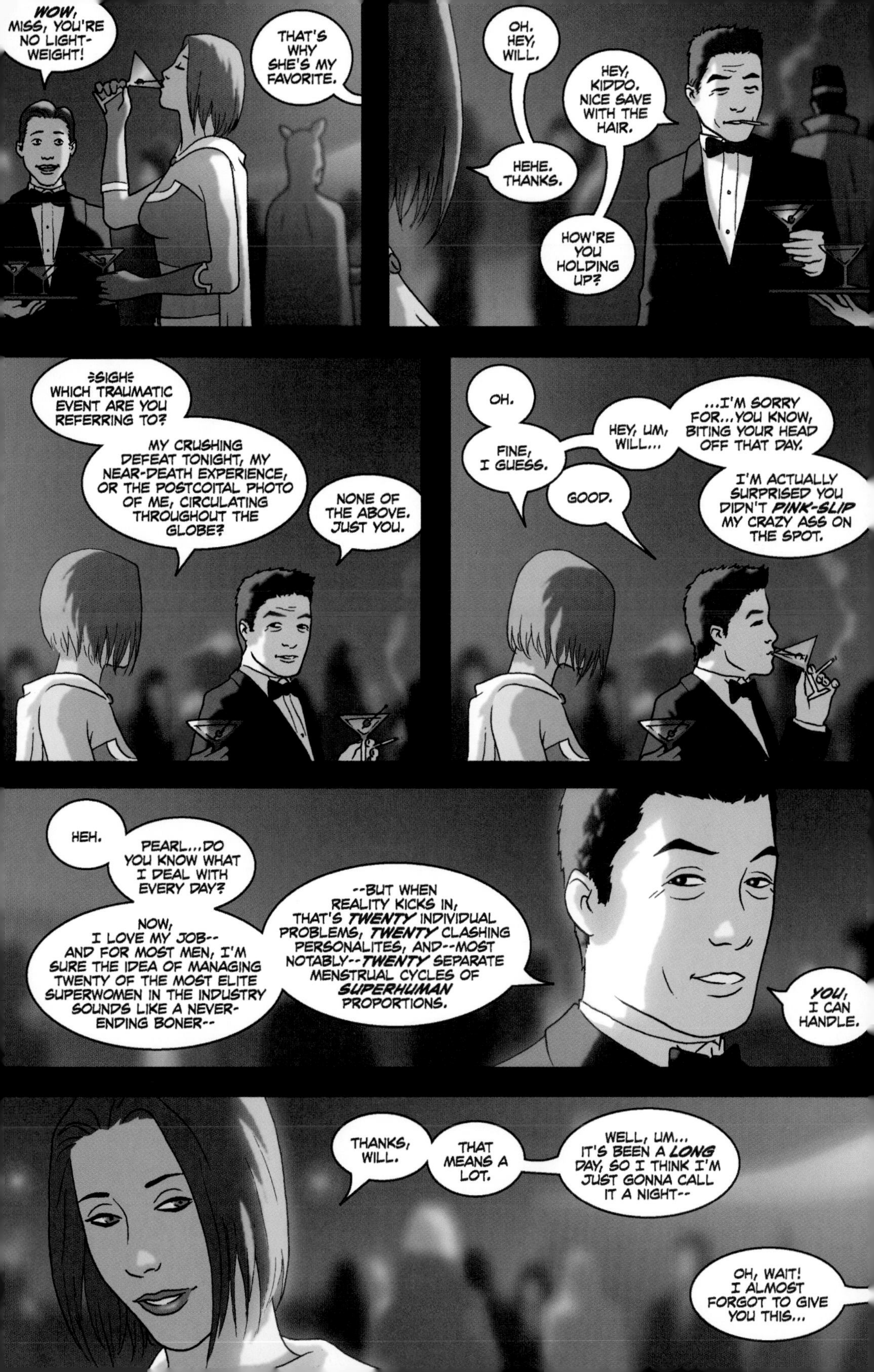
WOW, MISS, YOU'RE NO LIGHT-WEIGHT!
THAT'S WHY SHE'S MY FAVORITE.
OH. HEY, WILL.
HEY, KIDDO. NICE SAVE WITH THE HAIR.
HEHE. THANKS.
HOW'RE YOU HOLDING UP?
=SIGH= WHICH TRAUMATIC EVENT ARE YOU REFERRING TO?
MY CRUSHING DEFEAT TONIGHT, MY NEAR-DEATH EXPERIENCE, OR THE POSTCOITAL PHOTO OF ME, CIRCULATING THROUGHOUT THE GLOBE?
NONE OF THE ABOVE. JUST YOU.
OH.
FINE, I GUESS.
GOOD.
HEY, UM, WILL...
...I'M SORRY FOR...YOU KNOW, BITING YOUR HEAD OFF THAT DAY.
I'M ACTUALLY SURPRISED YOU DIDN'T PINK-SLIP MY CRAZY ASS ON THE SPOT.
HEH.
PEARL...DO YOU KNOW WHAT I DEAL WITH EVERY DAY?
NOW, I LOVE MY JOB-- AND FOR MOST MEN, I'M SURE THE IDEA OF MANAGING TWENTY OF THE MOST ELITE SUPERWOMEN IN THE INDUSTRY SOUNDS LIKE A NEVER-ENDING BONER--
--BUT WHEN REALITY KICKS IN, THAT'S TWENTY INDIVIDUAL PROBLEMS, TWENTY CLASHING PERSONALITES, AND--MOST NOTABLY--TWENTY SEPARATE MENSTRUAL CYCLES OF SUPERHUMAN PROPORTIONS.
YOU, I CAN HANDLE.
THANKS, WILL.
THAT MEANS A LOT.
WELL, UM... IT'S BEEN A LONG DAY, SO I THINK I'M JUST GONNA CALL IT A NIGHT--
OH, WAIT! I ALMOST FORGOT TO GIVE YOU THIS...

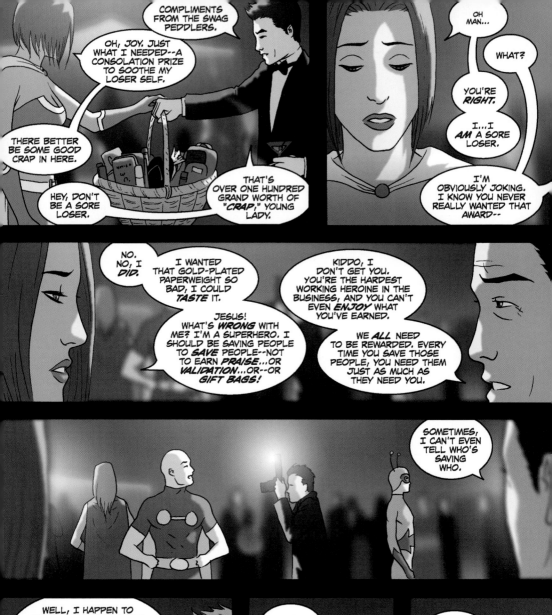

COMPLIMENTS FROM THE SWAG PEDDLERS.

OH, JOY. JUST WHAT I NEEDED--A CONSOLATION PRIZE TO SOOTHE MY LOSER SELF.

THERE BETTER BE SOME GOOD CRAP IN HERE.

HEY, DON'T BE A SORE LOSER.

THAT'S OVER ONE HUNDRED GRAND WORTH OF "CRAP," YOUNG LADY.

OH MAN...

WHAT?

YOU'RE RIGHT.

I...I AM A SORE LOSER.

I'M OBVIOUSLY JOKING. I KNOW YOU NEVER REALLY WANTED THAT AWARD--

NO. NO, I DID.

I WANTED THAT GOLD-PLATED PAPERWEIGHT SO BAD, I COULD TASTE IT.

JESUS! WHAT'S WRONG WITH ME? I'M A SUPERHERO. I SHOULD BE SAVING PEOPLE TO SAVE PEOPLE--NOT TO EARN PRAISE...OR VALIDATION...OR--OR GIFT BAGS!

KIDDO, I DON'T GET YOU. YOU'RE THE HARDEST WORKING HEROINE IN THE BUSINESS, AND YOU CAN'T EVEN ENJOY WHAT YOU'VE EARNED.

WE ALL NEED TO BE REWARDED. EVERY TIME YOU SAVE THOSE PEOPLE, YOU NEED THEM JUST AS MUCH AS THEY NEED YOU.

SOMETIMES, I CAN'T EVEN TELL WHO'S SAVING WHO.

WELL, I HAPPEN TO BELIEVE IN A THANKLESS DEED. WE SHOULDN'T FEEL THE NEED TO HELP PEOPLE JUST SO WE CAN HOARD ALL THIS...THIS JUNK.

LOOK AT THIS. DO WE REALLY NEED ANY OF THIS? CAN THIS TRULY FULFILL OUR--?

OH. THAT'S...

WELL, THAT'S INTERESTING...

WHAT IS IT?

NOTHING.

GOODNIGHT, WILL.

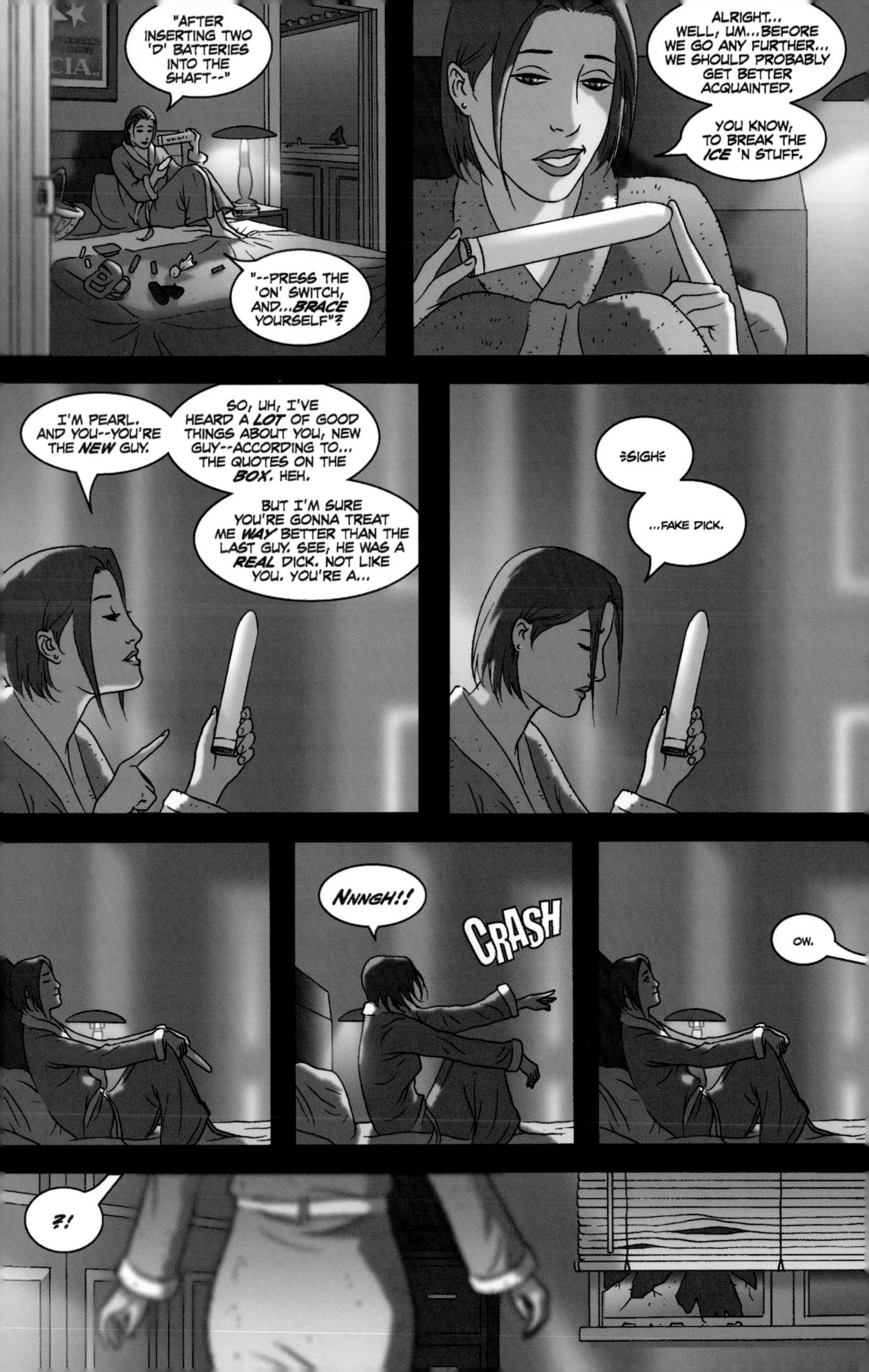
"AFTER INSERTING TWO 'D' BATTERIES INTO THE SHAFT--"
"--PRESS THE 'ON' SWITCH, AND...BRACE YOURSELF"?
ALRIGHT... WELL, UM...BEFORE WE GO ANY FURTHER... WE SHOULD PROBABLY GET BETTER ACQUAINTED.
YOU KNOW, TO BREAK THE ICE 'N STUFF.
I'M PEARL. AND YOU--YOU'RE THE NEW GUY.
SO, UH, I'VE HEARD A LOT OF GOOD THINGS ABOUT YOU, NEW GUY--ACCORDING TO... THE QUOTES ON THE BOX. HEH.
BUT I'M SURE YOU'RE GONNA TREAT ME WAY BETTER THAN THE LAST GUY. SEE, HE WAS A REAL DICK. NOT LIKE YOU. YOU'RE A...
SIGH
...FAKE DICK.
NNNGH!!
CRASH
OW.
?!

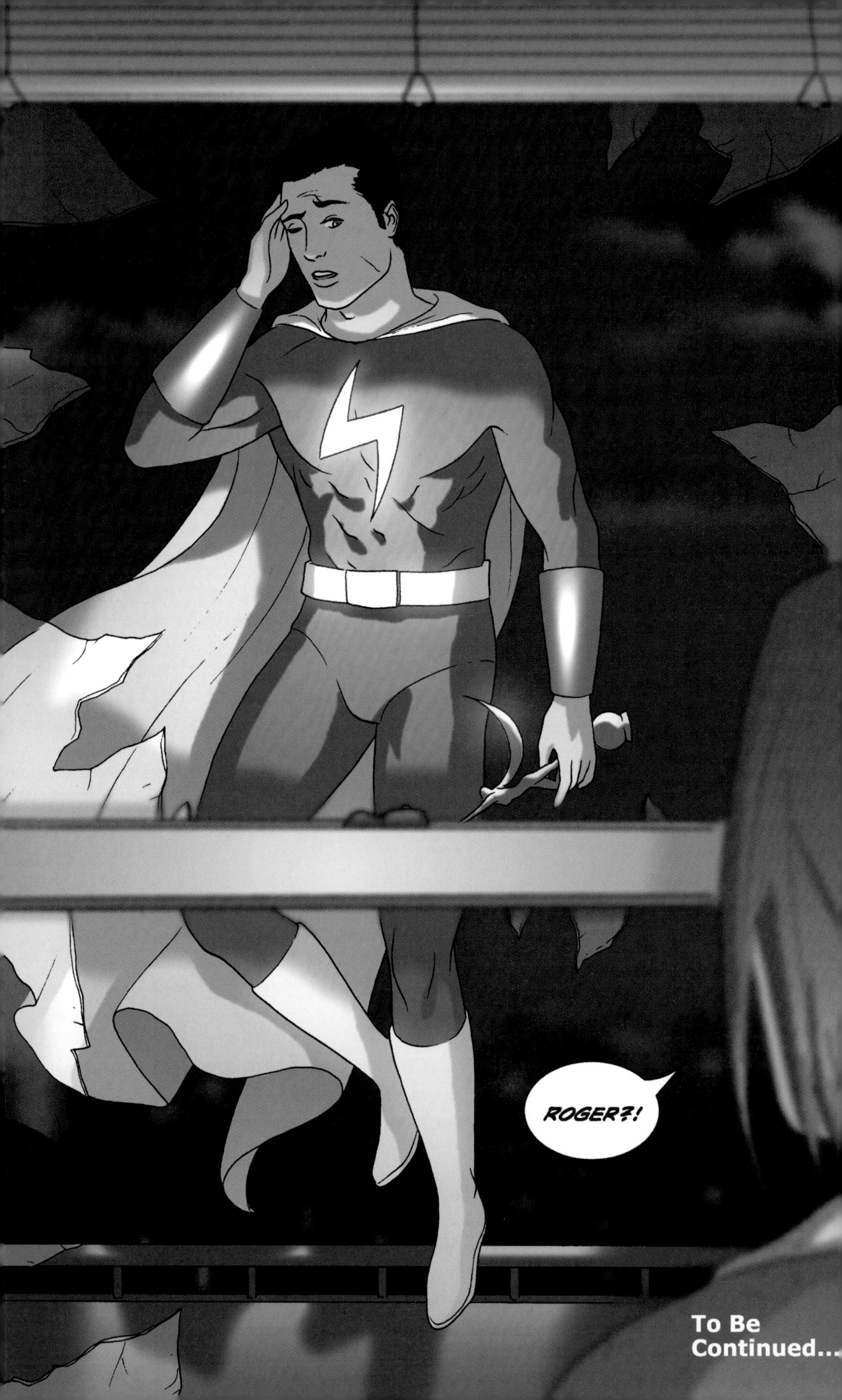
ROGER?!

To Be
Continued...

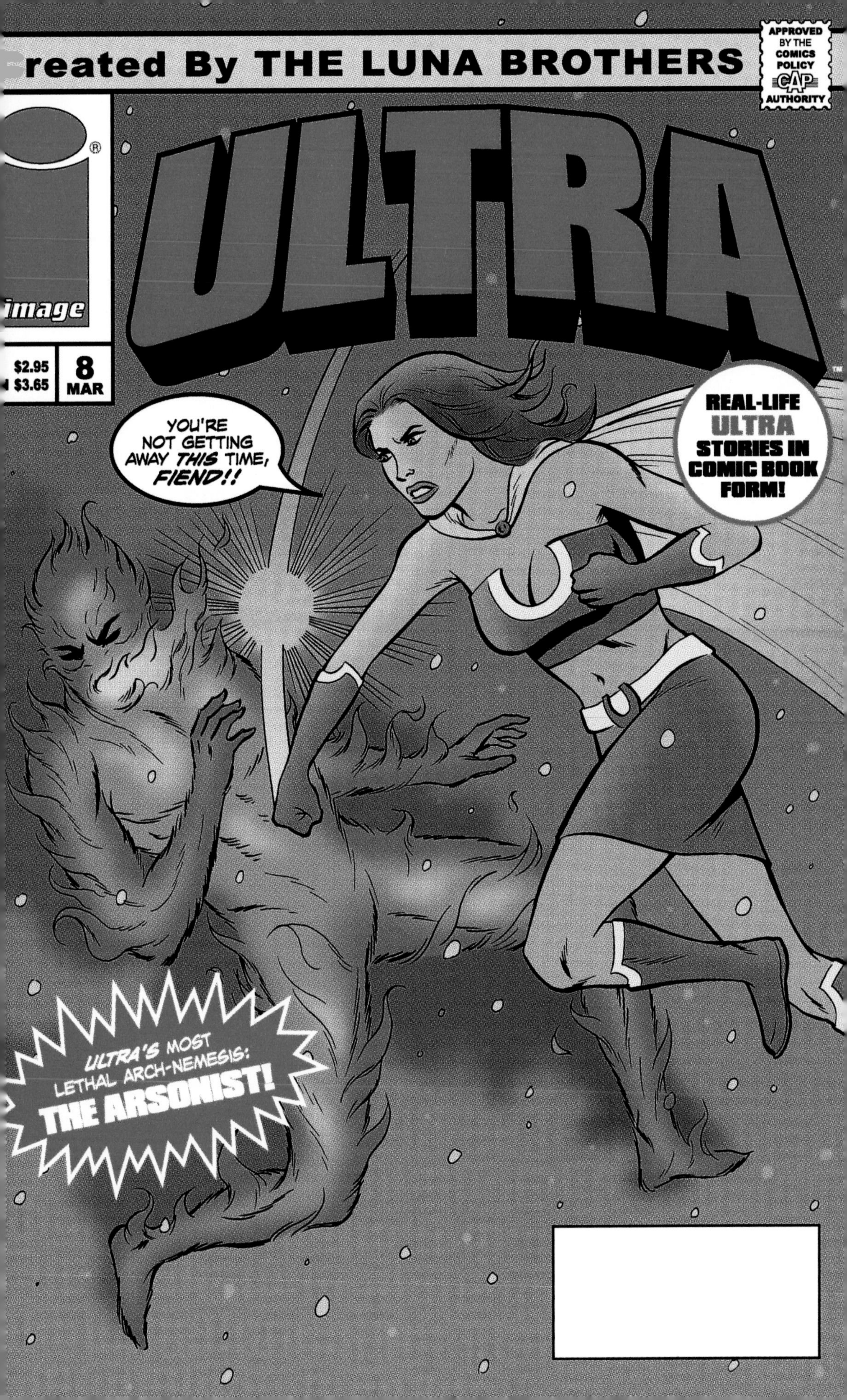

reated By THE LUNA BROTHERS
APPROVED BY THE COMICS POLICY CAP AUTHORITY
image
ULTRA
$2.95
$3.65
8
MAR
YOU'RE NOT GETTING AWAY THIS TIME, FIEND!!
REAL-LIFE ULTRA STORIES IN COMIC BOOK FORM!
ULTRA'S MOST LETHAL ARCH-NEMESIS: THE ARSONIST!

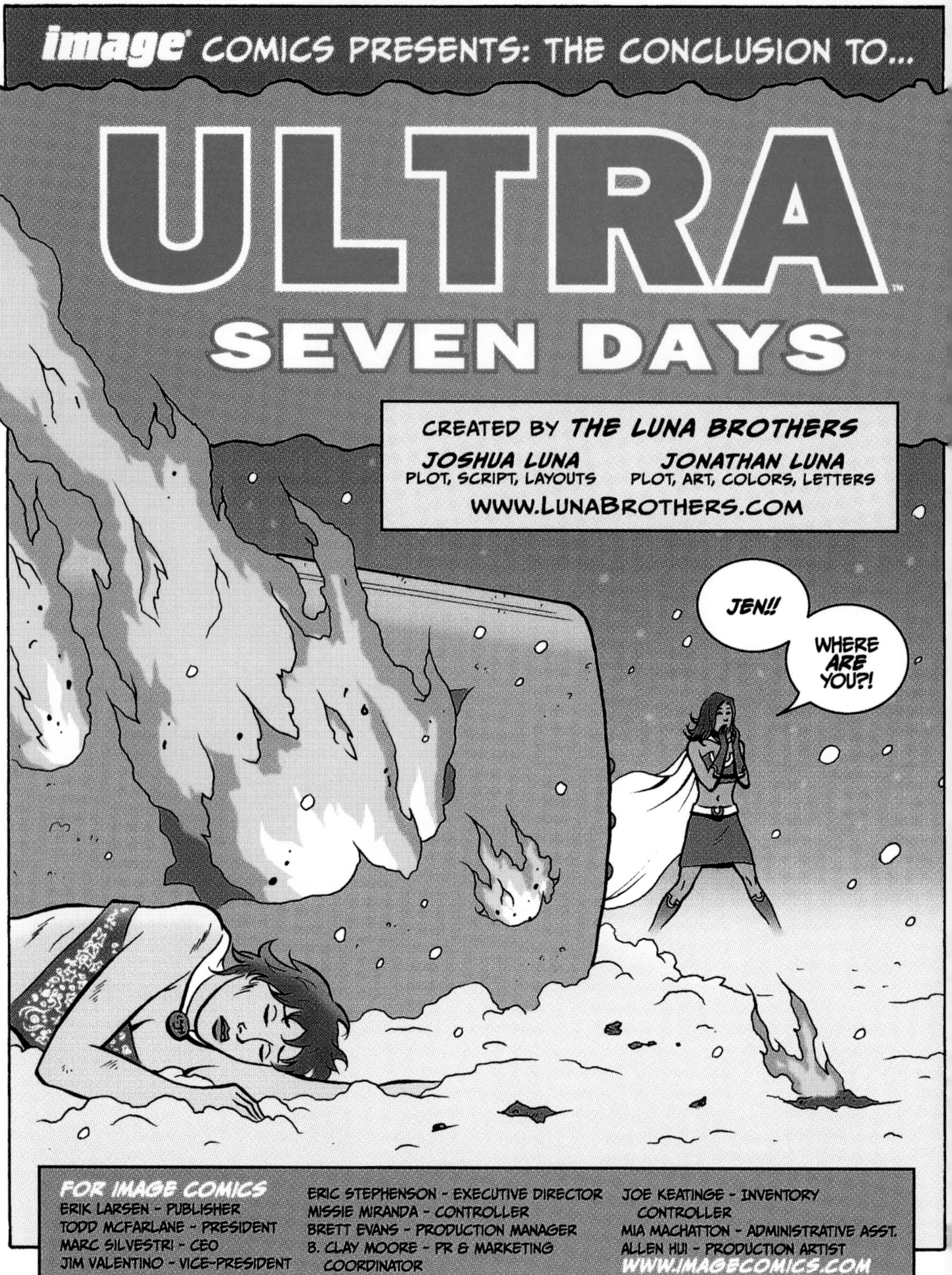
image COMICS PRESENTS: THE CONCLUSION TO...
ULTRA
SEVEN DAYS
CREATED BY THE LUNA BROTHERS
JOSHUA LUNA
PLOT, SCRIPT, LAYOUTS
JONATHAN LUNA
PLOT, ART, COLORS, LETTERS
WWW.LUNABROTHERS.COM
JEN!!
WHERE ARE YOU?!
FOR IMAGE COMICS
ERIK LARSEN - PUBLISHER
TODD MCFARLANE - PRESIDENT
MARC SILVESTRI - CEO
JIM VALENTINO - VICE-PRESIDENT
ERIC STEPHENSON - EXECUTIVE DIRECTOR
MISSIE MIRANDA - CONTROLLER
BRETT EVANS - PRODUCTION MANAGER
B. CLAY MOORE - PR & MARKETING COORDINATOR
JOE KEATINGE - INVENTORY CONTROLLER
MIA MACHATTON - ADMINISTRATIVE ASST.
ALLEN HUI - PRODUCTION ARTIST
WWW.IMAGECOMICS.COM

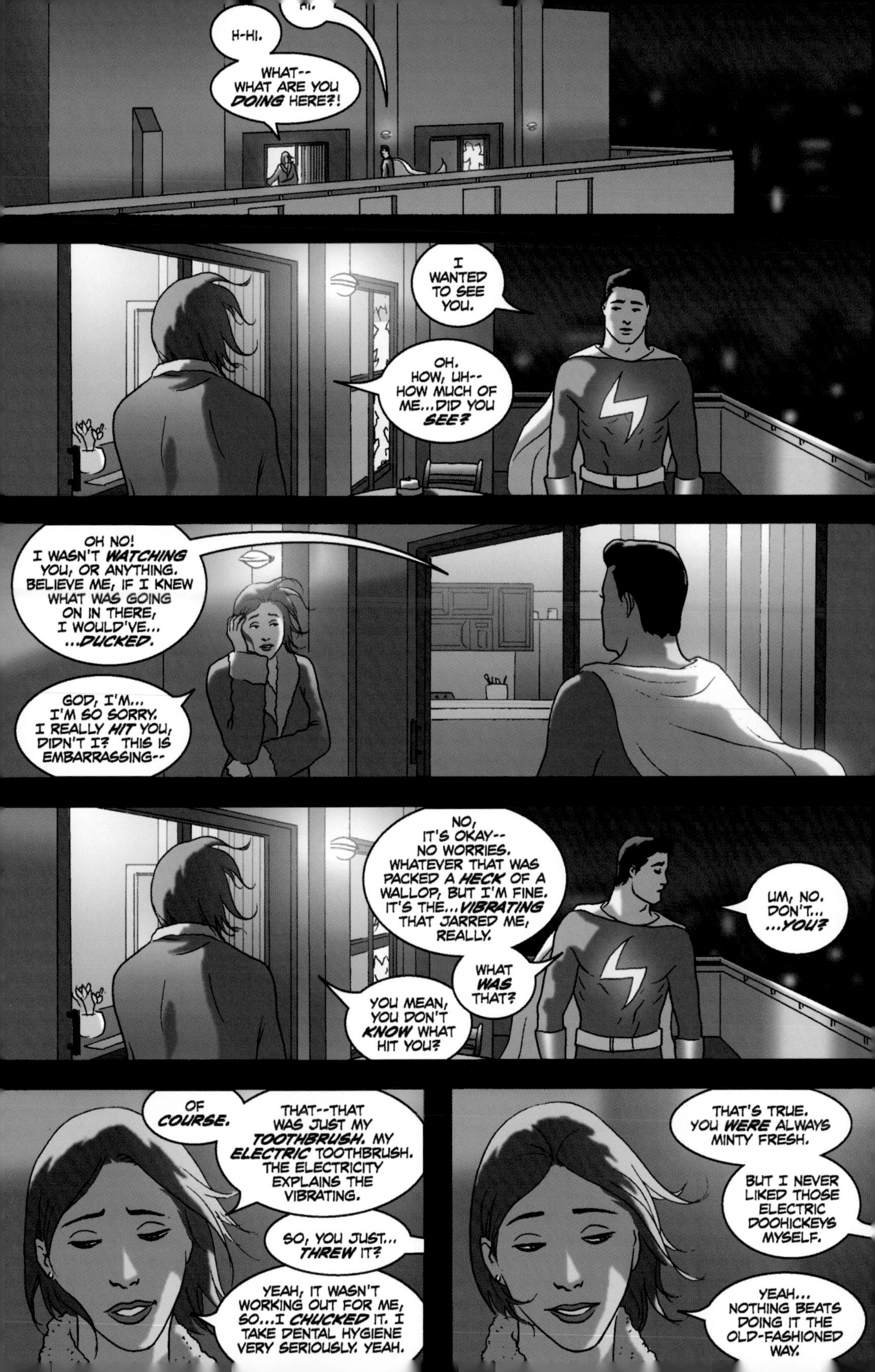
H-HI.
WHAT-- WHAT ARE YOU DOING HERE?!
I WANTED TO SEE YOU.
OH. HOW, UH-- HOW MUCH OF ME...DID YOU SEE?
OH NO! I WASN'T WATCHING YOU, OR ANYTHING. BELIEVE ME, IF I KNEW WHAT WAS GOING ON IN THERE, I WOULD'VE... ...DUCKED.
GOD, I'M... I'M SO SORRY. I REALLY HIT YOU, DIDN'T I? THIS IS EMBARRASSING--
NO, IT'S OKAY-- NO WORRIES. WHATEVER THAT WAS PACKED A HECK OF A WALLOP, BUT I'M FINE. IT'S THE...VIBRATING THAT JARRED ME, REALLY.
WHAT WAS THAT?
YOU MEAN, YOU DON'T KNOW WHAT HIT YOU?
UM, NO. DON'T... ...YOU?
OF COURSE.
THAT--THAT WAS JUST MY TOOTHBRUSH. MY ELECTRIC TOOTHBRUSH. THE ELECTRICITY EXPLAINS THE VIBRATING.
SO, YOU JUST... THREW IT?
YEAH, IT WASN'T WORKING OUT FOR ME, SO...I CHUCKED IT. I TAKE DENTAL HYGIENE VERY SERIOUSLY. YEAH.
THAT'S TRUE. YOU WERE ALWAYS MINTY FRESH.
BUT I NEVER LIKED THOSE ELECTRIC DOOHICKEYS MYSELF.
YEAH... NOTHING BEATS DOING IT THE OLD-FASHIONED WAY.

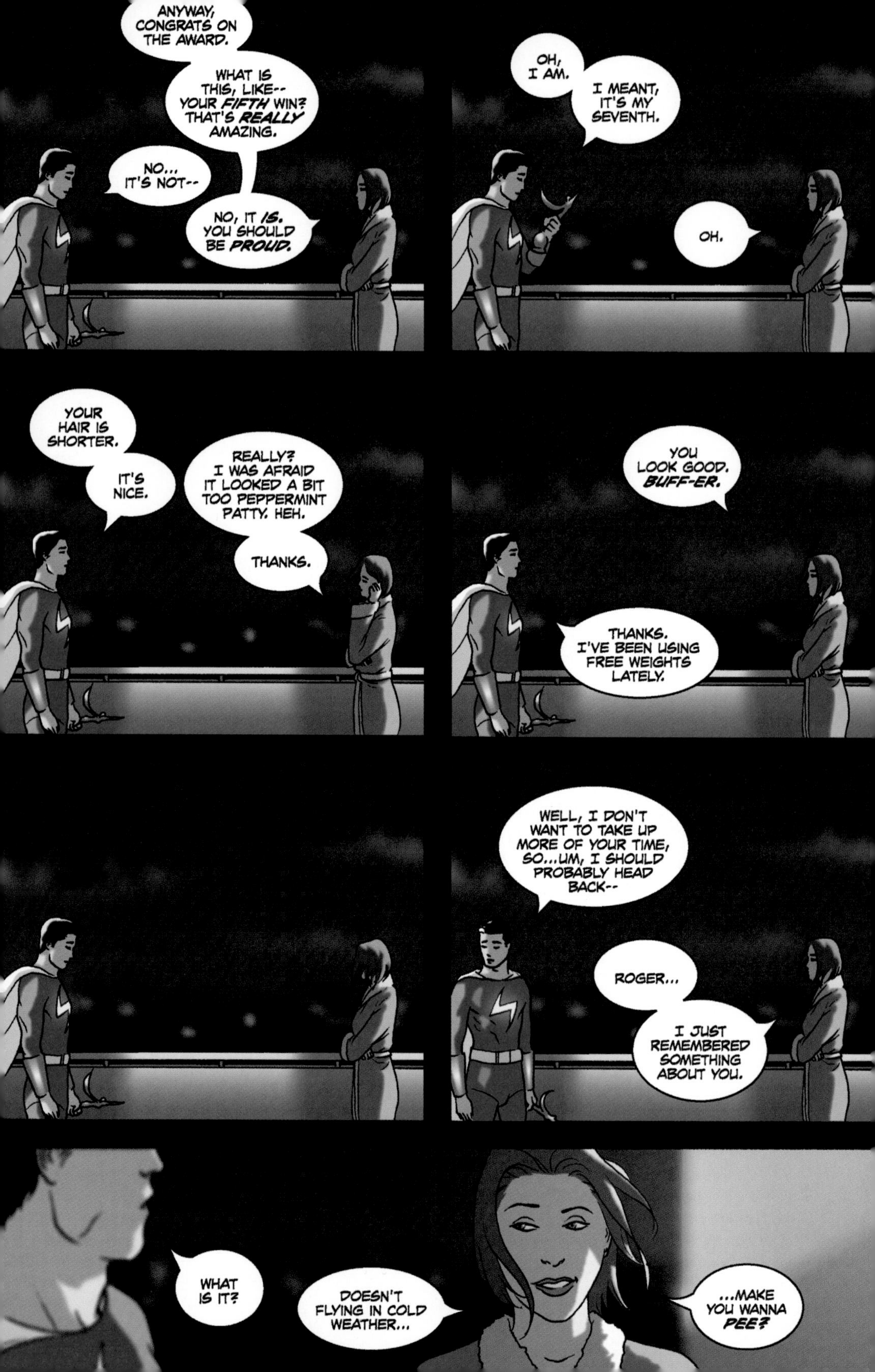
ANYWAY, CONGRATS ON THE AWARD.
WHAT IS THIS, LIKE-- YOUR FIFTH WIN? THAT'S REALLY AMAZING.
NO... IT'S NOT--
NO, IT IS. YOU SHOULD BE PROUD.
OH, I AM.
I MEANT, IT'S MY SEVENTH.
OH.
YOUR HAIR IS SHORTER.
IT'S NICE.
REALLY? I WAS AFRAID IT LOOKED A BIT TOO PEPPERMINT PATTY. HEH.
THANKS.
YOU LOOK GOOD. BUFF-ER.
THANKS. I'VE BEEN USING FREE WEIGHTS LATELY.
WELL, I DON'T WANT TO TAKE UP MORE OF YOUR TIME, SO...UM, I SHOULD PROBABLY HEAD BACK--
ROGER...
I JUST REMEMBERED SOMETHING ABOUT YOU.
WHAT IS IT?
DOESN'T FLYING IN COLD WEATHER...
...MAKE YOU WANNA PEE?

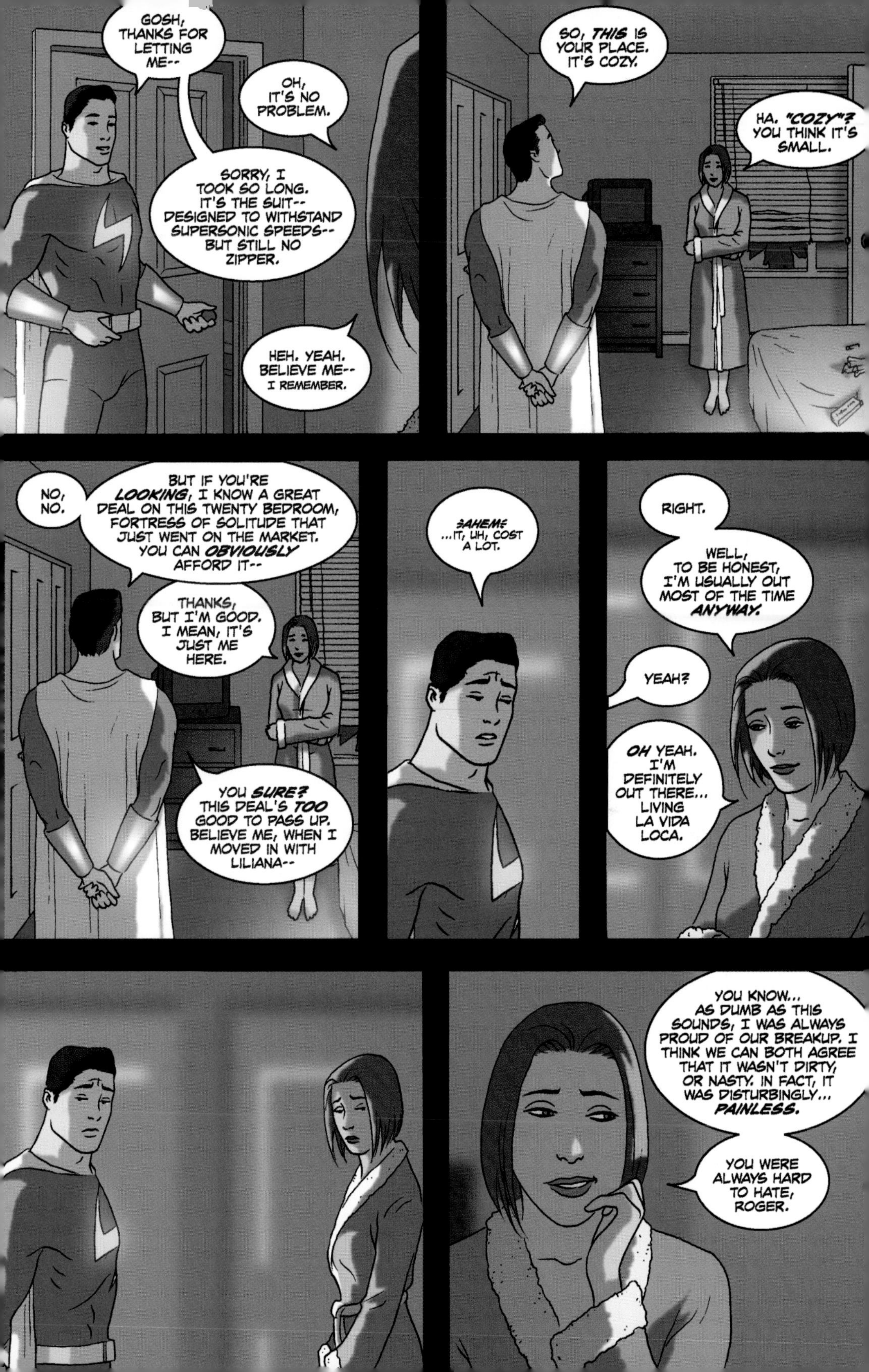
GOSH, THANKS FOR LETTING ME--
OH, IT'S NO PROBLEM.
SORRY, I TOOK SO LONG. IT'S THE SUIT-- DESIGNED TO WITHSTAND SUPERSONIC SPEEDS-- BUT STILL NO ZIPPER.
HEH. YEAH. BELIEVE ME-- I REMEMBER.
SO, THIS IS YOUR PLACE. IT'S COZY.
HA. "COZY"? YOU THINK IT'S SMALL.
NO, NO.
BUT IF YOU'RE LOOKING, I KNOW A GREAT DEAL ON THIS TWENTY BEDROOM, FORTRESS OF SOLITUDE THAT JUST WENT ON THE MARKET. YOU CAN OBVIOUSLY AFFORD IT--
THANKS, BUT I'M GOOD. I MEAN, IT'S JUST ME HERE.
YOU SURE? THIS DEAL'S TOO GOOD TO PASS UP. BELIEVE ME, WHEN I MOVED IN WITH LILIANA--
AHEM ...IT, UH, COST A LOT.
RIGHT.
WELL, TO BE HONEST, I'M USUALLY OUT MOST OF THE TIME ANYWAY.
YEAH?
OH YEAH. I'M DEFINITELY OUT THERE... LIVING LA VIDA LOCA.
YOU KNOW... AS DUMB AS THIS SOUNDS, I WAS ALWAYS PROUD OF OUR BREAKUP. I THINK WE CAN BOTH AGREE THAT IT WASN'T DIRTY, OR NASTY. IN FACT, IT WAS DISTURBINGLY... PAINLESS.
YOU WERE ALWAYS HARD TO HATE, ROGER.

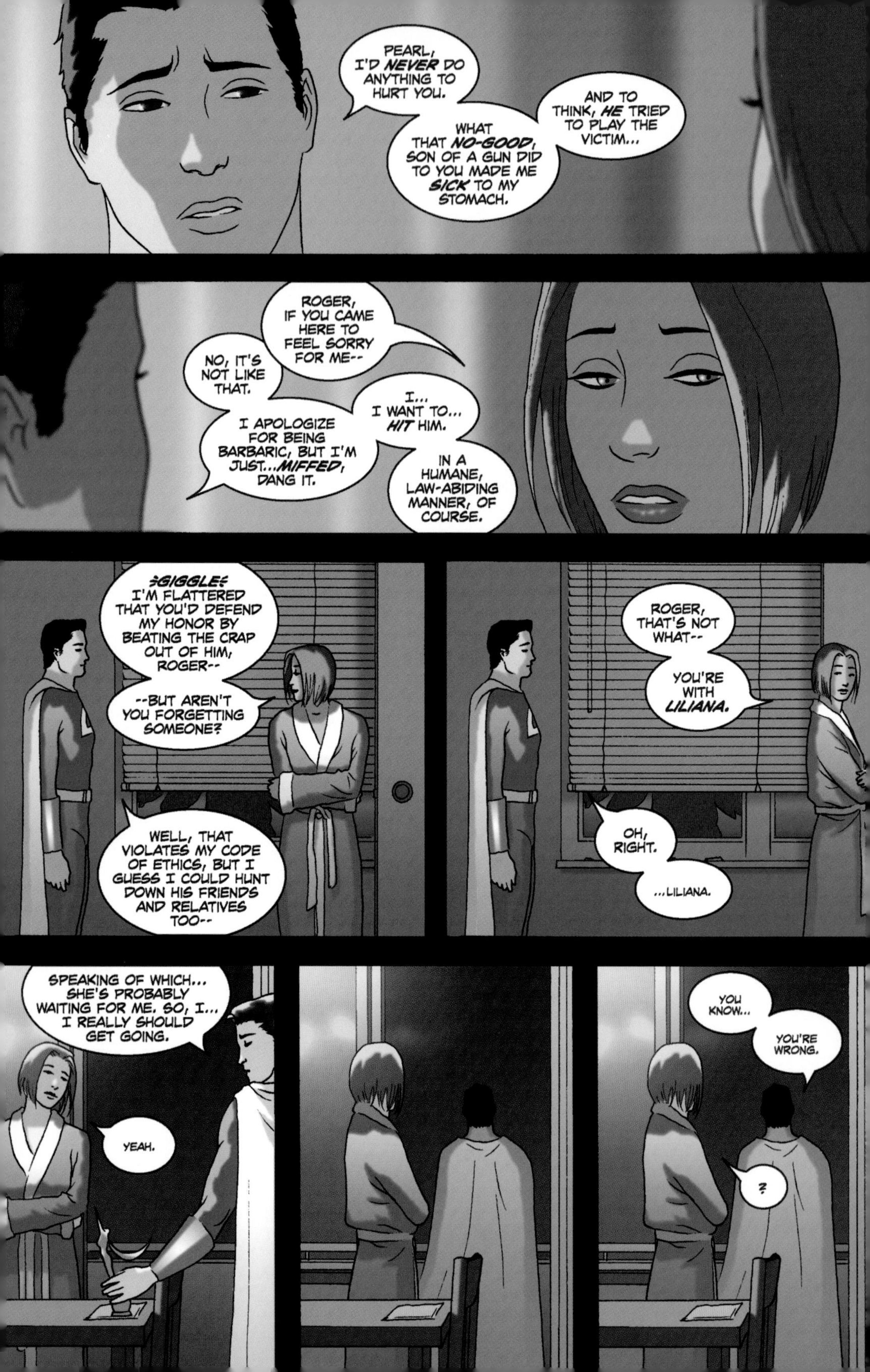
PEARL, I'D NEVER DO ANYTHING TO HURT YOU.
WHAT THAT NO-GOOD, SON OF A GUN DID TO YOU MADE ME SICK TO MY STOMACH.
AND TO THINK, HE TRIED TO PLAY THE VICTIM...
ROGER, IF YOU CAME HERE TO FEEL SORRY FOR ME--
NO, IT'S NOT LIKE THAT.
I... I WANT TO... HIT HIM.
I APOLOGIZE FOR BEING BARBARIC, BUT I'M JUST...MIFFED, DANG IT.
IN A HUMANE, LAW-ABIDING MANNER, OF COURSE.
:GIGGLE: I'M FLATTERED THAT YOU'D DEFEND MY HONOR BY BEATING THE CRAP OUT OF HIM, ROGER--
--BUT AREN'T YOU FORGETTING SOMEONE?
WELL, THAT VIOLATES MY CODE OF ETHICS, BUT I GUESS I COULD HUNT DOWN HIS FRIENDS AND RELATIVES TOO--
ROGER, THAT'S NOT WHAT--
YOU'RE WITH LILIANA.
OH, RIGHT.
...LILIANA.
SPEAKING OF WHICH... SHE'S PROBABLY WAITING FOR ME. SO, I... I REALLY SHOULD GET GOING.
YEAH.
YOU KNOW...
YOU'RE WRONG.
?

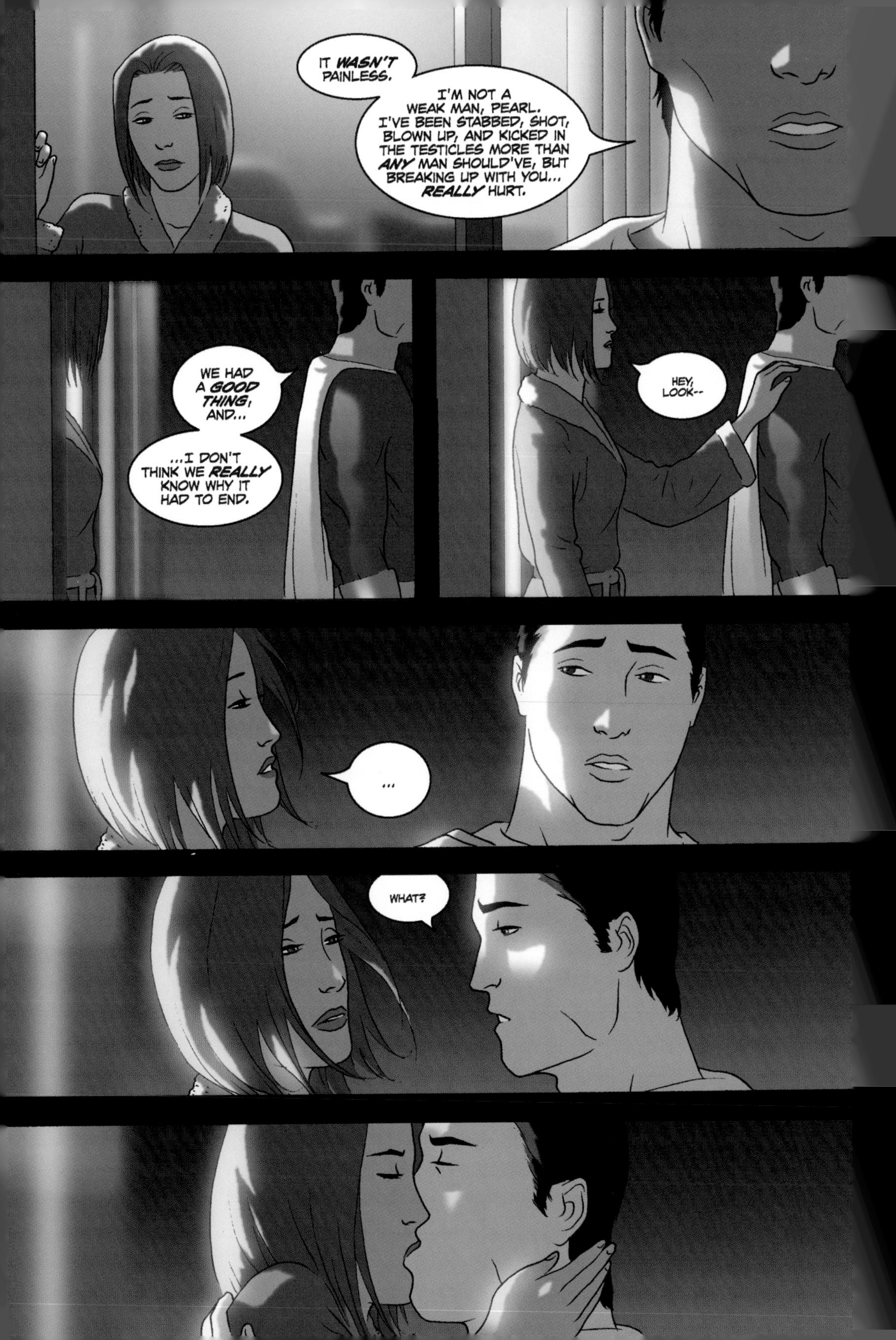
IT WASN'T PAINLESS.
I'M NOT A WEAK MAN, PEARL. I'VE BEEN STABBED, SHOT, BLOWN UP, AND KICKED IN THE TESTICLES MORE THAN ANY MAN SHOULD'VE, BUT BREAKING UP WITH YOU... REALLY HURT.
WE HAD A GOOD THING, AND...
...I DON'T THINK WE REALLY KNOW WHY IT HAD TO END.
HEY, LOOK--
...
WHAT?

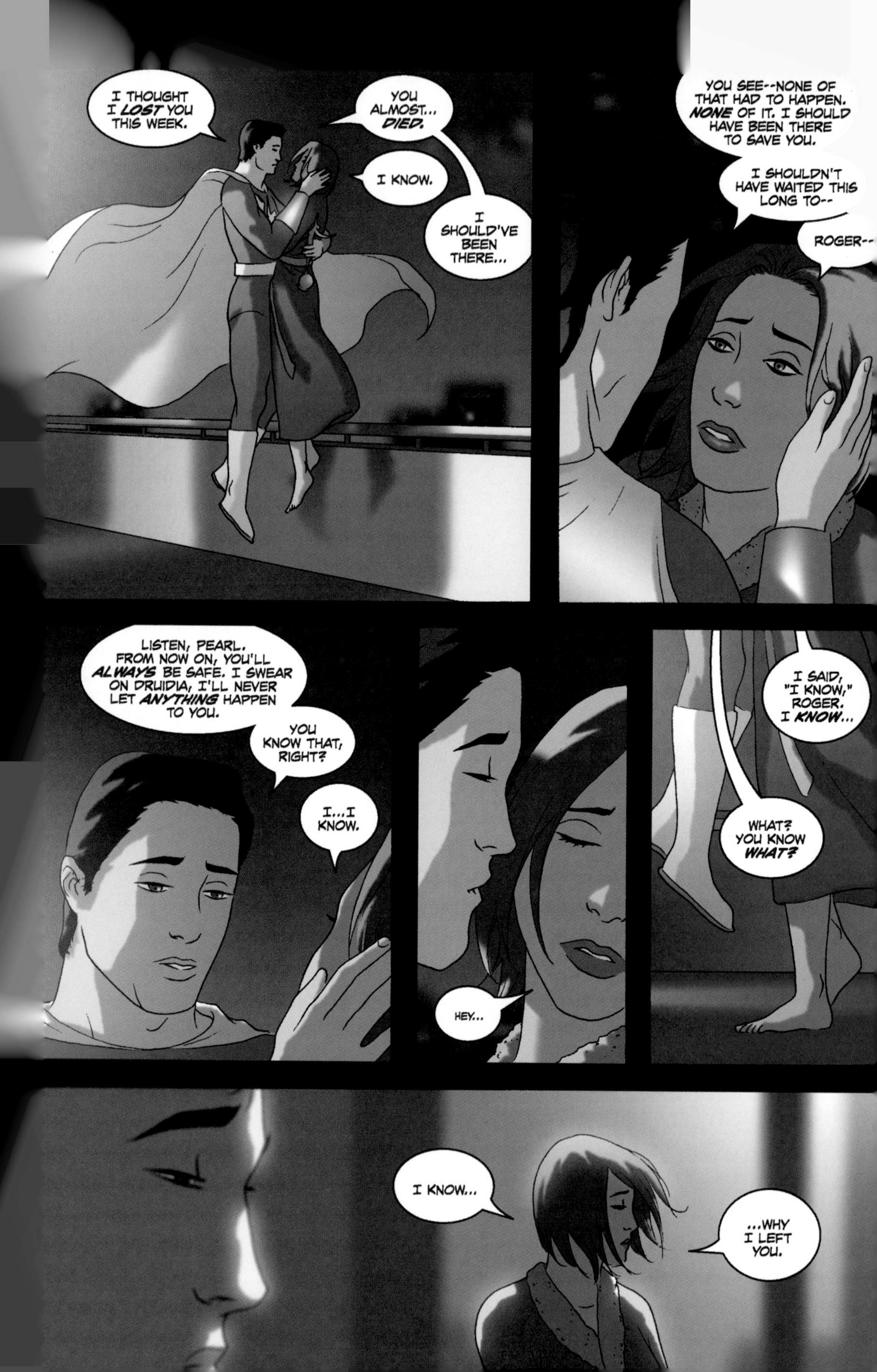
I THOUGHT I *LOST* YOU THIS WEEK.
YOU ALMOST... *DIED.*
I KNOW.
I SHOULD'VE BEEN THERE...
YOU SEE--NONE OF THAT HAD TO HAPPEN. *NONE* OF IT. I SHOULD HAVE BEEN THERE TO SAVE YOU.
I SHOULDN'T HAVE WAITED THIS LONG TO--
ROGER--
LISTEN, PEARL. FROM NOW ON, YOU'LL *ALWAYS* BE SAFE. I SWEAR ON DRUIDIA, I'LL NEVER LET *ANYTHING* HAPPEN TO YOU.
YOU KNOW THAT, RIGHT?
I...I KNOW.
HEY...
I SAID, "I KNOW," ROGER. I *KNOW*...
WHAT? YOU KNOW *WHAT?*
I KNOW...
...WHY I LEFT YOU.

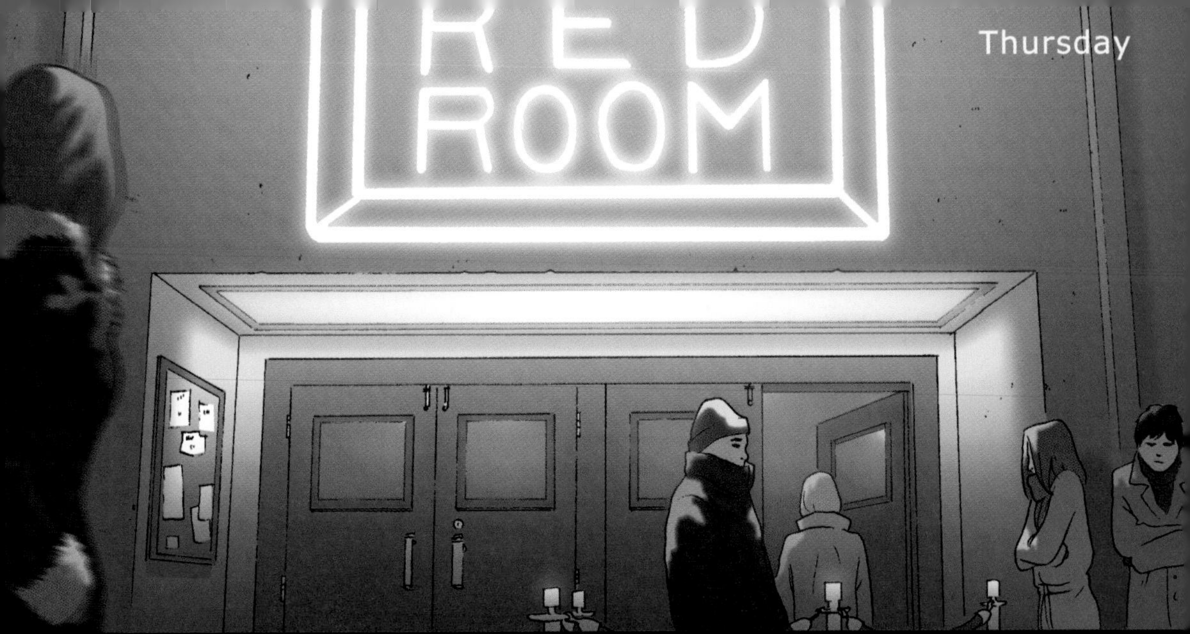
Thursday
RED
ROOM

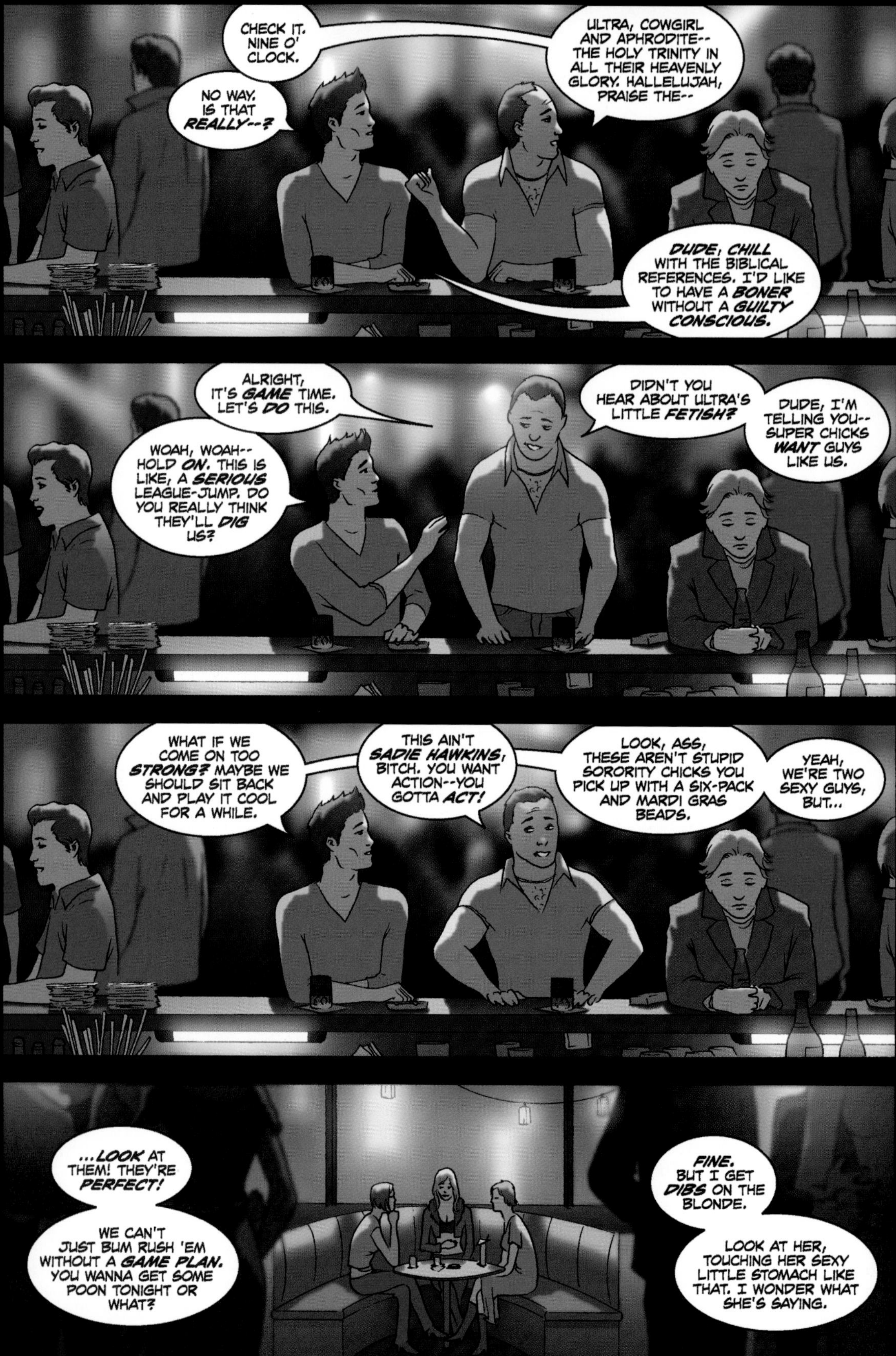
CHECK IT. NINE O' CLOCK.
ULTRA, COWGIRL AND APHRODITE-- THE HOLY TRINITY IN ALL THEIR HEAVENLY GLORY. HALLELUJAH, PRAISE THE--
NO WAY. IS THAT REALLY--?
DUDE, CHILL WITH THE BIBLICAL REFERENCES. I'D LIKE TO HAVE A BONER WITHOUT A GUILTY CONSCIOUS.
ALRIGHT, IT'S GAME TIME. LET'S DO THIS.
WOAH, WOAH-- HOLD ON. THIS IS LIKE, A SERIOUS LEAGUE-JUMP. DO YOU REALLY THINK THEY'LL DIG US?
DIDN'T YOU HEAR ABOUT ULTRA'S LITTLE FETISH?
DUDE, I'M TELLING YOU-- SUPER CHICKS WANT GUYS LIKE US.
WHAT IF WE COME ON TOO STRONG? MAYBE WE SHOULD SIT BACK AND PLAY IT COOL FOR A WHILE.
THIS AIN'T SADIE HAWKINS, BITCH. YOU WANT ACTION--YOU GOTTA ACT!
LOOK, ASS, THESE AREN'T STUPID SORORITY CHICKS YOU PICK UP WITH A SIX-PACK AND MARDI GRAS BEADS.
YEAH, WE'RE TWO SEXY GUYS, BUT...
...LOOK AT THEM! THEY'RE PERFECT!
WE CAN'T JUST BUM RUSH 'EM WITHOUT A GAME PLAN. YOU WANNA GET SOME POON TONIGHT OR WHAT?
FINE. BUT I GET DIBS ON THE BLONDE.
LOOK AT HER, TOUCHING HER SEXY LITTLE STOMACH LIKE THAT. I WONDER WHAT SHE'S SAYING.

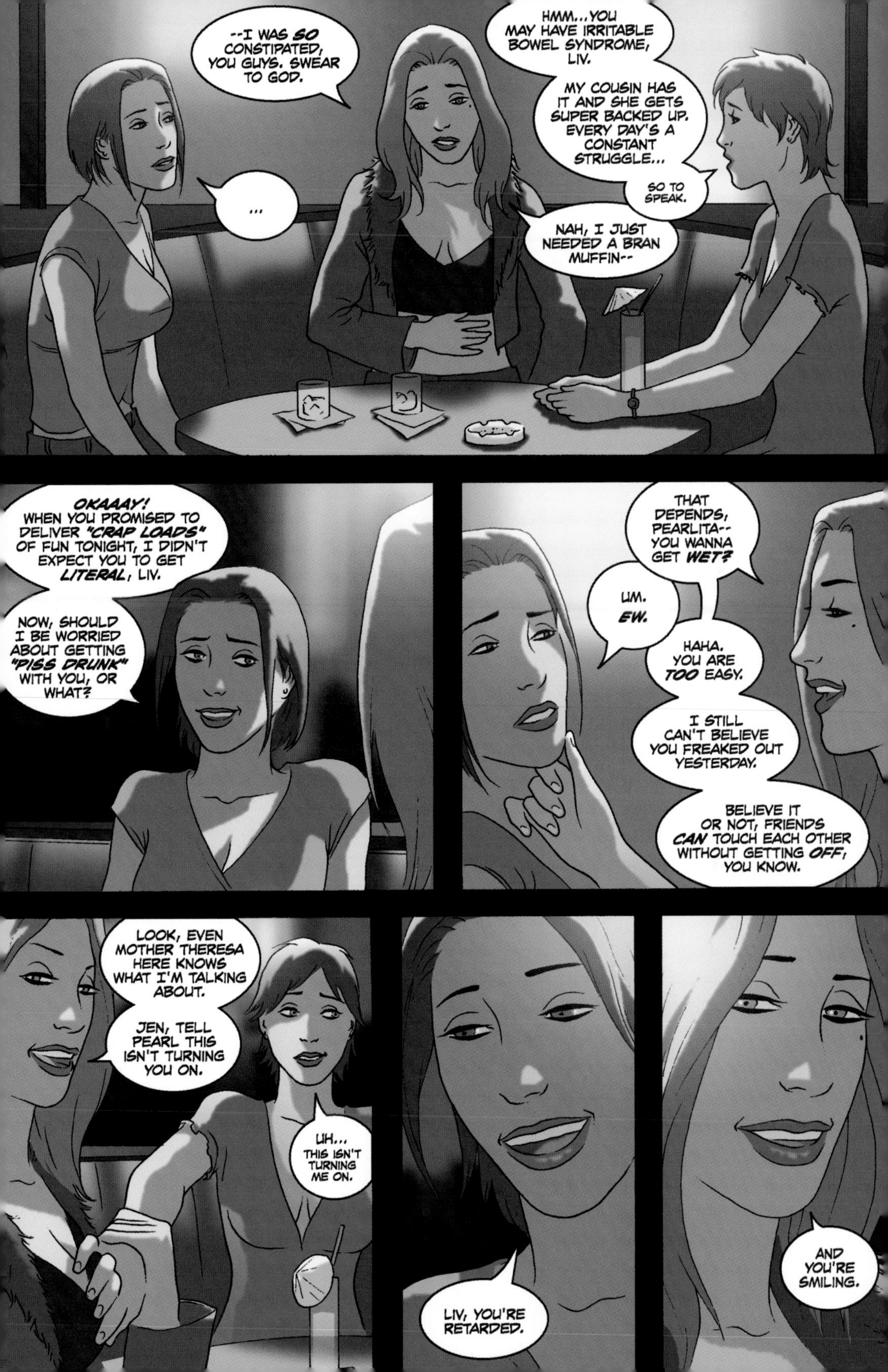
--I WAS SO CONSTIPATED, YOU GUYS. SWEAR TO GOD.
HMM...YOU MAY HAVE IRRITABLE BOWEL SYNDROME, LIV.
MY COUSIN HAS IT AND SHE GETS SUPER BACKED UP. EVERY DAY'S A CONSTANT STRUGGLE...
SO TO SPEAK.
...
NAH, I JUST NEEDED A BRAN MUFFIN--
OKAAAY! WHEN YOU PROMISED TO DELIVER "CRAP LOADS" OF FUN TONIGHT, I DIDN'T EXPECT YOU TO GET LITERAL, LIV.
NOW, SHOULD I BE WORRIED ABOUT GETTING "PISS DRUNK" WITH YOU, OR WHAT?
THAT DEPENDS, PEARLITA--YOU WANNA GET WET?
UM. EW.
HAHA. YOU ARE TOO EASY.
I STILL CAN'T BELIEVE YOU FREAKED OUT YESTERDAY.
BELIEVE IT OR NOT, FRIENDS CAN TOUCH EACH OTHER WITHOUT GETTING OFF, YOU KNOW.
LOOK, EVEN MOTHER THERESA HERE KNOWS WHAT I'M TALKING ABOUT.
JEN, TELL PEARL THIS ISN'T TURNING YOU ON.
UH... THIS ISN'T TURNING ME ON.
LIV, YOU'RE RETARDED.
AND YOU'RE SMILING.

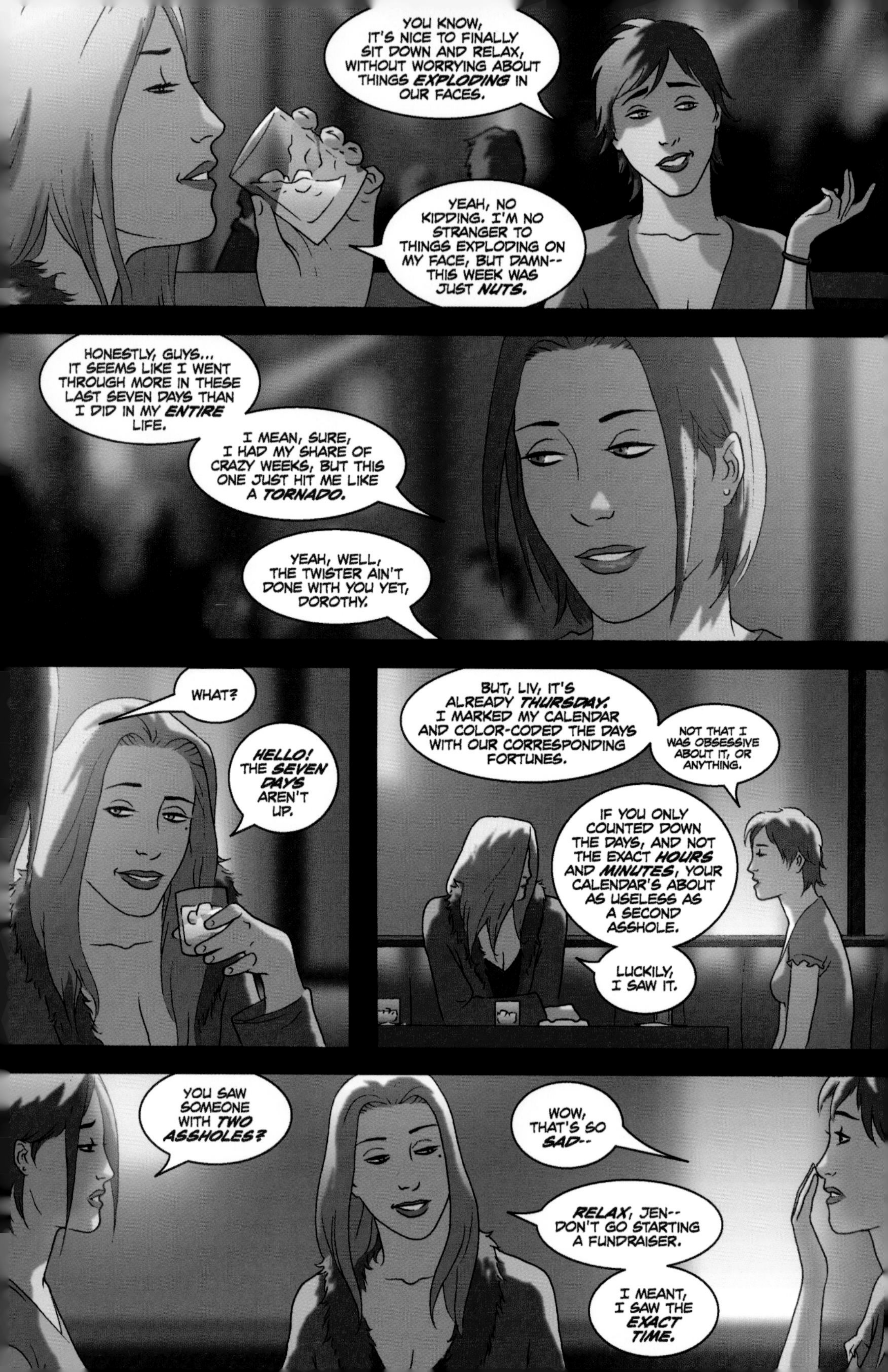
YOU KNOW, IT'S NICE TO FINALLY SIT DOWN AND RELAX, WITHOUT WORRYING ABOUT THINGS *EXPLODING* IN OUR FACES.
YEAH, NO KIDDING. I'M NO STRANGER TO THINGS EXPLODING ON MY FACE, BUT DAMN-- THIS WEEK WAS JUST *NUTS.*
HONESTLY, GUYS... IT SEEMS LIKE I WENT THROUGH MORE IN THESE LAST SEVEN DAYS THAN I DID IN MY *ENTIRE* LIFE.
I MEAN, SURE, I HAD MY SHARE OF CRAZY WEEKS, BUT THIS ONE JUST HIT ME LIKE A *TORNADO.*
YEAH, WELL, THE TWISTER AIN'T DONE WITH YOU YET, DOROTHY.
WHAT?
HELLO! THE *SEVEN DAYS* AREN'T UP.
BUT, LIV, IT'S ALREADY *THURSDAY.* I MARKED MY CALENDAR AND COLOR-CODED THE DAYS WITH OUR CORRESPONDING FORTUNES.
NOT THAT I WAS OBSESSIVE ABOUT IT, OR ANYTHING.
IF YOU ONLY COUNTED DOWN THE DAYS, AND NOT THE EXACT *HOURS* AND *MINUTES*, YOUR CALENDAR'S ABOUT AS USELESS AS A SECOND ASSHOLE.
LUCKILY, I SAW IT.
YOU SAW SOMEONE WITH *TWO ASSHOLES?*
WOW, THAT'S SO *SAD--*
RELAX, JEN-- DON'T GO STARTING A FUNDRAISER.
I MEANT, I SAW THE *EXACT TIME.*

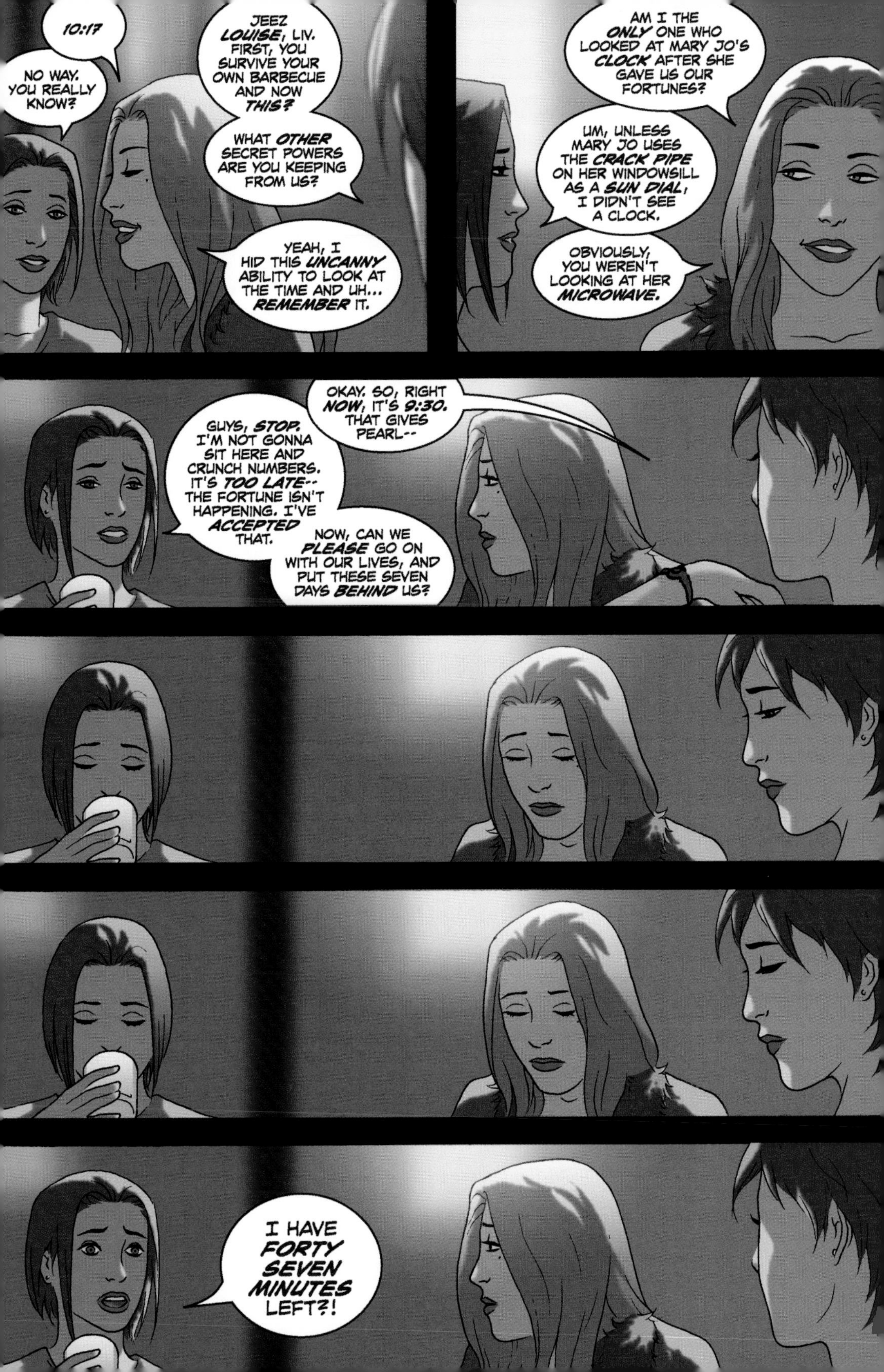
10:17
NO WAY. YOU REALLY KNOW?
JEEZ LOUISE, LIV. FIRST, YOU SURVIVE YOUR OWN BARBECUE AND NOW THIS?
WHAT OTHER SECRET POWERS ARE YOU KEEPING FROM US?
YEAH, I HID THIS UNCANNY ABILITY TO LOOK AT THE TIME AND UH... REMEMBER IT.
AM I THE ONLY ONE WHO LOOKED AT MARY JO'S CLOCK AFTER SHE GAVE US OUR FORTUNES?
UM, UNLESS MARY JO USES THE CRACK PIPE ON HER WINDOWSILL AS A SUN DIAL, I DIDN'T SEE A CLOCK.
OBVIOUSLY, YOU WEREN'T LOOKING AT HER MICROWAVE.
OKAY. SO, RIGHT NOW, IT'S 9:30. THAT GIVES PEARL--
GUYS, STOP. I'M NOT GONNA SIT HERE AND CRUNCH NUMBERS. IT'S TOO LATE-- THE FORTUNE ISN'T HAPPENING. I'VE ACCEPTED THAT.
NOW, CAN WE PLEASE GO ON WITH OUR LIVES, AND PUT THESE SEVEN DAYS BEHIND US?
I HAVE FORTY SEVEN MINUTES LEFT?!

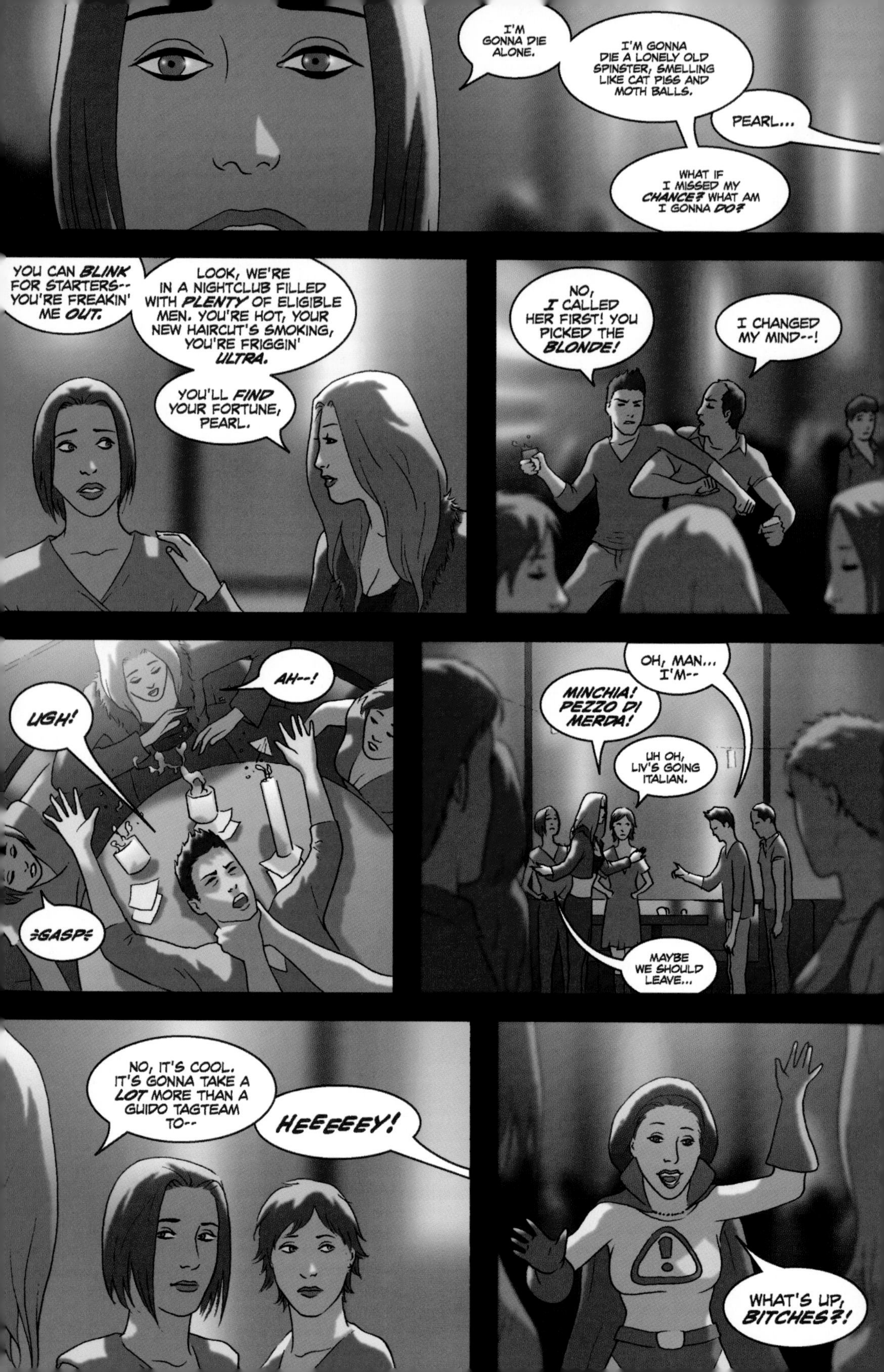
I'M GONNA DIE ALONE.
I'M GONNA DIE A LONELY OLD SPINSTER, SMELLING LIKE CAT PISS AND MOTH BALLS.
PEARL...
WHAT IF I MISSED MY CHANCE? WHAT AM I GONNA DO?
YOU CAN BLINK FOR STARTERS-- YOU'RE FREAKIN' ME OUT.
LOOK, WE'RE IN A NIGHTCLUB FILLED WITH PLENTY OF ELIGIBLE MEN. YOU'RE HOT, YOUR NEW HAIRCUT'S SMOKING, YOU'RE FRIGGIN' ULTRA.
YOU'LL FIND YOUR FORTUNE, PEARL.
NO, I CALLED HER FIRST! YOU PICKED THE BLONDE!
I CHANGED MY MIND--!
UGH!
AH--!
GASP
OH, MAN... I'M--
MINCHIA! PEZZO DI MERDA!
UH OH, LIV'S GOING ITALIAN.
MAYBE WE SHOULD LEAVE...
NO, IT'S COOL. IT'S GONNA TAKE A LOT MORE THAN A GUIDO TAGTEAM TO--
HEEEEEY!
WHAT'S UP, BITCHES?!

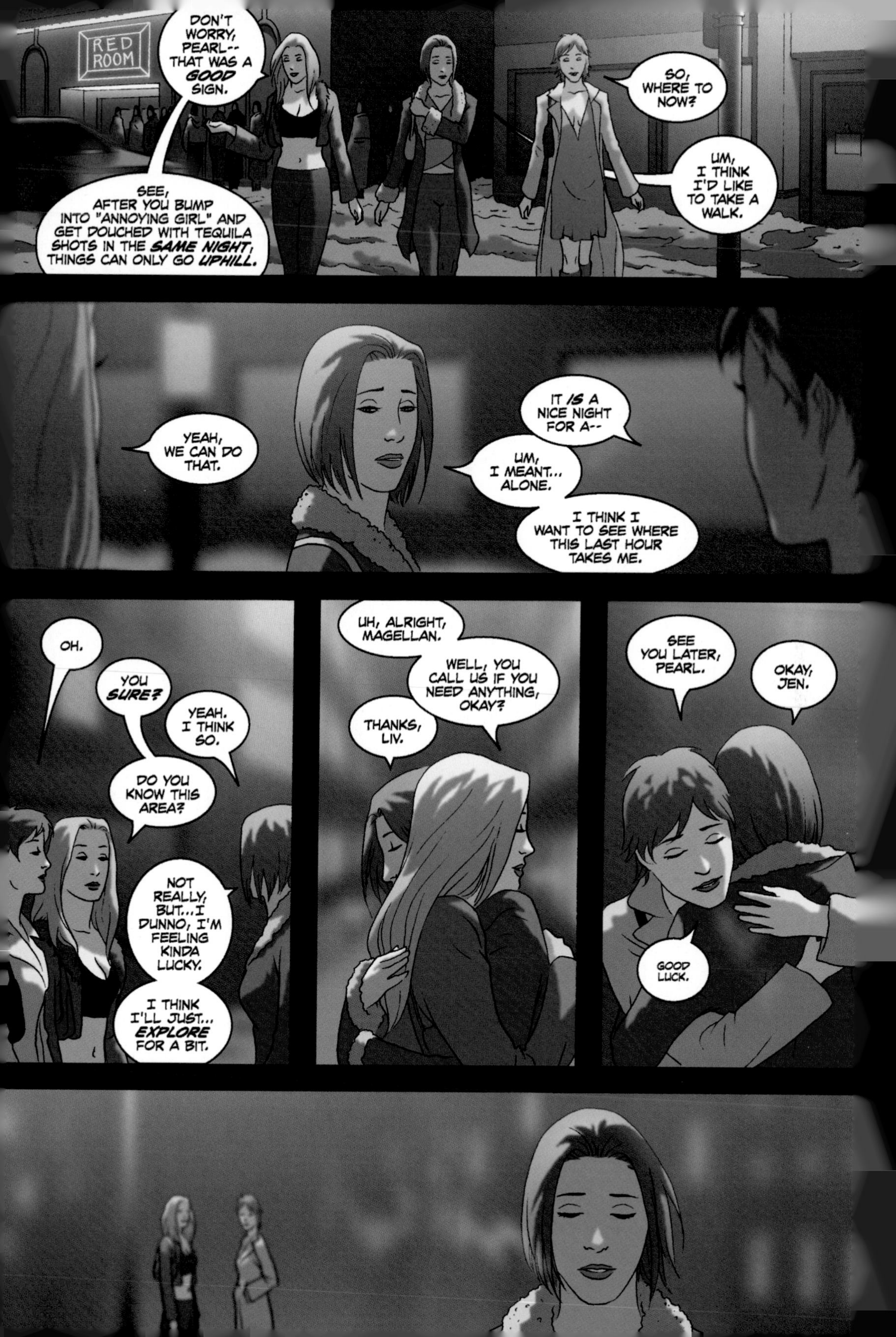
RED ROOM
DON'T WORRY, PEARL-- THAT WAS A GOOD SIGN.
SEE, AFTER YOU BUMP INTO "ANNOYING GIRL" AND GET DOUCHED WITH TEQUILA SHOTS IN THE SAME NIGHT, THINGS CAN ONLY GO UPHILL.
SO, WHERE TO NOW?
UM, I THINK I'D LIKE TO TAKE A WALK.
YEAH, WE CAN DO THAT.
IT IS A NICE NIGHT FOR A--
UM, I MEANT... ALONE.
I THINK I WANT TO SEE WHERE THIS LAST HOUR TAKES ME.
OH.
YOU SURE?
YEAH. I THINK SO.
DO YOU KNOW THIS AREA?
NOT REALLY, BUT... I DUNNO, I'M FEELING KINDA LUCKY.
I THINK I'LL JUST... EXPLORE FOR A BIT.
UH, ALRIGHT, MAGELLAN.
WELL, YOU CALL US IF YOU NEED ANYTHING, OKAY?
THANKS, LIV.
SEE YOU LATER, PEARL.
OKAY, JEN.
GOOD LUCK.

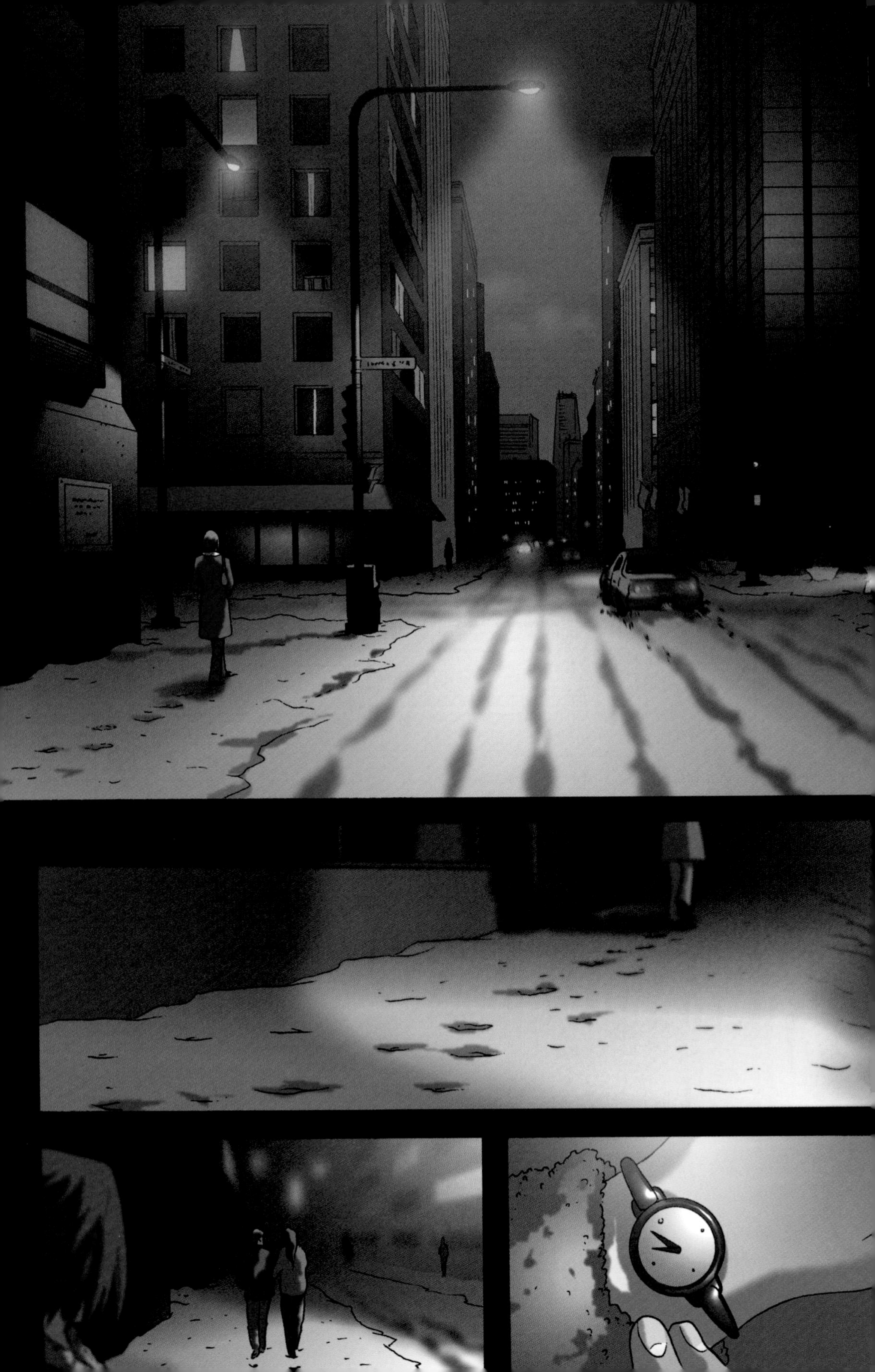

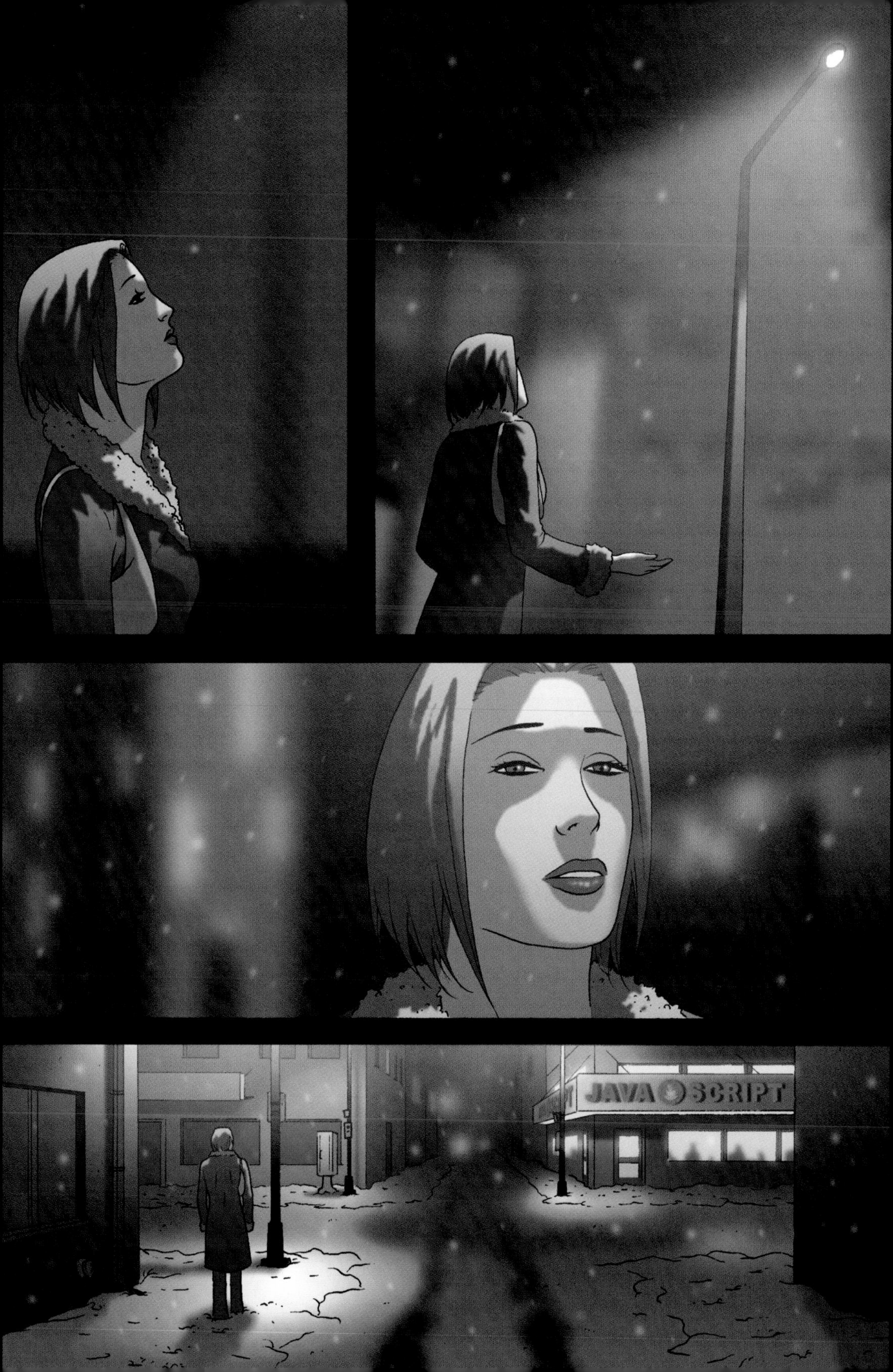
JAVA SCRIPT

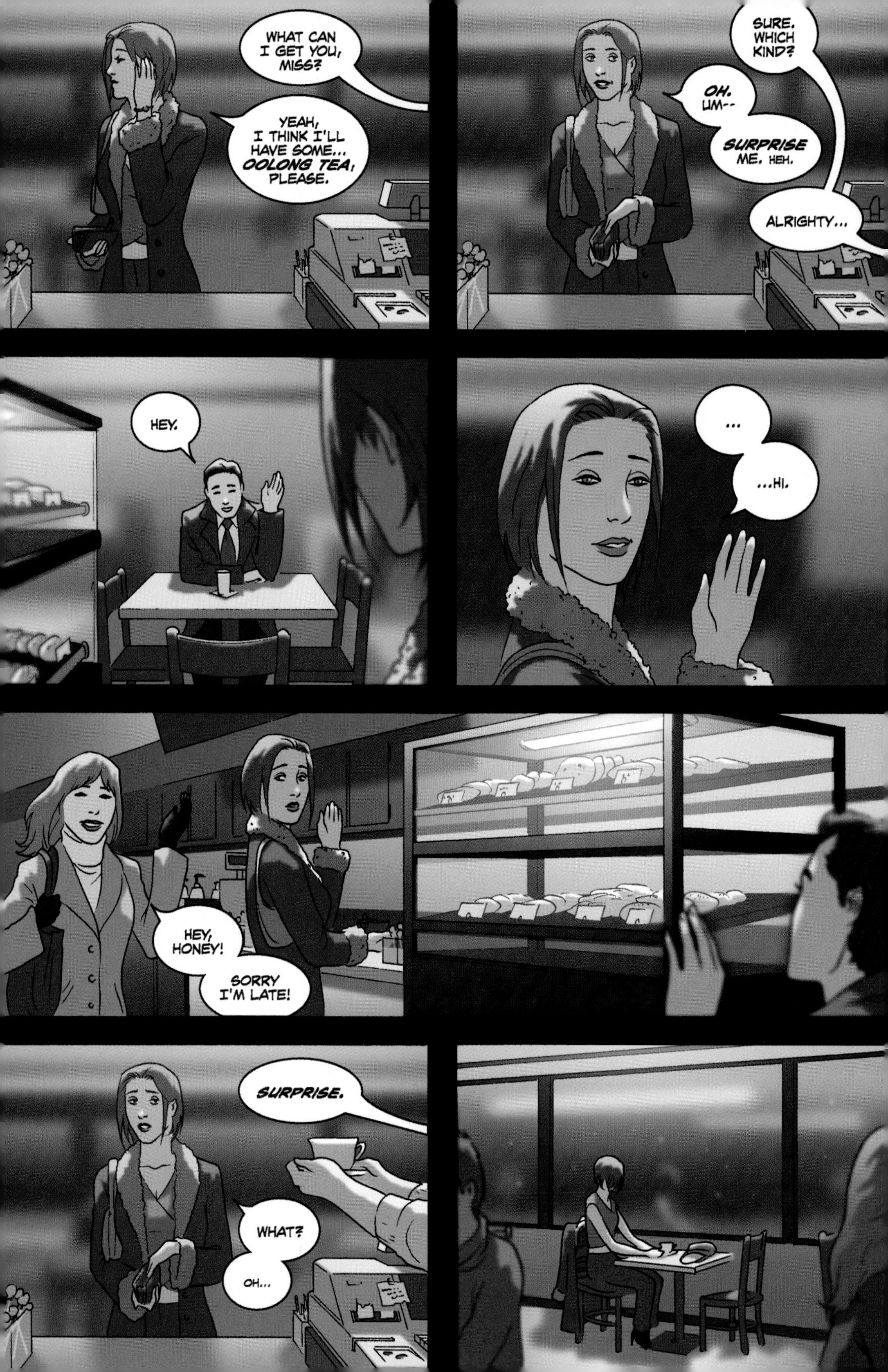
WHAT CAN I GET YOU, MISS?
YEAH, I THINK I'LL HAVE SOME... OOLONG TEA, PLEASE.
SURE. WHICH KIND?
OH. UM--
SURPRISE ME. HEH.
ALRIGHTY...
HEY.
...
...HI.
HEY, HONEY!
SORRY I'M LATE!
SURPRISE.
WHAT?
OH...

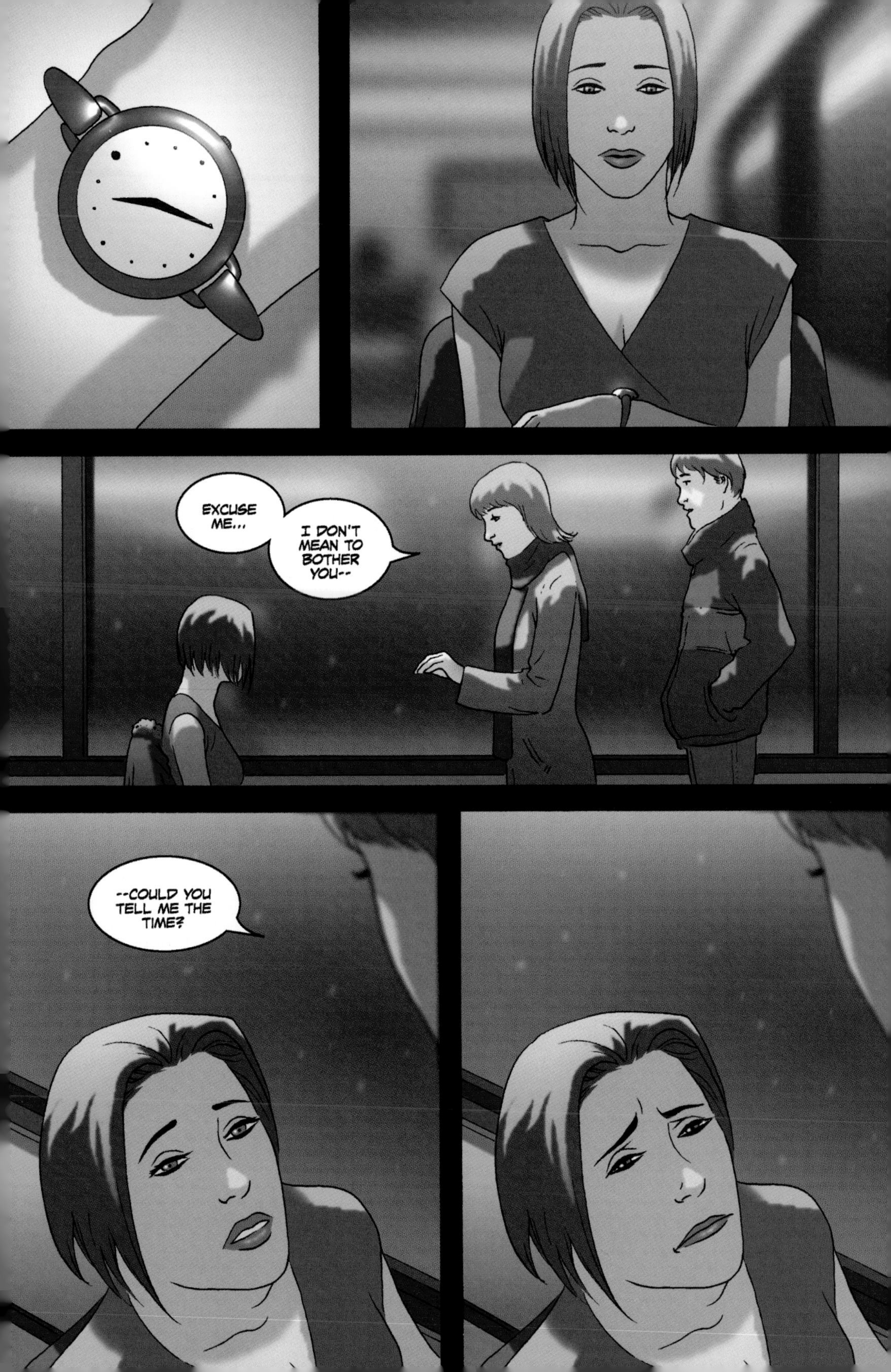
EXCUSE ME...
I DON'T MEAN TO BOTHER YOU--
--COULD YOU TELL ME THE TIME?

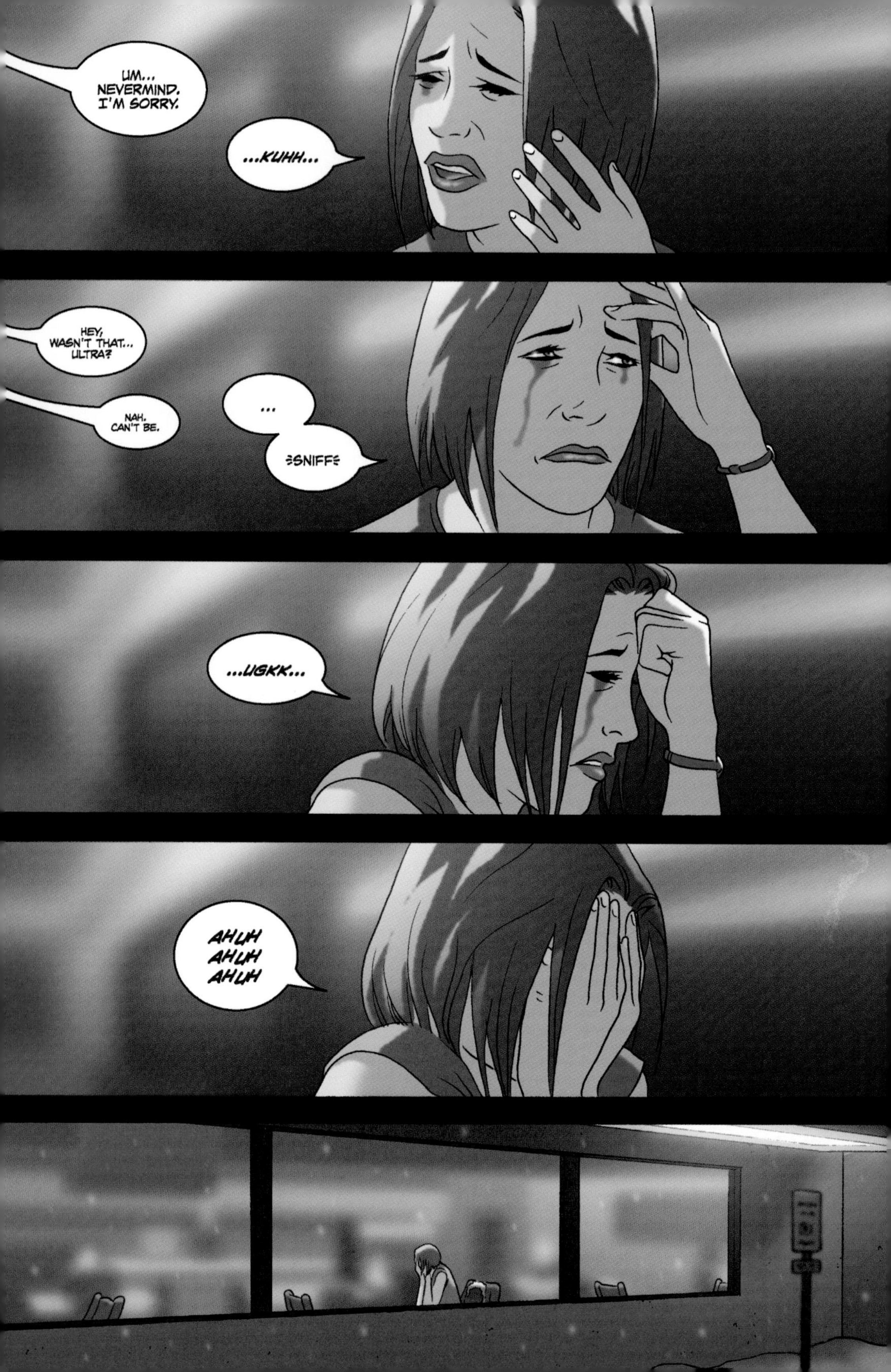
UM... NEVERMIND. I'M SORRY.
...KUHH...
HEY, WASN'T THAT... ULTRA?
NAH. CAN'T BE.
...
SNIFF
...UGKK...
AHUH AHUH AHUH

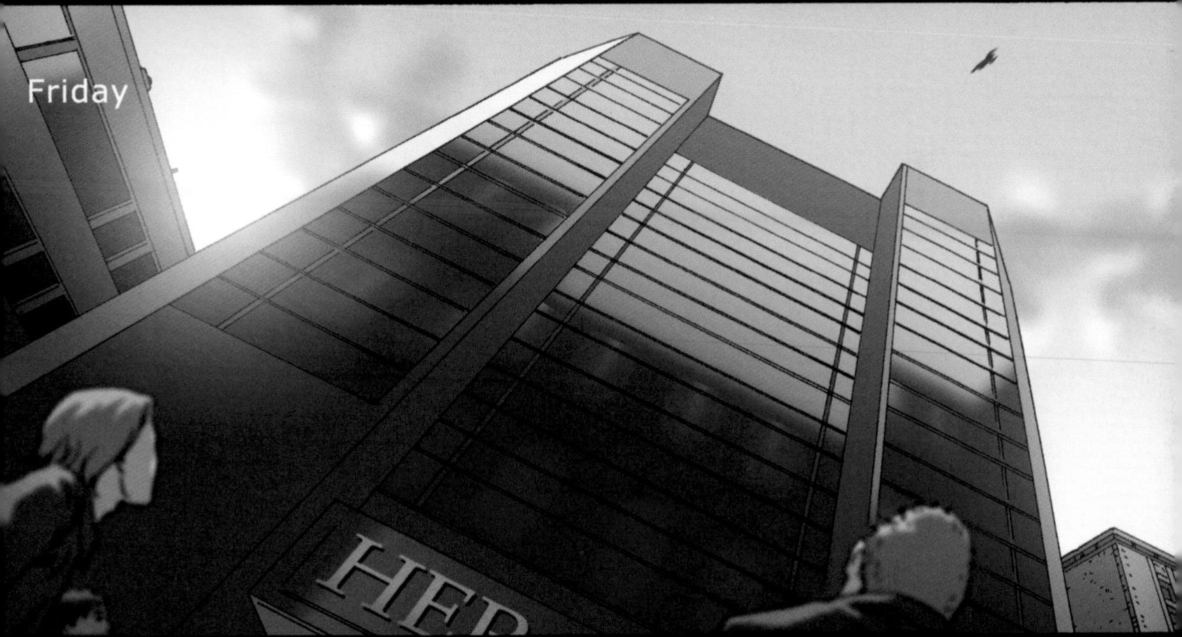
Friday

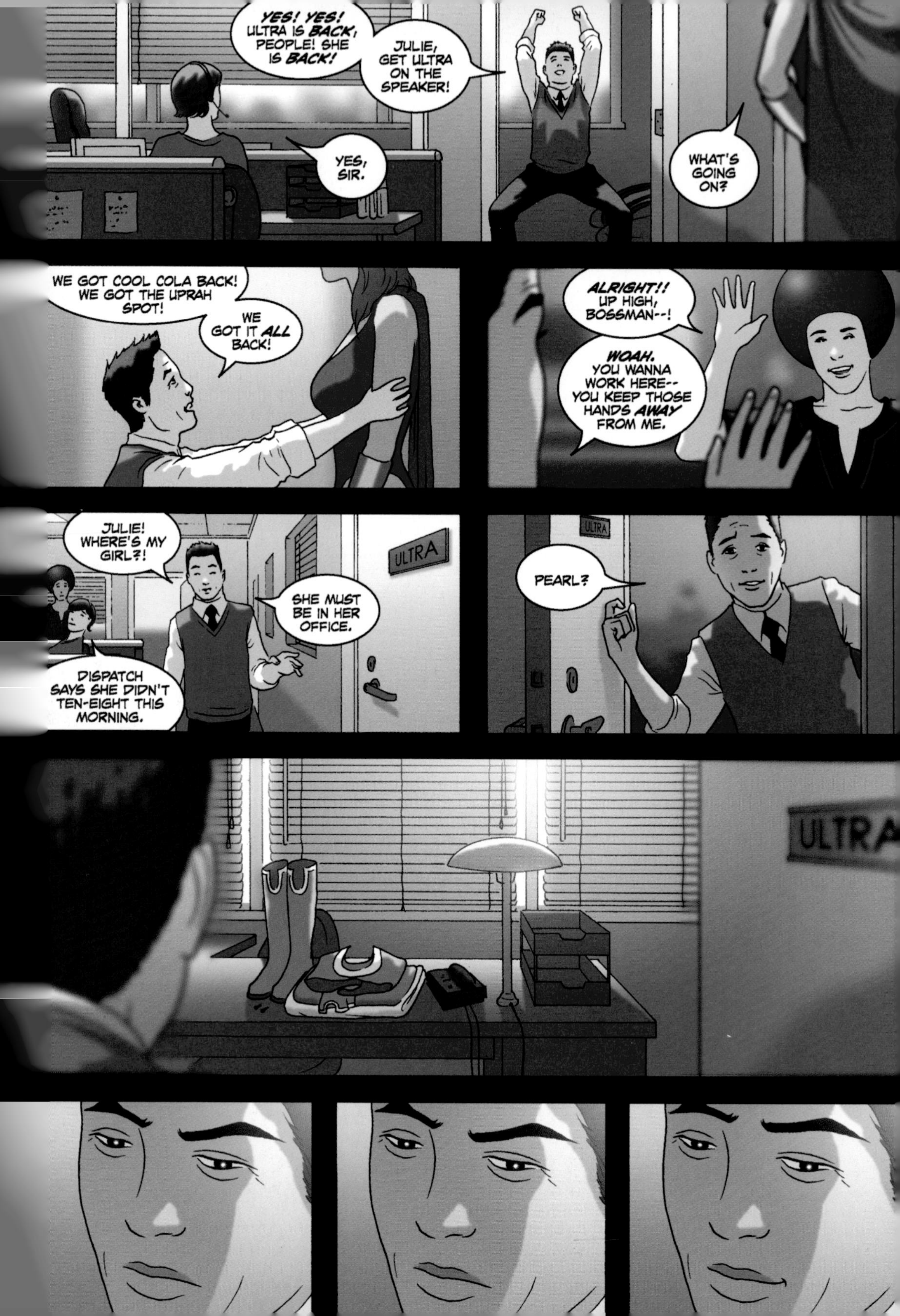
YES! YES! ULTRA IS BACK, PEOPLE! SHE IS BACK!
JULIE, GET ULTRA ON THE SPEAKER!
YES, SIR.
WHAT'S GOING ON?
WE GOT COOL COLA BACK! WE GOT THE UPRAH SPOT!
WE GOT IT ALL BACK!
ALRIGHT!! UP HIGH, BOSSMAN--!
WOAH. YOU WANNA WORK HERE-- YOU KEEP THOSE HANDS AWAY FROM ME.
JULIE! WHERE'S MY GIRL?!
ULTRA
SHE MUST BE IN HER OFFICE.
DISPATCH SAYS SHE DIDN'T TEN-EIGHT THIS MORNING.
ULTRA
PEARL?
ULTRA

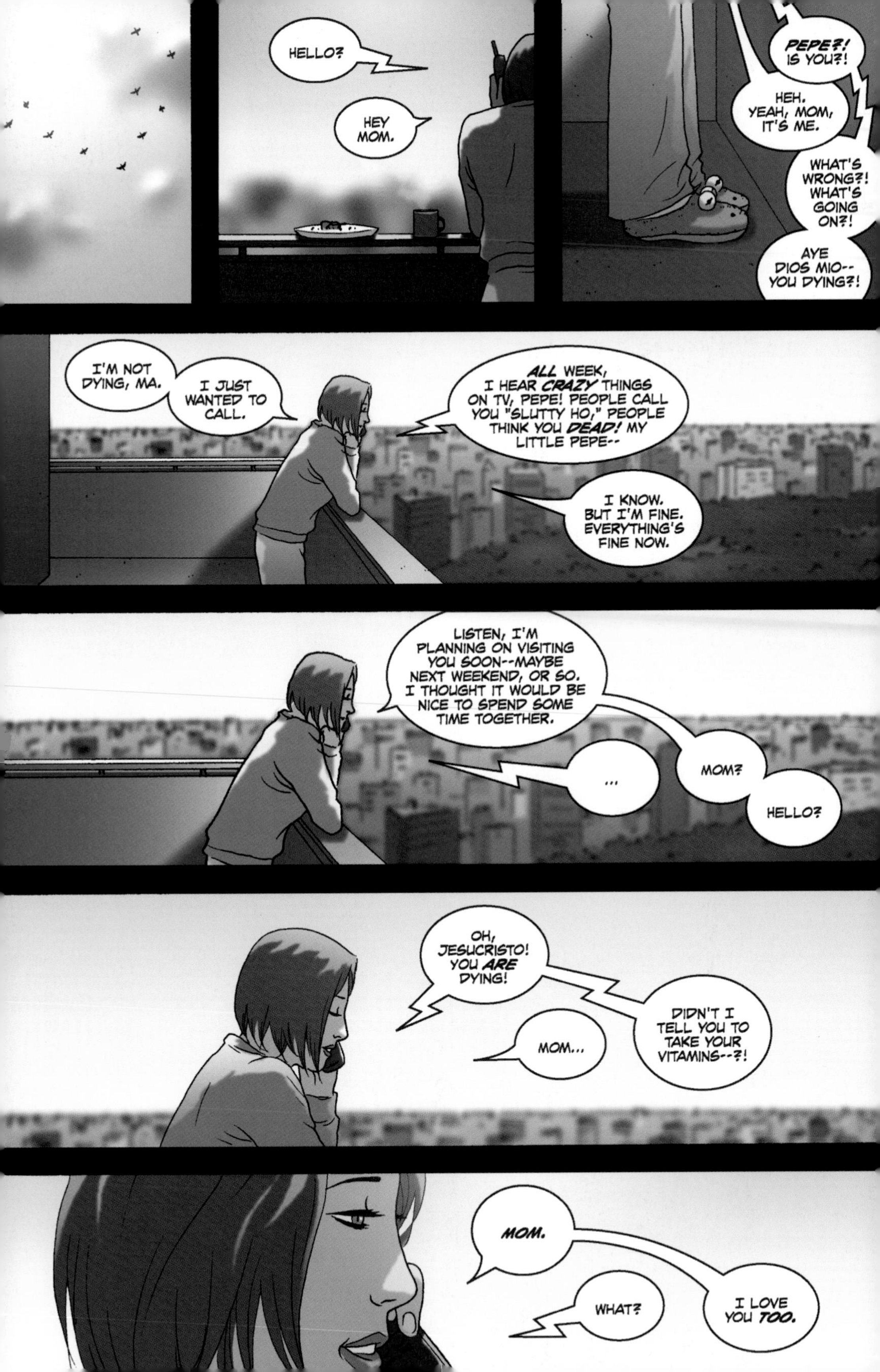
HELLO?
HEY MOM.
PEPE?! IS YOU?!
HEH. YEAH, MOM, IT'S ME.
WHAT'S WRONG?! WHAT'S GOING ON?!
AYE DIOS MIO-- YOU DYING?!
I'M NOT DYING, MA.
I JUST WANTED TO CALL.
ALL WEEK, I HEAR CRAZY THINGS ON TV, PEPE! PEOPLE CALL YOU "SLUTTY HO," PEOPLE THINK YOU DEAD! MY LITTLE PEPE--
I KNOW. BUT I'M FINE. EVERYTHING'S FINE NOW.
LISTEN, I'M PLANNING ON VISITING YOU SOON--MAYBE NEXT WEEKEND, OR SO. I THOUGHT IT WOULD BE NICE TO SPEND SOME TIME TOGETHER.
...
MOM?
HELLO?
OH, JESUCRISTO! YOU ARE DYING!
MOM...
DIDN'T I TELL YOU TO TAKE YOUR VITAMINS--?!
MOM.
WHAT?
I LOVE YOU TOO.

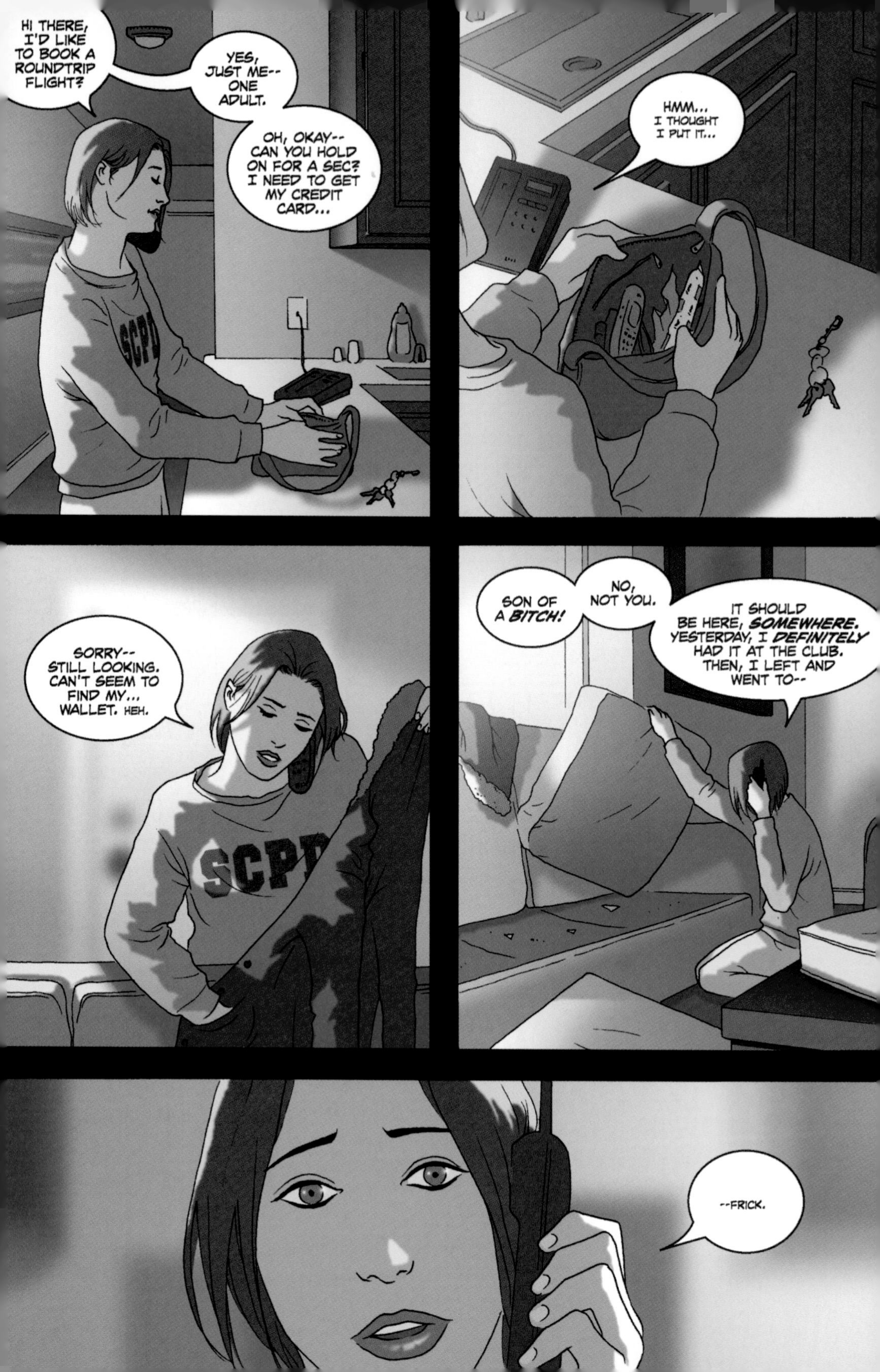
HI THERE, I'D LIKE TO BOOK A ROUNDTRIP FLIGHT?
YES, JUST ME-- ONE ADULT.
OH, OKAY-- CAN YOU HOLD ON FOR A SEC? I NEED TO GET MY CREDIT CARD...
HMM... I THOUGHT I PUT IT...
SORRY-- STILL LOOKING. CAN'T SEEM TO FIND MY... WALLET. HEH.
SON OF A *BITCH!*
NO, NOT YOU.
IT SHOULD BE HERE, *SOMEWHERE.* YESTERDAY, I *DEFINITELY* HAD IT AT THE CLUB. THEN, I LEFT AND WENT TO--
--FRICK.

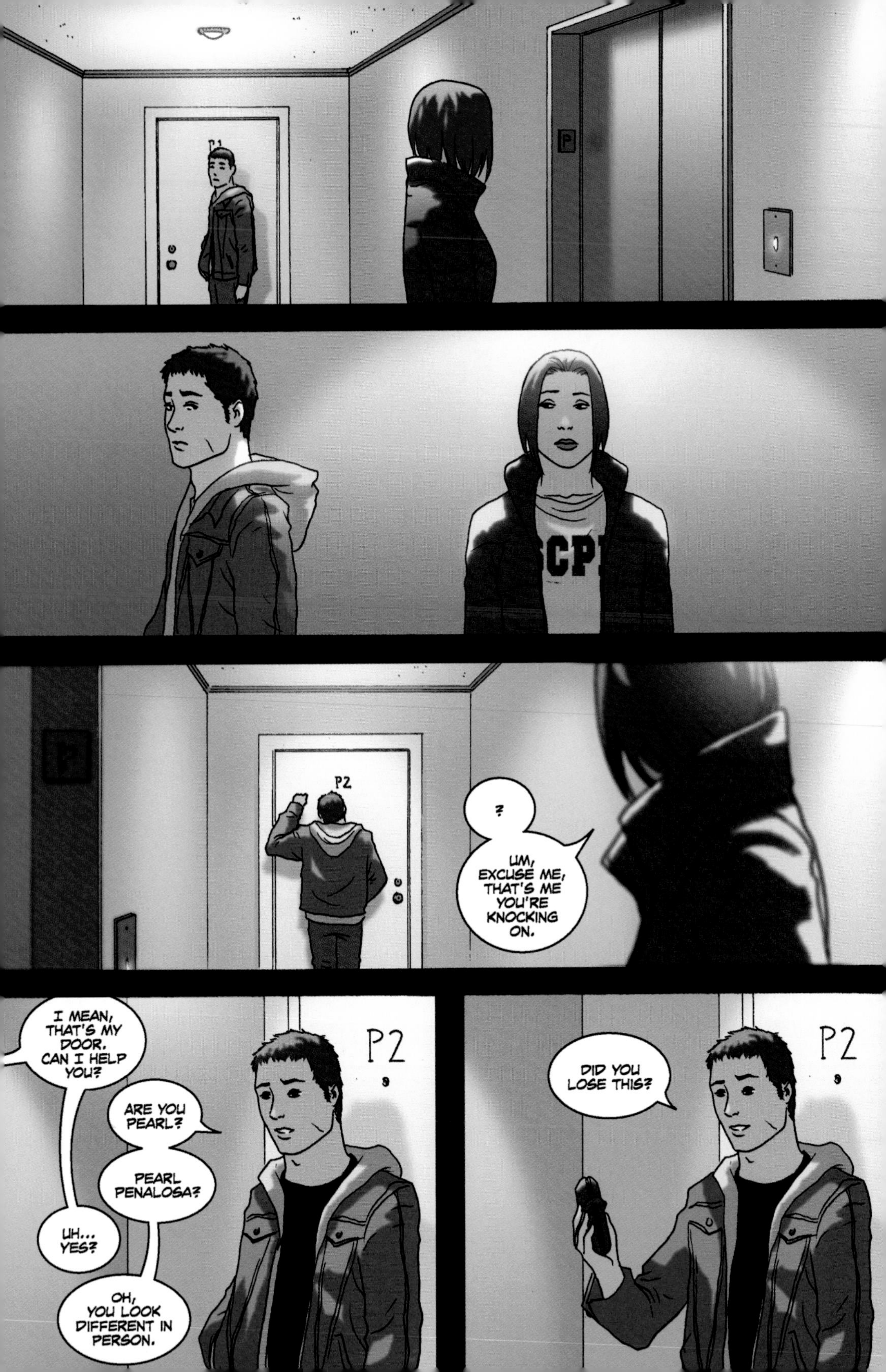
P1
P
SCPI
P
P2
?
UM, EXCUSE ME, THAT'S ME YOU'RE KNOCKING ON.
P2
I MEAN, THAT'S MY DOOR. CAN I HELP YOU?
ARE YOU PEARL?
PEARL PENALOSA?
UH... YES?
OH, YOU LOOK DIFFERENT IN PERSON.
P2
DID YOU LOSE THIS?

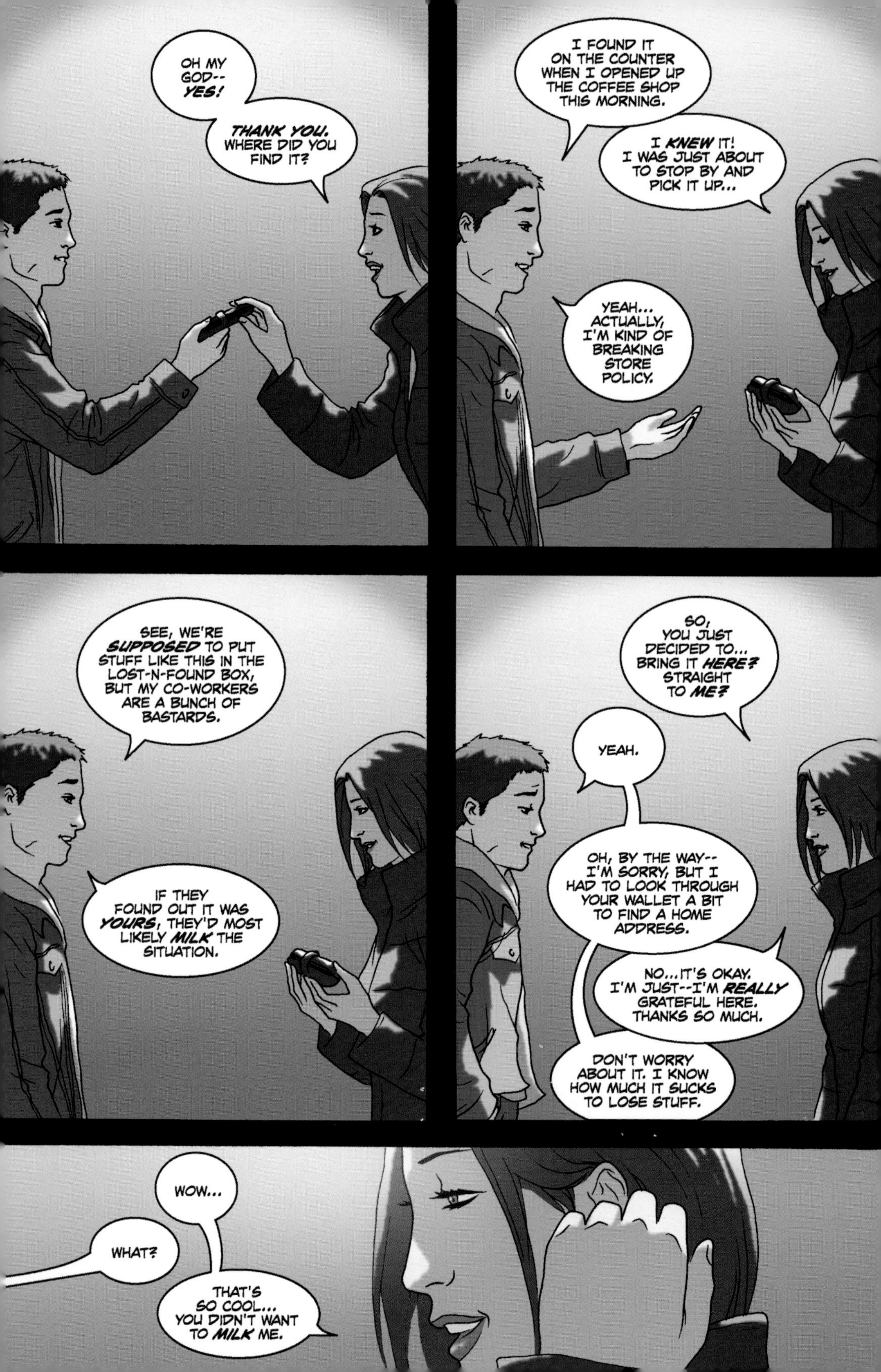
OH MY GOD-- YES!
THANK YOU. WHERE DID YOU FIND IT?
I FOUND IT ON THE COUNTER WHEN I OPENED UP THE COFFEE SHOP THIS MORNING.
I KNEW IT! I WAS JUST ABOUT TO STOP BY AND PICK IT UP...
YEAH... ACTUALLY, I'M KIND OF BREAKING STORE POLICY.
SEE, WE'RE SUPPOSED TO PUT STUFF LIKE THIS IN THE LOST-N-FOUND BOX, BUT MY CO-WORKERS ARE A BUNCH OF BASTARDS.
IF THEY FOUND OUT IT WAS YOURS, THEY'D MOST LIKELY MILK THE SITUATION.
SO, YOU JUST DECIDED TO... BRING IT HERE? STRAIGHT TO ME?
YEAH.
OH, BY THE WAY-- I'M SORRY, BUT I HAD TO LOOK THROUGH YOUR WALLET A BIT TO FIND A HOME ADDRESS.
NO...IT'S OKAY. I'M JUST--I'M REALLY GRATEFUL HERE. THANKS SO MUCH.
DON'T WORRY ABOUT IT. I KNOW HOW MUCH IT SUCKS TO LOSE STUFF.
WOW...
WHAT?
THAT'S SO COOL... YOU DIDN'T WANT TO MILK ME.

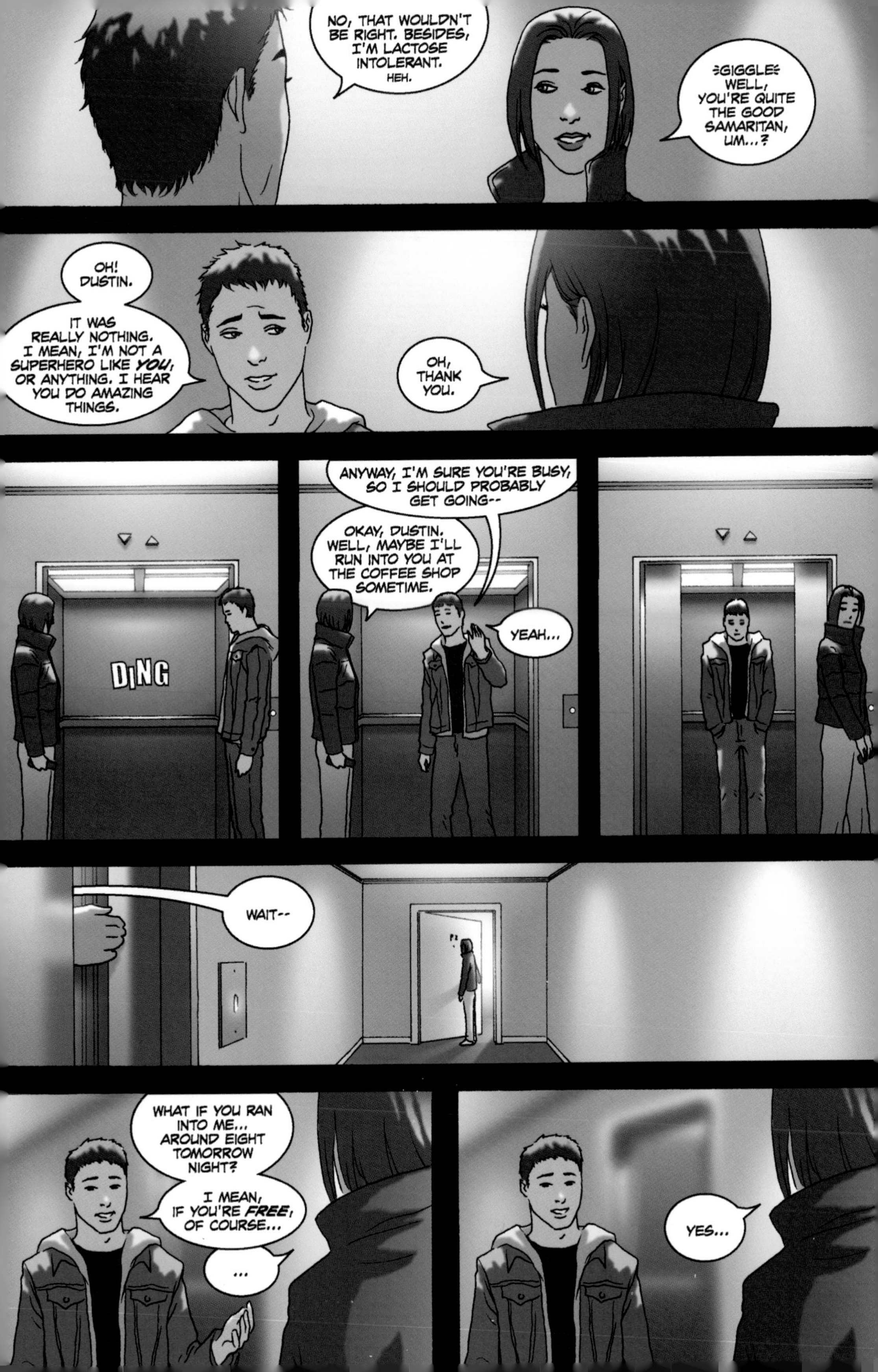
NO, THAT WOULDN'T BE RIGHT. BESIDES, I'M LACTOSE INTOLERANT. HEH.
≡GIGGLE≡ WELL, YOU'RE QUITE THE GOOD SAMARITAN, UM...?
OH! DUSTIN.
IT WAS REALLY NOTHING. I MEAN, I'M NOT A SUPERHERO LIKE *YOU*, OR ANYTHING. I HEAR YOU DO AMAZING THINGS.
OH, THANK YOU.
DING
ANYWAY, I'M SURE YOU'RE BUSY, SO I SHOULD PROBABLY GET GOING--
OKAY, DUSTIN. WELL, MAYBE I'LL RUN INTO YOU AT THE COFFEE SHOP SOMETIME.
YEAH...
WAIT--
WHAT IF YOU RAN INTO ME... AROUND EIGHT TOMORROW NIGHT?
I MEAN, IF YOU'RE *FREE*, OF COURSE...
...
YES...

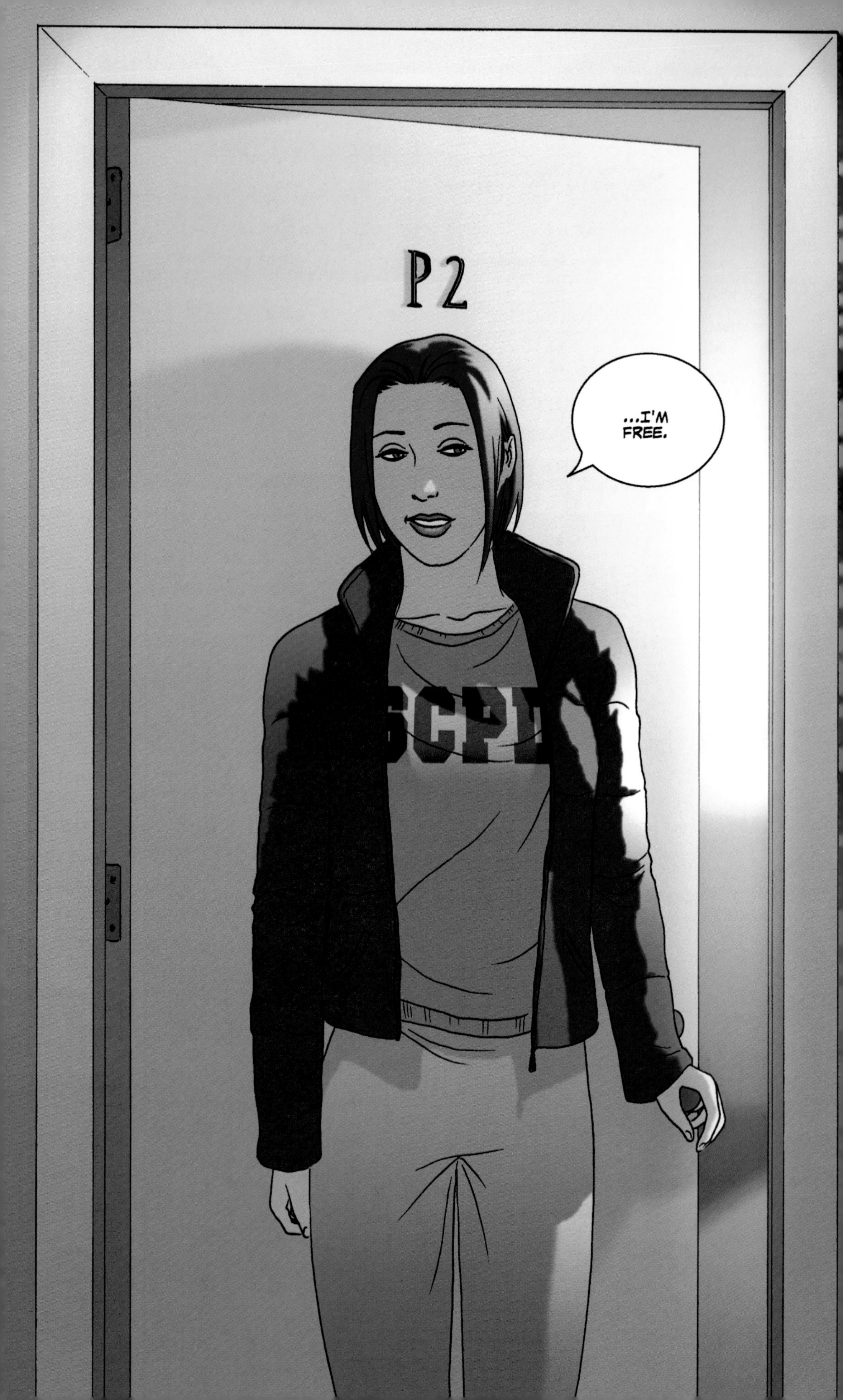
P2
...I'M FREE.
SCPD

ULTRA

SEVEN DAYS

SKETCHES

Commentary by
Jonathan Luna

The following pages actually contain the only preliminary sketches I've done for ULTRA. Most of the designing is done in my head, and I like to attack the pages before I get bored with the idea.

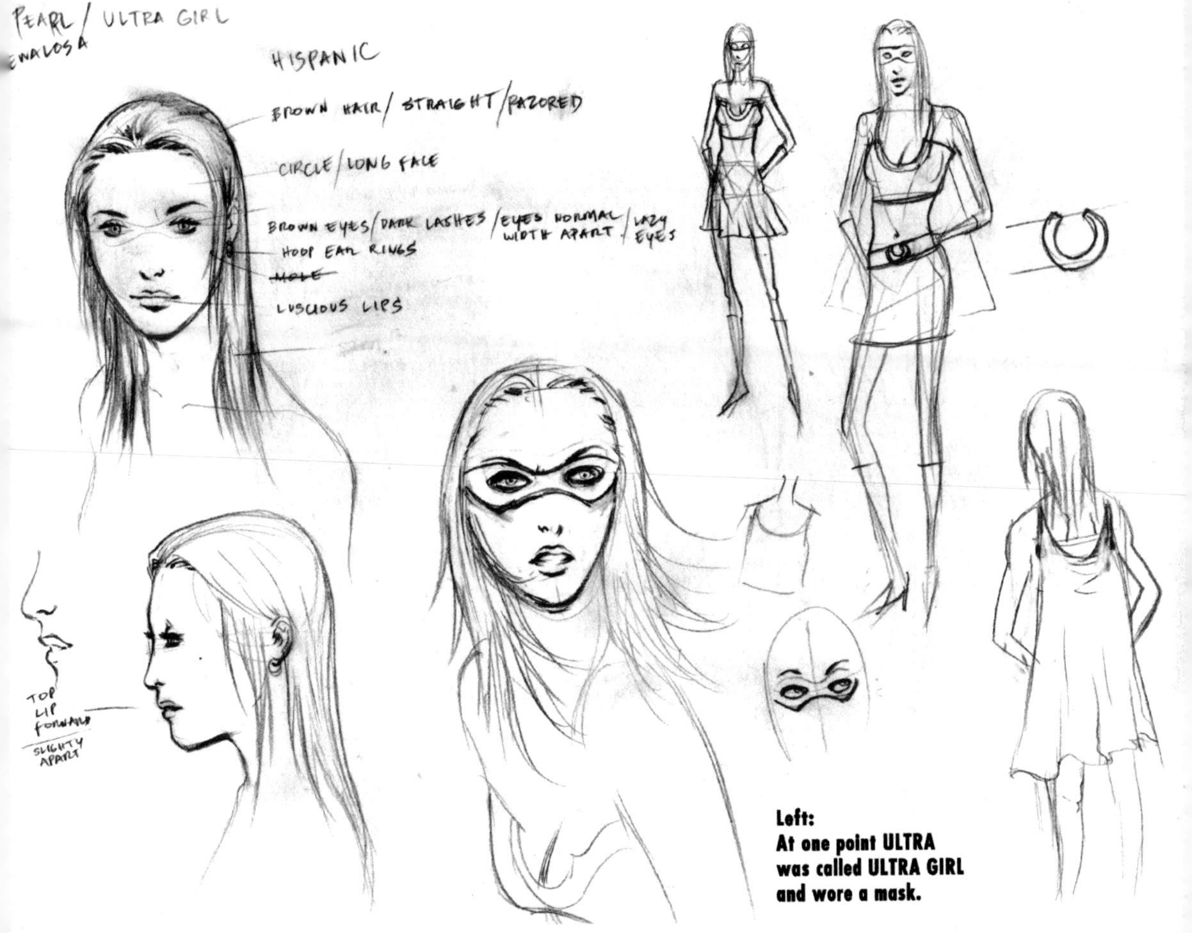
PEARL / ULTRA GIRL
HISPANIC
BROWN HAIR / STRAIGHT / RAZORED
CIRCLE / LONG FACE
BROWN EYES / DARK LASHES / EYES NORMAL WIDTH APART / LAZY EYES
HOOP EAR RINGS
MOLE
LUSCIOUS LIPS
TOP LIP FORWARD
SLIGHTY APART

Left:
At one point ULTRA was called ULTRA GIRL and wore a mask.

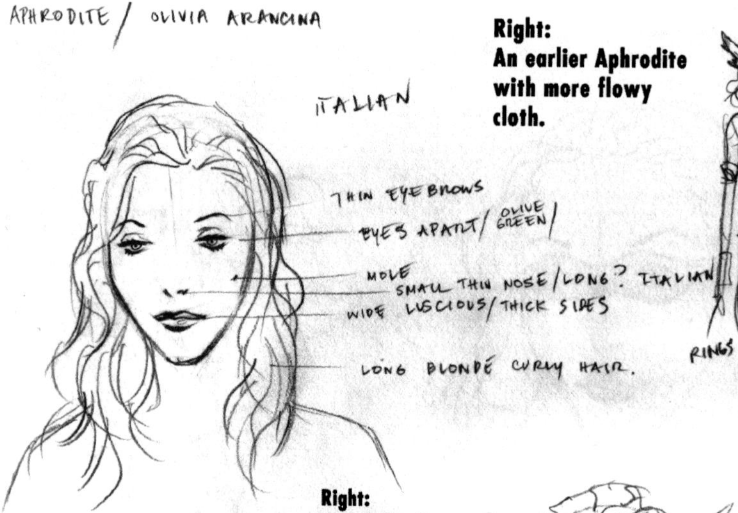
APHRODITE / OLIVIA ARANCINA
ITALIAN
THIN EYEBROWS
EYES APART / OLIVE GREEN /
MOLE
SMALL THIN NOSE / LONG? ITALIAN
WIDE LUSCIOUS / THICK SIDES
LONG BLONDE CURLY HAIR.

Right:
An earlier Aphrodite with more flowy cloth.

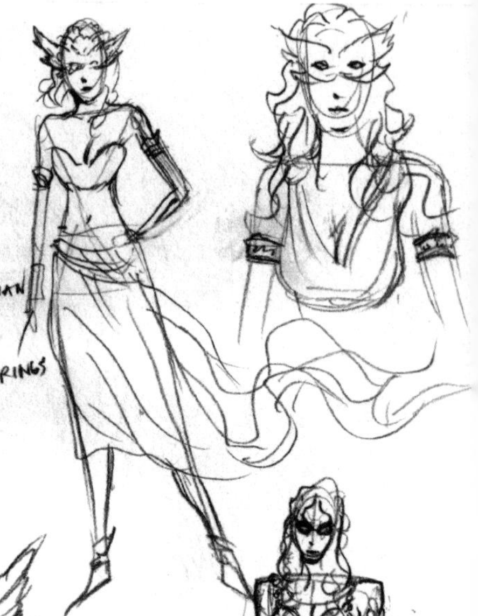
RINGS

Right:
We used to live in Italy, and this mask was inspired by the ones I used to see at Carnivale, a yearly event.

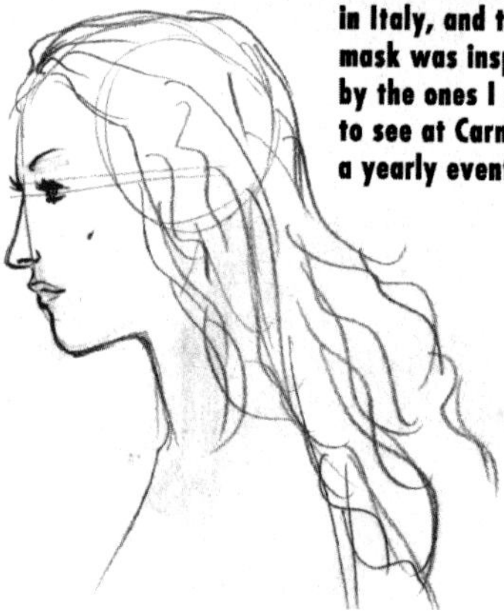

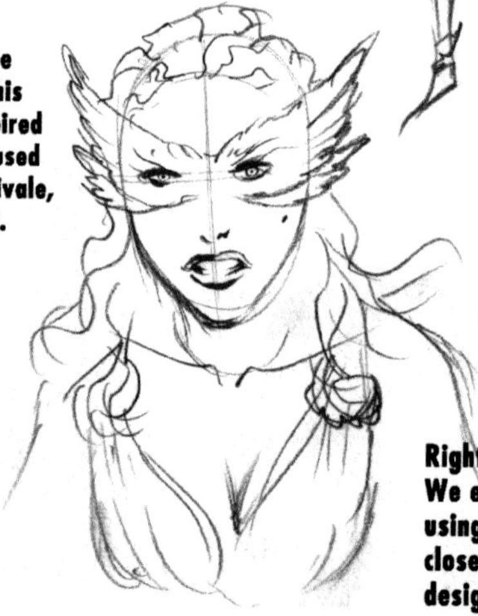

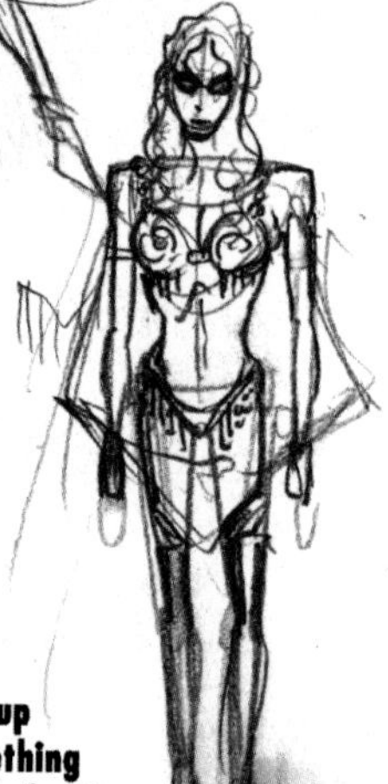

Right:
We ended up using something closer to Joshua's design--more metal, less cloth.

Joshua didn't like Cowgirl at first, and the design was almost scrapped. But I think it grew on him. I liked how silly it was--it shows how absurd marketing can be sometimes.

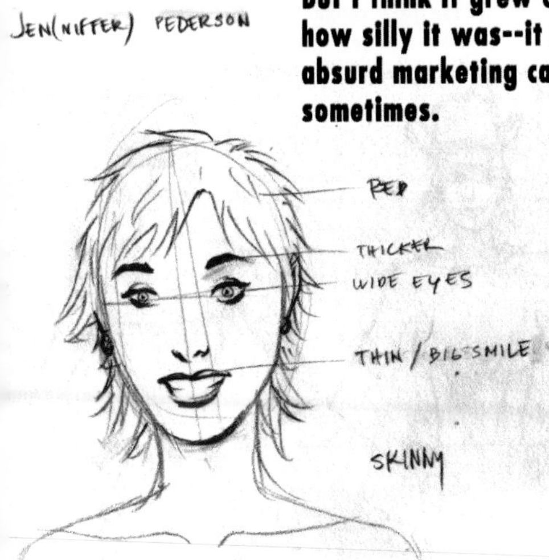
JEN(NIFFER) PEDERSON
RED
THICKER
WIDE EYES
THIN / BIG SMILE
SKINNY

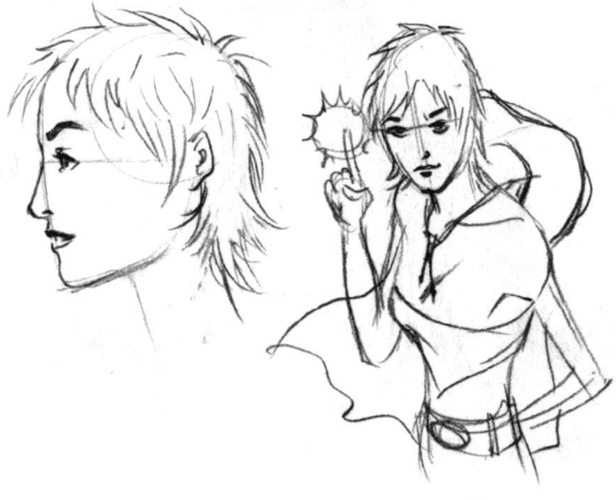

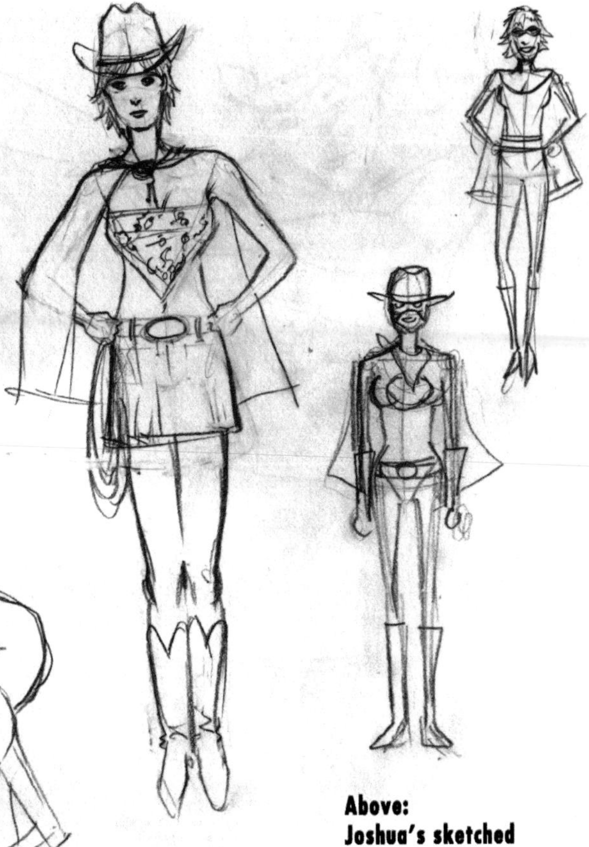

**Above:
Joshua's sketched version of Cowgirl.**

I paid a lot of attention to the colors of the girls' civilian wear--they share similar schemes with their costumes.

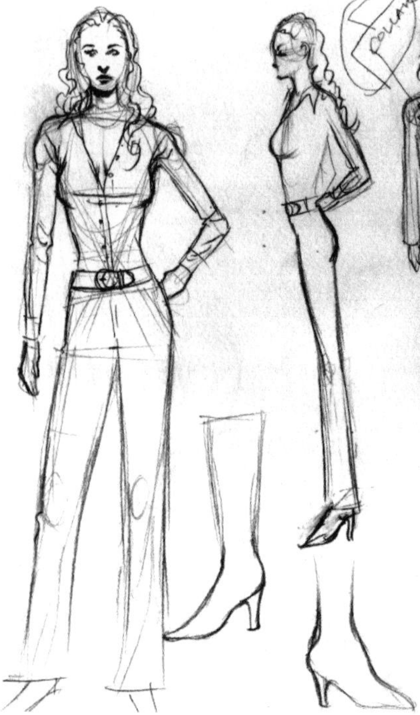

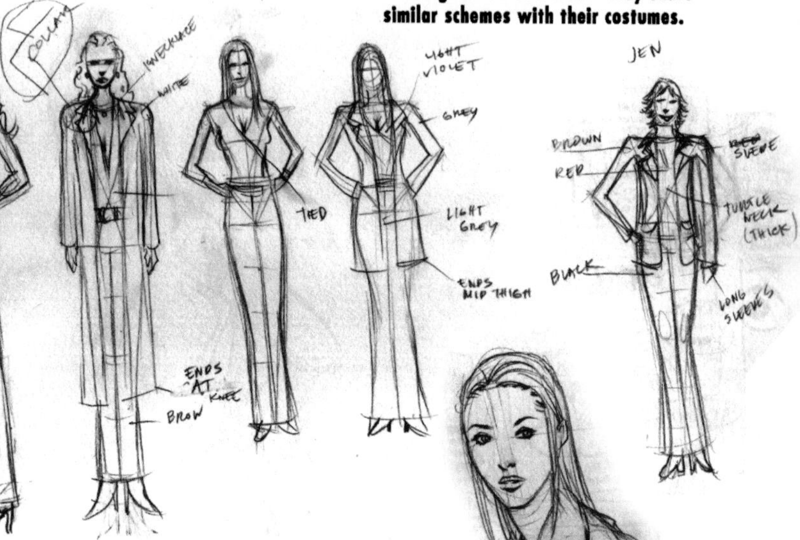
COLLAR
NECKLACE
WHITE
ENDS AT KNEE
BROW
TIED
LIGHT VIOLET
GREY
LIGHT GREY
ENDS MID THIGH
JEN
BROWN
RED
SUEDE
TURTLE NECK (THICK)
BLACK
LONG SLEEVES

The girls in their attire for issue #1. The cold doesn't bother them as much as the average person, but I clothed them in heavy wear to contrast with their ridiculously skimpy superhero costumes.

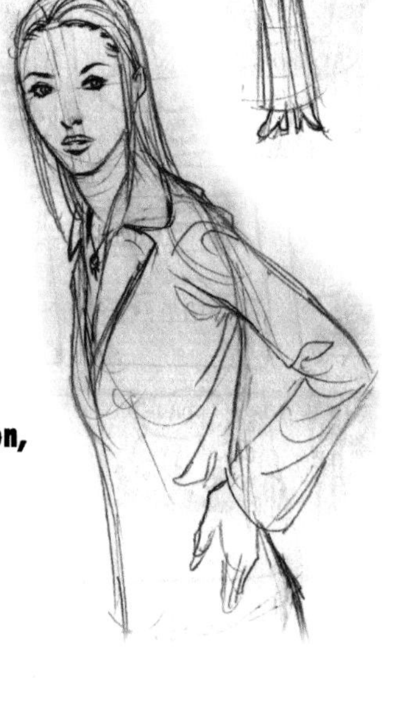

This was my color guide for the girls.
It's surreal to see how a simple drawing in my sketchbook became what ULTRA is today.

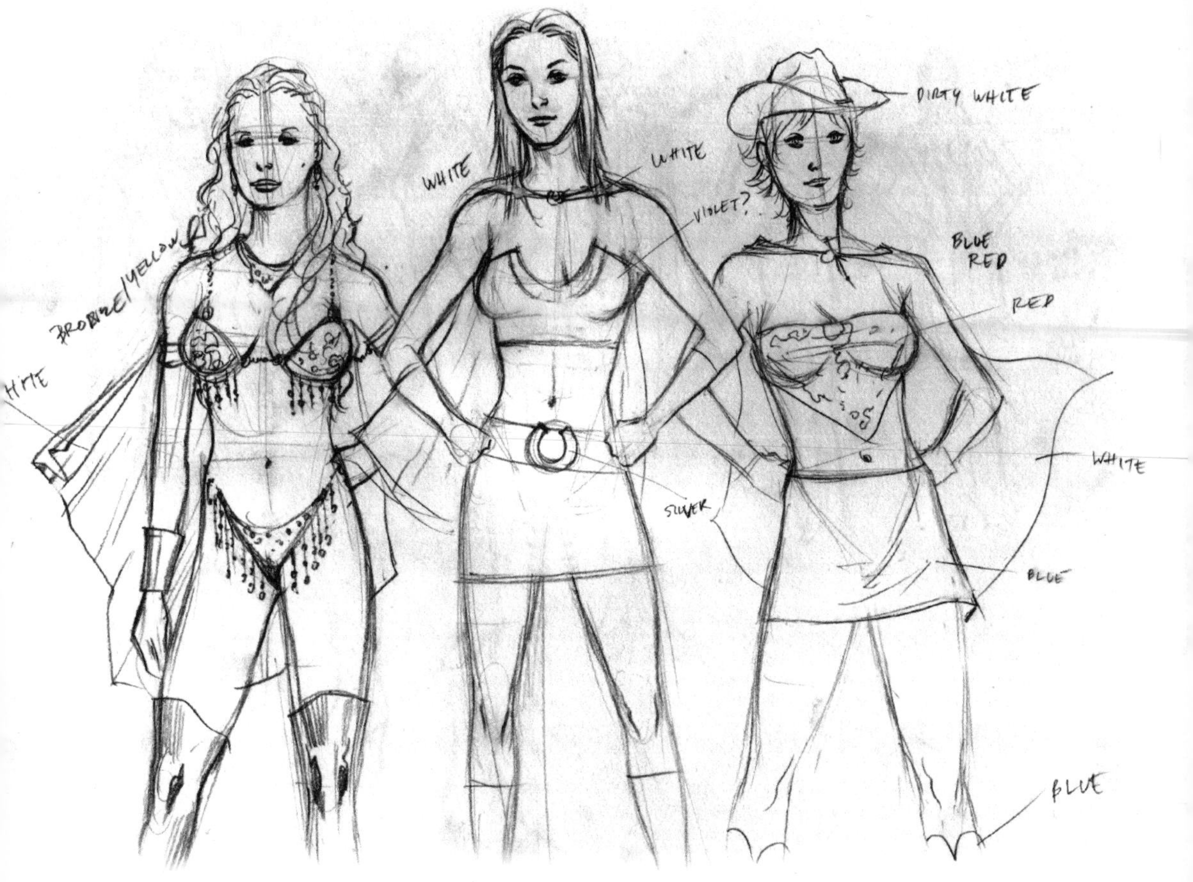
DIRTY WHITE
WHITE
WHITE
VIOLET?
BLUE
RED
RED
BRONZE/YELLOW
WHITE
SILVER
BLUE
BLUE

TRY A TASTY GRAND SLAM PIE!

APPLE
made with artificial flavoring
GRAND SLAM PIE

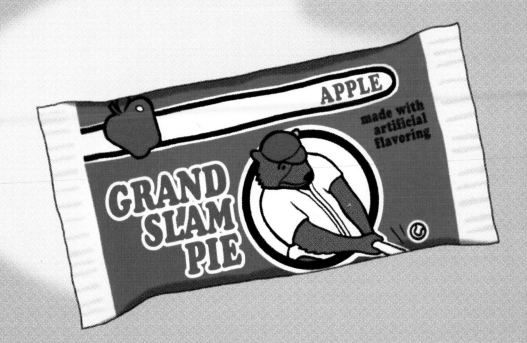

In 5 Yummy Flavors!

- Apple
- Chocolate
- Berry
- Vanilla
- Cherry

SUNSET
SNACK FOODS

The Best Pies In Spring City.

Not an actual product.

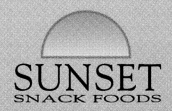

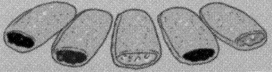

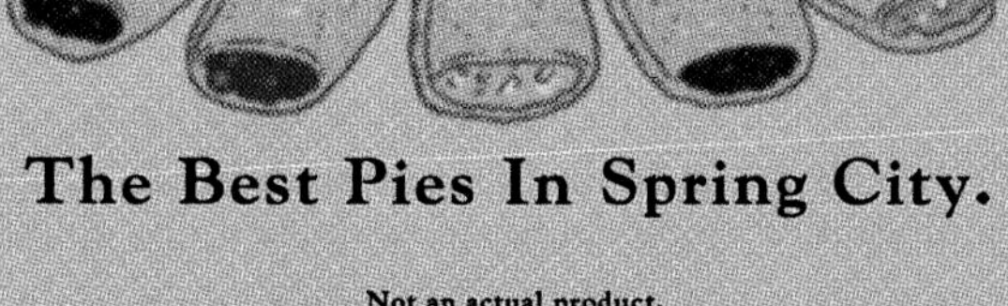